AN AMERICAN GLOSSARY

AN AMERICAN GLOSSARY

Being an Attempt
to Illustrate Certain Americanisms
Upon Historical Principles

RICHARD H. THORNTON

Volume III

Edited by
LOUISE HANLEY

FREDERICK UNGAR PUBLISHING CO.
NEW YORK

This volume is compiled from material published
posthumously in the publication *Dialect Notes*.

Printed in the United States of America

Library of Congress Catalog Card No. 61-13641

AN AMERICAN GLOSSARY

The following abbreviations are used throughout:

    H. R. = House of Representatives
    C. G. = Congressional Globe
    C. R. = Congressional Record.
    App. = Appendix (to C. G. or C. R.)

Figures in brackets, following the definitions, give the dates of first and last citations under the indicated head-words in Volumes I and II of "An American Glossary," by R. H. Thornton, Francis & Co., London, 1912.

A

A. B. papers, A. B. plot. These papers were written by Ninian Edwards of Illinois, in the early part of 1824, and were signed "A. B." They charged illegality and misconduct upon W. H. Crawford, Secretary of the Treasury. The charges were not substantiated. See Benton's "Thirty Years' View," I, ch. xiv.

Abolitionists. Extreme anti-slavery men. [1790-1840.]

1866 *Abolitionists,* Black Republicans, fanatics, disunionists, amalgamationists, woolly heads, negro worshipers, were the gentlest terms employed, and these were howled out as incessantly as dogs bay at the full moon.—Mr. R. W. Clarke of O., H. R., Feb. 24: *C. G.,* p. 1014/2.

Abolitionize. To imbue with abolition ideas. [1860.]

1860 The Methodist General Conference have defeated the Anti-slavery resolution, which proposed to *abolitionise* the general discipline.—Corr. *Richmond Enquirer,* June 1, p. 2/4.

1860 The Emigrant Aid Societies of Leavenworth are using great efforts to *abolitionize* the State by getting hold of the Literary Institutions.— *Id.,* July 31, p. 2/7.

About and about. As much on one side as on the other.

1867 Men were created equal. That is, at the very outstart the cytoblast, the primal cell, ... was *about and about.* I suppose it was. I doubt whether the best microscopes would detect any difference there.— Mr. Edgar Cowan of Pa., U. S. Senate, Jan. 8: *C. G.,* p. 331/2.

Abutter. An adjoining proprietor.

1874 The concrete walks on Depot Court and Pleasant Street have been wholly paid for by the *abutters.—Fitchburg City Documents,* p. 220. (N. E. D.)

1896 One half ... should be paid by the *abutters,* and the other half from the revenues of the District.—Mr. N. Dingley of Me., H. R., May 11: *C. G.,* p. 5083/2.

1896 The present law requires only one consent of the *abutters* to the establishment of a saloon, and that consent may last to the resurrection.— Mr. E. A. Morse of Mass., H. R., Dec. 14: *Id.,* p. 154/1.

Abutter. Land which abuts on the land in question.

1877 The boundaries of the land will become the property of the U. S., and the *abutters* will be defined in the records.—Mr. H. L. Dawes of Mass., U. S. Senate, Nov. 9: *C. R.,* p. 303/1.

Acequia. A canal. Spanish.

1868 We saw wheat, corn, &c., about three thousand acres, which had been sown, planted, and cultivated by these [Navajo] Indians; we saw these *Acequias:* .... We contemplate opening other large *acequias* and feeders, to bring another large tract under cultivation.—Testimony of Major Bristol, *C. G.,* March 20, p. 2018/2.

1

Acknowledge the corn. To yield the point. [1840-1888.]

1862 Mr. Kellogg of Ill.:—The modesty of my colleague is greater this morning than I ever knew it to be before. Mr. Richardson:—*I acknowledge the corn.* (Laughter.)—H. R., Jan. 30: *C. G.,* p. 566/2.

Address a man out of office. To force his removal by an address to the appointing power.

1872 I ask [Senator Cameron] if he would *"address"* a *man out of office,* because he is stricken down by sickness and unable to hold court. Would that be a reason for *"addressing"* him out? . . . There must be some cause to impeach him or *address him out;* but then the Constitution does not provide for *addressing a judge out of office.* It can only be done by impeachment.—Mr. Lyman Trumbull of Ill., U. S. Senate, Apr. 17: *C. G.,* p. 2500/2.

Administration measure, man, &c. One that supports the existing administration. [1827-1850.]

1869 Before the corrupting influence of patronage the genius and statesmanship of the Republic went down, until only the driveling diatribes of conspirators or the idiotic plaints of doughfaces were heard within this Capitol. No measure could pass here, unless it was an *administration measure.*—Mr. W. G. Brownlow of Tenn., H. R., March 18: *C. G.,* p. 137/3.

1870 "Mr. President," I said, "I am an *administration man,* and whatever you do will always find in me the most careful and candid consideration."—Mr. Charles Sumner of Mass., U. S. Senate, Dec. 21: *Id.,* p. 243/2.

Advance agent. An agent who goes before to make necessary arrangements; especially for travelling lecturers, operatic or theatrical companies when "on the road," and circuses.

1897 That great priest and apostle of protection, and that grand *advance agent* of prosperity, William McKinley.—Mr. H. R. Gibson of Tenn., H. R., March 23: *C. R.,* p. 177/1.

1897 [Mr. Bell of Colorado] said that McKinley was elected, the *advance agent* of prosperity, as [Mr. Dolliver] denominated him.—Mr. C. H. Grosvenor of O., H. R., March 24: *Id.,* p. 238/1.

Affiant. One who makes an affidavit.

1850 Burrill's Law Dictionary. (N. E. D.)

1868 In nearly all cases where this *affiant* challenged persons [as not being lawful voters] no attention was paid to the challenges, but on the contrary this *affiant* was told . . . . that this *affiant* must leave the window; that they were going to let them vote.—Affidavit of John Stauffer, Oct. 19: *C. G.,* Apr. 2, 1869, p. 452/2-3.

1870 The affidavit is what the Senator from Maryland was discussing, and what the *affiant* is required . . . . to state; and there is not a single word requiring the *affiant* to state that he is a qualified voter.—Mr. Eugene Cassidy of Calif., U. S. Senate, May 19: *Id.,* p. 359/1, App.

1878 When *affiant* went before Commissioner Hunter, he was told by Hunter that the person who made the affidavit against *affiant* . . . said that he (*affiant*) was "the wrong man."—Deposition taken in Alabama: *C. R.,* p. 2041/1, June 16, 1879.

Affiliate. Erroneously used instead of *fraternize.* [1852-1879.]

1843 Our cabin passengers . . . . are as diverse in characters and pursuits, as in birth and language. But we all *affiliate* and harmonize wonderfully.—Thurlow Weed "Letters," p. 9 (1866).

1866 In some respects I differ from many with whom I am *affiliated* here. —Mr. Ashley of Nev., H. R., March 10: *C. G.,* p. 1314/1.

1868 Mr. Burleigh of Dak.:—Does the gentleman suppose for a moment that I advocate the [Democratic] party? I would sooner *affiliate* with the devil and his host. Mr. Washburn of Ind.:—I am glad to hear the gentleman say he does not *affiliate* with that party.—H. R., July 13: *Id.,* p. 4016/2.

1868 See DEAD RABBITS.
1869 See BORDER RUFFIANS.
1891 Our nearest neighbors live several miles away, and we don't *affiliate* with them much.—W. B. Harben, "Almost Persuaded, p. 27. (N. Y.)

Affiliations. Friendly relations. [1852.]
1862 I am here almost without any *affiliation* in political sentiment.—Mr. Anthony Kennedy of Md., U. S. Senate, Jan. 31: *C. G.,* p. 589/2.
1879 Mr. Wallace of Pa.:—I presume the Senator from Me. understands what *"party affiliation"* is. He is a party man. Mr. Blaine:—I do, perfectly. Mr. Wallace:—He knows what *"party affiliations"* are.— U. S. Senate, June 14: *C. R.,* p. 2000/1.
1888 These workmen have no *affiliation* with gentlemen of infinite leisure, unbounded wealth, and great admiration for all things foreign.—Mr. W. McAdoo of N. J., H. R., May 8: *Id.,* p. 3853/1.
1890 The appointment of a jury commission, one of whom should be the clerk of the court, the other a citizen appointed, of opposite political *affiliations.*—Mr. J. H. Rowell of Ill., H. R., July 2: *Id.,* p. 6927/2.
1893 The black man has been moving in the procession; he is being educated, and can see where his political *affiliation* can best be allied.—Mr. T. H. Paynter of Ky., H. R., Feb. 28: *C. R.,* p. 2301/1.

Africanization. Subjection to negro supremacy.
1890 I said I was not in favor of the *Africanization* of this continent or of any part of it.—Mr. J. J. Ingalls of Kan., U. S. Senate, Jan. 23: *C. R.,* p. 806/2.
1890 The principal influence which holds the white people of the South together is the o!d Democratic war-whoop of "negro supremacy" and *"Africanization."*—Mr. H. D. Coleman of La., H. R., June 30: *Id.,* p. 6773/1.

After-form. The subsequent shape of a measure.
1871 It is the original draft of a proposition which determines its *after-form* in all the stages through which it may pass.—Mr. James G. Blaine, Speaker of the House, March 20: *C. G.,* p. 182/2.

Agreement railroads. Those with which the quartermaster general makes contracts for carriage of freight from time to time.
1901 Requests for travel over so-called *"agreement railroads."*—'Amendment to an Act,' Feb. 23: *C. R.,* p. 2899/2.

Air line. A direct or "bee" line. [1840-1853.]
1863 This is a proposition to construct an *air-line* railroad between Washington and New York.—Mr. Albert G. Porter of Ind., H. R., Feb. 7: *C. G.,* p. 873/1.
1864 I invite any gentleman who supposes that by voting for this bill he is voting for an *air line,* to look at [these maps] and see the kind of *air line* it is proposed to establish.—Mr. Broomall of Pa., H. R., March 24: *Id.,* p. 1264/2.
1870 What has been called the *"air-line* road" from Washington to New York was the offspring of the war, suggested as a means of cheap transportation between the national capital and the chief commercial center of the Atlantic seaboard.—Mr. Thomas Swann of Md., H. R., March 10: *Id.,* p. 1846/1.

Albany beef. The cured flesh of the sturgeon, which was formerly caught [in fyke-nets] and prepared near Albany, N. Y. (Century Dict.)

Albany cutter. A style of sleigh first built by James Goold in Albany, N. Y. Its characteristic features are a light bent-wood frame for the body, well-curved panels, and full-sweep outlines. An enlarged size has seat-room for four or six passengers. (Century Dict.)

Albany lead, in whist. An opening to show four trumps and three of each plain suit: so named because made popular by the Albany (N. Y.) Whist Club. (Century Dict.)

Albany regency, the. See quotation. Martin Van Buren was the chief leader; others being William L. Marcy, John A. Dix, and Silas Wright.

1882 After the council of appointment had been abolished, there soon arose in Albany what every student of American history knows to have been the *Albany regency*. It was a body of able and astute politicians of the Democratic party, who attempted to do privately and without warrant of law what the old council of appointment had substantially done. It undertook to control all the patronage of the party.—Mr. Warner Miller of N. Y., U. S. Senate, Dec. 14: *C. R.*, p. 282/1.

Albright Methodists. A body organized about 1800, in Pennsylvania, by one Jacob Albright (1759-1808) who was previously a Lutheran. It styles itself "The Evangelical Association," having assumed that name in 1818. Albright assumed to be a bishop, and was elected under that title the year before he died.

Alewife. The *Clupea serrata,* a fish like a herring. [1678-1824.]

1670 Big-bellied *Alewives,* Mackrils richly clad With Rainbow colours.— Samuel Clarke, "Account of the Plantations," p. 37.

Algerine. A pirate. [1844.]

1885 Bitterly as the conflict was waged between the "Dorrites" and the *"Algerines,"* as the contending parties were called, &c.—Mr. Spooner on the death of Senator Anthony of R. I., U. S. Senate, Jan. 21: *C. R.*, p. 912/1.

Aliunde Joe. A nickname applied to the Hon. Joseph P. Bradley (N. J.) of the Supreme Court of the U. S. It arose from the decision of the Electoral Commission in 1877, not to consider evidence *"aliunde* the certificates." (C. L. Norton, "Political Americanisms.")

All creation, all nature, all wrath. Everybody, everything. [1819-1862.]

1850 [The barber] began to rub my head like *all wrath.*—Wilmington (N. C.) *Commercial,* May 30, p. 2/3.

1863 Go to Wilmington, and telegraph *all creation.*—Edward Kirke, "Life in Dixie's Land," p. 215.

1878 The doctor used to give Cuff his cast-off clothes, and Cuff would prance round in 'em and seem to think he was a doctor of divinity himself, and had the charge of *all natur'.*—Harriet B. Stowe in the *Atlantic Monthly,* Oct., p. 472/2.

1891 A bombardment hurts, and a blow may hurt; but John L. Sullivan has endured a great many hurts of that kind, and has whipped *all creation* so far.—Mr. H. W. Blair of N. H., U. S. Senate, Feb. 3: *C. R.*, p. 2088/2.

1894 We declare it to be the part of wisdom to quit raising and making things here, which we can not make and raise in fair and honest competition with *all creation.*—Mr. Champ Clark of Mo., H. R., Jan. 19: *Id.,* p. 1077/1.

All to pieces. Completely, thoroughly. [1839-1847.]

1863 I know you Yankees *all to pieces;* I've lived among you.—Edmund Kirke, "My Southern Friends," p. 86.

All wool and a yard wide. A phrase expressive of excellence and thoroughness.

1892 I desire this House to understand that the people of the State of O. are *"all wool and a yard wide"* on the subject of sustaining this Government, its glory, and its character.—Mr. George W. Ray of N. Y., H. R., Feb. 10: *C. R.*, p. 1039/1.

Almighty. Monstrous. [1824-1857.]

1890 I think every man in this House whose olfactory nerves are in a healthy condition can smell an *almighty* lot of "smoke" in this bill.— Mr. S. L. Milliken of Me., H. R., June 23: *C. R.*, p. 6393/1.

Amalgamation. The mingling of the black and white races. [1839-1847.]

4

1837 *Amalgamation.* A black man and a white woman were lately brought before the Police Court in Boston, charged with unlawfully marrying. —*Baltimore Commercial Transcript,* June 8, p. 2/1.

Amanist. A member of a German religious community settled near Cedar Rapids, Ia. For the tenets of this odd little sect, see the Century Dict.

Ambulance chasers. See quotation.

1897 In N. Y. City there is a style of lawyers known to the profession as *"ambulance chasers,"* because they are on hand whenever there is a railway wreck, or a street-car collision, or a gasoline explosion, with their tender of consolation and their offers of professional service.— Mr. J. P. Dolliver of Ia., H. R., July 24: *C. R.,* p. 2961/1.

Amen corner. That part of a meetinghouse occupied by persons who assist the preacher with occasional and irregular responses. [1904- 1910.]

1884 One of the recent members of the Senate, when commiserated upon the fact that he was compelled to go to what is commonly known here as the *amen corner,* frankly said that any seat in the Senate was better than none.—Mr. J. J. Ingalls of Kan., U. S. Senate, Apr. 22: *C. R.,* p. 3207/1.

1894 One of those saintly Republican monopolists who sit in the *"amen corner"* of protected privilege, and who . . . even open oysters with prayer.—Mr. W. L. Terry of Ark., H. R., Jan. 26: *Id.,* p. 1502/2.

1902 I got a seat in the *amen-corner,* whar I could see him, an' all through preachin' I watched 'im like a hawk.—W. N. Harben, "Abner Daniel," p. 207.

American, as applied to the Colonists. [1647-1795.]

1796 The name of American, which belongs to you in your national capacity, must always exalt the just pride of patriotism more than any appellation derived from local discriminations.—'Farewell Address' of George Washington, Sept. 19.

1818 The *Americans* are at the forks of the river Appalachicola . . . . . The *Americans* have been very cruel since they commenced.—Robert C. Ambrister to Major E. Nicholls: Norfolk (Va.) *Beacon,* Dec. 17, p. 2/3.

American party. See quotation for 1870.

1863 I am glad to find that a gentleman who belonged to the *American party,* and a Democrat, and a Black Republican, all agree upon [the necessity of a conscription].—Mr. John Sherman of O., U. S. Senate, Feb. 5: *C. G.,* p. 737/1.

1864 I was a member of the *American party* . . . . The *American party* had men up for office, and I supported them, not because they were pro-slavery or anti-slavery, but because they were the choice of the *American party.* It was well known that the *American party* was neutral upon that subject.—Mr. Blow of Mo., H. R., March 7: *Id.,* p. 979/2. (See also PRO-SLAVERY.)

1864 In the fall of 1854, the *American party* organized in Baltimore city, and by the secrecy of its organization it threw an unprecedented vote, and swept the Democrats from power in that city.—Mr. Davis of Md., H. R., May 9: *Id.,* p. 2190/2.

1870 After the old Whig party was destroyed, and the Democratic party very much weakened and disorganized by *the American or Know-Nothing party,* the detached political elements in the northern States floated together and organized what they afterward called the Republican party.—Mr. W. E. Niblack of Ind., H. R., March 14: *Id.,* p. 1936/1.

Americanize. To make American. [1802-1824.]

1824 It is time we should become a little more *Americanized,* and, instead of feeding the paupers and laborers of Europe, feed our own.—Speech of Andrew Jackson, quoted in the *C. R.,* March 25, 1897: p. 66/2, App.

1866 If there be any people of our own race of whom it could not be predicated that in a few generations they would become homogeneous, or in other words *Americanized,* I would, if I had the power, deny to that people the right of suffrage.—Mr. Hubbard of W. Va., H. R., Jan. 18: *C. G.,* p. 310/2.

1866 [If the South] would prosper, she must *Americanize* her system of life, abandon her contempt for labor; and her habits of violence and disregard of law.—Mr. Kelley of Pa., H. R., Jan. 31: *Id.,* p. 559/1.

Anaconda. This term was applied to General McClellan's army, which was expected to "crush the rebellion." [1862-1879.]

1862 My colleague wound up his speech by the figure of the *anaconda,* in which he tried to be humorous at the expense of General Scott, who originated the trope.—Mr. S. S. Cox of O., H. R., Jan. 30: *C. G.,* p. 569/2.

1863 I want [our western boys] to go where there is something to do, where they may assist in opening the great river of the West, so that the cotton, the rice, and the sugar may pour out, and we may cut off the wealth of the rebellion from its heart, and then, with our *boa-constrictor* around them, drawing it closer and closer, ... we may see daylight before six months.—Mr. Joseph A. Wright of Ind., U. S. Senate, Jan. 6: *Id.,* p. 204/1.

1866 [Under General Grant] the *anaconda* of which so much had been said early in the war was no longer a myth.—Mr. Richard Yates of Ill., U. S. Senate, July 17: *Id.,* p. 3857/2.

Angle, v. To move in an angular fashion.

1876 The road *angles* itself up the . . hillside.—Mrs. A. D. T. Whitney, "Sights and Insights," p. 198. (N. E. D.)

1890 Mr. MacBride then *angled* up to me and [made a remark].—Statement of Mr. Clayton in Fort Smith *Daily Times: C. R.,* Feb. 18, p. 1464/1.

Annuity Indians. Those receiving pensions from the U. S. Government.

1870 The law [has been] in existence almost from time immemorial, that when a tribe of *annuity Indians* take a frontiersman's cattle and kill and eat them, on proper proof being made, a deduction shall be made from the next annuity to be paid to those Indians, and turned over to the man who has been despoiled of his property.—Mr. M. S. Wilkinson of Minn., H. R., June 30: *C. G.,* p. 5010/2.

Antagonize. To place or use in opposition.

1879 Senators will remember that the tobacco-tax bill was very strongly *antagonized* against this [anti-Chinese] bill.—Mr. A. A. Sargent of Calif., U. S. Senate, Feb. 13: *C. R.,* p. 1276/1.

Ante, ante up. To pay up. [1857-1888.]

1854 See Appendix VIII, Vol. II.

1861 [Senator Polk] is not familiar with scenes where hundreds of dollars are *"anted up."*—Mr. Willard Saulsbury of Del., U. S. Senate, Dec. 18: *C. G.,* p. 126/1.

Ante-bellum. Before the Civil War.

1881 [Pfaff talked] about *ante-bellum* times, '59 and '60, and the jovial suppers at his then Broadway place, near Bleecker Street.—Walt Whitman, "Specimen Days" (1887), p. 291.

1894 Sugar production in Louisiana steadily increased from the time when sugar-making first began, away back in *antebellum* times, until 1861.— Mr. N. C. Blanchard of La., U. S. Senate, June 5: *C. R.,* p. 5765/2.

Anthony Rule, The. An order of business framed by Senator Henry B. Anthony of R. I. (1815-1884.) It was worded as follows: *"Resolved,* That at the conclusion of the morning business for each day, unless upon motion the Senate shall at any time otherwise order, the Senate will proceed to the consideration of the Calendar of bills and resolutions, and continue such consideration until two o'clock; and bills and resolutions that are not objected to shall be taken up in their order: and each Senator shall be entitled to speak once and for five minutes only upon any question; and the objection may be interposed at any stage of the proceedings, unless upon motion the Senate shall otherwise order; and this order shall commence immediately after the call for 'concurrent and other resolutions,' and shall take precedence of the unfinished business and other special orders. But if the Senate shall proceed with the consideration of any matter notwithstanding an objection, the foregoing provisions touching debate shall not apply, but the subject shall be proceeded with under the standing rules of the Senate."

1870 The Chair will state the distinction between this and what was popularly known in the Senate as the "*Anthony rule*," under which the Calendar was gone over, subject to objection. That order stated that no other business whatever should be entertained.—U. S. Senate, June 17: *C. G.*, p. 4541/3.

1871 It has been said that the test-oath act has been repealed. How was it done? . . . Why, sir, without the knowledge of three men upon this floor. It was passed under what was called the *Anthony rule*, under which bills unobjected to were taken up and disposed of. It was called up here and passed in less than one minute.—Mr. O. P. Morton of Ind., U. S. Senate, Feb. 13: *Id.*, p. 1178/3.

1876 I will see whether I cannot get the approbation of the Senate to take up the Calendar under the *Anthony rule*.—Mr. Roscoe Conkling of N. Y., U. S. Senate, Aug. 8: *C. R.*, p. 5299/1.

1879 What is known as the *Anthony rule* can only be suspended on one day's notice given, or by unanimous consent.—Vice-President W. A. Wheeler, U. S. Senate, Feb. 5: *Id.*, p. 995/1.

1882 [This proposition opposes] what is called the *Anthony rule*. That rule has been usually adopted at each session of the Senate for a number of years. It was first adopted ten or twelve years ago, and it has operated very well. A great number of bills were passed under the five-minute rule and the docket was very largely reduced.—Mr. John Sherman of O., U. S. Senate, Feb. 3: *Id.*, p. 870/2.

1882 The *Anthony rule*, ... whether it be sufficient to accomplish all we desire or not, so far as it has gone has been productive of good. Hundreds of cases have been disposed of under it.—Mr. G. F. Hoar of Mass., U. S. Senate, *Id.*, p. 872/1.

Antifogmatic. A dram to keep the fog out of one's throat. [1788-1855.]

1815 A club of Virginia politicians met . . . . to take their *antifogmatics* alias *Mint Sling*.—Norfolk (Va.) *Public Ledger*, Apr. 10, p. 2/2. (From the *Alexandria Gazette*.)

Antipode. A direct opposite.

1848 In politics [Mr. Fulton] was our *antipode*.—Wilmington (N. C.) *Commercial*, Dec. 21, p. 2/1.

Anti-Renters. Those tenants in several counties of N. Y., holding land from the "patroons," who on the death of Stephen van Rensselaer in 1839 refused to pay rent: Stephen himself having in many instances failed to collect. They made a forcible resistance, and the dispute was compromised in 1850. (Brown's "Dict. of American Politics," 1892.)

Anti-scalping. Scalping is the selling at a profit, by speculators; it is also dealing in transportation tickets at less than official prices.

1897 Sundry petitions for the passage of the "*anti-scalping* railroad ticket bill" were presented.—Feb. 19: *C. R.*, pp. 1989-91, &c. The bill itself is to be found on p. 2466.

Anti-slavery. Opposed to slavery: the opposite of Pro-slavery. The American use is rather more extended than the English.

1823   *Anti-Slavery* Committee, *Anti-Slavery* Society. (N. E. D.)

1827   The *Anti-Slavery* Monthly Reporter was published in London; and followed by the *Anti-Slavery* Reporter, 1833, the *Anti-Slavery* Record, 1835, and the *Anti-Slavery* Examiner, 1836: all of New York.

1863   Men undervalue the *antislavery* movement.—Wendell Phillips, 'Speeches,' iii, 36.

1865   An *anti-slavery* man in sentiment, and yet heretofore a large owner of slaves. . . . The American sentiment is decidedly *anti-slavery*. . . . I say now from my own experience that the public sentiment of the southern people is *anti-slavery*. And I assert a proposition which may startle some gentlemen, but which I believe in my heart to be true, that the State of S. C. is *anti-slavery*.—Mr. Rollins of Mo., H. R., Jan. 13: *C. G.*, pp. 260-1.

1865   The gentleman from Ky. [Mr. Mallory, may pass on this reconstruction bill] in such manner as he may deem best, whether it be *anti-slavery* or pro-slavery.—Mr. James F. Wilson of Ia., H. R., Feb. 22: *Id.*, p. 1001/1.

Anxious seat. This expression explains itself. [1835-1857.]

1894   I am glad to see so many gentlemen "on the *anxious seat*."—Mr. T. B. Reed of Me., H. R., Feb. 23: *C. R.*, p. 2382/1.

Any. At all. [1817-1888.] Cf. *none* for *not at all.*

1866   There are houses now upon [League Island] with brick chimneys, that have stood the storms of years, and have not settled or sunk *any*.—Mr. Leonard Myers of Pa., H. R., June 7: *C. G.*, p. 3014/3.

1868   [He said] that he had not gambled *any* since he was eighteen years old.—Mr. W. P. Fessenden of Me., U. S. Senate, June 29: *Id.*, p. 3581/2.

1870   I did volunteer and stay here, though I did not fight *any*.—Mr. J. W. Nye of Nev., U. S. Senate, Apr. 5: *Id.*, p. 2420/3.

1871   We tell [our people we have made a railroad] away up near the north pole, running from Duluth to the Pacific ocean. That does not help them *any*.—Mr. B. F. Rice of Ark., U. S. Senate, March 3: *Id.*, p. 1957/3.

1894   I mentioned that to the committee, but it did not seem to move them *any*.—Mr. Thomas B. Reed of Me., U. S. Senate, Jan. 24: *Id.*, p. 1348/1.

Anywheres for *anywhere*. [1856-1858.]

1815   Seems to me I can get my living easier by my wits, a-most *ennywheres*.—David Humphreys, "The Yankey in England," p. 49.

A. P. A., The. The "American Protective Association," a body organized first in Ia. in 1887. Its principles were substantially those of the "Know-nothings." It aimed at the restriction of immigration, the refusal of subsidies to all religious and charitable corporations, and the overthrow in particular of the Roman Catholic Church. Harper's "Encycl. of U. S. History" (1902) states that it then held the political balance of power in the U. S., a statement open to grave doubt.

1894   I am not in the councils of the *A. P. A.*, and I do not know whether or not [Mr. W. S. Linton of Mich.] is their chosen mouthpiece.—Mr. T. A. E. Weadock of Mich., H. R., June 13: *C. R.*, p. 6239/1.

1896   There have been men making *A. P. A.* capital on your side, and all sorts of capital, out of this bill.—Mr. J. S. Williams of Miss., H. R., Feb. 4: *Id.*, p. 1309/1.

1896   This organization . . . is known as the "*American Protective Association*,"—a secret, oath-bound, red-lettered, left-handed, dark-lanterned organization, organized lately by a resident of Clinton, Ia. . . . . "America for Americans," and undying hatred to foreigners, are the

first and governing principles . . . . of this order.—Mr. C. H. Gibson of
Md., U. S. Senate, May 14 : *Id.,* p. 5219/2. (Copies of the oaths and
declarations of the *A. P. A.* are appended.)

1900 [It is said that there was] intimidation from a certain organization
known as the *A. P. A.*—Mr. J. H. Gallinger of N. H., U. S. Senate,
Apr. 7 : *Id.,* p. 3887/1.

Apple-butter. See quotation. [1832-1880.]

1870 *Apple-butter* is a substitute for butter ; it is spread upon bread and
eaten in like manner.—Mr. Robert C. Schenck of O., H. R., Apr. 14 :
C. G., p. 2685/1.

1880 If I draw my finger across the page, the ink comes off as though it
were printed with *apple-butter.*—Mr. E. B. Finley of O., H. R.,
March 12 : *C. R.,* p. 1534/2.

Applejack. Apple-brandy. A friend, brought up in Md., writes to me
thus: "To make *applejack* you take a modicum of whiskey, some
sweetening, a dash of spice, a little water, into which you drop a
small, thoroughly roasted, hot apple. If there is any cider about it,
you squeeze it out with your teeth. The idea is to permit the apple
to absorb enough of the delicious compound, and it of course is
bitten and swallowed last." The citations however indicate something different. See also Vol. I. [1865-1885.]

1865 The genuine Virginia stimulant known as *applejack,* or apple whisky.
—*N. Y Tribune,* about March. (N. E. D.)

1868 Mr. Sherman:—Do not they make any *apple-jack* [in Calif.]?
Mr. Stewart:—I never heard that they did. Mr. Davis:—The fruit
[of the apple orchards of the Alleghanies] is mostly applied to the
distillation of apple brandy.—U. S. Senate, July 6 : *C. G.,* pp. 3740-1.

1880 You will have distilleries on every farm, I may say in every cellar :
you will permit the old woman to fill her wash-tub with whisky, and
her milk-pail and tin cans and teapots with *apple-jack* to nourish the
children upon, all under the shade of their own "vine and fig tree,"
and without taxation.—Mr. D. C. Haskell of Kan., H. R., May 1 :
C. R., p. 2934/2.

1880 I wish my friend much success in his temperance work in the good
old North State, if he can get two barrels of untaxed peach brandy
and *apple-jack* in every household for family use.—Mr. Thos. Updegraff of O., H. R., *Id.,* p. 2936/1.

1890 I had had some experience with Ky. *apple-jack,* which was popularly
believed among the boys would dissolve a piece of the fattest pork
thrown into it.—Statement of John McElroy, Apr. 21 : *Id.,* p. 3636/2.

Apple-trees, within two rows of. See quotation.

1869 It does not come, if I may use the expression. *within two rows of
apple-trees* of the point here at all.—Mr. Roscoe Conkling of N. Y.,
U. S. Senate, March 2 : *C. G.,* p. 1793/2.

Appreciate, appreciation. To raise in value. [1779-1789-96.]

1864 The terms of this letter certainly *appreciate* General Butler in my
estimation.—Mr. Garrett Davis of Ky., U. S. Senate, June 8 : *C. G.,*
p. 2796/2.

1865 A Federal victory *appreciates* our currency ; but a Federal disaster
depreciates it.—Mr. Edgar Cowan of Pa., U. S. Senate Feb. 7 : *Id.,*
p. 639/1.

1869 The business of this Congress ought to be to adopt a policy which will
appreciate greenbacks, and do away with the difference between specie
and paper.—Mr. Shelby L. Cullom of Ill., H. R., Jan. 27 : *Id.,* p. 653/1.

1869 I was glad to see our bonds *appreciate* in the market, and that the
holders should get the benefit of the *appreciation.*—Mr. John Sherman
of O., U. S. Senate, Feb. 27 : *Id.,* p. 1669/1.

1874　It is admitted on all hands that if you receive a portion of the customs duties in greenbacks, you will *appreciate* the value of the greenbacks.— Mr. A. G. Thurman of O., U. S. Senate, Apr. 2: *C. R.,* p. 2725/2.

1878　If silver has depreciated, gold has correspondingly *appreciated.*—Mr. A. S. Merrimon of N. C., U. S. Senate, Feb. 13: *Id.,* p. 980/2.

Approach. To come near a man for the purpose of bribery. As a noun, access for that purpose.

1893　Nearly every bit of everything that is said about public men being corrupted or *approached* is false. . . . The idea that [Mr. Hooper] was subject to *approach* is ridiculous.—Mr. D. W. Voorhees of Ind., U. S. Senate, Sept. 28: *C. R.,* p. 1874/1.

Approbate, approbating. To approve. [1802-1861.]

1782　The authority [of Brooklyn] have run into a great error in *approbating* an additional number of public-houses.—Letter of Israel Putnam, Feb. 18. (Harper's "Encycl. U. S. Hist.," vii, 335.)

1870　While it is true that [polygamy] did prevail to some extent in ancient times, yet in no single instance does Holy Writ *approbate* it.—Mr. S. M. Cullom of Ind., H. R., Feb. 17: *C. G.,* p. 1373/2.

Arbor day. A day set apart annually for the planting of trees by school-children. The custom was begun in Neb. in 1872. (Century Dict.)

1892　[We are] causing such rapid depletion of our forests, that in every quarter of the country *"arbor days"* are days named by law, and also by custom, for planting forest trees to make lumber for the generations yet to come.—Mr. W. J. Stone of Ky., H. R., June 18: *C. R.,* p. 5404/2.

Argonauts. Adventurers who went to Calif. in 1849. See also Vol. I.

1892　He must have had the mental power and balance which "the *Argonauts*" termed a level head.—Mr. John T. Morgan of Ala., U. S. Senate, March 25, in his eulogy of Senator George Hearst: *C. R.,* p. 2565/1.

Arid belt. A rainless tract of land.

1894　In this entire *arid belt* nature has provided in one way or another a sufficient amount of water, and all the necessary material for the construction of dams, basins, and reservoirs.—Mr. W. V. Lucas of S. D., H. R., Aug. 11: *C. R.,* p. 8430/1.

Arkansas toothpicks. See quotation. [1840-1869.]

1837　Act of the Ala. legislature, approved June 30:—"That if any person carrying any knife or weapon, known as Bowie knives, or *Arkansaw toothpicks,* on a sudden rencounter shall cut or stab another with such knife, by reason whereof he dies, it shall be adjudged murder."— *Baltimore Commercial Transcript,* Sept. 21, p. 2/4.

1882　Things supposed to be required by "honor" will coarsen as they descend among the vulgar; . . . . the duel will develop into a street or bar-room fight with *"Arkansas toothpicks"* as the weapons.—*The Nation,* Dec. 7, p. 485. (Century Dict.)

Arm-in-arm Convention, The. This was the Republican convention which met in Philadelphia in 1866, and supported Andrew Johnson's reconstruction policy. "Its name arose from the fact that the members from Mass. and from S. C. entered [the hall] together." (Brown, "Dict. of American Politics," 1892.)

Armpits, to the. Completely, utterly.

1869　[The U. P. R. R.] Company is steeped in fraud *to the very armpits.* —Mr. J. W. Nye of Nev., U. S. Senate, Apr. 6: *C. G.,* p. 549/1.

1871　A poor mistaken man, who had been steeped in this rebellion to *his armpits* for years.—U. S. Senate, Feb. 17: *Id.,* p. 1343/1.

1878　There certainly has been a purgatory in the vicinity of this chamber, and I know that Colonel Polk has been in it *up to his armpits.*—Mr. H. B. Wright of Pa., H. R., Feb. 1: *C. R.,* p. 713/1.

Army worm. The larva of the cotton moth.
1852 [They] lay millions of eggs, and thus they increase until they deserve
the name of *army worm.*—Letter in DeBow, "S. and W. States," I,
171. (N. E. D.)
1864 The crops are poor, and every cotton-field destroyed by the *"army
worms,"* as if in imitation of its more intelligent namesakes.—Letter to
the *Sumter Watchman,* n. d. See *C. R.,* Apr. 21, 1890, p. 3643/1.
[Compare with this "Joel," ii, 25.]
1865 Seriously injured by the *army-worm.*—*Pall Mall Gazette,* No. 192,
p. 6/1. (N. E. D.)
At that. "Into the bargain." [1830-1906.]
1863 [This would be] to suppose the gentleman from Ill., is a dog, and
a very mean dog *at that.*—Mr. Shellabarger of O., H. R., Jan. 27:
C. G., p. 68/3, App.
1864 [They] were advocating the election of a man for the gubernatorial
office in my State, who was an open and avowed advocate of the
right of secession,—an outlaw *at that* [*i.e.,* Mr. Vallandigham].—Mr.
Rufus P. Spalding of O., H. R., Jan. 22: *Id.,* p. 315/3.
1865 What kind of a torpedo-boat would a vessel make, that cannot go
faster than three and a half miles an hour, and cannot be trusted by
herself *at that?*—Mr. Benjamin Wade of O., U. S. Senate, Feb. 17:
Id., p. 868/2.
1867 I have seen him with two different hats,—a slouched hat, and a silk
high-crowned hat with a medium brim, and not very sleek *at that.*—
Exam. of D. A. Hull, March 19: *Id.,* p. 296/1.
1870 See BUNCOMBE.
1871 I am not prepared to censure the people of Georgia, or of any other
southern State, because they have not been able to detect those who,
under the cover of night, and masked *at that,* go about the country
doing individuals wrong.—Mr. Joshua Hill of Ga., U. S. Senate,
Apr. 7: *Id.,* p. 536/2.
1872 To that class of men there is only one plat of ground that they are
willing to give to an Indian, and that is about six feet, and at least
six feet underground *at that.*—Mr. Lot M. Morrill of Me., U. S.
Senate, Apr. 5: *Id.,* p. 2197/1.
1877 The Senate will have to feed by platoons, and rather small ones *at that,*
if the feeding is to be done here.—Mr. Róscoe Conkling of N. Y., U. S.
Senate, Nov. 26: *C. R.,* p. 651/1.
1878 [A proposition] which would shock the sense of a child, and a young
child *at that.*—U. S. Senate, Apr. 4: *Id.,* p. 2268/1.
1879 They want hundreds of millions of money, and short dollars *at that.*
—Mr. Wilber, H. R., May 16: *Id.,* p. 1408/2.
1900 See ENGINEER. See OCTOPUS.
1905 Fifty years of age, and young *at that.*—Percy White, "The Patient
Man," ch. 3.
Atherton Gag, The. A name applied to a resolution introduced into
Congress in 1838, and in force for six or seven years, declaring that
all bills or petitions on the subject of slavery should be tabled without debate. The mover of it, Mr. Charles G. Atherton (1804-1853)
was a U. S. Senator from N. H. from 1843 to 1849.
1865 [Slavery] demanded silence in this House and in the Senate, and we
adopted the *"Atherton gag."*—Mr. Scofield of Pa., H. R., Jan. 6:
C. G., p. 144/3.
1867 The Senator from Me. [Mr. Fessenden] cannot have forgotten the
Atherton gag. . . . . How was it regarded at the time? Was it not
justly an offense and a stench in the nostrils of every patriot citizen?
—Mr. Charles Sumner of Mass., U. S. Senate, July 5: *Id.,* p. 493/2.

Augusta Boys. This name was assumed by a body of citizens of Augusta County, Va., who opposed the efforts of Governor Francis Fauquier and Col. Andrew Lewis to bring to justice the murderers of certain Cherokee Indians. The "Augusta Boys" issued a proclamation, June 4, 1765; and the "Paxton Boys" of Pa. offered to help them. See *Journal of House of Burgesses,* 1765, p. xxiv. (Richmond, 1907.)

Auntie. Applied to an old negro woman. [1852.]
1879 See UNCLE.

Available, availability. An available person or thing is one that can be used. [1840-1909.]
1837 The New York papers are discussing whether the most talented, or the most *available* man, shall be reëlected as candidate for the next presidency.—*Baltimore Commercial Transcript,* June 20, p. 2/2.
1844 The traits of character which, in the estimation of the Whigs, constitute the *ne plus ultra* of *"availability."*—Speech of Mr. Bidlack of Pa., H. R., June 4: p. 12/1 of the same as separately published.

Ax to grind. A purpose to serve. [1815-1869.]
1854 In passing the White House a few days ago, a friend, looking at its graceful columns and fine proportions, suddenly exclaimed, *"Axes ground here."*—Mr. John Wheeler of N. Y., H. R., Feb. 15: p. 3 of the speech as separately published.

Axeman. See quotations. [1777-1854.]
1818 Four likely Negro Men, Three of them very good *Axemen* and Sawyers.—Norfolk (Va.) *Beacon,* Dec. 29, p. 1/2. (Advt.)
1888 Scarcely an ax is swung today in a New England forest that is not swung by a Canadian, hired through the winter to take the place of a Yankee *axman.*—Mr. J. E. Russell of Mass., H. R., May 5: *C. R.,* p. 3764/1.
1888 There are times when the touching appeal to the *axman* to spare the tree is not founded in wisdom.—Mr. J. D. Taylor of O., H. R., May 31: *Id.,* p. 4790/1.

B

Babe. An infant. [1798-1842.]
1863 In some instances, after having murdered the parents, the savages placed *babes* in cooking-stoves, built fires, and left them to roast to death.—Mr. W. Windom of Minn., H. R., Feb. 28: *C. G.,* p. 141/3, App.
1894 See INFANT INDUSTRIES.
1895 There are Indians today in the U. S. who are just as helpless in respect to the arts of civilization as a *babe.*—Mr. D. T. Flynn of Okla., H. R., Jan. 16: *C. R.,* p. 1041/1.

Babiche. A rawhide thong. Canadian Fr., perhaps from Micmac *ababich.*
1902 The trader brought along with him the gun and the curved knife, with which men built better canoes and the women cut the finest leather, called *babiche.*—O. T. Mason in *Popular Science Monthly,* p. 340. (Century Dict.)

Baby act, the. Pleading the baby act is primarily setting up the legal defence of infancy in an action *ex contracta.* The term is applied also to some other evasions of responsibility to which the speaker objects.
1873 [Mr. Bingham] did not plead ignorance or *the baby act.*—Mr. C. A. Eldredge of Wisc., H. R., Feb. 28: *C. G.,* p. 191/1, App.
1882 We ought not to complain that the instrumentalities that we have set up, of which we have control, are being daily used and manipulated for the purpose of defrauding the Government. It is *pleading the baby act.*—Mr. P. B. Plumb of Kan., U. S. Senate, Feb. 9: *C. R.,* p. 1011/1.

1888 [Mr. S. S. Cox] admits the authorship of that infamous work, "The Buckeye Abroad," but *pleads the baby act* and says he was a boy when he wrote it, though the year after its publication he represented the Government in Peru.—Mr. W. Woodburn of Nev., H. R., Aug. 18: *Id.*, p. 440/1, App.

1891 [These men] are *pleading the baby act,* . . . saying that they were under duress.—Mr. F. M. Cockrell of Mo., U. S. Senate, Feb. 7: *Id.*, p. 2329/1.

1894 I am not disposed to *plead the baby act;* but when I state that I was born [in] Oct., 1850, [it] may perhaps explain any dereliction on my part as to bearing arms in the war of the rebellion.—Mr. H. U. Johnson of Ind., H. R., May 25: *Id.*, p. 5310/1.

1894 See INFANT INDUSTRIES.

1896 Let these claims be met upon their merits. Do not *plead the "baby act"* by saying that they are thirty years old, and therefore must not be paid.—Mr. T. M. Mahon of Pa., H. R., Dec. 18: *Id.*, p. 285/2.

Back and forth. To and fro. [1653-1878.]

1872 Various propositions were made [between the U. S. and France] *back and forth.*—Mr. John Sherman of O., U. S. Senate, Dec. 17: *Id.*, p. 243/1.

1874 Almost the only time the Attorney-General could get to read his official mail was while he was going *back and forth* in that carriage. [This was the landaulet that occasioned so much discussion.]—Mr. E. R. Hoar of Mass., H. R., Apr. 25: *C. R.*, p. 3379/1.

1893 Through North River, at the place to which I am referring, the tide sweeps *back and forth* twice every day.—Mr. J. D. Warner of N. Y., H. R., Dec. 20: *Id.*, p. 452/1.

1898 Take the State of Ky., never out of the Union, yet the armies fought *back and forth* over the territory of that State a score of times.—Mr. J. G. Cannon of Ill., H. R., June 21: *Id.*, p. 6215/1.

1899 Some of you . . . . remember when at Vicksburg our boys got so close to the Confederates that they talked *back and forth.*—Mr. W. E. Mason of Ill., U. S. Senate, Feb. 11: *Id.*, p. 1743/1.

Backbone. Firmness, courage, determination, moral principle.

1861 If the Republican Senators insist upon fighting, and they can get the *backbone* again put into their President-elect, and can get Mr. Chase reinstated in the Cabinet, I do not know but that we shall have to fight.—Mr. Louis T. Wigfall of Tex., U. S. Senate, March 2: *C. G.*, p. 1399/1.

1865 There is something ineffably mean in asking a soldier to go and fight for you, when you have not nerve and *backbone* enough to stand by and protect him.—Mr. Daniel Clark of N. H., U. S. Senate, Jan. 28: *Id.*, p. 473/2.

1867 If there is anything for which [Mr. R. C. Schenck of O.] has been noted ever since I first knew him, it is a determined will and *"backbone,"* which would bear him through anything he might undertake.—Mr. Thaddeus Stevens of Pa., H. R., July 10: *Id.*, p. 560/3.

1867 We want men for foreign ministers of more *backbone* and stiffer knees than some we have had. We want such men of *backbone* for Congressmen and committees.—Mr. W. E. Robinson of N. Y., H. R., Nov. 25: *Id.*, p. 791/1.

1870 I think a little Jacksonian *backbone* would be beneficial to some of the gentlemen . . . . who are at the head of our Government.—Mr. H. C. Calkin of N. Y., H. R., Feb. 15: *Id.*, p. 1300/3.

1871 I hope this committee will have *backbone* enough and independence enough to defeat this attempt to increase salaries.—Mr. J. F. Farnsworth of Ill., H. R., Jan. 17: *Id.*, p. 558/2.

1890 We have made no fair trial, we have made no determined effort, we have shown no *backbone.*—Mr. F. M. Cockrell of Mo., U. S. Senate, July 9: *C. R.*, p. 7052/1.

1893   Mr. Dolph:—I think it is about time that the Senate shall show a
little *backbone,* because it has never had any on such questions. . . .
I never claimed that the Senate had any *backbone.* That is not the
first instance in which the Senate has shown it had no *backbone.* They
authorized me to proceed, and then backed squarely down. Mr.
Butler:—The Senator from Ore. showed a good deal of *backbone* at
that time, but his *backbone* gave way, and I think his *backbone* will
give way now.—U. S. Senate, Oct. 17: *Id., p.* 2576.

1900   The Republicans who stand by the Constitution, though Republicans
with *backbones* not made out of angle worms.—Mr. D. A. deArmand
of Mo., H. R., Feb. 27: *Id.,* p. 98/1, App.

1912   The Colonel [Mr. Roosevelt] was charged with saying that McKinley
had no more *backbone* than a chocolate éclair. But his own spinal
column has appeared just a bit flexible in this affair of Senator Root
as temporary chairman.—*N. Y. Evening Post,* June 6, p. 4/6.

Backbone Company, The.   The New Orleans, Baton Rouge, and
Vicksburg R. R. Co.

1884   Mr. Oates:—Here was the grant to the *Backbone company;* the
five years' limit had about expired. . . . Mr. Van Eaton:—Grant
for the sake of argument that the *"Backbone" corporation* was [a] corrupt and swindling body . . . . Grant that in all the "carpet-bag" era
there was no worse corporation than this; yet if the company com-
plied with its agreement, what has its moral character to do with the
[matter]? It is true that the *Backbone people* were unable, either
from poverty, rascality, or I care not what, to construct their road.—
H. R., June 26: *C. R.,* pp. 5639, 5645. See also 5695.

Back country.   The interior. [1755-1845.]

1876   West Point for all practical purposes is an isolated place. There is
no *back country* to speak of. All supplies to it come from Albany or
New York by the boats.—Mr. S. A. Hurlbut of Ill., H. R., Jan. 26:
C. R., p. 668/2.

Backing and filling.   The alternate movement of a steamboat. Literal
and metaphorical. [1848-1887.]

1876   Notwithstanding all of his [Mr. E. A. Rollins's] *"backing and filling,"*
his testimony . . . was calculated. to leave the impression that there
was "something rotten in the state of Denmark."—Mr. J. Proctor
Knott of Ky., H. R., Aug. 3: *C. R.,* p. 5125/1.

1897   [The Government will appear] oscillating, imbecile, and uncertain in
its politics, *backing and filling,* to suit the circumstances of the politics
in the country.—Mr. J. T. Morgan of Ala., U. S. Senate, Jan. 22: *Id.,*
p. 1056/2.

Backings.   See quotation.

1867   What run [in distilling, after the doubling tub is removed], are called
"backings." . . . . These *backings* are too valuable to be lost, and
are placed back into the still, run through again, and come out doublings, or proof whisky.—Mr. Samuel McKee of Ky., H. R., Jan. 21:
C. G., p. 60/1, App.

Back inhabitant.   A dweller in the back country.

1757   The Petition of sundry *Back Inhabitants* of the said county of Fairfax.
—*Journal of House of Burgesses of Va.,* Apr. 22: Vol. VIII, 432.
(Richmond, 1909.)

Back lands.   Lands in the interior. [1681-1797.]

1842   When this Government acquired title to the *back lands,* as they were
called, . . . they became a permanent source of revenue.—Mr. Jacob
Thompson of Miss., H. R., Jan. 10, p. 4/1 of the speech as separately
published.

Back number, a.   One who is behind the times. [1910-1911.]

1892   We have not many Indians left in Minn. The Indian is a *back number* there.—Mr. W. D. Washburn of Minn., U. S. Senate, Apr. 5:
C. R., p. 2964/1.

1892 The Indian is in a state of desuetude. He is not of use to the white man. He is not exactly in innocuous desuetude, but still he is a *back number*, as it were.—Mr. D. W. Voorhees of Ind., U. S. Senate, Apr. 6: *Id.*, p. 2990/1.

1893 I heard [it said] that these election laws were a *"back number."* .... If they are a *"back number,"* why should not [both parties unite in expunging them]?—Mr. B. E. Russell of Ga., H. R., Oct. 5: *Id.*, p. 2161/2.

1893 [The Republicans have seldom of late] waved the "ensanguined garment," because it is a *"back number."*—H. R., p. 2163/1.

1893 See PICAYUNE.

1894 The precedent-hunter is a *back number*, stale and moss-grown, standing in the shade of the glory which belongs to dead ages.—Mr. O. M. Kem of Neb., H. R., Aug. 10: *Id.*, p. 8397/1.

1896 The election of 1892 is a *"back number,"* and the men who were elected in that contest have now been condemned to private life.—Mr. R. Pearson of N. C., H. R., March 19: *Id.*, p. 2980/1.

Back of. Behind, in the rear of. [1774-1910.]

1840 If he misstated, he asked his friends from Georgia, *back of* him, to correct him.—Mr. John C. Calhoun, U. S. Senate, Apr. 1. ("Works," 1856, III, 492.)

1857 The country which stretches *back of* Shanghai.—Robert Tomes, "The Americans in Japan," p. 83. (N. E. D.)

1866 The Government has been forced to send [its ironclads] up the Delaware river, and place them in the channel *back of* League Island.— Mr. A. H. Rice of Mass., H. R., June 7: *C. G.*, p. 3020/2.

1874 The question has been put to me by members, "Is there anybody speculating *back of* this bill?"—Mr. John A. Kasson of Ia., H. R., June 16: *C. R.*, p. 5058/1.

1875 The home lies *back of* the Sunday School.—E. H. Sears, "Sermons and Songs," p. 287. (N. E. D.)

1892 The ground is directly *back of* the statue.—Mr. E. O. Wolcott of Colo., U. S. Senate, June 1: *C. R.*, p. 4888/2.

1893 This movement is being engineered and backed up by the same parties who engineered the raid on the Reading Railroad a few days ago. The great public philanthropist, J. Pierpont Morgan, was *back of* that end, and he and his gambling friends are *back of* this.—Mr. Abner Taylor of Ill., H. R., Feb. 27: *Id.*, p. 2238/1.

Back seat, to take a. To occupy an inferior position. [1863-1907.]

1866 [That the seceders] should expect, or dream, or imagine that they have any other right but to *take a back seat* [until reconstruction is accomplished] is an instance of impudence having no parallel in profane history.—Mr. John Baker of Ill., H. R., Jan. 27: *C. G.*, p. 462/3.

1866 When [Andrew Johnson] was acting with the Union party, he proclaimed to the world that "traitors should *take a back seat.*" Now he proclaims that traitors shall have a front seat. He would give them front seats in this Hall!—Mr. Ebon C. Ingersoll of Ill., H. R., May 5: *Id.*, p. 2402/2.

1866 I would disfranchise every voluntary rebel in the land, and place him where ... Andrew Johnson of Tennessee, at a time when the patriotic predominated over the sinister elements of his nature, said he should be placed, "on the *back seats,*" in the great work of restoring the body politic to health and vigor.—Mr. John W. Longyear of Mich., H. R., May 10: *Id.*, p. 2536/3.

Backset. A reverse; a rebuff. [1721-1816.]

1878 We [in the South] cannot afford that there shall be another financial *backset.*—Mr. John W. Johnston of Va., U. S. Senate, Feb. 7: *C. R.*, p. 823/1.

1911 The labor union leaders see in the present outcome of the McNamara affair a distinct *backset* to the principle of labor unionism. But there is no disposition on the part of a fair-minded public to discourage the plan or policy of labor organization on lawful lines.—*Sunday Oregonian*, Dec. 3, p. 8/1.

Backset. To re-plough in the autumn. [1883.]

1894 In some cases it will pay to "break and *backset*" the roadway to kill out the weeds.—'Report on the Russian Thistle,' *C. R.*, July 31, p. 8047/2.

Back settlements. Those in the interior.

1763 Measures are at this time concerting, for the relief and protection of the *back settlements.*—The *New York Gazette*, quoted in the *Gentleman's Magazine*, Sept., p. 456/1.

Back-spring. The spring at the rear of the body of a vehicle.— (Century Dict.)

1890 Anybody who went into a place where he did not know everybody, and know what were the *back springs* of consideration.—Mr. G. F. Edmunds of Vt., U. S. Senate, July 19: *C. R.*, p. 7463/2.

Back taxes. Here, taxes already paid. [1788.]

1869 I do not like this changing of the laws to return *back taxes* which may be millions in value.—Mr. B. F. Butler of Mass., H. R., March 30: *C. G.*, p. 379/2.

Back track, to take the. To retreat from one's position. Possibly also to retrograde, and figuratively, to betray. [1802-1857.]

1869 We all have occasionally to *take the back track.* None of us are so proud as never to confess that we are wrong.—Mr. Rufus P. Spalding of O., H. R., Feb. 26: *C. G.*, p. 1606/1.

1888 If the gentleman . . . desires now to *take the back track;* if he desires to modify [his] statement, I have no objection.—Mr. A. J. Hopkins of Ill., H. R., June 9: *C. R.*, p. 5077/2.

1892 You are arresting progress and *taking the back track* on civilization.—Mr. A. J. Cummings of N. Y., H. R., June 6: *Id.*, p. 444/2, App.

Backwoodsmen. Dwellers in the backwoods. [1803-1848.]

1814 We are charged with being *backwoodsmen*, men who never saw a ship till convened here.—Mr. John C. Calhoun, H. R., Feb. 25: "Works" (1856), II, 79.

1824 Plain unsophisticated *backwoodsmen* like plain and open dealing.—*Cincinnati Gazette*, Apr. 30, p. 1/2.

Bacon, v. To turn into bacon.

1890 We consumed or sold our own pork, and we *baconed* it ourselves.—Mr. J. B. Morgan of Miss., H. R., Aug. 20: *C. R.*, p. 8887/1.

Badger, v. To hesitate, to shilly-shally. Rare.

1862 Then what are we *badgering* about [it] here for? [The bill for calling out the state militia.]—Mr. Edgar Cowan of Pa., U. S. Senate, July 11: *C. G.*, p. 3250/3.

Bagasse. Refuse of cane stalks. [1835-1875.]

1888 Even the refuse stalks, or *bagasse* . . . cannot be utilized [as common fuel].—Mr. John H. Gear of Ia., H. R., May 11: *C. R.*, p. 4015/1.

Baggage. This word, in the U. S., has superseded *luggage*. [1812-1860.]

1815 [You have] to get the *baggage* aboard; and help about the house.—David Humphreys, "The Yankey in England," p. 31.

[1875 The Pinchback swindle has been postponed, and this resolution ought to be kept as *luggage* to go with it . . . for it is a part of the *luggage* belonging to the swindle.—Mr. W. W. Eaton of Conn., U. S. Senate, March 20: *C. R.*, p. 118/2.]

Bagworm. Any one of several insects which, in the larval state, construct a baglike case and carry it about for protection.

1862　On the avenue and in the parks you will find the evergreen trees . . . .
being destroyed by the *bagworm.* . . . We have no bird that can tear
or penetrate the tough cocoon or covering in which it lives.—Mr.
William M. Davis of Pa., H. R., Jan. 8 : *C. G.,* p. 232.

Balance. The remainder of anything. [1819-1882.]

1807　The whole of the Danish fleet had arrived in England, with part of
the British ships; the *balance* was daily expected.—Norfolk (Va.)
Gazette, Dec. 15, p. 3/2.

1845　See App. XV, Vol. II.

1866　This road to the extent of six or seven miles is in Oregon; the
balance of it is in Washington Territory.—Mr. Hiram Price of Ia.,
H. R., Dec. 18 : *C. G.,* p. 173/1.

1875　Not a man of them was hung. Only five were shot, and the *balance*
escaped.—Mr. J. D. C. Atkins of Tenn., H. R., Feb. 27 : *C. R.,*
p. 1920/2.

1876　See MOSSBACK.

1892　The vice of the gentleman's position is that he wants to construe part
of the Constitution and ignore the *balance.*—Mr. W. C. Oates of Ala.,
H. R., Aug. 4 : *Id.,* p. 7046/1.

1892　See WHAT IS IT.

Bald Eagle of Rhode Island, The. Tristram Burges, 1770-1853.

1893　Fifty years ago, John Randolph of Roanoke . . . . denounced New
England and New England institutions. The grand old man, known
as *the Bald Eagle of Rhode Island* (Tristram Burges) rose to reply.—
Mr. J. L. Wilson of Wash., H. R., Oct. 16 : *C. R.,* p. 2561/1.

Bald-face. Old brown whiskey.

1849　If you 'er got any more of that *bald-face,* pour it out.—Wilmington
(N. C.) *Commercial,* Oct. 27, p. 1/6.

Ballot-box stuffers. Intriguers who tamper with the returns.

1866　A few years since, we heard much of a set of fellows in San Francisco who were designated as *ballot-box stuffers.*—Mr. Timothy O.
Howe of Wisc., U. S. Senate, Jan. 10 : *C. G.,* p. 166/1.

1869　Between the rule of an emperor and the rule of a clique of *ballot-box
stuffers,* every intelligent man must prefer the former as less rapacious
and more responsible.—Letter of Horace Greeley to Samuel J. Tilden
(Oct.) quoted in the *C. R.,* Apr. 22, 1879 : p. 681/2.

1882　One mode of ballot-box stuffing was thus described by Mr. Benjamin
Butterworth of O. :—They had been accustomed to have a box so
constructed that the lid would pull out in a groove part of the
way, and on election morning pulling the lid part way back, so the
bottom of the box could be seen, the judge, or one of them, would say,
"You see there is nothing in the box." The box would be closed, and
the balloting proceed. True, the box would appear to be empty, while
under the lid in the top of the box two or three hundred tickets would
be fastened. The box being shut with a thud, the tickets would fall
down.—H. R., July 7 : *C. R.,* p. 5738/2.

Baltimore-bird. The oriole. [1775.]

1715　Baltemore-bird, a beautiful Bird in Maryland, with black and yellow
Feathers.—Kersey, "Dictionarium Anglo-Britannicum."

Baltimore plan, the. See quotation.

1895　Briefly summarized, the *Baltimore plan* proposed, in order to procure
a "safe and elastic currency" :—Repeal the provision requiring the
deposit of bonds to secure circulation; allow the issue of circulation
to 50 per cent of paid-up unimpaired capital, &c., &c. . . . . . Those
who argue that the *Baltimore plan* is good, because the present system
of national banking has proved so under the stress of thirty years'
experience, are [greatly] astray.—Remarks of Mr. J. H. Wellock,
quoted by Mr. W. A. Stone of Pa., H. R., Jan. 8 : *C. R.,* pp. 168-9.
[The whole extract deserves examination.]

1896 What has become of the *"Baltimore plan"* and the "Carlisle plan" for banking currency? The Egyptian mummies across yonder in the Smithsonian Institution are not more dead than these plans.—Mr. S. C. Hyde of Wash., H. R., Feb. 6: *Id.*, p. 489/1, App.

Baltimore platform, the. See first quotation.

1866 I desire to present here the *Baltimore platform* upon which Andrew Johnson was elected. [It is accordingly set forth.]—Mr. Randall of Pa., H. R., May 5: *C. G.*, p. 2406/3.

1866 I propose to return to the Senator from Wisc. (Mr. Doolittle) and the Senator from Pa. (Mr. Cowan) for the purpose of determining whether they or others stand upon this *Baltimore platform*. . . . If that platform is large enough, if there is any room for others, I propose to stand there with them for awhile, until they push me off or leave it. The *Baltimore platform* was the political direction . . . upon which the last battle was fought and won, and I propose to hang to it.—Mr. James W. Nye of Nev., U. S. Senate, May 10: *Id.*, p. 2522/3.

Banco. A tract of land transferred by the shifting of a river. Spanish. See quotation.

1888 Sometimes the stream will suddenly cut a new channel, ... and in a single day, by a cut off, a tract of *"banco"* of a hundred acres will be found to be on the other side of the river. . . . When a man smuggles from a *banco*, it is almost impossible to catch and convict him. . . . Some *bancos* increase by deposit; some wear away till they are entirely swept off.—Mr. R. R. Hitt of Ill., H. R., Sept. 25: *C. R.*, p. 8937/1.

Bandore. See quotation. See Vol. I under **Banjo.** [1764-1836.]

1615 A woman loves to heare sweet musick on the Lute, Cithern, or *Bandora.*—Joseph Swetnam, "Arraignment, &c.," p. 38.

1715 *Bandore,* a Musical Instrument.—Kersey, "Dictionarium Anglo-Britannicum."

Band-wagon. One fitted up to carry a band, commonly used in circus processions.

1893 It is a lamentable fact that, as this country had been climbing the hill of prosperity for the last twenty years, and as we were viewing our possessions with complacency from the sunlit peaks of national greatness,—that at such a time our commercial enemy from across the water, with the Cobden Club and the free trader on this side, should come along with a *bandwagon* loaded with hobgoblins, and break up our picnic and obscure the sun.—Mr. John W. Moon of Mich., H. R., Aug. 25: *C. R.*, p. 897/1.

Banian. A loose shirt or undervest. See **Banyan,** Vol. I. [1725-1867.]

1732 I found him in a Night-Cap and *Banian,* which is his ordinary dress in that retired part of the Country.—W. Byrd, "Writings," p. 381. (1901.)

Bank, v. To form a bank at a gaming-table; hence colloquially, to wager with security: [to] trust as certain or sure: as, I would *bank* on his honesty; I'm not *banking* on that. (Standard Dict.)

1892 Mr. O'Ferrall:—I think the gentleman is succeeding mighty well in impeaching his own witness. Mr. Cobb:—O, I am not *banking* heavily on [him] as an honest man.—H. R., Apr. 20: *C. R.*, p. 249/2, App.

Bank-barn. A barn built on sloping ground, so that three sides of the lower story are surrounded by earth, the fourth being unbanked.— (Century Dict.)

1894 On my father's farm, when I was a boy, there stood a big *bank-barn,* and at the back of the barn there was a pool which in the summer was a hog-wallow.—Mr. J. C. Sibley of Pa., H. R., Jan. 18: *C. R.*, p. 1036/1.

1903 Advertisement in *Forest and Stream,* Feb. 21. (Century Dict.)

Banner county. That one which surpasses the others. See **Banner State**, Vol. I. [1840-1909.]

1866 I have shown that [Mr. Price] came within a few votes of losing the *banner county* of his own State and of his own residence.—Mr. John A. Kasson of Ia., H. R., Jan. 15: *C. G.*, p. 241/3.

1875 Barbour County can be safely put down as the *banner county.*—*Clayton* (Ala.) *Courier*: cited in *C. R.*, Feb. 4, p. 19/1, App.

1888 Clay County is the *banner Democratic county* of my Congressional district.—Mr. A. M. Dockery of Mo., H. R., Aug. 15: *Id.*, p. 7598/1.

1890 In the *banner county* in that Territory (Wyo.), the election was held in a back room of a store by three men who had a cigar box [to put the ballots in].—Mr. J. K. Jones of Ark., U. S. Senate, June 26: *Id.*, p. 6517/2.

1890 One of the arguments used before the Legislature in favor of Weston County [Wyo.] is that Newcastle is the *banner* town of Crook County. —Wyo. paper, cited *Id.*, p. 6522/1.

Barbecue. A feast on what is barbecued; a social entertainment at which one or more large animals are roasted or broiled whole.— (Webster.) [1690-1852.]

1864 Seldom has the Senate of the U. S. been compelled to listen to such a farrago of brutality, indecency, treason, and falsehood. This exhibition would not elevate even the Senator [Mr. Garrett Davis] in a Kentucky *barbecue.*—Mr. Henry Wilson of Mass., U. S. Senate, Jan. 13: *C. G.*, p. 182/3.

Barber shop. [1857-1910.]

1862 Our mails have been filled with useless books, sent to barrooms and *barber shops.*—Mr. Theodore M. Pomeroy of N. Y., H. R., Jan. 9: *C. G.*, p. 258/3.

1876 Mr. Mulligan was in the *barber-shop* . . . . and Mr. Blaine followed him into the *barber-shop,* and commenced to entreat . . . . that Mulligan would give up those letters which Blaine had addressed to Warren Fisher.—Mr. Eppa Hunton of Va., H. R., June 5: *C. R.*, p. 3611/2. [These were the well-known "Mulligan letters."]

[1878 Prosperity to the laboring man, to the agriculturist, to the man who works in the *blacksmith shop* and in the *shoemaker shop.*—Mr. S. B. Chittenden of N. Y., H. R., Feb. 26: *C. R.*, p. 1357/1.]

1911 On the morning that Taft arrived Huffman went into a *barber shop* to get shaved.—*The Argonaut*, December.

Bargain counter. A counter at which remnants or other so-called bargains are exposed for sale.

1890 You may go into any of the large mercantile establishments, even that of my respectable friend, Mr. John Wanamaker of Philadelphia, the Postmaster-General, and you will find what they call a *bargain counter.* —Mr. G. G. Vest of Mo., U. S. Senate, Aug. 28: *C. R.*, p. 9258/1.

1894 Circumstances are so changed that we may get some bargains at the *"bargain-counter";* but that does not affect the question of general prices.—Mr. H. D. Money of Miss., H. R., Jan. 24: *Id.*, p. 1346/2.

1900 Were the Spaniards right in their derisive epithets, calling us "pigs" and a *"bargain-counter nation"*?—Mr. J. A. Norton of O., H. R., Feb. 28: *Id.*, p. 77/2, App.

Bark-mill. A mill for grinding bark. [1829-1885.]

1824 Samuel Andres, Jr., of L'Acadie, near Montreal, advertised for lease "a Bark-house, and a good iron *Bark-mill,* &c."—*Rouse's Point Harbinger*, Feb. 17, p. 4/2.

Barlow knife. This knife is not mentioned in a long list of articles advertised in the Norfolk (Va.) *Beacon*, Dec. 18, 1818, p. 4/1, including "Jack, Pruning, Pen, and 2 to 12 Blade Knives." In 1827, *Id.*, July 3, p. 3/4, C. Hall advertises "Rodgers' Pen, Pocket, Virginia, desk, fruit, camp, trinket, scissor, Spanish, grafting, pruning, farrier's, nail and woodman's Knives." See Vol. I. [1779-1819.]

a.1860 A *Barlow knife,* which I always carry, because I am a Virginian.— G. W. Bagby, "Writings," I, 185 (1884).

1890 The little boy with his *Barlow knife* has to pay nearly twice as much per cent as [the purchaser of a] two dollar and a half Rodgers knife. He did not want to carry a cheap and nasty knife, but the little fellow has to carry a ten cent *Barlow.*—Mr. Z. B. Vance of N. C., U. S. Senate, Aug. 19: *C. R.,* p. 8812/2.

Barnburners. Radical Democrats. [1845-1909.]

1848, 1849 See HUNKER.

1876 The *"barnburner Democrats"* in 1853 tried very hard to adhere to their anti-slavery principles in N. Y., and still support the Pierce administration, and Mr. Greeley, with that inimitable humor which he possessed, said that they found it a very hard road to straddle, like a militia general on Broadway, who finds it an almost impossible task to follow the music and dodge the omnibuses.—Mr. James G. Blaine of Me., H. R., Jan. 13: *C. R.,* p. 404/1.

Barnstorm, v. To make popular addresses in small towns.

1896 [One Cabinet official], the last I heard of him, was *barnstorming* down in Ga. in favor of gold monometallism.—Mr. E. O. Wolcott of Colo., U. S. Senate, Apr. 7: *C. R.,* p. 3661/1.

Barrel of money. A large amount. Here a supply of money for political purposes. Another term is the "pork barrel." [1884.]

1876 In this year "Uncle Sammy's Bar'l" with its contents being poured out by its owner, formed the subject of one of Thomas Nast's cartoons.

1877 To secure the inauguration of his man, who once had a *"bar'l of money."*—Mr. John D. White of Ky., H. R., March 2: *C. R.,* p. 193/2, App.

1879 Facts show that the party trusted for success more in Tilden's *barrel* than in the humbug cry of reform.—Mr. P. C. Hayes of Ill., H. R., Apr. 24: *Id.,* p. 894/1.

1880 [They were] ready to do all they could toward placing in the presidential chair the man [Mr. Tilden] whose *barrel* had been so freely opened to supply the wants of the whisky-loving voters.—H. R., March 10: *Id.,* p. 1451/2.

1880 [They are] establishing "peace on earth" among Democrats . . . . by a liberal use of the contents of Tilden's *"bar'l."*—Mr. L. C. Houk of Tenn., H. R., Apr. 3: *Id.,* p. 2110/1.

1880 In the very instant of one of their [the Democrats'] cataleptic spasms of virtue let Samuel J. Tilden . . . . [point] his finger to the very least of his *"barrels,"* and straightway there would leap into that old, wizened, decrepit, and paralyzed frame a . . . . vigor mightier than "the might of France."—Mr. Thomas B. Reed of Me., H. R., Apr. 23: *Id.,* p. 2691/2.

1893 The Republican party has no organization in Ala. The People's party captured the entire "gang" last fall, Chris McGee and his *"barrel"* included.—Mr. J. F. Stallings of Ala., H. R., Oct. 9: *Id.,* p. 2347/2.

1912 With Hinman's name is coupled usually that of Stephen Clark, of Cooperstown, for Lieutenant-Governor. Hinman is a relatively poor man, and could bring no money for the campaign. Clark has the requisite *"barrel,"* and is credited with political ambitions.—*N. Y. Evening Post,* Sept. 23, p. 1/1.

Barroom. A taproom. [1809-1855.]

1879 Major Morgan . . . . stated that there are more than 500 licensed *barrooms* in the District [of Columbia].—Mr. Monroe of O., H. R., May 16: *C. R.,* p. 1396/2.

Baseballist. A baseball player.

1886 [He is well known] as a *baseballist* among constitutional lawyers, and a constitutional lawyer among *baseballists.*—Mr. J. M. Glover of Mo., H. R., Apr. 2: *C. R.,* p. 3043/2.

Basket clause. An omnibus clause, to include everything not previously specified.

1883 This *basket clause* seems to be a sort of prophetic fine comb with which to search all the possibilities of the future. . . . . It seems to me that there should be a line drawn somewhere in these *basket clauses*, which shall have some reference to the protection of the people. . . . Presently you will find prices raised upon the people, which would not be done were it not for these *basket clauses.*—Mr. John A. Anderson of Kan., H. R., Feb. 13: *C. R.,* p. 2580/1.

1884 Mr. Herbert of Ala.:—Will the gentleman allow me to ask him what became of that *"basket clause"* of 35 per cent? Mr. Russell of Mass.:— The *"basket clause"* in the new law was raised for good and sufficient reasons. The old law gave importers an opportunity to evade the law; that is, to change the styles or names of goods, and then throw them into the *"basket clause"* at lower rates than they would otherwise pay. —H. R., Apr. 16: *Id.,* p. 3015/1.

1897 Mr. Bailey:—If we strike [an item] from the dutiable list, we transfer it to the *"basket clause"* at 25 per cent. Mr. Dingley:—There is no *"basket clause"* to the free list. Mr. Bailey:—I understand that; but if you strike out an article absolutely, and do not transfer it to the free list, it would go to the *"basket clause."*—H. R., March 26: *Id.,* p. 367/2.

Basket of chips, a. See quotations. [1806-1908.]

1819 On which the whole populace flash'd the white grin
Like *a basket of chips,* and poor Georgy gave in.
—T. Moore, "Tom Crib's Memorial to Congress."

1892 My ticket was handed me at once, and the seller looked as pleasant as a *basket of chips.*—Mr. W. W. Bowers of Calif., H. R., March 22: *C. R.,* p. 2367/1.

Basket party. See quotation. Not in N. E. D.

1868 In the southern part of Ill. . . . . they have what they call *basket parties,* where every man carries his own refreshments, and they generally have a very good time. Every man brings his basket and his provisions, and is entirely welcome to the feast.—Mr. Zach. Chandler of Mich., U. S. Senate, Feb. 6: *C. G.,* p. 1008/3. [This is similar to a DUTCH TREAT.]

Basswood township. An extremely bucolic region.

1882 Every man who has practiced before a justice of the peace in a hog case in a *basswood township* would know, &c.—Mr. John J. Ingalls of Kan., U. S. Senate, Feb. 2: *C. R.,* p. 832/1.

Bat one's eyes. To wink. [1851-1867.]

1856 In another column Mr. M. V. Snell gives notice of his Daguerrian Room. We should advse those who desire to have their exact likeness preserved, to be looked at by their children and grandchildren, to go at once to Snell's finely fitted up rooms in the City Hotel. Have on your best look and best clothes and such jewelry as you have paid for, take a seat in Snell's artistic chair and before you can *bat your eye* he will have your face transferred on a nicely polished plate, ready for such a case as you choose yourself—sealed up for all coming time.— The *Weston Weekly Platte Argus,* Sept. 10: cited in the *Kansas City Star,* Nov., 1911.

1867 [President Andrew Johnson] stood like a rock upon the firm base of his own strong convictions when the strong billows of secession lashed around him. He will not swerve from that conviction now, nor even so much as *bat his eye.*—Mr. T. E. Noell of Mo., H. R., Feb. 12: *C. G.,* p. 106/3, App.

1890 He said, "Mitchell, shoot the [rascal] if he *bats his eye* or resents it." —Letter to the Secretary of the Treasury, May 22: *Id.,* June 6, p. 5689/1.

Battle of the Kegs. See quotation. [1778-1833.]

1778 "The *Battle of the Kegs:*—a song. Tune, Moggy Lawder," by Francis Hopkinson, is printed in Col. David Humphreys' 'Life of Putnam,' "Misc. Works" (1790), pp. 279-283.

Bay. See quotation.

1744 In a deed of conveyance, Bellinger to Buchanan, a street in Edmondsbury, S. C., is called *the Bay:* a term applied at that time to streets which fronted directly on the water.—*S. C. Hist. Mag.,* xi, 44 (1910).

Bay State. Massachusetts. [1773-1863.]

1864 The Chairman of the Committee of Elections has no doubt heard of a serious outbreak that was known as "Shay's Rebellion." It occurred in Massachusetts. The old *"Bay State"* has known what it was to nourish traitors.—Mr. Chandler of Va., H. R., May 17: *C. G.,* p. 2319/2.

Bayou. [In La.] an alluvial stream with but little current. [1812-1888.]

1864 [This circumstance] was communicated to me by a citizen of one of the parishes on that *bayou* [the Bayou Tèche], a Mr. Carlie, a Spanish Creole.—Mr. Garrett Davis of Ky., U. S. Senate, Feb. 17: *C. G.,* p. 704/2.

Bean-shooter. The same as a pea-shooter.

1890 Nobody saw anyone shoot, and it is well understood that some boy, with a *bean-shooter* or a little flipping affair, struck Mr. Benjamin and made a little skin wound. . . . I have not excused this rudeness or shooting with a *bean-shooter.*—Mr. C. R. Breckinridge of Ark., H. R., March 4: *C. R.,* p. 1920/1.

1890 This is the organized crowd of white men armed with Winchester rifles—I beg the pardon of the gentleman from Ark., I should have said *"bean-shooters."*—Mr. F. T. Greenhalge of Mass., H. R., March 4: *Id.,* p. 1921/2.

1890 He was . . . knocked down, kicked, and bruised, and shot in the forehead with a leaden bullet from a weapon known as a *"bean-shooter."*—Mr. John Dalzell of Pa., H. R., Sept. 5: *Id.,* p. 9744/2.

Bear a bead. See quotation.

1866 As we say out West, that kind of an argument will not *bear a bead;* it will not bear the touchstone of truth; it has neither rhyme nor reason nor justice in it.—Mr. Ebenezer Dumont of Ind., H. R., June 4: *C. G.,* p. 2955/2.

Bear tree. See quotation.

1832 Their only resource was to hunt *bear trees;* that is, large hollow trees in which bears lay concealed during the winter.—John A. McClung, "Sketches of Western Adventure," p. 24. (Philadelphia.)

Beat. In Ala. and Miss., the principal subdivision of a county: a voting precinct. (Century Dict.)

1893 The evidence shows that his tickets were brought to the polls by friends of Turpin, and peddled there by them. This is shown to have been the case at Steep Creek *beat,* in Lowndes County; . . . . at Hopewell *beat,* in Lowndes County; . . . and at Sandy Ridge, in the same county.—Mr. H. U. Johnson of Ind., H. R., Feb. 28: *C. R.,* p. 2298/1.

1896 He testified that [such men] lived in Lexington precinct, eight miles away. He says:—I am very well acquainted with Lexington *beat,* and only tolerably so with Orrville *beat.*—Mr. C. L. Bartlett of Ga., H. R., March 12: *Id.,* p. 2747/1.

1896 Testimony was taken to show that fraud was committed in certain *beats,*—the River *beat,* Union and one or two others,—no matter what *beat.*—Mr. H. A. Dinsmore of Ark., H. R., March 13: *Id.,* p. 2788/1. [And see the rest of the debate.]

Beat the Dutch. To surpass everything. [1775-1862.]

1831 If this dont *beet the duch* my name aint Enoch.—*The Georgian* (Savannah), Jan. 22, p. 2/5. (From the *Constellation.*)

1850 A dealer advertises "Great tribulation among the *Dutch and Jews,*" on account of his low prices.—Wilmington (N. C.) *Commercial,* Feb. 9, p. 4/4.

Beau ideal. The perfect type or model of the thing in question. [Washington Irving seems to have introduced this expression.]

1820 Wonderfully captivated with the *beau ideal* which they have formed of John Bull.—W. Irving "Sketch-Book." (N. E. D.)

1833 It may be said to be the opinion of the age, that the very *beau ideal* of a perfect government is the government of a majority, acting through a representative body.—Mr. John C. Calhoun, U. S. Senate, Feb. 16: "Works," II, 245 (1856).

1856 That *beau ideal* of a Whig unity,—"Whig President, Whig Congress, and Whig people," . . . . vanished [in 1841].—T. H. Benton, "Thirty Years' View," II, 373/1.

Beaver, busy as a. See **Work like a beaver,** Vol. II. [1775-1888.]

1879 A member of my society was *as busy as a beaver* circulating statements [concerning me].—Letter from Me., Oct. 21: cited in *C. R.,* Apr. 28, 1881, p. 419/1.

Bedizzened. Made dizzy. A nonce-word.

1867 What . . . . if some poor fellow, blinded with dust and *bedizzened* with [the flag's] splendor, had a miscalculation of steps?—Mr. W. E. Robinson of N. Y., H. R., July 12: *C. G.,* p. 8/3, App.

Bed-rock. The ultimate stratum or foundation.

1873 An opinion that stands upon the *bed-rock* of hard logic.—Mr. Smith of N. Y., H. R., Jan. 18: *C. G.,* p. 696/1.

1879 Encycl. Brit. X, 745/1. (N. E. D.)

1881 The transactions [were] based on *bed-rock* prices.—*Chicago Times,* June 11. (N. E. D.)

1883 The family is about down to *bedrock.*—*Century Mag.,* p. 581. (N. E. D.)

1892 We should follow the rule of a State, if at all, not simply because it is a rule of a State, but because it is grounded upon the *bed-rock* of eternal truth.—Mr. J. B. Brown of Ind., H. R., Feb. 25: *C. R.,* p. 1458/1.

1893 We [in the South] have become so poor that we have struck *bedrock,* and had mighty little to pay off.—Mr. M. C. Butler of S. C., U. S. Senate, Oct. 4: *Id.,* p. 2110/1.

1894 [Andrew Jackson and other pioneers] laid the foundation stones of proud and splendid commonwealths upon the enduring *bedrock* of popular liberty.—Mr. H. C. Snodgrass of Tenn., H. R., Jan. 10: *Id.,* p. 662/1.

1896 Taxation and representation must go together, according to the very *bedrock* definition of republican government.—Mr. J. W. Daniel of Va., U. S. Senate, Feb. 5: *Id.,* p. 1329/1.

Beecher's bibles, Beecher's rifles. Firearms furnished to anti-slavery men in Kansas.

1879 The gentleman wonders why, in my review of one of the early elections in Kan., I did not speak of *"Beecher's rifles,"* and did not tell of the organization on our side for the protection of our homes. There never was a *"Beecher's rifle"* sent to Kan., until you had marched armed men into that Territory, . . . and forced upon us thereby a bogus Territorial government. . . . You marched an armed body of men into my town before ever a *"Beecher's bible"* was sent to Kan. . . . I saw a blood-red flag run up the flagstaff, bearing on its crimson folds a single white star. It was the colors of a company of S. C. militia sent to my Territory to destroy the freedom of elections. Then, thank God, Beecher did send his *"bibles."*—Mr. D. C. Haskell of Kan., H. R., Apr. 5: *C. R.,* p. 262/1.

Beef. Any animal of the ox kind. [1821-1904.]

1862 Every slaughtered *beef* [the farmer may sell] is subject to a tax.— Mr. William Allen of O., H. R., July 12: *C. G.,* p. 3305/1.

1879 Would [this fact] convince the Senator from Ind. [Mr. Voorhees] that one *beef* was better than another?—Mr. McPherson of N. J., U. S. Senate, May 27: *C. R.,* p. 1620/1.

Beef-fat. In fit condition to be made into beef.

1901-2 It was no uncommon sight to see five- and six-year-old Texas steers coming into market *beef-fat* off the range.—Rep. Kan. State Bd. Agric., p. 60. (Century Dict.)

Beef issue. A government issue of cattle to the Indians for food.

1895 A *beef issue* is not a pretty thing to watch.—Mr. Marriott Brosius of Pa., H. R., Jan. 15: *C. R.,* pp. 1005-6. [A full description of this brutal proceeding, quoted from Mr. Richard H. Davis follows. The animals were hunted with arrows and with dogs, and finally shot down.]

Bee-gum. A section of a hollow tree, used as a beehive. [1835-1851.]

1850 M. A. received twenty lashes on Saturday, for stealing a *bee-gum* and its contents.—Wilmington (N. C.) *Commercial,* March 28, p. 2/5.

Bee line. A direct line. [1830-1867.]

1875 When George Washington left Virginia, and the boys made a *bee line* for Boston, there was then no row between Mass. men about slavery.— Mr. Thomas Whitehead of Va., H. R., Feb. 3: *C. R.,* p. 954/1.

1880 If he thought he could have bettered his fortune by going the same distance east or north, he certainly would not have made a *bee line* for the State of Ill.—Mr. Roscoe Conkling of N. Y., U. S. Senate, May 12: *Id.,* p. 3269/2.

Begin to. Used with a negative to express the extreme of impossibility. [1842-1856.]

1849 We can't *begin to* come up to the prospectus.—Wilmington (N. C.) *Commercial,* Apr. 5, p. 2/1.

1865 N. Y. does not *begin to* have sixty-nine thousand square miles—Mr. James W. Grimes of Ia., U. S. Senate, Feb. 8: *C. G.,* p. 664/1.

1867 We came to the conclusion . . . . that this building would not *begin to* stand, if erected upon the foundation.—Mr. Thomas A. Hendricks of Ind., U. S. Senate, Dec. 20: *Id.,* p. 298/2.

1870 Our railroads have not *begun to* realize for the community the benefit they are capable of producing.—Mr. Sidney Clarke of Kan., H. R., June 6: *Id.,* p. 4122/1.

1907 Often there's a . . . . dinner that you couldn't *begin to* get for the same price anywhere else.—W. D. Howells, "Through the Eye of the Needle," p. 43.

Belauded. Loaded with praise.

a.1849 [He] was *belauded* by the universal American press.—E. A. Poe, "Works" (1864), III, 139. (N. E. D.)

1870 The old statesmen of Va. who were so *belauded* by [Mr. J. S. Cox.] —Mr. B. F. Butler of Mass., Jan. 24: *C. G.,* p., 717/2.

Belittle. To depreciate. [1796-1842.]

1836 It is not long since ye have been disposed to *belittle* the constitution of the Christian priesthood.—Dr. G. T. Chapman, "Sermons," p. 12. (Hartford, Conn.)

1861 That is a poor reason why we are to be scaled, diminished, decreased, *belittled,* demeaned, &c.—Mr. Edward D. Baker of Ore., U. S. Senate, Feb. 22: *C. .G.,* p. 1114/1.

1911 The process of *belittling* [President Taft] has been carried to wholly unjustifiable extremes; and the result is really to *belittle* the men who are responsible for it.—*N. Y. Evening Post,* Dec. 18, p. 4/3.

Bend. Power, ability: as, "that is above my bend." Colloq., Western. —(Century Dict.) Perhaps this is a relic of the old Scottish *Bend,* a leap or bound. (See N. E. D.)

Better. More.

1814 Something *better* than fourteen years since, I . . . had money to spare.—Norfolk (Va.) *Public Ledger,* Nov. 26, p. 2/1.

Betterment. See quotations. [1809-1910.]

1877 The word *"betterments"* . . merely means the improvements or the buildings on the land.—Mr. W. P. Whyte of Md., U. S. Senate, Nov. 12: *C. R.,* p. 344/1.

1878 In 1808 Governor Sullivan [of Mass.] signed "the *betterment* act," humanely providing that in all actions instituted to recover lands, holden six years or more by possession, or improvement, whenever the jury found for the demandant, they should, at the tenant's request, also ascertain the increased value of the premises at the time of the trial, in virtue of his buildings and improvements.—Remarks of Mr. Wm. P. Frye of Me., on the presentation of the statue of Wm. King: *Id.,* Jan. 22, p. 470/1.

B'hoy. A town rowdy; a gay fellow. [1846-1866.]

1847 All the *b'hoys* will vote, aye, more than all. Let every Whig do his duty. Another year with a Democratic mayor—and such a mayor as the *b'hoys* would force upon the city! Who can tell what the taxes will be?—*N. Y. Comml. Advertiser,* Apr. 12. (Bartlett.)

1848 Mike Walsh, ... a *b'hoy* of the first water, was recently converted, and it is said intends to attach himself to the ministry.—*Id.,* Oct. 19, p. 2/4.

1848 Abby Folsom no doubt considers herself one of the *"b'hoys."*—Wilmington (N. C.) *Commercial,* March 30, p. 2/1. (From the Boston *Bee.*)

Big bugs. People of consequence. [1831-1861.]

1830 We never heard of anything that passed, nor any remarks made by them about him—honor among *big bugs!*—Lorenzo Dow, "A Cry from the Wilderness" (1850), p. 140/2.

Big Four, The. Any powerful fourfold combination. The term seems to have been first applied to four packing companies in Chicago; but latterly and specially to the Cleveland, Cincinnati, Chicago and St. Louis railroad company.

1890 A confidential clerk in the house of one of the *"big four"* can, smoking his cigar leisurely, pass by the confidential man representing another of the *"big four"* and say, "Charlie, I suppose cattle ought to be about a cent and a half lower today"; the answer is, "Yes, I suppose so," and he walks on. He meets another confidential clerk, and they exchange similar remarks.—Mr. D. B. Henderson of Ia., H. R., May 10: *C. R.,* p. 4524/2.

1890 The monopolist who usurps and controls the markets, as the *"big four"* have controlled the beef market of the country.—Mr. Marriott Brosius of Pa., H. R., *Id.,* p. 4540/1.

1890 [Mr. Mason] represents Chicago, where the *"Big Four"* reside.—Mr. R. P. Bland of Mo., H. R., June 11: *Id.,* p. 5960/2.

1892 Will [free coinage of silver] stop the *big four* of Chicago from putting down in every city market of the South beef that ought to be fed at home?—Mr. B. G. Stout of Mich., H. R., March 23: *Id.,* p. 2430/1.

1894 The conferees on the part of the House reported a disagreement and went back and reconferred with the *"big four"* of the House. It is said that the *"big four"* of the Senate told them that they must take the Senate bill or nothing.—Mr. John H. Gear of Ia., H. R., Aug. 13: *Id.,* p. 1355/1, App.

1900 What rival concern can compete against the Standard Oil Company, the *big four* slaughter and packing companies, the grain elevators, &c.?—Mr. Rudolph Kleberg of Tex., H. R., May 31: *Id.,* p. 6330/1.

1913 Middletown, O., May 1.—Eleven persons were injured, two probably fatally, in a head-on collision between a *Big Four* passenger train and a freight train near here today.—*N. Y. Evening Post,* May 1, p. 1/6.

1913 *Big Four* Rear-End Crash. Stalled diner splintered and sleeper telescoped.—*N. Y. Evening Post,* July 21, p. 2/1.

Big head. An inflated opinion of oneself. [1805-1896.]

1896 There are men holding subordinate places in the government of the U. S. today, men sitting with their feet on the mantlepiece, with cigars in their mouths, who are as difficult of access as the Mikado of Japan. They have got the *"big head,"* and got it bad.—Mr. J. S. Willis of Del., H. R., March 20: *C. R.,* p. 3030/2.

Big Muddy, The. The Missouri River. [1863-1870.]

1868 The train that brings the rich ore to Ind. carries back to Mo. coal superior even to that of the *Big Muddy.*—Mr. W. D. Kelley of Pa., H. R., June 1: *C. G.,* p. 2755/1.

Biggest toad in the puddle. The most consequential person.

1893 What kind of a fellow is Senator Gorman—*biggest toad in the Democratic puddle?*—Mr. La Moure, in the Minneapolis *Daily Tribune,* Apr. 10: see *C. R.,* Apr. 14, p. 153/2.

Bile for **boil.** [1778-1848.]

1803 He has a scar on his left cheek, occasioned by a *bile.*—*Georgia Republican,* May 19, p. 1/3.

Bill, v. To announce on placards.

1879 At a large popular meeting at Topeka . . . . I had been erroneously *bill'd* to deliver a poem.—Walt Whitman, "Specimen Days" (1887), p. 218.

Bill, v. To enter in a waybill.

1867 The station agent . . . . *billed* the goods through to C.—*Vt. Reports,* xl, 326. (N. E. D.)

1873 A car ticketed and *billed* from Boston, Mass., bound for Atlanta, Ga.—Mr. O. J. Dodds of O., H. R., Feb. 22: *C. G.,* p. 136/2, App.

1881 There were four hundred cars of grain *billed* to St. Louis.—*Chicago Times,* Apr. 16. (N. E. D.)

1884 A shipper who *bills* two cars could get a different rate from the shipper who *bills* one car.—Mr. John H. Reagan of Tex., H. R., Dec. 20: *C. R.,* p. 398/2.

1890 [The goods] are *billed* to him at that price, and then 50 per cent discount is allowed. . . . The article costs the American dealer exactly the same—that is, the *billed* price—that it costs the Southern dealer.—Mr. F. B. Stockbridge of Mich., U. S. Senate, Aug. 22: *Id.,* p. 9013/2.

1894 The evils of under-classification and false *billing* and false weighing prevail to an alarming extent.—Mr. John Dalzell of Pa., H. R., Dec. 8: *Id.,* p. 136/1.

Billion. A thousand million. The American meaning is taken from the French. [1840.]

1869 I suppose it safe to say that ten *billions,* or ten thousand millions in value, were destroyed in one way and another [during the Civil War]. —Mr. Cornelius Cole of Calif., U. S. Senate, Jan. 11: *C. G.,* p. 274/1.

1879 N. Y. has now more than two and one-half *billions* of dollars of property, real and personal, and all of these twelve [cotton] states have not as much.—Mr. Jno. T. Morgan of Ala., U. S. Senate, May 8: *C. R.,* p. 1153/2.

1888 I find that the total estimated true valuation of all property in the country in 1880 was about forty-four *billions* of dollars, the assessed valuation being seventeen *billions,* or about 39 per cent of the whole.— Mr. J. H. Gallinger of N. H., H. R., Apr. 30: *Id.,* p. 3541/2.

1888 The cotton production in this country is not only enough to offset the wool crop, but it is some three *billion* pounds—more than ten times the wool crop.—Mr. C. R. Breckinridge of Ark., H. R., May 17: *Id.,* p. 186/2, App.

1892 A *billion* dollars for two years, half of which is $500,000,000.—Mr. Richard P. Bland of Mo., H. R., Feb. 3: *Id.,* p. 812/2.

Billion Dollar Congress. A name applied especially to the Fifty-first Congress, because of its large appropriations.

1893   My Democratic friends, you can now change the old tune of "a *billion-dollar Congress*," and tell the story of a billion-dollar Democratic House. . . . . . The Democratic press, after the work of the Fifty-first Congress was completed, came out with such headlines as these: "The Billion Congress," "The Great Financial Spree," "The Indelible Billion," "The Tom Reed Robbers," "The Treasury Raiders." These are a few of the sample headlines in 1891.—Mr. D. B. Henderson of Ia., H. R., March 3: *C. R.*, pp. 102-3, App.

1897   Mr. Dockery:—After the wasteful appropriations of the *"billion-dollar Congress,"* the average annual expenditures of the government leaped from $303,792,115.07, as they were from 1887 to 1891, to $365,342,188.30 during the fiscal years from 1892 to 1894 inclusive. Mr. Lacey:—Which *"billion-dollar Congress"?* Mr. Dockery:—The first *"billion-dollar Congress."* Mr. Maguire:—This is the second. Mr. Dockery:—No; the last Congress was the third.—H. R., March 19: *Id.*, p. 89/1.

Binder twine, Binding-twine. A kind of twine made for use in connection with "harvesters" or reaping-machines.

1890   The observations of [Senator Davis] in respect to *binding-twine* are very important to the people of La. That article ought to be put on the free list.—Mr. R. L. Gibson of La., U. S. Senate, Aug. 28: *C. R.*, p. 9260/1. [See also pp. 5223, 9652-58, 9707.]

Bishop. See quotation. [1790-1848.]

1819   See INDISPENSABLE.

1848   [A lady] wearing what we call a bustle, then called a *bishop*, ... padded and stuffed with horse hair.—Wilmington (N. C.) *Commercial*, Sept. 7, p. 1/5. (From the *Sunday Messenger*.)

Bit, a. Usually one-eighth of a dollar. [1683-1860.]

1863   Two were small groceries, in which the vilest alcoholic compounds were sold at a *bit* (ten cents) a glass.—Edmund Kirke, "Life in Dixie's Land," p. 206. (Lond.)

1863   See TOTE.

Blab school. See quotation. Local.

1890   [In the mountains of the South] you are riding along a mountain road, and you hear a humming noise in the distance, coming through the trees. You go a little farther, and distinguish human voices mingling together in loud discord. What is the matter? Nothing but a school at study, and all studying together at the top of their voices. Such a din! This is a *"blab" school*, though the modern advocates of this kind of school sometimes dignify them with the more elegant term, vocal schools.—Magazine article, quoted in the U. S. Senate, Feb. 10: *C. R.*, p. 1165/1.

Black Belt. That strip of land, running across the Southern States, in which the negroes are most numerous; or any corresponding strip on a smaller scale.

1875   During this campaign I made a number of speeches in Ga. I spoke in what is known as the *"Black Belt."*—Mr. John B. Gordon of Ga., U. S. Senate, Jan. 8: *C. R.*, p. 342/1.

1878   There is one region of country to which no man emigrates, and that is what is called *"the black belt,"* where the negro population is very dense.—Mr. John T. Morgan of Ala., U. S. Senate, Dec. 17: *Id.*, p. 241/2.

1889   After two decades of negro suffrage, the white Democratic representatives in Congress from *the Black Belt* declare that the blacks are to be forever servile.—Mr. L. E. McComas of Md., H. R., Feb. 12: *Id.*, p. 1801/1.

1890   This district is commonly known as the *"Black Belt"* or the "Black District" of Ala., for the reason, I suppose, that its population, as shown by the last census, comprised 135,893 colored people and only 32,824 whites.—Mr. S. G. Comstock of Minn., H. R., June 3: *Id.,* p. 5543/1.

1890   This paper has never complained that the *Black Belt* Democrats maintain their supremacy. . . . The negroes are incapable of self-government; they are not fit to be intrusted with the control of public affairs, and the salvation of the *Black Belt country* depends on the upholding of white supremacy.—*The Age-Herald* (Ala.) n. d. See *C. R.,* June 3, p. 5546/1.

1890   General Pettus means that the *Black Belt counties* must reduce their representation in State conventions.—*Wilcox Progress* (Ala.) n. d. See *C. R.,* June 3, p. 5546/1.

1898   Dallas County was formerly a part of the Fourth Ala. Congressional district, which was composed entirely of *black-belt counties.*—Mr. E. E. Settle of Ky., H. R., Feb. 9: *Id.,* p. 1594/1.

Black code, the. See quotation.

1876   I hold in my hand the laws of the Legislature of S. C. passed in the session of 1865-66. . . . . Among the very first acts that they passed was the act which is known all over this country and all over the world as the *"black code"* of S. C., a code that should disgrace every one of its authors.—Mr. Patterson of S. C., U. S. Senate, Aug. 9: *C. R.,* p. 5347/1.

Black counties. Those in which negroes predominate.

1888   Justices of the peace in the *black counties* . . . converted their offices into engines of oppression to both races.—Mr. J. Z. George of Miss., U. S. Senate, Sept. 26: *C. R.,* p. 8947/1.

1893   The Democratic party [in Ala.], controlling the Legislature, threw all these *black counties* into this one Congressional district, which was denominated *"the black fourth."*—Mr. H. U. Johnson of Ind., H. R., Feb. 28: *Id.,* p. 2294/1.

Black Eagle of Illinois, The. A name given to Gen. John A. Logan in the National Republican Convention of 1884. He was also called "Black Jack."

Black eye, to give a. To defeat; to discredit. [1795.]

1876   The Senator from N. Y. [Mr. Conkling] was very much exercised . . . . somebody was threatening *to give a black eye* to these 3.65 bonds. —Mr. M. C. Hamilton of Tex., U. S. Senate, Feb. 3: *C. R.,* p. 854/1.

1892   You, Mr. Chairman, gave that precedent *a very black eye.*—Mr. A. N. Martin of Ind., H. R., Apr. 18: *Id.,* p. 231/2, App.

1892   The attempt was made to give this enterprise *a black eye,* by saying that we have granted [too much land already].—Mr. C. E. Hooker of Miss., H. R., Apr. 27: *Id.,* p. 3718/2.

1896   Men who knew better . . . . shook hands with Populism in order to give this nation of ours *a black eye.*—Mr. D. T. Flynn of Okla., H. R., Dec. 10: *Id.,* p. 79/2.

1900   I hope the Pension Committee will give *a black eye* to every bill of that kind.—Mr. T. M. Mahon of Pa., H. R., Jan. 19: *Id.,* p. 1004/2.

Blackguardism. Vile language. [1799-1826.]

1866   I use the word *blackguardism,* not in its offensive sense, but as indicating that kind of offensive language that has no relation to any matter before the House, and is personal in its character.—Mr. Philip Johnson of Pa., H. R., July 17: *C. G.,* p. 3881/3.

Black Hawk war. Black Hawk (1767-1838) was the chief of the Sacs and Foxes.

1879   Mr. Saunders:—The war with the Winnebagos occurred, I think, in 1828; the *Black Hawk war* was in 1831 and 1832. . . . . The *Black Hawk war* was the war in which the late President Lincoln served as a soldier. . . . . Mr. Thurman:—If we pension the soldiers in the *Black Hawk war,* then we must pension the soldiers of the Creek war in Fla., &c. . . . . and where are we to end?—U. S. Senate, March 1: *C. R.,* pp. 2224-5.

Black horse, Black horse cavalry. Those legislators who are accused of acting together for purposes of extortion. See Brown's "Dict. of Am. Politics," 1892.

1893 Mr. Dunn:—Speaking for N. J., I know something of the *black-horse cavalry* force and the way they do their work at Trenton sometimes. I know . . . the way the *black horse* does business round about legislatures, because I have been there, and have helped to run them out. Mr. Fellows:—I am not acquainted with the mysteries of N. J. politics. I do not know how far the *black-horse cavalry* may intervene in pushing measures through the legislature.—H. R., Dec. 20: *C. R.,* pp. 453/2, 455/2.

Black jack. The dwarf or scrub oak. [1792-1904.]

1874 These men would think it an improvement if they could bring down all the trees to the level of the *black-jack,* and all the stars to the size of the north star.—Mr. W. M. Robbins of N. C., H. R., Jan. 24: *C. R.,* p. 898/1.

Black Republican. A member of the Republican party considered as favoring the negroes. [1856-1861.]

1861 The *Black Republicans* are proficients in the game of delusion.—*New Orleans Picayune,* Jan. 16.

1861 The *Black Republicans,* exultant over their recent success, are not disposed to concede anything.—Letter of Jefferson Davis, Jan. 8: see *C. G.,* Feb. 17, 1868, p. 1209/2.

1862 Mr. Howard of Mich.:—Milton was a Republican poet. Mr. Morrill of Me.:—Yes, sir; a Republican poet. Mr. Garrett Davis of Ky.:—Not a *Black* one, though.—U. S. Senate, Apr. 2: *Id.,* p. 1503/1.

1864 [Senator Henry Wilson of Mass.] has been a sort of general whipper-in, not only of the *Black Republican* party, but of the whole Senate.—Mr. Garrett Davis, U. S. Senate, Feb. 17: *Id.,* p. 704/3.

1864 Hamblin (*sic*) was as *Black* a *Republican* as anybody.—Wilmington (N. C.) *Journal,* June 17, p. 2/1.

Black-sampson. The *Brauneria purpurea,* the thick black roots of which were supposed to have powerful medicinal virtues. (Century Dict.)

Bland dollars. They were named after Mr. Richard P. Bland of Mo. See quotations.

1878 On the 5th day of last November, upon a suspension of the rules and without debate, by a vote of 163 to 34, this House passed what is known as the *Bland silver bill,* containing as one of its main features the free-coinage clause.—Mr. A. S. Willis of Ky., H. R., Feb. 21: *C. R.,* p. 38/2, App. [The bill was amended by the Senate, vetoed by President Hayes, and carried over his veto by majorities of 46 against 19 and 196 against 73.]

1879 Notwithstanding this sad fate of the *Bland silver dollar,* it is now seriously proposed to repeat that folly on a much larger scale.—Mr. Deuster of Wisc., H. R., May 15: *Id.,* p. 1369/2.

1882 Take the *Bland dollar,* which is worth in the market some 20 cents more than the trade dollar.—Mr. Chas. N. Brumm of Pa., H. R., May 16: *Id.,* p. 303/2, App.

1883 On our latest dollar will be found the *blandest* and possibly, where all are ugly, our most abominable eagle, unless we except the one on the wing which once appeared as a scarecrow on the silver dollar, afterwards belittled as the eagle *volant* on the copper cent.—Mr. J. S. Morrill of Vt., U. S. Senate, Dec. 5: *Id.,* p. 41/2.

1890 I was a member of this House in 1878, when what is known as the *Bland* bill passed the House. It was then a bill for free coinage, pure and simple. The silver bullion then in the dollar provided for was worth 92 cents.—Mr. M. S. Brewer of Mich., H. R., June 7: *Id.,* p. 5810/2.

1894 The gentleman from Mo., the author of the Bland bill and father of the *Bland silver dollar,* the only citizen of the United States who has ever impressed his name upon one of our coins.—Mr. M. N. Johnson of N. D., H. R., March 1: *Id.,* p. 2517/1.

1896 Now we are asked that the holders of these securities shall be compelled to accept a *Bland dollar* authorized in 1878, which itself is not a legal tender.—Mr. John Sherman of O., U. S. Senate, May 7: *Id.,* p. 4935/2.

Blanket bid. A comprehensive bid.

1896 Mr. D. B. Hill:—Messrs. Morgan & Co. had given a *blanket bid* to cover the whole amount. . . . . Under the terms of the *blanket bid,* which covered all bids where there was a failure to take the bonds, Morgan & Co. obtained [these particular bonds]. . . . Mr. G. G. Vest:—The Secretary of the Treasury, under what is called by the Senator from N. Y. this *blanket bid,* turned over all the unfulfilled bids to J. Pierpont Morgan & Co.—U. S. Senate, May 4: *C. R.,* pp. 4783-4.

Blanket Indians. See quotations.

1875 [This] argument applies to reservations made for what we call in the West *"blanket Indians."* It applies to reservations set apart by the Government as temporary homes for the wild Indians of the prairies, and not for Indians like the Senecas, who are somewhat advanced in civilization.—Mr. Lewis V. Bogy of Mo., U. S. Senate, Feb. 2: *C. R.,* p. 912/2.

1878 A colony of Dakotas, who fifteen years ago were *"blanket Indians,"* busy over their war-dances and heathen mysteries, but who are now citizen farmers.—*The Word Carrier,* a Sioux newspaper, quoted in *Id.,* May 27: p. 203/2, App.

1886 [The young Indians, leaving school], go back to barbarism, back to the tepee, back to the *blanket Indians.* What have you done to enable him (*sic*) to go back to anything but a *blanket Indian*?—Mr. B. M. Cutcheon of Mich., H. R., March 10: *Id.,* p. 2273/1.

1889 Although these are *blanket Indians,* although they are uncivilized, although they are wards under the guardianship of this nation [yet we should keep faith with them].—Mr. W. C. P. Breckinridge of Ky., H. R., Feb. 6: *Id.,* p. 1585/1.

1891 Even among the *blanket Indians* you find men . . . of great thought, of reasoning minds, of wonderful conceptions; and I never saw that illustrated in a more striking manner than when I listened to the *blanket Indian* Joseph, of the Nez Percé tribe.—Mr. C. E. Hooker of Miss., H. R., Feb. 14: *Id.,* p. 2697/1.

1892 It is not a vain appeal to the Indian of the lower, the *blanket* order, the savage Indian, when you ask him to enlist in the military service, because it suits his tastes.—Mr. J. T. Morgan of Ala., U. S. Senate, March 23: *Id.,* p. 2403/1.

1897 See Buck.

1892 [These people] are *blanket Indians.* They follow their stock. They cannot be induced to turn their minds and industry towards agriculture. —Mr. E. O. Wolcott of Colo., U. S. Senate, March 29: *Id.,* p. 2637/1.

1898 Even among Indians there are two parties. There is the *"hat"* Indian and the *"blanket"* Indian. The Indian who believes in progress, who wears a blanket is called a *"blanket"* Indian. We have similar examples here in the House [reactionists and progressives] . . . .

Without any reference to which side of the House we find the *hat Indians* upon, or which side we find the *blanket Indians* upon, we all recognize [the distinction].—Mr. J. F. Lacey of Ia., H. R., Jan. 26: *Id.,* p. 1048/1.

Blast, in full. Energetically at work. [1850-1858.]

1890 Cities like Topeka, where the schoolboys never saw saloons, and where the jails are empty, now have these original-package saloons *in full blast.*—Mr. E. A. Morse of Mass., H. R., July 18: *C. R.,* p. 7436/2.

Blaze. To chip off a piece of the bark of a tree. [1737-1841.]

1878 I would as soon think of *blazing* the shade-trees along the avenue, to enable the judges of [the S. C. U. S.] to find their way to the court-room, as to go to the trouble of citing cases to establish [well-known principles].—Mr. Isaac P. Christiancy of Mich., U. S. Senate, March 18: *C. R.,* p. 1830/2.

1886 We have *blazed* a way for men like the knights [of labor] and for other great organizations. . . . These organizations are controlled by conservative, brainy, patriotic men.—Mr. Farquhar of N. Y., H. R., Apr. 2: *Id.,* p. 3043/1.

1913 And we may be sure that wide-awake and younger railroad men, more sensitive than he could be to the present-day conditions under which they must do their work, will be careful to avoid walking in the path which Mr. Mellen has *blazed* with failure.—*N. Y. Evening Post,* July 21, p. 4/7.

Bleachers. The uncovered benches for spectators at an athletic field. [1909.]

1911 The democracy of the game is at its best on the *bleachers* and in the grandstand. There the wealthy banker, straight from downtown by the "Wall Street subway special," hobnobs with the office-boy for once, on terms of perfect equality. Both "root" together, &c.—*N. Y. Evening Post,* Sept. 14.

Bleeding Kansas. An epithet applied to that state because of its sanguinary history in the eighteen-fifties.

1891 [I refer] to the treatment of the colored man in the State of Kan., sometimes called *"bleeding Kansas."*—Mr. James D. Richardson of Tenn., H. R., Jan. 17: *C. R.,* p. 97/2, App.

1896 Kan., *"bleeding Kansas,"* pays $277,634 internal revenue, and she gets back in the form of pensions $6,084,592.—Mr. R. Z. Linney of N. C., H. R., Jan. 16: *Id.,* p. 748/1.

Blind. A compulsory bet in the game of poker.

1894 [A school-boy], when told to illustrate the word blind,—the words deaf, dumb and lame being given to others,—wrote, "Put up your *blind.* It's my deal."—Mr. A. S. Berry of Ky., H. R., May 4: *C. R.,* p. 4408/2.

Blind bridle. A driving bridle, having attached to it blinders or blinds. See Vol. I, **Blinders.** [1809-1848.]

1894 The old farmer . . . . went in to the barnyard, and, an old *blind bridle* being the first hangman's rope he could find, he tied one end of it around his neck.—Mr. W. J. Talbert of S. C., H. R., Jan. 20: *C. R.,* p. 1148/2.

Blind tiger. A private residence, office room, shed, or tent, occupied temporarily for the sale of liquor. [1909.]

1892 The proprietor of a *"blind tiger"* (an illicit drinking place) has been fined in 577 cases.—*Evening Echo,* June 30, p. 1/7. (N. E. D.)

1912 [They] are in a mysterious place called a *"blind tiger,"* drinking the very bad whiskey for which Prohibition is indirectly responsible.—*Atl. Monthly,* Feb., p. 206.

1913 Dublin, Ga., Jan. 29. Norman Jackson, a negro preacher of this city, was fined by the city recorder Monday for running a *blind tiger.* Jackson was caught in the act of selling the whiskey.—(Press dispatch.)

Blizzard. An intolerable snowstorm, with high wind. [1834-1902.]

1886 It is not surprising, when a speaker attempts to make an oratorical path through a *blizzard*, with buzzards flying around his head, that he loses his way, and finally arrives at his goal in inextricable confusion. —Mr. G. G. Symes of Colo., H. R., Apr. 7: *C. R.*, p. 96/2, App.

1888 My advent in Wall Street was on the heels of the panic of 1857. That panic was known as the "Western *blizzard.*"—Henry Clews, "Twenty-Eight Years in Wall Street," p. 5. (N. Y.)

1900 [Mr. Reeder's jokes] are as clear as a northwest Kansas *blizzard*, translucent as a block of granite, bright as midnight in a billy goat's stomach, as pointed as a steam hammer.—Mr. P. T. Otey of Va., H. R., Feb. 28: *C. R.*, p. 2408/2.

Bloat. A bloated person. Slang.

1871 Wife-whippers, penitentiary birds, street vagabonds, beastly *bloats,* and convicted felons thronged Chambers Street, three thousand and more, for some days.—Mr. S. S. Cox of N. Y., H. R., Feb. 15: *C. G.*, p. 129/1, App.

Block. The aggregation of houses enclosed by four streets. [1796-1909.]

1867 He noticed a builder, as the flames were flying rapidly from *block* to *block*, coolly standing upon the pavement and watching their progress. —Mr. G. W. Scofield of Pa., H. R., Jan. 28: *C. G.*, p. 873/2.

1870 The notices of these sales were very full and complete, describing . . . . the *blocks* and lots by letters and numbers.—Mr. F. A. Sawyer of S. C., U. S. Senate, July 2: *Id.*, p. 556/3, App.

1894 He has gone past *block* after *block* of residences, and has not heard a word of English spoken.—Mr. J. H. Gallinger of N. H., U. S. Senate, July 16: *C. R.*, p. 6396/2.

Block. A large quantity of negotiable securities.

1870 Great *blocks* of this debt [the national debt of Great Britain] are now held by aristocratic families of great wealth.—Mr. Justin S. Morrill of Vt., U. S. Senate, March 3: *C. G.*, p. 1656/1.

1876 The combination began by selling large *blocks* of the stock for future delivery.—J. G. Holland, "Story of Seven Oaks," p. 331. (N. E. D.)

Blockade. Whiskey on which no duty has been paid. [1867.]

1896 [Is it not] better that we should have a little *blockade whisky* occasionally, than that the Gov't should go in partnership with a force which deals in lies?—Mr. R. Z. Linney of N. C., March 31: *C. R.*, p. 3408/2.

Block a game, to. To hinder a mischievous scheme.

1869 I invoke Congress to *"block this game"* [of appropriations], and bring the Government face to face with this great responsibility of properly caring for these Indians.—Mr. S. B. Axtell of Calif., H. R., March 19: *C. G.*, p. 166/2.

1884 Their little *game was blocked.*—*Boston Journal,* Dec. 20, p. 2/2. (N. E. D.)

Block out. To design in the rough. [1829-1837.]

1868 When the Territory of Mont. was organized, as chairman of the committee I *blocked out* the present Territory, gave it the name of Wyo., and attached it to the Territory of Dak.—Mr. James M. Ashley of O., H. R., July 22: *C. G.*, p. 4344/2.

Blocks of five. See first quotation.

1888 Divide the floaters into *blocks of five,* and put a trusted man with necessary funds in charge of these five, and make him responsible that none get away, and that all vote one ticket.—Circular letter of W. W. Dudley, Oct. 24: see *C. R.*, Jan. 8, 1890: p. 450/2.

1888 See FLOATER.

1890 During the last campaign money was used without stint; votes were bought in *"blocks of five."* Some of the people who put up the "boodle" to buy the *"blocks"* have been rewarded with fat offices.—Mr. Benton McMillin of Tenn., H. R., May 8: *Id.,* p. 4326/2.

1890 The last Presidential election, with its *"blocks of five,"* its vast corruption funds, and multifarious questionable methods, is too fresh in the minds of the people.—Mr. J. B. McCreary of Ky., H. R., June 28: *Id.,* p. 6730/2.

1890 See FRYING THE FAT.

1890 Those partisan manufacturers from whom "the fat was fried" for political purposes in 1888, or in other words, from whom vast sums of money were obtained with which to buy voters in *"blocks of five."*—Mr. D. W. Voorhees of Ind., U. S. Senate, Sept. 3: *C. R.,* p. 9594/2.

1892 Those who had conducted the disgraceful scheme set forth in the *blocks-of-five* letter discovered that it was not only an expensive one, but that it was hazardous.—Mr. J. B. Brown of Ind., H. R., Feb. 25: *Id.,* p. 1455/2. [See the whole speech.]

Blood-and-thunder stories. Those of a horrid and savage kind.

1875 All the rest of these *blood-and-thunder* stories he does not profess to know; he says they are told to him.—Mr. T. F. Bayard of Del., U. S. Senate, March 20: *C. R.,* p. 106/1.

1876 They desire . . . a row occasionally to give their *blood-and-thunder* friends in the North a little more electioneering capital.—Mr. Hartzell of Va., H. R., July 20: *Id.,* p. 4767/1.

1900 This bill . . . . fosters the *blood-and-thunder* stories which inflame the minds and allure the hearts of the youth of the land.—Mr. W. D. Vandiver of Mo., H. R., March 21: *Id.,* p. 3144/2.

Blooded. Of a particularly good stock. [1778-1888.]

1870 While Canada is a foreign country to us, yet they have thoroughbred animals there as pure and as good *blooded* as there are in England or anywhere else.—Mr. S. C. Pomeroy of Kan., U. S. Senate, June 29: *C. G.,* p. 4984/3.

1879 The *blooded* beast, if uncared for and left to run at will, will either perish or degenerate to the level of the common herd.—Mr. John P. Jones of Nev., U. S. Senate, Feb. 14: *C. R.,* p. 97/2, App.

Bloody chasm, The. The rift between North and South, viewed in relation to the Civil War.

1876 This measure is one of conciliation. It reunites; it fills up the *"bloody chasm."*—Mr. Felton of Ga., H. R., June 14: *C. R.,* p. 3791/1.

1878 Mass. and Maine are getting nearer together. They have already closed up the *bloody chasm.*—Mr. H. L. Humphrey of Wisc., H. R., Jan. 26: *Id.,* p. 599/2: the allusion being to Mr. Blaine's spiteful remarks, made four days previously.

1879 While I am pleased to see the North and South shaking hands over *"the bloody chasm,"* while I am pleased to see New Orleans and New York lying down in peace, I do hope my poor city [Baltimore] may not be ground between the upper and nether millstone of this reconciliation—Mr. W. P. Whyte of Md., U. S. Senate, Feb. 20: *Id.,* p. 1638/1.

1879 The President of the U. S. [Mr. Hayes] has clasped the endearing hand of friendship "across the *bloody chasm.*" He took into his Cabinet a Confederate soldier.—Mr. A. H. Coffroth of Pa., H. R., Apr. 18: *Id.,* p. 562/2.

1879 If abuses have crept into our judicial administration, it is to be hoped that in this era of peace and reconciliation, when we are all drawn so near together, when we are "shaking hands over the *bloody chasm,*" and all that kind of thing,—when you see here Confederate brigadiers and Union soldiers joining in the work of legislation—the "era of good feeling" will very soon enter the jury-box at the South.—Mr. Calkins of Ind., H. R., June 10: *Id.,* p. 1901/2.

1881 I hope the day has come when we have bridged *the bloody chasm,* and when we shall fold up that old *bloody shirt* that we have heard so much about, and bury it beneath the reach of resurrection.—Mr. Joseph E. Brown of Ga., U. S. Senate, March 24: *Id.,* p. 49/1.

1888 I hope I will be excused today from again shaking hands across the *"bloody chasm."* I have done that until I have corns on my hands.— Mr. John M. Allen of Miss., H. R., Dec. 11: *Id.,* p. 161/1.

Bloody shirt. "To wave the bloody shirt" was a phrase much used during Grant's second term, in allusion to popular harangues based on the incidents and consequences of the Civil War. The two words are collocated in Sidney's "Arcadia" (1598) and in Gibbon (ab. 1783) and were used by Lewis Cass in 1840.—(Century Dict.)

1876 There are gentlemen . . . . who seem to think that whenever I rise upon this floor, it is for the purpose of discussing State rights, ... because that is one of the great bugaboos which is to go along with the *"bloody shirt"* in the great contest which is approaching. . . . . The *"bloody shirt"* is freely used at one end of the Capitol, and here at this end is the bugaboo of State rights.—Mr. Tucker of Va., H. R., Apr. 17: *C. R.,* p. 2523/2.

1876 I have all this winter heard talk of the *"bloody shirt."*—Mr. Townsend of N. Y., H. R., Apr. 19: *Id.,* p. 2596/1.

1876 Whenever we talk on this side of the House about retrenchment and reform, the *"bloody shirt"* is an answer to us. If we talk about peculations and frauds in high places or in low places, the answer is the *"bloody shirt."*—Mr. Hereford of W. Va., H. R., June 17: *Id.,* p. 3860/1.

1876 This Tex. border bill [is introduced] to stimulate malignancy, and shake the *bloody shirt* in the face of the people.—Mr. S. S. Cox of N. Y., H. R., July 15: *Id.,* p. 4643/2.

1876 [Mr. Lamar] and others, who wanted to dress up in a nice starched and ironed shirt that would shame the *bloody shirt,* established a laundry at Jackson on the 4th of Aug. [1875], and a great many patronized it. . . . . In their party pow-wow, . . . they declared by formal resolution against the white-line policy.—*Meridian* (Miss.) *Mercury,* July 29: see *C. R.,* Aug. 4, p. 5183/2.

1876 I do not want to see the Presidential Mansion made the point from which the *bloody shirt* shall wave. Rather let the ensign of our freedom, the Stars and Stripes, float from the Presidential Mansion; but tell me not that the home which Washington filled, which Jefferson filled, which Jackson filled, which Polk filled, which a long line of illustrious Presidents has filled, has become the center wheel from which is to flaunt the *bloody shirt* that has waved from this Capitol for the last several years.—Mr. Saulsbury of Del., U. S. Senate, Aug. 5: *Id.,* p. 5207/1.

1876 It has come to be a saying in this chamber and in some . . . newspapers, that we are *"shaking the bloody shirt,"* if we call attention to brutal wholesale murder of colored republicans. All I have to say in answer to that is that, when democrats will stop staining the shirt with blood, we will quit shaking it. Until then it will be shaken in the faces of an indignant people.—Mr. John A. Logan of Ill., U. S. Senate, Aug. 7: *Id.,* p. 5258/1.

1879 See WALL STREET.

1890 The song of the *bloody shirt* is still sung into their ears by unscrupulous politicians, the hirelings of monopoly . . . but the taxpayers will wash that *bloody shirt* in the tears of disappointed politicians, and hang it on Mason and Dixon's line to dry.—Mr. B. A. Enloe of Tenn., H. R., May 8: *Id.,* p. 4353/2.

1890 [The phrase] means that, whenever you complain that an honest voter has his ballot counted in a different way than it was cast, that is "waving the *bloody shirt.*" It means that, if you object to reversing majorities, and to electing men by the counters, instead of by the voters, that is "waving the *bloody shirt.*" If you complain about stuffing ballot-boxes, that is "waving the *bloody shirt.*"—Mr. J. H. Rowell of Ill., H. R., June 4: *Id.,* pp. 5598-99.

1893 See BACK NUMBER, A [reference to the "Ensanguined garment."]

Blow. To brag, to boast. Scottish. [1840.]

1789 He brags and he *blaws* o' his siller.—R. Burns, "Tam Glen," iii. (N. E. D.)

1863 I am continually lost at the absence of *blowers* and *blowing* among these old-young American militaires.—Walt Whitman, "Specimen Days," (1887) p. 70.

1890 You know that years ago, when we [in the South] were boasting, you were building factories. Now we are building factories, and you are doing the *blowing.*—Mr. C. W. McClammy of N. C., H. R., May 19: *C. R.,* p. 4933/1-2.

Blow-hard. A boaster; a braggart. [As adj. 1855-1894.]

1894 Anyone who will read the whole testimony will see that [this man] was a mere braggart, a pretender, a *blow-hard,* a man who it seems was a hanger-on of Gen. Grant.—Mr. W. E. Chandler of N. H., U. S. Senate, Jan. 23: *C. R.,* p. 1238/2.

Blow in. To waste one's cash riotously. Modern slang.

1892 The best record made by any two Congresses in America was that made by the 49th and 50th Congresses, when they amassed a surplus of more than $100,000,000, and quietly turned it over to our Republican friends to *blow it in* the next year.—Mr. Thos. Lynch of Wisc., H. R., Feb. 2: *C. R.,* p. 784/1.

Bludgeoning. Beating with a bludgeon. The N. E. D. cites Dr. Doran (1868) for the use of *bludgeon* as a verb.

1864 Can we forget the *bludgeoning* of the distinguished Senator from Mass., Mr. Sumner, in the other end of the Capitol, because he . . . . spoke freely his opinions?—Mr. Schuyler Colfax of Ind., H. R., Apr. 14: *C. G.,* p. 1627/3. [The weapon savagely used by Mr. Brooks may have been a loaded cane; it was certainly not a bludgeon.]

Blue dog, Blue pup. See Appendix LXXI. 1893 See **Detector.**

Blue grass. Any of several grasses having bluish-green stems including the Kentucky blue grass, *Poa pratensis.* [1784-1909.]

1862 *Blue grass* has done for Ken. what turnips have done for Flanders, ... not only arrested the old process, which wore out the land, but restored the soil, and brought large profits to graziers.—Mr. Joseph A. Wright of Ind., U. S. Senate, Apr. 17: *C. G.,* p. 1692/1.

1879 The most valuable herds of cattle to be found anywhere in this country perhaps are to be found in the *"blue-grass"* pastures of [Ky.]. Their value is almost incalculable.—Mr. J. G. Carlisle of Ky., H. R., Apr. 12: *C. R.,* p. 402/1.

1886 Having been born in a city, I was carried . . . into the *blue-grass* region of Ky. in the exquisite month of May.—Mr. W. C. P. Breckinridge of Ky., H. R., May 13: *Id.,* p. 4489/1.

1898 Can you think of the *blue grass* of Ky., which when more grazed is always better, where you can run a case knife down among the roots and never touch the bottom of it, and talk of this stuff in Alaska as being *blue grass,* with a root an inch and a half long, and an enormous top to it?—Mr. G. G. Vest of Mo., U. S. Senate, March 3: *Id.,* p. 2417/2.

Blue hen's chickens. The people of Delaware. [1840-1861.]

1864 I remember the early history of the *"Blue Hen's Chickens,"* and it is a proud one; the record is as proud as that of the early "Jersey Blues."—Mr. Ten Eyck of N. J., U. S. Senate, June 15: *C. G.,* p. 2968/2.

Blue Hen State. Delaware.
1897 [I thank] the gentleman from the *"Blue Hen State"* for his suggestion.—Mr. J. F. Lacey of Ia., H. R., March 23: *C. R.,* p. 68/2, App.
Blue jay. The common jay (*Cyanocitta cristata*) of the Eastern United States; also in the Western United States any of several other jays.—(Webster.) [1792-1847.]
1871 Rufus Choate said, in speaking of the R. I. boundary, that it might as well be bounded on the north by a *blue jay,* on the east by a swarm of bees, south or west by three hundred foxes with firebrands tied to their tails.—Mr. S. W. Kellogg of Conn., H. R., Feb. 18: *C. G.,* p. 154/2, App.
1888 A day school is a good thing in some places, and it is not good in [others]. Take a day school among the Comanches, and it would not be any better than having a school of *blue jays.*—Mr. H. L. Dawes of Mass., U. S. Senate, June 1: *C. R.,* p. 4810/2.
Blue laws. Certain laws of Conn. not having the force of statute. Some of the Blue Laws are printed in the *Analectic Magazine* (Phila.) for July 1814, IV, 56-57: "No one shall run of a sabbath day, or walk in his garden or elsewhere, except reverently to and from church. No one shall travel, cook victuals, make beds, sweep houses, cut hair, or shave, on the sabbath day. No woman shall kiss her child on the sabbath or fasting day. No minister shall keep a school. Married persons must live together, or be imprisoned. Every male shall have his hair cut round, according to a cap." The code is said to have been administered as a part of the common law of Conn. [1775-1854.]
1829 Yea, one of the *blue laws* of Conn. was, neither to give meat, drink, or lodging to a Quaker, or to tell him the road.—Lorenzo Dow, "Omnifarious Law Exemplified," p. 13. (New London, Conn.)
1861 *The blue laws of Conn.* were a squib written by one Peters, which was passed off as history; . . . . and no witch was ever burned in the State of Mass.—Mr. G. F. Hoar of Mass., U. S. Senate, March 30: *C. R.,* p. 131/1. [But witches were hanged in that state in the seventeenth century.]
Blue lights. See quotation. [1844-1858.]
1866 Now we understand why, in the late war with old England, New Englanders sent up rockets and *blue lights* to apprise the enemy of an opportunity to capture them. They were tired of our, to them, imperfect form of government.—Mr. Philip Johnson of Pa., H. R., Jan. 29: *C. G.,* p. 55/1, App.
Bluenose. A native of Nova Scotia or New Brunswick. [1830-1859.]
1894 A *"bluenose."* I do not use that phrase disrespectfully, because the Nova Scotia people are among the most highly respectable people we have on the coast.—Mr. G. F. Hoar of Mass., U. S. Senate, June 6: *C. R.,* p. 5860/1.
Bluff. A high, steep bank. [1737-1841.]
1861 We were exposed to a heavy fire from Columbus, occupying a strong natural position upon a *bluff* immediately opposite.—Mr. Philip B. Fouke of Ill., H. R., Dec. 16: *C. G.,* p. 99/2.
1876 The Cuyahoga River [at Cleveland], coming in contact with the lake, passes around the foot of a great *bluff;* I do not know how high, but I will say 100 to 150 feet high,—quite a *bluff.*—Mr. John Sherman of O., U. S. Senate, Aug. 3: *C. R.,* p. 5112/1.
1896 It is said that the *bluff* near San Pedro, Calif., some sixty feet high, presents insuperable obstacles to reaching the shore.—Mr. S. M. White of Calif., U. S. Senate, May 9: *Id.,* p. 5023/1.
Bluff. A pretence at having more force than one really has, as in the game of poker. [1850-1910.]

1876 I should like to inquire of the Senator from Maine whether he thinks the action on the part of the railroad companies was simply a *"bluff game."*—Mr. J. H. Mitchell of Oregon, U. S. Senate, Aug. 11: *C. R.,* p. 5438/1.

Bluff, to call the. To recognize deception and demand acknowledgement.

1893 Mr. Bowers:—They attempted to work a little *bluff* on that Republican Senate. I suppose some of you will understand that. It is a common term. Mr. Wilson:—You do not understand the word *bluff*? Mr. Bowers:—I do not think I do in all its meanings. I know some of them. Mr. Wilson:—And you from the West! Mr. Bowers:—Yes, I say I do not understand it, but I have read about it. The Republican Senate *saw their bluff, called them, and made them show down.*—H. R., Oct. 13: *Id.,* pp. 2492-3.

1896 In this *bluff* that we are playing with the nations of the earth, somebody may *call* us, and where shall we be *when the bluff is called?*—Mr. G. L. Johnson of Calif., H. R., March 26: *Id.,* p. 3248/1.

Boat. To convey by boat. The N. E. D. furnished instances of the verb used intransitively, 1610-1871. "Discourse of Tanger," p. 22. (N. E. D.)

1681 The Horses . . . . were *boated* ashore.

1866 He had become captain of a company which he had raised and *boated* down to Pittsburg.—Mr. W. D. Kelley of Pa., H. R., July 24: *C. G.,* p. 4098/1.

Boatable. Navigable by boats. [1683-1830.]

1882 The forty-odd thousand miles of *boatable* streams of the Mississippi Valley.—Mr. J. F. King of La., H. R., Jan. 18: *C. R.,* p. 493/2.

Bob, v. To cut short.

[1709 A Mare . . . with a grisled Mane and Tail full *bob.*—*Lond. Gazette,* No. 4571/4. (N. E. D.)]

1894 [They] have adopted every English "fad," from a gold standard down to *"bobbing"* their horses' tails.—Mr. J. V. Cockrell of Tex., H. R., Jan. 11: *C. G.,* p. 43/1, App.

Bobolink. An American song bird. [1792-1870.]

1850 The black-and-white-coated *Bob-o-Lincoln* is wheeling his musical flight, while his quieter mate sits swaying on the topmost twigs.—Donald G. Mitchell, "Reveries of a Bachelor," pp. 151-2. (Lond., 1852.)

1886 See RICE-BIRD.

Bobtail. As an adj., maimed or imperfect.

1880 The Territories have only a part of what is called here *"bobtail"* representation, a power to speak but not to vote.—Mr. Roger Q. Mills of Tex., H. R., May 6: *C. R.,* p. 3078/2.

Bodyaceously. An absurd exaggeration of *bodily.* [See **bodaciously,** 1833-1904.]

1866 S. C. . . . . is where she always was: that is to say, when she went out of the Union, she did not pick herself up *bodyaceously,* walk off, and locate in some . . . . . other hemisphere.—Mr. Dumont of Ind., H. R., March 17: *C. G.,* p. 1473/3.

Body and breeches. Altogether, entirely. A decidedly colloquial expression.

1878 The Yankee notions produced by Newark every year will buy out, *body and breeches,* any thoroughly Democratic State in the Union.—Mr. Martin I. Townsend of N. Y., H. R., Apr. 12: *C. R.,* p. 2492/1.

Bog. A little elevated piece of earth in a marsh or swamp, filled with roots and grass.—(Webster.)

Bogus. Anything sham or forged. [1827-1867.]

1864 [The men of Kan.] denied that resistance to the *bogus* laws forced upon them by a legislature elected by a Mo. mob was rebellion; but the [Pierce] Administration claimed that it was.—Mr. John R. McBride of Ore., H. R., Feb. 17: *C. G.*, p. 718/1.

1867 It cannot be denied that all these *bogus* governments in the rebel States—I call them *bogus* only in the sense of their being unconstitutional—rest upon the military edicts of the President of the U. S. [Andrew Johnson].—Mr. Jacob M. Howard of Mich., U. S. Senate, Feb. 15: *Id.*, p. 1365/2.

1868 [President Johnson] had hatched out a brood of *bogus* governments.— Mr. F. C. Beaman of Mich., H. R., March 18: *Id.*, p. 1969/2.

1870 [These circulars] were sent from various *bogus* offices in the large cities, professing to be from agents of some enterprise or other, which are well enough upon their face, but upon examination are found to be entirely *bogus*.—Mr. John F. Farnsworth of Ill., H. R., Dec. 7: *Id.*, p. 35/2.

1879 See BEECHER'S BIBLES.

Boiled crow. To eat crow. 'The defeated party in an election is said to eat crow. [1872.]

1888 Other representatives of the Democracy from O. are taking this enforced "dish of *crow*," but they are doing it in silence. . . . I refer to my colleague from the central district because he not only takes his dish of *crow*, but deliberately turns around and assets that he always liked *crow* and always takes it in that form.—Mr. C. H. Grosvenor of O., H. R., Juìy 14: *C. R.*, p. 6314/2.

1894 Mr. Chairman, I am like the man who *could* eat *crow*. I will vote for this bill if I can get nothing better.—Mr. T. L. Johnson of O., H. R., Jan. 10: *Id.*, p. 639/2.

Boiler plates. Stereotyped material furnished by interested parties to country papers.

1893 The news and editorial columns of the metropolitan papers have contained the paid advertisements of the gold clique. The country weeklies have been sent tons of *"boiler plates,"* accompanied by courteous and wily letters, asking the editors to use the matter as news, "for the good of the country"; and, if they refused, they were allowed to publish it at advertising rates.—Mr. J. C. Sibley of Pa., H. R., Aug. 18: *C. R.*, p. 465/1.

1894 [These people] had hardly become rested from their efforts to assist the country onto a solid gold-standard system, until again they are called upon to send out *boiler-plate editorials.*—H. R., Jan. 18: *Id.*, p. 1032/1.

1897 Your *"boiler-plate"* literary bureau seems to have syndicated the "protest" business.—Mr. R. B. Mahany of N. Y., H. R., Jan. 6: *Id.*, p. 518/1.

Boiling, the. "The whole lot." Cf. the word *batch.*

1786 The d---l ran ahunting with the *boiling* of them.—*New Haven Gazette*, Apr. 13, p. 75/3.

1837 N. E. D. (Marryat.)

Boll-worm. "The *Heliothis armigera*, very destructive in some seasons to the cotton crop. . . . It also molests other plants, and is known under varying circumstances as the boll-worm, corn-worm, ear-worm, tassel-worm, and tomato-fruit worm."—(Century Dict.)

1880 It appeared strange to a great majority of our members that, if the producers of cotton were greatly suffering from the ravages of *boll-worms* and caterpillars, complaint and petition should not come from them, but [from speculators].—Mr. Henry Persons of Ga., H. R., May 10: *C. R.*, p. 3216/1.

1882 [One poor person] comes on a mortgaged mule, or with a lien on his crop, or assailed by the grasshopper and *boll-worm,* and threatened with foreclosure, &c.—Mr. W. M. Lowe of Ala., H. R., June 2, *Id.,* p. 334/1, App.

1888 See FRENCHING.

Bolt. To desert one's party by opposing it. [1812-1909.]

1867 This *bolting convention* of radicals at Cleveland was condemned . . . by the great mass of the Union party.—Mr. James R. Doolittle of Wisc., U. S. Senate, Feb. 16: *C. G.,* p. 1445/2.

1867 I did not follow [Mr. Fessenden] in his leadership on that occasion. I have no recollection of ever having *bolted my leader* until that time, but then I did.—Mr. Zach. Chandler of Mich., U. S. Senate, Apr. 16: *Id.,* p. 847/1.

Bomb-proof. A shelter proof against bombs.

1809 And housed in *bomb-proof* all the host she bore.—J. Barlow, "Columbiad," vii, 618. (N. E. D.)

1811 I do not think *bomb proof* absolutely necessary—Duke of Wellington, "Letters." (N. E. D.)

1861 We entered a lofty *bomb-proof,* which was the bedroom of the commanding officer.—W. H. Russell in *The Times,* June 11. (N. E. D.)

1865 "Earthworks alone without *bomb-proofs* [said General Delafield], requiring a very heavy expenditure, are worth nothing. The enemy can throw up earthworks as well as you, and he can shell you out of your earthworks unless you have expensive *bomb-proofs* built."—Mr. Conness of Calif., U. S. Senate, Feb. 24: *C. G.,* p. 1050/3.

Bomb-proof, adj. and n. Those Confederates who stayed in a safe place during the Civil War. [1877.]

1869 There is no man who has a greater respect for the Army than I have; but so far as regards these sleek, *bomb-proof* patriots, who fight the battles of their country by strutting about the avenue here, I say we should get rid of them as soon as possible.—Mr. John T. Deweese of N. C., H. R., Feb. 6: *C. G.,* p. 950/2.

1870 Why does [Mr. B. F. Butler] reserve all his fire, most of his fire, as he did in the war, for his own friends in the army, and then when attacked why does he retreat like a *"bomb-proof"* soldier and hide himself?—Mr. S. S. Cox of N. Y., H. R., Feb. 10: *Id.,* p. 1198/3.

1870 The active Kuklux are, for the most part, young men who held *bomb-proof* positions during the rebellion, and men formerly overseers of slaves.—Letter from N. C., March 20: *Id.,* p. 2742/3.

1871 [If ex-Confederate soldiers] cannot be found, *"bomb-proofs"* are patronized in their stead [in Va.] in preference to Union men.—Mr. Lewis Mackenzie of Va., H. R., Jan. 21: *C. G.,* p. 656/3.

1890 [Their] principal service . . . consisted in working themselves into *"bomb-proof"* places and forcing those whom they displaced into the field.—Statement of John McElroy, *C. R.,* Apr. 21: p. 3638/1.

1893 My experience is, generally, that the men who today abuse the South most vigorously were either camp-followers during the war, or gentlemen who occupied *bomb-proof positions.*—Mr. J. D. Alderson of W. Va., H. R., Oct. 7: *Id.,* p. 2326/2.

1895 He asked to be relieved from a *bombproof* situation under the Government in order to join his regiment and go out with Custer to fight Indians.—Mr. J. F. Stallings of Ala., H. R., Jan. 11: *Id.,* p. 887/2.

Bonanza. A profitable mine; any piece of good luck in an investment. [1866-1881.]

1876 See PETER OUT. See RINGMASTER.

1879 The *bonanzas* and rich placers of the golden shores of the Pacific would not surpass in value the annual productions [of the delta of the Mississippi].—Mr. J. D. C. Atkins of Tenn., H. R., Feb. 10: *C. R.,* p. 1175/1.

1882 If some old woman who raises a little tobacco should dare to violate this law by selling a pound or two to a neighbor, it is a perfect *bonanza* for the marshals who are prowling over the country to hunt down just such persons.—Mr. John D. White of Ky., H. R., June 22: *Id.*, p. 5230/2.

1883 These mines in Kan. and Mo. are not owned by *"bonanza* kings." Every miner there gets every dollar that the lead yields.—Mr. D. C. Haskell of Kan., H. R., Feb. 1: *Id.*, p. 1920/1.

1886 The *bonanza* farms, as they are called, that is to say the farms of a thousand acres or more, have increased many hundred per cent during the last decade.—Mr. H. W. Blair of N. H., U. S. Senate, June 22: *Id.*, p. 6001/2.

1892 I have seen a poor unfortunate driven from his boarding house, kicked out of saloons, and who would cringe to everybody; but let him strike a *bonanza*, and come into town, and he would sacrifice his life for his honor. The transformation would be miraculous.—Mr. W. M. Stewart of Nev., U. S. Senate, June 1: *Id.*, p. 4902/2.

Bone yard. A place where worn-out ships, machines, etc., are broken up. Colloq.

Bonnet leaf. A water lily.

1822 The *bonnet leaf,* a species of lotus, abounds in the dead water formed by the meeting currents of the river and the creeks that fall into it.— "Notices of East Florida," p. 29. (Charleston, S. C.)

Boodle. Money stolen by politicians. [1858-1909.]

1887 [In R. I.] the man who is bribed you could not punish, while the man who furnished the *"boodle"* was liable to indictment.—Mr. H. G. Turner of Ga., H. R., Jan. 25: *C. R.*, p. 1025/1.

1889 Make our friends in each precinct wake up to the fact that only *"boodle"* and fraudulent votes and false counting of returns can beat us.—Circular letter of W. W. Dudley, *C. R.*, Jan. 8, 1890, p. 450/2.

1890 See Blocks of Five.

1894 Republican conventions have always "pointed with pride" to any channel that floated *boodle* their way.—Mr. H. C. Snodgrass of Tenn., H. R., Jan. 10: *Id.*, p. 667/2.

1894 What we call the government of the people has become rotten to the core. It has become a government of *boodlers,* by the use of *boodle,* for the benefit of *boodleism.*—Mr. T. L. Johnson of O., H. R., Aug. 13: *Id.*, p. 1229/1, App.

1898 The barking of this mangy Wall-Street *boodleistic* cur . . . . reminds me of a lonely coyote baying the moon.—Mr. J. H. Stephens of Tex., H. R., Apr. 28: *Id.*, p. 4385/1.

Boodleize. To corrupt with "boodle."

1886 [The *Cincinnati Commercial* says in effect that] we seven men have been *boodleized,* and there are no seven men in the State of O., unless they were *boodleized,* who would agree to any such proposition.—Mr. John A. Logan of Ill., U. S. Senate, July 21: *C. R.*, p. 7266/1.

Boodler. One who handles boodle.

1894 Every nook and corner of the country . . . . was visited by the *boodlers* who were organizing for the defeat of Cleveland.—Mr. W. T. Crawford of N. C., H. R., Jan. 25: *C. R.*, p. 171/1, App.

Book concern. An establishment for printing and handling books. [1851.]

1872 Every book published by the Methodist *Book Concern,* every Bible, ... is published on sized paper.—Mr. John A. Logan of Ill., U. S. Senate, May 27: *Id.*, p. 3909/3.

1878 There has been a special order made with regard to a bill for the Southern Methodist *Book Concern.*—Mr. W. B. Allison of Ia., U. S. Senate, Apr. 17: *C. R.*, p. 2604/1.

1898   I keep in my house a pair of old saddle bags carried for more than fifty years by an old Methodist preacher who used them to distribute the . . . documents issued by the *Book Concern* of the Methodist Episcopal Church.—Mr. J. P. Dolliver of Ia., H. R., Jan. 28: *Id.,* p. 1183/1.

1898   [My object was] to expose . . . scandalous methods employed by a lobbyist and by two representatives of the Methodist *Book Concern,* in getting a great claim through the Senate.—Mr. J. T. Morgan of Ala., U. S. Senate, June 14: *Id.,* p. 5857/1.

1900   The little fellow who is attempting to establish a *book concern* at another place might be crushed.—Mr. J. S. Little of Ark., H. R., March 20: *Id.,* p. 3096/2.

Boom, Booming. See quotation. [1850-1890.]

1715   A ship is said to come Booming, when she makes all the sail she can.—Kersey, "Dictionarium Anglo-Britannicum."

1879   The word was first applied to the Grant movement, which on account of its sudden, rushing character, was aptly termed a *boom.* The papers took it up, . . cautiously at first, . . . but gradually [it] was taken into favor, until all the papers were talking about the Grant *boom.* . . . . Then came the Sherman *boom,* the Blaine *boom,* the Tilden *boom,* and many others. . . From politics the word passed into general use, and we had the business *boom,* the wheat *boom,* the iron *boom,* &c.—*Indianapolis Journal,* Oct. [W. S. Walsh, Handy-Book of Literary Curiosities": Philadelphia, 1893].

1884   Such outlays of money are . . . inexcusable, and their only purpose seems to be to *"boom"* the members securing them, when they ask for a second term.—Mr. D. W. Connolly of Pa., H. R., June 10: *C. R.,* p. 4977/1.

1890   See POST-TRADER.

1896   The object here is simply to *"boom"* one kind of dairy cattle as against the other breeds.—Mr. S. E. Payne of N. Y., H. R., Feb. 18: *Id.,* p. 1897/2.

Boost. To shove up; to lift up from below. [1825-1910.]

1815   It was rather unpossible for me to climb up to the tiptop of the mast without being *boosted* over the lubber-hole, as they tarm it.—David Humphreys, "The Yankey in England," p. 41.

1815   To *boost* my sperits up a leetle higher, I'll e'en sing.—*Id.,* p. 77.

1870   I have never had around me any toadying clique or mutual admiration society to *"boost"* me higher than I could "clemb" myself.—Mr. B. F. Butler of Mass., H. R., Jan. 28: *C. G.,* p. 864/2.

1891   The very purpose of *boosting* the price of just such books as are in the American market.—Mr. J. W. Daniel of Va., U. S. Senate, Feb. 13: *C. R.,* p. 2612/1.

1894   You may as well say you help a man support his family by first cutting off his right arm, then give him another *boost* toward fortune by cutting off his left arm.—Mr. M. D. Harter of O., H. R., Jan. 11: *Id.,* p. 742/1.

Bootee. A small boot. [1799-1844.]

1822   "Coarse Laced Pegged Bootees" for sale.—*Am. Beacon* (Norfolk, Va.), Jan. 4, p. 1/4.

Border ruffians. Those living on the border of civilized settlements. See also second quotation. [1856-1863.]

1864   We in Kan. have carried on a war for years against Indians, against *border ruffians,* and against rebels.—Mr. Pomeroy of Kan., U. S. Senate, June 24: *C. G.,* p. 3234/2.

1869   This claim is for property destroyed by the *"border ruffians,"* as they were called in the troubles of 1856. At that time a raid was made into the southern portion of Kan., by an armed band from Mo., and in consequence of Mr. Jones affiliating with the "Free State" party they . . . destroyed his residence.—Mr. Sidney Clarke of Kan., H. R., March 19: *Id.,* p. 171/1.

1870   History records the fact that, while Senators were denying the existence of *border ruffianism* in Kan., *border ruffians* were laying waste and murdering people for no other offense than that they were in favor of making Kan. a free state.—Mr. Henry Wilson of Mass., U. S. Senate, Apr. 4: *Id.,* p. 2391/1.

1877   In 1856 . . . I was sent on a mission to inquire into the conduct of the *border ruffians* of Mo.—Mr. John Sherman of O., U. S. Senate, Jan. 19: *C. R.,* p. 746/2.

Borer.   A wood-boring insect or worm.   [1789-1867.]

1878   Every practical lumberman knows that, if you allow the logs to lie on the ground one year, one-third of the value of your logs has disappeared.   . . . The *borers* have taken out one-third of the value of your logs.—Mr. W. P. Frye of Me., H. R., Feb. 5: *C. R.,* pp. 772-3.

Boss.   An employer.   As an adjective, principal.   [1806-1862.]

1863   Not uncommonly [in the U. S.] you will see the boy at the grindstone saying to the *boss workman,* this cog is a little too short, or that is a little too long.—Mr. Joseph A. Wright of Ind., U. S. Senate, Jan. 6: *C. G.,* p. 201/3.

1883   When he saw two *"bosses"* running after one workman, wages were high; but when he saw two workmen running after one *"boss,"* wages were low.—Mr. R. Q. Mills of Tex., H. R., Jan. 26: *C. R.,* p. 1643/2.

Boss, a political.   The leader of a corrupt following.   [1908-1911.]

1882   These [political] managers are popularly known now by the name of *bosses.*   There is a chief *boss,* who is over all.   Then there are subsidiary *bosses,* whose grades vary with their power and efficiency. . . The discipline among the commissioned officers, who are the *bosses,* big and little, is almost perfect—obedience is rewarded; disobedience is punished.—Mr. T. M. Bayne of Pa., H. R., July 6: *Id.,* p. 5706/2.

1894   Why is Tenn. marble specific, and Conn. limestone ad valorem? *Locutus bos.*   The *boss* has given orders. . . . Why do you give duty and bounty both to the sugar trust? *Locutus bos.*   The *boss* has given orders.—Mr. G. F. Hoar of Mass., U. S. Senate, July 12: *Id.,* p. 6154/2.

1911   *Boss* Murphy was most solemnly virtuous in denouncing the Putnam County Democrats who have driven a bargain with the Republicans that they shall elect the supervisors while their opponents choose the Assemblyman.   Deals like this are particularly offensive to any *boss*— when not arranged by himself and under cover.   Murphy, however, had no opinion to express of his *brother-boss* in Rochester.   That *boss* so clearly represents all that is politically odious that he cannot get men to run for office on his ticket.—*N. Y. Evening Post,* Oct. 19.

Boss.   To control.   [1867-1909.]

1869   [Mr. Butler speaks of the Me. Corps] contemptuously as the "horse marines," and speaks of "one brigadier-general to *boss* one colonel, and one colonel to *boss* somebody else."—Mr. W. E. Robinson of N. Y., H. R., Feb. 19: *C. G.,* p. 1388/2.

1878   [Mr. Thurman] was putting a finger in everybody's pie, correcting Mr. Stevenson on one point, suggesting another point to my friend from Vt., prompting the Senator from Del. in another place, and generally, if I might use a coarse phrase, *bossing* the debate.—Mr. James G. Blaine of Me., U. S. Senate, Apr. 8: *C. R.,* p. 2337/2.

1892   Mr. Walker:—If the gentleman from Tenn. will just keep still for a minute, and just quit *bossing* the House and everybody else. . . . I will explain.   Mr. Richardson:—I do not want to *boss* anybody.   I just want the gentleman to give that information.   No man needs *"bossing"* more than the gentleman from Mass.—H. R., March 18: *Id.,* p. 2196/1-2.

Bossism.   The rule, practices, or system of bosses, especially political bosses.—(Webster.)

1893 No party leader could have been freer [than Senator Barbour] from just imputaton of attempting *bossism.*—Mr. J. W. Daniel of Va., U. S. Senate, Feb. 3 : *C. R.,* p. 1144/2.

Bottle up. So to shut in as to prevent safe egress. Admiral Cervera's squadron was "bottled up" in Santiago Bay.

1890 [It would] take just forty-eight hours for a British fleet to come from Halifax through Long Island Sound and down to Sandy Hook, and effectually *bottle up* the commerce of [New York], including the navy yard,—so effectually *bottle it up* that they could not get out with anything but a submarine vessel or something of that kind.—Mr. J. R. Hawley of Conn., U. S. Senate, May 24 : *C. R.,* p. 5227/1-2.

Bottom disease. See **Crotalism.**

Bottom dollar. One's last dollar. [1882-1904.]

1866 His opinion is that a State can go out of the Union, and he is willing to bet his *bottom dollar* on his judgment.—Mr. Dumont of Ind., H. R., March 17 : *C. G.,* p. 1474/1.

Bottom facts. The real and full truth. [1877-1884.]

1896 I am only giving what I believe to be the *bottom facts.*—Mr. C. G. Burton of Mo., H. R., Feb. 26 : *C. R.,* p. 2182/2.

Bounced. Ejected summarily. [1882-1890.]

1876 Where are the soldiers of the Union army, many of them wounded and disabled? Nearly all gone, a clean sweep; to use a phrase that I never heard before, although I am told it is common in some sections of the country, they are *"bounced."* —Mr. John Sherman of O., U. S. Senate, Aug. 10; *C. R.,* p. 5403/1.

1881 It now seems probable that the Senate will never be organized till Gorham is *"bounced."—Daily Oregonian,* March 30 : cited, *C. R.,* Apr. 22, p. 389/1.

Bound boys. Apprentices. [1846.]

1891 [In the House of Commons] it rarely happens that more than two-thirds of the members are present, and, when they are, all but 360 must stand round like *"bound boys,"* as that number exhausts the sitting space on the floor.—Mr. Marriott Brosius of Pa., H. R., Jan. 27 : *C. R.,* p. 1890/1.

Bounty broker. See quotations.

1864 A *bounty-broker* is simply a crimp, or what the recruiting sergeants [here] call a "bringer."—G. A. Sala in the *Daily Telegraph,* Aug. 9. (N. E. D.)

1865 There has been a great deal of rascality perpetrated by *bounty brokers* and other persons of that description.—Mr. James W. Grimes of Ia., U. S. Senate, Feb. 7 : *C. G.,* p. 633/2.

Bounty jumpers. See second quotation. [1875-1889.]

1865 [We have been] putting *bounty jumpers* into the army as substitutes, to desert from time to time, leaving their regiments as small as when they went in.—Mr. John F. Farnsworth of Ill., H. R., Feb. 24 : *C. G.,* p. 1083/2.

1881 We had in some of our large cities men who were pursuing the very profitable industry of *"bounty jumping":* enlisting today and taking the oath of allegiance to the Government as a soldier, getting the bounty, and deserting tomorrow, and the next day enlisting again and taking another bounty. We had them by scores and hundreds; I am afraid by thousands.—Mr. S. J. Kirkwood of Ia., U. S. Senate, Feb. 7 : *C. R.,* p. 1292/2.

1884 I shall not vote for [this bill] until I am ready to put the man upon the pension-roll "who broke his leg attempting to *jump a bounty."*—Mr. T. M. Browne of Ind., H. R., March 28 : *Id.,* p. 2388/1.

1896 See Coffee-cooler.

1911 "Historically speaking," writes Mr. [Charles Francis] Adams, "it is a fact not to be denied that the bounty-bought material constituted a large percentage of the whole Civil War levy." What the *bounties* were, and how often they were *"jumped,"* may be seen by any one who will look at Mr. James Ford Rhodes's patient investigations.— *N. Y. Evening Post,* Dec. 28, p. 4/4.

Bourbon. A "dyed-in-the-wool" Democrat. [1859-1907.]

1875 If any American looks back to and longs for something like the republic of the fathers, he is hooted at as a *"Bourbon."*—Mr. W. M. Robbins of N. C., H. R., Feb. 10: *C. R.,* p. 37/2, App.

1875 Baxter's success depended upon the influence of his *Bourbon* allies.— Mr. W. J. Hynes of Ark., H. R., March 2: *Id.,* p. 2111/1.

1877 See Appendix.

1879 If I [still] believed, as the *Bourbons* do, that slavery was right, best for the master and best for the slave, and the true and rightful order of society, then, if I had the power, I would restore slavery. . . . . . The money king of the North has the same contempt for the Irishman who blacks his boots and drives his carriage, as the Southern *Bourbon* for the negro who works in his sugar field. . . . The white men of the South are not all *Bourbons.*—Mr. D. L. Russell of N. C., H. R., Apr. 17: *Id.,* p. 21, App.

1881 I am not sufficiently acquainted with history to know why a man should dislike to be called a *"Bourbon"* democrat.—Mr. N. J. Hammond of Ga., H. R., Feb. 7: *Id.,* p. 1305/2.

1881 I can tell [Mr. Johnston] what a *Bourbon* is. It was a man who never learnt anything or forgot anything; but the *Bourbons* are advancing, and now it is a man who never learns anything and forgets a great deal.—Mr. Geo. F. Hoar of Mass., U. S. Senate, March 25: *C. R.,* p. 61/1. [See also the remarks of Mr. Hill of Ga., March 30, pp. 128-9; and those of Mr. Pendleton of O., Apr. 13, p. 278/1.]

1882 I suppose that in this day [George Washington] would be read out of all parties as a miserable old *Bourbon,* an intolerable *Bourbon.*—Mr. B. H. Hill of Ga., U. S. Senate, Jan. 19: *Id.,* p. 511/2.

1882 The Bourbons of France were said "never to forget and never to learn anything"; but the *Bourbon* of the South, the average Alabama *Bourbon,* is eager to learn anything that will put him in power, and prompt to forget anything that will put him out.—Mr. W. M. Lowe of Ala., H. R., June 2: *Id.,* p. 330/1, App.

1882 I am met on every hand with *Bourbons* of the deepest dye: men who never learn and who never forget; envious, morose, implacable, wrapped up in their own sordid selfishness; men who never placed themselves in harm's way, and yet boast of their prowess.—Mr. Theron M. Rice of Mo., H. R., June 23: *Id.,* p. 549/2.

1892 See Wild and Woolly West.

Bourbon. Kentucky whiskey, from Bourbon County. [1857-1859.]

1862 The liquor that is termed "old *Bourbon*" had its origin in the county in which I reside, and a great deal of the genuine article is distilled there. . . . . One barrel of genuine *Bourbon* liquor taken to the city of Cincinnati will produce from three to four barrels of rectified whisky.—Mr. Garrett Davis of Ky., U. S. Senate, May 22: *C. G.,* p. 2288/3.

1868 The whisky that is manufactured in Ky. is called old *Bourbon.* It is taken to Cincinnati and New York, and even to Boston, and out of one barrel of *old Bourbon* the rectifiers there make three barrels of your Red Head.—U. S. Senate, March 19: *Id.,* p. 1983/2.

1880 [Every man who] makes, deals in, or drinks *Bourbon whisky* knows very well that it requires nearly three years to produce a *Bourbon whisky* which is ready for consumption.—Mr. Benj. Butterworth of O., H. R., May 1: *C. R.,* p. 2938/2.

1882 See Burgoo.

Bowery, the. See Vol. I. [1803-1832.]
1870 The Fifth Avenue and *the Bowery* are happily united in my person. The one raises oranges, grapes, and lemons under glass, while as an article of consumption (*sic*) there is no locality where more peanuts are consumed than in the dramatic precincts of the Bowery.—Mr. S. S. Cox of N. Y., H. R., May 13: *C. G.,* p. 3468/2.

Bowie knife. A knife with a blade ten inches in length. It was named for Col. Bowie. [1836-1889.]
1866 [We can remember] when weapons were drawn, and Barksdale's *bowie-knife* gleamed before our eyes.—Mr. Thaddeus Stevens of Pa., H. R., May 10: *C. G.,* p. 2544/3.

Box rent. Rent for a pigeon-hole in a post office. [1841.]
1862 What class of people is it who [read the papers]? It is the class of men who have *boxes* in post offices, who go there regularly, who pay postage.—Mr. Roscoe Conkling of N. Y., H. R., Jan. 9: *C. G.,* p. 258/1.
1864 [The local postmaster] receives the pay for the *box rents* in the estimate of his salary.—Mr. Collamer of Vt. In the small towns, the postmaster puts up these boxes as a matter of convenience to the inhabitants, and he puts the pay and emoluments from that source in his own pocket.—Mr. Hale of N. H., U. S. Senate, June 25: *Id.,* p. 3253/1.
1875 I cannot understand [how we can increase the pay of the postmaster of New York] unless we impose a new tax by increased *box-rent.*—Mr. C. L. Merriam of N. Y., H. R., Feb. 10: *C. R.,* p. 1126/1.
1881 Postal funds are such funds as arise from *box rents* and from the sale of postage stamps.—Mr. Eli Saulsbury of Del., U. S. Senate, March 1: *Id.,* p. 2283/1.

Box-wagon. An oblong wagon, sometimes provided with seats. This word seems to have eluded all the dictionaries.
1874 [It] was a small . . covered carriage, sufficient to enable a Bureau officer to come to the Capitol . . . . upon a rainy day like this, and not be soaked in a "*box-wagon.*"—Mr. S. Y. Kellogg of Conn., Apr. 25: *C. R.,* p. 3377/2.

Boys in blue. The Union soldiers.
1866 The brave "*boys in blue*" fought manfully, and through their efforts the Union has been preserved.—Mr. E. R. V. Wright of N. J., H. R., Jan. 27: *C. G.,* p. 460/1.
1866 See BUTTERNUTS. See JOHNNY REB.
1868 [The negroes] might have piloted the *boys in blue* into ambush and battery; . . . . but they toiled by day and traveled by night to warn us of danger.—Mr. T. W. Tipton of Neb., U. S. Senate, Feb. 10: *C. G.,* 1079/2.
1893 I do not wonder that there is great dissatisfaction among the *boys in blue,* the men who fought to sustain the Union.—Mr. J. N. Dolph of Ore., U. S. Senate, Sept. 30: *C. R.,* p. 1971/1.

Brain fag. Mental exhaustion.
1876 Whether [Mr. Blaine] has been actually prostrated by a protracted attack of "*brain fag,*" or has been merely playing the part of the "old soldier" in order to postpone investigation . . . . I do not know.—Mr. J. Proctor Knott of Ky., H. R., Aug. 3: *C. R.,* p. 5124/1.

Brain, on the. To have a subject on the brain is to be crazy about it. The N. E. D. gives no example.
1869 The Gazette seems to have the franking privilege "*on the brain.*"—Mr. Samuel F. Cary of O., H. R., Jan. 5: *C. G.,* p. 182/2.
1870 [This] is a volunteer statement from one of the somewhat notorious "peace commission," who seem to have "Indian *on the brain,*" and who appear to have less knowledge of Indian character and less sympathy for white men . . . . than any class of professed philanthropists of the day.—Mr. Jas. M. Cavanaugh of Mont., H. R., March 2: *Id.,* p. 1643/3.

Brainy. Possessing brains; quick-witted. [1874-1904.]

1879 Allow me to quote from the greatest, the *brainiest,* and ablest colored leader in the U. S. I refer to Hon. P. B. S. Pinchback.—Mr. B. B. Ellis of Ala., H. R., Apr. 25: *C. R.,* p. 932/2.

1886 We have blazed a way for men like the Knights [of labor] and for other great organizations. . . . These organizations are controlled by conservative, *brainy,* patriotic men.—Mr. Farquhar of N. Y., H. R., Apr. 2: *Id.,* p. 3043/1.

1893 The Secretary of the Interior . . . is a big, broad-gauged, *brainy* man, as honest and just as God makes men.—Mr. M. R. Baldwin of Minn., H. R., Dec. 18: *Id.,* p. 359/2.

1896 Mr. [Thomas B.] Reed, in my judgment the *brainiest* leader the Republican party has known on this floor for many years.—Mr. A. M. Dockery of Mo., H. R., June 10: *Id.,* p. 6430/2.

Brakeman. The man who handles the brake on a train.—(Webster.)

1861 A *brakeman* told me this delay was not very unusual.—Olmsted, "Cotton Kingdom," I, 161. (N. E. D.)

1872 The conductors who order and the *brakemen* who execute the ejectment of an insolent, presuming colored man from a . . . sleeping car.—Mr. J. C. Harper of N. C., H. R., May 4: *C. G.,* p. 371/1, App.

1883 The *brakeman* bawled out, "Tannery Town!"—*Harper's Mag.,* p. 212/2. (N. E. D.)

Branch. A stream smaller than a "creek"; a brook. [1817-1852.]

1878 I do not want the Senate to vote under the misapprehension that this river is a creek or a *spring branch.* . . . . It is a river of very considerable size. I know it well: I was raised upon its banks.—Mr. A. S. Merrimon of N. C., U. S. Senate, June 10: *C. R.,* p. 4377/1.

Bran dance. A Western dance at which the ground is generally sprinkled with Indian meal. [1833-1851.]

1883 "The *Bran Dance* at the Apple Settlement."—Sherwood Bonner, "Dialect Tales," pp. 151-161.

Branding-chute. A narrow lane or guideway through which cattle are driven one at a time to be branded.—(Century Dict.)

1900 [Judge Greene of Neb.] was just as much at home standing on a *branding shute* backed up against a sod corral out on the range, as some gentlemen are in making a political speech in an opera house.—Mr. W. L. Stark of Neb., H. R., Jan. 10: *C. R.,* p. 22/1, App.

Brash, Brashness. Foolishly impetuous. [1824-1837.]

1890 Lieut. Davis went into the war with great *brashness.*—Statement of John McElroy, *C. R.,* Apr. 21: p. 3638/1.

1897 [The duties under the Dingley bill] are too low and mild on the things of the South, and too high and *brash* on the things of the North.—Mr. John L. McLaurin of S. C., H. R., March 23: *Id.,* p. 190/2.

Brave. An Indian warrior. The word is used as a noun in a general sense by Chapman and others.—(N. E. D.)

1837 The *braves* following in a long line, painted and decorated.—W. Irving, "Captain Bonneville" (1849), p. 96. (N. E. D.)

1841 A Blackfoot *brave* whose portrait I have painted.—George Catlin, "N. Am. Indians" (1844), I, 35. (N. E. D.)

1886 The *braves* are there, . . actuated by the same desire to distinguish themselves in battle that actuated those who fought at the Custer massacre.—Mr. C. F. Manderson of Neb., U. S. Senate, March 23: *C. R.,* p. 2647/2.

Breachy. Apt to break through fences. Eng. dial. [1800-1846.]

1879 There are one or two *breachy* men who will insist upon leading your party into the very jaws of death and destruction; and would do so if it were not for the wiser heads of the party.—Mr. McMahon of O., H. R., June 10: *C. R.,* p. 1895/2.

Bread and butter brigade. A term derisively applied to the appointees of President Andrew Johnson.

1866 There are gentlemen here, who in the last political contest went over the country saying that a certain party was a *"bread and butter brigade."* . . . Who constitute the *"bread and butter brigade"?* Why, sir, the very Constitution is stricken down, all the powers that have been conferred upon the President of the U. S., and exercised since the foundation of the Government, are to be upturned, and for what? For the purpose of saving the *"bread and butter"* to the party here who seek to control matters in their own way, right or wrong.—Mr. Le Blond of O., H. R., Dec. 19: *C. G.,* p. 206/3.

1867 The only way in which we can get [at] Mr. Harvey [the minister to Portugal] is to "starve him out." And there is a peculiar propriety in our taking this course, when it affects one of this *"bread and butter brigade."*—Mr. R. C. Schenck of O., H. R., Jan. 29: *Id.,* p. 847/3. [See also the rest of this debate.]

[1867 You know that one of his Cabinet ministers was said to have proclaimed during the last session of Congress that no man could partake of the President's *bread and butter* unless he would support the President's policy.—Mr. Timothy O. Howe of Wisc., U. S. Senate, Feb. 6: *Id.,* p. 1041/1.]

1867 [What Senator Howe] said nearly a year ago, when he invented . . . . . a phrase, when he spoke of the *"bread and butter brigade."*—Mr. James Dixon of Conn., U. S. Senate, Apr. 12: *Id.,* p. 834/2.

1867 [These offices] were filled by Mr. Lincoln with good, responsible, reliable Union Republicans. [They] were removed by Andrew Johnson to make place for unreliable, irresponsible Copperheads in most cases, or *bread-and-butter men,* who are worse.—Mr. Zach. Chandler of Mich., U. S. Senate: *Id.,* p. 835/3.

Bread and butter, to quarrel with one's. To find fault with one's means of livelihood. [1820-1884.]

1884 Industries were not so plenty . . that men could afford . . to *quarrel with their bread and butter.*—*Harper's Mag.,* Dec., p. 92/2. (N. E. D.)

Breadstuffs. Cereal products. [1793-1852.]

1863 We want the handiwork of New England, and they want our *breadstuffs.* . . . . We want to furnish *breadstuffs* to New England and N. Y. The statistics show that N. Y. raises *breadstuffs* enough only to feed her population for four months in the year.—Mr. Elihu B. Washburne of Ill., H. R., Feb. 7: *C. G.,* p. 815/3.

Break. A blunder.

1890 That was a terrible *break* for us to make upon the law.—Mr. J. T. Morgan of Ala., U. S. Senate, July 17: *C. R.,* p. 7350/1.

1897 I believe [Mr. Hopkins of Ill.] made a bad *break* as a lawyer, but I believe him to be a good lawyer.—Mr. J. W. Miles of Md., H. R., Feb. 26: *Id.,* p. 2364/1.

Break. A Virginia term for a regular sale of tobacco at the time when the hogsheads are first opened.—(Century Dict.)

Break. To start off suddenly.

1892 When a man is working for wages out in the hot harvest field, there is nothing more delightful to him than a little fall of rain which will drive him in. So these harvesters *broke* for the barn.—Mr. J. M. Allen of Miss., H. R., Jan. 28: *C. R.,* p. 655/2.

Breakhead. The forward end or bow of a vessel, powerfully built in order to break through ice.

1904 In order to be able to maintain this ferry service in winter, the "Mecklenburg" has been constructed as an ice-breaker. The hull has a *breakhead* such as is usually only carried by ice-breakers.—*Sci. Amer. Supp.,* p. 23422. (Century Dict.)

Breaking team. A team that breaks up new ground.
1896 I do not brag of my voice. I came honestly by it driving *breaking teams.* It is the best voice I have.—Mr. D. B. Henderson of Ia., H. R., May 5: *C. R.,* p. 4843/2.

Breast, v. To oppose manfully. In its figurative sense, the word seems to be originally American.
1850 Prepared to *breast* the difficulties of the Sierra.—W. H. Prescott, "Peru," II, 29. (N. E. D.)
1888 Gentlemen . . . may lash themselves into a fury, . . . and talk about *breasting* the Senate. Why you cannot *breast* anybody on that.—Mr. Thomas B. Reed of Me., H. R., July 31: *C. R.,* p. 7104/1.

Breast of wheat. See quotation.
1868 In some sections of the country, a spikelet is better understood if it is spoken of as a *breast of wheat.*—S. E. Todd, "American Wheat Culturist," p. 24.—(Century Dict.)

Brick, like a thousand of [or **a ton of brick**]. See quotation.
1867 I had no expectation . . . . of bringing down upon myself, *"like a thousand of brick,"* the torrent of [Senator Saulsbury's] indignant eloquence.—Mr. Garrett Davis of Ky., U. S. Senate, Feb. 18: *C. G.,* p. 1513/3.

Brick pond. A pond in a bricked-in excavation. [1811.]
1850 Water [was] brought from the neighboring *brick ponds* in buckets.— Wilmington (N. C.) *Commercial,* Sept. 5, p. 2/3. (From the *Phila. Ledger.*)

Brief. A summary of arguments and cases. [1821.]
1877 The Ore. *brief* . . . . comes up again to prove that, when an ineligible person is elected, there is no election.—Mr. W. M. Evarts before the Electoral Commission, Feb. 15: 'Proceedings,' p. 108/1.
1892 I had the honor to be one of the attorneys in the case, and filed a *brief* against the bonds.—Mr. W. J. Bryan of Neb., H. R., March 16: *C. R.,* p. 2130/1.

Brighamites. See **Josephites.**

Bright. Quick-witted, intelligent.
1730 Against Challoner's name Mr. Mayes wrote, "He is said to be one of y⁰ *brightest* men that was ever bred in Douay College."—"Life of B. P. Challoner," I, 63 (1909).
1824 I began life unluckily by being the wag and *bright* fellow at school.— W. Irving, "Tales of a Traveller," I, 203. (N. E. D.)
1880 I recognize [Mr. Harris] as one of the *brightest* gentlemen on the floor; but I must decline to be interrupted further.—Mr. W. P. Frye of Me., H. R., Jan. 22: *C. R.,* p. 483/1.
1882 See DRUMMER.
1890 Every *bright* mechanic in his shop . . . . is inventing and improving every day in the processes.—Mr. J. R. Hawley of Conn., U. S. Senate, Aug. 12: *Id.,* p. 8469/1.

Bright mulatto. A quadroon or octoroon.
1831 For Sale, A *Bright Mulatto* Man.—*The Georgian* (Savannah), Apr. 5, p. 3/3. (Advt.)

Brindle-tails. The nickname of a political party in Arkansas.
1871 The Republican party in the State of Ark. was divided, and the *"Brindle-tail party,"* as it is called, headed by Senators Rice and McDonall, went off and opposed Governor Clayton's usurpations of power. . . . The Lieutenant-Governor, Mr. Johnson, . . . still remains in the Republican party, but belongs to the *"Brindle-tail"* wing of that party.—Mr. A. A. C. Rogers of Ark., H. R., Jan. 7: *C. G.,* p. 350/1.
1872 In the township of Ashley, more than in any other township in Pulaski County, did the *"Brindle-tail"* mob hold high carnival.—Mr. John Edwards of Ark., Feb. 9: *Id.,* p. 935/2.

Broad aisle. The middle passage of a meetinghouse or church. [1776-1872.]

1830 A respectable black man and his numerous family were seen advancing up the *broad aisle.—Am. Beacon,* July 7, p. 4/1. (From a Boston paper.)

Broadax. A large ax used by woodmen. [1779-1857.]

1844 I bid [these men] remember the fate of the fellow who "swallowed the *broad-axe,* but got choked with the handle."—Mr. Dawson of La., H. R., Jan. 2: p. 3 of speech as separately published.

1862 I do not like the idea that we are bound to go ahead with a *broadax,* and cut, and cut, and cut, merely for the sake of cutting, without regarding the consequence.—Mr. W. P. Fessenden of Me., U. S. Senate, March 6: *C. G.,* p. 1096/2.

1873 We gained in tonnage during the war of 1812. But those were the days of timber, of the *broadax,* the saw, and the adze.—Mr. A. H. Cragin of N. H., U. S. Senate, Feb. 6: *Id.,* p. 1146/2.

Broad-gauged. Liberal and open-hearted.

1870 In our *broad-gauged* and reckless way of counting cost and reckoning money, three cents is a sum hardly counted as anything.—Mr. Timothy O. Howe of Wisc., U. S. Senate, June 18: *C. G.,* p. 4578/2.

1881 Everything *broad-gauged* and in liberal proportions.—*Chicago Times,* June 4. (N. E. D.)

1882 [Mr. Vest of Mo.] is generally . . liberal and *broad-gauged* on questions of this sort.—Mr. J. S. Williams of Ky., U. S. Senate, July 10: *C. R.,* p. 5833/2.

1884 The value and importance of a *broad-gauge,* extensive system of harbor and waterway improvements.—Mr. P. Dunn of Ark., H. R., June 10: *Id.,* p. 4971/1.

1893 See BRAINY.

Broad-horn. An "ark" or flatboat. [1820-1850.]

1849 [He] hailed from Ark., and had just arrived on board a *broad-horn.—* Wilmington (N. C.), *Commercial,* March 29, p. 2/2.

Broiler. A fomenter of quarrels. Probably obs. in England.

a.1660 What doth he but turn *broiler* and boutefeu.—Hammond, "Works," iv, 544. (N. E. D.)

1841 Due impression alike on the civil and military *broiler.—*J. W. Orderson, "Cresleana," p. 91. (N. E. D.)

1888 A *broiler,* [a] deadbeat, and a fraud.—Affidavit cited in the *C. R.,* Sept. 24: p. 8894/1.

Broncho. See quotation. [1878-1883.]

1894 [The man said to me:] I had last winter a span of *broncos* that cost me about $75, and an old wagon and harness worth $25. That is all I had to begin with.—Mr. W. W. Bowers of Calif., H. R., Jan. 22: *C. R.,* p. 1197/2.

1894 We have in all the States men who are experts as judges of horseflesh, men who can tell at a glance whether a horse is a *broncho* or an Indian pony or a blooded horse.—Mr. J. C. Kyle of Miss., U. S. Senate, June 6: *Id.,* p. 5862/1.

1903 See CROW-HOP. See BUSTER.

Bronzer. One who works a bronzing machine.

1865 The *bronzer* then [in the Treasury Department of the U. S.] puts the paper through his bronzing machine, and when it is all bronzed it is counted again by the man bronzing it.—Mr. Daniel Clark of N. H., U. S. Senate, Feb. 9: *C. G.,* p. 682/1.

Brummer. A mill whistle.

1898 Our people can again hear the sweet familiar sounds of the *"brummer,"* which to many is more agreeable music than any of the Wagner compositions.—*Lebanon* (Pa.) *Daily News,* Jan. 20: see *C. R.,* Feb. 7, p. 1506/1.

Brush. Underwood, whether growing or cut down. [1774-1854.]

1860 I then, Sir, removing the *brush* from the way as well as I can, and beating about through the labyrinth, . . . have come to the conclusion &c.—Mr. Wigfall of Tex., U. S. Senate, Dec. 5: *C. G.,* p. 14/2.

1863 I would very much prefer to sleep on a bed of *brush* than a bed of boards. It is very far from being an uncomfortable bed, if men know how to make it. Soft *brush,* covered with straw or blankets, makes an excellent couch.—Mr. James Harlan of Ia., U. S. Senate, Jan. 23: *Id.,* p. 470/1.

1864 Jo. Hart, with his marauding band, went to the court house, ... removed these depositions, and took them to the *brush.*—Mr. King of Mo., H. R., June 1: *Id.,* p. 2647/3.

Brush meeting. One held in the woods.

1890 I remember in 1887 attending a great prohibition meeting that was held over in Virginia, called a *brush meeting.*—Mr. Cockrell of Mo., U. S. Senate, May 9: *C. R.,* p. 4376/2.

Bub. Small brother. [1835-1890.]

1876 You [addressing Mr. Eugene Hale of Me.] have been known in the last three or four Congresses as "Blaine's little *bub.*"—Mr. S. S. Cox of N. Y., H. R., Jan. 28: *C. R.,* p. 725/2. [He was called to order.]

Buck, v. See quotations.

1865 He saw men *bucked* by order of Wirtz for attempting to escape.— *Morning Star,* Oct. (N. E. D.)

1869 [He ordered] Private Franklin to be *"bucked"* in a cruel manner, with his hands tied together and stretched over his knees with a pole passing through under his knees. . . . [He ordered] Private Minnegan to be *"bucked,"* and the pole that passed through under his knees to be placed on two stakes, leaving his body swinging above the ground. Charges against Captain Conner, May 10: see *C. G.,* March 31, 1870, p. 2323/1.

1879 Dragging the minsters from the pulpit, *bucking* them across a log, and beating them.—A. W. Tourgee, "A Fool's Errand," p. 73. (N. E. D.)

Buck. A male Indian. [1860-1878.]

1869 I want to see Mr. Mix on a high horse, booted and spurred, with a big cocked hat on, with a bucktail in it, chasing the fourteen year old *buck Indians* across the plains, for the purpose of catching them and putting blue breeches on them.—Mr. John A. Logan of Ill., H. R., Feb. 27: *C. G.,* p. 1707/3.

1876 As soon as these *buck warriors* smell the warpath, they go off and assist the Sioux Indians to put our citizens to death.—Mr. S. J. Randall of Pa., H. R., June 2: *C. R.,* p. 3505/1.

1882 Maddened with pain [from arrow-wounds], the cattle stampede out over the prairies, when they are pursued in turn by the Indians armed with rifles, who shoot them down in their track, where they are left by the *bucks* until the squaws can go to them, who skin and dress the animals and pack the meat into camp, while their lieges bask leisurely in the shade . . . of their tents, conscious of having done their manly duty to their families.—Mr. R. F. Pettigrew of Dak., H. R., July 11: *Id.,* p. 5921/2.

1882 [Not long ago] a treaty was made with the Ute Indians in regard to their reservation; and to induce the agreement the commissioners provided a pound of striped candy for each *buck Indian* in order to be certain of his assent.—Mr. Scales of N. C., H. R., July 26: *Id.,* p. 6540/1.

1892 The pride of the *buck* was the chase and the warpath. The women bore the children and did the drudgery.—Mr. Ezra B. Taylor of O., H. R., Jan. 30: *Id.,* p. 7/2, App.

1897 All of these Indians,—the *bucks,* the squaws, and the papooses,—were blanket Indians.—Mr. J. K. Jones of Ark., U. S. Senate, Apr. 14: *Id.,* p. 715/2.

Buckboard. A four-wheeled vehicle having a long elastic board or frame bearing the seat.—(Webster.) [1839-1888.]

1878 Upon the whole of that route there was only one mule and a *buck-board,* or perhaps sometimes a horse.—Mr. H. D. Money of Miss., H. R., March 20: *C. R.,* p. 1915/2.

1879 Four years ago the Department made a contract for carrying the mail in Tex. on a route on a part of which the only conveyance was a *"buck-board"* wagon.—Mr. A. M. Waddell of N. C., H. R., Feb. 28: *Id.,* p. 2112/2.

1880 The mail [in Kan.] is carried in *buckboards* drawn by one or two mules. . . . Two horses or ponies in that country can draw a light *buckboard* twenty miles a day with perfect ease.—Mr. S. S. Cox of N. Y., H. R., Feb. 26: *Id.,* p. 1165/2.

Bucket letters. See quotation.

1865 Dave Holt [about 1840] was the author of the letters signed "Ned Bucket," and published all over the country. . . . . Anonymous letters came to be called *"Bucket letters."*—Alex. H. Stephens, "Diary," July 26, p. 380. (1910.)

Bucket shop. See Vol. I. [1881-1910.]

1879 See SHOULDER-HITTER.

1884 As between a *bucket-shop* and a put-and-call establishment, as between a margin-dealer and a roulette player, there is little or no moral difference. If there be any, it is in favor of the *bucket-shop* and the roulette-wheel.—Mr. S. S. Cox of N. Y., H. R., June 9: *C. R.,* p. 406/2, App.

1886 Rid the land, we beseech Thee, of all gamesters, whether they gamble with dice or cards or chips or with wheat or sticks or corn or cotton. Deliver us from the influence and power of robbers who, enticing their victims to boards of trade and stock exchanges and *bucket-shops,* name their practices of plunder "shearing the lambs."—Prayer by the Chaplain of the House of Representatives, one W. H. Milburn, March 22: *Id.,* p. 2626/1.

1892 We do not call [these places] casinos, but *bucket shops.* The *bucket shop* does not have the green cloth, but the blackboard.—Mr. W. D. Washburn of Minn., U. S. Senate, July 11: *Id.,* p. 5990/2.

1894 The *bucket-shops* . . . have demoralized more youth than all the gambling dens of the universe. Men who would not touch a pack of cards, or risk a dollar upon a horse race, will buy a put, a call, or a straddle, and salve their consciences with the certainty that they are business men.—Mr. J. C. Sibley of Pa., H. R., June 19: *Id.,* p. 934/2, App.

1898 When before we vote we listen to the ticker to know the state of the market, when the vicious people of the nation write the songs, and the trusts and the *bucket-shops* write the laws, the dawn of our day of decay is upon us.—Mr. W. E. Mason of Ill., U. S. Senate, Feb. 9: *Id.,* p. 1582/1.

Buckeye. Ohio is called the Buckeye State; an Ohioan is colloquially termed a Buckeye. [1784-1896.]

1862 See Mr. Hutchins's sarcastic allusions to Mr. Cox, and to his *"Buck-eye Abroad,"* H. R., July 5: *C. G.,* pp. 3130-33.

1882 [I knew] that the regenerated statesmanship of the modern *Buckeye* could be aroused by nothing less than the Presidency of the U. S.—Mr. A. S. Willis of Ky., H. R., July 8: *C. R.,* p. 5811/1.

1894 The very author of the tariff plank in the Chicago platform was last fall buried beneath more than 80,000 votes in that grand old *"Buckeye"* State.—Mr. W. R. Ellis of Ore., H. R., Jan. 16: *Id.,* p. 79/1, App.

Buck nigger. A male negro. [1842-1860.]

1880 I told the boys that we wanted 20,000 "bucks," *buck niggers,* in Ind. this year.—Testimony of Thomas P. Mills of Indianapolis: *C. R.,* June 4, p. 4147/1.

Buckshot war. An outbreak in Pa. (1838) arising out of election disputes. [1842.]

1868 Porter beat Ritner in 1838, and then Mr. [Thaddeus] Stevens made the capital mistake of his life, in determining to treat the election as if it had not occurred. This brought on the *"buckshot war."*—Mr. G. W. Woodward of Pa., H. R., Dec. 17: *C. G.,* p. 141/1.

1875 This *buckshot war* was a ridiculous affair from beginning to end. I am only sorry that the use of types has carried the history of it down to this time. Everybody laughed at it. I was in Harrisburgh at the time, and I was rather friendly to old Ritner, but nobody disturbed me.—Mr. Simon Cameron of Pa., U. S. Senate, March 12: *C. R.,* p. 38/1.

Buckskin. A Virginian. [1755-1837.]

1766 "An honest Buckskin" wrote to the *Virginia Gazette,* Aug. 1, in defence of John Robinson, Speaker and Treasurer of the House of Burgesses, who died May 11, 1766.

Bucktails. Name given to a Pa. regiment during the Civil War. [1863-1876.]

1864 General Crawford led the famous Pennsylvania Reserves, shouting to them, as amid shot and shell they rushed up a steep hill, and took an important battery, "Don't let the *Bucktails* (another Pa. regiment) beat you."—Mr. L. Myers of Pa., H. R., Jan. 12: *C. G.,* p. 172/2.

Budge, the. Nervousness. Local.

1824 Madame Neckar was a very sincere and excellent woman, but she was not very pleasant in conversation, for she was subject to what in Va. we call the *"budge,"* that is, she was very nervous and fidgety. She could rarely remain long in the same place, or converse long on the same subject.—Thomas Jefferson: see "Private Corresp. of Daniel Webster" (1857) I. 373.

Budge-barrel. See quotation. See also Vol. I, **Bludge barrels.**

1715 *Budge-barrel,* a little Tin-Barrel to hold Gun-powder, generally us'd aboard a Ship.—Kersey, "Dictionarium Anglo-Britannicum."

Buffalo chips. Dry buffalo manure. [1846-1893.]

1850 The young man had gathered some *buffalo chips* to make a fire to cook with.—Wilmington (N. C.) *Commercial,* Feb. 2, p. 1/5.

1878 Of course an officer on the plains, who is picking up *buffalo chips* with which to boil his teakettle, takes his commutation for fuel in money.—Mr. B. F. Butler of Mass., H. R., Feb. 5: *C. R.,* p. 778/1.

Buffalo grass. [1893.] 1863. See **Gramma.**

Buffalo platform. [1850.] See also Vol. II, **Platform, 1850.**

1863 [I think the people of the vicinage ought] to say who shall be postmaster. I do not care whether that doctrine is in the *Buffalo platform* or anywhere else.—Mr. S. S. Cox of O., H. R., Feb. 20: *C. G.,* p. 1154/1.

1864 Was he an unwilling advocate of emancipation, who first unfurled that banner in Mo. on the *Buffalo platform* in 1848, in defiance of the pro-slavery sentiment of his State, and in opposition to the views of . . . Colonel Benton?—Mr. F. P. Blair of Mo., H. R., Feb. 27: *Id.,* p. 49/2, App.

Buffalo tug. A long strip of buffalo hide.

1832 [The mother said] a *"buffalo tug"* was no weapon with which the son of a warrior ought to be struck.—John A. McClung, "Sketches of Western Adventure," p. 29. (Phila.)

1832 [The Indian conducted John S.] into a strong block house, pinioned his arms until the *buffalo tug* was buried in the flesh, and [passed] another thong round his neck.—*Id.,* p. 165.

Buffalo-wallow. See quotation.
1887 They had come to an alkali mud-hole, an old *buffalo-wallow,* which
had filled up, and was covered with a sun-baked crust, that let them
through as if they had stepped on a trapdoor.—Theodore Roosevelt,
Century Mag., xxxv. 658.
Bug. By the beginning of the eighteenth century, the word seems to
become specialized. Kersey (1715) says, "a well-known noisome
Insect." [1642-1867.]
1873 What is this [agricultural] bureau? It is in fact the bureau of
bugs. . . . I always supposed entomology did refer to *bugs.*—Mr.
S. S. Cox of N. Y., H. R., Jan. 10: *Id.,* p. 499/1.
1879 What an idea! Pay these scientific men to hunt *bugs,* pay them to
get up fancy colored maps, and yet charge the settler with the expense
of defining the boundaries of his little homestead!—Mr. D. C.
Haskell of Kan., H. R., Feb. 11: *C. R.,* p. 1211/2.
Bugaboo. A terrific vision. Scotland, Ireland, and Cheshire. See
Eng. Dial. Dict. and Notes and Queries 11, S. vii, 89. [1740-1860.]
1787 The maid threatens to leave them in the dark for the *bug-a-boos.*—
Columbian Mag., (Phila.), p. 464/2.
1865 All these *bugaboos* that [Senator Johnson of Md.] raises to fright us
from our purpose.—Mr. Benjamin Wade of O., U. S. Senate, Jan. 9:
C. G., p. 164/2.
1866 I have no fear for the liberties of the people from the President
[Andrew Johnson]. That is a *bugaboo.*—Mr. James Guthrie of Ky.,
U. S. Senate, Apr. 5: *Id.,* p. 1786/3.
1876 See BLOODY SHIRT, first quotation.
1878 All the imaginary *bugaboos* which [Mr. Edmunds] has constructed
out of his fertile imagination . . . I propose to cut up by the roots.—
Mr. James G. Blaine of Me., U. S. Senate, Apr. 9: *C. R.,* p. 2365/2.
[The compiler would gladly "give a fip" to see the process carried out.]
1879 First, as to this great *bugaboo,* John Roach. Who is John Roach?
. . . He is today the greatest American shipbuilder.—Mr. A. M. Waddell of N. C., H. R., Feb. 28: *Id.,* p. 2112/1.
1883 Let me call the attention of the Senate to the *bugaboo*—and I beg
pardon for calling it so—in regard to the duties placed on German
silver.—Mr. J. S. Morrill of Vt., U. S. Senate, Jan. 29: *Id.,* p. 1717/1.
1884 The stalwart pauper *bugaboo* of king-ridden, down-trodden Europe.—
Mr. S. S. Cox of N. Y., H. R., March 20: *Id.,* p. 7/1, App.
1888 As to "watering stock," that can take care of itself; I would not
raise a *bugaboo* of that kind in reference to this bill.—Mr. C. O'Neill
of Pa., H. R., June 11: *Id.,* p. 5122/2.
1890 You use the "trust" as a *bugaboo* to frighten the people away from the
Republican party into your ranks.—Mr. W. E. Mason of Ill., H. R.,
May 1: *Id.,* p. 4100/1.
1893 The fear and cry of negro domination was fitly named by a gentleman
from the South, who said it was a *"bugaboo."*—Mr. G. W. Ray of
N. Y., H. R., Oct. 6: *Id.,* p. 2231/1.
Buggy-plow. 1876. See **Gang-plow.**
Bugology. A slang term for entomology.
1893 Two volumes on what the scientists call entomology, but what we plain
people call *bugology.*—Mr. Champ Clark of Mo., H. R., Oct. 18:
C. R., p. 2667/2.
1898 Those of you who are acquainted with *bugology* know there is rather a
disreputable bug that looks one way and rolls the other.—Mr. J. M.
Allen of Miss., H. R., Apr. 22: *Id.,* p. 455/2, App.
Bug under the chip. A concealed purpose to secure an advantage.
1885 I know as well *what the bug is under this chip* as I know that the
resolution is pending here.—Mr. H. H. Riddleberger of Va., U. S.
Senate, Jan. 26: *C. R.,* p. 998/1.

Bulldoze. To restrain or coerce by intimidation.—(Webster.) [1842-1889.]

1876 The scenes that occurred in those parishes [of La.] that are called *"bull-dozed,"* where thousands of negroes fled from their cabins, slept at nights in the swamps, and worked at picking cotton in the daytime, were disclosed by that testimony.—Mr. John Sherman of O., U. S. Senate, Dec. 6: *C. R.,* p. 59/2.

1876 [Senator Sherman] is making a great effort to sustain the *bull-dozing* of the State of La. I do not think he will succeed.—Mr. L. V. Bogy of Mo., U. S. Senate, Dec. 20: *Id.,* p. 320/2.

1876 Some time in Sept. or Oct., 1875, a band of *bull-dozers* came into Saint Francisville, and by their yelling and hallooing through the streets . . . . put the inhabitants in a mortal terror.—Affidavit cited, *Id.,* p. 500/1.

1876 For the three months just before the election, the parish [of W. Feliciana] has been patrolled by the *bull-dozers.*—Another affidavit, *Id.,* p. 500/2.

1877 See MISSISSIPPI PLAN.

1877 [Anderson] is the fellow that shot himself to make it appear that his life was in danger from Democrats. It is proven that he shot through his own clothes, trying to *bulldoze* himself.—Mr. Lewis V. Bogy of Mo., U. S. Senate, Jan. 19: *Id.,* p. 748/1.

1879 [These men] have—I will not use the slang language of the day, I will not talk about *bulldozing*—but have coerced the Executive.—Mr. A. G. Thurman of O., U. S. Senate, June 6: *Id.,* p. 1823/2.

1880 A mighty effort was made to *bulldoze* Congress into counting Tilden in.—Mr. Philip C. Hayes of Ill., H. R., March 10: *Id.,* p 1451/2.

1881 Whatever may have been done elsewhere to cause the coinage of that brutal word, *bull-dozing*—and I ask pardon for using it—Senators are not likely to be *bull-dozed.* Their votes will be free.—Mr. Justin S. Morrill of Vt., U. S. Senate, Apr. 22: *Id.,* p. 377/2.

1882 Every art of persuasion, and I might say of *bulldozing,* has been brought to bear [upon us in the matter of the issue of 3 per cent bonds].—Mr. P. B. Plumb of Kan., U. S. Senate, Feb. 3: *Id.,* p. 863/1.

1890 The negro leader Neeley [in 1888] undertook to *bulldoze* such of the colored Republicans as would not follow him.—Mr. T. C. McRae of Ark., H. R., June 30: *Id.,* p. 6805/1.

Bullfrog. See quotation. [1705-1856.]

1715 Virginia-Frog, a kind of Frog that is eight or ten times as big as any in England, and makes a noise like the bellowing of a bull.—Kersey, "Dictionarium Anglo-Britannicum."

Bull-nettle. A weed with silvery leaves: *Solanum elæagni-folium.*

1876 [He] beat down the wild-brier and *bull-nettle,* . . . . felled the forest, and hewed out his humble home.—Mr. Philips of Mo., H. R., May 18: *C. R.,* p. 3166/2.

Bull pen. Primarily, a pen for the enclosure of bulls. Then it came to mean a place in which to pen convicts or other refractory subjects.

1879 If you give [such a man] authority about the cow-yards and the *bull-pens* . . . about the shipping ports, he will with the power become very offensive.—Mr. Voorhees of Ind., U. S. Senate, May 27: *C. R.,* p. 1626/1.

1891 [They] would coax these illiterate white men, weeks before election, and cage them in places called *bull pens,* drug them with bad whisky, and keep them there to vote against their convictions.—Mr. T. E. Miller of S. C., H. R., Feb. 14: *Id.,* p. 2693/2.

1912 Jackson, Mich., Sept. 3.—Rioting convicts who broke out of *"bull pens"* here are gathered in the prison yard, considering further steps. Officers of the prison are exerting every effort to keep them from scaling the walls.—*N. Y. Evening Post,* Sept. 5, p. 2/5.

Bull-trains.   Trains of ox-wagons.
1889   [They had] no means of getting to and from N. M. except what
used to be called . . . . *"bull-trains,"* which would only carry a person
from our Mo. frontier to N. M., in a period of from six to ten weeks.—
Mr. C. S. Voorhees of Wash., H. R., Jan. 16: *C. R.,* p. 869/2.

Bully boy.   A jovial, dashing fellow.
1609   Wee be three poore Mariners, newly come from the seas,
         Wee spend our lives in ieopardy, whiles others live at ease;
         Shall we goe daunce the round, the round, the round,
                 and shall we goe daunce the round?
         And he that is a *bully boy,* come pledge me on the ground.
    —Song for Treble, Tenor, and Bassus: T. Ravenscroft, "Deutero-
    melia," No. 6.

Bullyragging.   Scolding with threats.   [1807-1870.]
1881   [These men] who put the claims of their locality above the nation's
need and the nation's honor, began at once a course of *bully-ragging*
to get in their protective items.—Mr. S. S. Cox of N. Y., H. R.,
Feb. 7: *C. R.,* p. 149/2, App.

Bumblebee checks.   See quotation.
1880   Mr. M. C. Butler of S. C.:—[Mr. Teller] has said a good deal about
tissue ballots. Now, will he tell us something about the *bumblebee
checks* and soup-tickets used in R. I. in some elections there? Mr.
Teller of Colo.:—I know nothing about that.—U. S. Senate, May 25:
C. R., p. 3758/1.

Bummer.   A worthless, lazy fellow. A special meaning, a lone raider
and forager, became attached to the word during the Civil War.
[1856-1885.]
1868   [The lobbying on account of Wyo.] has all been in the interest of
paper-city proprietors and political *"bummers."*—Mr. James M. Ashley of O., H. R., July 22: *C. G.,* p. 4344/3.
1873   There was a sort of stampede of loafers and *bummers* and vagabonds
from eastern cities, who expected to go out [to Colo.] and pick up a
fortune in 1859 and 1860.—Mr. Taffe of Neb., H. R., Jan. 21: *Id.,*
p. 745/2.
1876   The hirelings and *bummers* of party have kept up their dirty work
of defamation and slander.—Mr. G. W. Cato of Wisc., H. R., May
20: *C. R.,* p. 3234/2.
1878   See DEADBEAT.
1879   A regular double-and-twisted, strong-fisted ward *bummer,* a fellow
that is around in party caucuses and conclaves.—Mr. James G.
Blaine of Maine, U. S. Senate, June 6: *Id.,* p. 1823/1.
1879   See SHOULDER-HITTER.
1890   A *bummer* so full of whisky that one could see the bead standing in
his eye, and hear it slosh in him as he trotted up and down.—Mr.
Z. B. Vance of N. C., U. S. Senate, July 1: *Id.,* p. 6833/2.
1892   I would refuse [a pension] to a man who followed the wake of the
army as a *bummer.*—Mr. E. E. Meredith of Va., H. R., March 18:
Id., p. 2215/2.

Bumper.   A buffer. See quotations.
1839   The *bumpers* or elastic cushions are to be attached &c.—*Journal,*
Franklin Institute, xxiv, 156. (N. E. D.)
1864   The *Bumper* is surrounded by a stiff spring, which prevents the
communication of the jar.—*Sanatory Commission, U. S. Army,* p.
110, note. (N. E. D.)
1868   Mr. W. E. Robinson:—There were India rubber springs at the end
of the car,—I do not know what you call them. A Member:—
Bumpers.—H. R., May 13: *C. G.,* p. 2453/3.

Bunch.   To group together.
1881   When trees are *bunched* together, they are scrubs.—*Chicago Times,*
Apr. 16. (N. E. D.)

1885   [The hogs] stand *bunched* around at the root of the tree.—*Milnor* (Dak.) *Free Press,* Aug. 18, p. 3/5.   (N. E. D.)

1888   [I wish to know whether these motions] may not be *bunched* and voted on all at once.—Mr. C. S. Baker of N. Y., H. R., Apr. 10: *C. R.,* p. 2841/1.

1890   Mr. McKinley *bunches* all these articles, such as coffee, tea, etc., under the head of agricultural products.—Mr. J. R. Williams of Ill., H. R., May 19: *Id.,* p. 4941/1.

Bunch grass. See Vol. I.   [1846-1878.]

1872   The vegetation of this section [from Ogden to Boise City] is principally sage-brush, interspersed with *bunch-grass.*—Mr. James H. Slater of Ore., H. R., Jan. 27: *C. G.,* p. 660/2.

Buncombe.   Claptrap.   See Vol. I.   [1827-1909.]

1848   The Rhodeislanders have no notion of taxing the people for *"Buncombe"* speeches.—Wilmington (N. C.) *Commercial,* May 16, p. 2/3.

1849   The *"Buncombe"* politicians—those who go for reëlection merely.—*Id.,* Jan. 27, p. 2/2.

1861   I have neither any speeches to make for *Buncombe,* nor any extraordinary protestations.—Mr. William M. Gorin of Calif., U. S. Senate, Feb. 23: *C. G.,* p. 1128/1.

1870   The speeches which have been made . . . on this subject [of mileage] are all *"buncombe,"* and the smallest kind of *"buncombe"* at that.—Mr. Chas. A. Eldridge of Wisc., H. R., Feb. 10: *Id.,* p. 1198/2.

1878   [In N. C.] many years ago there occurred an incident that has given us a word familiar in our American vocabulary. A representative was making a loud harangue in the house of delegates, but was not disturbed by the impatience or inattention of his fellow-members, because he was talking for *"Buncombe."*—Mr. James G. Blaine of Me., U. S. Senate, Dec. 17: *C. R.,* p. 238/2.

1882   [In this bill to reduce internal-revenue taxation], matches were cunningly flung in for *buncombe.*—Mr. J. B. Beck of Ky., U. S. Senate, July 17: *Id.,* p. 6134/2.

1883   This House, while very fast when it means *buncombe,* is very slow when it means business.—Mr. Phelps of N. J., H. R., March 19: *Id.,* p. 2080/2.

1890   [Senator Teller] says, with a little pardonable *buncombe,* that the State of Kan. depends entirely upon Colo., and that Colo. has made Kan. all it is.—Mr. P. B. Plumb of Kan., U. S. Senate, Aug. 26: *C. R.,* p. 9158/1.

Bundling.   Passing the night together, with clothes on.   [1775-1844.]

1884   Upon mattresses laid on the bare ground within this tent twenty-five of us were *"bundled"* in true Knickerbocker style, without regard to sex, side by side.—Mr. Lewis Beach of N. Y., H. R., June 25: *C. R.,* p. 343/1, App.

1888   That curious custom of courting termed *bundling* still survives in a few isolated localities along the eastern foothills of the Blue Mountains.—Dr. W. J. Hoffman, 'Folk-lore of the Penna. Germans,' *Journal of Am. Folk-lore,* I, 1331-2.

Bunglesome.   Bungling.   Clumsy.

1897   This shows an inexcusable and *bunglesome* fraud or mistake on the part of some one handling [the ballots].—Mr. J. M. Kendall of Ky., H. R., Feb. 18: *C. R.,* p. 55/1, App.

Bungtown copper.   A worthless copper coin.   [1840-1853.]

1848   The farmer took out what he called a *Bung town copper* and dropped it into the hat.—Wilmington (N. C.) *Commercial,* Aug. 29, p. 1/6.

Bunko.   To swindle.   [1887.]   [Usually *bunco,* despite the dictionaries.—Ed.]

1892   The farmer is always *buncoed* by the three-card monte, green-goods protection shouter.—Mr. M. D. Harter of O., H. R., March 29: *Id.,* p. 2651/2.

1892 I believe [Secretary Rusk] had been *"buncoed,"* so to speak,—had been imposed upon by these designing fellows.—Mr. Jerry Simpson of Kan., H. R., Aug. 5: *Id.,* p. 7084/2.

1895 If the old farmer goes to the city, and is *buncoed* once, I have considerable sympathy for him. If he is *buncoed* twice, I will help to keep the men off him, if I observe it; but when he is *buncoed* three or four times, if he is so ignorant, ... I think it is not my duty to interfere.—Mr. J. C. Sibley of Pa., H. R., March 2: *Id.,* p. 3215/1.

Bunko game. A swindling game.

1888 A *bunco game* is a sort of mysterious game that is played by certain sharpers to filch honest people out of their money. That is what a *bunco game* is as interpreted in the city of New York by the police courts there. It is a kind of gudgeon used as bait to entrap the greenhorns.—Mr. F. B. Spinola of N. Y., H. R., Dec. 14: *C. R.,* p. 260/2.

Bunko-steerer. See quotations.

1888 I have been told that there is a game of cards from which the player against the dealer can by no possibility ever rise a winner; but that poor deluded victim of a *bunco-steerer* is not more certain to lose or more helpless to obtain fair play than is the farmer as he struggles in the toils and meshes of Republican tariff legislation.—Mr. D. W. Voorhees of Ind., U. S. Senate, Dec. 19: *Id.,* p. 346/1.

1890 My first thought was that such a man would certainly become the victim of a *bunko-steerer* or a confidence swindler before he got out of town.—Mr. D. W. Voorhees of Ind., U. S. Senate, March 19: *Id.,* p. 2378/2.

Buntline. The original "Ned Buntline" of politics was E. Z. C. Judson, who organized the "Know-nothings" in 1853. [1855.]

1849 Great Riot in New York. Arrest of *Ned Buntline* [Edward Z. C. Judson].—Wilmington (N. C.) *Commercial,* May 15, p. 2/3.

1849 Sentence of the Opera House Rioters. E. Z. C. Judson (*Ned Buntline*) was sentenced to 12 months' imprisonment &c.—*Id.,* Oct. 4, p. 2/2.

Bureau. A department of the administration.

1872 I think the Senator from O. [Mr. Sherman] should have put in the head of the Agricultural Department, or *bureau,* or agency, or whatever you may call it. It is a *bureau,* call it what you please. It is a separate, independent machine, and therefore it is a *bureau* in the strictest sense and meaning of the word *"bureau,"* as applicable to an office.—Mr. John A. Logan of Ill., U. S. Senate, March 12: *C. G.,* p. 1604/3.

1872 A *bureau office* is any department within a department that reports to a chief; whether it is called a *bureau* or anything else makes no difference.—U. S. Senate, March 13: *Id.,* p. 1631/2. [See also p. 1637.]

Burglarize. To break in with burglarious intent.

1876 I found [in a San Francisco paper] that the house of a lady moving in good society had been *burglarized.*—Mr. A. A. Sargent of Calif., U. S. Senate, July 6: *C. R.,* p. 4419/2.

1883 The man who had a contempt for a petty theft will *burglarise* the wheat-bin of a nation.—Mr. Talmage in *Chr. Globe,* Sept. 13, p. 829/2. (N. E. D.)

1884 The house of John Fuller was *burglarized* on Wednesday night.—*Boston Journal,* Feb. 7, p. 1. (N. E. D.)

1894 The gentleman is speaking of a case where the post office was *burglarized.*—Mr. B. H. Bunn of N. C., H. R., Aug. 9: *C. R.,* p. 8350/1.

Burgoo. A kind of thick soup much used at open-air feasts.

1795 Is it any thing to us whether he prefers Charley to George, or George to Charley, any more than whether he used to eat his *burgoo* with his fingers or with a horn spoon? . . . As bad as serving up a mess of *burgoo* after a cranberry tart.—W. Cobbett, "A Bone to Gnaw," pp. 2, 17. (Phila., 3d ed.)

1882 The fatted calf,—the Kentucky ox,—was killed for the returning prodigals. They were feasted on Bourbon and *burgoo*.—Mr. John D. White of Ky., H. R., June 22: *C. R.,* p. 5229/2.

Burgoyne, v. To capture entirely. [1779-1820.]

1787 Help us to *burgoyn* Lincoln and his army.—*New Haven Gazette,* March 8, p. 22/3.

Burn. To waste, as in the slang phrase, "money to burn."

1897 Mr. Simpson:—You have plenty of time. Mr. Payne:—No; I have not got time *"to burn."*—H. R., March 27: *C. R.,* p. 400/1.

Burners. Swindlers. [1842-1845.]

1859 Matsell, in his "Vocabulum; or, Rogue's Lexicon," defines *Burners* as rogues who cheat countrymen with false cards or dice.

Burning bush. The *Euonymus atropurpureus.*

1883 The Euonymus, or *burning bush,* clothed in the autumn with its brilliant scarlet berries.—*Harper's Mag.,* p. 726/1. (N. E. D.)

1893 He hid himself in a thicket of plums and *burning bush* (bittersweet). —Mary A. Owen, "Old Rabbit &c.," p. 71.

Burnsides. A style . . such as that affected by General Burnside (1824-81) consisting of a mustache, whiskers, and a clean-shaven chin.—(Century Dict.)

Burr-oak. The overcup oak. [1833.]

1873 [In La. and Tex.] there are large quantities of live-oak, white-oak, *burr-oak,* poot-oak, beach (*sic*), holly, sugar maple, cherry, walnut, and magnolia.—Mr. W. S. Herndon of Tex., H. R., Jan. 11: *C. R.,* p. 7/3, App.

Burr patch. A piece of ground abounding in burrs.

1866 The gentleman [Mr. Andrew J. Rogers of N. J.] is like an unbroken colt in a *burr patch,* you can neither catch him nor hold him.—Mr. L. H. Rousseau of Ky., H. R., June 5: *C. G.,* p. 2973/3.

Bushel up. To patch up. The N. E. D., referring to Worcester, gives *Busheler, Busheller, Bushelman* (from Germ. *bosseln, bossler*) i.e., a man who does small repairs for tailors.

1893 To allow [this building] to be *"busheled up"* or repaired by a private purchaser would be to court inevitable disaster.—Report of Supervising Architect on the Federal Building in Chicago, Sept. 28: *C. R.,* Aug. 8, 1894, p. 8327/1.

Bushwhacker. A guerilla, a sharpshooter. [1809-1888.]

1865 I concede that the *bushwhackers* may be shot down, and that they ought to be shot down without being captured: that prisoners should not be taken from *bushwhackers* at all, because they are a lawless set of robbers, assassins, and murderers, who ought to be hunted down in that summary form. I concede further that if a man is a *bushwhacker,* and our authorities desire to make an example by way of retaliation, a *bushwhacker* may be taken as the subject of that retaliation. But I would qualify that concession in this wise: I would not allow any commanding general by his own order to determine who was and who was not a *bushwhacker,* and [to] order that man . . . . to be summarily executed. I would require the *bushwhacker* to be tried by a military court.—Mr. Garrett Davis of Ky., U. S. Senate: *C. G.,* p. 427/1.

Bust. A burst, a riotous time, a "spree." [1850-1859.]

1873 There are some men that seek their Christmas holiday for other purposes than *"busts"* or *"sprees."*—Mr. J. P. Stockton of N. J., U. S. Senate, Dec. 19: *C. R.,* p. 334/2.

Bust, Buster. A buster is a horse-breaker, one who "busts" bronchos. Western slang.

1903 It is upon the cowboys that the task falls of breaking to the saddle, or *busting,* the almost untractable "bronchos" that are raised both for this purpose and for the open market. . . . Naturally, on a large ranch which employs many cowboys, there is much rivalry among them as to who is the best rider, or *buster.—Wide World Mag.,* p. 545. (Century Dict.).

Bust-head. A low grade of strong whiskey.

1883 A man in this country cannot take a drink of American whisky, be it the Cincinnati *bust-head* or the N. C. pine-top, however distilled, without paying 200 per cent on it.—Mr. John S. Williams of Ky., U. S. Senate, Feb. 1: *C. R.,* p. 1898/2.

Butcher knives. [1822-1853.]

1868 On *"butcher knives,* cooks' and shoe knives, and spatulas and palettes," the advanced duties proposed are enormous.—Mr. James Brooks of N. Y., H. R., Dec. 15: *C. G.,* p. 66/3, App.

Buttermunk. A local New England name of the night heron, *Nyctiardea grisea nævia.—*(Century Dict.)

Butternuts. Here Confederate troops. [1781-1865.]

1866 A bill to give bounty land to the "boys in blue" could not be defeated, nor the *"butternuts"* included, without [Southern votes].—Mr. G. W. Scofield of Pa., H. R., Apr. 28: *C. G.,* p. 2248/2.

Buttes. See quotation. [1838-1878.]

1873 On appelle *"buttes"* les collines détachées et quelquefois complêtement isolées, qui se rencontrent fréquemment dans la "prairie."—G. N. Barringer, "Actes de la Société Philologique," III, 301.

1886 It is admitted that there are [in the Yellowstone Park] hot springs and soda *buttes.—*Mr. W. D. Kelley of Pa., H. R., Dec. 14: *C. R.,* p. 153/2.

Buzz saw. A circular saw. The caution, "Don't monkey with the *buzz saw,"* is not uncommon. *Noli simiare cum serrâ susurrante.*

1882 Gentlemen may commiserate the South . . . and wish they might hear the *"buzz saw"* humming and the spindle twirling there.—Mr. Aiken of S. C., H. R., June 22: *C. R.,* p. 5240/2.

1886 The characteristic and picturesque Americanism for a circular saw— "a *buzz-saw."—Saturday Rev.,* July 31, p. 142. (N. E. D.)

By and large. Comprehensively. [1833-1906.]

1890 In the larger towns and cities [of Me.] it has been found impossible . . . . to extirpate this traffic. But *by and large* all of us who live there and have memories going back for 40 years or more know the immense benefit that has been derived from [the prohibition law.]— Mr. Eugene Hale of Me., U. S. Senate, May 9: *C. R.,* p. 4376/2.

1913 Taken *by and large,* up and down, and hither and yon, the Senate lobby investigation has probably done more to upset one of Washington's most important industries than anything that has happened within the memory of the oldest Congressional inhabitant.—*Indianapolis News,* June.

By the name of. Now colloquial and U. S. [1676-1859.]

1807 A stranger was introduced to me by Col. Cushing, *by the name of* Swartwout.—Affidavit of Gen. Wilkinson, Norfolk (Va.) *Gazette,* Feb. 8, p. 3/3.

1818 His father is a ship carpenter, *by the name of* Harry Hall.—Norfolk (Va.) *Beacon,* Nov. 18, p. 3/2. (Advt.)

1890 See ORIGINAL PACKAGE.

1896 This lady married a man *by the name of* Madigan in 1846 or thereabouts.—Mr. F. C. Layton of O., H. R., Apr. 10: *C. R.,* p. 3863/2.

C

C. O. D. Cash on delivery. See also first quotation. [1863-1909.]

1866 I was informed that many hundred pardons had been sent by [the Adams] Express Company, . . . that each one had marked upon it "C. O. D. $300."—"C. O. D." meaning, I believe, "collect on delivery." —Mr. G. W. Scofield of Pa., H. R., Dec. 19: *C. G.,* p. 204/1.

1892 It was a transaction payable on sight,—a C. O. D. transaction, so to speak,—payable on the very day.—Mr. J. J. Little of N. Y., H. R., July 25: *C. R.,* p. 6722/2.

Cablegram. A message by cable.

1868 The new word *cablegram* is used by a N. Y. contemporary to characterize a telegraphic despatch.—*Daily News,* Sept. 26. (N. E. D.)

1873, 1880, 1883. N. E. D.

1890 These are the latest quotations by *cablegram.*—Mr. J. H. Gear of Ia., H. R., May 9: *C. R.,* p. 4390/1.

Caboose. A car used on freight or construction trains for workmen or the train crew.—(Webster.) [1839-1888.]

1869 [They] obliged us to take a *caboose* car, hitched on to a freight train. —Letter to Chicago *Tribune,* March 10: *C. G.,* p. 536/1.

1894 See VESTIBULE.

Cæsarism. Absolute power.

1857 Monarchial absolutism, or what I choose to call modern *Cæsarism.*— O. Brownson, "Works," V, 192. (N. E. D.)

1858 *Westminster Review.* (N. E. D.)

1875 *Cæsarism,* a modern word, has become very common to express individual power. . . . What is meant by *Cæsarism?* By it is meant power in the hands of one man, and it had its origin two thousand years ago. Cæsar himself attempted to establish *Cæsarism.*—Mr. Andrew Johnson of Tenn., U. S. Senate, March 22: *C. R.,* p. 129/1.

Cahoot, *v.* To club together.

1857 They all agree to *cahoot* with their claims against Nicaragua and Costa Rica.—*N. Y. Herald,* May 20. (Bartlett).

Cahoot, cahoots. Partnership, partners. [1834-1892.]

1869 Fisk and his *"cahoots"* have got at cross purposes, and he has been put out of bed.—Mr. James W. Nye of Nev., U. S. Senate, Apr. 6: *C. G.,* p. 538/3.

1882 [They were] dictating their terms to the White House, when not acting in *"cohoot"* [*sic*] with the President himself.—Mr. P. B. Thompson of Ky., H. R., June 21: *C. R.,* p. 5197/1.

1892 A white boy said to a colored boy. "Let's go into *cahoots* and go a coon hunting; you furnish the dog and climb the tree, and I'll do the hollering." They went. The white boy "hollered"; the colored boy furnished the dog and climbed the tree. They caught three coons. When they came to divide, the white boy took them all. The colored boy asked, "What am I going to have?" "Why," said the white boy, "you get the *cahoots.*"—Mr. W. J. Bryan of Neb., H. R., March 16: *Id.,* p. 2133/1.

1892 Indian agents are in *"cahoots,"* as they say out [West] with certain parties . . . who are buying cattle for the Government.—Mr. J. H. Kyle of S. D., U. S. Senate, March 23: *Id.,* p. 2400/2.

Cahot. A surface undulation or ridge-like inequality which, with the corresponding depression, is known in [New England] as a "thank-you-ma'am."—(Century Dict.) Candian-French.

1902 Corresponding undulations sometimes produced by sledge-driving on snow-covered roads are familiar in Canada, where they are called *cahots.*—*Rep. Brit. Ass'n. for the Advancement of Science,* p. 731. (Century Dict.)

Cake, to take the. To surpass all competitors. [1886.] The belle of the innkeepers congress, held at Rothenburg in 1610, was the daughter of the innkeeper at Bourgoin, near Chambéry, and in the English transcript of the original MS. there is a marginal note, "Ista capit biscottum," which appears to have been retained from the original. See Mr. E. S. Bates's "Touring in 1600," p. 275 (1911). The expression also means "to win a prize for a cakewalk."

Calamity howlers. Those who constantly prophesy disaster.

1892 It seems to me that we had some *"calamity howlers"* here in Washington as well as in Kan.—Mr. Jerry Simpson of Kan., H. R., March 2: *C. R.*, p. 1654/1.

1892 I have a sort of suspicion that [they] were of the stripe of *calamity-shouters* whose occupation is gone, unless they can prove that calamity stalks abroad by noonday as well as by night in this country.—Mr. S. E. Payne of N. Y., H. R., March 17: *Id.*, p. 2160/2.

1892 We are like most of the farmers of the country, who, if the *calamity howlers* had not shown them their rags, would never have known that they had any.—Mr. Ezra B. Taylor of O., H. R., June 16: *Id.*, p. 5348/2.

1893 You charged us with being *calamity howlers.* Yet if there has been more calamity howled than has been howled by our distinguished friends of the other side, I do not know where . . . to find it.— Mr. J. C. Sibley of Pa., H. R., Aug. 18: *Id.*, p. 465/1.

1893 The calamity struck us some five years ago in Kan., and we were the best *calamity howlers* of the country; but I say now, with all due respect, that we take off our hats in acknowledgment of the superiority of the New England *calamity howlers.*—Mr. Jerry Simpson of Kan., H. R.: *Id.*, p. 487/2.

1894 The country needs certainty as to our tariff policy, and rest from croakers and *calamity howlers.*—Mr. J. B. McCreary of Ky., H. R., Jan. 22: *Id.*, p. 1215/1.

1894 If all the *calamity howlers* in the trans-Mississippi were boiled down . . . into one *calamity howler,* and that *calamity howler* was run by the highest grade of electrical engine to be found, his howling would not equal in intensity and grandeur the howl of my eloquent friend from Pa., Mr. Brosius.—Mr. T. J. Hudson of Kan., H. R., Jan. 15: *Id.*, p. 54/1, App.

1897 At last our President [Mr. Cleveland] has become a *calamity howler.* He has pointed out to us the dire distress, the poverty, and the misery of our people.—Mr. W. L. Greene of Neb., H. R., March 22: *Id.*, p. 144/1.

Calf-wrestler. 1887. See **Work Like Beavers** and **Bluff, to call the.**

Call, v. In poker, to require one's opponents to show their hands.

1896 Mr. Milliken:—I do not know how great the amount of our saving might be, if [Mr. Cummings] should consult all of his colleagues on this floor. Mr. Cannon:—Do you think we had better *call* him? Mr. Milliken:—The gentleman is using language peculiar to a certain pursuit that I am not so familiar with as he is.—H. R., May 23: *C. R.*, p. 5634/1.

Call to (the) book. To call to account. The N. E. D. has **Bring to Book,** with examples 1870 and 1879.

1867 We are *calling to the book* men who have been in arms against us.— Mr. Jacob M. Howard of Mich., U. S. Senate, March 16: *C. G.*, p. 138/2.

Cama. A prairie-like basin-floor inclosed by hills or uplands.—(Century Dict.) Spanish: used in the Southwest.

Camas. A root somewhat resembling the sweet potato in taste and nutritive properties. [1837-1845.]

1899 See KOUSE ROOT.

Camas rat. A rodent of the family *Geomyidæ*, and genus *Thomomys*, which lives for the most part on the roots of the camas.— (Century Dict.)

Camerist. A photographer. Uncommon.

1900 When a high wind is encountered, the cloth at one end can be buttoned around the camera, and at the other end around the head or face of the *camerist.—Boston Transcript*, Feb. 23. (Century Dict.)

Campaign. An election contest, sometimes lasting several weeks.

1884 The attempt of the Republicans to introduce the tariff as one of the issues of the *campaign.—Boston Journal*, Sept. 20. (N. E. D.)

Campaign button. A badge worn by a campaign partisan.

1900 The wearing of a *campaign button* is a harmless sort of decoration, but a social condition that dictates to a man what kind of a button he shall wear approaches a condition of tyranny, and makes a man want to stick *campaign buttons* all over him, and protect his privilege with a Gatling gun.—Mr. E. L. Hamilton of Mich., H. R., March 8: *C. R.*, p. 2670/2.

Campaign documents. Those distributed during a political campaign.

1871 I want ten thousand copies of [this resolution] .... as a *campaign document;* and as it is said that we get all our *campaign documents* from the public printer and at the public expense, here is an opportunity where I can lawfully get a small quantity.—Mr. G. F. Edmunds of Vt., U. S. Senate, Dec. 20: *C. G.*, p. 236/1.

1876 [Mr. Eaton] is the last man who would think of getting up a *campaign document*, or making a speech for campaign purposes.—Mr. W. Windom of Minn., U. S. Senate, June 2: *C. R.*, p. 3543/1.

1879 See TAFFY.

Campbellite. A follower of Alexander Campbell. [1830-1908.]

1892 James A. Garfield was preaching in *Campbellite churches* after driving mules upon the towpath of an Ohio canal.—Mr. Amos J. Cummings of N. Y., H. R., Jan. 30: *C. R.*, p. 695/1.

Camp hunt. A hunting expedition lasting several days.

1889 He enjoyed no recreation as much as he did the *"camp hunts"* for deer, which in his day, as now, were in vogue in La.—Mr. N. C. Blanchard of La., H. R., Jan. 19: *C. R.*, p. 1010/2.

Canada thistle. The *Cirsium arvense*. [1799-1850.]

1894 Then we have the *Canada thistle*, which ... is said to be [as] destructive to agriculture as the Russian thistle is. I believe there are a number of states which have special laws compelling every owner of land and every road overseer to destroy the *Canada thistle.—Mr.* F. M. Cockrell of Mo., U. S. Senate, July 17: *C. R.*, p. 7578/1.

Canaigre. A tuberous plant indigenous to the Southwest, the roots of which contain about 35 per cent of tannic acid. They have been long used by the Mexicans as a medicine, and for tanning saddle leather.—(See the Century Dict., which furnishes a picture.)

Canary slips. A term applied to certain official forms supplied through the War Department to the Pension Office; the examiner signing a "face brief" and a "case slip," and pronouncing upon the application.

1894 These slips have an official nomenclature. They are called *"canary slips,"* in distinction from full record slips. Thousands of cases were adjudicated, that contained three documents alone. First, the claimant's application; . . . second, this *"canary slip,"* which contained the date of his entering the service and leaving it; . . . and the third paper, the medical examination. . . . [This slovenly method led to] a carnival of looseness and wrongdoing.—Mr. J. C. Black of Ill., H. R., March 3: *C. R.*, pp. 624-5, App.

Candle lighting. The time of lighting up. [1784-1888.]

1596 He wil hold you prattle from morningsberie to *candle lighting.*— Thos. Lodge, "Wits Miserie," p. 32.

Canebrake. A thicket of cane bushes. [1787-1838.]
1804 Here was plenty of grass, and a *cane brake.*—Lorenzo Dow, "Journal" (1850) p. 100/2.
1864 I would ask [Mr. Mallory] if the perfect terror of the larger plantations of La. and Miss. is not a runaway negro hid in the *canebrakes.*— Mr. James G. Blaine of Me., H. R., June 25: *C. G.,* p. 3274/2.
1875 [These men] have been grievously persecuted, horse-whipped, driven into *canebrakes,* or murdered.—Mr. John Coburn of Ind., H. R., Feb. 26: *C. R.,* p. 1827/1.
1896 The counties of Hale and Perry . . . are what is known as the *"canebrake* section" of Alabama.—Mr. J. F. Stallings of Ala., H. R., June 9: *Id.,* p. 6343/2.

Canuck. In Canada, a French Canadian; in the U. S. often any Canadian.—(Webster.) [1855-1884.]
1862 They went from St. Louis to Canada to buy the little *Canuck* ponies at $130 apiece, which would have been [useless].—Mr. E. B. Washburne of Ill., H. R., Apr. 29: *C. G.,* p. 1867/3.

Canvasback ducks. A species much valued by epicures. [1784-1839.]
1865 Upon the Eastern Shore of Md. it is not beef, but oysters, terrapins, and *canvasback ducks* which make our people equal to the beef-eaters of Calif.—Mr. E. H. Webster of Md., H. R., Feb. 23: *C. G.,* p. 1039/3.
1866 As far as climate is concerned, and as far as the wealth of the soil is concerned, I do not think [the State of Me.] altogether equal to the State of Md., to say nothing of our fine oysters and soft crabs, and last, but by no means least, terrapins and *canvasback ducks.*— Mr. Reverdy Johnson of Md., U. S. Senate, May 29: *Id.,* p. 2875/1.
1873 I boarded at Gadsby's, and we had *canvasback ducks* every day in the season.—Mr. Simon Cameron of Pa., U. S. Senate, March 1: *Id.,* p. 2046/2.
1893 Good citizenship does not necessarily mean great riches and clipping coupons and eating terrapin and *canvasback ducks,* though some people seem to think so.—Mr. Champ Clark of Mo., H. R., Dec. 15: *C. R.,* p. 275/1.

Cap the climax, to. To surpass everything. [1804-1861.]
1814 *Capping the climax* of atrocity.—Norfolk (Va.) *Public Ledger,* Oct. 26, p. 3/1.
1863 *To cap the climax,* the Southern members from the two branches of the last Congress took themselves away from their seats here, when they had it in their power to prevent any ultra measures upon the part of gentlemen from the North.—Mr. Thomas H. Hicks of Md., U. S. Senate, Feb. 28: *C. G.,* p. 1371/3.
1863 Mr. Field [recently a Senator from N. J.] *caps the climax* of folly and presumption when he declares . . . that the only safe depositary of this power to suspend the privilege of [the writ of habeas corpus] is the Executive—Mr. James W. Wall of N. J., U. S. Senate, March 2: *Id.,* p. 1463/2.
1864 A thing so abhorrent to humanity [as arming the negroes] was *capping the climax* of all that is absurd.—Mr. Dumont of Ind., H. R., March 12: *Id.,* p. 1073/2.
1869 The American people have dignified Ulysses S. Grant so that he can look the proudest monarch in the face. In view of his achievements upon the battlefield, kingdoms and despotisms are quaking as did Belshazzar. (Laughter.) Ulysses S. Grant has *capped the climax* of grandeur.—Mr. James Mullins of Tenn., H. R., Feb. 23: *Id.,* p. 1460/1.
1870 To *cap the climax* of extravagance and absurdity, $100,000 is appropriated to pay the expenses of an expedition "toward the north pole."— Mr. G. W. McCrary of Ia., H. R., June 10: *Id.,* p. 466/2, App.

1879 To *cap the climax* of absolutism, the votes of those States were stolen.—Mr. M. P. O'Connor of S. C., H. R., Apr. 5: *C. R.,* p. 261/2.

Cap-sheaf. The crowning point. [1800-1873.]

1834 This is indeed the *cap sheaf* of outrage.—*The Georgian* (Savannah), July 26, p. 3/2.

Cap-sheet. See quotation.

1867 Building the foundation upon the voice of the people, and putting the superstructure up with the same voice, and putting the very *cap-sheet* [*sic*] to the structure with that same voice.—Mr. Charles D. Drake of Mo., U. S. Senate, March 15: *C. G.,* p. 117/3.

Caption. A title or heading. [1821-1908.]

1836 The result Mather gives us under this *caption:*—"Determination given by a late assembly &c."—Dr. G. T. Chapman. "Sermons," p. 256. (Hartford, Conn.)

1848 My eye was directed to the *caption* "Kidnapping."—Wilmington (N. C.) *Commercial,* Oct. 12, p. 2/5.

1888 I send to the clerk's desk a letter which I ask that he will read, including the printed *caption* at its head.—Mr. John H. Rogers of Ark., H. R., July 14: *C. R.,* p. 6295/1.

Captivate. To capture. [1825-1840.]

1815 May I be *captivated* by the Algerines, if &c.—David Humphreys, "The Yankey in England," p. 34.

Card. A special notice in the nature of an advertisement. [1769-1813.]

1860 We the undersigned, citizens of Woodsfield, hereby certify that we were present at the Douglas ratification meeting in said town on the evening of the 26th day of June, 1860; that we heard the speech of James R. Morris; that it breathed the utmost defiance and contempt for his fellow Democrats who refused to support Mr. Douglas; that Mr. Morris characterized them as a set of mad fanatics, fire-eaters, and disunionists; said they and the Republicans had one common end—a dissolution of the Union; and wound up his speech by saying: "If the devil don't get such men, there is no use in keeping a devil."— [Mr. Morris produced this handbill, signed by six persons, in the House of Repr., July 7, 1862: *C. G.,* p. 3159/3.]

Cargo, v. To load as with a cargo.

1580 The Persian galleys, being high *cargued,* heavy, and not yare of sterage.—North's "Plutarch" (1676), p. 105. (N. E. D.)

1892 The wagon itself, the horses and harnesses, the pelts and peltries, and anything else the teamster may be *cargoed*‧with.—Mr. D. W. Voorhees of Ind., U. S. Senate, March 18: *C. R.,* p. 2188/1.

Carotte. A cylindrical roll of tobacco.—(Webster.)

1890 I have here some *carots* of Cuban tobacco; they look alike, and a customs inspector would readily class them as wrapper leaf; but one *carot* is not suitable for wrappers.—Testimony of F. A. Schroeder, *C. R.,* Aug. 27, p. 9213/2.

Carpetbag, v. To travel with a carpet-bag. See **Carpetbagger.**

1890 It has been stated that Mr. McDuffie *carpetbagged* from somewhere down into Ala. ... Now I will tell the House how Judge McDuffie happened to *carpetbag* down into that district. He happened to be a Union soldier.—Mr. J. H. Rowell of Ill., H. R., June 4: *C. R.,* p. 5598/2.

Carpetbagger. A term of contempt originally for itinerant wildcat bankers of the West, later for Northerners who went South after the Civil War to live, especially to seek profit under the often corrupt Reconstruction governments.—(Webster.) [1857-1904.]

1868 The men of northern birth who have gone into the South since the war, the *"carpetbaggers,"* as they are sneeringly called.—Mr. Horace Maynard of Tenn., H. R., July 16: *C. G.,* p. 457/1, App.

1868 I was born in the State of Me., and went to New York with a trunk thirty years ago. I did not go there three months ago *with a carpet-bag.*—Mr. James Brooks of N. Y., H. R., July 21: *Id.,* p. 4295/1.

1868 [This proposition of adjournment] is for the purpose of carrying out the Blair letter of the 3d of July, for the purpose of stamping out the loyal State governments of the South, and dispersing us *"carpetbaggers."*—Mr. John T. Deweese of N. C., H. R., July 23: *Id.,* p. 4379/1.

1868 I glory in that progressive spirit which made me a *carpetbagger.* . . . I will say that I followed the lead of that great *carpetbagger* [Gen. Grant] whom the people of the U. S. have selected for their Chief Magistrate.—Mr. Willard Warner of Ala., U. S. Senate, Dec. 15: *Id.,* p. 86/1.

1868, 1869, 1870. See Scalawag.

1869 A young man raised in my immediate neighborhood,—a *"carpetbagger,"* I may say, he having gone to Ga. somewhere about the year 1859.—Mr. Warner, U. S. Senate, Jan. 28: *Id.,* p. 676/1.

1871 The favorite name applied to our southern governments by our Democratic friends is that of *"carpet-bag governments";* and the northern men, mostly soldiers, who went to the South after the war, are called *"carpetbaggers."*—U. S. Senate, March 3: *Id.,* p. 273/2, App.

1871 These *carpetbaggers* are the veriest scoundrels that God ever made. They are a burlesque upon humanity, and they deserve to be denounced. —Mr. Willard Saulsbury of Del., U. S. Senate, Apr. 12: *Id.,* 603/1.

1872 When I speak of *carpet-baggers,* I do not allude to northern men who have come and settled among us. . . . We object to the man who comes for office only, and who, when the office ceases, ceases to exist there; the man who has no residence there; who pretends to represent the sovereignty of [a southern state], and has no identity of interest, no stock in common, pays no taxes, belongs not to our society, and remains with us for the [sole] purpose of enjoying office; . . . the man who lives on the passions of the people, who seeks to keep up the strife that exists between the colored race and the white race.—Mr. James S. Alcorn of Miss., U. S. Senate, May 21: *Id.,* p. 3704/1.

1875 These adventurers were the cuckoos who sat upon the eggs of other birds—the scum which rose to the top of political reconstruction. They were called *carpetbaggers,* not because they always carried one of those indispensable articles of travel, for many of them were not even provided with that article, but [because] they moved in a mysterious way, with no fixed mode of life or the *animus manendi.* The *carpetbagger* had little to go on and much to get. He made out of negro credulity a living, and he made the negro his prey. He began as a sharper, and was reconstructed as a statesman.—Mr. S. S. Cox of N. Y., H. R., Feb. 27: *C. R.,* p. 1918/1.

1876 See Freedman's Bureau.

1876 When [Mr. Greeley] returned to New York, they asked him . . . if what was reported about the *carpetbagger* was true. His response was, "Yes, gentlemen, I regret to say to you that he is a mournful fact; and the attitude in which I have most generally found him is with both arms around the negro's neck and both hands in his pocket." —Mr. Hooker of Miss., H. R., June 15: *Id.,* p. 3821/1.

1879 You sent *carpet-baggers* and scalawags to wield this [negro] power which you had created in the interest of the Republican party. You put them there with their feet upon the neck of your Anglo-Saxon and Caucasian people, blood of your blood, bone of your bone, ... and yet you have never lifted a finger to protect them.—H. R., Apr. 24: *Id.,* p. 897/1.

1881 [Mr. Calkins] asks, What is a *carpetbagger?* In reply I say he is a political legalized burglar; that is just what a *carpetbagger* is.—Mr. D. W. Aiken of S. C., H. R., Feb. 5: *Id.,* p. 1276/1.

1881 You make a mistake when you speak of the *carpetbagger* as a Republican. He is not a Republican; he is a bird of prey; he is a thief and nothing but a thief, as a general rule.—Mr. Wade Hampton of S. C., U. S. Senate, *C. R.,* p. 372/2.

1891 When I went West as a *carpetbagger* in 1858, St. Louis was an outpost of civilization. Jefferson City was the farthest point reached by a railroad.—Mr. J. J. Ingalls of Kan., U. S. Senate, Jan. 14: *Id.,* p. 1282/1.

Carpetbagism. Carpetbag rule.

1896 An attempt to repeat the criminality of *carpetbagism* would have stirred the Union to such an extent that election cyclones would not have been causes of discomfort.—Mr. S. M. White of Calif., U. S. Senate, Jan. 10: *Id.,* p. 554/2.

Carry. To lead or guide one, on foot. This use seems to be peculiar to S. C.—(See N. E. D., p. 135/1.)

Carryall. A term for a carriage of a useful rather than handsome kind, variable in capacity. [1814-1857.]

1868 Whether she can .. swear that her old *carryall* is not worth $300.— Mr. W. D. Kelley of Pa., H. R., June 1: *C. G.,* p. 2756/1.

1870 We are to pay for clerks to committees, pages, horses, and *carryalls* $20,000 by way of deficiency.—Mr. Allen G. Thurman of O., U. S. Senate, Apr. 6: *Id.,* p. 2449/2.

Case slip. See **Canary slips.**

Casket. A coffin of an elaborate and costly kind. [1881-1910.]

1874 At half past twelve o'clock the *casket* containing the remains [of Charles Sumner] was brought in to the Senate Chamber.—*C. R.,* March 12: p. 2143/1.

1913 For Cheaper Funerals. Motor 'Buses to hold *Casket* and Twenty-seven Mourners. Chicago, July 19.—The high cost of dying is to be lowered in Chicago with the advent of motor 'buses. The funeral coach will have a compartment to the right of chauffeur's seat for the coffin and above it a place for flowers. Near the driver will sit the minister and undertaker, and there will be accommodations for twenty-seven mourners.—*N. Y. Evening Post,* July 21, p. 2/6.

Cassaba. The manioc from which tapioca is made. [1777-1837.]

1671 See **Mush.**

1715 *Cassave,* an American Root, the Juice of which is rank Poison, but the dry Substance is the general Bread of that Country.—Kersey, "Dictionarium Anglo-Britannicum."

Cat in the meal tub. A concealed reason for what is done. [A similar expression is "a nigger in the woodpile."]

1878 When I find Republicans coming up and voting solidly for an Irish-Catholic Democrat, then I know there is *"a cat in the meal tub."*—Mr. John A. McMahon of O., H. R., Apr. 8: *C. R.,* p. 2350/1.

1879 It was the second resolution that had *"the cat in the meal tub."*—Mr. W. P. Whyte of Md., U. S. Senate, Feb. 5: *Id.,* p. 1000/2.

1879 O, there is *the cat in the meal tub.* The gentleman wants to kill the bill, and I do not propose to consent to that.—Mr. Harris of Va., H. R., May 22: *Id.,* p. 1523/2.

1880 Is this *the cat in the meal tub* of refunding?—Mr. A. H. Buckner of Mo., H. R., May 10: *Id.,* p. 3193/1.

Catch on. To apprehend; to grasp the point. [1884-1894.]

1884 Mr. Browne of Ind.:—But here is an idea. Mr. Cox of N. Y.:— Thank God for the idea. Mr. Browne:—It is very seldom that my friend from N. Y. *catches on* to an idea, . . . for ideas come to him like angels' visits, few and far between.—H. R., June 28: *C. R.,* p. 5758/1.

1890 The trouble with the constituents of the Senator from Tex. is that they have been asleep; they have not fully *"caught on"* to the movement.—Mr. John P. Jones of Nev., U. S. Senate, Sept. 10: *Id.,* p. 780/1, App.

Cat-face. A mark in lumber, disfiguring it.

1879 Logs that have *cat faces* or burnt places.—*Lumberman's Gazette,* Dec. 3. (N. E. D.)

Cat-haul, v. To haul a cat over a slave's bare back. See Vol. I. [1816-1847.]

1881 You begin to ransack and examine and *cat-haul* the whole navy, big and little.—Mr. Roscoe Conkling of N. Y., U. S. Senate, Feb. 28: *C. R.,* p. 2202/2.

Caucus, v. (of politicians). To meet in order to settle upon their combined plan of action. [1774-1888, noun.]

1822 It is the next Congress that is to *Caucus* and nominate candidates for the Presidency and Vice-Presidency.—*Am. Beacon* (Norfolk, Va.), July 11, p. 3/2.

1879 See BUMMER.

Cause. Because. [1798-1884.]

a.1594 *Cause* I know thee secret as my soule.—Thos. Kyd, "Spanish Tragedie," E3.

1599 All this broile was *cause* he could not enter.—"The Sinner of Wakefield," C1.

1604 Thy M. hates me, *cause* my bloud hath ranged.—Dekker, "Honest Whore," E2.

1613 I morne thus fervent *cause* he di'd no sooner.—Marston, "Insatiate Countess," A2.

1615 Food I want not, *cause* the sea yeelds fish.—W. Smith, "Hector of Germanie," F4.

Caution. An example; usually in a ludicrous sense. [1834-1862.]

1848 The way locofocoism was done up by the orator was *a caution* to political sinners.—Wilmington (N. C.) *Commercial,* Oct. 14, p. 2/2.

Cavort. To prance about. [1834-1882.]

1880 [I concluded] that it was not wise to allow the wild colt of the prairies to *cavort* around without a curb.—Mr. W. P. Frye of Me., H. R., Jan. 22: *C. R.,* p. 483/2.

Cayuse. A native pony in the Western country. [1857-1909.]

1885 With one last wicked shake of the head the wiry *cayuse* breaks into his easy lope, and away go horse and rider.—*Harper's Mag.,* lxxi, 190. (Century Dict.)

Centralism. Centralization.

1837 The tendency of our system to *centralism,* with its ruinous consequences.—John C. Calhoun, "Works," II, 638. (N. E. D.)

1871 Nor am I deterred from this conclusion by any cry of *centralism,* or it may be of imperialism.—Mr. Charles Sumner of Mass., U. S. Senate, Apr. 13: *C. G.,* p. 651/1.

1872 See FRAZZLE.

Chair post. The leg of a chair. [1788.]

1911 Mr. John S. Coleman was in town last Monday evening, and gave us this very remarkable snake story: "A Mr. Vaughan, who lives near Moriah, had a rat trap, one of these little snap fellows, set in his smokehouse for mice. One morning recently he went in the smokehouse and found his little trap had clamped down on a big highland moccasin, killing him dead. The snake was as large around as a *chair post* and about three feet long."—*Roxboro* (N. C.) *Courier,* November.

Chalk. A quarter of a dollar. Southern, and nearly obs.*

* Is this expression still used? W. Himes heard it once only, about 1850, used by an uncle who lived in La.

1805 A girl, bringing . . . . a hog to sell, asked one dollar, and three quarters, which they call seven *chalks.*—Lorenzo Dow, "Journal," Jan. 10 (1850), p. 102/1.

Chalking on a barn door. Calculating roughly. It is not equivalent to "splitting the difference," which is an easier process.

1880 Mr. Matt. Carpenter of Wisc.:—[The Geneva arbitrators] took the two statements, varying seven millions in amount, they went up into a mountain and *chalked on a barn door,* and split the difference. Mr. Blaine of Me.:—[The Senator has used] the phrase, well known in the country, *"chalking on the barn-door,"* for splitting the difference. Mr. Thurman of O.:—That was no *marking on a barn-door:* that was no guessing.—U. S. Senate, Apr. 19: *C. R.,* pp. 2478/2, 2518/2, 2557/1.

Changa. The mole-cricket, *Scapteriscus didactylus,* found in Georgia, though properly belonging to Porto Rico.

1901 The *"changa,"* . . . a kind of a mole-cricket, which has become very troublesome. It is believed this insect was introduced from South America in guano. It is very destructive to a wide range of plants during the period of their early growth, especially to vegetables on sandy soils; it is also destructive on the sugar and tobacco plantations. —*Yearbook U. S. Dept. Agr.,* p. 510. [Century Dict. furnishes a picture of this formidable insect.]

Chaparejos or Chaps. Leather breeches or overalls, worn by horsemen for protection against bushes and thorns. Southwestern Spanish.

1903 A bit farther on we saw some cowpunchers, or what seemed to be such, for they sat in cow saddles and wore *chaparejos.*—*Forest and Stream,* p. 147. (Century Dict.)

Chaparral. A thicket of cactus, mesquite, and various spiny shrubs. [1846-1888.]

1878 They . . . imagine they see in every Democratic Representative upon this floor a Mexican bandit skulking in the political *chaparral.*—Mr. Casey Young of Tenn., H. R., June 15: *C. R.,* p. 453/2, App.

1883 Enormous clouds of dust are raised. Much of it is alkali. . . . . If a civilized man should unexpectedly meet one of [the shepherds] coming around the corner of a *chaparral,* . . . he would take to his heels.—Mr. John T. Morgan of Ala., U. S. Senate, Feb. 6: *Id.,* p. 2144/1.

Chaqueta. A jacket, usually of leather, worn by cowboys in going through the chaparral. Southwestern.—(Century Dict.)

Charlie-on-the-spot. A punctual person; one to be depended on. [1805-1835.] Johnny-on-the-spot is a somewhat common variant.

Chattelhood. The condition of being a chattel.

1870 A race has been elevated from *chattelhood* to all the rights of humanity.—Mr. Henry Wilson of Mass., U. S. Senate, Feb. 25: *C. G.,* p. 1561/3.

1871 The last great country in which human *chattelhood* exists as an institution.—*The Echo,* Aug. 15. (N. E. D.)

Check, v. To crack or split without falling apart.

1902 Wherever they have been opened, the coal beds of the Washington Creek Basin show no evidence of faulting, and the coal is not crushed, but can be obtained in large pieces, which *"check,"* but do not break up readily, on exposure to the air.—*U. S. Geological Survey,* p. 277. (Century Dict.)

Check. A ticket given as a temporary receipt for a piece of baggage. [1847-18—.]

1850 Porters will receive *checks,* take charge of the baggage, and convey it to the Hotel.—Wilmington (N. C.) *Commercial,* Feb. 28, p.3/3. (Advt.)

Check baggage, v. To deliver to a transportation company in exchange for a ticket or token. See Vol. I.

1860 It is a great convenience to the traveling public to be able to *check baggage* through, and make connections right through, without, in the night, being compelled to get into omnibuses, exposed to the weather.— Mr. Stephen A. Douglas of Ill., U. S. Senate, Dec. 21: *C. G.*, p. 177/2. [See the remainder of the debate.]

1866 I do object to one thing that the Baltimore road is guilty of, and that is that they will not *check baggage* from here to any point in the West. They . . . compel you to *recheck your baggage.*—Mr. John B. Henderson of Mo., U. S. Senate, July 20: *Id.*, p. 3972/3.

Checks and balances. See second quotation. [1796-1821.]

1866 I have heard it said that this is a world of *checks and balances.* I believe it, and it is well that it is.—Mr. S. M. Cullom of Ill., H. R., June 16: *C. G.*, p. 254/2, App.

1871 The theory of our fathers was that this was a Government of *checks and balances;* not that one Department was independent of the other by any means; but that, where there was danger of concentration of power in one Department, there was power given to another Department by way of a check, by way of a balance.—Mr. Richard Yates of Ill., U. S. Senate, Jan. 23: *Id.*, p. 668/1.

Cheesedom. A name facetiously applied to the cheese-producing part of the "Western Reserve."

1867 I am very sorry that my colleague and friend [Mr. James A. Garfield] is not here to defend his butter and cheese, representing as he does what in O. we call "*Cheesedom.*"—Mr. Robert C. Schenck of O., H. R., Feb. 14: *C. G.*, p. 1253/3. [Continuing the debate, Mr. Schenck said, I have no idea of attacking the interests of "*Cheesedom*"; far from it. Whether there be any connection between butter and cheese and political questions, I will not attempt to determine; but I know that, where they make the most cheese and butter in O., they are sounder, politically, than in other parts of the State. Mr. Garfield:—The cream of the State. Mr. Schenck:—Well, the cream and the skim milk together. *Id.*, p. 1254/2.]

Cheesery. A cheese factory.

1883 From the upper stories of these *cheeseries* were long wooden gutters leading to the ships in dock, and along these troughs trickled a never-ceasing rill of the ripened and matured article.—Mr. G. H. Boughton, *Harper's Mag.*, p. 692. (Century Dict.)

Cherokee Strip or Outlet. A tract of land once occupied by the Cherokee Indians, running along the western line of Arkansas Territory. See quotations. The patent of the U. S. to this and other lands is to be found in *C. R.*, Feb. 18, 1890, pp. 1456/7. The term has been applied facetiously to the back seats in the House of Representatives. (See 1894.)

1869 [In March last] a joint resolution was passed through Congress, providing for the sale of certain lands known as the "*Cherokee strip.*"— Mr. Edmund G. Ross of Kan., U. S. Senate, Dec. 8: *C. G.*, p. 29/2.

1871 I ask unanimous consent to [present] a bill to provide for the sale of certain Indian lands in Kan., known as the "*Cherokee strip,*" to the settlers on the same.—Mr. David P. Lowe of Kan., H. R., March 16: *Id.*, p. 123/1.

1871 The land is what is called the *Cherokee strip* along the Kan. southern line. It is about one mile wide at one end, and two miles at the west end. The council and representatives of the Cherokees themselves want the land sold.—Mr. Garrett Davis of Ky., U. S. Senate, Apr. 17: *Id.*, p. 729/3.

1888 A debate which took place touching the *Cherokee Strip,* or *Outlet,* as it is sometimes called.—Mr. J. H. Rogers of Ark., H. R., July 24: *Id.*, p. 6756/1.

1888 We can not afford to relegate Tex. back to Mexico because she blocks the *Cherokee Outlet.*—Mr. T. R. Stockdale of Miss., H. R., July 26: *Id.,* p. 473/2, App.

1888 [Mr. Hooker] seems to have slept an absolute Rip Van Winkle sleep upon the history of the title to the *Cherokee Strip.* With all his pretended knowledge in behalf of these Indians, he seems not to know that they absolutely ceded this *Cherokee Strip* to the U. S. Government in 1866.—Mr. G. G. Symes of Colo., H. R., Dec. 13: *Id.,* p. 244/1.

1889 The large body of agricultural lands constituting what is known as the *"Cherokee Outlet"* ought not to be, and indeed cannot long be, held for grazing.—Message of President Benjamin Harrison, Dec. 3: *Id.,* p. 88/2.

1890 The *Cherokee Outlet* is a strip 50 miles wide, 150 miles long, and embraces 6,022,244 acres.—Mr. J. E. Washington of Tenn., H. R., Feb. 19: *Id.,* p. 1509/1. [This seems to be a miscalculation.]

1890 This *"outlet"* cut the Okla. Territory into two parts.—(*C. R.,* p. 1509/2.) It was so named because it afforded an *outlet* to the west, and was an *outlet* merely.—Letter of John C. Calhoun, Sec. of War, Oct. 8, 1821: *Id.,* p. 1513/1.

1891 Mr. Teller :—I do not know what you call the *Cherokee Outlet.* That is an ambiguous term. Mr. Jones of Ark.:—It is in the *Cherokee Strip.* Mr. Teller :—Some people say that one place is called the *Cherokee Strip,* and some another place. It is sufficient to say it is within the limits of the Indian Territory, practically in the northwest corner.—U. S. Senate, Feb. 28: *Id.,* p. 3532.

1892 [I wished], if possible, to pass a bill, known as the "Peel bill," to open up the *Cherokee Strip* or *Outlet.*—Mr. Jerry Simpson of Kan., H. R., Aug. 5: *Id.,* p. 7084/1.

1894 I rise to a point of order in behalf of members who occupy seats over here in the *"Cherokee Strip."*—Mr. T. R. Stockdale of Miss., H. R., June 7: *Id.,* p. 5928/2.

1901 If the Republican majority increases in size, the size of the *"Cherokee Strip"* [in the House] increases.—Mr. C. E. Littlefield of Me., H. R., Jan. 5: *Id.,* p. 598/1.

Cherry Hill. See Murray Hill.

Chess. A weed, or species of broom, resembling wheat, and very frequently mingled with it. [1805-1843.]

1898 [The sample] did not contain a particle of rye grass, but was composed entirely of *chess,* one of the most vile weeds known to the farmer.—Mr. J. H. Davidson of Wisc., H. R., Jan. 13: *C. R.,* p. 463/1, App.

Chestnut. A stale anecdote or joke. The term came into use about 1886. Mr. Joseph Jefferson attributed its origin to Mr. William Warren, the famous actor of the Boston 'Museum.' A captain, in the play of "The Broken Sword," in relating his exploits, speaks of the thick boughs of a cork tree. Pablo says, "A chestnut, captain, a chestnut." "Booby," he replies, "I say a cork tree." "A chestnut," reiterates Pablo, "I have heard you tell that tale these twenty-seven times." Mr. Warren, who had often played Pablo, was at a dinner where a story of doubtful originality was told. *"A chestnut,"* he murmured; "I have heard you tell the tale these twenty-seven times."—W. S. Walsh, "Handy-Book of Literary Curiosities," Philadelphia, 1893. [1886.]

1888 This reminds me of the old *chestnut* . . . of the young fellow who took his daddy out to help him train his dog to be a bear dog. The old fellow acted as the bear; the puppy got [him] by the nose, and was giving him fits, when he shouted to the boy, "Help, come take him off." "O," said the boy, "daddy, hold on, stand it; it is hard on you, but it is the making of the pup."—Mr. E. P. Allen of Miss., H. R., May 12: *C. R.,* p. 4070/2.

1888 Those remarks were uttered in years past, and are the oldest kind of *chestnuts* in Ia.—Mr. J. B. Weaver of Ia., H. R., July 11: *Id.,* p. 6147/1.

1890 [Mr. Walker of Mass.] says, "that is an old *chestnut.*" Well, say that it is. It is a good illustration of the point.—Mr. J. H. Outhwaite of O., H. R., May 14: *Id.,* p. 4661/1.

1890 The "damnable iteration" with which the Montgomery Advertiser mouths out its *chestnuts* about the representation question . . . must be very wearying to its limited number of readers.—Birmingham (Ala.) *Age-Herald,* n.d. See *Id.,* June 3, p. 5546/2.

1890 [They] see enough . . . to think about and contend for, without appealing to the worm-eaten *chestnut* of bloody shirts . . . to arouse discord. —Mr. Nathan Frank of Mo., H. R., June 30: *Id.,* p. 6815/1. [See BLOODY SHIRT.]

1890 If I should call up what might be called an old *chestnut,* I would bring up in this connection Banquo's ghost.—Mr. John F. Lacey of Ia., H. R., Sept. 3: *Id.,* p. 9626/2.

1890 See WOODEN NUTMEG.

Chevals. Riding breeches.

1803 My pantaloons were worn out; my riding *chevals* were worn through in several places.—Lorenzo Dow, "Journal," Oct. 28, (1850), p. 81/1.

Chewing gum. [1836-1882.] 1897 See **Chicle.**

Chicago, v. In card-playing and other games, to "skunk" or whitewash (an opposing side): that is, to prevent it from scoring any runs or points. Slang.—(Century Dict.)

Chicago platform. The declaration of principles enunciated at a convention of either party, meeting in Chicago. The most celebrated of these conventions were those of 1860 and 1864, both Republican. At the former, Lincoln and Hamlin were nominated; at the latter, Lincoln and Johnson. [As to the Convention of 1860, see Mr. Arnold's graphic account in *C. G.,* Feb. 20, 1865, pp. 70-71, App.] In later years, the National Democratic Convention assembled in Chicago in 1884, 1892, 1896; and the National Republican Convention in 1884, 1888 &c.

1863 You are ready [to vote for] a proposition utterly unconstitutional and in violation of the *Chicago platform,* which your President [Lincoln] declared was a law unto him.—Mr. Lazarus W. Powell of Ky., U. S. Senate, Feb. 7: *C. G.,* p. 801/1.

Chicken. See quotation.

1890 In the hospital I saw an admirable illustration of the affection which a sailor will lavish on a ship's boy to whom he takes a fancy, and makes his *"chicken,"* as the phrase is. The U. S. sloop Water Witch had recently been captured in Ossabaw Sound, and her crew brought to the prison. One of her boys, a bright, handsome little fellow, of about fifteen, had lost one of his arms in the fight. He was brought into the hospital, and the old fellow whose *"chicken"* he was was allowed to accompany him. This old "barnacle back" was as surly a growler as ever went aloft, but to his *"chicken"* he was as tender and thoughtful as a woman.—Statement of John McElroy, *C. R.,* Apr. 21: p. 3637/1.

Chicle. The gum of the naseberry, *Sapota zapotilla.*

1897 *Chicle* is the basic material from which common chewing gum is made. It is raised only in Mexico. . . . *Chicle* is a purely raw material.—Mr. E. D. Cooke of Ill., H. R., March 26: *C. R.,* pp. 382-3.

Chilly day, to be a. A facetious way of expressing extreme infrequency of occurrence is to say that "it is a chilly day" or "it is a cold day in January" when the occurrence takes place.

1893 If I might adopt [Mr. Cannon's] simile, under the present low temperature in the Pension Office, it is *a chilly day* when a Congressman goes to the Pension Office now, looking up the rights of an old soldier. —Mr. J. F. Lacey of Ia., H. R., Dec. 16: *C. R.,* p. 290/1.

Chimney rock. Stone for building chimneys.

1870 The marbles of our western border have heretofore served as *"chimney rock"* for the cabin of the luxurious border farmer, and for fencing for his field.—Mr. S. S. Burdett of Mo., H. R., March 26: *C. G.,* p. 225/2, App.

Chinch bug. The bedbug; a fetid hemipterous insect very destructive to grass and grains.—(Webster.) [1705-1910.]

1872 I might as well talk about defending the king of the forest from the attack of a *chinch bug,* as to talk about defending the judiciary of Virginia from the assaults of my colleague.—Mr. R. T. W. Duke of Va., H. R., Apr. 6: *C. G.,* p. 2244/1-2.

1880 This commission maliciously, feloniously, and without warrant of law laid bloody and murderous hands upon the *"chinch bug."* . . . It was not that *chinch bugs* were killed, but illegally killed.—Mr. Henry Persons of Ga., H. R., May 10: *C. R.,* p. 3217/2.

Chinee, the heathen.

1871 *"The heathen Chinee* is peculiar."—Bret Harte.

1877 [The army is maintained] to put down the *"heathen Chinee."*—Mr. Townsend of N. Y., H. R., Nov. 8: *C. R.,* p. 296/1.

Chink. A Chinaman. Slang.

1912 Agents Baffle Government Officials and Bring *"Chinks"* Across Border in Coffins, Ice Chests and Box Cars.—Head-lines, *N. Y. Evening Post,* Aug. 26, p. 6.

Chinook salmon. See quotation.

1897 If the herd of sea lions which have their headquarters at Seal Rocks, just south of False Tillamock, were exterminated, the number of fat *Chinook salmon* coming into the Columbia would be greatly increased. —*The Oregonian.* See *C. R.,* Dec. 16, p. 221/2.

Chinook wind. A warm, moist wind from the south west, blowing on the Oregon and Washington coast. [1884-1910.]

1889 Not a signal station has been established . . . to give warning of approaching storms, or study the characteristics and effects of the *Chinook winds.*—Mr. Binger Hermann of Ore., H. R., Jan. 29: *C. R.,* p. 1300/1.

1900 If we get wind in winter, it is the soft, warm *Chinook,* coming up the mighty Columbia from the sea, making the daisies smile in the lap of winter.—Mr. W. L. Jones of Wash., H. R., May 15: *Id.,* p. 5556/2.

Chinquapin, Chinkapin. A kind of nut growing in a burr like a chestnut. Chinkapin whistles, made of bark, are still well known in Va. [1624-1856.]

1670 [In Va.], many goodly Groves of, *Chincomen-Trees,* that have husks like a Chestnut, and are good meat either raw or boiled.—Samuel Clarke, "Account of the Plantations," p. 12.

1807 For Sale, 2,000 Cedar and *Chinquepin* Posts.—Norfolk (Va.) *Gazette,* Nov. 13, p. 4/3. (Advt.)

1884 The diagnosis of an ailing calf . . . . towers over the educational question like Jumbo over a narrow-gauge mule, or a cedar of Lebanon over a *chinkapin-bush.*—Mr. Z. B. Vance of N. C., U. S. Senate, March 24: *C. R.,* p. 2209/1.

1887 [I saw the girls in N. C. last summer] spending an entire day picking huckleberries and *chincapins.*—Mr. Allen of Miss., H. R., Feb. 12: *Id.,* p. 81/1, App.

Chip in, to. To interpose a remark. Colloq. [1870-1888.]

1894 I hope the time occupied by the gentleman from Me. [Mr. Thomas B. Reed] will not be taken out of my time, for he is in the habit of *"chipping in"* in everybody's time.—Mr. Robert Neill of Ark., H. R., Feb. 26: *C. R.,* p. 2437/2.

Chip on one's shoulder. One who seeks a quarrel is said to go about with a chip on his shoulder, daring others to knock it off. [1840-1901.]

1860 Let a boy at school put a *chip on his head,* and tell another that he must not knock it off, and he will be sure to do it.—Mr. James S. Green of Mo., U. S. Senate, Dec. 10: *C. G.,* p. 27/3.

1868 I have known a great many bold men to put *chips on their shoulders,* and ask somebody to knock them off.—Mr. Lyman Trumbull of Ill., U. S. Senate, Feb. 28: *Id.,* p. 1494/1.

1873 The time has passed when the American nation need go round *with a chip on its shoulder,* challenging everybody to fight.—Mr. Joseph R. Hawley of Conn., U. S. Senate, Dec. 12: *C. R.,* p. 182/2.

1879 In his peculiar manner [Mr. Blaine] sets a great big *chip on his shoulder,* and he invites some Southern Senator to knock it off.—Mr. W. A. Wallace of Pa., U. S. Senate, June 14: *Id.,* p. 2001/1.

1887 Members who . . carry *chips on their shoulders,* while all the while they have politics in their eyes.—Mr. Buck of Conn., H. R., Jan. 8: *Id.,* p. 470/1.

1896 Ever since this session began we have been acting like a boy at school *with a chip on his shoulder,* walking around and asking somebody to knock it off.—Mr. G. L. Johnson of Calif., H. R., March 26: *Id.,* p. 3248/1.

Chipper. To chatter, to twitter. As a noun, chattering. (East Anglian.)

1861 Always *chippering* and chattering to each other, like a pair of antiquated house-sparrows.—Harriet B. Stowe, "Pearl Orr's Island," p. 22. (N. E. D.)

1865 A mirthful *chipper* and laugh under the song of soaring larks. . . . The twitter and *chipper* of birds.—Elihu Burritt, "Walk to the Land's End," pp. 314, 411. (N. E. D.)

1900 Men can harp about the Constitution and *chipper* about the flag.—Mr. C. H. Grosvenor of O., H. R., Feb. 28: *C. R.,* p. 114/1, App.

Chippy, Chip-bird, Chipping bird. The *Spizella domestica.* Also called the hair-bird. [1824.]

1900 The ground *chippy* darted under the fences, and had its nest in the tall grass.—Mr. A. J. Cummings of N. Y., H. R., Apr. 30: *C. R.,* p. 4872/2.

Chirk. ·Cheerful. [1824-1878.]

1815 "How fare ye, Doolittle?"—"Cleverly. Stiddy, pritty stiddy, and quite *chirk* again."—David Humphreys, "The Yankey in England," p. 29.

Chirpiness. Cheerfulness. See Vol. I, **Chirpy.** [1838.]

1867 He saluted us with a cricket-like *chirpiness* of manner.—W. D. Howells, "Italian Journeys," p. 248. (Century Dict.)

Chivalry. See quotations.

1863 The blood of the *chivalry* was rising, and he replied, "Keep a civil tongue in your head."—Edmund Kirke, "My Southern Friends," p. 67. (N. Y.)

1866 This man Jackson is a clerk in the Second Auditor's office, one of the *"chivalry."*—Mr. Henry Wilson of Mass., U. S. Senate, June 5: *C. G.,* p. 2960/2.

1866 Tell the working men of the North that they are to be robbed of thirteen Representatives in Congress in order that the *"chivalry"* may have that much additional power.—Mr. W. Windom of Minn., H. R., June 14: *Id.,* p. 3170/1.

1866 [This language] savors a little of what the English are accustomed to call "bounce," and what in this country has hitherto been understood as *"southern chivalry."*—Mr. Henry J. Raymond of N. Y., H. R., July 17: *Id.,* p. 3875/2.

1868 He was one of the Hotspurs of the South, one of the pinks of *southern chivalry*, one of those who believed that one southern man could whip five northern men in a fair and equal fight.—Mr. Geo. F. Edmunds of Vt., U. S. Senate, Feb. 13: *Id., p.* 1153/3.

1876 The South is today ruled over by the miserable thrall of Yankeedom; but they cannot muzzle our *chivalry* and patriotic devotion to the "lost cause."—Speech attributed to Rev. Taylor Martin of Charlotte, N. C., May 5: see *C. R.*, Aug. 4, p. 5183/1.

1876 [The Democrats] made you believe that the war would begin in the streets of our northern cities; that we were a community of shopkeepers, of sordid money-getters, and could not stand against your *chivalry.*—Mr. James A. Garfield of O., H. R., Aug. 4: *Id.*, p. 5184/1.

Choke off. To silence, to put a stop to. [1841-1910.]

1864 If we are to be *choked off* from argument, I hope that the House will choke down the bill.—Mr. Moorhead of Pa., H. R., Apr. 19: *C. G.*, p. 1735/3.

1870 Who among this body of men is going to be *choked off* from saying . . . what he deems it his duty to say?—Mr. J. W. Nye of Nev., U. S. Senate, May 6: *Id.*, p. 3278/1.

1884 An attempt to pass any bill . . . under the whip and spur, and with an idea of *choking off* a full, fair, and free discussion of the merits . . . does not do credit to the intelligence of this House.—Mr. G. A. Post of Pa., H. R., June 18: *C. R.*, p. 5309/2.

Chore. A small job, particularly about a house or farm. [1820-1878.]

1815 Do a number of little *chores* about the house; in short, everything you are told; carry tidings, 'tend table, and milk the ducks; do you consent to all this?—David Humphreys, "The Yankey in England," p. 21.

1862 Whoever undertakes to labor under the whip of the distinguished chairman of the Committee on Finance has not any time to play, nor to do *chores.*—Mr. T. O. Howe of Wisc., U. S. Senate, May 5: *C. G.*, p. 142/2, App.

1870 To reloan $1,200,000,000 at a saving of from one-sixth to one-third of the interest, and at the same time to substitute nearly $400,000,000 of U. S. notes with national bank notes, to do all this at once, is no *chore* for a child.—U. S. Senate, March 7: *Id.*, p. 131/2, App.

1871 Every Senator will remember how I was made to plead yesterday in my effort to get through a couple of little *chores* lying on my desk now.—U. S. Senate, Feb. 4: *Id.*, p. 956/1.

1875 One other *chore* engaged the attention of a portion of the army in 1859.—U. S. Senate, Jan. 12: *C. R.*, p. 396/2.

Chowder. A substantial soup of clams or fish. [1762-1888.]

1870 This amnesty bill may be called a *"chowder"* of rare and varied ingredients, and of the purest water of the New England kitchen.—Mr. Thomas L. Jones of Ky., H. R., Dec. 22: *C. G.*, p. 281/2.

Chuck-a-luck. A game of chance. [1857.]

1864 [They were] engaged in the favorite out-door occupations of their class, such as "seven-up," "quoits," "pitch and toss," and *"chuck-a-luck."*—Edmund Kirke, "Down in Tenn.," p. 63. (N. Y.)

1898 [The Indian boy may be] taken back to Ariz., and thrown into association with the people who are playing *chuck-a-luck*, the gambling bucks of the Apache tribe.—Mr. John F. Lacey of Ia., H. R., Jan. 26: *C. R.*, p. 1048/1.

Chunk. A bit, as in "a chunk of a fight." [1833-1856.]

1894 Mr. Patterson:—Just one moment, my friend. You are a lawyer. Mr. Kilgore:—Yes, a *chunk* of a lawyer.—H. R., July 13: *C. R.*, p. 7445/1.

Chunky. Stocky. [1776-1833.]
1807 He is full-faced, and *chunky.—The Republican* (Savannah, Ga.), March 10, p. 4/1. (Advt.)
Church fair. A church bazaar.
1876 A *church fair,* or any fair in fact, always seems to me like a contrivance to get a great deal of money for very little value.—W. A. Butler, "Mrs. Limber's Raffle," p. 18. (N. E. D.)
1890 Sugar and molasses are put upon the free list. This reminds me very much of certain entertainments and *church fairs,* which I have attended, when the admission was free. They were very pleasant occasions, but I always found that, while we got in free, it generally took $2 or $3 to get out.—Mr. G. W. Cooper of Ind., H. R., May 8: *C. R.,* p. 4343/2.
Chute. A natural or artificial flume or rapid waterway. [1806-1839.]
1826 See RIFFLE.
1864 The draws are to be constructed at the head of two *chutes,* and there is only one *chute* through which boats can be passed under [ordinary] circumstances. These draws are to be large enough for the passage of the largest boats; and the draws will be an index to the boatmen as to where the *chute* is, by which they shall pass over the falls [of the Ohio River].—Mr. Mallory of Ky., H. R., Apr. 19: *C. G.,* p. 1735/2.
Cimarron. The Spanish-American name for the bighorn or Rocky Mountain sheep. The word was proposed as a name for the northwest corner of the Indian Territory, also called "No Man's Land."
Cinch. To fasten with a tight girth. Hence to have an advantage; to have a man "in a tight place." [1875-1878.]
1894 This bill is for the purpose of paying the corporations and speculators a premium for deliberately violating the law, . . . in cornering money last year, and *"cinching"* every debtor in the U. S.—Mr. W. W. Bowers of Calif., H. R., June 5: *C. R.,* p. 5780/2.
1897 This bill . . . has been killed and put into its coffin, and by the "eternal *cinch"* effect of the motion to reconsider and lay on the table the coffin has been nailed up.—Mr. W. L. Terry of Ark., H. R., Jan. 11: *Id.,* p. 690/2.
Cinch. A tight girth. Hence, an advantage over the one cinched. [1872-1909.]
a.1898 A man's son is entitled to a chance in his business, but not to a *cinch.—*G. H. Lorimer, "Gorgon Graham," p. 8.
Circuit rider. An itinerant preacher, usually Methodist or Baptist. [1838-1858.]
1864 [The Confederate legislatures of Ky. and Mo.] were as peripatetic as a tin-peddler's cart or a Methodist *circuit-rider;* still they claimed to be legitimate.—Mr. Chandler of Va., H. R., May 17: *C. G.,* p. 2317/3.
Circumstance, a. "Anything to speak of." [1836-1867.]
1893 The affection of Damon and Pythias, or that of David and Jonathan, is not a *circumstance* to the love of the white Republican for the negro while the ballots are going in.—Mr. Champ Clark of Mo., H. R., Oct. 2: *C. R.,* p. 2044/1.
City of Brotherly Love. Philadelphia. [1799-1850.]
1862 Is the *City of "Brotherly Love"* so full of kindness as its name implies? —Mr. John C. Ten Eyck of N. J., U. S. Senate, July 11: *C. G.,* p. 3247/1.
1867 I am suspicious of this [League Island] bill. I do not know when the *City of Brotherly Love* ever offered such a munificent gift to the Government before.—Mr. Garrett Davis of Ky., U. S. Senate, Feb. 14: *Id.,* p. 1301/2.
1876 What would [the Centennial Exposition] be without a wooden horse from Greece within thy gates, O *City of Brotherly Love?—*Mr. S. S. Cox of N. Y., H. R., Feb. 9: *C. R.,* p. 986/1.

1881   Did not the Huguenot and the Cavalier, the Quaker from the *City of Brotherly Love,* and the Puritan, furnish us our early settlers in the Far West?—Mr. W. H. Calkins of Ind., H. R., Feb. 5: *Id.,* p. 1274/2.

City of Churches.   Brooklyn, N. Y.

1893   The rights . . of the people are denominated by the accomplished gentleman from *the City of Churches* [Mr. J. C. Hendrix] as "rot."—Mr. T. R. Stockdale of Miss., H. R., Aug. 21: *C. R.,* p. 74/2, App.

City of Magnificent Distances.   Washington. [1835-1858.]

1862   We all know that this city has been called one of *magnificent distances.* Whether the first characteristic, with reference to its magnificence, is true or not, I am not prepared to say: but with respect to its distances, ... it is a striking feature that meets the eye.—Mr. John C. Ten Eyck of N. J., Apr. 4: *C. G.,* p. 1539/2.

1870   [Sandstone and granite have been transported] even in their rough state from their distant beds to this *"city of magnificent distances."*—Mr. John A. Logan of Ill., H. R., Jan. 22: *Id.,* p. 682/1.

1870   The City of Washington, I believe, is about four miles square; and the number of avenues and streets, their width and their length, in this *"city of magnificent distances,"* have no precedent on earth from the foundation of time.—Mr. Garrett Davis of Ky., U. S. Senate, June 21: *Id.,* p. 4650/3.

Civil Rights Bill.   A bill intended to equalize negroes with white men in respect of citizenship.   The original bill was passed over President Johnson's veto in April, 1866.   Nine years later, Mr. Charles Sumner introduced a more stringent bill, for the purpose of securing to negroes free access to hotels, schools, and public conveyances.   This bill was passed, but was declared unconstitutional by the Supreme Court of the U. S. in Oct. 1883.

1876   We have no desire to filibuster, although the *civil rights bill,* which was designed to give the rights of manhood to the colored members, was ordered to be reported regularly from a committee, and for seventeen successive Monday mornings filibustering cut off the chance to report it.—Mr. James G. Blaine of Me., H. R., Jan. 14: *C. R.,* p. 421/1.

Clam-bake.   A feast on clams and fish.   [1840-1888.]

1879   See Squantum.

1894   See Good Time.

Clapboard.   A weather-board.   [1632-1848.]

1670   Of Oakes there be three kinds, Red, White, and Black, whereof one kind is fittest for *Clap-board,* others for sawn-board, &c.—Samuel Clarke, "Account of the Plantations," p. 31.

Classhood.   The system of social grades.

1878   [Free labor in America] eliminated *classhood* in Society, and made opportunities for advancement, socially, politically, and financially equal among men.—Mr. A. A. Sargent of Calif., U. S. Senate, March 7: *C. R.,* p. 1551/2.

Clawhammer.   An evening dress coat.   [1869-1879.]

1880   Mr. Kirkwood of Ia.:—Suppose that, to offset the tax on tobacco, we put a tax on *claw-hammer coats,*—swallow-tails, I believe they are called.   Mr. Cameron of Wisc.:—They are tax enough on the men who wear them.   Mr. Kirkwood:—Suppose, in addition to that, we tax every man who wears a stove-pipe hat. . . . Something certainly ought to be done to discourage the use of these monstrosities.   Mr. Hamlin of Me.:—Why not tax frock-coats, and reach the Senator from Iowa?   Mr. Kirkwood:—No: I say tax *clawhammer coats* and stovepipe hats.—U. S. Senate, Apr. 16: *C. R.,* p. 2468/1.

Clay-dog.   See quotation.

1892   In the vicinity of Pleasant Plains, ... the low plain is covered to a considerable depth with similar laminated clay, . . rich in concretions,

which are locally known as "clay-stones," *"clay-dogs,"* "stone-dogs,"
&c.—R. D. Salisbury, "Genl. Survey of N. J.," p. 138. (Century
Dict.)

Clay-eaters. Certain "poor whites" in the South use a sort of semi-
edible clay. The term is one of reproach and scorn. [1841-1901.]

1863 On the top of the coach, coiled away on a pile of horse blankets, was
a woman whose dress and appearance designated her as one of the
species of "white trash" known in N. C. as *"clay-eaters."*—Edmund
Kirke, "My Southern Friends," p. 43.

1866 How many degrees are the "corn-crackers," the "sand-hillers," and
the *"clay-eaters"* above the "greasers" and "guerrillas" of Mexico?—
Mr. Ignatius Donnelly of Minn., H. R., June 5: *C. G.,* p. 2968/1.

Clean-cut. Sharply defined. [1876-1910.]

1894 This bill should have been a *clean-cut* bill for revenue, and revenue
only.—Mr. L. F. Livingston of Ga., H. R., Jan. 24: *C. R.,* p. 1343/2.

1894 This is simply a *clean-cut* exhibition to be made by the government
[at Atlanta].—H. R., Aug. 10: *Id.,* p. 8386/1.

Clean out. To demolish. [1812-1867.]

1866 I hope my colleague will be allowed to proceed, and that I may be
allowed to *clean him out.*—Mr. S. J. Randall of Pa., H. R., Dec. 19:
C. G., p. 205/2.

1870 I hope and believe that Colonel Baker's late *"cleaning out"* of the
Piegans in Montana . . . . will end Indian murders, robberies, and
other nameless outrages in my Territory.—Mr. James M. Cavanaugh
of Mont., H. R., March 2: *Id.,* p. 1644/1.

1871 The enemy did take possession of the house one day. They were
"cleaned out," as we say; they were compelled to leave the house.—
Mr. Timothy O. Howe of Wisc., U. S. Senate, Jan. 5: *Id.,* p. 316/1.

Clean-up. A periodical settlement of accounts.

1866 When what they technically call in mining the *clean-up* comes, very
often the *clean-up* exhibits the lofty sum of nothing, while thousands
have been expended in the effort. . . . . The next *clean-up* gives something, and so on until it begins to be remunerative.—Mr. John Conness
of Calif., U. S. Senate, June 18: *C. G.,* p. 3231/1.

Clever. Obliging, kind, pleasant, amiable. [1768-1878.]

1843 See Up to the Notch.

1849 Mr. Jones is a *clever* man, as we have said,—a kind neighbor.—Wilmington (N. C.) *Commercial,* May 5, p. 2/2.

1853 See Shinplaster.

1864 The gentleman says that [this hall] is an unfit place to live in, and I
do not think it is a very *clever* place to die in.—Mr. Thaddeus Stevens
of Pa., H. R., June 29: *C. G.,* 3395/2.

1869 See Collateral.

1872 A Methodist preacher, a very genteel, *clever* gentleman, as they usually
are, had got into some difficulty.—Mr. Justin S. Morrill of Vt., U. S.
Senate, March 12: *C. G.,* p. 1594/1.

1876 A *clever* man may keep a saloon, but I mention it as evidence that he
is not a man of high position.—Mr. Lewis V. Bogy of Mo., U. S.
Senate, Dec. 6: *C. R.,* p. 63/2.

1878 The other two were no doubt *clever* men, but comparatively ignorant.
—Mr. John T. Harris of Va., H. R., March 27: *Id.,* p. 2093/1. [For
fuller citation see Sportsman.]

1888 I love [Mr. O'Ferrall] almost like a brother, for he is a *clever*
fellow; but a worse misguided fellow, politically I mean, never lived.
—Mr. L. C. Houk of Tenn., H. R., March 6: *Id.,* p. 1795/2.

1893 See Not by a Jugful.

Climb down, to. To retreat from an untenable position. Colloq.

Clinton's ditch. A nickname for the Erie Canal, opened in 1825.

1879 *Clinton's ditch,* as it used to be called, was sneered at when it was an experiment.—Mr. James G. Blaine of Me., U. S. Senate, Jan. 22: *C. R.,* p. 629/2.

1880 The Erie Canal, which has made De Witt Clinton immortal, was derided as *Clinton's ditch,* and accepted as the evidence of a distempered mind.—Mr. William Kimmel of Md., H. R., May 20: *Id.,* p. 178/1, App.

Close. A close district is one in which the votes are almost evenly divided. Macaulay (1855) has close contest, close division. (N. E. D.)

1874 St. Helena is a very *close* parish. In 1870 it gave 30 democratic majority. It is considered a very *close* parish.—Testimony of State Secretary Bovee, *C. R.,* Jan. 30, p. 1042/1.

1887 See DOUBTFUL.

Close call. A narrow escape.

Cloud-burst. An overpowering deluge of rain. [1821-1881.]

1912 Rock Springs, Wyo., August 1.—A message just received from Point of Rocks, says that a *cloudburst* occurred there late last night, and that a forty-foot wall of water is headed toward this city.—*N. Y. Evening Post.*

Coachee. See quotation. [1796-1818.]

1804 For sale, a light well finished *Coachee,* and a pair of young Horses.— *Georgia Republican,* May 11, p. 3/2.

Coal-oil, v. To smear with coal oil before burning.

1894 [The negroes] are tortured; they are *coal-oiled* and burned.—Mr. W. E. Chandler of N. H., U. S. Senate, Feb. 5: *C. R.,* p. 1862/1.

Coast. To glide down an ice path on a bobsled. The path used to be called a coast. [1775-1909.]

1872 The sidewalk, the plankway, and the brickway were given up entirely as a *coasting-ground,* where the boys were *coasting* in what may be called a positively constitutional way: that is, without distinction of race, color, or previous condition of servitude.—Mr. H. B. Anthony of R. I., U. S. Senate, Feb. 7: *C. G.,* p. 869/2.

1889 The term *"coast"* is said to be known in Boston, but not in Salem or Plymouth.—*Journal of Am. Folk-Lore,* II, 155.

Coastwise. Lying on the coast, or sailing along it. The word, as an adverb, is more than two centuries old. (N. E. D.)

1856 During our *coastwise* drift.—Kane, "Arctic Expl.," I, 42. (N. E. D.)

1892 Mr. Gorman:—I would not open the door for a foreign vessel to engage in the *coastwise* trade. Mr. Mitchell:—What *coastwise* States on the Atlantic Coast have abandoned the compulsory pilot system? Mr. Gorman:—As the foreign commerce has grown in the great Northern States, they found it wise to reduce or to abolish compulsory pilotage on the *coastwise* vessels.—U. S. Senate, May 19: *C. R.,* pp. 4413-4.

Coatee. A coat. [1775-1852.]

1794 [He] had on when he eloped a blue *coatee* and trowsers.—*City Gazette* (Charleston, S. C.), Aug. 1, p. 4/4. (Advt.)

1827 Two of the men wore *coatees,* and the other a surtout.—*Nat. Gazette* (Phila.), Oct. 23, p. 2/4.

Cobb Dollars. Counterfeit money. [1786-1865.]

1786 [The robbers found] some small pieces of coin, and a *cobb dollar.*— *New Haven Gazette,* Apr. 6, p. 63/2.

Cob-house. A house built of corncobs. [1818-1857.]

1913 Mayor Gaynor made a statement, comparing the "Curran Scandal committee" to a *"cobhouse* of sensationalism, lying, and scandal. All *cobhouses* [he added] fall down at the first jar."—*N. Y. Evening Post,* June 5, p. 6/3.

Cockarouse. A captain or brave fellow. [1624-1731.] See *Journal of Am. Folk-Lore,* xv, 244.

1651 There was a Wainoake Indian told him that there was an Englishman a *Cockarous* hard by Captaine Floods.—"Discovery of New Brittaine," Aug. 28.

Cocked hat. To knock anyone into a cocked hat is to "use him up" completely. [1833-1858.]

1862 I think this argument is, as we say in Dixie, "effectually *knocked into a cocked hat*."—Mr. Joseph Segar of Va., H. R., Feb. 10: *C. G.,* p. 732/1.

Cocktail. A stimulating liquor, composed of spirits of any kind, sugar, water, and bitters. [1806-1861.]

1871 [The Sixteenth Amendment], it is of course understood, is to be appropriated to those blushing damsels who are, day after day, beseeching us to let them vote, hold office, drink *cocktails,* ride astraddle, and do everything else the men do.—Mr. J. Proctor Knott of Ky., H. R., Jan. 27: *C. G.,* p. 66/3, App.

Cocoa grass. See quotation.

1894 See JOHNSON GRASS.

1894 That extraordinary grass known as *cocoa grass,* which has spread over large areas in the States of La. and Miss., until to-day many of the richest lands of La. have been abandoned.—Mr. C. E. Hooker of Miss., H. R., July 31: *C. R.,* p. 8049/1.

Co-conspirator. A fellow conspirator.

1863 Jefferson Davis and his co-conspirators . . . . would be utterly undone.—Mr. Edwin H. Webster of Md., H. R., Feb. 28: *C. G.,* p. 1426/1.

1863 He has sought to become . . . . in the palace of the French emperor a *co-conspirator* with him.—Mr. John Bright, 'Speech on American Affairs,' June 30. (N. E. D.)

Codfish aristocracy. An opprobrious name for persons who have made money in trade. [1850-1865.]

1867 The *codfish aristocracy* had bounties for fishing, in order to build up a navy. [Here the allusion is specifically to the New Englanders.]— Mr. T. E. Noell of Mo., H. R., Feb. 12: *C. G.,* p. 105/3, App.

1874 This talk about "social equality" . . . is the cry of the old-time office-holder and *codfish aristocrat,* who uses the negro . . . to make capital of.—Mr. Charles Hays of Ala., H. R., Jan. 31: *C. R.,* p. 1097/1.

1876 In the Statehouse at Boston, in the house of representatives, ... there hangs, swimming in air, the well-mounted effigy of an enormous codfish, suggesting the origin and giving a typical representation of what is called there "the *codfish aristocracy*."—Mr. Banks of Mass., H. R., May 19: *Id.,* 3221/1.

1884 Some of those who devoted their time and money to this purpose [of maintaining fish-ponds] were satirized as "mullet millionaires." These old Romans are the archetypes of our *codfish aristocracy.*— Mr. S. S. Cox of N. Y., H. R., May 12: *Id.,* p. 313/2, App.

1888 [They wanted to get] into the society of the *codfish aristocracy* of the city of Columbus [Ohio.]—Mr. W. Woodburn of Nev., H. R., June 11: *Id.,* p. 5115/2.

1897 Just the other day England was the richest nation. To-day Uncle Sam could buy the whole of the tight little island and all that therein is, including her kings and queens and knaves, and all that they have, and hold it as a summer resort for our *codfish aristocracy.*—A Fourth of July oration, quoted July 7 in the *C. R.,* p. 2444/1.

Cod walloper. A cod-fishing vessel of the New England coast.

Coffee-cooler. See quotations.

1890 Those who in platform and in speech delight in characterizing the old soldiers as *"coffee coolers,"* "bounty jumpers," and "bummers,"

. . . are not those upon whom the soldier can rely for generous legislation.—Mr. Binger Hermann of Ore., H. R., Apr. 30: *C. R.,* p. 106/2, App.

1890 There the Indians went in their savage state, before they became mere *coffee-coolers,* wards of the Government, to procure their supplies.—Mr. G. C. Moody of S. D., U. S. Senate, July 17: *Id.,* p. 7344/2.

1893 A deserter or a bummer or a coward or a *"coffee-cooler"* or a hospital lounger.--Letter of July 29: *Id.,* Dec. 27, 1894: p. 10/1, App.

1895 I am opposed to giving pensions to deserters, and *"coffee coolers,"* and bounty jumpers, and camp followers.—Mr. W. J. Talbert of S. C., H. R., Jan. 18: *Id.,* p. 1129/2.

1896 They are men enough to turn their backs upon . . . deserters, *coffee-coolers,* bummers, and camp followers. . . . . [This section] opens up a wide field for granting pensions to bummers, *coffee-coolers,* and deserters.—H. R., March 20 and Apr. 23: *Id.,* pp. 3062/2 and 4336/1.

1896 Mr. Lewis:—I have heard a good many times in this discussion the phrase *"coffee-cooler."* . . . Who is the inventor of this expression, *"coffee-cooler"*? Mr. Milnes:—Grover Cleveland. (Laughter.) Mr. Lewis:—Did it come from the same source as that other phrase, "innocuous desuetude"? I want to say that the expressions *"coffee-cooler"* and "bounty jumper" have . . . fallen into innocuous desuetude. We had no bounty jumpers or *coffee-coolers* in Kentucky. The only sort of jumpers we had there were men who jumped over the enemy's works, and jumped to the top of the mountains and planted the Union flag there.—H. R., Apr. 27: *Id.,* p. 4492/1.

1896 I have stood here many a time, and heard the Union veterans called *"coffee-coolers,"* and "bummers," and all that class of pet names.— Mr. S. L. Milliken of Me., H. R.: *Id.,* p. 4493/1.

Coffee plant. See quotation.

1890 It has been shown . . . that anywhere on the Pacific coast, from Ore. down to the southern line of Calif., the climate is peculiarly adapted for the culture of [the wild silk-worm], which subsists upon an indigenous plant found on that coast, the common name of which is *"coffee plant,"* and which is entirely different from the mulberry.— Mr. S. R. Peters of Kan., H. R., June 12: *C. R.,* p. 5992/1.

Coho. A species of salmon found on the North Pacific coast. In the opinions of the canners . . . the *coho* should rank next after the king salmon in food value.—*Bulletin U. S. Fish Comm.,* xviii, 6. (Century Dict.)

Cohunk. See quotation.

1728 The Indians call [wild geese] *cohunks,* from [their] hoarse note.— William Byrd, "Writings," p. 146. (1901.)

Coin notes. Notes payable in coin.

1876 The first section of this bill requires *coin-notes* to be paid out, and consequently it involves the . . necessity of redeeming those *coin-notes.*—Mr. Kasson of Ia., H. R., July 25: *C. R.,* p. 4866/1. [See the rest of the debate.]

Cold facts, the. The facts without illustration or comment.

1892 It seems to me the only thing that should be permitted is to give the *cold facts* with fair comparisons, without comments and without opinions.—Mr. W. D. Washburn of Minn., U. S. Senate, June 23: *C. R.,* p. 5480/1.

Collah. A crab claw used as a charm.

1822 Put into your mouth this crab claw, and you can't be wounded. . . . . He said, give me back my corn, and *collah* (that is, crab's claw).— *Am. Beacon,* Sept. 5, p. 2/4. [Account of Denmark Vesey's insurrection in Charleston.]

Collar and Cuff District. 1894 See **Dicker.**

Collar, to wear someone's. To be slavishly subservient to someone. See **Collar-dogs,** Vol. I.

1862 I belong to no party. I am too old; my remaining years on earth are too few for me ever to expect to wear another *party collar.*—Mr. Garrett Davis of Ky., U. S. Senate, Jan. 23: *C. G.*, p. 452/1.

1866 I do not believe that [Mr. Lane's] constituents will be quite satisfied with so broad a declaration, that he is to wear any man's *collar,* and follow him wherever he may go.—Mr. B. F. Wade of O., U. S. Senate, Apr. 6: *Id.,* p. 1799/3.

1866 The Senator from O. has suggested that I have taken upon myself the *collar* of the President of the U. S. I hurl the suggestion in the teeth of the Senator from O., as unworthy of a Senator. I wear a *collar!*—Mr. Lane of Kan., U. S. Senate, Apr. 6: *Id.,* p. 1802/2.

1866 Do you want to wear *the collar and the harness* of a man superior over you? If you do, you are unworthy sons of revolutionary sires. . . . I will never submit to wearing *the collar or the harness* of any man.—Mr. Edgar Cowan of Pa., U. S. Senate, May 11: *Id.,* p. 2557/1.

Collards. Dial. & U. S. Coleworts or cabbage. [1818-1882.]

1863 "Do you raise anything else?" "Yas, I hab *collards* and taters, a little corn, and most eberyting."—Edmund Kirke, "Life in Dixie's Land," p. 118. (Lond.)

1898 I would not incite my friends . . . to riot, but I must say that a dinner of hog jowl and sweet Georgia *collards,* or bacon and tender spring turnip tops, or fried chicken and brown gravy, with the inseparable accompaniment of sugar yams, smoking corn pones, hot biscuit, and cold buttermilk, is better than all the pork and beans or corned beef and pickled cabbage, pumpkin pies, stale bread, and cider that can be spread on any table in New England.—Mr. J. M. Griggs of Ga., H. R., March 15: *C. R.,* p. 2830/2.

Collateral. Security for the repayment of a loan. [1847-1887.]

1869 Our friends who are engaged in banking down East are very clever fellows. When we want money to move our wheat, we understand we can go down there and borrow it. If we have got the *collaterals* to put up, we get it.—Mr. Timothy O. Howe of Wisc., U. S. Senate, March 25: *C. G.,* p. 273/2.

1893 Mr. Cannon:—I stepped into one of those great banks, and said, "I have such and such security as *collateral,* and want so much money," and I always got my answer at once. Mr. Springer:—Your *collaterals* were good. That is what helped you out.—H. R., Oct. 16: *C. R.,* p. 2574/1.

College scrip. A species of land scrip issued and sold in order to establish colleges.

1869 The *college scrip* of many of the eastern States was bought up on mere speculation for fifty or sixty cents an acre, and entered in large tracts throughout the new States, entirely excluding settlement, improvement, and taxation.—Mr. Alex. Ramsey of Minn., U. S. Senate, Feb. 4: *C. G.,* p. 874/2.

College widow. See quotation.

1887 That class of young ladies known among the students as *"college widows,"* and commonly supposed to have the acquaintance of several generations of collegians.—*Lippincott's Mag.,* p. 298. (N. E. D.)

Collide. To come into collision (with). [1700-1880.]

1863 This anomalous power [of liberating the slaves] . . . . . *collides* with many clauses of the Constitution.—Mr. Garrett Davis of Ky., U. S. Senate, Jan. 27: *C. G.,* p. 532/2.

Colloquy, v. To hold a colloquy. [1860-1868.]

1871 When I saw the speaker *colloquying* with the Democrats, I knew very well what was to come.—Mr. B. F. Butler of Mass., H. R., March 16: *C. G.,* p. 126/1.

Color line. A line of demarcation separating blacks from whites.

1875 We are in favor of the *color line* as a principle, a necessity, and a policy.—*Handsborough* (Miss.) *Democrat,* quoted in *C. R.,* App., p. 21/2. (Jan., 1876.)

1875 The grand result of the *color line* has been accomplished in organizing the white people of the State and placing them in a position to control the coming election.—*Columbus* (Miss.) *Index,* Aug. [See *Id.,* Aug. 4, 1876, p. 5182/1.]

1876 We discarded the *color line* yesterday. [Mr. Lamar] kicked the *color line* out of this House, and I hope it is not going to be brought back today.—Mr. Townsend of N. Y., H. R., July 26: *Id.,* p. 4890/1.

1878 We shall soon cease to hear of a *color line.*—*N. Am. Review,* cxxvii, 491. (N. E. D.)

Colorphobia. A dislike of negroes.

1862 There was a democratic *colorphobia*—as I believe it is described in some of our abolition prints—prevailing in the mind of the prosecuting attorney, and he would not [summon] colored witnesses to rebut what took place in the presence of colored people.—Mr. John P. Hale of N. H., U. S. Senate, July 3: *C. G.,* p. 3100/1.

1863 The Mayor and Aldermen . . . have been such slaves of *colorphobia,* that they did not choose to execute this law.—Mr. Wendell Phillips, "Speeches," iii, 48. (N. E. D.)

1869 There is no doubt that [the exclusion of negro surgeons] was accomplished by an organized effort, quickened by *colorphobia.*—Mr. Chas. Sumner of Mass., U. S. Senate, Dec. 9: *C. G.,* p. 46/3.

1886 *Colorphobia* in Chicago.—*Boston Journal,* Oct. 23, p. 6/6. (N. E. D.)

Columbiad. See first quotation.

1861 The *columbiad* is a kind of Dahlgren,—that is, a piece of ordnance very thick in the breech, and lightened off gradually from the trunnions to the muzzle.—W. R. Russell in *The Times,* May 14. (N. E. D.)

1870 I remember when treason placed its huge *columbiads* on the heights of Arlington.—Mr. William Williams of Ind., H. R., Jan. 29: *C. G.,* p. 870/2.

Combine. A combination. [1887-1888.]

1890 If you pass this bill you accomplish a great result; you give to the people cheap raw sugar and cheap refined sugar, and save to them untold millions of dollars annually; and in addition you destroy, root and branch, the greatest *"combine"* known to our people, a *"combine"* which was "conceived in sin and born in iniquity"; a *"combine"* which may be called the American "devil-fish."—Mr. J. H. Gear of Ia., H. R., May 9: *C. R.,* p. 4390/1.

1892 Every business [in England] almost is carried on entirely by *combines,* a toothpick combination, a skewer combination, a combination for making rattles for children.—Mr. Ezra B. Taylor of O., H. R., June 16: *Id.,* p. 5347/1.

1894 Let us see what the effect of a protective tariff is. It was very cogently stated by Mr. Henry George, who says that out of a protective tariff as naturally as grow toadstools out of a rotten log, grow the trusts and *combines.*—Mr. Jerry Simpson of Kan., H. R., Jan. 12: *Id.,* p. 774/1.

1894 [The protective system] has enriched our lexicography by attaching new and ominous meanings to the words *"combine,"* "lockout," "boycott," and "strike." It has helped to invest anthropology with new interest by adding to its classifications the "snob" and the *"tramp."*— Mr. A. J. Cummings of N. Y., H. R., Jan. 31: *Id.,* p. 1748/2.

1896 See DEVIL.

Come near. To come within a little of.

1877 An unlucky accident that *came near* ruining my spine makes it painful for me to stand and speak.—Mr. W. D. Kelley of Pa., H. R., Nov. 15: *C. R.,* p. 436/1.

1878 We *came very near* having a smash-up. *Scribner's Mag.,* p. 24/2.
(N. E. D.)

Comer. A promising animal.

1901-2 He has made good growth since he came before the public, ...
and still shows that remarkable looseness and elasticity of hide that
indicates a *"comer"* when he is put next to the feed-box.—*Rep. Kan.
State Bd. Agr.,* p. 202. (Century Dict.)

Come-uppunce. To get one's come-up-with means to meet with one's
deserts, more or less unpleasantly. See Vol. I, **Come up with.**
[1869-1897.]

1893 [Geese] git dey *come-uppunce* des lak [just like] folks.—Mary A.
Owen, "Old Rabbit, The Voodoo, &c.," p. 29.

Commoner, the Great. This term, originally applied to the elder
William Pitt, has been used with reference to Henry Clay, and to
Thaddeus Stevens of Pa. (1792-1868.) It was also applied to
Richard P. Bland of Mo. (1835-1899). See his eulogy by Mr.
S. W. T. Lanham of Tex., Apr. 7, 1900: *C. R.,* p. 3896/1.

1844 [Mr. Clay] was soon regarded as the leading spirit of the opposition
party; and it was about this time [1800] that the title of *"The Great
Commoner"* was bestowed upon him.—Epes Sargent, "Life etc. of H.
Clay," p. 6/2.

1868 The gentleman from Pa., the *"great commoner,"* as he is called, whose
power and influence we have felt and seen—Mr. Chas. A. Eldridge of
Wisc., H. R., Feb. 24: *C. G.,* p. 1397/3.

1868 With his own supporters his name was a household word. To them,
and among themselves, "Old Thad" was a phrase of endearment;
while even his foes spoke of him with pride as the *"great commoner."*
—Mr. Oliver J. Dickey of Pa., H. R., Dec. 17: *Id.,* p. 131/1.

1868 Mr. Stevens was in the latter part of his career sometimes pleasantly
called "the great *commoner"*; but this invitation to a comparison
between him and Chatham was not well advised.—Mr. Chas. R.
Buckalew of Pa., U. S. Senate, Dec. 18: *Id.,* p. 147/2.

1879 There was a man once . . . . that had the love of his party and the
respect of his opponents perhaps to as large a degree as any man
that has lived, unless it be Andrew Jackson. I speak of Henry Clay
of Ky. . . . Let me read what the *Great Commoner* said in 1833.—
Mr. Eaton of Conn., U. S. Senate, May 16: *C. R.,* p. 1381/2.

1882 The grandest man I have ever met in the American Congress, the
"old commoner" of Pennsylvania, Thaddeus Stevens.—Mr. W. D.
Kelley of Pa., H. R., Apr. 10: *Id.,* p. 2733/1.

1900 Here is the gentleman from N. Y. [Mr. Sulzer] who was created to
look like *the great commoner,* Mr. Clay. *The great commoner* from
Ky. . . . . has been reincarnated, so that we have my friend from
N. Y. as a foundation to go upon the ticket, to save the country,
to save the party, to save the world. He comes from Tammany, and
Tammany made him, and he jumps when Tammany pulls the string.—
Mr. J. G. Cannon of Ill., H. R., Feb. 17: *Id.,* p. 1901/2.

Commune. To communicate; especially in the sacrament. [1821-1856.]

1831 Some of our citizens . . . were carrying on the slave trade, while
with a smooth face they were praying in our religious societies, and
communing at the Lord's table.—*The Liberator,* Feb. 26, p. 34/1.

Complected. Complexioned. [1800-1896.]

1822 He is well made, light *complected,* &c.—*Am. Beacon* (Norfolk, Va.),
Jan. 8, p. 3/3. (Advt.)

1830 These signatures the dark *complected* gentleman had not been able
to obtain.—*Id.,* July 7, p. 4/2. (From a Boston paper.)

1868 [They were disfranchised] merely for the crime of being *darker complected* than the generality of men.—Mr. John A. Logan of Ill., H. R.,
Jan. 8: *C. G.,* p. 402/1.

1877 See Appendix.

Compromise used adjectivally. Not in N. E. D.

1867 [Are we] to sit here from day to day and make rejection after
rejection, and finally take somebody who is not the choice of the
Senate, but a sort of *compromise man,* who is neither Democrat nor
Radical?—Mr. Richard Yates of Ill., U. S. Senate, Apr. 16: *C. G.,*
p. 848/2.

Compromise tariff, the. Henry Clay's tariff, which was in force from
1833 to 1842. It provided for a gradual reduction of duties.

Concord wagon. See the second citation.

1870 [They were] building the famous *Concord wagons,* found in all parts
of the country, even in the cañons of the Rocky Mountains.—Mr.
Horace Maynard of Tenn., H. R., March 30: *C. G.,* p. 264/2, App.

1870 The Overland Mail vehicle of that description known as the *Concord
wagon,*—a stout oblong box on springs, painted red, with heavy
wheels and axles, having a flat arched roof of waterproof cloth erected
on strong posts, like those of a rockaway, and to this are attached
curtains of the same fabric.—F. H. Ludlow, "The Heart of the
Continent," p. 10.

Condemn. To condemn land is to take it, by proper proceedings, under
right of eminent domain.

1876 If we have a right to have a post office, and we cannot rent one, we
have a right to build one, and we cannot build one without buying
the land, and if we cannot buy the land voluntarily, we have the right
to take it. So with regard to a customhouse; so with regard to a
fort; so with regard to any public building or public work whatever.
If the Government has the right to make this improvement, and the
State of Ore. does not furnish the land, and the people will not
voluntarily sell it, the Government has a right to *condemn* it for
that purpose.—Mr. O. P. Morton of Ind., U. S. Senate, Aug. 2: *C. R ,*
p. 5079/1.

Condemnation. See quotation.

1911 The act of determining and declaring, after due process of law, that
some specific property is required for public use, and must be surrendered by the owner on payment of damages to be determined by
commissioners or a jury: as, the *condemnation* of private lands for a
highway, a railway, a public park, &c.—(Century Dict.)

Condition, Conditioned. A student, failing to pass an exam., is sometimes admitted to his degree on condition of further exam. He is
said to be conditioned, while still pursuing his study. [1849-1869.]

Condolence council. A tribal council of the Iroquois, held after the
death of a sachem.

1890 He was engaged on the Grand River Reservation in Canada, where
he successfully made [an] effort to obtain the chants and speeches
used in the *condolence council* of the league. *Smithsonian Rep.,* p.
49.—(Century Dict.)

Conductor. The "guard" of a train. [1839-1857.]

1865 [The company] should furnish the necessary hands to handle the
property, and the engineers, *conductors,* and brakemen to run the
trains.—Mr. Lyman Trumbull of Ill., U. S. Senate, Feb. 18: *C. G.,*
p. 900/1.

1865 [If black people] are excluded from the cars [on the street railways
in the District of Columbia], it is the result of the exercise of a
petty, arbitrary authority by some mean *conductor.*—Mr. Patterson
of N. H., H. R., Feb. 23: *Id.,* p. 1026/3.

Conepatl. A badger-like skunk. Mexican.

Conestoga horses. See quotations.

1814 Mr. McDuffie of S. C., in the H. R., May 31, alluded to Mr. James
Buchanan's "celebrated breed of *Conestoga dray horses,*" p. 9/2 of
the speech as separately published.

1862 We place you on a level with the owner of the turnpike and the *Conestoga team,* when the railroad and the locomotive were introduced.—Mr. W. M. Davis of Pa., H. R., March 6: *C. G.,* p. 1107/2.

1875 The *Conestogas* respond promptly to the whip, but if there should be in that team any high-mettled thoroughbred, the touch of the lash rouses him to resistance.—Mr. R. E. Withers of Va., March 22: *Id.,* p. 132/1.

1880 Kiskiminetas! There may be seen the *Conestoga team,* with its road wagon, its eight Norman horses, its bells, its tar-bucket and dog under the wagon, illustrative of the earlier days of Pa. enterprise.—Mr. S. S. Cox of N. Y., H. R., Jan. 22: *Id.,* p. 490/1.

Conestoga wagons. Wagons with broad wheels and characteristic canvas tops. They were named for a town in Pa. [1783-1846.]

1874 Sixty years ago . . . . . . transportation was carried on in long trains of *Conestoga wagons,* traveling only about three miles an hour.—Mr. F. T. Frelinghuysen of N. J., U. S. Senate, June 4: *C. R.,* p. 4544/1.

1880 A class of gentlemen reverently in love with the old system of *Conestoga wagons,* with a tar-bucket and a dog under each wagon.—Mr. John H. Reagan of Tex., H. R., Feb. 5: *Id.,* p. 732/2.

Confederate brigadiers. A term applied to those ex-confederate army officers who were returned to Congress.

1879 They were apparently saying to the *"brigadier generals"* of the South, "Come to us, come and help us."—Mr. A. H. Coffroth of Pa., H. R., Apr. 18: *C. R.,* p. 562/2.

1879 The *"confederate brigadiers,"* who allied themselves with [the republican] party are not only harmless, but the very quintessence of patriotism. They can be trusted as Cabinet officers and foreign ministers and Federal judges.—Mr. W. L. Steele of N. C., H. R., Apr. 19: *Id.,* p. 591/1.

1879 Unmanly and uncalled-for references to the presence of *"rebel brigadiers"* and *"ex-confederate colonels"* on this floor.—Mr. Jas. W. Covert of N. Y., H. R., Apr. 22: *Id.,* p. 683/1.

1879 There are on our side of the Senate several of these much-abused *"confederate brigadiers,"* who in the prime of their young manhood [served in the war with Mexico].—Mr. John S. Williams of Ky., U. S. Senate, Apr. 23: *Id.,* p. 720/1.

1879 *Confederate brigadiers* have yelled and howled with rage, and sawed the air &c.—Mr. J. R. Thomas of Ill., H. R., Apr. 24: *Id.,* p. 892/2.

1879 See BLOODY CHASM. See STALWART.

1881 My friend from Tex. [Mr. Maxey] referred to the fact that a great deal was said . . . during the last two years about *confederate brigadiers* having control of the democratic side of the House, the democratic side controlling the Senate, and therefore the *Confederate brigadiers* controlling the Senate. I have no taste for any of these matters.—Mr. Joseph E. Brown of Ga., U. S. Senate, March 24: *C. R.,* p. 48/1.

Confidence game. A species of swindle. **Confidence man.** A swindler.

1867 [This] is simply to place the U. S. Government in the position of a man playing a *"confidence game"* of the meanest description, in which the Treasury Department and Congress are the confederate knaves, and the whole mass of bondholders the unfortunate victims.—Mr. Jas. G. Blaine of Me., H. R., Nov. 26: *C. G.,* p. 801/2.

1873 [He], like a *"confidence-man"* as he is, endeavoring to hoist himself into respectability by referring to Chief Justice Chase.—Letter of Mr. G. B. Lamar, *C. G.,* Jan. 18, p. 692/1.

1884 For some weeks the newspapers here have waged a war of extermination against gamblers, *confidence men,* &c.—*Boston Journal,* Nov. 22, p. 6/5. (N. E. D.)

1890 See BUNKO-STEERER.

Conflagrated. Burned up. The verb *to conflagrate* is used in 1657. (N. E. D.)

1814 Rebellion, civil war, prostrated liberty, and *conflagrated* towns.— John C. Calhoun in the H. R., Feb. 25. ["Works" (1856), II, 102.]

1866 [His health] was in a strangely painful, and as if *conflagrated* condition.—T. Carlyle, "Reminiscences" (1881), II, 175. (N. E. D.)

Congressman. A member of Congress.

a.1850 Our *Congressmen,* my dear hearers, what are they? Nothing but bloodsuckers upon the cheek of the U. S.—Dow Jr., "Sermons," III, 137. (Bartlett.)

1888 The term *"Congressman"* is commonly used to describe a member of the House of Representatives, though . . . . it ought to include Senators also.—Bryce, "Am. Commonwealth," I, 197*n*. (N. E. D.)

Connections, to make. A traveller is said to do this, when, on alighting from any conveyance, he finds another ready to carry him onward, as he expected. When the first conveyance is delayed, he may fail to make connections, or to "connect."

Conniption. A fit of hysterics. [1833-1859.]

1888 This is not the first time I have seen gentlemen on the other side in a state of *"conniption."*—Mr. T. B. Reed of Me., H. R., June 9, *C. R.,* p. 5076/1.

1896 Somebody . . . that has *conniptions* and spasms over the guinea's stamp, and knows nothing about the guinea's gold.—Mr. J. S. Willis of Del., H. R., March 20: *Id.,* p. 3031/1.

Conquer-John. Solomon's Seal, *Polygonatum biflorum.* Southern.

1893 Er chunk ob er root ob *Conquer-John.*—Mary A. Owen, "Old Rabbit, The Voodoo, &c.," p. 67.

Conscience-Whig, Cotton-Whig. A *Conscience-Whig,* "in the last days of the Whig party, one of those northern Whigs who were indisposed to regard the [Clay] Compromise of 1850 as a final settlement of the slavery question." A *Cotton-Whig,* one who took the contrary part.—(Century Dict.)

Conscript. To conscribe, or enlist by compulsion.

1864 Go on then; *conscript* the negro; re-enslave the negro. . . . You have made this a negro abolition war.—Mr. Jas. Brooks of N. Y., H. R., Feb. 19: *C. G.,* p. 762/3.

1864 Every man *conscripted* must shoulder the musket and march.—Mr. Mallory of Ky., H. R., June 25: *Id.,* p. 3273/2.

1865 He was first *conscripted* for two years.—Walt Whitman, "Specimen Days" (1888), p. 62. (N. E. D.)

1880 I had been *conscripted* and forced into the army.—*Atl. Monthly,* p. 22, July. (N. E. D.)

Considerable. A great deal. [1816-1852.]

1872 I think you will not have [that land] *by considerable.* It was dedicated to the Indians 40 years ago solemnly; and they hold it in fee simple.—Mr. Lot M. Morrill of Me., U. S. Senate, Apr. 5: *C. G.,* p. 2198/1.

1875 I am sorry [that my time has expired], because I had *considerable* more to say.—Mr. G. F. Edmunds of Vt., U. S. Senate, Feb. 27: *C. R.,* p. 1870/2.

1884 *Considerable* has been said . . . concerning the English policy of railway amalgamations.—Mr. J. R. Glasscock of Calif., H. R., Dec. 11: *Id.,* p. 189/2.

Contestant, Contestee. A contestant is one who contests, in war or in politics; a contestee is one against whom a contesting claim is made. The N. E. D. gives an instance (1665) of the former, but states it to be unknown to Bailey, Johnson, Webster 1828, and Worcester 1846.

1861 A little after six o'clock the remaining *contestants* withdrew down the precipitous river bank.—*The Times,* Nov. 8. (N. E. D.)

1870   [It is stated] that so many voted for the *contestant* and so many for the *contestee* in that ward.—Mr. R. R. Butler of Tenn., H. R., Feb. 16: *C. G.,* p. 1349/3.

1876   *Contestant* makes him his witness . . . . [and he is] cross-examined by *contestee.*—Mr. House of Tenn., H. R., May 31: *C. R.,* p. 3429/2. [See also pp. 3430-37.]

1882   The *contestee,* Mr. Campbell, presented a certificate signed by the governor of Utah Territory.—Mr. W. H. Calkins of Ind., H. R., July 13: *Id.,* p. 6006/1.

1884   [Who are the witnesses?] First, the postmaster, who said he had been working for the *contestee* for two months; and secondly a man by the name of Evans, employed by the *contestee* as his counsel.—Mr. J. F. Follett of O., H. R., May 27: *Id.,* p. 4584/1.

1896   My friend put a question to the *contestee* which has not been answered, and never will be until Gabriel blows his horn.—Mr. R. Z. Linney of N. C., H. R., July 9: *Id.,* p. 6340/2.

Continental army. A name given to Washington's troops. See Vol. I for **Continental** (noun). [1778-1856.]

1778   An additional number [from R. I.] to make up their proportion to the *continental army.*—Letter of Gen. Varnum to George Washington, Jan. 2: see *C. G.,* Feb. 2, 1863, p. 681/2.

Continental money. The scrip issued by Congress during the Revolutionary War. As to the gradual depreciation of the "Continental Currency" from 1777 to 1780 inclusive, see an extract from an almanac of 1791, cited by Senator Powell, May 30, 1864; *C. G.,* p. 2574/2. The rate of depreciation then grew from 1½ to 75 per cent. But in May, 1781, one hundred paper dollars were equivalent to one dollar in coin, and after that the value of a "continental" became nominal. [1825-1888.]

b.1813   [My father] lost his property . . . by the sinking of *Continental money.*—"Journal of Peggy Dow," p. 199/1. (1851.)

Contoured. Naturally bounded.

1896   The land so *contoured* that extreme weather hardly ever lasts more than three days.—Sermon by Dr. Talmage, quoted in *C. R.,* May 14, p. 5218/1.

Contraband. In 1861 this term was applied to negroes escaping to the Union lines. [1861-1908.]

1861   There they stand with arms stretched out to us, ... *contrabands* heretofore, deodands now, ... anxious for service and ready to receive the hire which labor may always rightfully demand.—Mr. Thomas D. Eliot of Mass., H. R., Dec. 12: *C. G.,* p. 79/1.

1862   In this city, at any moment, we may look for an *emeute* occasioned by the crowding out of white labor by black *contrabands.*—Mr. S. S. Cox of O., H. R., June 3: *Id.,* p. 245/3, App.

1862   The government is incurring large expenditures in keeping these *contrabands.*—Mr. William Allen of O., H. R., July 12: *Id.,* p. 3304/3.

1862   What I have said of the proportion of free colored persons to the whites in the District [of Columbia] is from the census of 1869, having no reference to persons called *contrabands.*—President Lincoln's Message, Dec. 1: *Id.,* p. 4, App.

1863   I have a letter from Rear Admiral Porter, which says that he has shipped upon his squadron four hundred negroes, able-bodied *contrabands,* who work at the guns.—Mr. Charles B. Sedgwick of N. Y., H. R., Jan. 30: *Id.,* p. 630/1.

1863   In the place of the cargoes of Sea Island cotton which was to be produced by the *contrabands,* you have spent some millions in masterly inactivity, and we have heard nothing of cotton.—Mr. T. L. Price of Mo., H. R., Feb. 28: *Id.,* p. 137/3, App.

Contractionist. The opposite of an inflationist: one who is for contracting the paper currency.

1881 Whether the new Secretary [of the Treasury] . . . would be an expansionist or a *contractionist.*—N. Y. *Nation,* xxxii, 160. (N. E. D.)

1890 This distinguished Senator and *contractionist* [Mr. John Sherman].— Mr. J. C McRae of Ark., H. R., July 12: *C. R.,* p. 7208/1.

1892 It was the duty of Senators to return here when a bill of this kind was pending; but they can defeat the will of the people, and serve the gold-standard *contractionists;* they can serve Lombard and Wall Streets by being absent. They cannot however deceive the people.— Mr. W. M. Stewart of Nev., U. S. Senate, June 30: *Id.,* p. 5658/1.

Contraption. A contrivance. [1837-1909.]

1917 The natives had no notion that the word "train" did not stand for the same tiny *contraptions* the world over, as that to which they applied it.—H. A. Franck, "Vagabonding down the Andes," p. 17. (Century Co.)

Convention City. See quotation.

1912 Although Baltimore is best known as the "Monument City," it long ago achieved a wide distinction as the *"Convention City."* In fact, it can really be said to be the birthplace of the convention system for Presidential nominations. Here it was .that the first Democratic National Convention met in 1832; here in that year the famous but bothersome two-thirds rule was first adopted; here the first national political platform was put forth in 1840; and here the first "dark horse" made his appearance, in the person of James K. Polk, in 1844. Altogether, there have been eight national conventions of the Democratic party held in Baltimore—this present one will be the ninth. Three national conventions of the Whig party were held here and one of the Republican.—Newspaper item.

Cook book. A cookery-book.

1881 Miss Parloa's *New Cook Book,* a guide to marketing and cooking. (Boston.)

1889 We cannot supply the demand for *cook books* and elementary works on domestic economy.—Report of Am. Library. (N. E. D.)

Cook stove. A cooking stove.

1871 The vulgar words wash-tub, shoe-horn, brew-house, *cook-stove,* . . . . which are merely slovenly and uncouth abbreviations of washing-tub, shoeing-horn, brewing-house, and cooking-stove.—R. G. White, "Words and their Uses," p. 232. [The same objection might be raised to many useful words.]

1878 Every step in getting away from arbitrary power is a step toward communism in exactly the same sense and no other than you, sir [Mr. Oglesby of Ill. in the chair] building a fire in your small *cook-stove* on the prairies of Ill. to cook your dinner is a step toward incendiarism.—Mr. G. F. Edmunds of Vt., U. S. Senate, Apr. 9: *C. R.,* p. 2365/2.

Cool off. To cool oneself, especially after being angry.

1879 I am only going to get a drink of water. I must *cool off.*—Mr. William Windom of Minn., U. S. Senate, June 26: *C. R.,* p. 2353/1.

Coolieism. The coolie system.

1870 [To seek to encourage manufactures] by reductions on labor alone, or by unnatural foreign immigration, is to depress labor, not to protect it. To seek it by Chinese immigration in the form of *coolieism* is still worse.—Mr. Jacob H. Ela of N. H., H. R., Jan. 21: *C. G.,* p. 654/1.

1879 Asiatic *coolieism* is a form of human slavery, and is **for**ever prohibited in this State.—Constitution of Calif.

1882 According to the interpretation in this country, a *cooly* is a man whose passage is paid to the U. S. by some one who has the money, and who in return receives the promise of the emigrant to repay the advance with interest, either in money or in labor, after his arrival.— Mr. J. P. Jones of Nev., U. S. Senate, March 9: *C. R.,* p. 1742/1. [Under this definition, the "Redemptioners" (q. v.) were coolies.]

Coon, for Raccoon. [1839-1862.]

1844 The speech of Mr. Duncan of O. (March 6), as separately published, contains on p. 15 a full-page picture of a *coon* laid on his back and cut open. His internal organs are labelled "National Bank," "Hartford Convention," "Tippecanoe party, &c."

1897 We are told that a *coon* was first used as a campaign emblem in 1844; that "that same old coon," uttered in derision by his opponents, was adopted by the followers of Henry Clay as their slogan and emblem.—Mr. J. M. Kendall of Ky., H. R., Feb. 18: *C. R.,* p. 51/2, App. [This is not correct.]

1876 Mr. Hendricks was talking to the eastern democrats when at Saratoga. He was endeavoring to catch the eastern *coon.—Cincinn. Enquirer,* cited Aug. 5: *C. R.,* p. 5226/2.

Coon. A negro. Why so called, see the story in *Journal of Am. Folk-Lore,* xi, 13-14. (1898.)

1891 "A slick *coon*—aristocratic citizens object to a negro neighbor." After citing this heading of an item in an Illinois paper, Mr. Richardson of Tenn. said:—It will be observed that not only is this colored man treated [thus], but the people of Ill. denounce him as a *"coon."*— H. R., Jan. 17, *C. R.,* p. 100/1, App.

1892 Instead of seating one colored Representative, they seated two,—two *coons* in place of the elected Representatives of the people.—Mr. A. G. Caruth of Ky., H. R., Feb. 4: *Id.,* p. 856/2.

1896 Chief Justice Chase was talking to a nigger one day, ... He said to this *coon*—negro I mean—"I have always thought that it was very strange that a coon wore his fur on the outside. When I have a coat with fur on it, I generally put the fur on the inside. I find that it is warmer to wear it that way, and I do not see why a *coon* should not wear it in that way. Why is it?" "Well," said the negro, "you'd know if you was de *coon."*—Mr. P. J. Otey of Va., H. R., Apr. 4: *Id.,* pp. 3593-4.

1897 Even the darky will fight if you call him a *"coon."*—Mr. L. W. Royse of Ind., H. R., Feb. 18: *Id.,* p. 1970/2.

Coon-oyster. A small oyster, usually growing in clusters. Southern Coast.—(Century Dict.)

Coon song. A popular song, such as is common among the negroes in the Southern States.—(Century Dict.)

Cop. A policeman. Slang. The term is said to have been first applied to the N. Y. police under Fernando Wood, on account of their copper badges. But more probably from the verb to *cop.*

1859 And where [will be] the buffer, bruiser, blowen,
And all the *cops* and beaks so knowin',
A hundred stretches hence?
—G. W. Matsell, "Vocabulum," p. 124. (N. Y.)

1867 What's a *cop?* . . . That's what the boys call a policeman.—F. H. Ludlow, "A Brace of Boys," p. 262. (N. E. D.)

1896 The term "juvenile offenders" may include little chaps who have been arrested . . . . for being impudent to a majestic *cop,* or for trespassing upon forbidden grass.—Mr. C. H. Gibson of Md., U. S. Senate, May 14: *C. R.,* p. 5216/2.

Copperhead. A Northerner who was supposed to be a Southern sympathizer during the Civil War. [1863-1885.]

1863 The seat of the rebellion is to-day not in Richmond, it is among the *copperheaded* traitors of the North.—Mr. Zachariah Chandler of Mich., U. S. Senate, *C. G.,* p. 936/2.

1863   Who knows but this manifestation of profanity and pugnacity of the *copperheads* of the East may have been only a Yankee trick to commend Puritanic New England to the *copperheads* of the West, who prate about leaving New England out in the cold?—Mr. Henry Wilson of Mass., U. S. Senate, Feb. 21: *Id.,* p. 1163/3.

1863   These Indiana *copperheads* hiss their venomous slanders at the Commonwealth of Massachusetts.—U. S. Senate, Feb. 28: *Id.,* p. 1370/2.

1864   Who made [the draft law unpopular?] It is the declarations of such traitors as Chauncey C. Burr, Clement L. Vallandigham, John U. Andrews, and lately, as that word has been introduced here,—I did not introduce it,—lately the *copperhead* orator of the city of New York.—Mr. A. Myers of Pa., H. R., Feb. 3: *Id.,* p. 472/1.

1864   It is the dark, oozy, unwholesome soil, between the solid earth on either side, over which unclassified *copperheads* do creep, and mark their slimy and doubtful track.—Mr. Schenck of O., H. R., Apr. 11: *Id.,* p. 1538/1.

1866   I had hoped that when peace had returned, when passion had subsided, I never again in the Senate of the U. S. should hear the term *"copperhead"* drop from the lips of any Senator.—Mr. Willard Saulsbury of Del., U. S. Senate, May 7: *Id.,* p. 2427/1.

1867   See BREAD AND BUTTER BRIGADE.

1869   This man to whom I refer is the tail end of a *copperhead* law firm.— Mr. W. G. Brownlow of Tenn., U. S. Senate, Dec. 15: *C. G.,* p. 139/1.

Coppet. A knoll; a "hammock."

1904   These *"coppets,"* or "hammocks," as they are called in Florida, are areas devoid of either pines or palmettos, and often occupy isolated areas entirely surrounded by pine forests, as in southern Florida.— *Science,* p. 113. (Century Dict.)

Copyholder. A proofreader's assistant.—(Century Dict.)

1888   Persons employed in the Printing Office under the names of proofreaders and *copyholders.*—Mr. Eugene Hale of Me., U. S. Senate, Jan. 24: *C. R.,* p. 666/1.

Coquina. A conglomerate of sea-shells united by a calcareous cement, much used in Florida as a building material.

1883   St. Augustine, a still older settlement [with its] white *coquina* walls, quaint Peninsular houses, etc.—*Pall Mall Gaz.,* Oct. 20, p. 5/1. (N. E. D.)

Cord. A measure of four feet by four by eight. [1616-1845.]

1874   I will show [in canal construction] where we have taken out thousands upon thousands of *cords* of rock, not scratching dirt.—Mr. Zach. Chandler of Mich., U. S. Senate, June 3: *C. R.,* p. 4500/2.

Corn. Indian corn; maize. [1697-1888.]

1872   I am told that *corn* is now used as fuel even in the region of the great Iowa and Missouri coal-field.—Mr. M. M. Walden of Ia., H. R., Feb. 17: *C. G.,* p. 1101/1.

Corn-bread, Corn-cake. That made of the meal of Indian corn.

Corncob. The chaffy axis on which the kernels . . . . are arranged.— (Webster.) [1767-1856.]

1845   See SHUCKS.

1897   You might as well talk of corking up Vesuvius with a *corncob* as to talk about "opening the mills."—Mr. W. L. Greene of Neb., H. R., March 22: *C. R.,* p. 146/1.

Corn-cracker. A Kentuckian. [1837-1848.]

1866   See CLAY-EATER.

Corndodger. A cake made of the meal of Indian corn, baked hard under embers.—(Webster.) See Vol. I, under **Dodger.** [1834-1864.]

1877   Both hog and hominy, both patriotism and guts, both *corndodgers* and corn-juice.—Mr. S. S. Cox of N. Y., H. R., Nov. 19: *C. R.,* p. 534/1.

Corner. A temporary monopoly of some commodity. [1853-1888.]
1872 Who is there or what is there to prevent the manufacturers of tobacco from forming a *"corner,"* or combining to regulate the price at which leaf tobacco is to be bought or sold?—Mr. John M. Rice of Ky., H. R., Dec. 20: *C. G.,* p. 2/2, App.
1877 There is a set of gamblers in Wall Street, ... who make *corners* in wheat and corn, no matter what suffering it may cause the poor; they are the gamblers who make *corners,* and seek to control the price of cotton and tobacco.—Mr. J. J. Davis of N. C., H. R., Nov. 14: *C. R.,* p. 410/2.
1878 See INFLATIONIST.
Corner grocery, Corner groggery. A drinking place. See Vol. I, under **Grocery.** [1806-1909.]
1862 As to the policy and means used, men may well differ, without subjecting themselves to the charge of disloyalty by every *corner-grocery* politician in the land.—Mr. James R. Morris of O., H. R., July 7: *C. G.,* p. 3159/1.
1864 The hungry wife . . . . complains not of taxation, but that her wretched husband loiters in the schoolhouse of modern Democracy,— the *corner groggery.*—Mr. W. D. Kelley of Pa., H. R., Jan. 19: *Id.,* p. 270/1.
1883 It must be admitted that our current small coins are suggestive of no nobler use than that found in paying a reckoning at a *corner grocery.*—Mr. J. S. Morrill of Vt., U. S. Senate, Dec. 5: *C. R.,* p. 42/1.
Corner lot. One facing on two streets. [1829-1852.]
1860 What about *corner lots* in St. Joseph?—Mr. Owen Lovejoy of Ill., H. R., Dec. 13: *C. G.,* p. 89/2.
1863 These early pioneers [in Colo.] at once pitched their tents, and commenced laying off *"corner lots,"* and holding elections.—Mr. H. P. Bennet of Colo., H. R., Feb. 28: *Id.,* p. 139/1, App.
1868 I was sent here by a gentleman who happens to own a *corner lot,* to whom great injustice was done, as he said, by making him improve on both sides of his lot.—Mr. Jas. W. Patterson of N. H., U. S. Senate, Apr. 7: *Id.,* p. 2265/1.
Corn high. As high as an ear of Indian corn.
1893 I was born in Chicago, . . . and railroaded ever since I was *corn high.*—A. C. Gunter, "Miss Dividends," p. 52.
Corning. A top-buggy with deep sides and the part forward of the seat cut down square. Named after Erastus Corning of Albany, N. Y.—(Century Dict.)
Corn-shuck. The envelope, or husk, of an ear of Indian corn. See Vol. II, under **Shuck.**
1866 I found myself riddled with bullets from every quarter, until, as the boys say, my hide would not hold *corn-shucks.*—Mr. Ebenezer Dumont of Ind., H. R., June 4: *C. G.,* p. 2953/2.
Cornstalk as a depreciatory epithet.
1898 I was a tin soldier—a kind of a *cornstalk* captain—but I have had [some] experience.—Mr. Chas. K. Wheeler of Ky., H. R., Apr. 23: *C. R.,* p. 4216/1.
Corn-stealers. The hands. [1827-1857.]
1880 His phalanges or metacarpus, or rather *corn-stealers,* are bigger than those of any other member [of the House].—Mr. S. S. Cox of N. Y., H. R., Jan. 22: *C. R.,* p. 488/1.
Corral. An enclosure for horses or cattle. Spanish. [1845-1860.]
1876 The general shout which [the Democracy] sent up shook the whole country from sea to sea, and completely stampeded the party of the Administration. Everywhere they broke from their *corrals,* snapped their halters, and went wild in scattered confusion.—Mr. Black, Apr. 27: "Trial of W. W. Belknap," p. 12/2.

1883 [There was] a man on the Santa Fé road who slept one night in a *corral*. He awoke along in the middle of the night, feeling that the air was a little close, and he got up and found the gate of the *corral* closed; he opened it, and was all right again.—Mr. P. B. Plumb of Kan., U. S. Senate, March 1: *C. R.*, p. 3485/2.

1888 See SNUBBING-POST.

Corral, v. To enclose or capture. [1860-1888.]

1879 That party which has *corraled* courts of justice with national bayonets. —Mr. Roscoe Conkling of N. Y., U. S. Senate, Apr. 24: *C. R.*, p. 805/2.

1894 The Indian rides on horseback; yet the Secretary of War sends down a lot of infantry to *corral* him if he gets out on the war path.— Mr. D. T. Flynn of Okla., H. R., Dec. 17: *Id.*, p. 374/2.

1898 [This man] *corralled* the judges of election . . . and gave them instructions.—Mr. Jacob Yost of Va., H. R., Apr. 25: *Id.*, p. 4261/1.

Co-State. A word coined by Jefferson. A fellow state. [1798-1841.]

1857 Va. exercises the right that pertains to a State . . . . in declaring her views, and inviting the like action of her *co-States*.—T. H. Benton, "Thirty Years' View," p. 349.

Cottondom. The cotton-producing region.

1863 I want to see La., Tex., Ark., and Mo. cut off from the cotton region. I know that there is not a foot of grazing land in the southern confederacy when you cut those States off from *cottondom*. . . . . Then I want to see those rivers which go up into the heart of *cottondom* lined with our gunboats.—Mr. Joseph A. Wright of Ind., U. S. Senate, Jan. 6: *C. G.*, p. 203/3.

Cotton States. Those raising a great deal of cotton and using negro labor very largely.

1858 If we organize "committees of safety" all over the *cotton States* . . . . . we shall fire the Southern heart.—Wm. L. Yancey, "Cradle of Confederacy," p. 393. (N. E. D.)

1891 Ala. is called the *Cotton State* because it is the central State of the Cotton Belt.—M. Townsend, "The U. S.," p. 66. (N. E. D.)

Cottontail. Sometimes "Molly Cottontail." The common American rabbit.—(Webster.)

1885 A *cottontail* rabbit rose.—*Harper's Mag.*, p. 828/2. (N. E. D.)

Cottonwood. Any of various American species of poplar having a cottony tuft about the seeds.—(Webster.) [1817-1847.]

1878 The *cottonwood* is the pioneer tree of the plains; its growth is rapid, its shade is delightful; it is a valuable tree for lumber and for fuel.— Mr. A. S. Paddock of Neb., U. S. Senate, March 20: *C. R.*, p. 1894/2.

Cotton-worm. See first quotation.

1870 The *cotton-worm* (*Anomis xylina* Say) is very generally known by the name of the *Cotton Army worm*, in the South.—Riley, "Mo. Rep. Insects," p. 37. (N. E. D.)

1879 The beginning of this investigation into the grasshopper and *cottonworm* was in the summer of 1876 by the Senate, and the policy was adopted of having an investigation into the habitat of both the *cottonworm* and the grasshopper.—Mr. S. D. Maxey of Tex., U. S. Senate, March 1: *C. R.*, p. 2162/1.

Cough up. To pay up. Slang.

1912 (Western Ind.) He *coughed up* forty dollars for us before we left him.—*Dialect Notes*, III, 573.

Count out. To exclude. See Vol. I, **Count in or out.** [1808-1859.]

1863 Perhaps [Mr. Vallandigham supposed I wished] to immortalize myself by coupling my name with so distinguished a person as himself. If that is the gentleman's idea, I beg him to *count me out*.—Mr. John A. Bingham of O., H. R., Feb. 23: *C. G.*, p. 1227/3.

1890　It is commonly understood among men of all parties [in Ala.] that the election machinery being wholly within the hands or under the control of the Democratic party, they, to rid themselves of what they are pleased to term "negro domination," habitually *count out* the negro vote.—Mr. S. G. Comstock of Minn., H. R., June 3: *C. R.*, p. 5545/1.

Country, in my, in his country, &c. A particular section of country, frequently of indefinite extent. [1780-1855.]

1775　See SAVANNAH.

1856　See RED CENT.

1867　In my portion of the country we have got over those principles a long time ago. The husband has no right to flog the wife *in my country*.— Mr. Lot M. Morrill of Me., U. S. Senate, Feb. 9: *C. G.*, p. 1115/1.

1869　The gentleman says that *in his country* the deacons always used to get into these difficulties, and to have distilleries also. Now *my country* is better off than that.—Mr. Nathaniel Boyden of N. C., H. R., Feb. 12: *Id.*, p. 1154/1.

1874　See TUNKER.

1875　See FORTY ACRES AND A MULE.

1876　*In my country*, when we want a Fourth-of-July celebration, we usually go out among the neighbors, and some will supply a little money, and some a quarter of mutton or of beef, and some bread, and we meet together and have a social Fourth of July at our own expense.—Mr. Bland of Mo., H. R., June 19: *C. R.*, p. 3894/2.

1878　See GAS.

1880　See BUCKBOARD. See JACKPOT.

1886　See COWBOY.

1888　See UNLOAD. See OLD SLEDGE.

1890　If we could see a dozen old women from the mountains of *my country* come here and tackle the committee in regard to the duty on tin cups and coffeepots, the Lord have mercy on them.—Mr. Z. B. Vance of N. C., U. S. Senate, Aug. 12: *C. R.*, p. 8464/1.

1894　See DRUMMER.

County house. A poorhouse.

1872　[Mr. Willard of Vt.] feels that any one who would recommend him for any office ought to go to the *county-house*.—Mr. B. F. Butler of Mass., H. R., Apr. 18: *C. G.*, p. 269/1, App.

1888　An exceedingly singular character has just died at the Hillsdale *county house*.—*The Press*, Phila,, Jan. 29. (Farmer.)

County ranger. A county officer who takes charge of strays . . In Miss. the coroner is also the *county ranger,* and performs the duties of that office. (It is the duty of the *county ranger* to take charge of stray horses, mules, jacks, cattle, sheep, or hogs.)—Buck, "Med. Handbook," III, 295. (Century Dict.)

Courtesy of the Senate. This relates particularly to two customs; that of yielding to the wishes of senators from a particular State with regard to the confirmation or rejection of appointments to office, within that State, made by the President; and that of confirming the nomination to an office by the President of a member or former member of the Senate, without the usual reference to a committee.—(Century Dict.)

Cover money into the Treasury. To pay into. [1884.]

1868　It not unfrequently happens that money lies in the hands of the Treasurer [of the U. S.] for a very considerable time, small sums of money, because they cannot ascertain to what particular account to carry it. As soon as they do, the warrant is drawn. These covering warrants are not drawn every day, but once a week or once a fortnight or once a month, as the case may be. . . . They are drawn in this way, and receipted by the Treasurer. And this is technically called *covering money into the Treasury.*—Mr. W. P. Fessenden of Me., U. S. Senate, Feb. 17: *C. G.*, p. 1211/3.

1868   The measure providing for the *covering* of the cotton money *into the Treasury.*—Mr. Geo. F. Edmunds of Vt., U. S. Senate, Feb. 28: *Id.,* p. 1489/1.

1870   Either this money must be *covered into the Treasury,* ... or the fund will be very soon exhausted.—Mr. B. F. Butler of Mass., H. R., Jan. 19: *Id.,* p. 583/2.

1870   The amendment proposes to *"cover in"* to the Treasury every dollar resulting from [the sale of the navy-yard].—Mr. Chas. O'Neill of Pa., H. R., Jan. 25: *Id.,* p. 741/2.

1874   The balance of the money would have to be *covered back into the Treasury.*—Mr. B. F. Butler of Mass., H. R., March 10: *C. R.,* p. 2117/1.

1876   Here is money received under a treaty. When money is received from an individual in the nature of taxes it is *covered into the Treasury.* This money was received under a treaty, and the law required it to go into the Treasury of the U. S.; and when it is *covered into the Treasury,* it is under the seal and sanction of Congress.—Mr. John Sherman of O., U. S. Senate, May 31: *Id.,* p. 3410/1.

1892   Within the last ten years, $92,000,000 of appropriations ... had come within the terms of the *Covering-in Act,* [and] have been *covered back into the Treasury.*—Mr. D. B. Henderson of Ia., H. R., Jan. 14: *C. R.,* p. 319/1.

1913   Washington, May 8.—Republican Senators today began to look into Postmaster-General Burleson's plan to require 50,000 fourth-class postmasters *covered into* the civil service by Presidents Roosevelt and Taft to pass competitive examinations or lose their places.—*N. Y. Evening Post,* May 8, p. 1/4.

Cow.   To cower. South Cheshire (E. D. S.).

1844   He now *cowed* before me quite spirit-broken.—*Fraser's Mag.,* xxix, 561. (N. E. D.)

1863   [Senator Henry Wilson] says that the Democrats ... are now cowering before the people. I should like to know where they have ever *cowed* before the people. Did they *cow* in N. Y., when they elected Seymour Governor, when all your party was denouncing him as a traitor? Did they *cow* in N. J., when they elected a State ticket the other day? Did they *cow* in Ind.? Did they *cow* in Ill.? Did they *cow* in O.? Did they *cow* in Pa.?—Mr. Lazarus W. Powell of Ky., U. S. Senate, Feb. 21: *C. G.,* p. 1166/3.

Cowboy.   At first meaning simply a boy who looks after cattle, this word acquired an opprobrious meaning in the Revolutionary War. It now usually means a mounted herdsman on the cattle ranches of the West. [1725-1884.] Tusser (1573) has *Oxboy.*

1863   I grant you that the *Cowboys* of the Revolution might have been very respectable people, if King George had but succeeded in maintaining his government over the Colonies; but, as he did not happen to be successful, the name of *Cowboys* and Tories has become somewhat disreputable.—Mr. H. B. Wright of Pa., H. R., Jan. 14: *C. G.,* p. 319/3.

1879   Mr. Wallace:—[Mr. Blaine] is for the Republican party pure, simple, and stalwart. He does not want any of these fellows who are between the parties. Mr. Blaine:—I do not. They are the *cow-boys* of modern days, as they were in the Revolution.—U. S. Senate, June 14: *C. R.,* p. 2001/2.

1883   Wyo. and Mont. and other places where the cattle kings who live at Chicago and elsewhere own the cattle, and send their *cowboys* there to attend to them.—Mr. J. B. Beck of Ky., U. S. Senate, Jan. 29: *C. R.,* p. 1697/2.

1884   These homestead entries imply not *cowboys,* not ranchmen, not cattle-herders on the public domain, but farmers.—Mr. Benj. Harrison of Ind., U. S. Senate, Dec. 11: *Id.,* p. 185/1.

1886 The *cowboy* of the Eastern newspaper is largely a creature of the imagination. [Those who are] known as *"cowboys"* are young men, the sons for the most part of farmers of the Eastern, Western, and Southern States. . . . In my country it is not a disgrace to be called a *"cowboy."*—Mr. J. M. Carey of Wyo., H. R., June 28: *Id.,* p. 241/1, App.

Cowcatcher. A fender placed in front of an engine. [1838-1888.]

1853 To be thrown off the track by every buffalo-calf that gets in the way of the *cow-catcher.*—*Putnam's Mag.,* II, 33. (July.)

1886 You jump aboard of our train, run through and get out on the *cow-catcher,* and, as we move up to the station, shout, "Here we are!" —Mr. Butterworth of O., H. R., March 2: *C. R.,* p. 1980/1.

Cow-puncher. A cowboy. Colloq.

1903 See CHAPAREJOS.

Cows come home, till the. An indefinite time. [1610-1860.]

1616 Kisse *till the Cow come home,* kisse close, kisse close, Knaves.— Beaumont and Fletcher, "The Scornful Ladie," sig. D.

1878 You may enact laws *"until the cows come home,"* and you cannot remove these prejudices by those laws alone.—Mr. A. E. Burnside of R. I., U. S. Senate, Apr. 2: *C. R.,* p. 2191/1.

1896 We will drive from the American barnyard the horde of counterfeiters and cheats . . . and keep them out *"till the cows come home."*—Mr. J. P. Dolliver of Ia., H. R., Apr. 10: *Id.,* p. 3851/2.

Coyote. The prairie wolf. [1628-1899.]

1874 I believe it would be as wise to treat with and place upon a reservation the rattlesnake and *cayote* as the Apache and the Cheyenne.— Mr. J. J. Ingalls of Kan., U. S. Senate, Apr. 20: *C. R.,* p. 3188/1.

1877 See Appendix.

1886 *Coyotes,* skunks, foxes, squirrels, mice, and gophers are passionately fond of ripe raisin-grapes . . . . *Coyotes* live on grapes from the time they get sweet until the last raisin is taken off the trays and put into boxes.—Statement of Robert Kennicott: see *C. R.,* June 10, p. 5499/1.

1888 We will all lie down in peace and kick our heels in the daisies, or join in chasing a lonely *coyote* for a winter overcoat in his skin.— Mr. W. McAdoo of N. J., H. R., May 8: *Id.,* p. 3853/1.

1897 Persons gifted, like the *coyote,* with leather lungs, innate wickedness, and an infernal desire to injure all that they cannot control.—Mr. G. L. Johnson of Calif., H. R., Jan. 8: *Id.,* p. 592/2.

1911 A western Kansas man, who was in Topeka the other day, tells of running down *coyotes* with motor cars in his section of the State. The dogs rout out a *coyote* and the motor car heads for him. He dodges and gains on the car, but if he stays in smooth country— and the other kind is hard to find in western Kansas—the motor car finally runs him down. The man who told the story said the *coyote* finally came to bay and wanted to fight the motor car, but although the man is an eminent jurist, not much credence has been placed in that statement.—*Hutchinson* (Kan.) *News,* Oct.

Crab the deal. To spoil the whole transaction. Colloq. See quotation.

1901 The conditions of the race laid down definitely that every part of a competing [automobile] must be built in the country by it repre- sented, and the use of foreign tires of course *crabbed the deal.*— *N. Y. Independent,* Dec. 12. (Century Dict.)

Cracker. A poor southern white. So named from the use of whips with a piece of buckskin at the end, a "cracker." [1784-1902.]

1772 Persons who have no settled habitation, and live by hunting and plundering the industrious Settlers. . . . . The People I refer to are really what you and I understand by *Crackers.*—James Habersham to Governor Wright, Aug. 20: "Habersham Letters," p. 204. (1904.)

1865 The Georgia *"cracker,"* as I have seen him since leaving Milledgeville, seems to me to lack not only all that the negro does, but also even the desire for a better condition.—Letter in the *Boston Daily Advertiser,* Nov. 15: *C. G.,* Jan. 1866, p. 552/1.

1873 This being inhabits the Southern States under various names. . . . . In Va. he is known as the "mean white" or "poor white," and among the negroes as "poor white trash." In N. C. he flourishes under the title of "conch." In S. C. he is called "low-downer." In Ga. and Fla. we salute him with the crisp and significant appellation of *cracker.*—J. S. Bradford, *Lippincott's Mag.,* vi, 457.

Crack up. To brag, to boast; to praise extravagantly. [1835-1909.]

1850 The scenery in the vicinity of Cape Horn is all it is *cracked up* to be. —Wilmington (N. C.) *Commercial,* March 7, p. 1/6. (From the *Yankee Blade.*)

Crank. An eccentric person. Don Piatt applied the term to Horace Greeley, alluding to the crank of a hand organ: after which it became popular. [1888-1910.]

1882 I am not ashamed of the distinction, if it be a distinction, of being the target for the folly of every *crank* in this House.—Mr. Robeson of N. J., H. R., Feb. 14: *C. R.,* p. 1138/2.

1884 Temperance *cranks* and temperance fanatics were assailed in the opening of [this] discussion, without even stopping to inquire whether there was any such thing as a whisky *crank* or whisky fanatic.—Mr. J. D. Taylor of O., H. R., March 26: *Id.,* p. 2300/2.

1884 The two things that puzzle me most are the damnable rules of the House, and the "talking *cranks."*—Mr. J. J. Kleiner of Ind., H. R., Apr. 19: *Id.,* p. 126/1, App.

1884 Had any member in 1868 introduced a bill reducing these [railroad] rates, he would have been denounced as a *crank,* and his bill been cited as proof of lunacy.—Mr. J. H. Budd of Calif., H. R., Dec. 10: *Id.,* p. 169/2.

1890 Mr. Rogers:—We have almost reached the point in this great body, that if a man refers to the Constitution he is regarded either as a pedant or a bore— Mr. Oates: Or a *crank.* (Laughter.) —H. R., May 24: *Id.,* p. 5253/2.

1890 The *cranks* of one generation become the philosophers of the next. The *cranks* of this generation will be the philosophers of the generation to succeed us.—Mr. L. C. Houk of Tenn., H. R., May 27: *Id.,* p. 5346/2.

1893 Any man who stands in advance of the present is called a *crank.* They did not then have the name invented, but I fancy Columbus, Luther, Galileo, Garrison, Lowell, Patrick Henry, ... were all denominated *cranks,* or the equivalent term therefor.—Mr. J. C. Sibley of Pa., H. R., Aug. 18: *Id.,* p. 466/2.

1898 The person who adopts "any presentiment, any extravagance as most in nature," is not commonly called a transcendentalist, but is known colloquially as a *crank.*—O. W. Holmes, "Emerson," p. 150. (Century Dict.)

Crank-boxes. See quotation.

1873 Washington adopted the electric fire-alarm many years ago, and the now old-fashioned *crank-boxes* furnished us (then the best in use) are not always reliable. An alarm turned in from them by ignorant, careless, or reckless hands may strike the wrong number and mislead the firemen.—Report of Fire Commissioner, May: see *C. R.,* June 17, 1874, p. 439/1, App.

Crankism. Eccentricity, crankiness.

1882 Such mathematics [in relation to congressional districts] is contaminated with congenital infirmity. No vaccination will save it from confluent smallpox. It is *crankism* applied to figures.—Mr. McClure of O., H. R., Feb. 13: *C. R.,* p. 1106/2.

1890 The epidemic of *crankism* which has prevailed.—*Troy Daily Times,* Nov. 15, p. 2/3. (N. E. D.)

Crappie. A sunfish found in the Mississippi, *Pomoxys annularis.* Also called *campbellite, new light,* and *bachelor.*—(Century Dict.)

Craps. A game of chance played with dice [popular among negroes and low whites]. The players bet as much as they choose, and the caster covers the amount he is willing to risk. If the first throw is 7 or 11, it is a nick or natural, and the caster wins everything. If 2, 3, or 12 is thrown, it is a *crap* and the caster loses everything. Any other number thrown is the caster's point, and he must continue throwing until he brings the same number again and wins, or throws 7 and loses.—(Century Dict.)

Crawfish, crayfish. Any of a family (*Astacidæ*) of numerous fresh water crustaceans closely resembling the lobster but much smaller.— (Webster.) [1805-1826.]

1875 No man is more anxious to escape peril than I am myself, but I cannot turn back in order to avoid it. I am not constructed upon the *crawfish* plan. My way must be on.—Mr. Timothy O. Howe of Wisc., U. S. Senate, Jan. 12: *C. R.,* p. 397/1.

1878 See CREVASSE.

Crazy quilt. A quilt of patchwork. [1886--1908.]

1894 In the Old Dominion constitutional *crazy-quilt* makers would not have U. S. Senators chosen by the legislatures of States, but would have them . . . . elected as quick as lightning by the people.—Mr. J. S. Morrill of Vt., U. S. Senate, Dec. 11: *C. R.,* p. 197/2.

Creditive. Implicitly assenting. Rare.

1846 Simple human reason is not the *creditive* subject.—O. Brownson, "Works," V, 498. (N. E. D.)

1868 This faith . . . . is no mere *creditive* assent or conviction.—H. Bushnell, "Sermons on Living Subjects," p. 58. (N. E. D.)

Creek. A stream of water, smaller than a river. [1737-1869.]

1653 Walton. 1671 "Par. Regained," II, 25. 1674 Penna. Archives. (N. E. D.)

1881 Mr. Robeson:—Cohansey River is in my district. Mr. Townshend of Ill.:—Cohansey *Creek,* not river. Mr. Robeson:—We call it "river" down in N. J. Mr. Townshend:—The committee calls it *"creek."*—H. R., Feb. 15: *C. R.,* p. 1647/1.

1883 [Cheesequake's Creek, N. J.] is a *creek,* not in the sense in which we denominate the small streams and *creeks* of the Northern States; but it is a tidal stream.—Mr. H. F. Page of Calif., H. R., Feb. 28: *Id.,* p. 3442/1.

Creole. See quotations. [1851.]

1841 [The young lady] was a *Creole,* that is to say, born in the country, of parents from Europe.—Mr. Thos. H. Benton of Mo., U. S. Senate, Aug. 25: *C. G.,* p. 379.

1886 *Creole*—Strictly, one born in America of European parents. In La., and elsewhere down South they apply the term to any native productions, so that we hear of *Creole* cattle, *Creole* cabbages, and so forth. In New Orleans the term *Creole* is limited to persons of pure French extraction, so that Mr. Cable's mistake in applying the term to mulattos and quadroons has given great offence there.—R. A. Procter in "Knowledge," ix, 180.

Creolization. The development of characteristics of a Creole race.

1890 The subject race had . . . been physically refined by those extraordinary influences of climate and environment which produce the phenomena of *Creolization.—Harper's Mag.,* p. 416. (Century Dict.)

Crescent City. New Orleans. [1835.]

1844 I am proud of our *crescent city.* I am grateful to a kind Providence that my home is on the banks of that mighty and majestic river, that pours her broad and deep and rapid current onward to the Gulf.—Mr. Dawson of La., H. R., Jan. 2: p. 2 of speech as separately published.

1874 The *Crescent City,* queen of that realm of trade and chivalry.—Mr. J. Y. Brown of Ky., H. R., Feb. 28: *C. R.,* p. 1866/2.

1890 Whatever prominence New Orleans possesses is due to the fact that it is located near the mouth of the Mississippi River; this city, bearing the title of the beautiful "Crescent," taking its name from a conformation of that majestic inland sea whose importance as a national natural artery of commerce gives to the *"Crescent City"* the second position in the list of export cities of this western hemisphere.—Mr. H. D. Coleman of La., H. R., May 27: *Id.,* p. 5349/1.

Crevasse. A breach in a levee. [1819-1888.]

1849 In this year there was a destructive flood of the Mississippi, and several *crevasses* are particularly described in the *New Orleans Com. Bulletin,* May 14.

1867 Floods do not come every year. *Crevasses* in levees do not come every year, destroying vast regions of country.—Mr. Chas. D. Drake of Mo., Dec. 20: *C. G.,* p. 305/1.

1878 A *crevasse* in the levees of the Mississippi River is something of which the imagination, unaided by observation, can scarcely form any accurate conception. At first it may be but a slender thread of water percolating through a crayfish hole, or a slight abrasion in the upper surface caused by the waves set in motion by a passing steamer or by a sudden storm; but in a few hours the seemingly innocent rill is swollen to a resistless torrent, the great wall of earth has given way before the tremendous pressure of the mighty river, and the waters rush through the opening with a force which soon excavates it to a depth of 30 or 40 feet, with a roar which rivals the voice of Niagara, and with a velocity which is great enough to draw an incautious steamer into the boiling vortex.—Mr. J. B. Eustis of La., U. S. Senate, Dec. 12: *C. R.,* p. 120/1.

Crib. See quotation.

1876 The *crib,* as it is called, is a house built out in [Lake Michigan] some two and a half miles from [Chicago], ... and in times of very heavy fog it stands out there so as to be in the way of vessels passing; . . . The *crib* is right opposite the harbor, and it is very necessary that a light or something to give notice to vessels should be on the *crib* in times of very heavy fogs.—Mr. John A. Logan of Ill., U. S. Senate, July 1: *C. R.,* p. 4327/1.

Crib, the public. The U. S. Treasury, or that of a State. The figure is that of hungry animals at the grain shed.

1857 They have no other view . . . than to get one elected who will enable them to eat out of *the public crib,*—who will give them a key to *the public crib.*—T. H. Benton, "Thirty Years' View," I, 49.

Crime of 1873, the. A term used by the Democrats in denouncing the "demonetization" of silver.

1897 Mr. Lacey:—I want to know if all this great growth . . . . occurred since *"the crime of 1873."* Mr. Wheeler:—The depression occurred immediately after *"the crime of 1873,"* and [it] continued until we rebuked *the crime of 1873* by enacting the law of 1879 for the coinage of silver.—H. R., Feb. 24: *C. R.,* p. 45/1, App.

Cripple land. See quotation. See Vol. I, under **Cripple.** [1705-1832.]
1866 In 1690 the London Land Company acquired title to League Island, known in the language of the day as *"cripple land,"* signifying land which is in part covered by the tide, and in part overgrown with sturdy oaks and other trees of the forest.—Mr. W. D. Kelley of Pa., H. R., June 6: *C. G.,* p. 2995/2.

Crittenden Compromise, Crittenden Resolution, The. In the session of 1860-1, Senator John J. Crittenden of Ky. (1787-1863) introduced a measure reëstablishing the Missouri Compromise and a fourfold resolution supporting the Fugitive Slave Law. These propositions were rejected.
1863 [Senator Henry Wilson] says the President [Lincoln] has faithfully carried out the *Crittenden resolution.* If this emancipation policy is a faithful carrying out of the *Crittenden resolution,* I should like to know upon what process of reasoning you arrive at it.—Mr. Lazarus W. Powell of Ky., U. S. Senate, Feb. 21 : *C. G.,* p. 1166/1.
1866 Five years ago, when these Halls rang with angry menaces of incipient treason, five amendments to the Constitution were proposed in what is called the *Crittenden compromise:* an amendment to recognize and establish slavery, and protect it south of 36° 30′; an amendment forbidding the nation to prohibit slavery where it possessed exclusive jurisdiction; an amendment forbidding Congress to abolish slavery in the District of Columbia without the consent of Md. and Va.; an amendment to allow the slave-masters to take their slaves with them, and range all over the loyal States, and hold them manacled and chained in the face of a Christian people; and an amendment to pay for fugitive slaves that had escaped from the U. S. marshals, or were taken from them.—Mr. Henry Wilson of Mass., U. S. Senate, March 8: *Id.,* p. 1254/3.
1870 Both Houses of Congress passed unanimously, with one or two exceptions, the celebrated *Crittenden resolutions* at the very commencement of the war, to the effect that the war was prosecuted on our side to keep these States within the Union.—Mr. Fernando Wood of N. Y., H. R., Jan. 13 : *Id.,* p. 435/1.

Critter, Crittur, Creature. This term was especially applied to a horse; then to other animals; and finally to a contemptible person. See Vol. I. [1782-1862.]
1815 I compounded the matter to work my way by cooking for the crew, and taking care of the dum *critturs.*—David Humphreys, "The Yankey in England," p. 41.
1848 See SHAW.

Croatans, The. A race of people still extant in Eastern North Carolina, who occupied Croatan Island, Carteret County, in the reigns of Elizabeth and James the First. They seem to be a mixed product of the Indians and of those Englishmen who founded the "lost colony" of Roanoke in 1587, with a later infusion of French blood. There is a tradition that some of them, including the Durrs of Lincoln County, are descended from Virginia Dare, the first English child born (1587) in America. The family names of the Croatans are nearly all English or French.

Crook. A sharper. [1886.]
1912 Everything can be condoned in a wicked boss or a business *crook* if he is only for Roosevelt. There is but one unpardonable sin, and that is the sin of being against him.—*N. Y. Evening Post,* June 6, p. 4/6.

Crooked. Dishonestly made or sold.

1876 [He has had] a full knowledge that such persons were continually manufacturing *crooked whisky.*—Mr. G. W. Cate of Wisc., H. R., May 20: *C. R.,* p. 3236/2.

1876 The fact that a company [of soldiers] has been stationed in Ky. to look after their *crooked whisky* . . . . is no reason why, &c.—Mr. Hancock of Tex., H. R., June 16: *Id.,* p. 3846/2.

1876 In the city of Brooklyn, Government troops have had to clear out the *crooked* stills and to fight the people in the streets, who were pelting them with stones and other missiles.—Mr. W. D. Kelley of Pa., H. R., *Id.,* p. 3847/2.

1876 Another house testified that half its entire annual product was *"crooked."*—*N. Am. Rev.,* cxxiii, 301. (N. E. D.)

1891 *Crooked whiskey.* Illicitly distilled whiskey, upon which no excise has been paid. (Farmer.)

Cross cut, sawing a. Sawing across the grain of the wood with a two-handled saw. See Vol. I, **Crosscut saw.**

1861 In the West, where my friends Senator Douglas and Senator Bright are familiar, we sometimes do what we call "sawing a *cross cut.*" It always requires two to perform the operation well.—Mr. Andrew Johnson of Tenn., U. S. Senate, March 2: *C. G.,* p. 1354/2.

Cross-town. That which crosses the town.

1894 I do not believe that on the L street, or, as it is called, this *crosstown* road, it is possible for a cable or electric motor to be sucessfully used.—Mr. Richardson of Tenn., H. R., May 28: *C. R.,* p. 5413/1.

Crotalism. A disease of horses, known chiefly in the valley of the Missouri river, due to eating the rattlebox, *Crotalaria sagittalis.* Also called "bottom disease," because it occurs on bottom-land.

1900 The diseases resulting from plant poisoning known as locoism and *crotalism,* which prevail in some parts of the West and Northwest, are caused respectively by the continued eating of some one of the several locoweeds (*Astragalus* and *Aragallus* species) and of the rattleweed or rattlebox (*Crotalaria sagittalis*) either in the field or in hay.—*Yearbook, U. S. Dept. Agr.,* p. 308. (Century Dict.)

Crout. See **Sour-crout.**

Crowd. Any company of people; the following of a political "boss." [1840-1910.]

1865 [I found] the ice cream good, the punch good, the music good, and the ladies handsome,—upon the whole a very civilized *crowd.*—Mr. Yeaman of Ky., H. R., Feb. 9: *C. G.,* p. 710/1.

1896 [Mr. Parker of N. J.] is more honest than most of his *crowd.*—Mr. John M. Allen of Miss., H. R., June 10: *C. R.,* p. 6403/1.

Crowding, Crowding the mourners. Exerting unwelcome pressure. Bartlett (1877) says of the second, "In political slang, it means adding some further embarrassment to politicians laboring under difficulties."

1865 [To bring the motion up at this time] is, I will not say reprehensible or outrageous, but it is at least *crowding* the good nature of this body.—Mr. Zach. Chandler of Mich., U. S. Senate, Feb. 23: *C. G.,* p. 1007/3.

1868 [Such an argument as] this is *"crowding the mourners."*—Mr. Jacob M. Howard of Mich., U. S. Senate, Feb. 19: *C. G.,* p. 1263/3.

1912 Western Indiana. *Dialect Notes,* III, 574.

Crow-hop. The action of a horse in endeavoring to throw a rider by arching the body, holding the legs stiff, and bucking vigorously.

1903 All bronchos are different individually, but the ways they try to throw their riders may be classed under three heads. The first is known as the *crow-hop.* The rider gets on a wild horse, and immediately the steed bunches itself up like a goat, holds itself stiff in limb and body, and bucks promiscuously. It jars the rider; but the horse that only does this is considered easy and tame.—*Wide World Mag.,* p. 548. (Century Dict.)

Cubby, Cubbyhole. A narrow, contracted space. Somerset and Wiltshire dialect. (N. E. D.)

1853 One little fellow . . scampered back again to his *cubbyhole* on the deck.—Elisha K. Kane, "Grinnell Exped." (1856), p. 226. (N. E. D.)

1868 [Many of the national banks] keep a little *cubby* of an office, loan no money, render no facilities, and yet draw interest on their circulation.—Mr. John Sherman of O., U. S. Senate, June 2: *C. G.,* p. 2762/3.

1878 [Mr. Durham] knows that on the cars that run along the border of [Ky.] there is a little *cubby-house* that the drovers of cattle occupy as they go with their droves to the East, and he thinks those are postal cars.—Mr. O. D. Conger of Mich., H. R., Dec. 17: *C. R.,* p. 262/2.

1882 I called attention to that little *"cubby"* hole which is behind that clock.—Mr. R. M. McLane of Md., H. R., Dec. 12: *Id.,* p. 219/2.

1884 *Cubby holes,* dark cellars, uninspected closets.—*Century Mag.,* xxix, 45/1. (N. E. D.)

Cuckoo. A follower who merely echoes his leader's cry.

1895 The democracy of Grover Cleveland and his *cuckoos* and the democracy of S. C. are as wide apart as the poles.—Mr. W. J. Talbert of S. C., H. R., Jan. 4: *C. R.,* p. 65/1, App.

1895 You *cuckoo Democrats* are against [this measure] because the President has sent down his order for you to be against it.—Mr. J. G. Cannon of Ill., H. R., Dec. 28: *Id.,* p. 388/1.

1894 See MUGWUMP.

1897 See WHOOP IT UP.

1897 A Democratic paper, and I may say the *cuckoo* of the present administration in Mich.—Mr. J. A. Hemenway of Ind., H. R., Jan. 27: *Id.,* p. 17/2, App.

1898 When he was reëlected in 1892, Mr. Cleveland fell into the arms of the Republicans of this body, ... and it was Republicans, aided by a few *cuckoos* and *pie-eaters,* who furnished a majority [for him].—Mr. C. F. Cochran of Mo., H. R., Jan. 25: *Id.,* p. 996/1.

1898 Mr. Grosvenor spoke of Mr. Barrett of Mass. as "suddenly born into the kingdom of the *personal cuckoo party."* He explained the phrase by alluding to the aggressiveness of that "very peculiar bird." See *C. R.,* pp. 4-6, App.

Cuesta. See quotation.

1899 An upland of this kind may be called a *cuesta,* following a name of Spanish origin used in New Mexico for low ridges of steep descent on one side and gentle slope on the other.—W. M. Davis, "Phys. Geog." p. 133. (Century Dict.)

Cundurango. A Peruvian shrub, the bark of which began to be used in medicine in 1871. (N. E. D.)

1871 The *Cundurango* or Condor vine . . . [resembles] much in its habits the grapevine of our own forests.—*N. Y. Pharm. Journal,* Nov. 18. (N. E. D.)

1872 It has remained for the honorable Senator from Mo. [Mr. Schurz]
. . . to discover the real political *cundurango* that is to cure all our
evils.—Mr. James W. Nye of Nev., U. S. Senate, Jan. 30: *C. G.*,
p. 705/1.

Cunner. The cunner or Sea Roach is mentioned in Josselyn's "New
England's Rarities," p. 25. (1672.)

Cupshake. (1905.) See **Ringshake.**

Curbstone operator. A small dealer in stocks. See Vol. I, **Curbstone
broker.**

1868 It is rather a habit with the *curbstone operator,* when he gets
severely winged, to go into the cigar business.—R. B. Kimball,
"Undercurrents," p. 321. (N. Y.)

Curly top. See quotation.

1901 Sugar beets in N. Y., O., and Mich. suffered severely from leaf spot.
In Utah, Colo., Neb., and to a slight extent in the Middle States the
disease known as *"curly top"* was prevalent.—*Yearbook, U. S. Dept.
Agr.,* p. 671. (Century Dict.)

Curmurging. A grumbling or disturbance. The word is a variant of
the Sc. *Curmurring,* used by Burns and Scott. (See N. E. D.)

1898 If you want to have a watch doctored, you take it to a silversmith.
If you want to have your horse shod, you take it to a blacksmith.
If unfortunately there should be a *"curmurging"* within you, you go
to a doctor.—Mr. E. W. Pettus of Ala., U. S. Senate, July 1: *C. R.*,
p. 6574/2.

Currency. That which circulates as money.

1729 Money . . . . by being coined is made a *currency.*—B. Franklin,
"Works" (1840) II, 270. (N. E. D.)

1869 If we do not get any more *currency,* I shall be sorry for it.—
Mr. Timothy O. Howe of Wisc., U. S. Senate, March 31: *C. G.*,
p. 385/2.

1869 [The Committee] do not doubt that some kind of a man might be
hired for $750 in *currency* on the Pacific Coast, who would undertake
to act as farmer for the Indians.—Mr. Jas. Harlan of Ia., U. S.
Senate, March 31: *Id.*, p. 389/3.

Currency Sixes. See quotation.

1895 That subsidy was to be secured by certain bonds which the Govern-
ment would issue, bearing 6 per cent interest, and which are known in
Treasury parlance as the *"currency sixes."*—Mr. H. H. Powers of
Vt., H. R., Jan. 31: *C. R.*, p. 1594/1.

Cush. N. C. The crumbs and scrapings of cracker- or meal-barrels,
fried with grease.—(Century Dict.)

Cushaw, Cashaw. The winter crookneck squash.

1868 The best variety [of squash] for family use is the *Cashaw,* a long,
cylindrical, curved variety, swollen at one extremity, of fine, creamy
yellow color, and solid.—W. N. White, "Gardening for the South,"
p. 214. (Century Dict.)

Cusk. The burbot, *Lota maculosa.*

1624 *Cuske* or small Ling, Sharke, Mackarell.—Capt. Smith, "Virginia,"
vi, 216. (N. E. D.)

1843 I will bring you a *cusk* if there shall be one in our market. (Note—
A species of fish, sometimes spelt Torsk.) —D. Webster to Edward
Curtis, Dec. 16: 'Private Corresp.' (1857) II, 178.

1867 Tough and dried As a lean *cusk* from Labrador.—J. G. Whittier,
"Tent on Beach," xxi. (N. E. D.)

Cuspidor. A spittoon. See Vol. I under **Cuspadore.** [1779-1902.]

1893 [The negro legislature of S. C., in 1871-2, substituted] for forty-cent
spittoons, eight-dollar *cuspidors.*—See *C. R.,* Oct. 5, 1893, p. 2164/2.

1898 The man is . . . . cleaning *cuspidors* . . . and dusting desks.—
Mr. G. H. White of N. C., H. R., Jan. 11: *Id.*, p. 542/1.

Cussedness. Mischief, malignity. [1866-1877.]

1879 What Miss. needs to-day is more corn and cotton and less *cussedness;* more mills, more manliness; less murders, less moonshiners.—
Mr. R. G. Horr of Mich., H. R., Apr. 26: *C. R.,* p. 951/2.

1890 Mr. McMillin:—Did you put in the *"cussedness"* that is in that
letter, or did he? Mr. Kelley:—I want to inform the gentleman from
Tenn. that the *"cussedness"* was not put into this letter, but was in
the facts.—H. R., Apr. 23: *Id.*, p. 3732/2.

1896 Unless we, just out of pure *cussedness,* so to speak, and aggres-
sion, . . . shall go forth to force other people to fight.—Mr. B. R.
Tillman, U. S. Senate, May 1: *Id.*, p. 4658/1.

1897 I want to know if it would be in order to submit a few remarks on
the general perversity and *cussedness* of human nature in general,
and of [Mr. Erdman] in particular.—Mr. A. M. Hardy of Ind., H. R.,
Jan. 8: *Id.*, p. 604/1.

Cut. A reduction in prices, rates, or charges.

1881 Supplemented by a still further *"cut"* of two cents.—*Chicago Times,*
June 17. (N. E. D.)

1888 The gentleman says there has been a small *cut* on sugar and on
rice. Now the *cut* on sugar is infinitely greater than the *cut* on . . . .
iron. [So is] the *cut* on rice.—Mr. B. McMillin of Tenn., H. R.,
May 31: *C. R.,* p. 4786/1.

1888 Where is the *cut* coming first, if the duty is taken off lumber? It
is coming upon labor.—Mr. M. M. Boothman of O., H. R., June 2:
Id., p. 4857/1.

1888 Stocks declined . . because of a radical *cut* in the freight rates between
Chicago and the sea-board.—*The Times,* Nov. 13, p. 5/1. (N. E. D.)

Cut eyes, to. To meet someone's gaze and look quickly away.

1827 Went to New York, took steamboat to New Brunswick, thence Stage
No. 7, strangers crossed words and *cut eyes.*—Lorenzo Dow, "Journal"
(1850) p. 177/2.

Cut in two, to. To halve. This term is used even when the two por-
tions are unequal.

1898 Let us not send [these men] to battle, and at the same time *cut in
two* their petty compensation.—Mr. D. B. Henderson of Ia., H. R.,
Apr. 28: *C. R.,* p. 4364/2.

Cut no ice. To be of no consequence. See Vol. I.

1898 Mr. Shafroth:—Does not the line end at a point five miles west of
the city of Ogden? Mr. Powers:—It does; but that *"cuts no ice."*
—H. R., Feb. 4: *C. R.,* p. 1452/1.

Cut rates. To lower prices.

1884 If one road *cuts the rates,* it will get the freight, unless the other
roads *cut the rates* too; and then when another road *cuts* a little
lower the others must follow, or lose the business.—Mr. Chas.
Stewart of Vt., H. R., Dec. 10: *C. R.,* p. 164/1.

Cut up. To play pranks. [1859.]

1893 If anybody *"cuts up"* before the referee, sitting on a log somewhere,
or at a country schoolhouse, if any man does anything unbecoming
to the dignity of that referee, then &c.—Mr. T. R. Stockdale of
Miss., H. R., Dec. 5: *C. R.,* p. 50/1.

Cute. Clever or shrewd.—(Webster.) Acute, smart. [1779-1856.]

1884 The inventive genius of a Yankee nation, as represented in some
cute applicant at the door of the Patent Office.—Mr. Chas. A. Sumner
of Calif., H. R., March 8: *C. R.,* p. 1734/2.

Cut-nail. Nail-cutting. Not in the dictionaries.

1878 An improvement nearly as important in cheapening the production of silver as was the *cut-nail* machine in making nails.—Mr. Justin S. Morrill of Vt., U. S. Senate, Jan. 28: *C. R.,* p. 612/1.

Cut-off. A short cut, by land or by water. [1818-1881.]

1869 If Dewitt Clinton had never lived, some other man [would have] initiated a *cut-off* from Lake Erie to the Hudson.—Mr. H. E. Paine of Wisc., H. R., Jan. 14: *C. G.,* p. 373/3.

1874 In cases where the river has, for ages perhaps, cut away the bank on one side, making a bend of 20 or 30 miles shaped like an enormous horseshoe, sometimes in a great flood it cuts across and makes a new channel, through which it tears its way and rushes down, a mad torrent, with fearful speed and violent turmoil. Such *"cut-offs,"* as they are called, for a time lower the water above them, as it now has to run only a mile perhaps, or less, where it used to run 25; but they make an awful destruction of the banks on one side or the other, both below and above.—Mr. Barbour Lewis of Tenn., H. R., June 6: *C. R.,* p. 4655/2.

1897 In 1876 there occurred at Vicksburg what is called in river parlance a *"cut-off."* The river at that point made a great bend; . . . . . the peninsula inclosed was about 4 miles long, and the river cut its way—"caved"—through the center of this peninsula.—Mr. T. C. Catchings of Miss., H. R., Feb. 13: *Id.,* p. 1805/1.

Cut-off. An attachment to a magazine firearm, enabling the user of it to fire single shots.

1903 The new [Springfield rifle] is what is known as the clip-loading magazine gun, being provided with a *cut-off* which enables the firer to use it as a single loader.—*Review of Reviews,* p. 570. (Century Dict.)

Cutthroat mortgage. One which practically deprives the mortgagor of his equity.

1894 Mr. Allen:—The trust deeds are used as a mere *cut-throat* affair. . . . There are very few States in the Union to-day that permit a sale under a trust deed by mere notice. . . . . Mr. Hawley:—I suggest that [our Conn. method] is much less liable to cruel abuse than this system, which we in the East have the fashion of calling *cut-throat mortgages.*—U. S. Senate, March 19: *C. R.,* pp. 3082-3.

Czar, Czarism. One who assumes absolute power; the assumption of such power. Mr. Thomas B. Reed of Me. was called a Czar by the Democrats, because of his rulings as Speaker of the House of Representatives. See **Dictator.**

1892 See TIME AND AGAIN.

1896 Bedlam itself was outdone in that notorious madhouse of 1890, when the whole Democratic party were railing against our benign and amiable *"Czar,"* now everywhere accepted as the reformer of old, absurd, and worthless Parliamentary usages.—Mr. J. P. Dolliver of Ia., H. R., Jan. 23: *C. R.,* p. 936/1.

D

Dablet. A little dab; a small amount.

1897 These driblets and *dablets* [of concession] are expected to float $113,000,000 of oppressive taxation.—Mr. B. McMillin of Tenn., H. R., March 24: *C. R.,* p. 231/1.

Dago. A foreigner of the working class and of Latin race, usually an Italian or a Spaniard. [1832-1888.]

1896 Q.:—Is it not a fact that the men that were employed on that sewer were a class of men who moved around wherever they could get a job? A.:—I should say, mostly *dagos.*—Testimony cited Feb. 26: *C. R.,* p. 2180/1.

Daily. A daily newspaper. [1833-1858.]

1874 [The rates] ought not to be higher than one cent for weeklies and *dailies,* and two cents for magazines.—Mr. E. H. Roberts of N. Y., H. R., June 19: *C. R.,* p. 5207/2.

Daisy. A choice specimen. Slang. [1888.]

1894 In regard to robber protection, the Democratic tariff reformer . . . . is "a *daisy,*" whether in embryo, in the egg, or as the finished article.— Mr. W. W. Bowers of Calif., H. R., June 5: *C. R.,* p. 5780/1.

Dander. Anger, passion, temper. [1801-1860.] Some have derived the word from *tander=tinder*: which I doubt. See *N. & Q.,* 11 S. vi, 468; vii, 15, 52, 153.

Danger line. A line to pass which is dangerous. (Not in N. E. D.)

1890 I believe the good sense of our law-makers will still hold us inside the *"danger line* of peril."—Mr. E. H. Conger of Ia., H. R., June 5: *C. R.,* p. 5654/2.

1902 A line, real or imaginary, marking the boundary between apparent safety and danger, as the fire-lines of a conflagration, or the line or level on a riverbank above which the rising waters of a river in flood may overflow, or burst the banks.—*Monthly Weather Review,* Jan., p. 3. (Century Dict.)

Dangerous. Dangerously ill.

a.1616 Beaumont and Fletcher. (N. E. D.)

1884 He's *dangerous;* they don't think he'll live.—"Breadwinners," p. 244. (N. E. D.)

Danite. A member of a secret military organization of the Mormons. [1857-1870.]

1900 Mr. Eldredge was not a polygamist, but Mr. Eldredge was a *Danite.* Mr. Eldredge was a Blood Atoner.—Mr. C. B. Landis of Ind., H. R., Jan. 24: *C. R.,* p. 1131/1.

Dark and bloody ground. Kentucky. [1833-1838.]

1899 A genuine son of the *"Dark and Bloody Ground"* is in his normal condition only when fighting.—Mr. Champ Clark of Mo., H. R., Feb. 4: *Id.,* p. 1468/1.

Dark horse. A candidate who unexpectedly comes to the front. Phrase taken from the racing vocabulary, as used in England by Disraeli in 1831. (N. E. D.) Therefore not of American origin but especially used in America.

1880 My friend from S. C. whispers to me that my friend from Tex. may be the *"dark horse."* There are a great many *dark horses* that I see all around here.—Mr. W. W. Eaton of Conn., U. S. Senate, June 3: *C. R.,* p. 4109/2.

1884 A simultaneous turning toward a *"dark horse."—Harper's Mag.,* p. 472/1. (N. E. D.)

1884 Mr. Eaton of Conn.:—N. Y. elects her electoral ticket for John Smith or James G. Blaine or anybody—I will say John Smith. Mr. Browne of Ind.:—Yes, he is the *dark horse.*—H. R., June 12: *C. R.,* p. 5078/2.

1888 That a *dark horse* is likely to come out of such a complicated situation is most probable.—*Boston Journal,* June 19, p. 5/4. (N. E. D.)

1912 See CONVENTION CITY.

Darky, Darkey. A negro. [1775-1864.]

1864 Did these abolitionists affect the institution of slavery? They affected it just as much as a large humble-bee could affect the skull of a *darkey* through its curly tonsorial luxuriance.—Mr. A. Myers of Pa., H. R., Apr. 12: *C. G.*, p. 1588/2.

1867 Congress backs the Freedmen's Bureau, the bureau backs the *darkey*, and the negro gives the white man the devil; and this is your perfect Republic!—Mr. A. H. Ward of Ky., H. R., Jan. 19: *Id.*, p. 62/2, App.

1876 We are not familiar with the names of all the leading *darkies* of Buena Vista.—*Chicasaw Messenger,* January: see *C. R.,* Aug. 4, p. 5182/2.

1890 Many years ago there was an old *darky* who used to fish on a rock in the Miss. River. He would get out upon his rock and take his seat and light his pipe and fish for catfish. One day he swung an unusually big cat, and in the struggle the cat pulled him off the rock and he was drowned; and the poet of the local newspaper had the following couplet:

> The neighbors never could make out,
> By the aid of all their figuring,
> Whether the nigger went a-fishing,
> Or the catfish went a-niggering.

—Mr. Z. B. Vance of N. C., U. S. Senate, Aug. 30: *C. R.*, p. 9404/1.

1898 Still gentlemen come here and speak about the "negro" and the "*darky*," and talk of him in dialect and old plantation language.— Mr. G. H. White of N. C. (a mulatto), H. R., Apr. 22: *Id.*, p. 4194/2.

Deadbeat. A worthless fellow who tries to exist on other people's resources. [1877-1882.]

1878 Thomas O'M. was, as I claim, a sort of make-up, *dead-beat*, tramp, and fraud.—Mr. John T. Wait of Conn., H. R., Feb. 6: *C. R.*, p. 809/1.

1878 [Mr. Foster] is exceedingly nervous about a few "*dead-beats*" from the State of O. . . . . Let him look at the army of "*dead-beats*" that he may have had put into the Departments.—Mr. John A. McMahon of O., H. R., March 7: *Id.*, p. 1566/1.

1878 Mr. P. agreed, before he was elected to the office of doorkeeper, that he would divide among the bummers and "*dead-beats*" he had, working up his cause, the offices in his department.—Mr. John H. Baker of Ind., H. R., Apr. 4: *Id.*, p. 2281/2.

1878 [Mr. Foster] characterized the portion of [these men] belonging to his own State as "Ohio *dead beats.*" It was a throng evidently like that described by a late English novelist, who says of one of his characters that "to meet him was to know him, to know him was to drink with him, and to drink with him was unfortunately to pay for him."—Mr. Eugene Hale of Me., H. R., *Id.*, p. 2282/1.

1879 See FLYER.

1880 See RUN.

1894 [My constituents] don't believe, sir, in *deadbeat* industries any more than they do in *dead beat* men.—Mr. J. D. Warner of N. Y., H. R., Jan. 10: *C. R.*, p. 657/2.

1882 [Are we] going to put a premium on judicial trampery and *deadbeatism?*—Mr. Benton McMillin of Tenn., H. R., Jan. 25: *C. R.*, p. 615/1.

Deadening. A field in which the majority of the trees are girdled with deep cuts. [1800-1850.]

1864   A poor white man, who could be trusted, had a small *"dead'nin'"* about a mile away.—Edmund Kirke, "Down in Tennessee," p. 100. (N. Y.) See also p. 91.

Deadfall. A trap for large animals. [1611-1909.]

1879   If we do [this] we shall set a *deadfall* to catch and ruin honest importing merchants.—Mr. W. M. Robbins of N. C., H. R., Feb. 26: *C. R.,* p. 1963/1.

1893   The amount expended upon the building is prodigious, but nevertheless it stands to-day a veritable *deadfall,* the hour of whose crumbling into ruin can not be foreseen.—Letter of Members of Cong. from Ill., Sept. 16: *Id.,* Aug. 8, 1894, p. 8326/1.

Deadhead. One who does not pay. To deadhead is to secure transportation and the like without paying. [1849-1903.]

1869   I do not feel that I shall prove a *dead-head* in the enterprise if I once embark in it.—Letter of James G. Blaine to Warren Fisher, June 29. [This was one of the "Mulligan letters" used against Mr. Blaine in the Presidential campaign of 1884.]

1874   It is proposed to crown the weekly newspapers as *"dead-heads,"* and in that way to separate them [in respect of transmission by mail] from the great metropolitan journals.—Mr. E. H. Roberts of N. Y., H. R., Feb. 24: *C. R.,* p. 1755/2.

1876   [The Lieut.-Gen'l's staff] must go with him. They are obliged to live at hotels, and . . . . to pay their bills. They cannot *dead-head* it.—Mr. G. F. Edmunds of Vt., U. S. Senate, June 26: *C. R.,* p. 4151/2.

1892   The free-delivery service is burdened by the collection and delivery of thousands of tons of *dead-head* matter under the "penalty postage system."—Mr. John L. Wilson of Wash., U. S. Senate, May 31: *Id.,* p. 385/1, App.

1894   Who pays the taxes for the support of the army, the police, and militia? Clearly the laborer; and the wealth of the country, like a *"deadhead,"* refuses to pay a single cent.—Mr. Edward Lane of Ill., U. S. Senate, Jan. 31: *Id.,* p. 1754/2.

Dead line. A line in a military prison, not to be passed under risk of death. The term is used to mean in general, also, "the extreme limit of safety." In newspaper language, it means the time after which no more copy may be handed in.

1864   A railing around the inside of the stockade, and about 20 feet from it, constitutes the *"dead line,"* beyond which the prisoners are not allowed to pass.—Report of the Assistant Adjutant of Andersonville, Jan. 5: see *C. R.,* Jan. 12, 1876, p. 384/1.

1867   They were not only starved, but we recollect the *"dead line,"* to which they were induced to crawl with the offer of food, and if they passed the line they were shot dead for thus transgressing the rules.— Mr. Rufus P. Spalding of O., H. R., March 21: *C. G.,* p. 257/2.

1868   Seventeen feet from the inner stockade was the *"dead line,"* over which no man could pass and live.—Lossing, "History of the Civil War," iii, 600. (N. E. D.)

1888   [The law governing the national banks, as it concerns their reserve funds] establishes a *"dead line"* which is so dreaded when approached, that it becomes almost a panic line.—Henry Clews, "Twenty-Eight Years in Wall St.," p. 161. (N. Y.)

Dead rabbits. A gang of ruffians who infested New York about 1855-60. [1858-1859.]

1868   [The Democratic party] met lately in national convention in the city of New York. It had in that great city for auditors the *"dead rabbits,"* and the asylum-burners they had affiliated with in 1863.— Mr. Austin Blair of Mich., H. R., July 13: *C. G.,* p. 415/3, App.

1880 [We should] protect the ballot-box from violence, from bull-dozing, from the "short boys" and *"dead rabbits"* of this country.—Mr. Hiram Price of Ia., H. R., Apr. 12: *C. R.,* p. 2327/1.

Dead-rent. A payment made in order to keep an industry closed, thus destroying competition.

1883 I asked my companion what was the history of those dismantled huts and those ruined manufactories. I was told that they were the salt-works of the Kanawha Valley that were under what was called *dead-rent.* *Dead-rent* to whom? Never was there a fitter phrase than *dead-rent.* I was then informed . . . . . . that those salt-works had been stopped by the action of the New York companies, ... and were paid so much income not to make salt.—Mr. Thos. F. Bayard of Del., U. S. Senate, Feb. 9: *C. R.,* p 2352/2.

Deadwood, to have the, on someone. To have him in one's power, because of possessing special knowledge. [A similar expression is "to have the goods on" someone.] To have an advantage over him or be superior to him. See second quotation. [1857-1872.]

1888 Most of the members of the Legislature thought they had got the *"deadwood"* on the Commodore.—Henry Clews, "Twenty-Eight Years in Wall St.," p. 349. (N. Y.).

1909 So we've put our bid in heavy for free seeds from Uncle Sam,
   And we're goin' to have a college an' an irrigatin' dam;
   We'll show 'em that for farmin' that is scienced and way up
   Cactus Center's got the *deadwood* on that measly Spotted Pup.
   —Arthur Chapman in *Denver Republican,* Feb. 2.

Deal. A transaction, a bargain. Also an underhand bargain. See **Crab the deal.**

1881 [The party boss's] power of making *"deals"*—*N. Y. Nation,* p. 487. (N. E. D.)

1882 The shifts and expedients and *"deals"* which had illustrated his rise to political prominence.—*N. Y. Nation,* p. 411/1. (N. E. D.)

1888 Bryce, "Am. Commonwealth," II, 461. (N. E. D.)

1890 I never knew the time when the Senate did not get in a little railroad *"deal"* somewhere in a conference report. That is what they are there for.—Mr. John A. Anderson of Kan., H. R., June 11: *C. R.,* p. 5959/1.

1891 It is not known who are Deacon White's heirs in this corn *deal.*— —*Boston Journal,* Nov. 27, p. 6/4. (N. E. D.)

1892 An alleged *deal* between the Republicans and the Democrats.—*Id.,* Nov. 5, p. 12/7. (N. E. D.)

Dear kens, dear knows. A euphemism for "The dear Lord knows." "The dear kens" and "Guid kens" are still used in the south of Scotland. [1814-1876.]

1839 See GUID KENS.

Death-a-cold. Deadly cold. Colloq. and nearly obs. (N. Eng.)

1851 Her feet and hands . . had never seemed so *death-a-cold* as now.— N. Hawthorne, "House of the Seven Gables," p. 287. (Century Dict.)

Death on. Exceedingly fond or addicted to. Also fatal to. [1842-1850.]

1863 [The Carolina swine] have their uses; they make excellent bacon, and are *"death on snakes."*—Edmunk Kirke, "Life in Dixie's Land," p. 191. (Lond.)

Decedent. A deceased person. See Vol. I.
   No debts of a *decedent,* except they are secured by a mortgage, &c.— Act of Assembly of Pennsylvania.
   A personal representative may sue and be sued upon . . . . any contract of or with his *decedent.*—Act of Assembly of Virginia.

1890 While the *decedent* was upon the usually traveled road, on legitimate business, duly sober, in broad daylight, he accidentally fell into a pool of water.—Report of Committee on Invalid Pensions: *C. R.*, June 13, p. 6070/1.

Deck of cards. A pack of cards. [1853-1858.]

1609 Ile deale the Cards and cut ye from the *decke,* you understand me, go. —Robert Armin, "Two Maids," D.

1872 I for one will sit here for the next month, ... before [the Liberal Republicans] shall thus go off with their stacked *deck,* if I may say so without cutting in and breaking their lead.—Mr. J. W. Flanagan of Tex., U. S. Senate, June 1: *C. G.*, p. 4147/2.

1873 Just as a gambler would [produce] an old greasy *deck* of cards, and be ready to turn a jack with it at any time.—U. S. Senate, Feb. 27: *Id.*, p. 1887/1.

Deck-pot. A large iron pot or kettle used on whalers to receive scraps from the try-pots.

1904 The oil flows freely between their fingers into the pots, while the refuse, called *"twitter,"* is thrown into another receptacle, called the *deck-pot,* or perhaps into scrap-tubs.—*Sci. Amer. Suppl.*, p. 23, 551. (Century Dict.)

Deed. To convey by deed. [1816-1861.]

1870 I saw in the State of Calif. . . . as pretty land as ever I saw, and dry and nice, that had been *deeded* under the swamp and overflowed land law.—Mr. W. M. Stewart of Nev., U. S. Senate, Feb. 19: *C. G.*, p. 1424/1.

Deedy. A chicken. Southern.

1888 They disputed about the best methods of tending the newly hatched *deedies.*—C. E. Craddock, *Harper's Mag.*, lxxvi, 67. (Century Dict.)

Deliver the goods. See **Goods.**

Demagogue, v. To play the demagogue. [1656-1854.]

1867 What I said was this: that there was a great temptation presented to members of the Republican party now to *demagogue.*—Mr. Henry Wilson of Mass., U. S. Senate, March 16: *C. G.*, p. 146/1.

1876 I have not been one of those representatives of the people who have always been talking about high salaries, and trying to cut down a few dollars for the purpose of *demagoging* before the country.—Mr. John A. Logan of Ill., U. S. Senate, July 1: *C. R.*, p. 4338/1.

1892 You want to destroy the [hemp] industry because of a little *demagoguing* in the next election.—Mr. S. E. Payne of N. Y., H. R., March 17: *Id.*, p. 2164/1.

1897 Here is a plain, common-sense question, not to be *demagogued* in any way.—Mr. J. R. Hawley of Conn., U. S. Senate, Feb. 20: *Id.*, p. 2041/2.

Democrat. See quotation.

1890 The vehicle was, in the language of the country, a *"democrat,"* a high four-wheeled cart, painted and varnished, with double seats, one behind the other.—S. J. Duncan, "Social Departure," p. 26. (N. E. D.)

Dengue. The breakbone fever. [1828-1847.] See Vol. I, under **Dengue** and **Break-bone fever.** [1862-1888.]

1828 The Dengue. This . . . epidemic exists at this time in our city.— Charleston *Courier,* July 15.

1828 The *Dengue* seems to have become prevalent throughout the southern country.—Mobile *Commercial Register,* Aug. 9.

1830 The other vessels are quite healthy, with a few exceptions of *Dengue.* —*Am. Beacon* (Norfolk, Va.), Sept. 30, p. 2/1.

1830 A rheumatic fever, pronounced by the physicians to be the celebrated *Dengue* of 1818, made its appearance [in Baton Rouge].—*Id.*, Nov. 9, p. 2/2.

1869 "Dandy fever" or break-bone (*Dengue*) has prevailed several times. —E. A. Parkes, "Pract. Hygiene," p. 573. (N. E. D.)

1898 He had *dengue* or breakbone fever, and it left him with rheumatism.— Mr. G. G. Vest of Mo., U. S. Senate, Dec. 14: *C. R.*, p. 170/1.

Department store. A store keeping a great variety of goods arranged in departments.—(Webster.)

1896 [Senator Nelson of Minn.] seems to think that a *department store* is the great curse of the country, and the devilfish which ought to be killed.—Mr. E. O. Wolcott of Colo., U. S. Senate, Apr. 7: *C. R.*, p. 3661/2.

Depot. A railway station. [1836-1866.]

1861 A man, standing on the platform at the *depot*, announced, "I am just from the seat of war."—Mrs. Chestnut, "A Diary from Dixie," p. 104. (1905.)

1877 See SHADOW.

1885 Flour is being shipped from Chicago to New York for a less sum than it costs a man who buys it in the market at New York to carry it from the *depot* to his residence in that city.—Mr. S. M. Cullom of Ill., U. S. Senate, Jan. 14: *C. R.*, p. 687/2.

1895 See GRIP.

Desk. A pulpit: occasionally "the sacred desk." [1770-1863.]

1866 I have seen in *the sacred desk* what were called eloquent clergymen, full Africans.—Mr. McDougall of Calif., U. S. Senate, Jan. 24: *C. G.*, p. 401/3.

Desk-room. Hired space for a single person in a business office. [1870-1910.]

1868 I occupied an office—no, I had "*desk-room*" in a basement office.— R. B. Kimball, "Undercurrents," p. 9. (N. Y.)

Detector. A published list of current bank notes, intended to serve as a guide to their value, and much used when the State banks issued notes; i.e. before 1864.

1893 Then we had the Mich. wild-cat money; then we had throughout Ind., Ill., and O., what is known as blue-dog and yellow-pup, where every man had to carry a *detector* with him.—Mr. John L. Wilson of Wash., H. R., Aug. 25: *C. R.*, p. 936/2.

1894 Among the archives of the Philadelphia Library I have been enabled to obtain one of the old bank-note *detectors* which have been so often referred to.—Mr. Robert Adams of Pa., H. R., June 5: *Id.*, p. 5790/2.

Devil. To bedevil; to plague; to ruin. [1652-1823.]

1896 [When Mr. Quigg was speaking], all the members of what [is called] the "hog combine" were on their feet, *deviling* him and asking him questions. The combine was there in full feather.—Mr. A. J. Cummings of N. Y., H. R., Dec. 21: *C. R.*, p. 384/2.

Devil round the stump, to whip the. To get round a difficulty by an artful excuse or evasion.

1857 There, you are now *whipping the devil around the stump*.—*N. Y. Evening Post*, n.d. (Bartlett.)

1863 I "*whipped the devil round the stump*" by hiring a white distiller, and calling him "overseer."—Edmund Kirke, "My Southern Friends," p. 128. (N. Y.)

1866 The mode in which this is got up is only what is commonly called *whipping the devil around the stump*. It is a mere evasion—Mr. W. P. Fessenden of Me., U. S. Senate, July 3: *C. G.*, p. 3551/2.

1869 [The use of revenue-cutters] was a sort of *beating the devil round the stump.*—Mr. F. A. Pike of Me., H. R., March 1: *Id.,* p. 1748/1.

1871 This gentleman, who is familiar with all the ropes [in the P. O. Department] can show him how to *"whip the devil round the stump."* —Mr. G. F. Edmunds of Vt., U. S. Senate, Feb. 16: *Id.,* p. 1311/2.

1874 This is *whipping the devil around the stump,* but it is *whipping him constitutionally around the stump.*—Mr. Matt. H. Carpenter of Wisc., U. S. Senate, Jan. 6: *C. R.,* p. 401/1.

1876 Let us not *"whip the devil round the stump"* any longer, in this era of reform.—Mr. J. G. Cannon of Ill., H. R., March 29: *Id.,* p. 2052/1.

1878 Let me state how these marshals and clerks *"whip the devil round the stump"* [in the matter of fees].—Mr. John Hanna of Ind., H. R., March 19: *Id.,* p. 1879/1.

1891 In some instances there has been what the boys used to call *"whipping the devil around the stump,"* and copyright given when the residence has been very slight indeed.—Mr. O. H. Platt of Conn., U. S. Senate, Feb. 13: *Id.,* p. 2606/1.

Devil's corkscrew. A name locally applied to a great spiral fossil, found in Neb., Wyo., and S. D., and known scientifically as the *Daimonelix.* It was first definitely described by Mr. E. H. Barbour, State geologist of Neb., in 1891. (Century Dict.)

Deviltry. Mischief. [1788-1888.]

1870 Let the troops go [into Ga.], declare martial law, and operate upon those who sustain those midnight *deviltries.*—Mr. C. D. Drake of Mo., U. S. Senate, March 18: *C. G.,* p. 2066/3.

1872 Fisk and McComb [were] not co-partners in business, but co-partners in general *deviltry.*—Mr. James Brooks of N. Y., H. R., Dec. 17: *Id.,* p. 257/3.

1873 The man who seems to have been the presiding genius of this *deviltry.* —Mr. Roscoe Conkling of N. Y., U. S. Senate, Feb. 27: *Id.,* p. 1882/2.

1879 All the *deviltry* which made the elections in the city of New York for years a wretched, guilty farce.—U. S. Senate, May 16: *C. R.,* p. 1388/2.

Diamond hitch. An arrangement of ropes in packing goods on the back of a mule.

1887 The Missourian was an expert packer, versed in the mysteries of the *diamond hitch,* the only arrangement of the ropes that will insure a load staying in its place.—T. Roosevelt, *Century Mag.,* xxxvi, 202.

Diamond State, the. Delaware.

1869 Pass this bill [for the reconstruction of Ga.], and you strike down the sovereignty of the States, ... and my own little *"Diamond State"* is crushed.—Mr. Benjamin T. Biggs of Del., H. R., Dec. 20: *C. G.,* p. 262/2.

Dick Smith. See **Play Dick Smith.**

Dicker. A bargain. To dicker is to chaffer. [1802-1910.]

1863 If the Government would honestly execute this confiscation bill, you would not need this trading sort of *dicker* [in cotton principally]. You could take the property of rebels, and protect loyal citizens; and there is the difficulty. [The] Government wants to trade and barter and *dicker* and compromise.—Mr. Daniel Clark of N. H., U. S. Senate, Feb. 27: *C. G.,* p. 1339/3.

1869 If we can pass the bill to put an end to secret gold sales and other *dickers* by which the market is manipulated, ... we may hail that as a newness of life leading toward a sound and safe condition.— Mr. Roscoe Conkling of N. Y., U. S. Senate, Feb. 11: *Id.,* p. 1075/1.

1871 You are not content with our buying icebergs, seals, Indians, and misery at one end of the world, but you are *dickering* for earthquakes, hurricanes, negroes, and bananas at the other.—Mr. S. S. Cox of N. Y., H. R., Feb. 15 : *Id.,* p. 129/3, App.

1873 [The Federal Govt.] had no right to drive bargains and *dickers* with States for the purpose of requiring them to pay a part of [this road.]—Mr. O. P. Morton of Ind., U. S. Senate, Feb. 19 : *Id.,* p. 1487/2.

1888 When [the Democratic party] wants to dodge, and *dicker,* and crawl, and creep into power, ... I do not care anything more about it.—Mr. J. B. Morgan of Miss., U. S. Senate, Aug. 20 : *C. R.,* p. 7721/1.

1890 This argument . . . might have applied to the conditions of trade as they existed when the Iroquois bartered the bearskin for the Algonquin's basket, when all trade was *dicker* and "swap."—Mr. R. M. LaFollette of Wisc., H. R., May 10 : *Id.,* p. 4481/2.

1892 Mr. Speaker, truck, traffic, and *dicker* greatly distinguish man from other animals. Here is the point where civilization begins and savagery wanes.—Mr. A. J. Cummings of N. Y., H. R., June 6 : *Id.,* p. 442/1, App.

1894 Pennsylvania's representatives occupied a different position from the gentlemen representing the "Collar and Cuff" district of New York, and were not willing to *dicker* and trade their votes for any local concession.—Mr. C. W. Stone of Pa., H. R., Jan. 20 : *Id.,* p. 1151/1.

1897 We can not afford to higgle, *dicker,* and deal, as hucksters would, respecting the disposition of public lands.—Mr. W. V. Allen of Neb., U. S. Senate, Jan. 12 : *Id.,* p. 716/1.

Dictator, The. A term applied to Mr. Thomas B. Reed of Me., on account of his vigorous management while he was Speaker of the House, especially in 1890. See **Czar.**

1894 The distinguished gentleman who was . . . . known throughout the country as the *"dictator"* and the "czar" of legislation.—Mr. B. A. Enloe of Tenn., H. R., January 13 : *C. R.,* p. 7441/2.

Die, v. To form by means of a die.

1885 Every machine-made shoe also has an "inner-sole" *died* out or moulded to correspond in shape with the "outer sole."—*Harper's Mag.,* lxx, 282. (Century Dict.)

Diff. A blow. Southern. Cf. the word *biff,* slang term for a blow.

1889 He got a big scyar [scar] on de side er his neck now whar somebody hit 'im a *diff.*—Joel C. Harris, "Balaam and his Master."

Digger. A Digger Indian. [1837-1855.]

1876 The lizard-fed *Diggers* that follow in the train or hang about the stations of our railroad civilization.—Mr. S. S. Cox, H. R., June 3 : *C. R.,* p. 3569/2.

Dime novel. A romance of the lurid kind. [1879-1890.]

1865 A little primer-looking sort of a child's book. . . . It was a *dime novel,* "The Black Ship."—Alex. H. Stephens, "Diary," Aug., p. 424 (1910).

Diner. A dining car.

1913 See **Big Four.**

Dingley tariff, the. The tariff which became law in 1897, being highly protective. Its framer was Mr. Nelson Dingley, Jr., of Lewiston, Me.

Dip. The better sort of turpentine. See **Scrape.**

1863 [The Abolitionists have] long, lean, tommerhawk faces, as white as vargin *dip.*—Edmund Kirke, "Life in Dixie's Land," p. 226. (Lond.)

Dipping. Chewing snuff. [1853-1857.]
1868 The mean whites [said Mr. Gilmore recently] are far below the slaves in morals and civilization; are indolent, shiftless, thieving, lying; given to whisky-drinking, snuff-*dipping*, clay-eating, incest, and all manner of social vices.—Mr. W. D. Kelley of Pa., H. R., Jan. 31: *C. G.,* pp. 551-2.

Disgruntled. Offended, discontented, dissatisfied. [1682-1909.]
1848 The Locofoco leaders are hugely *disgruntled.*—Wilmington (N. C.) *Commercial,* Oct. 26, p. 1/6.
1877 This continual grasping after authority for the purpose of meeting the individual case of some *disgruntled* persons should receive the stamp of this committee's disapprobation.—*Providence* (R. I.) *Journal,* March 1. (Century Dict.)
1886 Those that were *disgruntled,* because Dutch and German were dropped [in the names of certain denominations] staid where they were.—*The Churchman* (N. Y.), Oct. 30, Suppl. (Century Dict.)
1891 These men [were] *disgruntled* that they should turn from the sweet sound of harmony to the discords of an ax upon a frozen log.—Mr. W. McAdoo of N. J., H. R., Jan. 28: *C. R.,* p. 1938/1.
1911 A presidential election always makes a strong appeal to party loyalty. In "off" years *disgruntled* citizens may take their fling in large numbers, but the tradition of party regularity and obligation is much more compelling when it is a question of electing a President.—*N. Y. Evening Post,* Oct. 5.

Dished face. One that is concave in profile.
1901-2 There was a time when swine-breeders had a delusion for *"dished faces"* and heavy jowls.—*Rep. Kan. State Bd. Agr.,* p. 52. (Century Dict.)

Dish-faced. See quotation.
1912 Applied especially (in Western Indiana) to a face that lacks individuality.—*Dialect Notes,* III, 574.

Disloyalist. A disloyal person.
1870 The county of Monroe [in Missouri] was the place where *disloyalists* fleeing from other counties took shelter all the time.—Mr. John F. Benjamin of Mo., H. R., July 7: *C. G.,* p. 5310/3.
1885 Pall Mall Gazette. (N. E. D.)
1886 As dangerous in his character of a *disloyalist* as [in] that of a polygamist.—Joseph Cook in *The Advance,* Boston, Feb. 18, p. 99. (N. E. D.)

Disrupt. To break asunder. [1860-1861.]
1860 Senators on the other side suppose that when "this glorious Union" is *disrupted,* it will be in blood, and that our negroes will rise in insurrection.—Mr. Wigfall of Tex., U. S. Senate, Dec. 12: *C. G.,* p. 73/2.
1861 The Democratic party permitted itself to be *disrupted* by the nullifiers and seceders at Charleston and Baltimore.—Mr. John A. Gilmore of N. C., H. R., Jan. 26: *Id.,* p. 580/2.
1892 It was the action of Germany alone that *disrupted* the former ratio between [gold and silver].—Mr. Lind of Minn., H. R., March 24: *C. R.,* p. 2521/1.

Ditch-rider. A man who inspects an irrigation canal, with a view to the prevention of waste.—F. H. Newell, "Irrigation in the U. S.," p. 107. (Century Dict.)

Ditty-box. See quotations.
1883 A *"ditty-box"* is an American fisherman's receptacle for all sorts of odds and ends, together with implements of every-day use.—*Pall Mall Gazette,* June 2, Suppl. (N. E. D.)

1886   In the small stores account we find that Paymaster Smith . . . purchased over five thousand *ditty-boxes*. It was supposed that the sailors would want them to hold their needles and tobacco and pipes and such things.—Mr. H. A. Herbert of Ala., H. R., June 17: *C. R.*, p. 5836/1.

Dive.   A low resort, devoted to drinking, gambling, etc. [1882-1909.]

1890   Adventurers and political outcasts, who, from their nests and *dives* in our large cities, breed and swarm out as anarchists.—Mr. L. E. Payson of Ill., H. R., Aug. 20: *C. R.*, p. 8879/1.

Divide.   A watershed. [1807-1899.]

1868   This doctrine of political equality forms the great *"divide"* between parties, now as heretofore.—Mr. G. W. Scofield of Pa., H. R., July 14: *C. G.*, p. 4068/1.

1897   McKinley prosperity is a myth. It is always just over the *divide*— in the next county—on the other side of the hill.—Mr. Champ Clark of Mo., H. R., May 6: *C. R.*, p. 937/2.

Divide.   A division of plunder. Cf. Vol. I, and below, the word **Divvy.**

1880   A vast number of public building provisions were grouped together on what is called the log-rolling principle, and I think the wags called it *"the little divide,"* to distinguish it from the river and harbor bill, . . . which goes by the very appropriate title of *"the great divide,"* division in this sense not being what the geographers or the geodetic people . . . mean by that word as a watershed, but a method of apportioning out the public money into where there is not water or anything else,—into private hands.—Mr. G. F. Edmunds of Vt., U. S. Senate, May 27: *C. R.*, p. 3854/1.

1891   I am afraid that these gentlemen who own these ships . . . . will not give a fair *"divide"* with the boys who do the work.—Mr. G. W. Fithian of Ill., H. R., Jan. 8: *C. R.*, p. 1049/1.

Divvy.   A dividing up of profits. [1890-1909.]

1890   But, above all, accept my thanks and the thanks of my farmer friends for free divi-divi [in the tariff bill]. I am afraid there is some mistake about this. . . . My Republican brethren, do you really mean to *"divvy"*?—Mr. C. W. McClammy of N. C., H. R., May 19: *C. R.*, p. 4933/2.

1890   [There is nothing to be had] out of the Treasury of the U. S., upon which these men can get a *"divvy."*—Mr. John T. Morgan of Ala., U. S. Senate, July 7: *Id.*, p. 6992/1.

1893   What I want is a square deal and a fair *"divy"* all around.—Mr. Champ Clark of Mo., H. R., Oct. 18: *Id.*, p. 2667/1.

1894   Here we have "divi divi" on the free list. During the 33 years of Republican ascendency in this country there was always work at fair wages, and something to *"divvy"* between labor and capital, and something in the workingman's pantry for the housewife to *"divvy"* among the children.—Mr. M. N. Johnson of N. D., H. R., Jan. 24: *Id.*, p. 1354/2.

Dixie.   The Southern States. [1863-1901.]

1862   [The Continental currency of 1776] bears small resemblance to the delicate paper issues . . . . of the present day in the U. S. It smacks a little of the poverty of *"Dixie,"*—as is said.—Mr. C. L. Vallandigham of O., H. R., Feb. 3: *C. G.*, p. 44/2, App.

1862   The men over here in the land of *Dixie,* who had raised . . . . the most wicked and gigantic rebellion that history has yet made record of.—Mr. George P. Fisher of Del., H. R., May 2: *Id.*, p. 1934/3.

1863   When the million of armed colonists from Yankeedom have driven the people all out of *Dixie,* and have entered upon the quiet possession of their lands and negroes, may I be there to see.—Mr. T. L. Price of Mo., H. R., Feb. 28: *Id.*, p. 138/3, App.

Do. To suffice, to answer. [1846.]

1880 I should like to have ten minutes, but it will *do me* just as well in the morning.—Mr. R. G. Horr of Mich., H. R., Jan. 22 : *C. R.,* p. 491/1.

Doated. Discolored by incipient or partial decay;—used of timber, especially birch, beech, and oak. (Cf. **Doaty,** Webster.)

a.1860 [England] is, as we Virginians say of a tree, *doted,* and Englishmen are but the fungoid remains of what was once a people.—G. W. Bagby, "Writings," I, 172. (1884.)

Dobber. The cork or float of a fishing line.

1812 He floated on the waves like a merman, or like an angler's *dobber,* until he landed safely on a rock.—W. Irving, "The Knickerbockers," ii, 5. (Century Dict.)

Docket. A list of causes set down for trial. [1790-1846.]

1818 The *docket* is not quite so formidable as was expected.—D. Webster to J. Mason, Feb. 22 : "Private corresp." (1857), I, 2/1.

1862 You will please mark down the leaves covering the *docket,* so far as it is the *docket* of the confederate court. . . . . You say that is the trial *docket* of the confederate court of that district?—Examination of Jacob McGavock before the U. S. Senate, June 26 : *C. G.,* p. 2945/3.

1866 Suitors in the Supreme Court are now compelled to wait two or three years before their cases can be reached upon the *docket.*—Mr. James Guthrie of Ky., U. S. Senate, Apr. 2 : *Id.,* p. 1717/1.

1872 It is not convenient or proper that the Supreme Court of the U. S. should have its *docket* loaded down with controversies involving cases of only $1,000.—Mr. B. F. Butler of Mass., H. R., Jan. 31 : *Id.,* p. 734/1.

1879 It is usual in every court, I suppose, for the names of witnesses summoned to be placed on the subpoena *docket.*—Mr. H. A. Herbert of Ala., H. R., Feb. 19 : *C. R.,* p. 1603/1.

1880 The *dockets* of the Supreme Court and of the circuit courts in the greater number of the circuits are encumbered with the constant accession of cases.—Annual message of President R. B. Hayes, Dec. 6 : *Id.,* p. 8/1.

1895 For years the *dockets* in the Federal Courts in Chicago have been running further and further behind. . . . The maritime *docket* has not been called in more than two years.—Mr. R. A. Childs of Ill., H. R., Feb. 1 : *Id.,* p. 1652/2.

Document, v. To provide with ship's papers.

1828 Webster's Dict.

1879 Printed decision No. 3717, Sept. 5, 1878, in relation to *documenting* canal-boats.—John Sherman, Secretary of the Treasury, May 17 : see *C. R.,* p. 2337/1.

1893 In the valley of the Miss. River alone last year there were used, for transporting the products of the farm, *documented* and *undocumented* vessels with a tonnage of 3,500,000 tons.—Mr. W. P. Frye of Me., U. S. Senate, Feb. 13 : *Id.,* p. 1516/2.

Dodge. To evade. See Vol. I, **Dodge the question.** [1846.]

1861 The Senator will get an answer. I never *dodge* a question—Mr. Lyman Trumbull of Ill., U. S. Senate, Jan. 10 : *C. G.,* p. 315/1.

1861 I am not here to palliate or to *dodge* one of the inevitable dangers that beset us.—Mr. John H. Reagan of Tex., H. R., Jan. 15 : *Id.,* p. 392/1.

1866 I said to the Senator from Delaware, "No *dodging* of my question by putting another case about peace"; but I said nothing about *dodging* to the Senator from Connecticut, and I did not mean the word in any offensive sense to the Senator from Delaware.—Mr. Lyman Trumbull of Ill., U. S. Senate, Feb. 27 : *Id.,* p. 1049/2.

Dodgeful. Full of devices. A "nonce-word."

1889 [He] was just as *"dodgeful"* as one of those partridges down our way—what you call quails in the North.—Mr. Robert Smalls of S. C. before H. R., Feb. 12 : *C. R.,* p. 1810/1.

Doggery. A low drinking place. [1835-1864.]

1849 If we were a man—if we were a voter—we would vote down the *doggeries* [says Mrs. Swisshelm.]—Wilmington (N. C.) *Commercial,* July 10, p. 2/4.

1877 The other day my friend abused one of the returning boards as keeping a *doggery* or grocery. The truth is that he keeps an eating-house. If all the men in the democratic party in the city of New York who keep a *doggery* or an eating-house or anything of that kind were turned out as rascals and thieves and scoundrels, I am afraid that the democratic majority would fade away.—Mr. John Sherman of O., U. S. Senate, Jan. 19: *C. R.,* p. 750/1.

Doggone it or **Dog on it.*** A piece of vulgar profanity, common in mining camps. [1834-1851.] It occurs ten times in D. M. Moir's "Mansie Wauch," 1839.

Dog-leg tobacco. That of a low quality.

1863 The other [half of the store] was densely crowded with logwood, *"dog-leg,"* strychnine, juniper berries, New England rum, and cistern water.—Edmund Kirke, "My Southern Friends," p. 49 (N. Y.).

1868 [They] are wearing holes in their coats, and particularly in their trousers, sitting on store-boxes and horse-blocks about the country-seats (*sic*) and cross-road groceries, watching the neighbors pitch horse-shoes for *dog-leg tobacco,* for want of better employment.— Mr. H. P. H. Bromwell of Ill., H. R., March 18: *C. G.,* p. 287/1, App.

Dog town. A community of prairie dogs. See Vol. II, **Prairie Dog.**

1887 The black-footed ferret [will] work extraordinary havoc in a *dog town,* as it can follow the wretched little beasts down into the burrows. —Theodore Roosevelt, *Century Mag.,* xxxv, 666.

Dog towns. Towns in which plays are tested.—(Frank J. Wiltsach, "Stage Dict.") [The companies "try the play on the dog."]

Dog warriors. See Vol. I, **Dog soldier.**

1880 The young men, the *dog warriors* of all these tribes, as they are termed, as soon as they are fed by the U. S. and armed by traders, stay upon their reservations not one single minute longer than they can mount their horses and join some Indian chief then upon the war path. —Mr. G. G. Vest of Mo., U. S. Senate, Jan. 26: *C. R.,* p. 522/2.

Dogwood winter. See quotation. Southern.

1907 A man from N. C., who was visiting in Philadelphia, in the course of conversation used the expression *dogwood winter.* "What do you mean by *dogwood winter*?" asked his host. "Don't you know what *dogwood winter* is?" demanded the man from Hickory, N. C.—"There is always a spell of it in May, when the dogwood tree is in bloom. For several days there is cold, disagreeable, cloudy weather, and often a touch of frost. Down our way it never fails, and we call it *dogwood winter.* I thought the phrase was general."—*Journal of Am. Folk-Lore,* p. 235. (Century Dict.)

Dollar of our fathers, the. See first quotation.

1878 This bill proposes to coin pieces of silver of a standard nine-tenths fine, weighing 412½ grains, and to call them dollars and units of value in the American currency, and make them unlimited legal tender for all debts. This is called in debate a restoration of the silver dollar, *"the dollar of our fathers."*—Mr. Thos. F. Bayard of Del., U. S. Senate, Feb. 4: *C. R.,* p. 729/2.

---

* [Dr. Moir ("Delta" of the "Blackwood Wits") published his fanciful *Life of Mansie Wauch* in Blackwoods, 1824-7. I have used the N. Y. ed. of 1828, in which I have noted *dog on it* on pp. 34, 46, 127, 136, 151, 180, 200, and 206. For an unconvincing attempt to defend *dog on it* as the original form of the phrase, see *The Nation* (N. Y.) Apr. 21, 1892, p. 303.—Ed.]

1878 The advocates of the remonetization of *"the silver dollar of the fathers,"* as it is fondly called, assign just two reasons in behalf of their claim. .... Is there any foundation for the claim that the additional coinage of that almost mythical token, *"the loved dollar of the fathers,"* would [make things any better]? ..... Catch terms, *"dollar of the daddies,"* violent adjectives, can have no weight in a discussion of this character.—Mr. W. W. Eaton of Conn., U. S. Senate, Feb. 5: *Id.,* p. 753/1.

1878 There was not [in 1873] a man that ran a peanut stand in the U. S., who based his stand on the silver dollar. There were none. Why, sir, *"the dollar of the fathers"* had gone into the melting-pot of the sons, and it was used in works of adornment, of luxury, and of art; and I beg to say right here that we have heard enough about this "glorious *dollar of the fathers."* Let us now have the dollars of the sons, that weigh something like one hundred cents in gold.—The same, p. 756/1-2.

1878 Shall we .... continue to disown and disinherit the silver *dollar of our fathers,* sometimes in latter days facetiously called the *"dollar of our daddies"?*—Mr. David Rea of Mo., H. R., Feb. 21: *C. R.,* p. 57/2, App.

1879 The *"dollar of the fathers"* was an honest dollar, ... and stood even at a premium in the market, ... unlike our "standard silver dollar," which promises more than it gives, it gave more than it promised.—Mr. Deuster of Wisc., H. R., May 15: *Id.,* p. 1368/2.

1889 *Dollar of the Fathers,* a catch cry, turned by opponents into the "dollar of our daddies," which was used during the remonetization agitation of 1877-8.—(Farmer.)

1890 If the silver-producer, when he puts his silver in the mint and has it coined into the *"dollar of his daddies,"* should be compelled to lug back the *dollars of his daddies* into his cart, and take [them] home with him, it would not be so objectionable. But no, [the bill] does not do that. He says he has no use for the *dollar of his daddies* after it is coined. He wants to compel the Government to purchase these dollars that he has been so anxious to have coined.—Mr. Abner Taylor of Ill., H. R., June 25: *C. R.,* 6498/2.

1896 "We want *the dollar of the daddies,"* is your cry. What was *the dollar of the daddies?* It was the dollar of 412½ grains of standard silver ... That was *the dollar of the daddies.* Restore its quality— restore its value as silver bullion, and we stand ready to restore *the dollar of the daddies.*—Mr. W. P. Hepburn of Ia., H. R., Feb. 8: *Id.,* p. 127/1, App.

Doll baby. A doll. [1795-1887.]

1875 Did you ever see [a darky] who believed in black angels? Did you ever hear of one who wanted a black *doll-baby?*—Mr. Thomas White- head of Va., H. R., Feb. 3: *C. R.,* p. 953/1.

Dominie. A parson or settled minister. [1680-1831.]

1834 They desired the *Dominie* to tie them in wedlock's holy bond.—*The Georgian* (Savannah), July 10, p. 2/3.

Donate. To give. [1846-1859.]

1868 [This] is no more and no less than a plan to get a bridge built across the Mississippi River by the U. S., and then to *donate* it to a railroad company.—Mr. G. W. Scofield of Pa., H. R., Feb. 10: *C. G.,* p. 1086/2.

Donation Act. The Act of 1850, providing for the acquisition of titles to U. S. land by actual settlers thereon.

1894 Certain lands disposed of under the act of Congress approved Sept. 27, 1850, and the acts amendatory and supplemental thereto, ... com- monly known as the *"donation act."*—Message from the House to the Senate, July 17: *C. R.,* p. 7572/2.

Donation parties. See quotation.

1911 The minister is [now] better paid; he depends less on *donation parties,* with their heterogeneous collection of undesirable provender, and receives his salary with greater regularity.—*Atlantic Monthly,* June, p. 801/2.

Do-nothing. Indolent, ineffective. The word occurs as a noun in 1579 and 1624. (N. E. D.)

1832 The invalids, old women, and other curious *do-nothing* folk.—W. Irving, "Alhambra," II, 84. (N. E. D.)

1839 Thomas Carlyle. (N. E. D.)

1862 Your *do-nothing* policy gives us no title, no possession, no guarantee. —Mr. Aaron A. Sargent of Calif., H. R., March 31: *C. G.,* p. 1460/3.

1862 *Do-nothing* strategy gave way to an "immediate advance upon the enemy's works."—Mr. Zach. Chandler of Mich., U. S. Senate, July 16: *Id.,* p. 3390/3.

1874 [These things] have come to pass under that identical *do-nothing* policy which [Mr. Boutwell] advocates.—Mr. Carl Schurz of Mo., U. S. Senate, Jan. 14: *C. R.,* p. 642/2.

Doodle-bug. The larva of any cicindelid beetle. Southern. (Century Dict.)

Door-facing. The woodwork at the side of a doorway.

1877 This man . . . . was sitting up in the door with his feet on the *door-facing.*—Testimony from S. C., *C. R.,* Nov. 26: p. 705/1.

Dope. To adulterate.

1898 They will run their flutter mills and mixers, and *dope* the flour to suit themselves.—Letter from Tenn., *C. R.,* p. 223/1, App.

Dope mill. One that grinds up corn meal with flour.

1898 The *dope mill* gets the pure flour price for its product.—Mr. J. W. Gaines of Tenn., H. R., Feb. 22: *C. R.,* p. 220/2, App.

Dornick. An irregular bit of stone. [1840-1878.]

1893 Aunt Kate, she des [just] fell back in 'er cheer lak [like] some un hit 'er wid er *dornick.*—Mary A. Owen, "Old Rabbit, the Voodoo, &c.," p. 13.

Dorrite. A partisan of "Dorr's Rebellion," in Rhode Island, 1840. [1844-1857.]

1875 The *Dorrites* of that day, like the Garlandites of this day, were not without their supporters.—Mr. W. J. Hynes of Ark., H. R., March 2: *C. R.,* p. 2114/1.

1885 See ALGERINE.

Dorr's Rebellion. See Vol. I, quotations under **Dorrite.**

1865 *Dorr's rebellion* arose against the existing government. They had their two legislatures and their two executives, and were ready to enter into a conflict of arms. An appeal was made to the President of the U. S. [John Tyler] to put down the insurrection; and [he] decided that Dorr's party were the party in rebellion; . . . and that ended the controversy.—Mr. James R. Doolittle, U. S. Senate, Feb. 3: *C. G.,* p. 577/2.

Dot, to a. Exactly, minutely.

1866 He understands it *to a dot.*—Mr. John Conness of Calif., U. S. Senate, June 18: *C. G.,* p. 3235/3.

1881 Mr. Burnside:—[The question] is as to whether a majority shall rule or not. Mr. Butler:—No, sir. Mr. Burnside:—That is the question. That is it *to a dot.*—H. R., Apr. 20: *C. R.,* p. 356/1.

Double ender. A gunboat rounded at each end.

1864 I have a petition from contractors for the machinery of the side-wheel gunboats known as *"double enders."*—Mr. John P. Hale of N. H., U. S. Senate, Feb. 24: *C. G.,* p. 786/1. [See also p. 2221, May 11.]

1865 The *double-ender* Sassacus . . . caught one of the shells, which carried away the skylight of the cabin.—*Star,* Feb. 3. (N. E. D.)

1865 The gentleman from Maryland directed his animadversions against another class of vessels, the *double-enders,* or ferry-boats, as he was pleased to term them.—Mr. A. H. Rice of Mass., H. R., Feb. 3: *Id.,* p. 45/1, App.

1865 Suppose it to be true that the *double-enders,* which have been used for the shallow rivers and narrow inlets of the South, are exposed in their machinery on account of their light draught of water, is that anything to be wondered at? Was not the expenditure upon them made for a temporary purpose?—Mr. F. A. Pike of Me., H. R., Feb. 4: *Id..* p. 48/2, App.

Double-team. To make a joint attack. [1860.]

1865 Beauregard and Lee were expected, but Grant had *double-teamed* on Lee.—W. Chestnut, "A Diary from Dixie," p. 346. (1905.)

Doubletree. A bar moving on a pivot, intended to equalize the draft of two horses pulling together; the crosspiece to which the singletrees are attached.

1886 If we be upon the right line, then I will pull with the gentleman from Kansas and the gentleman from Michigan just as hard as I can, to keep up my end of the *doubletree.*—Mr. J. G. Cannon of Ill., H. R., March 10: *C. R.,* p. 2273/2.

Doublings. See quotation. The term was originally used with reference to brewing: N. E. D., with citation 1743.

1867 *Doublings* is only a technical distillers' phrase for whisky. In the language of the [Treasury] department, *doublings* are high wines, and singlings low wines.—Mr. Samuel McKee of Ky., H. R., Jan. 21: *C. G.,* p. 60/1, App.

Doubtful. The term "doubtful" or "close" is specially applied to a state, county, or voting district in which the vote usually approaches a tie.

1887 Mr. Grosvenor:—They may appoint an agent in every *doubtful* county, in every *doubtful* State of the Union. Mr. Goff:—What do you mean by *"doubtful"* counties? Mr. Grosvenor:—Close counties, like some of those in the State of my friend from West Virginia.—H. R., Jan. 20: *C. R.,* p. 50/1, App.

1888 See FLOATER.

Doughbird. The Eskimo curlew, *Numenius borealis.* (Century Dict.)

Doughfaces. Northern men who were for maintaining slavery in the South. See Vol. I. [1820-1861.]

1861 From every press and husting which a Democrat could command, this evil day was prophesied. But we were Cassandras. Unbelieving men derided us as *doughfaces,* and sneered at us as Union-savers.—Mr. S. S. Cox of O., H. R., Jan. 14: *C. G.,* p. 374/2.

1862 Even those slimy *"doughfaces"* and creeping things that still continue to hiss at "abolitionism" betray a tormenting apprehension that their day and generation are rapidly passing away.—Mr. G. W. Julian of Ind., H. R., May 24: *Id.,* p. 186/1, App.

1869 See ADMINISTRATION MEASURE.

1888 In the bitter sectional times of the past, the stinging taunt was often flung at the Northern Democracy, that they were submissive to the South in public affairs, that they were *doughfaces* on the subject of slavery. With infinitely more of truth and justice that taunt can now be returned against the leaders of the Republican party in their servile obedience to every demand of tariff monopoly and protected trusts. They are the *doughfaces* of a financial slavery . . . more heartless and cruel than any other form of human servitude ever known in our midst.—Mr. D. W. Voorhees of Ind., U. S. Senate, Dec. 19: *C. R.,* p. 348/1.

1894 Again the *"doughfaces"* of the North fawn at the feet of those who in the sixties sought to destroy our nation, and now seek to wreck our industries.—Mr. E. J. Hainer of Neb., H. R., Jan. 26: *Id.,* p. 1488/1.

Doughnut. See V.ol. I. [1809-1857.]

1866 [There was] an ancient enactment [of Conn.] that no girl should get married until she could bake a *doughnut* that would preserve its twist for a year.—Mr. Edgar Cowan of Pa., U. S. Senate, Dec. 13: *C. G.,* p. 102/1.

Down East. In New England. [1825-1861.]

1860 I have spoken for myself and a very small State away *down East,* and only for half of her.—Mr. John P. Hale of N. H., U. S. Senate, Dec. 5: *C. G.,* p. 10/2.

1867 When the gentleman from Maine [Mr. Pike] said that the country did not want impeachment, he must have meant the country "away *down East."*—Mr. Thad. Stevens of Pa., H. R., July 11: *Id.,* p. 588/1.

Down town. In the business district. [1870-1888.]

1891 The Second ward of the city of New York . . . is what is called a *down-town* ward, a business ward. I may be mistaken, but I apprehend that there is not a dwelling or a tenement house in it.—Mr. Frank Hiscock of N. Y., U. S. Senate, Jan. 28: *C. R.,* p. 1906/1.

Draw. A drawbridge, or its movable part. [1786-1856.]

1862 I think it utterly impossible to construct on this river [the Ohio] a drawbridge. I was referring to the spaces between the spans, not to the *draw.*—Mr. Edgar Cowan of Pa., U. S. Senate, June 21: *C. G.,* p. 2852/2. [The word is much used in this debate.]

1862 Where the bridge is to be built ninety feet above low water mark [this bill] does not contemplate a *draw,* because vessels can go under the bridge whenever they please.—Mr. B. F. Wade of O., U. S. Senate, July 5: *Id.,* p. 3112/1. [See also Mr. Collamer's remarks, p. 3112/3.]

1864 See CHUTE.

1865 There is no necessity for a *draw.* [The bridge] is to be one hundred feet above low water mark in the center.—Mr. Jacob Collamer of Vt., U. S. Senate, Feb. 9: *Id.,* p. 672/2.

Drawbar. A bar sustaining train couplings.

1839 The bumpers or elastic cushions are to be attached . . . . to the front and rear *drawbar.*—*Journal,* Franklin Institute xxiv, 156. (N. E. D.)

1861, 1889 English citations. (N. E. D.)

1893 Why is it necessary for Congress to bother itself as to how and when the railroad companies shall adopt a *drawbar* of uniform height, if they must have a *drawbar* of uniform height before they can adopt this coupler?—Mr. Joseph N. Dolph of Ore., U. S. Senate, Feb. 10: *C. R.,* p. 1418/2.

1893 The *drawbar* and the coupler are one and the same thing. They are interchangeable terms for that appliance by which one car is attached to another and the train is drawn. To raise or lower the *drawbar,* you must raise or lower the entire coupler.—Mr. Joseph E. Washington of Tenn., H. R., Feb. 27: *Id.,* p. 2242/2.

Draw game. A drawn game.

1890 Better call a halt and declare the business a *draw game.*—Greensborough (Ala.) *Watchman,* n. d.—See *C. R.,* June 3: p. 5546/1.

Draw out. To withdraw, to retire.

1894 [As regards government appropriations for Indian schools], the Methodist denomination *drew out,* if I may use that expression, in 1892.—Mr. O. H. Platt of Conn., U. S. Senate, July 18: *C. R.,* p. 7620/2.

Draw poker. The card game usually called poker.

1882 I do not know [how] the question was determined, whether it was by a game of *draw poker* or by throwing coppers.—Mr. R. G. Horr of Mich., H. R., July 13: *C. R.,* p. 6014/1.

Draw span. The movable part of a drawbridge. Not in the dictionaries.

1892 Said bridge [over the Missouri River] shall be constructed as a pontoon bridge, and shall contain a *drawspan* giving a clear opening of not less than 300 feet in length.—Amendment to a bill: U. S. Senate, Jan. 14: *C. R.,* p. 312/2.

Dressed. Made ready for market or for immediate use.

1526 Delycates or deynty *dressed* meates.—"Pilgrim Perf.," p. 99. (N. E. D.)

1775 Shirts, made of *drest* deer-skins.—Adair, "Amer. Indians," p. 7. (N. E. D.)

1896 I have known pork, *dressed* hogs, at St. Louis, to sell for $1.50 net.— Mr. J. M. Palmer of Ill., U. S. Senate, May 7: *C. R..* p. 4928/1.

Drib. A driblet. The N. E. D. cites Ramsay and Swift (ab. 1730-1745).

1862 [Taxes in Great Britain] are collected "by *dribs* and drabs," . . . . from day to day and from month to month.—Mr. Albert S. White of Ind., H. R., March 13: *C. G.,* p. 1225/3.

1862 We are sending such regiments and *dribs* from here and Baltimore as we can spare.—Abraham Lincoln to Gen. McClellan, May 25. (N. E. D.)

1902 See KEEP TAB.

Drives, to join. To unite forces. New England.

1880 Mr. Morrill accepted [the amendment] so as to *join*—I will use a legal phrase for the benefit of the Senator from Wisconsin, *"jine drives,"* as the lumbermen say.—Mr. James G. Blaine of Me., U. S. Senate, Apr. 19: *C. R.,* p. 2520/1.

Driveway. A road for driving.

1870 I doubt as to the policy of allowing this railroad to go along exactly in the track of where we propose to have a public *driveway.*—Mr. Justin S. Morrill of Vt., U. S. Senate, Feb. 2: *C. G.,* p. 966/3.

1884 Winding *driveways* lead up to it from the road.—*Harper's Mag..* p. 184/2. (N. E. D.)

1889, 1895. (N. E. D.)

Drive-way. A way along which animals are driven by hunters.

1875 Capturing both larger and smaller sorts by means of *drive-ways,* and in rude traps and yank-ups.—"Hist. of Northfield, Mass.," p. 46. (N. E. D.)

Driving. Energetic.

1870 I think the tax on sugar is a greater oppression to the young and *driving,* as well as the old and decrepit, than the tax on sales.—Mr. G. F. Edmunds of Vt., U. S. Senate, June 28: *C. G.,* p. 4923/2.

Drop letters. Letters "dropped" or deposited in the post office for delivery. [1844-1888.]

1863 I believe no *drop letter* is delivered at all, unless a stamp is on it at the time it is placed in the post office.—Mr. Charles J. Biddle of Pa., H. R., Feb. 20: *C. G.,* p. 1153/1.

1863 This bill . . . . has a two-cent rate for *drop letters,* and a one cent rate for drop letters in small towns where the carrier system is not adopted. The rate on *drop letters* is one hundred per cent higher in large cities than in small ones.—Mr. John Hutchins of O., H. R., Feb. 21: *Id.,* p. 1168/3.

1871 A *drop-letter* is a letter to be delivered within the delivery of the particular office in which it is placed.—Mr. Alex. Ramsey of Minn., U. S. Senate, Feb. 4: *Id.,* p. 960/2.

1878 In cities having the carrier system one-cent *drop-letters* are rare. A two-cent stamp gives the *drop-letter* to the carrier, and in consideration of the extra stamp he delivers the letter at the place to which it is addressed.—Mr. C. H. Harrison of Ill., H. R., June 7: *C. R.,* p. 295/1., App.

Drudge. Whisky in the raw state, as used in the manufacture of alcohol. (Century Dict.)

Drummer. A commercial traveller. [1827-1910.]

1882 The merchants of the city of New York have many thousands of the brightest men in the country *drumming* for business in every town and village in the land.—Mr. Jas. B. Beck of Ky., U. S. Senate, Jan. 10: *C. R.*, p. 315/1.

1894 The "commercial tourists," as I believe they are called now,—down in my country we call them *"drummers."*—Mr. W. J. Stone of Ky., H. R., Feb. 14: *C. R.*, p. 2186/1.

Drunk. A drinking bout. Colloq.

1862 Both Houses immediately adjourned and made preparations for a *"general drunk."*—*The Times* corresp., Apr. 10. (N. E. D.)

1879 When I come out of one of my *drunks*.—W. D. Howells, "Lady of the Aroostook" (1883), II, 44. (N. E. D.)

1893 He could put up with an occasional *drunk* in a man who promised to make as good a trooper.—Capt. King, "Foes in Ambush," p. 39 (N. E. D.)

1894 I was informed in the presence of the officer himself . . . that he was in the habit of going on periodical *drunks*.—Mr. J. D. Sayers of Tex., H. R., July 31: *C. R.*, p. 8052/2.

Dry. Without intoxicating liquors; forbidding the sale of intoxicants. [1888-1909.]

1869 I do not believe in a ball where there is nothing to make it joyful. A *dry* dance is no dance at all, according to my notion.—Mr. Simon Cameron of Pa., U. S. Senate, Jan. 13: *C. G.*, p. 331/2.

1890 See WET.

1912 West Virginia votes *dry*. Prohibition amendment stops liquor traffic July 1, 1914.—Headlines, *N. Y. Evening Post*, Nov. 7, p. 1/1.

Dry up. To cease speaking or writing. [1856-1869.]

1870 I want to see if I cannot get the gentleman from Illinois (Mr. N. B. Judd) *dried up* for once.—Mr. G. W. Scofield of Pa., H. R., June 23: *C. G.*, p. 4745/1.

1897 I have no doubt that, when Gabriel . . . begins to blow his tremendous trumpet [Mr. J. H. Walker of Mass.], will rise in his wrath, and say, in his off-hand way, *"Dry up,* Gabriel! *Dry up.* You don't know a thing about judgments, anyhow. Just give us a tariff on horns up in Mass., and we will show you how to run it."—Mr. Champ Clark of Mo., H. R., March 30: *C. R.*, p. 483/2.

Dry Whisky. See **Mescal-buttons.**

Dude. A dandy, an exquisite. [1883-1891.]

1883 The elderly club *dude* may lament the decay of the good old code of honor.—*Harper's Mag.*, lxvii, 632. (Century Dict.)

1884 In many of our cities some of the people are aping foreign manners. There are *dudes,* and a class who want to pronounce like Englishmen, to ride like Englishmen, to hold their arms like Englishmen, and all that.—Mr. S. B. Maxey of Tex., U. S. Senate, Jan. 23: *C. R.*, p. 590/1.

1884 A little less of the *dude* and more of the man is required.—Mr. J. R. Glascock of Calif., H. R., Dec. 11: *Id.*, p. 191/2.

1890 To a blind smoker a Sumatra-covered cigar is not distinguishable from a fine American product. Mr. Morse . . . aptly characterized it as a *"dude"* cigar, with nothing to recommend it but its appearance.—Mr. Marriott Brosius of Pa., H. R., May 10: *Id.*, p. 4539/1.

1892 My bill was thoroughly American. It sought to destroy the Anglo-mania bacteria . . . which are so rapidly undermining the feeble constitutions of our rich young men and maidens. It was a blow at the *dudes* and *dudines,* "don't ver know."—Mr. O. M. Hall of Minn., H. R., July 15: *Id.*, p. 481/2, App.

1896 See STORE CLOTHES.

Duebill. See quotation, 1850.

1836 I'll give you my *dubisary;* I don't know that I can pay it this year, unless the crap of hemp turns out well.—"A Quarter Race in Ky.," p. 24. (1846.)

1850 A brief written acknowledgment of a debt, not made payable to order. —Burrill, "Law Dict.," cited by Webster, 1864.

1863 Persons having claims against the estate will be allowed to pay by authenticated accounts and *duebills.*—Edmund Kirke, "My Southern Friends," p. 263. (N. Y.)

1874 [Mr. Boutwell has said] that the Government is . . . not bound to pay its legal-tender *duebills* on demand.—Mr. Carl Schurz of Mo., U. S. Senate, Jan. 14: *C. R.,* p. 635/2.

1878 Mails are quite as necessary for your merchants who wish to send out their circulars or their *duebills,* as for ours to send orders or drafts for payment in reply.—Mr. Martin Maginnis of Mont., H. R., Apr. 13: *Id.,* p. 2506/1.

1894 [The money] was accounted for . . . . in memorandum checks and *duebills.*—Mr. Cogswell of Mass., H. R., March 19: *Id.,* p. 3117/1.

Dugout. An artificial cave. [1860-1888.]

1885 I would as much resist injustice to railroads as I would resist injustice to the humblest dweller in the remotest *dugout* upon the frontier of the West.—Mr. J. J. Ingalls of Kan., U. S. Senate, Jan. 7: *C. R.,* p. 518/1.

Dugout. A boat made by hollowing out a log. [1819-1866.]

1886 [To certain landsmen] a clumsy *dugout* propelled across some muddy bayou, or down some snaggy stream winding sluggishly through a cottonwood bottom, is the climax of navigation.—Mr. James Buchanan of N. J., H. R., Apr. 10: *C. R.,* p. 402/1, App.

1902 See Wokas.

Dumb-bell district. An electoral district shaped like a dumb-bell, created for "gerrymandering" purposes.

1882 Mr. McDuffie and Mr. Webster and their cotemporaries would have lost faith in public virtue and the success of free institutions, and stood paralyzed with disgust, if you had shown them the *dumb-bell district* of Pa., and told them that sworn legislators . . . had made such a district, and . . . called it contiguous territory.—Mr. Beltzhoover of Pa., H. R., Feb. 13: *C. R.,* p. 1104/2.

1882 If gentlemen want to exhibit the districts by illustrations, ... I ask them to go over to my district in Brooklyn, and that I suppose may be called the *"dumb-bell district."* It has been made up by a Republican Legislature more out of all reasonable shape than any other district that has been presented here . . . . And go across into New York, ... and you will find that they have made that into a regular "grasshopper district."—Mr. W. E. Robinson of N. Y., H. R., July 19: *Id.,* p. 6222/2.

Dump. See quotations. Chiefly U. S. (N. E. D.) [1851.]

1828 Webster. *Dump, v. t.,* to throw or drop, as a load from a cart.

1856 Loading [the carts] with dirt, and *dumping* them upon the road.— Olmsted, "Slave States," p. 387. (N. E. D.)

1870 I see . . . California quartz-mountains *dumped down* in New York.— Emerson, "Works" (Bohn), III, 13. (N. E. D.)

1878 Mails carried on one line of road, which traverses the entire length of my State, are carried to Kansas City in Missouri, and *dumped out* there to remain 24 hours frequently,—they cannot be distributed on the train.—Mr. P. B. Plumb of Kan., U. S. Senate, March 22: *C. R.,* p. 1973/1.

1879 Presently the carcasses . . . were carried up and *dumped* into the water.—H. C. MacCook, "Nat. Hist., &c.," p. 139. (N. E. D.)

1881 They made a mob, they seized those two white men, *dumped* them into a buggy, and drove them off.—Mr. Wm. P. Frye of Me., U. S. Senate, Apr. 20: *C. R.*, p. 350/1.

1882 [The sediment was taken] down below Alexandria, and then, when that was found to interfere with the channel [of the Potomac], it was carried by a tedious process far down the river, . . . and there *dumped.*—Mr. O. D. Conger of Mich., U. S. Senate, July 10: *Id.*, p. 5831/2.

1884 In the States of New Jersey, Delaware, and Maryland, the peach-growers, when their crop is so great as to affect unfavorably the price of peaches, *dump* their surplus into the Delaware River or Bay. Time and again have these farmers *dumped* their peaches. . . . The surplus *dumped* from foreign pauper markets is the great bane of our industries. It is this *dump* that we want to stop; it is protection against this *dump* that the protective system seeks to accomplish.— Mr. C. N. Brumon of Pa., H. R., May 1: *Id.*, p. 3663/1.

Dump. A place where rubbish is shot down.

1883 We sat by the margin of the *dump* and saw, far below us, the green tree tops standing still in the clear air.—*Century Mag.*, xxxii, 38.

1883 A sort of platform on the edge of the *dump.* There, in old days, the trucks were tipped and the loads sent thundering down the chute.— *Id.*, 191.

1890 Gentlemen who favor this bill make this country the *dumping-ground* for all the silver in the world. It can not be *dumped* here without taking from this country the gold.—Mr. Abner Taylor of Ill., H. R., June 25: *C. R.*, pp. 6498-9.

Dumpage. The right to dump loads of material on a particular spot; also the fee paid for such privilege. (Century Dict.).

Dunfish. See quotation.

1819 I have heard you Boston folks brag that the codfish we get are not the thing; but you have a certain animal called a *"Dun fish,"* much superior. Can you procure me a box?—J. Hopkinson to D. Webster (1857), I, 305, Apr. 19.

Duress, v. To constrain.

a.1626 If the party *duressed* doe make any motion or offer.—Bacon "Maxims, &c." (1636). p. 81. (N. E. D.)

1870 I never heard of a man who was *duressed* into an office to hold and exercise the functions of it during a period of four years by *duress.*—Mr. Luke P. Poland of Vt., H. R., July 5: *C. G.*, p. 5197/3.

Dutch. German.

1639 Frequent mention hath been made of the Teutonic order, or that of *Dutch* Knights . . . . The greater number of the *Dutch* Knights, in Prussia, did Knight-service against the Tartarians.—Thomas Fuller, "The Holy War," Book V, ch. iv.

1863 A gentleman . . . . told me that he saw a squad of *Dutch* soldiers, many of whom could hardly speak the English language, take possession of the polls. . . . . They were a crowd of Germans who could say nothing but "yaw."—Mr. Lazarus W. Powell of Ky., U. S. Senate, Feb. 7: *C. G.*, p. 793/3.

1870 I care little whether you call me Hollander or German. I know that *"Dutch"* is a geographical error, probably originating in the similarity of the sounds "Dutch" and "Deutsch." . . . The Germans are a reflective people.—Mr. Edw. Degener of Tex., H. R., May 23: *Id.*, p. 3730/1.

Dutchman. A German. [1778-1859.]

1513 To thraw . . . The casting speris on the *Duche mennis* gys [manner]. Lat., *Teutonico ritu soliti torquere cateias.*—Douglas, "Eneados," ed. Small, 1874, Bk. VII, p. 135.

1804 Forty miles, stayed with a *Dutchman* who was reasonable in his charges.—Lorenzo Dow, "Journal," Sept. 11 (1850), p. 98/1.

1807 Mr. Blannerhasset (*sic*) said to me, "You are a *Dutchman,* and a common man; and as the *Dutch* are apt to be scared by high men, if you'll go to New Lancaster, where the *Dutchmen* live, and get me 30 or 40 men to go with us, I will give you as many dollars."—Testimony of Jacob Allbright at Aaron Burr's trial. Norfolk (Va.) *Gazette,* Sept. 2, p. 1/3.

1848 A *Dutchman* smiles when he sees snits and scralls, and tastes sourkrout.—Wilmington (N. C.) *Commercial,* Apr. 27, p. 1/6.

1866 I met a *Dutchman* in my State during that [1864] canvass.—Mr. Edgar Cowan of Pa., U. S. Senate, May 11: *Id.,* p. 2558/1.

1886 [Mr. R.] is a native of Bavaria, a crout-eating, pretzel-stuffing, beer-swilling *Dutchman,* who has about as much conception of the spirit of our institutions as a pickaninny on the Congo of the philosophy expounded in the "Novum Organum."—Correspondence of the Louisville *Courier-Journal,* Feb. 21: See *C. R.,* p. 117/1, App.

1892 You ought to know by this time that, if you allow a *Dutchman* to come in among you, he will not only make a living but get rich, where a white man would starve to death.—Mr. F. E. White of O., H. R., June 15: *Id.,* p. 5312/1.

1892 I am not a Yankee, and only claim the right of a *Dutchman* when I ask the gentleman a question.—Mr. M. D. Harter of O., H. R., Feb. 19: *Id.,* p. 1343/1.

Dutch treat. See Vol. I. Compare this with **Basket party.**

Dutch uncle. To talk to anyone like a Dutch uncle is to reprehend him. [1837.]

1889 You were just about drunk enough . . . to look after me *like a Dutch uncle.*—J. C. Harris, "Balaam and his Master."

Dyed-in-the-wool. Thorough-going, without compromise. [1579-1904.]

1866 All the frenzied people of the North, all the strong-minded spinsters of New England, all the fighting clergy of the northern States who are for letting slip the dogs of war and crying havoc, all the Black Republican party, *dyed in the wool,* who hold office obtained in this crusade against slavery, &c.—Mr. Garrett Davis of Ky., U. S. Senate, Jan. 24: *C. G.,* p. 395/2.

E

Eagle. A ten dollar gold piece. [1789-1888.]

1871 That happier and better era when once more the silver dollar will be seen, and the golden *eagle* be exhibited to all our people, and be in the pockets of all our laboring men.—Mr. James Brooks of N. Y., H. R., March 20: *C. G.,* p. 186/1.

1878 In 1834 the Gold *Eagle,* which by act of 1792 had been made to contain 270 grains, with its fineness fixed at 916⅔, was reduced to 258 grains in weight, and the fineness was also reduced to 899.225. The fineness was again changed in 1837 to 900, 9 parts pure gold to 1 part alloys.—Mr. D. C. Haskell of Kan., H. R., Feb. 9: *C. R.,* p. 908/2.

Ear, on one's. In fighting attitude. Slang.

1879 [I once] thought I could understand why some members of this House always *"got up on their ear"* whenever anything relating to the U. S. Army was presented.—Mr. M. I. Townsend of N. Y., H. R., Feb. 4: *C. R.,* p. 965/1.

Easily. Beyond controversy. The N. E. D. very happily suggests the Latin *Facile princeps.*

1883 Harvard has . . . . *easily* the finest gymnasium in the world.—*Harper's Mag.,* p. 907/1. (N. E. D.)

1894 Chicago is today *easily* the second great postal point in the Union.—Memorial concerning the Federal Building, Jan. 17: *C. R.,* Aug. 8, p. 8326/2.

Easterner. A person belonging to the Eastern States, from Maine to Delaware. [1864.]

1887 Nothing can be more foolish than for an *Easterner* to think he can become a cowboy in a few months' time.—Theo. Roosevelt. *Century Mag.,* xxxv, 502.

Eastern Shore. Of Maryland, that part lying between the ocean and Delaware Bay. Term apparently extended to include Virginia. See Vol. I, **Eastern Shore, the.** [1777-1784.]

1676 It is ordered that William Niccolls Tayler liveing on the *Easterne shore,* his Account . . . Bee payde.—*Journals of House of Burgesses of Virginia,* Feb. 20: Vol. II, p. 76. (Richmond, Va., 1914.)

1776 As a Virginia regiment was ordered up from *the Eastern Shore,* they were directed to halt at Dover for the further orders of Congress.— Robert Morris to George Read, Apr. 12: See *C. G.,* Apr. 12, 1871, p. 600/2.

1812 [In reply to] "A Citizen of the *Eastern Shore* of Virginia," what has the malversation of embargo breakers and smugglers to do with the integrity and patriotism of the citizens of the *Eastern Shore?*—Norfolk (Va.) *Herald,* July 10, p. 3/1.

1865 See CANVASBACK DUCKS.

1889 See a paper by Mrs. Bergen, *Journal of Am. Folk-Lore,* II, 295-300.

Eat crow. To submit to, or put up with, something offensive, humiliating, or the like. (Webster.)

1894 As I said when voting for the Wilson bill, I can *eat crow.* But this crow that I am now asked to eat is too big and too black for me to swallow.—Mr. T. L. Johnson of O., H. R., Aug. 13: *Id.,* p. 1229/1, App.

Eat dog. An Indian custom, from which a phrase sometimes used in politics is derived. [1775-1902.]

[1673 A feast followed. A large dog, boiled was the "pièce de résistance." This did not tempt the travellers (Marquette and his companions), and they were allowed to regale themselves on fat buffalo meat.—Mr. J. L. Mitchell of Wisc., U. S. Senate, Apr. 29, 1896: *C. R.,* p. 4547/1.]

Ebo. Ebony(?).

1822 Monday [Gell] is an *Ebo,* and now in the prime of life.—*Am. Beacon* (Norfolk, Va.), Sept. 3, p. 2/1.

E'ena'most. Even almost; nearly. [1834-1856.]

1844 A carpenter, being informed that the model of the house he was building was planned by a woman, exclaimed in astonishment, "Why, I declare, she knows *e'en-a'-most* as much as some men!"—Lydia M. Child, "Letters from N. York," Second S., p. 133. (Lond., 1845.)

Effectuate. To effect; to make effective. [Am.?]

1894 You want to *effectuate* your reform at the expense of a Democratic State.—Mr. C. J. Boatner of La., H. R., Jan. 22: *C. R.,* p. 1186/1.

Egypt. Southern Illinois. So called derisively with reference to the supposed intellectual darkness of the inhabitants. [1855-1888.]

1863 Illinois is a western State, and of course she is entitled to be benefited. If I had my way, I would give her another grant of land for the purpose of enlightening *Egypt,* where we all know there is so much darkness. (Laughter.)—Mr. Thaddeus Stevens of Pa., H. R., Feb. 7: *C. G.,* p. 811/3.

1864 [This bill was to give Mr. Washburne] a solid political foothold in that part of the great State of Illinois known as *"Egypt,"* in which Cairo is a favorite city.—Mr. Rollins of Mo., H. R., June 24: *Id.,* p. 3249/1.

1866 A great many [Kentuckians] settled nearly the whole of the lower part of my State. . . . But, now that *Egypt* is redeemed, I do not think, &c.—Mr. Lyman Trumbull of Ill., U. S. Senate, Feb. 2: *Id.,* p. 600/2.

1872 The Ohio river circles around *Egypt;* not the Egypt of antiquity, but the *Egypt* which is adorned by the residence of my friend from Ill. [Mr. Crebs].—Mr. O. D. Conger of Mich., H. R., March 13: *Id.,* p. 1654/1.

1879 Take the Barringers; one of them is a U. S. judge in *Egypt.* They were confederates; they are republicans now, and they are cared for. —Mr. D. W. Voorhees of Ind., U. S. Senate, June 18: *C. R.,* p. 2119/2.

1892 Hardin County, a southern county that . . . is a part of *Egypt,* . . . a county which is very poor.—Mr. W. C. Newberry of Ill., H. R., May 27: *Id.,* p. 4777/2.

1894 One thing is true, Mr. Speaker, the cities farther west than *Egypt,* Ill., will not be ungrateful . . . if such a favor as this shall be given.— Mr. Lafe Pence of Colo., H. R., Aug. 10: *Id.,* p. 8385/1.

Eight-by-seven. This phrase was used with reference to the decision of the Electoral Commission in the Hayes-Tilden controversy.

1880 My colleague [Mr. McMahon] declares "that . . . the Supreme Court of the U. S. has decided that the election law is constitutional by a sort of *eight-by-seven* decision, &c." He undertakes to throw contempt on that decision by styling it "a sort of *eight-by-seven* decision."—Mr. J. A. Garfield of O., H. R., March 17: *C. R.,* p. 1639/1.

1891 There was a monotonous *"eight to seven, seven to eight,"* from the beginning to the end of the chapter.—Mr. John W. Daniel of Va., U. S. Senate, Jan. 16: *Id.,* p. 1446/1.

Elbow neighbor. One who sits close by.

1895 My objection . . . . would have come just as soon if the suggestion had been made by my *elbow neighbor,* with whom I am on the most intimate and kindly terms.—Mr. I. G. Harris of Tenn., U. S. Senate, Feb. 7: *C. R.,* p. 1899/1.

Electrocute. To kill by an electrical shock. A hybrid word. Sometimes spelled "electricute."

1890 The issuance of such an order as that is no more warranted than it would be if the Speaker should issue his order that the gentleman from Arkansas should be *"electrocuted"* by the Kemmler process recently adopted in the State of N. Y.—Mr. B. A. Enloe of Tenn., H. R., Aug. 9: *C. R.,* p. 8375/1.

1890 *Electrocution* offers a far more decorous, humane, certain, and painless method of doing away with murderous criminals than any other means . . . and . . . *electrocution* should have a fair trial.—*Illustrated Home Journal,* Sept., p. 4/2. [Standard Dict.]

1890 Mr. Morse:—[The hogs] were not *electricuted,* then? Mr. Houk:— No, sir; that highly civilized method had not then been invented.— H. R., Aug. 21: *C. R.,* p. 8965/1.

Elegant. Excellent, fine, and the like. [1765-1856.]

1866 The people of New England have given their children a very *elegant* education.—Mr. Andrew J. Rogers of N. J., H. R., June 5: *C. G.,* p. 2969/2.

1892 [The general superintendent of Indian schools] is a most *elegant* gentleman and a most efficient officer.—Mr. S. W. Peel of Ark., H. R., Feb. 18: *C. R.,* p. 1305/2.

Element. A component part of a community.

1864 A section where the secession *element* is so strong.—Edmund Kirke, "Down in Tennessee," p. 31. (N. Y.)

1869 There was imminent danger that the rebel *element* would snatch from the midst of defeat all the nefarious ends at which it had aimed by armed rebellion.—Mr. A. A. Sargent of Calif., H. R., Apr. 1: *C. G.,* p. 435/2.

1869   I am far from being inclined to dwell on the . . . agonies we, the Union *element* in the South, had to suffer during the war.—Mr. Alex. H. Jones of N. C., H. R., *Id.*, p. 435/3.

1870   We have heard of "the Republican *element*"; we have heard of "the Democratic *element*"; we have heard of "the loyal *element*"; we have heard of "the disloyal *element*"; we have heard of "the Yankee *element*"; and very much in my colleague's newspaper of "the German *element*"; but it is a new thing under the sun in Missouri that papers should begin to talk there about "the Confederate *element*"; and yet such is the fact.—Mr. Chas. D. Drake of Mo., U. S. Senate, Dec. 16 : *Id.*, p. 5/3, App,

Elephant. The recognized symbol of the Republican party [the Grand Old Party]. The "Republican Elephant" was invented by Thos. Nast. It appeared in his cartoon of Nov. 7, 1874.

1894   Pretended fear of "tariff reform" is now agitating the huge frame of the G. P. O. [G. O. P.] *elephant* . . . . Old Jumbo was paralyzed in 1892, but by careful nursing he has been kept alive.—Mr. H. H. Powers of Vt., H. R., Jan. 15 : *C. R.*, p. 845/1.

Elevator. A lift for passengers or freight. [1883.]

1873   Mr. Farnsworth :—I do not believe in putting in an *elevator* [at the Capitol] for the benefit of a few decrepit Senators. Mr. Garfield :— One *elevator* will do for all these purposes. Mr. Farnsworth :— Gentlemen get sufficiently elevated here without any machinery.— H. R., March 3 : *Id.*, p. 2113/2.

1890   On this list there are firemen, watchmen, *elevator-men.*—Mr. Frank Lawler of Ill., H. R., Aug. 4 : *C. R.*, p. 8123/2.

Elevator. A building for elevating, storing, and discharging grain (Webster). [1795-1862].

1885   A short time ago we found the *elevators* along the New York and New Jersey shores filled with grain. The export demand had not enabled the grain to be shipped abroad, so that the *elevators* were filled.—Mr. J. R. McPherson of N. J., U. S. Senate, *C. R.*, p. 692/2.

1894   Sometimes, if the *elevator man* has a good deal of bad wheat, he gets some of a first-class article, and mixes the two in his *elevator.*—Mr. T. R. Stockdale of Miss., H. R., July 21 : *Id.*, p. 1087/2, App.

Emperor Nicholas. A nickname applied to Nicholas Biddle of Phila. (1786-1844) who from 1819 to 1839 was president of the U. S. Bank.

1856   [To whom did Mr. B. make these loans?] To members of Congress, to editors of newspapers, to brawling politicians, to brokers and job-bers, to favorites and connections; and all with a view to purchase a re-charter, or to enrich connections, and exalt himself,—having the puerile vanity to delight in being called the *"Emperor Nicholas."*— T. H. Benton, "Thirty Years' View," II, 366/1.

Empire City, The. New York.

1865   I do not represent the city of Boston, whose life is commerce. I do not represent the *Empire City*, whose daily food and daily breath is commerce.—Mr. John P. Hale of N. H., U. S. Senate, Jan. 11 : *C. G.*, p. 204/3.

1865   I am told that [General B. F. Butler] curbed the proud *Empire City* of New York; that he restrained it within proper bounds on the day of election; that but for him there was no knowing what might have passed.—Mr. James Brooks of N. Y., H. R., Jan. 24 : *Id.*, p. 398/3.

Empire State, The. New York. [1837-1909.]

1862   I need not say that the *Empire State* has no sympathy with this rebellion.—Mr. R. H. Duell of N. Y., H. R., Apr. 23 : *C. G.*, p. 1796/1.

1869 The cataract of Niagara has been a boon of Providence to the city and state of New York. It has made one the *Empire State* of the Republic, and the other the commercial metropolis of the New World.—Mr. H. E. Paine of Wisc., H. R., Jan. 14: *Id.*, p. 373/3.

Empire State of the South. Georgia.

1870 Georgia is a great State; it is the *Empire State of the South.*—Mr. Henry Wilson of Mass., U. S. Senate, Apr. 4: *Id.*, p. 2391/3.

1872 All Georgia wants is to let her alone, and in a few years she will get back to the proud position she occupied in former times, in being *the Empire State of the South.*—Mr. A. T. McIntyre of Ga., H. R., Feb. 2: *Id.*, p. 801/3.

1888 There are greater elements of strength in Georgia today than there were before the war. She can make an *"Empire State"* of herself, as she has chosen to call herself for many years, much more readily with free labor than she could with slave labor.—Mr. H. M. Teller of Colo., U. S. Senate, March 15: *C. R.*, p. 2102/2.

Empire State of the South. Texas.

1894 There is a story told of one of the States in that section of the Union in which I live, a State which is proud of being called "the *Empire State of the South,*" a State which has for its emblem a lone star:—I have heard it stated that sometimes down in that State a particular kind of firearm is wanted, and when it is wanted it is wanted like ——sheol.—Mr. N. C. Blanchard of La., U. S. Senate, May 25: *C. R.*, p. 5256/2.

Emptins, Emptyins. The lees of beer, and the like. [1848-1860.]

1881 Mr. Chairman, this bill is nearly played out, and is running *emptyings.* . . . [Mr. Robeson] asks for a little appropriation for a creek in N. J. called Cohansey. . . . Have we not run *emptyings* to come down to Cohansey?—Mr. S. S. Cox of N. Y., H. R., Feb. 15: *C. R.*, p. 1647/1.

1889 To run like a boy after *emptins.* Eastern Mass.—*Journal of Am. Folk-Lore*, II, 153.

Engineer. An engine-driver; one who manages a locomotive or a stationary engine.

1881 [A] spiteful *engineer* saw somebody at a way station [whom] he did not like, and when that person wanted to get aboard as a passenger, the *engineer* put on additional steam, and ran by with great velocity.—Mr. D. W. Voorhees of Ind., U. S. Senate, Apr. 1: *C. R.*, p. 166/2.

1900 [It was] stated that a head of department asked for an *engineer*, and a Methodist minister,—and a negro at that,—was certified.—Mr. J. J. Fitzgerald of Mass., H. R., Feb. 15: *Id.*, p. 1856/2.

Engineer, v. To carry a scheme through. [1859-1882.]

1864 When [Mr. Colfax] undertakes to *engineer* a resolution through this house for the expulsion of a brother member, he must take the consequences of the debate which he inaugurates.—Mr. S. S. Cox of O., H. R., Apr. 9: *C. G.*, p. 1510/1.

1888 See SOREHEAD.

1893 See BACK OF.

Enthuse. To kindle into enthusiasm. [1859-1884.]

1863 How many school boys have declaimed and have warmed and become *enthused* in the declamation of that great philippic [of Colonel Barré's] against the cruelty and inhumanity of the British Government in employing the savages against the colonists in the American war!—Mr. Garrett Davis of Ky., U. S. Senate, Feb. 7: *C. G.*, p. 800/1.

1882 [Mr. Pendleton of Ohio is] standing up here and proclaiming a sentimentalism upon this question [of political assessments] which he says thoroughly *enthuses* him.—Mr. Eugene Hale of Me., U. S. Senate, June 26: *C. R.*, p. 5336/2.

1892 A Democrat in my State last year, becoming *enthused,* vociferously proclaimed, "I was born a Democrat." "Yes," said a wicked fellow in the crowd, "born like a dog, blind."—Mr. R. E. Doan of O., H. R., Apr. 4: *Id.,* p. 2935/2.

1913 The power of the pure Gospel to *enthuse* men with a desire to help their brothers.—*English Churchman,* July 24, p. 480/2.

Enunciator. An automatic signal.

1888 Others of you set your watches by the street-car *enunciators.*—Mr. W. E. Mason of Ill., H. R., May 17: *C. R.,* p. 4348/2.

1889 An electric *enunciator* in the box-office.—*Pall Mall Gazette,* Jan. 21, p. 6/3. (N. E. D.)

Episcopal. This word, which properly means "of or relating to a bishop," has been grossly abused, first in Scotland, then in America. [1752-1843.]

1876 The testimony of Major Bascom . . . . was fully corroborated by the *Episcopal bishop* in La.—Mr. J. W. Stevenson of Ky., U. S. Senate, Dec. 6: *C. R.,* p. 2/2, App.

Era of good feeling. A term applied to the period of President Monroe's administration, and then used generally. [1817-1909.]

1868 It is the *"era of good feeling"* we want, such as existed in Monroe's administration, when all questions were settled, when all the States were in harmony each with the other.—Mr. Richard Yates of Ill., U. S. Senate, June 11: *C. G.,* p. 352/2, App.

1879 See BLOODY CHASM.

1889 There seems now to be an *era of good feeling* toward the Territories. . . . I trust this is not merely a "spurt," and that you will not "break and go to pieces" over . . . . New Mexico.—Mr. F. T. Dubois of Ida., H. R., Jan. 16: *C. R.,* p. 878/1.

Escrod. A small cod, broiled. New England. [Now generally *scrod.*]

1844 A good Boston breakfast! Only think of it. A glass of Daniels' cider, and that morsel for Monica, an *escrod!*—D. Webster to Mrs. Paige, March 26: "Private corresp." (1857), II, 186.

Essex Junto, The. The name was applied in 1781 by John Hancock to those who desired a strong Federal government. John Adams revived the nickname about 30 years later, applying it to the promoters of the Hartford Convention. [1801-1825.]

Eventuate. To turn out, to result, to come to a head. [1789-1860.]

1816 It is plain that the Great Being had a hand to attend, and superintend human affairs to *eventuate* the same.—Lorenzo Dow, "Journal," §1012 (1850), p. 157/2.

1836 If the bible does contain [these statements], the whole world cannot enter into such a solemn league and covenant as shall *eventuate* in their entire overthrow.—Dr. G. T. Chapman, "Sermons," p. 365. (Hartford, Conn.)

1895 See GRAB GAME.

Everglades. A district in Florida, partly covered by water. [1827-1841.]

1858 They traversed the forests . . . together, wading through swamps and *everglades,* groping their way through hommocks, and gliding over prairies.—Joshua R. Giddings, "The Exiles of Florida," p. 114.

1863 The only public lands of the U. S. [in Florida] are those great *everglades* of the Indian Billy Bowlegs, occupied so long in defiance of the power of the U. S.—Mr. Charles A. Wickliffe of Ky., H. R., Jan. 29: *C. G.,* p. 602/1.

Evolute. To evolve oneself.

1886 They expect [that he], being a Mugwump, will materialize and *evolute* into a full-blooded Democrat some time hereafter.—Mr. L. C. Houk of Tenn., H. R., March 30: *C. R.,* p. 2935/2.

1889   From the zoological garden, pure and simple, came the grandly organized boom for Rock Creek Park. The monkey-garden, true to its nature, has *evoluted* into this gigantic demand on the national taxpayer.—Mr. W. McAdoo of N. J., H. R., Feb. 27: *Id.*, p. 2424/1.

1891   There was a process of evolution, and by and by they *"evoluted"* into an effective organization.—Mr. J. G. Cannon of Ill., H. R., Feb. 7: *Id.*, p. 2358/2.

1893   While we have been *"evoluting"* toward a gold basis, we have been *"evoluting"* toward that condition which confronted all the nations of ancient times just before they lost their liberties.—Mr. J. C. Sibley of Pa., H. R., Aug. 18: *Id.*, p. 473/2.

Exchanges.   Interchanged newspapers.   [1848-1886.]

1870   I think that *exchanges* ought to be free. It will be a heavy burden upon county newspapers if they are required to pay postage on their *exchanges*. To enable their publishers to publish valuable papers, they must have numerous *exchanges* from all parts of their own State and from different parts of the country.—Mr. Oliver P. Morton of Ind., U. S. Senate, Feb. 11: *C. G.*, p. 1208/2.

Executive.   The chief magistrate.   [1787-1910.]

1802   Three or four private persons . . . . directing the *Executive* of the U. S. . . . . to make way for men without talents or respectability.— A letter to the President [Jefferson] by Noah Webster, p. 20. (New Haven.)

1862   I have watched the President of the U. S. with some disposition to find fault. It has been my misfortune through life, too often probably, to differ with the *Executive* which I had aided in placing in power.— Mr. W. A. Richardson of Ill., H. R., March 13: *C. G.*, p. 1218/1.

1862   How fine it will look, after emancipating the slaves in this District, to welcome here at the White House an African [from Hayti], full-blooded, all gilded and belaced, dressed in court style, with wig and sword and tights and shoe buckles and ribbons and spangles and many other adornments which African vanity will suggest! How suggestive of fun to our good-humored, joke-cracking *Executive!* With what admiring awe will the contrabands approach this ebony demigod! while all decent and sensible people will laugh the ceremony to scorn. —Mr. S. S. Cox of O., H. R., June 2: *Id.*, p. 2503/3.

1865   The *Executive* Mansion, and other *executive* buildings, were placed at one end of the city, while the Capitol was placed at the other, avowedly to avoid *executive* influence, and to escape any encroachment upon legislative deliberations.—Mr. Justin S. Morrill of Vt., H. R., Jan. 25: *Id.*, p. 423/3.

1866   The power of appointing these officers . . . . has been exercised by all the *Executives* from President Jackson down to the present time.— Mr. LeBlond of O., H. R., Dec. 19: *Id.*, p. 206/3.

1869   [Talk about Andrew Johnson] is not pertinent to this debate. It is sufficient that we now have as our *Chief Executive* a man (U. S. Grant) in political sympathy with the Congress and with the great body of the people. . . . He is now the *Executive* and political head of the nation.—Mr. Edmund G. Ross of Kan., U. S. Senate, March 24: *Id.*, p. 242/1.

1879   See BULLDOZE.

1896   See GOLDBUG.

Expansionist.   An advocate of an enlarged paper currency.

1868   I am no wild *expansionist*. I have been a hard-money man all my life. I am not in favor of a rag currency, as it is called.—Mr. John B. Henderson of Mo., U. S. Senate, Jan. 15: *C. G.*, p. 532/2.

1881   Whether the new Secretary . . . . would be an *expansionist* or a contractionist.—*The Nation* (N. Y.), p. 160. (N. E. D.)

Exploiter, v. To exploit; to draw an illegitimate profit from.
1853 It is sad to see [these men] *exploitered* by a two fold jesuitry.—Theodore Parker, "Theism, &c.," Introd., p. 41. (N. E. D.)
1864 [The idea] was repeated, diversified, and—to use an American adaptation of a French word—*"exploitered,"* till it became rather wearisome. —*Fraser's Mag.,* Apr., p. 406. (N. E. D.)
Exploiter. One who "exploits" a matter, in a good or bad sense.
1870 Happy mining company . . these fortunate *exploiters.*—*Fraser's Mag.,* March 10, p. 152/2. (N. E. D.)
1870 The pockets of all the railroad *exploiters* [have] been crammed with public money.—*The Nation* (N. Y.) Feb. 17, p. 101/2. (N. E. D.)
1883 *The Athenæum.* (N. E. D.)
1890 *Exploiters* are found hanging around amongst the mining camps, to try to get men to make false affidavits to impeach . . . election returns.— Mr. J. B. Morgan of Miss., U. S. Senate, Apr. 15: *C. R.,* p. 3383/2.
Express. Express companies undertake the conveyance of parcels, boxes, trunks, etc. [1846-1862.]
1863 *Express companies* do not always follow armies, nor can they always deliver packages to the soldiers. But the mail always follows the flag. —Mr. Schuyler Colfax of Ind., H. R., Jan. 6: *C. G.,* p. 209/2.
1874 We can reduce the cost of the [mail] service by lopping off excrescences. . . . . [Let us] free it from the characteristics of an *express.*— Mr. Lot M. Morrill of Me., U. S. Senate, Jan. 15: *C. R.,* pp. 666/7.
1885 An individual in the city of Boston conceived the . . . idea of delivering bundles in the surrounding towns in a one-horse wagon. The idea grew, and its author grew, until it has developed into the mammothian, monopolized devilfish known by its founder's name as *"The Adams Express,"* whose feelers extend across the continent lengthwise and breadthwise and whose age of life is not to be measured by that of the *Republic,* but of some succeeding despotism which may perchance arise out of its ruins.—Mr. W. J. Green of N. C., H. R., Jan. 7: *Id.,* 529/2.
Express. To send by express.
1894 A negro, who was employed as a general roustabout at a railroad station, saw a large dog brought in to be *expressed* to some distant point.—Mr. B. McMillin of Tenn., H. R., Jan. 23: *C. R.,* p. 1248/1.
Expressage. The cost of sending by express.
1864 Webster.
1888 The *expressage* or postage has not been prepaid.—*Harper's Mag.,* p. 161/1. (N. E. D.)
Expressman. A worker in an express company, employed in receiving and delivering.
1847 [He] tells the *expressman* that it is all right.—H. D. Thoreau, *Atlantic Monthly* (1892), p. 744. (N. E. D.)
1884 We stand in a crowd of . . . hack drivers and *expressmen* on the New York side.—*Harper's Mag.,* p. 270/1. (N. E. D.)
Express rider. A swift courier.
The marks of spurs [are] still to be seen on the side of the counter [in the Trumbull house at Lebanon, Conn.] where orderlies and *express riders* had sat awaiting the governor's orders during the war of independence.—Mr. O. S. Ferry of Conn., U. S. Senate, Feb. 27: *C. R.,* p. 1871/2.
Express wagon. A light wagon.
1875 They came in great squads [to vote], came in *express wagons* in great droves.—Testimony from Alabama, *C. R.,* Feb. 27, p. 1901/1.
Expunging Resolution, The. A resolution to expunge from the journal of the U. S. Senate a previous resolution, moved by Henry Clay, and dated March 28, 1834, which condemned the action of President Jackson in removing the deposit of the public money from the Bank of the U. S., sometimes called "Biddle's Bank." The expung-

ing resolution sustained the President's action, and was adopted Jan. 14, 1837, on the motion of Thomas H. Benton. See Benton's "Thirty Years' View" (1857), I, 402-436, 719-731; also the speech of James Buchanan, Jan. 16, 1837: "Works" (1908), III, 168-194.

Eye-opener. A startling occurrence.
1876 See RINGMASTER.
Eyeteeth, to cut one's. To learn wisdom by experience.
1837 Them are fellers *cut their eye-teeth* afore ever they sot foot in this country.—Haliburton, *"Clockmaker,"* p. 147. (N. E. D.)
1870 Like progress that is made by a boy 'when he *cuts his eye-teeth.'*—Emerson, "Works," III, 7. (N. E. D.)
1876 The war launched us in an almost fathomless sea of expenditure. . . . The things that we actually needed cost enormously. The things that we wasted in overcost and oversupply, in *"cutting our eye-teeth,"* to use a New England phrase,—by building up the fortunes and learning the ways of swindling contractors and thieves,—cost us nearly as much more.—Mr. Eugene Hale of Me., H. R., Jan. 26: *C. R.,* p. 660/1.

F

Face brief. See **Canary Slip.**
Face bricks. See quotation, 1911.
1877 In consequence of the limit placed upon the cost of the building, it was found necessary to adopt *face-bricks,* with limestone or sandstone trimmings, for the outside walls.—Letter from the Supervising Architect, in *C. R.,* Jan. 25, 1878, p. 548/1.
1911 In a brick wall, the face-work may be of what are called *face brick,* and laid with thinner joints.—(Century Dict., Supp., vol. iii, s. v. Face-work.)
Face the music. To do one's best in adverse circumstances; to meet difficulties bravely. [1850-1888.]
1866 We determined that they should *"face the music,"* as became men.—Mr. LeBlond of O., H. R., May 15: *C. G.,* p. 2602/2.
1869 [The question] is whether we must not *"face the music,"* and unseat some half dozen members from Georgia.—Mr. Rufus P. Spalding of O., H. R., Jan. 28: *Id.,* p. 677/2.
Faculty. See quotation, 1859.
1844 The want of self-reliance, and what in New England is called *"faculty"* about common things, was partly to be attributed to Miss Adams's delicate health.—Lydia M. Child, "Letters from New York," Second S., p. 134. (Lond., 1845.)
1859 *Faculty* is Yankee for *savoir faire,* and the opposite virtue to shiftlessness.—Mrs. H. B. Stowe, "Minister's Wooing," p. 2. (N. E. D.)
1876 Above all things [Winthrop] had what we Yankees call *faculty*—the knack of doing everything.—G. W. Curtis, Introd. to "Cecil Dreeme," p. 12.
1884 Lizzie had *"faculty,"* and proved a notable housekeeper.—J. D. Whiting in *Harper's Mag.,* p. 741/1. (N. E. D.)
Fairly and squarely. For "fair and square" the N. E. D. cites Friar Bacon's Prophecy (1604), Cromwell (1649), Wycherley and Arbuthnot (1712); but for "fairly and squarely," only W. A. Wallace (1890).
1862 [I doubt if these guns would] remain in their position if they were to be struck *fairly and squarely* by shot from the enemy.—Mr. John C. Ten Eyck of N. J., U. S. Senate, March 27: *C. G.,* p. 1402/2.
1864 Have the committee *fairly and squarely* rebutted the presumptions with which I come here?—Mr. Joseph Segar of Va., H. R., May 17: *Id.,* p. 2313/3.

1866   If Senators believe that . . . . they are supporting [this] amendment for the purpose of conferring the suffrage upon the negro, let us meet the question *fairly and squarely.*—Mr. John B. Henderson of Mo., U. S. Senate, March 9: *Id.,* p. 1283/3.

[1867   That is a *fair and square* proposition.—Mr. Thos. A. Hendricks of Ind., H. R., Feb. 27: *Id.,* p. 1879/1.]

Fair top boots. Those topped with light leather. [1826.]

1857   [Mr. Macon] was neat in his person, always wore fine linen, . . . a fine fur hat with a brim to it, *fair top boots.*—T. H. Benton, "Thirty Years' View," I, 118.

Fake. Any person or thing that, through trickery or device, is made to appear otherwise than he or it really is.

1897   The P. O. Department is powerless to stem the growth of the tide of "fake" newspapers.—Mr. E. F. Loud of Calif., H. R., Jan. 6: *C. R.,* p. 510/1.

Fakir. A common error for faker, a cant word used in Borrow's "Lavengro."

Fall. To let fall.

1594   As easie maist thou *fall*
                 A drop of water in the breaking gulfe.
                                      —Comedy of Errors, II, 2.   (1623.)

1594   Her mantle she did *fall.*—Midsummer Night's Dream, V, 1.   (1623.)

1604   Each drop she *falls,* would prove a Crocodile.—Othello, IX, 1.   (1623.)

Fallfish. See quotations.

1812   A delicious chub which we call a *fallfish.*—John J. Henry, "Campaign against Quebec," p. 32.   (Lancaster, Pa.)   (N. E. D.)

1857   There is a fish in these [Virginia] waters, called the *"Fallfish,"* resembling the English dace, or in some degree our chub.—D. Webster to Fletcher W., June 27: " Private Corresp." (1857), II, 448.

Fall of the leaf. The autumn.

1603   [Queen Elizabeth] came in *the fall of the leafe,* and went away in the Spring.—Dekker, "The Wonderful Yeare," B4.

1609   'Tis the time of yeare, *the fall of leafe* sir.—Robert Armin, "Two Maids," D.

1623   With me, 'tis *Fall o' the Leafe.*—Webster, "Devil's Law Case," B.

1848   We do not believe that the present government [in France] will go through the winter months, if it survives the *"fall of the leaf."*—Wilmington (N. C.) *Commercial,* Sept. 14, p. 2/3.

False-counter. A falsifier of election returns.   Not in the dictionaries.

1879   Let repeaters, *false-counters,* and ruffians no longer be employed to carry elections.—Mr. Roscoe Conkling of N. Y., U. S. Senate, Apr. 24: *C. R.,* p. 805/2.

Fan. An enthusiastic devotee of any sport.   Slang.   [1901-1910.]

1903   Cranks and *"fans"* of all degrees
                 Are there to howl and scream.
                      —*Kan. City Daily Times,* Apr. 23.   (Century Dict.)

1919   Portland baseball *fans* will miss the smiling countenance of the late Governor James Withycombe. . . .The late state executive was an ardent baseball *fan* and took a prominent part in the ushering in of the baseball season each year.—*The Oregonian,* March 4, p. 14/5.

Fast horse. A good trotter.   [1854-1857.]

1868   Men who, in the city of St. Louis, are rolling in wealth, building fine houses, riding in splendid carriages, and driving *fast horses.*—Mr. W. A. Pile of Mo., H. R., Jan. 9: *C. G.,* p. 432/2.

1882   Kentucky has always been noted for its *fast horses* and its lotteries, and some other things.—Mr. R. G. Horr of Mich., H. R., July 13: *C. R.,* p. 6015/2.

1888   See SPEED, v.

1894 It is the poor people, who are not able to drive *fast horses,* who have to ride on the street railways—Mr. J. D. Richardson of Tenn., H. R., May 14: *Id.,* p. 4742/1.

Fast land. The mainland. Germ. *Festland.*

1862 [League Island] is not an island that is overflowed by the tide . . . . I have spent many a day there, and I know that it has four hundred acres and more of high, dry, *fast land.*—Mr. W. D. Kelley of Pa. . . . [The idea entertained by Mr. F. A. Conkling] may have originated in the alarm which took place in the lower part of Delaware at the time that the Delaware and Chesapeake canal was to be cut through the State. The people objected to it for fear that it would let the sea in and carry away the lower part of Delaware, or forever prevent it from being connected with the *fast land* of the north.—Mr. W. M. Davis of Pa., H. R., July 11: *C. G.,* p. 3264/2.

1866 We have, and have had for a century at least, two hundred and thirty-five acres of *fast land* [at League Island] where there need be hardly any piling.—Mr. Leonard Myers of Pa., H. R., June 7: *Id.,* p. 3014/3.

1866 What [Mr. Brandegee of Conn.] calls three hundred acres of mud contains more than five hundred acres of natural *fast land.*—Mr. W. D. Kelley of Pa., H. R., June 7: *Id.,* p. 3022/3.

1867 Go for *fast land,* as you term (*sic*) near League Island, and where do you find it, except at Red Bank in the State of New Jersey?—Mr. Geo. R. Riddle of Del., U. S. Senate, Feb. 14: *Id.,* p. 1300/2.

Fatbird. The pectoral sandpiper, *Actodromas maculata*: New Jersey. (Century Dict.)

Fault, v. To blame, to find fault with. [1820-1907.]

1912 Mr. Figgis is less the adventurer than the scholar and thinker. He has not, indeed, any of the scholar's turn for the beauty and rightness of language, being often slovenly and obscure, and occasionally degrading English by the use of such hideous expressions as "to *fault* Hamlet," "more often Shakespeare succeeds in besting a character," "having glimpsed this sight of Shakespeare."—*The Times,* Feb. 1, p. 41/3.

Favorite son. A politician respected or admired in his own State, but little regarded beyond it. [1789-1888.]

1877 A title to the Presidency 50 years ago, tainted with the mere suspicion of fraud, consigned a great son of Mass. to comparative retirement and barred the doors of the executive department forever against the *favorite son* of Kentucky.—Mr. John R. Tucker of Va., H. R., Jan. 23: *C. R.,* p. 856/1.

Faze. To disconcert, worry, daunt. (Webster.)

1917 One day [Judge Gantt] sought to *feaze* Fiske with a historico-legal question.—J. S. Clark, "Life of John Fiske," II, 205. (Boston.)

Feather, in full. In high feather; in great power.

1896 The combine was there in *full feather.* [For ampler citation see DEVIL, (v.).]

Federal. Northern.

1870 A *Federal* officer bearing himself gallantly through the entire war.—Mr. Jacob S. Golladay of Ky., H. R., Jan. 29: *C. G.,* p. 881/1.

1874 During the late rebellion . . . great use was made of torpedoes by both *Federals* and Confederates.—Mr. S. S. Cox of N. Y., H. R., Jan. 14: *C. R.* p., 660/2.

1897 See YOU-UNS.

Federal City. Washington. [1793-1801.]

1805 The profits .. I designed to aid in erecting a meetinghouse in Washington, the *Federal City.*—Lorenzo Dow, "Journal," Jan. 27 (1850), p. 102/2.

Feed to, feed out to. To supply food to.

1862 Mr. Sherman :—Would it not be better to say "all grain consumed," so as to include not only what goes into the mash tub, but what is *fed out to hogs?*—Mr. Fessenden :—They *feed it out to hogs* afterwards. —U. S. Senate, May 26: *C. G.,* p. 2352/3.

1868 I suppose the stock would not starve if he . . . *fed the grain to the oxen* and to the hogs without running it through the mash tub at all.— Mr. Timothy O. Howe of Wisc., U. S. Senate, March 28: *Id.,* p. 2190/2.

1883 Mangel-wurzel . . . is *fed to the cows* in winter.—*Harper's Mag.,* p. 652/1. (N. E. D.)

1886 Corn [in Kansas] can not be exported at a profit. We are compelled to *feed it* to cattle and to swine.—Mr. J. J. Ingalls of Kan., U. S. Senate, May 6: *C. R.,* p. 4226/1.

1893 He has been *feeding* bread and butter *to the dog.*—*Atlantic Monthly,* p. 184/1. (N. E. D.)

Feel good. To be elated. [1854-1888.]

1879 When the bill passed which [John L. Davenport] got through Congress, he went back in high spirits to the city of New York and he *felt good,* for he foresaw what was coming.—Mr. A. G. Thurman of O., U. S. Senate, May 15: *C. R.,* p. 98/1, App.

1894 We had succeeded . . . in passing our bill for the reformation of the tariff in such magnificent shape that I *felt unusually good.*—Mr. T. C. Catchings of Miss., H. R., Feb. 2: *Id.,* p. 1812/1.

Feel like. To feel like doing a thing is to feel inclined to do it. [1855-1857.]

1870 Would any gentleman, after having done such a thing, *feel like* he could look an honest man in the face?—Mr. J. Proctor Knott of Ky., H. R., Feb. 2: *C. G.,* p. 984/1.

Feet, off one's. To be carried off one's feet is to be swept away with a sudden emotion, usually enthusiasm.

1869 Even the sedate, calm, and astute chairman of the Judiciary Committee is *taken right off his feet* at the mention of female clerks.—Mr. Justin S. Morrill of Vt., U. S. Senate, March 2: *C. G.,* p. 1779/1.

1889 He positively *carried me off my feet* for a few minutes that evening.— "Repentance of P. Wentworth," III, 145. (N. E. D.)

1894 I have heard of men by their eloquence carrying an audience *off its feet.*—Mr. W. H. Crain of Tex., H. R., May 7: *C. R.,* p. 4456/1.

Feet, on one's. In the act of speaking in public. The N. E. D. has examples, 1792, 1799, 1801, of the corresponding expression, "on one's legs."

1867 I propose to put to [Senator Howe] the inquiry which I proposed to put to him when he was *on his feet.*—Mr. Jas. W. Nye of Nev., U. S. Senate, Apr. 12: *C. G.,* p. 837/2.

1870 Here is a Senator *on his feet* who proposes to make a speech.—Mr. Lot M. Morrill of Me., U. S. Senate, May 12: *Id.,* p. 3405/3.

1891 The Senate . . . allowed the minority to talk, . . . and never attempted to take a Senator *off his feet.*—Mr. W. M. Stewart of Nev., U. S. Senate, Jan. 22: *C. R.,* p. 1656/2.

Fences, to look after one's. To guard one's own private or political interests.

1888 Mr. Dougherty :—I presume [the absent members] are at home seeking renomination or *looking after their fences.* . . . Mr. Weaver :— I have *"fences"* as well as other gentlemen; but my friends will look after my *"fences"* while I am here. . . . Mr. Springer :—I am very anxious that the public business should be dispatched as early as possible, and that we may return to our constituents; and then, if there are any *"fences"* to be mended, . . . we shall have our own time in which to attend to such matters.—H. R., Aug. 16: *C. R.,* p. 7646.

Fetch up. To come to a stop or standstill.

1858 When in quest of any particular point, [they] are likely enough to *fetch up* at some other.—N. Hawthorne, "Fr. and Ital. Journals," V, 705. (N. E. D.)

1864 That slavery-conserving sheet [the Missouri Republican] knew where the wandering gentleman [Governor King] would *"fetch up."*—Mr. Joseph W. McClurg of Mo., H. R., March 9: *C. G.,* p. 1014/3.

Few, a. Much, considerably, a good deal; also, a little. See Vol. I, **A few.** [1761-1862.]

1853 Mr. Smallweed bears the concise testimony, *"A few!"*—Dickens, "Bleak House," p. 199.

F. F. V. See first quotation. [1847-1870.]

1849 [Along the James River] were the ancient aristocratic families planted, from which comes the saying, still in use, and now always laughed at, "First Families in Va.," or *"F. F. V."*—D. Webster to Mrs. Paige, Apr. 21: "Private Corresp." (1857), II, 316.

1861 We taunted [Col. L. Q. C. Lamar] with his fine words to the *F. F. V.* crowd before the Spotswood [Hotel.]—Mrs. Chestnut, "A Diary from Dixie," p. 70. (1905.)

1861 Mr. [James M.] Mason is a manly old Virginian, straightforward, brave, truthful, clever, the very beau-ideal of an independent, high-spirited *F. F. V.*—The same, p. 125.

1881 American citizens, be they white or black, "respectable" or unrespectable, men who wore the gray or the blue, *F. F. V.'s* or carpetbaggers. —Mr. J. A. Anderson of Kan., H. R., Feb. 26: *C. R.,* p. 222/1, App.

Fiat money, Fiat dollars. Those made a legal tender by legislative fiat.

1879 You now have the *"fiat dollar,"* pure and simple, redeemable in pulp. If you can *"fiat"* 85 cents to be worth 100 cents, to an unlimited amount, you can *"fiat"* 42½ cents of silver to be worth 100 cents, or one cent's worth of silver, or one cent's worth of paper. You can *"fiat"* a piece of bark or a wooden shingle . . . . just as well.—Mr. Newberry, H. R., May 17: *C. R.,* p. 1438/1.

1880 We still hear echocs of the old conflict, such as the virtues of *"fiat money."*—E. Kirke, "Life of Garfield," p. 30. (N. E. D.)

1882 I challenge you to show me a dollar of money that is not *fiat money*— I care not whether it be made of gold or silver or nickel or copper, or whether it be made of paper.—Mr. Chas. N. Brumm of Pa., H. R., May 16: *C. R.,* p. 303/2, App.

Fice, fiste, fyst, &c. A worthless dog. Southern.

1583 With falling woommanish hearelocks. Like *fiest hound* . . .—Stanyhust, "Æneid," p. 68.

1600 You see [her] busied about that little *foisting curre,* rubbing and combing him.—Hospitall of Incurable Fooles, p. 148.

1600 Goe a Theater, and heare a Queenes *Fice,* and he make hur laugh.— Thos. Nashe, "Sumners Last Will," C.

1606 My Ladies *foisting hound.*—John Day, "Ile of Gulls," D4.

1805 Bob Sample, one of the most popular A-double-L-part preachers in the country, who like a little *fice* or cur-dog would rail behind my back.—Lorenzo Dow, "Journal," Oct. 3 (1850), p. 113/2.

Field hand. A darky doing agricultural work. [1835-1856.]

1862 [The slaves whom we propose to liberate] are the house servants and the *field hands* of those who now claim to be their owners.—Mr. James Harlan of Ia., U. S. Senate, March 25: *C. G.,* p. 1357/3.

1879 The *field hand* on the large plantation, who had no contact with the white owner or his family, remained the same, awkward, ignorant, and stupid from the day of his birth almost to the day of his death.—Mr. B. B. Ellis of Ala., H. R., Apr. 25: *C. R.,* p. 931/1.

Fieldman. A member of a field party; one who works in the open, especially in surveying.

1903 The *fieldmen* of the Geological Survey have been the pioneer surveyors of the natural features of the vast regions which constitute half the continent.—*Sci. Amer. Supp.*, p. 22, 647. (Century Dict.)

Fifty-four Forty or Fight. The motto of the war party of 1846, with reference to the Oregon question. '[1846-1854.]

1868 Let us be bold and do something that is here (*sic*) to *54° 40" or fight* on this subject.—Mr. Roscoe Conkling of N. Y., U. S. Senate, March 9: *C. R.*, p. 1754/1.

Fighting chance. A possibility of success. Colloquial.

1894 [The manufacturer] may be put to hard struggle, but he can not be beaten out of hand. He will have a *fighting chance.*—Mr. Thos. B. Reed of Me., H. R., Feb. 1: *C. R.*, p. 1786/1.

Fight it out on this line. A famous expression used by General Grant, which passed into common use. The phrase occurs in his dispatch to Secretary Seward, after the battle of Spottsylvania, May 11, 1864. [1910.]

1864 [On the Montana question] I adopt the language of our lieutenant general in the field, "I will *fight on this line* to the end, even if it takes all summer."—Mr. Sumner of Mass., U. S. Senate, May 19: *C. G.*, p. 2351/1.

1864 According to the modest but electric words of General Grant, he is to "*fight it out on this line* if it takes all summer."—Mr. Morrill of Vt., H. R., June 2: *Id.*, p. 2672/2.

1870 We will "*fight it out upon this line,*" if it takes all night.—Mr. C. A. Eldridge of Wisc., H. R., June 4: *Id.*, p. 4097/2.

1871 The Republican party is under . . . obligations which it has neither the will nor the power to ignore, "*to fight it out on this line,*" if it takes another decade.—Mr. H. W. Bany of Miss., H. R., Apr. 5: *Id.*, p. 267/2, App.

1872 I propose to vex the ear of this House till I touch its heart, if, in the language of a once popular but now somewhat disparaged individual, it takes not only "*all summer,*" but the ensuing winter besides.—Mr. John Ritchie of Md., H. R., Apr. 13: *Id.*, p. 2405/3.

Figure. To calculate. The N. E. D. cites Hugh Miller (1854) for the same verb used intransitively.

1865 I have not *figured* the number of square miles that there will be.—Mr. W. M. Stewart of Nev., U. S. Senate, Feb. 9: *C. G.*, p. 671/3.

1913 The mastodon is estimated to have been eleven feet high at the shoulder. Yale men *figure* that the bones have lain where found from 5,000 to 20,000 years.—*N. Y. Evening Post,* Sept. 8, p. 1/6.

File-mark. A mark put on a legal document when it is filed. **File-mark, v.** To mark on such a document the date, &c., of filing.

1871 The *file marks* of the mandate addressed by the supreme court of Columbia were erased. . . . . The *file marks* and indorsements on the final order of said district court were erased.—Mr. S. S. Marshall of Ill., H. R., Feb. 20: *C. G.*, p. 1449/3.

Filers. Persons filing claims for the allotment to them of government land.

1893 The purchase money was tendered by each one of these *filers*. . . . . I am personally acquainted with these *filers.*—Testimony cited in *C. R.,* Feb. 11, pp. 1469-70.

Filibuster. A freebooter, a marauder. [1835-1869.] As a verb, to rob.

1857 Mr. R. A. Proctor in "Knowledge," 1887, p. 113/2, quotes a letter of Gen. Henningsen to Senator Toombs of Ga., as follows: "What was Moses but a *filibuster,* whose mission was to dispossess tribes retrograding? . . . . What were the Normans from whom the sovereigns of Great Britain affect to derive their descent, . . but *filibusters?* What the Pilgrim Fathers but *filibusters?* What State, what territory in this Union has not been *filibustered* from the Indians, or purchased from those who had *filibustered* it? Have ever five years elapsed . . . since the landing of the Pilgrim Fathers, that some of the Monarchies of Europe have not, somewhere, been *filibustering* something?"

1870 The duty of opposition to *filibustering* has been admitted by every President. Washington encountered the efforts of Genet and the French revolutionists; John Adams, the projects of Miranda; Jefferson, the schemes of Aaron Burr.—Message of President U. S. Grant, June 13: *C. G.,* p. 4401/1.

Filibuster. An act of filibustering. (Political.)

1890 A *filibuster* was indulged in, which lasted . . . for nine continuous calendar days, only one or two recesses having occurred.—Mr. L. E. Payson of Ill., H. R., Feb. 11: *C. R.,* p. 1217/1.

Filibustering (in politics). Wasting time in the legislature, and obstructing progress. [1853-1889.]

1862 These two old men [Messrs. Mason and Slidell] were for many years Senators. One was the author of the fugitive slave bill, and the other was the chief author of the *fillibustering* system which has disgraced our national name and disturbed our national peace.—Mr. Charles Sumner of Mass., U. S. Senate, Jan. 9: *C. G.,* p. 241/1.

1863 I owe it in justice to [Mr. B. F. Thomas] to say that he was not engaged in voting with these *filibustering* gentlemen.—Mr. Owen Lovejoy of Ill., H. R., Jan. 29: *Id.,* p. 607/3.

1863 [Mr. S. S. Cox's] friends *filibustered* all night in this hall.—Mr. Colfax of Ind., H. R., Feb. 20: *Id.,* p. 1154/1.

1867 Mr. John Sherman of Ohio:—They might perhaps [stave off a final vote] by *filibustering.* Mr. G. H. Williams of Ore.:—That is a possible thing, as we all know.—U. S. Senate, Feb. 15: *Id.,* p. 1369/2.

1867 A fair opportunity for debate ought to be allowed, and it is not *filibustering* when [members] vote against the call for the previous question.—Mr. T. A. Hendricks of Ind., U. S. Senate, Feb. 20: *Id.,* p. 1639/1.

1870 It is Saturday afternoon and we are *"filibustering"* without any bad blood or any unkind feeling. . . . We *"filibuster"* because the previous question has been demanded, cutting off amendments.—Mr. C. H. Eldridge of Wisc., H. R., Feb. 19: *Id.,* p. 1388/2.

1872 *Filibustering* has at least the merit of courageous resistance on the part of a minority to what they regard as an attempt under the forms of parliamentary proceeding to deprive the minority of its rights.—Mr. Eugene Casserly of Calif., U. S. Senate, May 21: *Id.,* p. 3733/2.

1875 I do not at all find fault with the minority when they *filibuster* against an attempt to force them to a vote without debate.—Mr. James A. Garfield of O., H. R., Feb. 1: *C. R.,* p. 893/2. [See the rest of the debate.]

1875 The very origin of *"filibustering"* was on the Kansas-Nebraska bill, and it was resorted to by the minority to defeat what has gone into history as a parliamentary fraud. . . . . Against that the minority called the yeas and nays one hundred and thirty-eight times. That was the origin, if I mistake not, of *"filibustering."* [This was in 1854.] —Mr. James G. Blaine of Me., H. R., Feb. 1: *C. R.,* p. 899/1.

1876 See CIVIL RIGHTS BILL.

1890 When I came into the House, thirty years ago, the usual practice of *filibustering,* as it is called, for the purpose of obtaining time and securing "second sober thought" in legislation, was for a gentleman to ask to be excused from voting, and then for another member to move that he be excused; and successive motions of that kind were piled upon each other and voted upon for days at a time.—Mr. W. S. Holman of Ind., H. R., Feb. 11: *C. R.,* p. 1211/1.

1892 While I have seen *filibustering* here, and participated in it, I do not regard it as an unmixed evil. I believe that, while *filibustering* has been sometimes resorted to when it should not have been, yet in the main more good than harm has resulted from it.—Mr. W. C. Oates of Ala., H. R., Jan. 29: *C. R.,* p. 684/1.

1892   *Filibustering* is always by a minority; and if it is wrong to *filibuster* for a great length of time, it is wrong to clothe the minority with the power to *filibuster* for any length of time.—Mr. W. D. Bynum of Ind., H. R., Feb. 2: *Id.,* p. 772/2.

Fill.   The opposite of an excavation; an embankment.   [1850-1884.]

1886   Here is a picture of a *"fill,"* an embankment 420 feet in length, the filling of which is composed of logs and brush, and nothing else.— Mr. L. E. Payson of Ill., H. R., Dec. 11: *C. R.,* p. 92/1.

Fill an order.   To supply what is required.   [1860-1891.]

1861   I do not intend that merchants shall send orders out and have them *filled* before this bill takes effect.—Mr. Charles Sumner of Mass., U. S. Senate, July 29: *C. G.,* p. 319/1.

1864   The contractor . . . . . did not get his contract with any view of ever *filling* it.—Mr. Schenck of O., H. R., June 28: *Id.,* p. 3356/1.

Filled cheese.   See ·quotation.

1896   [Latterly the dairying] industry has been much hampered . . . by the manufacture of a spurious imitation of cream cheese, called *"filled cheese."* . . . . By the use of a . . 'cream separator the butter fat is extracted from the milk, and manufactured into good creamery butter; then the skimmed milk is taken, and . . . . lard and neutral oils are forced into it, to take the place of the butter fat.   From this skimmed milk, so "filled" with lard and neutral oils, *"filled cheese"* is made . . . . The cost of producing a pound of *filled cheese* is about 3½ cents.— Mr. E. Sauerhering of Wisc., H. R., Apr. 10: *C. R.,* p. 3847/2.   [See the rest of the debate.]

1896   The principal part of the *filled cheese* is made out of lard, instead of out of cream or the produce of the cow.—Mr. John Sherman of O., U. S. Senate, May 23: *Id.,* p. 5605/1.   [See also p. 5715/1.]

Filler, Filling.   The tobacco used for the inside of cigars.

1864   Nearly all cigars are made of Connecticut-grown wrappers, and the best qualities filled with Cuba *filling.*—Mr. Grimes of Ia., U. S. Senate, June 3: *C. G.,* p. 2706/3.

1874   There is a tacit agreement among all the manufacturers that they will not give beyond so much for a certain class of *fillers* and a certain class of wrappers.—Mr. Thomas Whitehead of Va., H. R., Jan. 10: *C. R.,* p. 558/1.

1884   A cigar consists of three parts, the wrapper, the bunch, and the *filler.—Pall Mall Gazette,* May 17.   (N. E. D.)

1890   The leaf which makes *fillers* and binders for cigars comes mainly from Cuba, and the leaf which makes wrappers comes mainly from Sumatra.—Mr. W. E. Simonds of Conn., H. R., May 8: *C. R.,* p. 4340/1.

1890   There are three general classes of cigars made in this country, "the clear Havana," "the seed and Havana," and "the clear seed." The clear Havana is made entirely of Havana tobacco, wrapper and *filler.* The seed and Havana is made with the Havana *filler* and a domestic or any other wrapper than Havana.   The clear seed cigar is made of all domestic *filler* and all domestic or other inferior wrapper.   The last class includes [about two-thirds] of the cigars manufactured in this country.—Mr. Samuel Pasco of Fla., U. S. Senate, Aug. 27: *C. R.,* p. 9213/1.

Fills.   The shafts between which a horse is hitched to a vehicle; properly **thills.**

1845   If [Mr. Polk's] volitions were the other way, he could not follow them, any more than a dray horse can jump out of the *fills.*—D. Webster to Edward Everett, Feb. 26: "Private Corresp." (1857), II, 202.

Fill the bill. To meet all requirements; to come up to the mark. [1862-1889.]

1882 Mr. Ford . . . *filled the bill* today, to the best of his ability, objecting to legislation of any kind.—St. Louis *Globe-Democrat,* Dec. 27: see *C. R.,* p. 887/2.

1894 [The Puyallups] are an educated, self-reliant, self-respecting people, and *fill the bill* completely when you come to require an educated, cultured red man.—Mr. W. H. Doolittle of Wash., H. R., July 13: *Id.,* p. 6250/1.

1898 "Populism in its later manifestations is something worse than the vain and incoherent babbling of queer freaks and low demagogues." I do not know whether the Populists on this floor can *fill that invoice* or not.—Mr. C. H. Grosvenor of O., H. R., Apr. 21: *Id.,* p. 4172/1.

Fine as a fiddle. In excellent condition. [1811.]

1815 Why, I am as *fine as a fiddle,*—and e'en-a-most as musical tu.—David Humphreys, "The Yankey in England," p. 37. [See E'ENA'MOST.]

Fine-cut. A kind of tobacco. [1854.]

1863 The duty "on tobacco, cavendish, plug, twist, *fine-cut,* &c.," under the Act of March 3, was fifteen cents per pound.—See *C. G.,* June 3, 1864, p. 2707/3.

1864 Sometimes just as fine tobacco is used in cavendish as in *fine-cut.*— Mr. Clark of N. H., U. S. Senate: *C. G.,* p. 2708/2.

1878 Gentlemen of fortune can very well afford to smoke their high-priced cigars and to chew their *fine-cut* tobacco.—Mr. A. L. Pridemore of Va., H. R., June 5: *C. R.,* p. 4164/2.

Fine-haired. See **Hoodlum,** 1901.

Fip. A "five pence" or "fippenny bit." [1822-1858.]

1841 See YORK SHILLING.

1850 I haven't hardly a hair left to my hide, or a pewter *fip* in my pocket.— S. Judd, "Margaret," II, 7. (Century Dict.)

1851 [The barber] had already earned two *fips* and a quarter, and he now thought another levy would make an even half.—Wilmington (N. C.) *Commercial,* Feb. 18, p. 4/1.

Fire break. A space cleared to prevent the spread of a fire. [1885.]

1894 Thus could the larger weeds, which develop in gopher mounds, *fire breaks,* and similar places on the prairies, be destroyed.—Report on the Russian thistle, *C. R.,* July 31: p. 8047/2.

Firebug. An incendiary. [1872-1909.]

1899 [Kentucky] swarmed with cutthroats, robbers, thieves, *firebugs,* and malefactors of every degree.—Mr. Champ Clark of Mo., H. R., Feb. 4: *C. R.,* p. 1468/1.

1912 *Firebugs* made a bold attempt to burn two residences in Westfield [N. Y.], a few nights ago.—*Living Church,* Aug. 31, p. 631/3.

Fire eater. A swaggerer; a braggadocio. The fire eaters of South Carolina and Georgia precipitated the Civil War. [1847-1910.]

1866 There were men in the southern States, known as *fire-eaters,* disturbers of the peace.—Mr. T. A. Hendricks of Ind., U. S. Senate, Jan. 23: *C. G.,* p. 368/2.

1867 In 1860 the *fire-eaters* of the South played smash, nominated Breckenridge, and elected Lincoln.—Mr. T. E. Noell of Mo., H. R., Feb. 12: *Id.,* p. 106/2, App.

Fire-froth. Ebulliency. A nonce-word.

1864 Out of the very burning and *fire-froth* of sectionalism springs the ideal of a new nation.—Mr. B. G. Brown of Mo., U. S. Senate, March 8: *C. G.,* p. 987/2.

Fire out. To eject; to expel. See *N. & Q.,* 10 S, viii, 37, 454. [1885-1887.]

1680 *Fire* Calvin and his nest of upstarts *out.*—John Oldham, Satire III.

Fire water. A term for strong liquor, attributed to the North American Indians.

1826 [They] taught him to drink the *fire water,* and he became a rascal.— J. F. Cooper, "Last of the Mohicans," ch. xi. (N. E. D.)

1849 Never taste of the strong *fire water.*—J. G. Whittier, 'Margaret Smith's Journal' (1809), "Prose Works," I, *32.* (N. E. D.)

1895 When you strike a full-blooded Indian, you generally strike an orderly, honest man, unless his brain is inflamed by *"fire water,"* as they call it,—whisky.—Mr. John S. Little of Ark., H. R., Jan. 15: *C. R.,* p. 1002/2.

First floor. The ground floor.

1663 The *first Floore* of a building should not lye level with the ground.— Sir B. Gerbier, "Counsel and Advise to all Builders," p. 101. (N. E. D.)

First-termer. One who is in for a first term.

1888 He was going upon the idea . . . . that a *first-termer* has not much standing in this House.—Mr. Cobb, H. R., May 25: *C. R.,* p. 4634/2.

Fish-cultural. Engaged or concerned in the culture of fishes.

1872 (Title.) Transactions of the American *Fish Cultural* Association.— (N. E. D.)

1897 I believe that in our part of the country *fish-cultural* stations are important . . . . We have a large sponge interest, and it is important that we should have a *fish-cultural* station in Fla.—Mr. Samuel Pasco of Fla., U. S. Senate, July 8: *C. R.,* p. 2464/1.

Fish hatchery. A place for hatching eggs.

1897 A bill granting to the State of Washington certain lands for the purpose of a *fish hatchery.*—*C. R.,* Jan. 8, p. 602/2.

Fish or cut bait. To adopt a definite course on this side or that. Not in the dictionaries.

1876 Now I want you gentlemen on the other side of the House to *"fish or cut bait."*—Mr. J. G. Cannon of Ill., H. R., Aug. 5: *C. R.,* p. 5226/1.

1882 This company should be made either *to fish or cut bait.* . . . The company can take just which horn of [the] dilemma it likes best.— Mr. John A. Anderson of Kan., H. R., Feb. 3: *C. R.,* p. 6/1, App.

1886 *"Fish or cut bait."* Subtitle in a speech by Mr. J. A. Anderson of Kansas, H. R., Apr. 1: in which he says, "The company must either perform its duty as a carrier, or it must go out of the business."— *C. R.,* p. 3017/1.

Fish story. An improbable tale; a cock-and-bull story. [1819-1857.]

1831 One is told in the *Wellsborough* (Pa.) *Phoenix,* and reprinted in *The Georgian* (Savannah), June 15, p. 2/5.

Fist, make a. To make a success, good or bad. [1834-1880.]

1869 I am afraid that the poor old lawyer . . . would *make but a bad fist of it* in either of those avocations.—Mr. Robert C. Schenck of O., H. R., Feb. 19: *C. G.,* p. 1388/2.

Five-twenties. Bonds issued by the U. S. in 1862, '64, and '65: redeemable after 5 years from date of issue, and payable at the end of 20 years.

1868 The Ten-Forty bonds have stood in the market at almost precisely the same figure as the *Five-Twenty* bonds.—*The Nation* (N. Y.), V, 296. (Century Dict.)

1868 We have the right to pay our debts, the *five-twenties* as they are called, in greenbacks, today or whenever they shall fall due.—Mr. Chas A. Eldridge of Wisc., H. R., July 21: *C. G.,* p. 4300/3.

1895 These fellows are like the Irishman when he heard of the first bonds issued, and said to his brother: "Jimmie, how about these bonds, the *foive-twinties,* the *siven-thirties,* and the *tin-forties?*" Jimmie says: "It is this way: The poor laboring mon hes to rise up at 5.20 in the marnin' an' worruk until 7.30 in the avenin', so that the bond holder can lie abid until 10.40 in the forenoon."—Mr. Jerry Simpson of Kan., H. R., Feb. 5: *C. R.,* p. 195/2, App.

Fix. To arrange, to place, to set right, to mend, to dress, to settle; a word of wide import. [1708-1870.]

1845 See SHAW.

1880 The first Indian who learned to raise corn in this country, after he had raised his crop under instructions of a white agriculturist, came to the white man and said: "I want to know how to *fix* this corn so I can eat it out of a bottle like the white man."—Mr. Hiram Price of Ia., H. R., May 1: *C. R.,* p. 2933/1.

Fixed. Prepared; in a position to do a stated thing.

1803 [The advertiser] is well *fixed* for heaving vessels down, &c.—*Georgia Republican,* May 19, p. 1/3.

Fixed fact. A matter admitting of no discussion. [1842-1866.]

1860 There is but one way, and that is to let the southern States go out of the Union; and when the northern people see that that is a *fixed fact,* .... a sound state of opinion may possibly arise.—Mr. Iverson of Ga., U. S. Senate, Dec. 11: *C. G.,* p. 50/1.

1861 I propose .... to recognize the existence of sections as a *fixed fact,* which can no longer be denied or suppressed.—Mr. Clement L. Vallandigham of O., H. R., Feb. 20: *Id.,* p. 241/1, App.

1864 [Mr. Davis] has occupied three long hours in running around it, in climbing over it, in crawling under it; but there stands the proposition, a *fixed fact.*—Mr. Henry Wilson of Mass., U. S. Senate, Jan. 13: *Id.,* p. 184/1.

1864 There are some things in this world which we Yankees have designated by the vigorous word "fixed," or what the French, in their philosophic phrase, call "fait accompli." Sir, the abolition of slavery is a *fixed fact,*" a fact accomplished—I must accept it.—Mr. Brooks of N. Y., H. R., Feb. 19: *Id.,* p. 762/1.

1867 The work of reconstruction is going on; its success is a certainty, a *fixed fact.*—Mr. Henry Wilson of Mass., U. S. Senate, Dec. 10: *Id.,* p. 99/2.

1870 [The enactments secured by the Republican party] are achieved results; they are *"fixed facts."* Men may dash their heads against them in the future, as they have in the past, but they will stand the shock.—The same, Feb. 25: *Id.,* p. 1562/1.

1882 Gentlemen will vote for this commission. I know it. The commission is a *fixed fact.* You have the men picked out.—Mr. S. S. Cox of N. Y., H. R., May 6: *C. R.,* p. 3676/1.

1890 The Long Bridge [at Washington] is there as a *fixed fact,* and was there long before the tracks of this railroad were laid.—Mr. Chas. O'Neill of Pa., H. R., June 23: *Id.,* p. 6392/2.

Fix up. To arrange, to patch clumsily together.

1861 There are too many .... who are overanxious, in the quaint language of the day, to *"fix up"* something to save the Union.—Mr. Thomas Ruffin of N. C., H. R., Feb. 20: *C. G.,* p. 226/1, App.

1866 When you have to *fix up* a Constitution to include some things and exclude others, for partisan purposes, you do find difficulties of phraseology. It cannot be made easy.—Mr. Thomas A. Hendricks of Ind., U. S. Senate, June 8: *Id.,* p. 3040/1.

Fix up. To arrange by conspiracy.

1896 They do not all swear to the same thing. If they did, I would think it was *fixed up.*—Mr. R. Z. Linney of N. C., H. R., June 9: *C. R.,* p. 6341/1.

Fizzle. A failure. [1847-1908.]

1872 The French arms case [San Domingo] is the greatest *fizzle,* over which numerous windy speeches were made, that the world ever knew. —Mr. Jesse H. Moore of Ill., H. R., Apr. 6: *C. G.,* p. 2229/3.

Flank. To escape, especially to evade military duty. [1866-1879.]

1865 I asked the Captain if he had Mr. Toombs. "No," he replied, "Mr. Toombs *flanked* us."—Diary of Alex. H. Stephens (1880), p. 103.

1888 These lumber operators never undertake to go to Canada and contract for the importation of Canadian laborers; but by means of deceptive advertisements they get them into the country, and thus *"flank"* the law, which is designed to keep such laborers out.—Mr. M. H. Ford of Mich., H. R., June 6: *C. R.*, p. 4966/1.

Flanker. One who outwits an opponent or outflanks an enemy.

1868 See GROUND AND LOFTY TUMBLING.

Flapdoodle. Empty talk, foolishness. [1862-1884.]

1897 Talk of this kind . . . . is mere *flapdoodle,* such as is fit only to be doled out to fools and idiots.—Mr. G. L. Johnson of Calif., H. R., Jan. 5: *C. R.*, p. 471/1.

Flat. See quotation.

1870 Ordinarily, I am told, [the three per cent certificates] in the N. Y. market have been sold *"flat,"* in the language of Wall Street: that is to say, without taking the interest into account. Where the interest was nearly due, it has sometimes been accounted for in the transaction, but generally not.—Mr. Oliver P. Morton of Ind., U. S. Senate, Jan. 25: *C. G.*, p. 733/2.

Flat. A boat with a flat bottom and square ends, used especially in shallow waters. (Webster.)

1791 Wanted to Purchase a Good *Flat,* That will carry from 70 to 80 Hogsheads Tobacco, for which prompt payment will be made Either in Cash or Negroes.—*Augusta* (Ga.) *Chronicle,* July 2, p. 4/2.

Flatfooted. Positive and uncompromising. [1846-1858.]

1913 Mr. Dan Hanna's Cleveland *Leader* has come out *flatfooted* for an amalgamation of Republicans and Progressives.—*N. Y. Evening Post,* May 5, p. 4/7.

Flathead. A snake which flattens its head, as a species of *Heterodon.* (Century Dict.)

1888 The blow-snake of Illinois is variously known in other localities as hog-nose, *flat-head,* viper, and puff-adder.—Bergen in *Pop. Sci. Monthly,* xxxiii, 660.

Flatman. The navigator of a flatboat, especially on the Ohio and Mississippi rivers. (Century Dict.)

Flatwoods. "1. A local name in Ohio for valleys formerly occupied by rivers, but now flats and covered with woods. 2. In Alabama, especially in the Coosa valley, a type of land consisting of an impervious clay derived from the Cambrian shales, supporting a dense growth of dwarf oaks, pines," &c. (Century Dict.)

Flicker-tail. 1. The gopher (Western). 2. An epithet sometimes applied to the State of North Dakota. (Century Dict.)

Flimflam. To humbug, to cheat. Hence flimflammer.

1660 None but Fools will by the flood of Words be *flim-flam'd* into.—Fisher, "Rustick's Alarm" (1679), p. 307. (N. E. D.)

1890 [Sent to jail] for *flimflaming* a . . . . saloon-keeper out of some money.—*Columbus* (O.) *Dispatch,* July 26. (N. E. D.)

1894 The New York *flimflammers* and green goods men . . are still out of the clutches of the United Secret Service.—*Id.,* Jan. 31. (N. E. D.)

1899 Senator Hale thinks that Columbia has been *flimflammed,* and that Uncle Sam has bought a gold brick in the Philippines.—Dunkirk (N. Y.,) paper, cited in *C. R.,* Jan. 26: p. 1065/1.

Flink. Originally a variant of *flinch.*

1583 Antenor was habil, from Greekish coompanie *flinking,* Too passe through Greceland.—Stanyhurst, "Æneid," p. 7.

Flitters. Tatters. [1789-1829.]

1863 We have got to fight this war out, or the northern part of the country, the loyal States, will go into *flitters* and anarchy.—Mr. Daniel Clark of N. H., U. S. Senate, Feb. 23: *C. G.,* p. 1197/1.

Float. A certificate preliminary to a purchase of government land. [1837-1841.]

1841 We have wisely determined to put down forever the practice of granting what are called *"floats,"* which was certainly productive of many and great [land] frauds.—Mr. James Buchanan, U. S. Senate, Jan. 5: "Works" (1908), IV, 345.

Floater. An uncertain, fluctuating voter. In Mississippi and Tennessee, a representative in the State legislature, who may be elected indifferently from either of two or more counties. (Century Dict.)

1888 [President Jackson, in his farewell address,] seems to have had in contemplation the Dudley scheme of purchasing *floaters* in "blocks of five" in the doubtful State of Indiana.—Mr. S. Z. Landes of Ill., H. R., Dec. 12: *C. R..* p. 8/1, App. [See BLOCKS OF FIVE.]

1897 It is perhaps unnecessary to explain that in Kentucky the word *"floater"* means vote seller.—Mr. J. M. Kendall of Ky., H. R., Feb. 18: *Id.,* p. 52/2, App.

Floater. A vagrant. [1878.]

1890 Those loose and worthless ravelings of human life, known as *"floaters."* —Mr. D. W. Voorhees of Ind., U. S. Senate, Jan. 8: *C. R.,* p. 454/2.

1897 This man is a soldier of fortune; . . . He is what we used to term in the army a *floater,* likely to turn up anywhere where it was safe to be. —Mr. E. F. Loud of Calif., H. R., Feb. 5: *Id.,* p. 1583/1.

Floater. A floating island. (Louisiana.)

1903 Occasionally some of the land is torn away, and becomes an island. Such islands are known as *flottants* or *floaters,* by the the Creoles, and are among the most picturesque sights of these La. lakes, sailing upon them, borne hither and thither by the winds or currents.—*Sci. Amer. Supp.,* p. 22, 9111. (Century Dict.)

Floodwood. Driftwood on a river. [1822-1860.]

1864 Leaders who aspire to control the country, as drifting *floodwood* tells the course of the stream.—Mr. Grinnell of Ia., H. R., March 5: *C. G.,* p. 955/2.

1866 Modern Democracy is but the *floodwood* that maddens the rushing waters, but cannot stay the flood.—Mr. Wm. M. Stewart of Nev., U. S. Senate, May 24: *Id.,* p. 2803/1.

1878 These irregular troops were what many years ago, when I was a boy in the State of New York, were called *"flood-wood."*—Mr. Angus Cameron of Wisc., U. S. Senate, March 11: *C. R.,* p. 1634/1.

Floor. The right to speak. [1774-1888.]

1861 The phrases, assigning *the floor,* being entitled to it, having it, obtaining it, resuming it, taking it, and yielding it, occur in a debate in the H. R., Jan. 22: *C. G.,* p. 512.

Floor leader. A manager of parliamentary debates.

1899 Congress has witnessed few more successful *floor leaders* than Mr. Dingley.—Mr. E. C. Burleigh of Me., H. R., Feb. 11: *C. R.,* p. 1764/2.

Floorwalker. One who walks about in a large retail store as an overseer and director. (Webster.) [1884.]

1911 "Am I required to exchange wedding gifts in the department from which they were purchased?" Not at all," said the *floorwalker.* "Thank you. I would like to exchange a rose jar for a frying pan."— *Washington Herald,* December.

Flouring mill. A mill for grinding wheat into flour. (Bartlett, 1859.)

1876 Is not a *flouring mill,* situated in an enemy's country, turning out flour for the enemy, contraband in that sense in which a wagon-train loaded with that flour is contraband?—Mr. Roscoe Conkling of N. Y., U. S. Senate, July 17: *C. R.,* p. 4651/1.

1888 The way from the mealing-stone to the *flouring-mill* is long.— *American Anthropologist,* p. 307. (N. E. D.)

Flume. A channel, natural or artificial, in which water flows rapidly. [1792-1878.]

1869 In mining operations there is a necessity for timber to support tunnels, for building mills, for *flumes,* and for blocks for the *flumes.*—Mr. Aaron A. Sargent of Calif., H. R., Dec. 22: *C. G.,* p. 318/2.

Flume, v. To carry by a flume; to build a flume.

1903 The original scheme was to develop the Coquitlam by *fluming* along the steep hillside a distance of about seven miles.—*Electric World,* p. 837. (Century Dict.)

Flurry. The death struggle of a whale. [1823-1849.]

1888 A mere makeshift, a fraudulent pretense, a sham assumed in the face of a dire emergency, a tub thrown to a whale in a *flurry.*—Mr. D. W. Voorhees of Ind., U. S. Senate, Dec. 19: *C. R.,* p. 344/1.

Flurry. A commercial panic.

1893 The *flurry* began, and the depositors demanded their money . . . . When this *flurry* came, the depositors became alarmed about the safety of their deposits.—Mr. M. C. Butler of S. C., U. S. Senate, Oct. 4: *C. R.,* p. 2110/1.

Flutter mill. A flour mill.(?)

1898 See Dope.

Fly. An appendage to a parliamentary act.

1870 [This provision] was put in as a *"fly"* in the act of 1869. It was not intended to mean anything there, but the people have accepted it to mean something, and have dealt with it as meaning something.—Mr. B. F. Butler of Mass., H. R., July 1: *C. G.,* p. 5062/1.

Flyer. A small venture in stocks, on the chance of a rise. [1870-1888.]

1879 The father of a family who teaches his sons to come late to breakfast, to study and work short hours, . . . to take *flyers* at the stock exchange . . . . will raise a family of deadbeats who will need and clamor for fiat money, &c.—Mr. S. B. Chittenden of N. Y., H. R., May 8: *C. R.,* p. 1171/1.

1893 A *"flyer"* is a small venture for amusement as well as profit.—Mr. Marriott Brosius of Pa., H. R., March 1: *Id.,* p. 72/1, App.

Flyer or **Flier.** A small handbill.

1888 [My opponent] placed upon every doorstep of every house in [the city of Saginaw] a *flyer,* "Do not vote for Tim Tarsney: he is a free-trader."—Mr. T. E. Tarsney of Mich., H. R., June 6: *C. R.,* p. 4966/2.

1889 Inserting gaily-colored advertising *fliers* in the body of the magazine. —*Literary World* (Boston), Dec. 21, p. 485/2. (N. E. D.)

1895 I have characterized [this paper] as a circular, a political *flyer,* sent out as an appeal to the people against the vote of Congress.—Mr. John T. Morgan of Ala., U. S. Senate, Dec. 9: *C. R.,* p. 75/1.

Fly off the handle. To go off in a great rage or great excitement. [1825-1888.]

1871 Mr. Beck:—I do not want the gentleman to *fly off the handle.* Mr. Stevenson:—But I want to fly on to the handle, and work with the gentleman.—H. R., March 14: *C. G.,* p. 102/2.

Fly round. To proceed quickly, to bestir oneself. [1833-1871.]

1851 Old 'ooman, *fly around,* git somethin' for the Squire and Dick to eat.— "Widow Rugby's Husband," &c., p. 44. (N. E. D.)

Fly round loose. To be easily seized or obtained.

1871 This stock must have been *flying round pretty loose* not to be better conserved.—Mr. A. A. Sargent of Calif., H. R., Feb. 20: *C. G.,* p. 1444/2. [Lie around loose?]

Fly time. The season when flies annoy cattle. [1706-1858.]

1868 As uncomfortable as that famous stump-tailed bull in *fly time.*—Mr. Ignatius Donnelly of Minn.. H. R., May 2: *C. G..* p. 2351/3.

Fly to pieces. To get in a violent rage.

1868 I saw Mr. Callaway, who *flew all to pieces* at me.—Testimony before a select committee: *C. G.,* Feb. 20, p. 1294/3.

Fogy ration. See quotation.

1879 The meaning of [the bill] then is that the officer is to have pay allowed him, computing all the time of service while in the Army, ... in addition to what is called the *fogy ration,* or longevity ration?— Mr. John A. Logan of Ill., U. S. Senate, Apr. 25: *C. R.,* p. 907/2.

1881 Hamersley, "Naval Encycl." (N. E. D.)

Folder. A folding-up sheet or map.

1887 The Fitchburg Railroad has just issued a local *folder* corrected to July 5. It [contains] well-arranged time-tables, a good map, &c.— *The Congregationalist,* July 14. (Century Dict.)

1889 The time-table sheets or *folders,* which every company must keep on hand at its stations.—*Scribner's Mag.,* p. 219/1. (N. E. D.)

1899 Mr. Loud:—Has the gentleman all the *folders* in this report? Mr. Odell:—There are four cases.—H. R., Jan. 24: *C. R.,* p. 997/2.

Folder. One employed to fold papers; also a mechanical device for the same work.

1837 Women are employed . . . as compositors, as well as *folders* and stitchers.—Harriet Martineau, "Soc. Amer.," III, 148. (N. E. D.)

1886 The press is a new Hoe perfecting machine, with a *folder* attached. —*N. Y. Herald,* Oct. 27, p. 6/3. (N. E. D.)

1899 This House should determine how many *folders* are necessary, and they should be put on the *folders'* roll. ... [One man] appearing on the roll as a *folder,* comes to us asking pay as a bookkeeper. And applications are made for additional folders to do the work, possibly .... these gentlemen . . . . are too gentlemanly, too aristocratic perhaps, to perform the duties of a *folder.*—Mr. E. F. Loud of Calif., H. R., Jan. 24: *C. R.,* p. 998/1.

Folks. Scottish. Respectable people in general. [1840-1867.]

1885 The right to sell the right to transport a poodle or a parrot, a monkey, a dude, or a donkey, implies the kindred right to carry *folks* at a corresponding increase of rate.—Mr. W. J. Green of N. C., H. R., Jan. 7: *C. R.,* p. 529/2.

Food-fishes. Those used for food.

1875 A good many States have already established a system for the introduction of *food-fishes.* We have such a system in Ohio.—Mr. John Q. Smith of O., H. R., Feb. 26: *C. R.,* p. 1804/1.

Fool. Foolish. O.E., now Sc. and dial., N. E. D.

1596 The *foole* multitude that choose by show.—Merchant of Venice, II, 9 (1623).

1805 I addressed a large congregation on Solomon's irony, in which I showed the contrast of a gentleman and a *fool* deist.—Lorenzo Dow, "Journal," March 16 (1850), p. 105/1.

1897 Mr. Stewart [to Mr. Vilas]:—If you had availed yourselves of the information, you would not have given the *fool* votes you did.—U. S. Senate, Jan. 21: *C. R.,* p. 1018/2.

Fool-fish. A kind of plaice, *Liopsetta putnami*: so called from the readiness with which it takes any bait. (Century Dict.)

1842 Our fishermen apply to it [*Monocanthus broccus*] the whimsical name of *fool-fish,* in allusion to . . its absurd mode of swimming.—DeKay, "Nat. Hist. of N. Y.," iv 335. (N. E. D.)

1888 The *Pleuronectes glaber,* which is called *fool-fish* at Salem. because they are easily decoyed.—"Riverside Nat. Hist.," III. 279. (N. E. D.)

Fool-killer. An imaginary person authorized to kill fools.

1863 Only a very small part of those in the galleries take part in these disturbances. The *fool-killer* will take care of them.—Mr. S. S. Cox of O., H. R., Feb. 23: *C. G.,* p. 172/2, App.

1888 Now and then Niagara has ably assisted the *fool-killer* by knocking out gentlemen who bid for fame by going over the Falls in a barrel.— *N. Y. Tribune,* Dec. 23. (Century Dict.)

Fool's hill. A fool's paradise.

1882 England . . . got upon the *"fool's hill"* of tariff protection, and there remained [for some time].—Mr. Townsend of O., H. R., Apr. 12: *C. R.,* p. 2825/2.

Footgear. Boots and shoes.

1872 Then, except the matter of gloves and mittens, it is *footgear* only that is made of kip skins?—Mr. Roscoe Conkling of N. Y., U. S. Senate, May 27: *C. G.,* p. 3917/1.

Foothill. A hill near the foot of a mountain range. [1873-1879.]

1873 [Mr. Sutro] saw at a glance that if a tunnel could be run through the mountains from the *foothills* seven miles distant, ... it would, &c.— Mr. Merriam of N. Y., H. R., Feb. 21: *C. G.,* p. 1595/2.

1884 In the State of California west of the Mohave Desert are valleys and *foothills* . . . . containing fine bodies of land.—Mr. P. B. Plumb of Kan., U. S. Senate, June 27: *C. R.,* p. 5682/2.

1886 [The table-lands extend] back from the Columbia River to the *foot-hills* of the Cascade Range, the Blue Mountains, and the Bitter Root Mountains.—Mr. Joseph N. Dolph of Ore., U. S. Senate, Apr. 1: *Id.,* p. 2990/2.

1888 In the State of California . . . . . the riparian proprietors passed up into the *foothills* of the mountains and commenced to dam the waters. —Mr. J. B. Morgan of Miss., U. S. Senate, July 30: *Id.,* p. 7019/1.

1888 You go on down the *foothills* of the Appalachian range, upon that bench of land that lies between that range and the South Atlantic Ocean, and you will find it a continuous cotton country until you come to Chattanooga in Tennessee.—Mr. J. T. Morgan of Ala., U. S. Senate, Dec. 12: *Id.,* p. 182/2.

Footstool (God's). The earth. [1821-1891.]

1861 They deserve expatriation from this the cushioned part of *God's foot-stool* given in high trust to their keeping.—Mr. S. S. Cox of O., H. R., Dec. 17: *C. G.,* p. 121/2.

1863 [Mr. Vallandigham of Ohio] is the last man *on this footstool* that I would want to have any wrangle with.—Mr. John A. Bingham of O., H. R., Feb. 23: *Id.,* p. 1227/2.

1866 I pretend to be as much a man as any on this part of *God's footstool.* —Mr. Ebenezer Dumont of Ind., H. R., June 5: *C. G.,* p. 2976/2.

1870 For one, I will not cease in this work until the life of the humblest individual who walks on *God's footstool* is as safe in Georgia, is as safe in Tennessee, is as safe in North Carolina, as it is in Iowa or New York.—Mr. J. M. Thayer of Neb., U. S. Senate, March 21: *Id.,* p. 2093/2.

1870 Who gave warrant to any man or party to beat out [Chinamen's] brains, . . . to deny them asylum, or to live on *God's footstool*?—Mr. A. A. Sargent of Calif., H. R., Apr. 8: *Id.,* p. 2531/1.

1874 [This] means more than your greenbacks and more than your gold. It means the only place [these early settlers] have on *God's footstool* to live.—Mr. John A. Kasson of Ia., H. R., June 16: *C. R.,* p. 5058/2.

1876 It is denied that [the money paid under the Geneva award] belongs to anybody upon *God's footstool.*—Mr. O. D. Conger of Mich., H. R., June 20: *Id.,* p. 4260/2.

1882 A vast region as desolate, as uninhabited, as uninhabitable as any region on *God's footstool.*—The same, July 10: *Id.,* p. 5832/2.

1884　It would be difficult indeed to find on *God's footstool* a more desolate region than these mountain tops. . . . It would take a ten-acre range to fatten a grasshopper.—Mr. Lewis Beach of N. Y., H. R., June 25: *Id.,* p. 342/1-2, App.

1894　It is greatly to be regretted that a system of taxation, which concerns the people of the greatest and grandest nation *on the footstool,* is to be formulated at the behests of a party caucus.—Mr. H. H. Powers of Vt., H. R., Jan. 15: *Id.,* p. 840/2.

1896　I do not believe in counterfeits anywhere. . . . I think that each entity upon *the Lord's footstool* should stand upon its own merits.—Mr. J. G. Cannon of Ill., H. R., Apr. 11: *Id.,* p. 3869/1.

1900　[This Republic] has done more toward the advancement of correct principles and the eradication of evil ones, than any other nation upon the *footstool.*—Mr. D. A. De Armond of Mo., H. R., Feb. 27: *Id.,* p. 95/2, App.

Foot the bill. To pay the account. [1844-1862.]

1861　It astonished me beyond measure to find that Uncle Sam *footed the bill.*—Mr. John P. Hale of N. H., U. S. Senate, Dec. 4: *C. G.,* p. 10/3.

1864　"Uncle Sam" is not the ultimate party *to foot all the bills.*—Mr. Howard of Mich., U. S. Senate, May 19: *Id.,* p. 2354/2.

1866　When the manufactured article reaches the poor man in the distant West, who has to buy a coat, he *foots the bill* for all this taxation.—Mr. John Hogan of Mo., H. R., March 7: *Id.,* p. 1248/2.

1866　Unless [the colonel] is willing to *foot the bill* himself, he has no business to have his family tagging on his heels. He has no right to billet them on the Government.—Mr. Ebenezer Dumont of Ind., H. R., June 4: *Id.,* p. 2953/3.

1866　This is what we are to say to the people who *foot the bill,* the hard-handed yeomanry of the country who furnish the money.—The same, p. 2956/1.

1867　Gentlemen smile at this thing; but perhaps they will smile out of the other corner of the mouth when they come to *foot the bills.*—Mr. James R. Doolittle of Wisc., U. S. Senate, Feb. 23: *Id.,* p. 1807/2.

1874　In the West we believe in the Fourth of July, and always celebrate it; but, in our homely phrase, *"we foot our own bills."*—Mr. L. B. Gunckel of O., H. R., May 6: *C. R.,* p. 3642/2.

1892　As the citizens of Washington are to reap the benefits arising from the encampment, let Washington *foot the bills.*—Mr. A. J. Cummings of N. Y., H. R., June 30: *Id.,* p. 5689/1.

Foot-washing Baptists. A sect in the South.

1872　*Q.* You yourself were once a Methodist preacher, were you not?
Ans. I was.
Q. You belonged to the Southern Methodist Church?
Ans. I belong now to the *Foot-washing Baptists*—the simplest form of the Christian faith.—Testimony of Augustus R. Wright of Ga., *C. G.,* May 30, p. 478/3, App.

Footwear. Boots, shoes, slippers, &c.

Force Bill, The. See quotation.

1872　In 1832 we were upon the brink of civil war. South Carolina had nullified the tariff acts, and was in arms for the purpose of resisting the Federal law. At that time Mr. Clay made up his mind that, in order to preserve the Union and avoid civil strife, it would be a wise measure to abolish the tariff and to accompany that abolition by what was called *"the force bill."* In other words, to use his own language, he proposed in the tariff bill to hold out the olive branch of peace to South Carolina, and in *"the force bill"* to hold out the sword.—Mr. James Brooks of N. Y., H. R., Apr. 2: *C. G.,* p. 2110/1.

1890　See Honey-fugle.

1893 [Under certain conditions] the infamous and odious *"force bill"* could be lawfully enacted, if the party in power should deem it expedient.— Mr. J. C. McDearmon of Tenn., H. R., Oct. 7: *C. R.,* p. 217/1, App.

1893 The so-called *"force-bill"* has been consigned to its political grave.— Mr. H. U. Johnson of Ind., H. R., Feb. 28: *Id.,* p. 2300/1.

1895 I call to mind the leading Republican paper of the Miss. Valley, the *Globe-Democrat* of St. Louis, which . . . denounced the *force bill,* and declared that it would ruin the Republican party to enact it.—Mr. G. G. Vest of Mo., U. S. Senate, Jan. 16: *Id.,* p. 1014/1.

Forehanded. Provident, thrifty, well fixed. [1650-1878.]

1616 Thou art a pretty *forehanded* fellow, would thou wert wiser.— Beaumont and Fletcher, "The Scornful Ladie," E.

1888 That [the holding of cotton for a better market] is done very frequently by planters who are *forehanded.*—Mr. J. T. Morgan of Ala., U. S. Senate, Dec. 12: *C. R.,* p. 183/2.

Forest culture. Growth and care of forests. Not in the dictionaries.

1878 It would be the severest hardship upon the *forest-culture* of [the western plains] if the cottonwood should be excepted.—Mr. A. S. Paddock of Neb., U. S. Senate, March 20: *C. R.,* p. 1894/2.

Forty acres and a mule. The proverbial goal of a negro's wishes.

1871 [The slaves] only appreciated the advantages of fighting for freedom when this privilege was accompanied with a present bounty or the future prospect of *"forty acres and a mule."*—Mr. A. B. Roosevelt of N. Y., H. R., Apr. 1: *C. G.,* p. 398/1.

1871 It has not been long since every negro in the country imagined he was to grow suddenly wealthy. O, they were to have *forty acres of land and a mule,* and every negro in the country was waiting for the *forty acres and the mule* to come.—Mr. B. T. Biggs of Del., H. R., Dec. 20: *Id.,* p. 254/1.

1875 There has always been a longing on the part of the colored man to get something he did not have, and a longing on the part of his white brother to pretend to give him something he did not have. In our country they had it that each colored man was to have *forty acres of land and a mule.*—Mr. Thos. Whitehead of Va., H. R., Feb. 3: *C. R.,* p. 953/1.

1875 Washington Jones, colored, testified to voting the Republican ticket, and being promised by Mr. Heyman and other Republicans bacon, *a horse or mule, and forty acres of land,* the day after election.—Mr. J. K. Luttrell of Calif., H. R., Feb. 27: *Id.,* p. 1888/2.

1879 [The negro] values the elective franchise because for eight consecutive years he had it incessantly preached to him that the ballot was a power, and should be sacredly preserved. So forcibly impressed are they with this idea, that they have often sewed the ballot in a rag and worn it as an amulet round their necks, as confidently believing that this little cabalastic charm would . . . buy them the long promised *"forty acres and a mule,"* as they believed then and do believe now that a horseshoe nailed over the door will keep witches out of the house.— Mr. D. W. Aiken of S. C., H. R., Feb. 19: *Id.,* p. 1619/2.

1891 When the war closed, these people were led to believe that the agents of the Freedmen's Bureau were going down amongst them with an immense drove of mules, with a surveyor along; that each darkey was to have the privilege of selecting his own *mule,* and the surveyor was going to stake out his *forty acres* of land.—Mr. F. B. Spinola of N. Y., H. R., Jan. 27: *C. R.,* p. 1885/2.

Forty-niners. The "Argonauts" of California. [1890.]

1892 Those old adventurous *"Forty-niners."*—Mr. D. W. Voorhees of Ind., U. S. Senate, March 25, in his Eulogy of Senator George Hearst: *C. R.,* p. 2563/2.

Forty rods. Some decoctions of strong drink are said to be strong enough to "kill at forty rods."

1862   Those who swallow that which is said to be "sure to kill at *forty rods*" will have it at any hazard of life or purse.—Mr. Justin S. Morrill of Vt., H. R., March 12: *C. G.,* p. 1195/2.

1863   The manufacturers of what they call rectified whisky, but what we call, in my country, whisky that *kills at sight,* spoil our whisky. They put a little coloring in it, and send it here, calling it old *Bourbon.* —Mr. Charles A. Wickliffe of Ky., H. R., Feb. 26: *Id.,* p. 1312/1.

1867   Instead of encouraging the manufacture of pure good whisky, made by the little distillers, whisky which a man can drink regularly three times a day and live to be a hundred years old, you allow the monopolists to make a sort of liquor that will poison and *kill* a man *at the distance of a hundred feet.*—Mr. Andrew H. Ward of Ky., Feb. 14: *Id.,* p. 1254/3.

1868   Old New England rum is a beverage that is well known. It will *kill around the corner* with the first distillation.—Mr. James W. Nye of Nev., U. S. Senate, June 18: *Id.,* p. 3251/1.

1896   That will kill [said the doctor] at *forty rods.* It is a compound of wood alcohol, whisky, and strychnine, sold under the label of Hennessey brandy.—Mr. A. J. Cummings of N. Y., H. R., March 24: *C. R.,* p. 3142/2.

Four Hundred, The. The socially elect, generally.

1892   We take these Indian children, put them in a palace car, transport them to a school at Carlisle, Pa., or to another school in Phila., and I suppose we will soon establish a curriculum to prepare them to enter the select *"Four Hundred"* in New York.—Mr. T. R. Stockdale of Miss., H. R., Feb. 17: *C. R.,* p. 5/1, App.

1894   Diamonds have gotten out of fashion among the rich. There are fewer diamonds among the *"four hundred"* of New York than among the saleswomen of the country and the actresses and the politicians.— Mr. J. G. Hendrix of N. Y., H. R., Jan. 26: *Id.,* p. 1465/1.

Fourth of July oratory. Oratory for effect, usually of an excessively patriotic type.

1879   Has the oratory that is peculiar to the Fourth of July come to be a hissing and a byword, a scorn and a reproach, . . . in this day and generation when we supposed that we had practically vindicated every abstract and elemental truth in the Declaration of our Independence? Is it enough to smother opposition and put down argument, to say that that is merely the sentimentality of a *Fourth of July oratory?*—Mr. Stanley Matthews of O., U. S. Senate, Feb. 13: *C. R.,* p. 1275/1.

Fox fire. Phosphorescent light. [1829-1853.]

1896   They have more sorts of fire in Alabama than in any place in the world. They have the *foxfire;* they have the common fire you light your cigar with; and if they do not stop stealing votes, they will, before this thing is over, have the biggest chunk of hell fire that ever struck the country.—Mr. R. Z. Linney of N. C., H. R., July 9: *C. R.,* p. 6340/1.

Fractional notes or currency. See quotation, 1879.

1878   [Silver] is not like our *fractional notes,* a promise to pay. It is payment.—Mr. W. A. Wallace of Pa., U. S. Senate, Jan. 29: *C. R.,* p. 638/2.

1878   The *fractional currency* had become so ragged and so dirty that people were willing to surrender it for almost anything, and we could not get a proposition through both Houses to print anything more of the *fractional currency.*—Mr. Justin S. Morrill of Vt., U. S. Senate, Feb. 4: *Id.,* p. 727/2.

1879   *Fractional currency,* small coin, or paper notes, in circulation, of less value than the monetary unit.—Webster's Dict., Supplement.

Frail.   To beat.   Southern.   [Possibly for flail?]

1889 I sorter sassed him about a gal he was flyin' around, an' he upped an' *trailed me out,* an' got the gal to boot.—Joel C. Harris, "A Conscript's Christmas."

Frame. Built of sawed wood instead of hewn timbers. [1784-1860.]

1875 *Q.* Were those *frame* or log churches? *Ans.* Two of them were *frame,* and the Wachoochee Valley church was a log church.—Testimony from Alabama, *C. R.,* Feb. 26, p. 1845/1.

Framed-up. Made by conspiracy or plot, especially for an evil purpose, as to incriminate a person on false evidence. Slang. (Cf. *Frame-up,* Webster.)

1913 They arrested our organizers, speakers and officials and, with the aid of their despicable tools, the county authorities, railroaded them to jail on trumped-up charges and *framed-up* evidence.—*Industrial Worker* (Spokane, Wash.), July 3.

Franklin stove. The story, told in Vol. I, 1841, is related also by Senator Howe of Wisc., June 18, 1870: *C. G.,* p. 4578/2.

Franklin, the State of. The name at first proposed for Tennessee.

1898 My own native State of Tennessee, first organized as the "*State of Franklin,*" but which afterwards became Tennessee. It was turned over as the territory of North Carolina, and generously placed in the lap of the Government in the U. S.—Mr. W. B. Bate of Tenn., U. S. Senate, June 30: *C. R.,* p. 6523/2.

Frazzled. Frayed out. [1882-1910.]

1872 *Q.* I notice the ends of these sticks are broken; did you find them broken in that way? *Ans.* Yes, sir; all *frazzled* like that.—Testimony of C. C. Hughes, *C. G.,* May 30, p. 576/2, App.

1872 The ends of the [hickory] switches were all *frazzled.*—Testimony of Mary Brown, *Id.,* p. 577/3, App.

1872 They went out and got great big long brushes, as big as these chair posts, and they whipped them all into *frassels.*—Testimony of Washington Eager. *Id.,* p. 578/2, App.

1893 Yo' kin brag on rattlesnake grease . . . twell yo' tongues is all wo' [worn] ter *frazzles.*—Mary A. Owen, "Old Rabbit, &c." p. 105.

1912 Curtis is so lost to all sense of shame as to be the Taft leader in Kansas. Opposed to him was the patriotic Stubbs, seeking elevation from Topeka to Washington. One would have thought that there could be no question of the result of such a contest. Yet the armies of the Lord were *beaten to a frazzle* in the popular vote, and only the vote by legislative districts can save Stubbs from retirement to private life.—*N. Y. Evening Post,* Aug. 8, p. 4/1. [This is sarcastically written. "The armies of the Lord" are the Roosevelt forces.]

Freedmen's Bureau, The. A branch of the U. S. War Department, organized early in 1865, to protect the liberated negroes.

1867 See DARKY.

1876 The *Freedmen's Bureau* was established as one of the inventions sent to plague us, the agents of which robbed the colored man with one hand and scattered the seeds of distrust between him and his former master with the other, thus destroying any system of labor by which we might hope to repair our waste places and rebuild our shattered fortunes. The carpetbaggers descended upon us like the locusts, and the scalawags sprung up among us like the lice of Egypt.—Mr. House of Tenn., H. R., May 18: *C. R.,* p. 3188/2.

Free Jacks. Emblems of independence and unconcern.

1886 Wherever the Army approached, wherever the flag of the country appeared, there were men who had not taken the oath of allegiance, who floated "*free jacks,*" as the phrase was.—Mr. John A. Logan of Ill., U. S. Senate, May 13: *C. R.,* p. 4455/1.

Free-soiler. One who was for excluding slavery from the Territories of the U. S. [1848-1884.]

1849 It is asserted that the *"free-soilers"* will be likely to break the regulation of neutrality.—Wilmington (N. C.) *Commercial,* March 24, p. 2/1.

Freeze, Freeze-up. Freeze as a noun occurs c. 1440 and 1630. (N. E. D.) A frost.

1866 You have had a *freeze* out of my ghost story.—C. Dickens, "Letters" (1880), II, 246. (N. E. D.)

1876 I have seen a building in Chicago thrown out of plumb six inches by one winter's *"freeze."*—Mr. Harrison of Ill., H. R., June 22: *C. R.,* p. 4044/1.

1879 Most of the sawmills . . . . get as much of their stock into lumber before the *freeze-up.*—*Lumberman's Gazette,* Dec. 19: (N. E. D.)

1891 During a *freeze* there is no comfort in a southern home.—Kate Field, "Washington," IV, 383/2. (N. E. D.)

Freeze out. To force to retire; to eliminate by pressure sometimes verging on threats. [1882-1910.]

1879 That is the condition of *freezing-out* our trade with the South American countries.—Mr. James A. Garfield of O., H. R., Feb. 28: *C. R.,* p. 2127/2.

1882 [The large tobacco manufacturers] *freeze out* the small fellows.—Mr. J. S. Williams of Ky., U. S. Senate, July 19: *Id.,* p. 6195/1.

1890 The judge, by standing in with his general assignee, was enabled to *"freeze out"* the assignee whom the creditors had appointed.—Mr. C. J. Boatner of La., H. R., July 22: *Id.,* p. 7579/1.

Freeze-out. The operation of freezing a man out.

1884 They organized a *freeze-out* against him.—"The Breadwinners," p. 144. (N. E. D.)

1896 That course which is known to many gentlemen engaged in corporate operations as *"freezing out"* the balance of the stockholders.—Mr. W. P. Hepburn of Ia., H. R., Dec. 17: *C. R.,* p. 253/2.

Free zone, the. The Mexican "zona libre," so called on account of its immunity from customs duties.

1895 The Mexican *free zone* includes a strip of territory varying in width from 3 to 12 or 13 miles. Into that territory all goods coming from any country in the world, whether from Japan, China, or the U. S., are entered by the payment of one-tenth of the regular Mexican tariff rate. After those goods leave that zone, they are compelled by each municipality, by each State, and by the Federal government . . . . to pay the regular tariff rate.—Mr. W. H. Crain of Tex., H. R., Feb. 27: *C. R.,* p. 2850/2. [See the rest of the debate, pp. 2851-2.]

1898 The Mexican Government . . . . has first established and then maintained a strip of country 13 miles wide, known as the *Free Zone,* or . . . the *"Zona Libre."*—Mr. C. H. Grosvenor of O., H. R., May 4: *Id.,* p. 4581/2. [See the rest of the debate.]

Free-willer. In Maryland during the colonial period, an immigrant who had voluntarily sold his labor under contract for a certain number of years. (Century Dict.)

Freighter. A carrier of goods, especially in the West; also an employee.

1881 An Indian was killed by a white man, a *freighter* on the road to the agency.—Mr. Hill of Colo., H. R., Jan. 28: *C. R.,* p. 1003/2.

1884 Men employed by the *freighters* to look after the mules.—*American,* ix, 110. (N. E. D.)

Freighting. Conveying heavy merchandise by land.

1856 The roads seemed to be doing a heavy *freighting* business with cotton. —Olmsted, "Slave States," p. 396. (N. E. D.)

1867 Is a lumber wagon, cart, or dray used for any purpose except for farming or *freighting*?—Mr. John F. Farnsworth of Ill., H. R., Feb. 22: *C. G.,* p. 1480/2.

1884 The water . . . . fills the arroyo, and renders *freighting* in wagons difficult.—L. Hamilton, "Mexican Hand-Book," p. 67. (N. E. D.)

1888 Very often it has not been possible to *freight* the mails . . . in the postal cars, but they were placed in the express car.—Mr. S. R. Peters of Kan., H. R., May 24: *C. R.,* p. 4592/1.

Frenching. The peculiar distorted and dwarfed condition of cotton, tobacco, corn, and other plants, due either to some fungus or to disturbed nutrition: often used synonymously for the mosaic disease. (Century Dict.)

1888 Then [the cotton plant] begins to blight; then comes *frenching* and the shedding of squares and forms; then comes the "army worm," and then the "boll-worm."—Mr. E. P. Allen of Miss., H. R., May 12: *C. R.,* pp. 4069-70.

Fresh. A freshet.

1814 [Much] damage had been done on [James] River by the late *fresh.*—Norfolk (Va.) *Public Ledger,* Aug. 3, p. 3/1.

1831 We have had a severe *fresh* in the Wateree [river].—*Charleston Courier,* Aug. 27.

Frills. Affectations, airs, things superfluous.

1889 He puts on too many *frills.*—Example suggested in Century Dict.

1895 Mr. Wolcott:—I think the restaurant could be improved so as to meet the needs of Western Senators. Mr. Hale:—Would the Senator have more liquids and less solids? Mr. Wolcott:—Not at all: but I would have less *frills.*—U. S. Senate, Jan. 3: *C. R.,* p. 580/2.

Fritter out. To vanish by degrees, to evaporate. The N. E. D. gives an example (1764) of the same phrase used actively.

1888 It is true the affair *frittered out* and did not amount to much. I would like to have a celebration that will not *fritter out.*—Mr. C. N. Brumm of Pa., H. R., Aug. 7: *C. R.,* p. 7316/1.

Froe, Frow. A wedge-shaped tool for cleaving staves, etc. Now chiefly U. S. (N. E. D.)

1573 to 1685. See N. E. D. (Fusser, &c.)

1775 A river or splitter, who rives [trees] with the *fro.*—Romans, "Hist. Fla.," p. 182. (N. E. D.)

1851 With *froe* in one hand and mallet in the other.—S. Judd, "Margaret" (1871), p. 137. (N. E. D.)

1897 The farmers will . . . . pulverize you with their disks, cut you down with their axes, split you to pieces with their *froes,* &c.—Mr. Champ Clark of Mo., H. R., March 31: *C. R.,* p. 551/2.

Frog. A grooved piece of iron placed at the junction of rails, where one track crosses another. [1860.]

1870 We have struck down the duty on steel railway *frogs,* &c., from 3¼ cents to 2½ cents a pound.—Mr. J. A. Peters of Me., H. R., May 4: *C. G.,* p. 3232/3.

Frog pond. A somewhat jocular term for a small body of water. [1799-1859.]

1874 I do not know that Congress has anything to do with the petty commerce carried within the limits of a *frog-pond* of a State.—Mr. S. A. Hurlbut of Ill., H. R., March 4: *C. R.,* p. 1968/1.

1881 When it comes to the farce of pretending, under the power for the regulation of commerce, to improve a *frog pond* or a trout stream in West Virginia or North Carolina, do you not feel some compunction of conscience?—Mr. A. G. Thurman of O., U. S. Senate, Feb. 26: *C. R.,* p. 2148/2.

1882 [The language of the amendment] is sufficiently precise to cut off headwaters and *frog-ponds,* the Kiskiminetas and even the Kanawha, and it applies to main rivers exclusively.—Mr. R. R. Dawes of O., H. R., Jan. 18: *C. R.,* p. 497/1.

Front office. The police headquarters. [Thieves' cant.]
1901. See GUN.
Frying of fat.* The extortion of money for political purposes.
1890 That process which in the U. S. is called the *"frying of fat"* out of
       people.—Mr. John T. Morgan of Ala., U. S. Senate, July 10: *C. R.,*
       p. 7088/1.
1890 I did not suppose there had been any authority of law for *"frying the
       fat"* out of the manufacturers in the last presidential campaign.—Mr.
       John H. Rogers of Ark., H. R., July 26: *Id.,* p. 7790/1.
1890 [This tariff question] has always had about it the unpleasant odor of
       frying fat, and its continuing to burn may after a while contaminate
       the entire atmosphere.—Mr. J. T. Morgan of Ala., U. S. Senate,
       Aug. 11: *Id.,* p. 8422/1.
1890 Those from whom, in current parlance, *"the fat was fried,"* whose
       "sinews of war" commanded "blocks of five," &c.—Mr. W. B. Bate of
       Tenn., U. S. Senate, Aug. 14: *Id.,* p. 8558/2.
1894 When, in 1888, an enormous campaign contribution was levied upon
       the sugar trust, it refused to pay it. Senator Plumb advised Chair-
       man Foster to "put it over the fire and *fry some of the fat out of it."*—
       Mr. Jerry Simpson of Kan., H. R., Jan. 12: *Id.,* p. 774/1.
1894 See MILK IN THE COCOANUT.
Fugacious. Fugitive. [1826-1860.]
a.1755 A few *fugacious,* deceitful pleasures—Laurence Sterne, 'Sermon X
       on Job,' XIV, 1-2.
1850 Let the *fugacious* slave run as far as he may, he must be still on land.
       —Mr. T. H. Benton in the U. S. Senate: "Thirty Years' View," II,
       755/1. (1856.)
Fugleman. (Originally *flugelman.*) In its applied meaning a political
       leader. [1802-1850.]
1896 [My remaining silent] might inure to the benefit of some *"fugleman,"*
       as somebody on this floor has been very politely called tonight,—
       some *fugleman* of some candidate for the presidency. I suppose we have
       a good many *fuglemen* here. I imagine that the gentleman who made
       the charge is a sort of a *fugleman,* possibly not a major general, pos-
       sibly only a corporal, but I think he will *fugle* some before he gets
       through.—Mr. C. H. Grosvenor of O., H. R., March 27: *C. R.,*
       p. 3307/2. [See also p. 3351/1.]
Funeral, not one's. Not one's affair. [1854-1896.]
1870 Mr. Painter, addressing you, said, "This is *not my funeral,"* repeating
       those words twice. You then asked, "There is to be a funeral then,
       is there?" Mr. Painter answered, "So they say."—Letter of H. V.
       Poor, Apr. 12: *C. G.,* p. 2780/3.
Fur fly, to make the. To make a big commotion; to whip one's
       opponent. [1825-1888.]
1865 I have been summoned before the select committee of the Senate for
       investigating frauds in naval supplies, and *if the wool don't fly* it will
       not be my fault.—Letter quoted by Senator Hale, Feb. 6: *C. G.,*
       p. 614/2.
1870 The puppy drove the cat away from the bowl of cream, and *made the
       fur fly* splendidly when the cat was licking off the cream; but no
       sooner had the cat got away than [he] himself went to licking out of
       the same bowl.—Mr. Justin S. Morrill of Vt., U. S. Senate, Jan. 26:
       C. G., p. 775/1.
1892 [The politicians suggest to the farmer] that if they were at Washing-
       ton *the fur would fly.*—Mr. E. O. Wolcott of Colo., U. S. Senate,
       Apr. 6: *C. R.,* p. 2984/1.

---

* This is quite distinct from the phrase in Chaucer, to make a man fry in his own
grease or fat.

Fuss and feathers. A tumult, unnecessary ado over trifles. See Vol. I. [1860-1861.]

1864 Let the Senate appoint the judge advocate and pay him, ... and not have the *fuss and feathers* of military parade brought into your judicial proceedings.—Mr. Hale of N. H., U. S. Senate, May 16: *C. G.,* p. 2287/3.

1895 A great deal of *fuss and feathers* is made by some gentlemen whenever the proposition of permitting State banks to issue their circulating notes is broached.—Mr. T. C. Catchings of Miss., H. R., Jan. 5: *C. R.,* p. 685/1.

Futures. Stocks and commodities sold nominally for future delivery, but really with an expectation of winning or losing the difference in values.

1880 American *futures* are in better demand.—*Daily News,* Nov. 10, p. 3/8. (N. E. D.)

1883 Amongst the new developments of the cotton trade, the buying of *futures* may be looked upon as the most prominent.—*Manchester Examiner,* Nov. 6, p. 4/4. (N. E. D.)

1884 The capitalist who deals in *futures* is in some respects better than he who speculates, to the ruin of innocent families, with money not his own. Yet both are gamblers—Mr. S. S. Cox of N. Y., H. R., June 9: *C. R.,* p. 406/2, App.

1892 Originally *futures* provided for delivery on a specified day. It was found, on the one hand, that this facilitated the operations of those who used them as a preparation for cornering the market, and, on the other hand, that the legitimate uses of contracts for future delivery could generally be subserved, provided the one who expected the delivery could be certain of receiving within some definite month the product contracted for. In order therefore to protect the seller against an attempt to corner against him for a single day the supply of the article in question at the particular place where he had to deliver it, there is now generally inserted in contracts for *futures* used by exchanges a clause providing that the delivery shall be at such time within a given month as, upon a given number of days' notice, the seller may choose to designate.—Mr. J. D. Warner of N. Y., H. R., June 6: *Id.,* p. 445/1, App.

1893 See Spot Cash, Spot Cotton, &c.

G

Gadsden Purchase, The. A tract of land containing 45,535 square miles, bought from Mexico in 1853, by the instrumentality of Mr. James Gadsden of South Carolina (1788-1858).

1872 These Indians are mostly in a territory purchased from the Mexican Republic for some $10,000,000, called *the Gadsden purchase.*—Mr. Cornelius Cole of Calif., U. S. Senate, Apr. 1: *C. G.,* p. 2063/3.

1894 When we found that our line was not exactly where we wanted it with Mexico, we added $10,000,000 more for the purchase of a little strip known as the *Gadsden purchase,* south of the Gila River in Arizona.—Mr. H. M. Teller of Colo., U. S. Senate, Jan. 29: *C. R.,* p. 1577/1.

1900 The *Gadsden treaty* settled disputes with Mexico as to the southern part of Arizona. Thereby the U. S. secured the disputed territory at the price of $10,000,000, and with it a right of transit for troops, mails, and merchandise over the isthmus of Tehuantepec.—Mr. R. R. Kenney of Del., U. S. Senate, Feb. 20: *Id.,* p. 1969/2.

Gag-law or **rule.** One limiting debate. [1798-1846.]

1861 The Pacific railroad bill, just passed through this House under the *"gag,"* and in violation of the Constitution.—Mr. I. N. Morris of Ill., H. R., Jan. 16: *C. G.,* p. 49/1, App.

1890 The resolution which I have opposed has the effect of a *"gag rule."* It shuts off discussion and prevents us from taking the action we desire.—Mr. W. J. Connell of Neb., H. R., Aug. 9: *C. R.,* p. 8380/1.

Gall. Impudence, effrontery. [1891.]

1623   All you women,
      Although you be of never so low stature,
      Have *gall* in you most abundant, it exceeds
      Your braines by two ounces.
                  —Webster, "Devil's Law Case," B 4.

1896 They have the *"gall"* and the assurance to deny the . . established facts of history.—Mr. S. L. Milliken of Me., H. R., Apr. 27: *C. R.,* p. 4493/1.

Gallowses. Braces, suspenders. [1806-1857.]

1839 A wheen ready made waistcoats, *gallowses,* leather caps, and Kilmarnock cowls.—D. M. Moir, "Mansie Wauch," ch. vi.

1882 I can see in my mind's eye . . . . those *one-gallows,* straw-hatted fellows flying from the revenue officials to their mountain fastnesses.—Mr. John S. Williams of Ky., U. S. Senate, July 19: *C. R.,* p. 6194/1.

Galoot. A fellow. Originally a raw young soldier. [1888.]

1909 We have had a hoss-thief raisin', and the neighbors all agree
    That a more upliftin' session this here place will never see;
    And we've painted, sence we started, sev'ral pairs of high-heeled boots,
    All the pairs containin' Trilbies of our gun-fightin' *galoots.*
          —Arthur Chapman in *Denver Republican,* Feb. 2.

Gang of saws. A set of saws sufficient in number to convert a log into boards by a single operation. [1821-1833.]

1863 Now some whittling, whistling Yankee . . . establishes a *gang of saws,* and competes with the old mill.—Mr. W. M. Davis of Pa., H. R., March 3: *C. G.,* p. 168/1, App.

1883 The Penobscot River at every fall has its sawmill, with its *gangs of saws;* the Kennebec River the same; the Androscoggin River the same.—Mr. W. P. Frye of Me., U. S. Senate, Jan. 22: *C. R.,* 1445/2.

1883 A *"gang,"* as a set of saws is called, ... arranged at different intervals.—*Harper's Mag.,* p. 824/2. (N. E. D.)

Gang plow. One with several shares, &c., in a series.

1856 I sow wheat and guano together, and plow them in with a *gang plow.*—Olmsted, "Slave States," p. 9. (N. E. D.)

1876 We are developing our wheat interest . . . by the addition of . . . the turning-plow, the *gang plows,* . . . the buggy plow, and so on.—Mr. Maxey of Tex., U. S. Senate, July 17: *C. R.,* p. 4656/1.

Gas. Empty talk. [1847-1855.]

1864 [The man] has the reputation of being a most notorious liar, so much so that he went by the name of *"Gassy* Brown."—Mr. Hubbard of Ia., H. R., June 11: *C. G.,* p. 2887/2.

1878 At six o'clock on a November evening in Louisiana, the sun has gone down, and darkness gathered about. There is no *gas* in that country, except in the mouths of certain politicians.—Mr. E. J. Ellis of La., H. R., Feb. 20: *C. R.,* p. 1223/2.

Gas tips. Tips for gas burners. (Not in N. E. D.)

1870 Yankee ingenuity converts the talc [produced in Tenn.] into *gas tips* which will not corrode.—Mr. W. D. Kelley of Pa., H. R., March 28: *C. G.,* p. 214/1, App.

Gate City, the. Atlanta, Ga.

1894 In the front, where the . . . enterprising citizens of Atlanta have put that beautiful *"Gate City"* of the South.—Mr. Cogswell of Mass., H. R., Aug. 10: *C. R.,* p. 8384/2.

1894 There is no place where I . . . would rather go than to Atlanta, the *"Gate City"* of the New South, and see the flag of my country waving over a great exposition, &c.—Mr. C. H. Grosvenor of O., H. R., Aug. 10: *Id.,* p. 8385/2.

Gee. To agree.

1889 Somehow . . me an' these here fine Seegyars [cigars] don't *gee.*— Joel C. Harris, "The Old Bascom Place."

Germantown carriage, Germantown wagon. One made in Germantown [Pa.(?)].

1874 That was when the democracy was getting beyond the days of its simplicity, and when it was becoming necessary to discard old wagons and ride in fine *germantown carriages.*—Mr. W. A. Wheeler of N. Y., H. R., Apr. 25: *C. R.,* p. 3377/2.

1885 Farmers came in their buggies, *germantowns* and farm waggons.— H. C. McCook, "Tenants of an Old Farm," p. 322. (N. E. D.)

Gerrymander. An artful mode of redistricting a portion of territory for political purposes. Also a verb. [1812-1881.] The G is properly hard. See also **Dumb-bell district** and **Shoestring district.**

1872 In the city of Norfolk there is a considerable Republican majority, but by an unholy *gerrymandering* the Legislature has thrown all the Republican majority into one part of the city.—Mr. Jas. H. Platt of Va., H. R., March 5: *C. G.,* p. 1439/2.

1875 I was *gerrymandered* out of my district by a Republican legislature.— Mr. S. S. Cox of N. Y., H. R., Feb. 20: *C. R.,* p. 1549/2.

1882 We have been bad enough in Indiana, but not quite so bad as that map indicates. We can sit at the feet of Mississippi and learn lessons in *gerrymandering.*—Mr. W. H. Calkins of Ind., H. R., Apr. 29: *Id.,* p. 3442/1.

1882 The *gerrymander* in South Carolina while it is bad enough, is only boy's play when you contrast it with the work of the master *gerry-manderer's* hand in Pennsylvania. No State in the Union can justly be mentioned in the same category with the old Keystone State [in this respect].—Mr. F. E. Beltzhoover of Pa., H. R., July 20: *Id.,* p. 522/2, App.

[1889 You will see [by the map] that the First district runs right across and through the Seventh, and up for 35 miles along the coast like the tail of a gigantic catamount rampant.—Mr. W. C. Cooper of O., H. R., Feb. 12: *Id.,* p. 1795/2.]

1890 The Republicans *gerrymander* Pennsylvania in a manner that is unfair. They *gerrymander* New York in a manner that is exceedingly unfair. But the Democrats *gerrymander,* when they get the power, Ohio and Indiana, and that is in some sense a set-off.—Mr. H. A. Herbert of Ala., H. R., June 30: *Id.,* pp. 6764-5.

1891 These *gerrymanders* for Congressional purposes are in most cases buttressed by a *gerrymander* of the legislative districts.—Message of President Harrison, Dec. 9: *C. R.,* p. 19/2.

1893 See where the hateful serpent of the *gerrymander* has wound his sinuous course; see where in his glittering folds he has strangled the life out of the spirit of liberty.—Mr. H. U. Johnson of Ind., H. R., Feb. 11: *Id.,* p. 1492/2.

1893 The Democrats of Ala. proceeded to *re-gerrymander* the State for the avowed purpose of dismembering the district.—The same, Feb. 28: *Id.,* p. 2298/2.

Get. To puzzle, to embarrass, to corner, to capture.

1887 Who was Navajo? Ah, that's where you've got me, young man.—
F. Francis, Jr., "Saddle and Mocassin," p. 236. (N. E. D.)

1888 Yes, . . . I did. I don't deny it. You've got me there.—H. F. Lester,
"Hartas Maturin," III, 157. (N. E. D.)

1890 I would swallow this free list entire, horns, hoofs, bones, and all,
if it were not for free ipecac. That is what *gets* me; I can not stand
that.—Mr. C. W. McClammy of N. C., H. R., May 19: *C. R.,*
p. 4933/2.

Get or git. To be off, to proceed.

1884 He presented a cocked revolver and told them to *get,* and they *got.*—
Graceville (Minn.) *Transcript,* Aug. 25. (N. E. D.)

1887 *Get up!—get up!* . . he says . . and once more the horses resume their
gait.—F. Francis, "Saddle and Mocassin," p. 123. (N. E. D.)

1889 I . . thought discretion the better part of valour, and the sooner I *"got"*
the better.—H. O'Reilly, "Fifty Years on Trial," p. 170. (N. E. D.)

1895 Our team proceeded with many a *"git"* and whip crack from their
dusky Jehu.—*Blackwood's Mag.,* p. 282. (N. E. D.) [The phrase
"Git up" or "Git ap" is frequently addressed by a driver to his horses.]

Get away with. To get the better of; to carry off as plunder.

1887 The boys *got away with* the . . road agents.—A. A. Hayes, "Jesuit's
Ring," p. 227. (N. E. D.)

1892 [These gentlemen] will have to be content with the pitiful $240,000
that they have already *"got away with."*—Mr. R. R. Hitt of Ill.,
H. R., Dec. 13: *C. R.,* p. 122/2.

Get left. The opposite of "to come out ahead." To be disappointed,
to be the loser.

1894 The gentleman from Illinois [Mr. Springer] was evidently afraid
that he might *"get left"* on this proposition.—Mr. E. F. Loud of Calif.,
Apr. 6: *C. R.,* p. 3513/2.

Get off. To utter, to publish. [1849-1858.]

1874 See GROSS.

1878 One thing I beg of [Mr. B. F. Butler], and that is never to repeat
the little piece of wit he *got off* about me a short time ago.—Mr. S. S.
Cox of N. Y., H. R., Apr. 5: *C. R.,* p. 2312/1.

1879 To *get off* some smart things for the amusement of the galleries.—
Mr. Hill of Ga., U. S. Senate, June 11: *Id.,* p. 1911/2.

Get religion. A jocular term for being converted. [1826-1908.]

1883 We had come to Andover to *get religion,* and the pursuit of this object
was seldom interfered with by such episodes as the one just related.—
Josiah P. Quincy, "Figures of the Past," p. 6. (Century Dict.)

Get round. To get about from place to place.

1884 A tough waggon, a moderate load, four good horses, and a skilled
driver, seem to be able in the West to go anywhere, or to *get round,*
which amounts to the same.—W. Shepherd, "Prairie Experiences,"
p. 71. (Century Dict.)

Get round [a person]. To circumvent him in any manner.

1849 One from the land of cakes sought to *get round* a right smart
Yankee.—G. F. Ruxton, "Life in the Far West," p. 89. (Century
Dict.)

Get there. To attain one's object.

1887 He said as he'd been gambling, and was two hundred dollars ahead of
the town. He *"got there with both feet"* at starting.—F. Francis, Jr.,
"Saddle and Mocassin," p. 144. (N. E. D.)

1888 Although not a delegate, he *got there all the same.*—*N. Y. Herald,*
July 29. (Farmer.)

1891 As the humorous American phrase goes, "he *gets there all the same."*—
Daily News, Nov. 18, p. 5/1. (N. E. D.)

1894 See HUSTLER.

Gibe. To work with, to work in harmony. [1857-1909.]

1911 Lawyers tell us that it is impossible to invent a lie which shall not somewhere jar with fact. It is just as impossible to conceive of a false belief which shall always and everywhere exactly *jibe* with the nature of things.—*The Oregonian,* Aug. 27.

Gig and saddle. See quotations.

1890 [In the La. lottery] by paying an extra 25 cents on a ticket you can put what is called a *"gig and saddle"* on it, and then in the event that two of the numbers on your ticket correspond with any two of the thirteen numbers drawn from the wheel, a prize of $2.45 is paid.— Mr. H. C. Evans of Tenn., H. R., Aug. 16: *C. R.,* p. 8713/2.

1911 Bets are made upon single numbers coming out, or upon the order or position they will occupy in the line, or upon combinations of numbers and their order, called *gigs and saddles.* The odds paid are in proportion to the improbability. The famous negro *gig,* 4-11-44, means that those three numbers will come in that order among those drawn.— Century Dict., s. v., *Policy,* 2.

Giggit. To convey or to move rapidly. (New England.)

1862 He nearly like to have got her eat up by sharks, by *giggiting* her off in the boat out to sea, when she warn't more'n three years old.— H. B. Stowe, *The Independent,* Feb. 27. (Century Dict.)

Gilderoy's Kite, as high as or **higher than.** See Vol. I. [1869.]

1888 The height which *Gilroy's kite* attained would have been nowhere in point of altitude to that which I should have reached, had I not had the good luck to have cleared my decks as I did.—Henry Clews, "Twenty-Eight Years in Wall St.," p. 79. (N. Y.)

Gilt-edged. Exceptionally good by way of security.

1867 Business is so much demoralized that speculative paper, backed up by collaterals ranging from gold bullion down to fancy copper stocks, drives even the *gilt-edged* business paper out of bank parlors on to curbstones.—Mr. Justin S. Morrill of Vt., U. S. Senate, Dec. 11: *C. G.,* p. 127/2.

1868 We must not conceal nor deny the fact that our paper in Europe is not *"gilt edged."*—Mr. Lewis Selye of N. Y., H. R., June 13: *Id.,* p. 346/2, App.

1868 [My] paper was considered, in the present parlance of the street, *"gilt-edged."*—R. B. Kimball, "Undercurrents," p. 130. (N. Y.)

1872 [The city of St. Joseph] pays her debts, and her credit today in the money markets of the East is first class, and her paper is *"gilt-edged."* —Mr. Isaac C. Parker of Mo., H. R., Apr. 6: *C. G.,* p. 2245/3.

1884 These bonds, hitherto marked doubtful, are now *gilt-edged securities.*— Mr. E. J. Lewis of La., H. R., June 26: *C. R.,* p. 401/2, App.

1892 Colonial and Indian securities, and other *gilt-edged* stock.—*Spectator,* Sept. 17, p. 374/1. (N. E. D.)

Gimcrack. A fop. Obs. in England. Examples 1618-1706, N. E. D.

1832 [Mr. Ogden] is an agreeable . . fellow, and something, I should suppose, of what we call "a *gimcrack"* in America.—Diary of James Buchanan, May 4: "Works" (1908), II, 184.

Gin mill. A saloon; a barroom.

1887 [They] could . . . choose only between the gutter and a *gin-mill.*— *Christian Union,* June 16. (Century Dict.)

1890 Three of them were sitting round a stove in a *gin-mill.*—Mr. F. B. Spinola of N. Y., H. R., March 29: *C. R.,* p. 2815/1.

Give, n. A capacity of bending or yielding.

1885 Compared to the Frenchman, the American is more loosely hung together, and has more swing and *give* in gait and gesture.—Albert Rhodes, "Monsieur at Home," p. 45. (Century Dict.)

1892 [He took the hoe and dug it in the floor] and there was no *give* about it.—Mr. S. E. Payne of N. Y., H. R., March 17: *C. R.,* p. 2156/1.

Give away. To betray, to expose to detection or ridicule. (N. E. D.) Hence a "give-away" is the act of thus giving away. [1862-1878.]

1878 Ye went back on her, and shook her, and played off on her, and *gave her away*—dead away !—*Scribner's Mag.*, xv, 812/1. (N. E. D.)

1883 I thought he would *give himself away.*—F. M. Crawford, "Dr. Claudius," ii. (N. E. D.)

1889 My closely cropped hair . . *gave me away.*—*Answers,* Apr. 20, p. 326. (N. E. D.)

1890 I wish our gold friends could be made to see [that they] unwittingly perpetrate a perfect *"give away"* of their case in stigmatizing silver as too cheap, &c.—Mr. C. P. Wickham of O., H. R., June 6: *C. R.,* p. 5752/1.

1891 Genl. Sherman would not be told a secret. He said he would *give it away* to the first person he met.—*Boston Journal,* Feb. 20, p. 4/1. (N. E. D.)

Glimpse, v. To see for a moment only. Now chiefly Am.

1779 Sometimes [he] would ask [us] to talk about religion; *glimpsing* in some things the difference between Romish and Protestant.—Forrest, "Voy. N. Guinea," p. 292. (N. E. D.)

1823 She *glimpsed* the peak of my mitre in the waters.—*New Monthly Mag.,* viii, 503. (N. E. D.)

1868   Like Helen's hair
       Glimps'd in Elysium, insubstantial gold.
—J. R. Lowell, "A June Idyl," *Atl. Mo.,* June, 1868. [Later called "Under the Willows."]

1883 De Soto merely *glimpsed* the river.—S. L. Clemens, "Life on the Mississippi."

Glittering generalities. See quotations.

1856 Rufus Choate, in his letter to the Maine Whig Convention, Aug. 9, spoke of "the *glittering and sounding generalities* of natural right which make up the Declaration of Independence."

1898 The gentleman from Minnesota said that the first sentence of the St. Louis platform was a *glittering generality.*—Mr. S. E. Payne of N. Y., H. R., March 10: *C. R.,* p. 2692/1.

Globe trotting. Travelling extensively. See Vol. I for **Globe-trotter.** [1880-1909.]

1897 The [experts] who are now *"globe-trotting"* at our expense, on a salary of $5,000 a year.—Mr. M. N. Johnson of N. D., H. R., Dec. 16: *C. R.,* p. 224/1.

Glorious Fourth, the. The Fourth of July. [1827-1862.]

1896 Go and see in our public schools the children of German, Irish, Bohemian, and Italian parents waving the Stars and Stripes on *the glorious Fourth.*—Mr. Richard Bartholdt of Mo., H. R., May 19: *C. R.,* p. 5422/1.

Gloves, without. Without apology or ceremony. [1828-1892.]

1872 Since 1868, when we handled this organization *without gloves,* we have had no Ku Klux in Arkansas.—Mr. Powell Clayton of Ark., U. S. Senate, May 21: *Id.,* p. 3707/3.

Go (or **come**), ellipsis of. A common construction. [1784.]

1864 As the Yankees say, *"he wanted in."*—Mr. Richardson of Ill., U. S. Senate, June 13: *C. G.,* p. 2902/2.

Go-as-you-please. Unconfined by rules. [1888-1890.]

1886 The best corps . . . . degenerates into a sort of *go-as-you-please* walking match along the line of march.—Mr. M. A. Haynes of N. H., H. R., Feb. 11: *C. R.,* p. 1353/2.

1893 The Senator who asserts that he is in favor of a single gold standard for the money of the country cannot belong to either of the great parties. He must be a no-party man, a free-thinker, a *go-as-you-please* politician.—Mr. David B. Hill of N. Y., U. S. Senate, Aug. 25: *Id.,* p. 869/2.

Go back on. To turn against one's former action or opinion. [1868-1882.]

1861 The clergyman assured him . . . if he married, it must be for better and worse; that he could not *go back upon* the step.—E. B. Ramsay, "Sc. Life and Character," p. 218. (Century Dict.)

1867 If you are wise, . . . you will endeavor to *go back upon* your past legislation, to mend, to repair, to heal, to cure, if you can.—Mr. Wm. Sprague of R. I., U. S. Senate, Dec. 20: *C. G.,* p. 304/2.

1870 I am sorry I [intimated] that the Senator from Wisconsin [Mr. Carpenter] intended to *go back,* or was *going back, upon* the Republican party.—Mr. Richard Yates of Ill., U. S. Senate, Feb. 16: *Id.,* p. 1323/1.

1890 There is no sufficient reason why this body shall *"go back"* (to use a vulgar phrase) *upon* its own action.—Mr. J. K. Jones of Ark., U. S. Senate, June 26: *C. R.,* p. 6518/1.

Go-backs, the. In the mountains of Va., a baby is said to have the go-backs when its size or weight does not correspond to what is expected. See a paper by J. Howard Gore, 1892, *Journal of Am. Folk-Lore,* V, 107-9.

Gobbler. A turkey cock. [1800-1890.]

1873 Do not undertake . . . to raise an excitement in this matter, like shaking a piece of red flannel at a mad bull. Indeed, it reminds me rather of shaking a piece of flannel at a turkey *gobbler.*—Mr. O. J. Dickey of Pa., H. R., Jan. 14: *Id.,* p. 576/1.

1896 These proud, supercilious pension examiners are no more to be compared to my mountain constituents than a jay bird to a turkey *gobbler.* —Mr. H. R. Gibson of Tenn., H. R., Feb. 29: *C. R.,* p. 2310/1.

Gobble up. To eat or swallow greedily or hastily; to capture. [1861.]

1844 "The *gobbling up* Texas," it is said by the [London] *Herald,* "only whets [the U. S. government's] appetite."—Speech of Mr. Belser of Ala., H. R., May 21: p. 10/1 of the same as separately published.

1868 Should these gallant colored politicians . . . make a raid and *gobble up* all the offices in the Northwest, that day would be a dark one indeed.—Mr. F. C. Beaman of Mich., H. R., March 18: *C. G.,* p. 1970/2.

1870 On the specious pretext that the coveted lands are really subject to overflow, the speculator literally *"gobbles"* hundreds of thousands of acres.—*Alta California* (S. F.), quoted July 6, *Id.,* p. 5245/1.

1871 [It is objected] that, if we make the donation in the shape of a land warrant to the soldier, he will not be able to take care of his interests, and the warrant will go into the hands of moneyed corporations who will *gobble up* the public lands and cheat the soldier.—Mr. John M. Crebs of Ill., H. R., Jan. 31: *Id.,* p. 860/1.

1874 There are only $18,000,000 that have not been *gobbled up,* to use a phrase that is employed here; all the rest has been used for the benefit of the country.—Mr. Simon Cameron of Pa., U. S. Senate, Apr. 6: *C. R.,* p. 2828/1.

1877 Last Tuesday Cole's circus exhibited in Charleston; I presume some of our friends have heard of that institution. The soldiers . . . . broke down the door, and made a great deal of trouble generally. The police . . . got after them, and did not call for any help, but *gobbled them up* and put them all in the guardhouse.—Mr. D. W. Aiken of S. C., H. R., Nov. 9: *Id.,* p. 322/1.

1884 There is an attempt being made, if I may use the expression, to *gobble up* everything in the [Yellowstone] Park by railroads and hotel companies and herders.—Mr. John A. Logan of Ill., U. S. Senate, May 27: *Id.,* p. 4549/1.

1887   Suppose the District engineer . . . . was *gobbled up* by opposing inter-
      ests, . . . what then?—Mr. J. G. Cannon of Ill., H. R., Feb. 14: *Id.*,
      p. 1747/1.

1895   England is engaged in a system of *gobbling up* territory in foreign
      countries, and therefore she has been compelled . . . to build this
      enormous navy.—Mr. Jerry Simpson of Kan., H. R., Feb. 15: *Id.*,
      p. 2242/2.

Go behind. To attempt to ascertain the facts. See Vol. I, **Go back of.**
    [1839-1890.]

1861   It is a thing settled, an award made, ... and therefore we cannot
      go behind it, and make any inquiry whatever.—Mr. William P. Fes-
      senden of Me., U. S. Senate, Feb. 2: *C. G.,* p. 705/3.

1869   Could the Vice President *go behind* and inquire into the character of
      the laws of the several States where the electors are chosen?—Mr.
      Francis Thomas of Md., H. R., Feb. 13: *Id.,* p. 1190/2.

1869   Governor Geary had no formal returns to *go behind.* But Governor
      Packer had the formal returns . . . . [And] he *went behind* those
      formal returns.—Mr. G. W. Scofield of Pa., H. R., Apr. 2: *Id.,*
      p. 455/1.

1877   It is claimed that Congress has no power to *go behind* the certificate
      of the canvassing officers of the State to see if what they certify is true
      or false.—Mr. Levi Warner of Conn., H. R., Feb. 24: *C. R.,* p. 119/2,
      App.

1877   Much has been said here . . . about *"going behind the returns,"* and
      the terrible consequences of such an act. You would suppose that if
      it was once established that so terrible a crime as to go for a moment
      "behind the returns" could be perpetrated, we should wander in the
      great wilderness. . . . . In no real, proper, true sense is it proposed
      to *"go behind the returns."* It is only proposed to go *to* the returns,
      not *behind* them.—Remarks of Mr. Commissioner Abbott: 'Proceed-
      ings of the Electoral Commission,' p. 232/2.

Go Democratic, Go Republican, &c. See second quotation.

1877   Had the State by unaccountable means really *gone Democratic,* we
      should have heard nothing of this flippant talk.—Mr. J. H. Rainey of
      S. C., Feb. 21: *C. R.,* p. 217/2, App.

1887   A State is said to *go Democratic,* or to *go Republican,* when it votes
      for one or the other cause after being for a time doubtful, or on
      the other side.—R. A. Proctor, 'Americanisms,' in *Knowledge,* Dec. 28.
      (N. E. D.)

1889   Marlborough was by no means unlikely to have *gone Jacobite* after
      all.—*Sat. Rev.,* p. 589/2. (N. E. D.)

1890   The constituency has alternately *"gone"* Gladstonian and Tory.—*Id.,*
      p. 213/2. (N. E. D.)

1897   [The other day] Chicago *went Democratic,* and St. Louis *went
      Republican.*—Mr. R. Bartholdt of Mo., H. R., Apr. 22: *C. R.,*
      p. 812/1.

Go-devil. A device for exploding a dynamite cartridge in an oil well.
    (Century Dict., with illustration).

1887   A queer-looking pointed piece of iron, called the *go-devil,* is dropped
      down the well, and [strikes] a cap on the top of the torpedo.—*St.
      Nicholas,* xiv, 48.

Go-devil. A rough sled used for hauling logs, one end of them dragging
    on the snow or ice: otherwise called a *tie-boy.* (Century Dict.)

God's country. A term sometimes applied to the U. S., or to some
    particular part thereof, according to the speaker's predilection.

1870   There was a crash of musketry, the rebel skirmishers gave way, and
      the first line of rebel works was transferred to *"God's country."*—Mr.
      Jasper Packard of Ind., H. R., Feb. 5: *C. G.,* p. 1057/2.

1896 I have a letter here which comes from *God's own country,* down in Mississippi.—Mr. David B. Hill of N. Y., U. S. Senate, Apr. 16: *C. R.,* p. 4047/2.

Go for. To be in favor of, to support. [1834-1846.]

1861 [The bill] provides for . . two railroads—a southern and a northern one—to terminate at San Francisco. I will *go for* both these roads at the proper time. I would *go for* two or three railroads to terminate at San Francisco.—Mr. Joseph Lane of Ore., U. S. Senate, Jan. 15: *C. G.,* p. 383/1.

1862 Mr. Fisher:—"I understand the gentleman from Ohio voted for Stephen A. Douglas." Mr. S. S. Cox:—"Voted for him! I *went for* him, heart, soul, and boots."—H. R., May 2: *Id.,* p. 1935/1.

1867 I can *go for* no such resolution as this, and I think it totally idle and unnecessary.—Mr. B. F. Wade of O., U. S. Senate, July 5: *Id.,* p. 492/2.

Go for. To attack. [1838-1888.]

1868 [He said] that in such a house was a Yankee officer, and suggested that they should *go for* him. Thereupon [they] went to the house, and captured the Union soldier.—Mr. B. C. Cook of Ill., H. R., June 20: *C. G.,* p. 3329/1.

1872 Do you not think [Mr. Beck] would . . . . *"go for"* the unlucky individual who should suggest such a thing?—Mr. R. T. W. Duke of Va., H. R., May 2: *Id.,* p. 3013/1.

Go, from the word. From the outset.

1866 *From the very word "go"* I have been a conservative.—Mr. Edgar Cowan of Pa., U. S. Senate, Dec. 11: *C. G.,* p. 61/2.

1874 There is no man so dear to me that I will not fight him *from the word "go"* until the election closes, if he is unsound on this question.— Mr. J. R. Hawley of Conn., H. R., Apr. 1: *C. R.,* p. 2708/2.

1885 He was a drag and a brake on me *from the word Go.*—W. D. Howells, "Silas Lapham" (1891), I, 82. (N. E. D.)

1888 He met with hosts of friends from the very start, and he prospered *from the word "go."*—Henry Clews, "Twenty-Eight Years in Wall St.," p. 417. (N. Y.)

Going. Condition of ways for travelling. Bartlett, 1859.

1887 The *going* was bad, and the little mares could only drag the wagon at a walk.—*Century Mag.,* xxxvi, 51.

1890 It was the spring of the year, and the *going* was dreadful.—S. O. Jewett, "Cunner-fishing." (Century Dict.)

Go it alone. To play the game single-handed,—a simile from the game of euchre. [1855.]

1874 Our forefathers [did not act] upon the idea that a member of Congress was to take his carpet-bag and *"go it alone"* [while in Washington].— Mr. G. F. Edmunds of Vt., U. S. Senate, Jan. 9: *C. R.,* p. 517/1.

Go it blind. To act without due consideration or information. [1846-1875.]

1842 See Locofoco.

1866 Mr. Thayer:—I have no idea of *"going it blind"* on the statement of any person. Mr. Hale:—What does the gentleman mean by *"going it blind"?* It is a thing strange to me. Mr. Thayer:—It is one of the expressions of the day, and means voting for a thing on the say-so of some other person when you do not know who the person is, or what he says.—H. R., May 23: *C. G.,* p. 2787/1.

1894 When you get your heads set, gentlemen, it does not make any difference where you are to be led, or into what kind of a pit you are to fall, you will *"go it blind"* when a Democrat is in the lead, regardless of consequences.—Mr. G. W. Ray of N. Y., H. R., July 16: *C. R.,* p. 7559/1.

Gold bugs. Those persons in favor of the gold standard. (?)
1879 I realize, Mr. Speaker, that when I shall have taken my seat fresh
raids upon *gold bugs* will be in regular order.—Mr. S. B. Chittenden
of N. Y., H. R., May 8: *C. R.,* p. 1170/2.
1886 At that time there was no prejudice for or against either gold or
silver. It was before the days of *"gold-bugs"* and "bloated bondholders."—Mr. G. W. Dargan of S. C., H. R., March 27: *Id.,* p.
2846/1.
1886 If a *gold-bug* will vote right, I am entirely willing he should do so.
It does not frighten me to see *goldites* voting to preserve greenbacks.—
Mr. J. B. Weaver of Ia., H. R., June 24: *Id.,* p. 6090/2.
1890 The *gold bugs* of the East and the silver kings of the West have come
to an understanding.—Mr. T. C. McRae of Ark., H. R., Jan. 28: *Id.,*
p. 366/1, App.
1890 The gentlemen on the other side . . . . care very little about American
"gold bugs," but they are deeply interested in the *"gold bugs"* of
Europe.—Mr. Joseph D. Taylor of O., H. R., May 17: *Id.,* p. 4856/1.
1890 Years ago you attempted to strangle the greatest industry of the
West by clandestinely demonetizing silver, the money of the Constitution, in the interest of the *gold-bugs.*—Mr. T. J. Clunie of Calif.,
H. R., May 19: *Id.,* p. 4921/1.
1892 Behind . . . all this talk about *"gold-bugs"* . . . . the fact is that there
is a class, represented here, who are looking for some device by which
an honest debt of 100 cents can be paid with 70 cents.—Mr. Chas. W.
Stone of Pa., H. R., March 23: *Id.,* p. 2410/1.
1892 [The farmer's] contracts and mortgages are today mostly payable in
gold. When they become due, with gold out of circulation, he would
be at the absolute mercy of the much-abused *gold-bug.* He must give
whatever the said *"bug"* requires for the gold.—Mr. James N. Castle
of Minn., H. R., March 24: *Id.,* p. 74/1, App.
1893 The *gold bug* and the *silver bug* are subject to the same fortune in
common. The financial blow which prostrates one can not fail to
shake, if indeed it does not shatter, the other.—Mr. S. L. Milliken of
Me., H. R., Aug. 24: *Id.,* p. 852/2.
1893 The American banker . . . . is pictured here as a shark in Wall Street;
a *gold bug* east of the Alleghenies; a vulture in Lombard Street; and
the incarnation of the rest of the odious part of the animal kingdom in
the various market places of the world.—Mr. J. C. Hendrix of N. Y.,
H. R., Aug. 26: *Id.,* p. 986/1.
1893 A man who has been born and reared in New York, if he is a pet
among the *gold bugs,* will be a *gold bug.*—Mr. B. F. Grady of N. C.,
H. R., Aug. 24: *Id.,* p. 3/2, App.
1896 Mr. Sherman:—He calls me, what is it?—a *gold bug.* Well, sir, I
am a *gold bug.* Mr. Teller:—I think, if the Senator from Ohio will
look over my speeches, he will find that I have never called him a
gold bug.—U. S. Senate, Apr. 29: *Id.,* p. 4561/1.
1896 Previous to the advent of the present Executive into national political
life, the voice of the *gold bug* was rarely . . heard in Democratic
ranks.—Mr. H. W. Ogden of La., H. R., Feb. 11: *Id.,* p. 148/1, App.
Golden State, The. California.
1874 From the hills of *the Golden State* we will send horses, mules, and
cattle of every breed, &c. [to the Centennial Exhibition].—Mr. John
K. Luttrell of Calif., H. R., May 7: *C. R.,* p. 246/2, App.
Gold fever. A mania for going in quest of gold.
1875 Everything indicates that we are on the eve of another of those subtle
contagions commonly called a *"gold fever,"* an epidemic that will result
perhaps in disaster and ruin to thousands of people, like that of Pike's
Peak in 1859.—Mr. J. J. Ingalls of Kan., U. S. Senate, March 15:
C. R., p. 55/1.

Goloid. A mixture of gold and silver: the "electrum" of the ancients.
1879   The Greeks and Romans descended to plated coin, and . . . tried at length the *"goloid,"* the very mixture which the distinguished gentleman from Georgia, the chairman of the Committee on Coinage, Weights, and Measures now admires and recommends. . . . . It is a reasonable assumption that "electrum" (our *goloid*) was popular, for the convenient reason that it favored rascals and fostered fraud.—Mr. S. B. Chittenden of N. Y., H. R., May 8: *C. R.,* p. 1171/1.

Goober. A peanut. Probably from African *ngooba.*
1885   Raking *goobers* out of the ground.—*U. S. Cons. Rep.,* liv., 382. (Cent. Dict.)
1887   Hogs that had been fed on acorns and *goobers.—Boston Journal,* Dec. 31, p. 2/4. (N. E. D.)
1888   Peanuts, known in the vernacular as *"goobers."—Century Mag.,* xxxvi, 770/2. (N. E. D.)
1888   Tennessee, Virginia, and North Carolina . . . . go for *"goobers"* at a cent a pound.—Mr. S. S. Cox of N. Y., H. R., May 17: *C. R.,* p. 4334/1.

Good enough Morgans. Fictions designed to serve a temporary use. [1856.]   The phrase has been attributed to Thurlow Weed (1797-1882), who was a prominent Anti-Mason. William Morgan of N. Y. State disappeared in Sept., 1826, after announcing his intention of publishing a book which should reveal the secrets of Masonry; and it was commonly reported that the Freemasons murdered him.
1827   The election of 1827 elicited an accusation against me which assumed [large] proportions. . . . Ebenezer Griffin, Esq., observed laughingly to me: "After we have proven that the body found at Oak Orchard is that of Timothy Monroe, what will you do for a Morgan?" I replied in the same spirit: "That is *a good enough Morgan* for us until you bring back the one you carried off."—Thurlow Weed, "Autobiogr.," I, 319. On the following day the Rochester *Daily Advertiser* gave what became the popular version of the story, namely, that Mr. Weed had declared that, whatever might be proven, the body "was *a good enough Morgan until after the election."*—C. L. Norton, "Political Americanisms."
[1829   So the affair of Capt. William Morgan—perhaps some few, who are called Masons, have killed him!—perhaps not. Who knows?—Lorenzo Dow, "Omnifarious Law Exemplified," p. 41. (New London, Conn.)]
1878   The decision of today . . . [may be] merely a sham, intended to delude the people; "a *good enough Morgan* until after the election."—Mr. John H. Baker of Ind., H. R., Apr. 4: *C. R.,* p. 2279/2.
1888   It makes no difference whether these facts are true or false, since he considers that, for the time being they will be *"good enough Morgan."* —*N. Y. Sun,* March 10: cited in *C. R.,* March 15, p. 2108/1.
1890   This bill is a mere makeshift, "a *good enough Morgan* until after election." It means nothing; it will do nothing; and in my judgment it is meant to do nothing.—Mr. J. L. Chipman of Mich., H. R., Aug. 30: *C. R.,* p. 9418/1.
1893   Is it the plighted word of men of honor to accomplish certain things, or is it only "A *good enough Morgan"* till after election?—Mr. Champ Clark of Mo., H. R., Aug. 19: *Id.,* p. 527/2.
1897   Mr. Hale:—I know about the case of John Scott. But they are Sanguilys, or Delgados, or Ruiz, or names of that kind. There is not one real Morgan among them. Mr. Platt of Conn:—"*A good enough Morgan until after the election."*—U. S. Senate, May 10: p. 947/2.

Good Indian. It has been said that an Indian is never good but when he is dead. See 1876.

1863 They will sign anything. They would all sign a paper today, stating that they were *good Indians.*—Mr. Henry M. Rice of Minn., U. S. Senate, Jan. 26 : *C. G.,* p. 511/1.

1863 In many cases those so-called *"good Indians,"* who had received the most favors and professed the warmest friendship, were the most brutal.—Mr. W. Windom of Minn., H. R., Feb. 28 : *Id.,* p. 143/2, App.

1868 I like an Indian better dead than living. I have never in my life seen a *good Indian* (and I have seen thousands) except when I have seen a dead Indian.—Mr. J. M. Cavanaugh of Mont., H. R., May 28 : *Id.,* p. 2638/3.

1870 A spirit of retributive justice and relentless hatred of the offending race, which . . . shocks the ears of uninformed civilization with the expression of its belief that the *good Indians* are the dead Indians. Sir, if we throw an iron lariat about this vicious beast, ... we shall speedily solve the problem of "what to do with the Indian." The Shoshone and the buffalo will be domesticated; the Apache and the panther will be destroyed.—Mr. Thomas Fitch of Nev., H. R., Apr. 29 : *Id.,* p. 3106/2.

1871 I never said that in my opinion "the dead Indians were the only *good Indians."*—The same, Jan. 25 : *Id.,* p. 731/1.

1876 I do not propose that the Indian shall ever be put under the control of any Army officer; I do not care whether it be General Sherman, or General Sheridan, whose only motto in regard to the Indian is that he did once see a *good Indian,* but he was a dead one. . . . He never saw a *good Indian* but what was dead.—Mr. Wilshire of Ark., H. R., Apr. 19 : *C. R.,* p. 2625/1.

1878 The reputed saying of General Sheridan that "the only *good Indian* is the dead Indian."—Mr. C. G. Williams of Wisc., H. R., May 27 : *Id.,* p. 467/1, App.

1878 The best wild Indian I ever saw was a dead one.—Mr. Thos. Ryan of Kan., H. R., Dec. 19 : *Id.,* p. 316/2.

1884 The old idea that "the only *good Indians* are dead Indians" has been given the lie at Carlisle, at Lincoln School, at Hampton, at Forest Grove, among the Dakota schools, and wherever the educational plan has been faithfully tried.—Mr. B. M. Cutcheon of Mich., H. R., Apr. 3 : *Id.,* p. 2567/2.

Goods, deliver the. Come up to requirements; make good one's statements.

1879 There are men in the North who walk around with ponderous brows and oracular utterance, saying, "See me; I am a statesman. The North will stand by you; put me forward, and I will take you to victory. They cannot *deliver the goods."*—Mr. J. R. Hawley of Conn., H. R., Apr. 4 : *C. R.,* p. 236/1.

1880 Mr. Teller of Colo. :—I will pledge every vote on our side of the Chamber. Mr. Eaton of Conn. :—You cannot *deliver the goods.*— U. S. Senate, May 25 : *C. R.,* p. 3758/1.

Goods, the. The thing bargained for. [1852-1911.]

1812 Federalists call the troops now raising "A Standing Army." They are mistaken in *the goods.*—Norfolk (Va.) *Herald,* May 29, p. 3/4.

1892 Mr. Vest :—The Mexican minister wanted to know what he was going to pay for. . . . . Mr. George :—He wanted to look at *the goods.* Mr. Vest :—Yes, he wanted to look at *the goods.*—U. S. Senate, Jan. 19 : *C. R.,* p. 405/1.

Good time, a. A time of enjoyment; sometimes of revelry. [1843-1874.]

1874 I believe in the Fourth of July all over, from the crown of my head to the sole of my feet. As a boy and young man I fired my guns and had my *good time.*—Mr. J. R. Hawley of Conn., H. R., May 7 : *C. R.,* p. 258/1, App.

1876 We [people from the interior of Ill.] like to travel around Chicago, to pay for our whisky and cigars, and *have a good time generally.*— Mr. Cannon of Ill., H. R., June 22: *Id.,* p. 4045/1.

1894 [Certain owners of yachts] want a stopping place somewhere between New York and New London, where they can stop and have a clambake and a *good time.*—Mr. G. W. Ray of N. Y., H. R., May 3: *Id.,* p. 4389/2.

Go (a person) **one better.** To excel, to play higher. [1859-1910.]

1866 I will say "amen to the eulogy" and *go* [the eulogist] *one better* on it, in the language of the West.—Mr. R. F. Spalding of O., H. R., July 14: *C. G.,* p. 3823/1.

1874 The Senator from North Carolina [Mr. Merrimon] proposes an increase of 46 millions of banking circulation. The Senator from Pennsylvania [Mr. Cameron] *goes him better,* and proposes an unlimited increase.—Mr. Timothy O. Howe of Wisc., U. S. Senate, Feb. 17: *C. R.,* p. 1556/1.

Goose creek. A very shallow creek; that is, a small stream. See **Creek.**

1878 Farther inland—you find little *"goose creeks,"* trout streams, and almost waterless rivers.—Mr. S. S. Cox of N. Y., H. R., Apr. 23: *C. R.,* p. 2747/1.

Goose (the) hangs high. Affairs are prosperous.

1874 Big riot today [in Enfaula]. Several killed and many others hurt, some badly, but none of our friends among them. *The white man's goose hangs high.*—*Morning News,* Montgomery, Ala., Nov. 4: See *C. R.,* Feb. 27, 1875, p. 1902/1.

1894 If you believe there is a plethora of money, if you believe everything is lovely, and *the goose hangs high,* go down to the soup houses in the city of New York.—Mr. W. J. Stone of Ky., H. R., Feb. 14: *Id.,* p. 2185/2.

1894 It does not look to me that just now the Democratic horizon is altogether lovely, or that *the antiquated bird is beautifully suspended at an elongated altitude.*—Mr. Robt. Neill of Ark., H. R., Feb. 26: *Id.,* p. 2438/1.

1894 We were going on in a way that might be satisfactory even to the Senator from Tennessee [Mr. Harris]; .... everything was lovely, and *every goose hung high.*—Mr. Eugene Hale of Me., U. S. Senate, June 11: *Id.,* p. 6106/2.

Gopher. The pouched rat; also a ground squirrel. [1812-1858.]

1789 [The dog] expired by the mouth of a *megopher's* hole.—Augusta (Ga.) *Chronicle,* July 11, p. 4/2.

1886 Instances are related in which potato heaps covered with earth and left out during winter have been entered by the *gophers* and the tubers carried off. They sometimes enter melons, pumpkins, and squashes through holes at the bottom, and eat out all the fleshy part, and then fill the hollow rind with earth, leaving it in a condition to create much astonishment, when harvested. They also feed upon the bark of the roots of trees, as well as upon the fleshy roots of herbaceous plants. Some of our prairie farmers are greatly injured by their destruction of osage orange hedges.—Statement of Robert Kennicott: see *C. R.,* June 10, p. 5499/1.

Gopher. A species of land turtle. [1791-1841.]

1894 Mr. Stockdale:—The *gopher* proper is not a ground squirrel at all. It is more like a terrapin. ... Mr. Cummings:—I want to say that the *gopher* [referred to] is a native of Florida; that it has a shell with a hinge in front: that it burrows in the ground; and that the darkies in Florida consider it very fine eating. They are very dangerous little animals, because they make great holes in the ground in the palmetto scrub, and the cowboys frequently, in rounding up their cattle, ride their horses into those holes and break their legs.—H. R., March 15: *Id.,* p. 2995.

Gospo. See quotation.

1894 Honest dealing was to be enforced, and the people permitted to buy pure *gospo,* instead of an alleged "impure mixture injurious to health and fraudulently branded."—Mr. C. J. Boatner of La., H. R., July 21: *C. R.,* p. 1085/1, App. [The allusion is to lard and cottonseed oil.]

Gostration. Bragging; showing off; vainglorious conduct. Colloquial.

1840 See HOOSIER.

1864 With the blustering *gostration* of the cock, [he] would scare the enemy to death without a fight, and save his powder.—Mr. Dumont of Ind., H. R., Apr. 11: *C. G.,* p. 1556/1.

Gotham. Usually New York. Here, apparently the North. [1800-1851.]

1863 In an evil hour the foolish, I will not say wicked, "men of *Gothem"* (*sic*) persuaded her merchant princes . . . that she could retain or force back the southern trade by war.—Mr. Clement L. Vallandigham of O., H. R., Jan. 14: *C. G.,* p. 58/2, App.

Go the limit. See **Limit.**

Go the whole hog. To proceed thoroughly and without reservations. [1821-1854.]

1832 [Mr. Felix Grundy] says, "I claim to be *a whole-hog Jackson man,* because I voted for that fellow Biddle."—Chas. Biddle, "Senator Grundy's Political Conduct Reviewed," p. 22. (Nashville, Tenn.)

1867 *Went the Whole Hog.* Henry Thompson, a stout, able-bodied, greasy-looking nig, was yesterday arrested . . . on a charge of having stolen and killed a hog weighing two hundred pounds.—Memphis paper, quoted Feb. 20 in the *C. G.,* p. 1631/3.

Go to Halifax.* See first quotation.

1876 [The tories or loyalists, after the revolution], went to England, to France, to Nova Scotia, to New Brunswick, and especially to Halifax; and that town was such a resort for them, that it became the swear-word of our boyhood. *"Go to Halifax"* was a substitute for a more impious, but not more opprobrious expression. The presence of tories made it opprobrious.—Mr. James A. Garfield of O., H. R., Aug. 4: *C. R.,* pp. 5184-5.

1882 He told them . . . . that he had no further use for them, and they could go home, ashore, or *to Halifax.*—Mr. A. S. Willis of Ky., H. R., July 13: *Id.,* p. 6015/1.

Go-to-meeting clothes, Sunday clothes. One's best clothes. [1825-1854.]

1815 Changing my old shabby duds for these new Sabbada close, fit for a *go-to-meeting* day, enny wheres.—David Humphreys, "The Yankey in England," p. 29.

Go to pieces. To become disintegrated and ruined.

1878 They are all *going to pieces.* . . . I should not be surprised to hear of their going up at any moment.—*Scribner's Mag.,* xvi, 864/2. (N. E. D. s. v. Go UP.)

1890 You have *gone to pieces* on the tariff. The people are repudiating your sham civil-service pretension; they are deserting you everywhere. —Mr. John M. Allen of Miss., H. R., Apr. 23: *C. R.,* p. 3740/2.

---

* The expression may perhaps be connected with Halifax and its gibbet in Yorks; but the connection is not clear. See *N. & Q.,* 5 S. iv, 66, 154.

Gotten. Archaic in England, but common in the U. S. **Got** is also used, however. [1769-1909.] "Gotten up" here is much the same as "stirred up" or "cooked up."

1880 I have seen the liveliest fights *gotten up* here upon pretended privileges that I ever saw anywhere in my life, beating even an Irish fair.— Mr. W. P. Frye of Me., H. R., Jan. 22: *C. R.*, p. 482/2.

Gouge. Punching holes; cutting roughly; scooping out as with a gouge. In second quotation *to gore.*

1616 I will save in cork . . . . by *googing* of them out Just to the size of my bottles.—Ben Jonson, "The Devil is an Ass," II, 1.

1863 If, like a pen of ill-managed cattle, one *gouges* one way, and one another, how are we to come together?—Mr. Thomas H. Hicks of Md., U. S. Senate, Feb. 28: *C. G.*, p. 1373/1.

Gouge. To cheat; to get what one wants "out of" some one else. [1845.]

1867 The East has the superior advantage of shrewdness in "*gouging.*" It has secured most of the benefits of the Government. It has the most of the patronage.—Mr. Thomas E. Noell of Mo., H. R., July 20: *C. G.*, p. 765/2.

1867 This whole thing goes on the ground that Senators are stealing, that they are committing petty larceny, *gouging* sheets of paper and quills, and all that sort of thing.—Mr. Wm. P. Fessenden of Me., U. S. Senate, Dec. 19: *Id.*, p. 274/3.

1883 As long as we have this system of funding and refunding and cheating and *gouging,* playing tricks upon one another, ... there is no use to talk about restoring our commerce.—Mr. G. W. Ladd of Me., H. R., Jan. 9: *C. R.*, p. 1027/2.

Gouger. An old-fashioned snow-plow.

1903 It consisted of a strongly built box-car which carried a plow at its head, set low enough to run under a drift and throw it over.—*Sci. Amer.*, p. 8. (Century Dict.)

Governmental. Pertaining to government. [1744-1850.]

1744 The *governmental* view . . was . . . well settled, &c.—"Coll. Ga. Hist. Soc." (1840), I, 96. (N. E. D.)

1781 One part out of seventy-three of all governmental taxes . . . . *governmental* employments in Conn.—S. Peters, "Hist. Conn.," pp. 171, 286. (N. E. D.)

1879 Not the Legislature of the State, not a *governmental* body to make laws for a State, but a legislature of the U. S.—Mr. Geo. M. Robeson of N. J., H. R., Apr. 23: *C. R.*, p. 751/1.

Grab bag. A mild form of lottery used at church fairs, &c. [1864-1879.]

1876 The game was a game of pure chance, just as at your fairs you put your hand in a "*grab-bag*" and pay for taking out all that your hand can include.—Mr. Whyte of Md., U. S. Senate, June 30: *C. R.*, p. 4263/1.

Grab game. A mode of stealing or grabbing; originated by swindlers.

1859 See Bartlett, who adds: "The term is . . used in a more general sense to signify stealing and making off with the booty."

1864 A bold, daring, unscrupulous man, who, in the language of his acquaintances, practised the *grab game*.—R. B. Kimball, "Was He Successful?" (N. Y.), ix, 116. (N. E. D.)

1872 Gentlemen talk about this being a *grab game*. Sir, what is a *grab game*? It is giving to a railroad corporation a strip of territory a hundred miles in width, and extending across this continent. That is a *grab game*.—Mr. John Coburn of Ind., H. R., May 7: *C. G.*, p. 3172/2.

1890 It is a *grab game* all around, and as usual the rich monopolists and manufacturers are given a greater scope to continue their system of robbery than was afforded them by the war tariff bill.—Mr. T. J. Clunie of Calif., H. R., May 19: *C. R.*, p. 4920/2.

1895   This eventuated in preventing the *grab game* of France.—*The Forum,* N. Y., p. 265. (N. E. D.)

Grade. The inclination of a road upward or downward. Hence to *grade* a road, to adjust its inclination. [1835.] [*At grade,* on the same level.]

1869   Mr. Dickey:—Does not the junction road to which the gentleman has referred cross the streets of Phila. *at grade?* Mr. O'Neill:—No, sir: it crosses them *above grade* in nearly every instance.—H. R., March 24: *C. G.,* p. 252/3.

1870   I have great respect for Minnesota, although I do not think much railroad is *graded* there in the middle of February.—Mr. Allen G. Thurman of O., U. S. Senate, Apr. 11: *C. G.,* p. 2581/1.

1890   Petition . . . . for leave to cross the Grand Trunk tracks at North Stratford *at grade.*—*Boston Journal,* Aug. 26, p. 4/2. (N. E. D.)

1894   It is difficult for trains to stop at these places on account of the *grades.*—Mr. J. H. Gear of Ia., H. R., Feb. 17: *C. R.,* p. 2259/2.

Grafter. One who receives an illicit commission or profit, particularly in connection with a political job. See Vol. I for **Graft.** [Thieves' cant.]

1901   See Gun.

Gramma or **Grama.** A kind of grass suitable for pasture.

1851   There the *grama grass* is longer and more luxuriant.—Mayne Reid, "The Scalp Hunters," ch. xxvi. (N. E. D.)

1863   The entire surface of the country [in Southern Colorado], with some slight exceptions, is covered with grass of a peculiar rich quality, known as *gramma or buffalo grass.*—Mr. H. P. Bennet of Colo., H. R., Feb. 28: *C. G.,* p. 140/3, App.

1869   There is very little land [between St. Joseph and Denver] which will not bear not only buffalo grass but *gramma grass,*—the *gramma* grass of Mexico, almost as nutritious as oats.—Mr. Roscoe Conkling of N. Y., U. S. Senate, Jan. 25: *Id.,* p. 579/1.

1870   The short, wiry *gramma* . . . is the main support of the herds along the Platte.—F. H. Ludlow, "The Heart of the Continent," p. 109.

1884   [These] are high table-lands, usually covered with a thin growth of *gramma* or mesquite grass.—Mr. P. B. Plumb of Kan., U. S. Senate, June 27: *C. R.,* p. 5682/2.

Grand Old Party, or **G. O. P.** Usually the Republican Party.

1879   This phrase was applied by Mr. Hill of Georgia to the Democratic party. "We are for national parties now. We come back to the *grand old party* of the North, that never went off after secession, that never went after the Baals of consolidation. If there are any men on this earth for whom I have a higher regard than others, they are the democrats of the North."—U. S. Senate, June 11: *C. R.,* p. 1913/1.

1888   Old Farmer:—Is this Democratic doings or Republican doings? Collector:—O, it is the doings of the *G. O. P.,*—the *grand old party,*—the Republican party.—Speech of Mr. C. T. O'Ferrall of Va., H. R., May 1: *C. R.,* p. 3598/1.

1888   I am glad that I am a member of that *grand old party* that assures a better trade to our people, larger wages, &c.—Mr. Edward Lane of Ill., H. R., May 10: *Id.,* p. 3981/1. [The Democratic party.]

1890   Hurrah for honest citizens who vindicate the right;
Hurrah for law and liberty, the people won the fight.
Republican corruptionists went weeping to their fate,
For the voters placed the brand upon the men who stole the State.
We whipped them in the north of town, we whipped them in the south,
We whipped the man who "worked" the State, and him who worked his mouth;

We whipped them in the west of town, we whipped them in the east,
And we've placed a little tombstone o'er the grave of the deceased.
The mourners speak in whispers, there's crape upon the door,
The *G. O. P.* was killed by stealing precinct thirty-four.
—Message from Butte, Mont.: *C. R.,* p. 3388/1, Apr. 15.

1890 Was it the object of the framers of this bill . . . . to provide places
for such workers and members of the *G. O. P.* as the present administration had failed to find "holes" to stick these "pegs" in?—Mr. J. A.
Geissenhainer of N. J., H. R., June 28: *Id.,* p. 6735/2.

1894 See ELEPHANT.

1898 Has the *Grand Old Party* (G. O. P.) so called never been corrupt?
Has it never had dishonest men in it?—Mr. E. H. Driggs of N. Y.,
H. R., Jan. 7: *Id.,* p. 444/1.

Grand Old Roman, The. Allen G. Thurman (1813-1895).

1893 He spoke . . . of the *grand Old Roman* from Ohio, who occupied a
seat in this Chamber for so many years.—Mr. David B. Hill of N. Y.,
U. S. Senate, Oct. 17: *C. R.,* p. 2594/1.

Grange, Granger. A grange is an agricultural society. Grangers are
members of such a society.

1874 I am glad to see *grangers* and other organizations—the people in their
primary capacity—holding frequent meetings . . . to discuss public
affairs.—Mr. David B. Mellish of N. Y., H. R., Jan. 10: *C. R.,*
p. 563/2.

1874 I am not a *granger,* and do not want to give them what they want.
I say it very boldly. I do not like *granger* principles. The *grangers*
did not nominate me; the *grangers* did not vote for me.—Mr. W. W.
Phelps of N. J., H. R., Feb. 24: *Id.,* p. 1754/1.

1875 The great convention of the *Granges* held at Springfield, Ill.—C. F.
Adams, *N. Am. Rev.,* cxx, 405. (N. E. D.)

1875 The time has now come when the *Granger* can be looked upon as a
phenomenon of the past.—*Id.,* p. 395. (N. E. D.)

Granite State, The. New Hampshire. [1830-1842.]

1872 The past summer I had occasion to visit my early home in the old
Granite State.—Mr. E. A. Hibbard of N. H., H. R., May 9: *Id.,*
p. 3235/2.

Grapevine telegram. A canard. [1864-1865.]

1890 [Alluding to a dispatch in the *N. Y. Sun*], Mr. Cutcheon:—That was
a heliogram—a "sun" dispatch. Mr. Williams:—What we used to call
a *"grape-vine."*—H. R., Aug. 22: C. R., p. 9049/2.

1909 We thought that the *"grapevine telegraph,"* by which news moves so
swiftly and mysteriously among the negroes, had warned the thief.—
H. H. Bennett, *Atlantic Monthly,* p. 713/1. (Nov.)

Grasshopper district. An electoral district of scattered parts, contrived
for political purposes. See **Gerrymander** and **Shoestring district.**

1882 See DUMB-BELL DISTRICT.

Grayback. A Confederate soldier. [1862-1882.]

1864 [Suppose Gen. Lee had been successful at Gettysburg], a considerable
portion of the State of Pennsylvania, for a longer or shorter period,
would have been overrun by *graybacks.*—Mr. Chandler of Va., H. R.,
May 17: *C. G.,* p. 2319/2.

1868 The rebel Democracy can only carry the Southern States for their
greenback and *grayback* ticket by menace, intimidation, and violence
at the polls.—Mr. Henry Wilson of Mass., U. S. Senate, July 21: *Id.,*
p. 4280/1.

1884 [Miss Dame] was always present where most needed, and to the suffering, whether "Yank" or *"Grayback,"* she was truly an angel of
mercy.—Letter by Gen. Gilman Marston of N. H., *C. R.,* p. 5709/1.

Gray Eagle of the Quinsigamond, The. Mr. Joseph H. Walker of Worcester, Mass.

1897 My venerable Republican friend, *"the gray eagle of the Quinsigamond,"* swooped down . . . with fierce beak and bloody talons.—Mr. G. D. Perkins of Ia., H. R., March 30: *C. R.,* p. 482/1.

Greased lightning. An emblem of rapidity. [1833-1888.]

1863 Vanish now, like *greased lightning.*—Edmund Kirke, "My Southern Friends," p. 250.

Greaser. A Mexican. [1849-1890.]

1849 [At Saltillo, Mexico] the *greaser* buys theatre tickets for one bit.—Wilmington (N. C.) *Commercial,* July 19, p. 2/2.

1862 My colleague [Mr. Biddle] felicitously interwove the pet phrases of the Mexican *greaser* and the barroom lounger . . . with the magnificent rhetoric of Chatham and Sumner.—Mr. W. D. Kelley of Pa., H. R., June 3: *C. G.,* p. 2528/2.

1864 In the frontier settlements . . . . there are a set of *greasers,* poachers, men that will not live by industry, but by Rob Roy practices.—Mr. Garrett Davis of Ky., U. S. Senate, March 9: *Id.,* p. 1003/2.

1866 See CLAY-EATERS.

1867 A great deal of sympathy is expended here upon that hybrid race of mixed breed Spaniards, Indians, and negroes, known by the generic name of *greasers,* headed by a mongrel president.—Mr. T. E. Noell of Mo., H. R., Feb. 12: *C. G.,* p. 105/3, App.

1884 [We ought to] preserve the good faith and fair fame of our Republic as well in regard to Mexican *greasers* as to our own people.—Mr. O. D. Conger of Mich., U. S. Senate, Feb. 4: *C. R.,* p. 850/2.

1890 He paid his laborers $15 per month, and hired *"greasers"* at that.—Mr. B. McMillin of Tenn., H. R., Jan. 23: *Id.,* p. 816/2.

1917 We were playing billiards, when some *greaser* said something about gringos, and I told him to shut up.—H. A. Franck, "Vagabonding down the Andes," p. 515. . (Century Co.)

Grease spot. An infinitesimally small quantity. [1836-1867.]

1894 See MILK IN THE COCOANUT.

Great Expounder, The. Daniel Webster.

1888 The celebrated controversy with Hayne and Calhoun . . won Webster the title of *"The Great Expounder of the Constitution."*—Mr. G. W. Dargan of S. C., H. R., May 10: *C. R.,* p. 3972/1.

1893 In the district which I represent . . lie buried the mortal remains of Daniel Webster, the *great expounder* and defender of the Constitution. . . . At Quincy, in my district, sleep the remains of John Adams, the second President of the U. S., and of John Quincy Adams, the old man eloquent.—Mr. E. A. Morse of Mass., H. R., Feb. 24: *Id.,* p. 2138/1.

Great Objector, The. W. S. Holman of Indiana. (1822-1897.)

1897 Having acquired the sobriquet of *"The Great Objector,"* it is generally supposed that his entire work was limited to vigilant watchfulness over public expenditures. Not so, however.—Mr. J. D. Sayers of Tex., H. R., July 8: *C. R.,* p. 2518/1.

Great Pacificator, The. A term applied to Henry Clay, especially with reference to the "Missouri Compromise."

Greenbackers. Those who advocated an over-issue of paper money. [1876-1878.]

1878 The millions who call themselves *Greenbackers.*—*N. Am. Rev.,* cxxvii, 103. (N. E. D.)

1879 In the Louisville district, Mr. Willis had to compete with a democrat, a *greenbacker,* and a republican.—Mr. Harris of Mass., H. R., Apr. 24: *C. R.,* p. 843/1.

Greenback party. See **Greenbackers.**

1880 Those who believe the greenback lion to be dead merely because he has ceased to roar for the present are sadly deluding themselves. The *greenback party* was the natural outgrowth of the depression which so long hung over our land, and now . . . the greenback lion slowly retreats, growling, to his den. But we must not flatter ourselves by thinking he is dead.—Mr. Hutchins of N. Y., H. R., June 11: *C. R.,* p. 4450/1.

1880 Be it known to the democratic side of the House and to the republican side of the House that the *greenback party* is not a republican party nor a democratic party, but it is a *greenback party,* separate and distinct in its organization.—Mr. J. B. Weaver of Ia., H. R., Dec. 21: *Id.,* p. 309/2.

Green goods. Counterfeit paper money.

1889 There are various terms used to avoid the use of the ugly words "counterfeit money," the most common one being *"green goods."*—Mr. B. A. Enloe of Tenn., H. R., Jan. 29: *C. R.,* p. 1307/2.

1894 See FLIMFLAM.

Green Mountain Boys. The Vermonters. [1775-1852.]

1775 Ethan Allen, foreseeing war with Great Britain, sent assurances to Oliver Wolcott of Conn., that "the regiment of *Green Mountain Boys* would assist their American brethren."—Geo. Bancroft, "Hist. of the U. S.," iv, 143. (1885.)

a.1775 The brave and impetuous Allen said in his letter to Congress: "I am as resolutely determined to defend the independence of Vermont as Congress is that of the U. S.; and rather than fail I will retire with the hardy *Green Mountain boys* into the desolate caverns of the mountains, and wage war with human nature at large."—Mr. Redfield Proctor of Vt. in his eulogy of John L. Chipman, U. S. Senate, Jan. 25, 1894: *C. R.,* p. 1387/1.

1876 No sooner had [Ethan Allen] reached his home than he took again his acknowledged place as the chief leader of the *Green Mountain Boys* in their unhappy contest with their neighbors of New York, and in the great cause of freedom for all the States.—Mr. G. F. Edmunds of Vt., U. S. Senate, June 10: *C. R.,* p. 3740/2.

Griddlecake. One baked on a griddle.

1783 Chas. Vallancey, "Collectanea," III, 460. (N. E. D.)

1852 Mary stood at the stove, baking *griddle-cakes.*—Mrs. H. B. Stowe, "Uncle Tom's Cabin," p. 118. (N. E. D.)

1877 [The] experiment was tried upon Humboldt. It failed; failed, sir, upon *griddle-cakes* for breakfast.—Mr. S. S. Cox of N. Y., H. R., Nov. 19: *C. R.,* p. 534/1.

Gringo. See quotation 1884.

1876 Cortina has never failed to rouse the hatred of the Mexican population against the *"gringos,"* and to incite their hopes that the hated Americans would one day be driven back beyond the Nueces.—Mr. Schleicher of Tex., H. R., June 30: *C. R.,* p. 4310/1.

1877 [The Mexicans] are aliens in every sense of the word, taught . . from childhood to hate the name of American, and contemptuously . . . . call Americans by the name *"Gringo."*—Mr. S. B. Maxey of Tex., U. S. Senate, Nov. 14: *Id.,* p. 392/1.

1884 *Gringo,* a term of ridicule and obloquy applied to Americans throughout all Mexico.—*Harper's Mag.,* p. 748/2. (N. E. D.)

1892 [He] satisfied his prejudice against these *"Gringoes,"* as the Mexicans call all Americans.—Mr. G. G. Vest of Mo., U. S. Senate, *Id.,* p. 367/2.

Gripman. The man who manipulates the grip of a machine.

1886 The driver, or *gripman,* then opened the valve.—*Science,* p. 275. (N. E. D.)

1897 Gentlemen will say, "We are compelled to have the motorman, or the *gripman,* and the conductor, under the requirements of municipal law." —Mr. E. F. Loud of Calif., H. R., Feb. 12: *C. R.,* p. 1779/1.

Gripsack or Grip. A handbag, a portmanteau. [1883.]

1895 [One day a young lady] came running to the depot in order to take a train. A big, stout fellow, very much I suppose as I am, also came running to the train; and when the train moved off, and left them both standing, the man put his *grip* down, and said, "Damn that train." The lady said sweetly to him, "I thank you."—Mr. J. M. Palmer of Ill., U. S. Senate, Jan. 17: *C. R.,* p. 1062/2.

1898 He saw there was going to be trouble, and he got his *gripsack* and went out.—Mr. S. Brundidge of Ark., H. R., Apr. 21: *Id.,* p. 4174/1.

Gripsack party, the. A term at one time used in Va., alluding to the "Carpetbaggers."

1881 [The resolution] speaks of the *"grip-sack republicans."* Is the Senator from Mass. enlightened? Does he now know which the *"grip-sack party"* is? Does the Senator belong to the *grip-sack party?* Is he a *grip-sack republican?*—Mr. B. H. Hill of Ga., U. S. Senate, March 30: *C. R.,* p. 124/1.

1881 The republican party in the U. S. have found at last their attempt to govern the Southern States through the *"grip-sack party,"* as Mr. Mahone calls them, or the carpet-bag party, as we call them, is a failure.—Mr. John T. Morgan of Ala., U. S. Senate, Apr. 14: *Id.,* p. 290/2.

Gritter. A grater. See quotation. Local.

1888 Now what is "the grate of the gritter"? That is heard in kitchens. The *"gritter"* is a piece of cast-away tin or sheet-iron, through which holes have been punched with a nail, so as to throw out the surface on one side and make it rough. In its use it is what we would call a grater. It is used by good Kentucky women, in the midst of such wealth of minerals and timber as Pennsylvania never had, for rubbing the green corn from the cob in order to cook it for a family meal.— Mr. W. D. Kelley of Pa., H. R., May 1: *C. R.,* p. 3587/2.

Grocery. A drinking place. [1806-1909.]

1863 See BIT, A.

1868 I am told that it is very common for southern gentlemen to meet at a *grocery* where they will stay from Monday morning until Saturday night, and fight, and shoot, and get up horse races and yet complain continually that negroes will not work.—Mr. Oliver P. Morton of Ind., U. S. Senate, Jan. 7: *C. G.,* p. 350/3.

1868 I was informed that two or three *groceries* had been open [in Lowell, Mass.] and free drinks had been given.—Mr. W. E. Robinson of N. Y., H. R., May 13: *Id.,* p. 2453/2.

1869 Every country store and every *cross-roads grocery* in the West and South has become a place for the sale of spirits.—Mr. Jas. R. McCormick of Mo., H. R., Feb. 12: *Id.,* p. 1154/1.

1869 In my section of the country the boys do not resort at night to the *groceries* of the neighborhood; they are otherwise engaged.—Mr. S. B. Axtell of Calif., H. R., Feb. 12: *C. G.,* p. 1156/2.

1872 [These men] may have been disorderly, but they were not drunken. There was not a *grocery* within forty miles of them.—Mr. W. L. Stoughton of Mich., H. R., Feb. 23: *Id.,* p. 1194/2.

Groggery. A low drinking den. [1824-1858.]

1862 There are all around in the towns [of Maine] these little *groggeries,* and the difficulty is in finding where they are.—Mr. William P. Fessenden of Me., U. S. Senate, May 28: *C. G.,* p. 2396/3.

1864 He had been frolicking, and he may have been to an ale-house or *groggery*,—they call them *groggeries* in the West,—or some such place. —Mr. Garrett Davis of Ky., U. S. Senate, Jan. 13: *Id.*, p. 179/2.

Grogman. A seller of liquor.

1805 Satan hoisted his standard near by, as a *grogman* brought his liquors for sale.—Lorenzo Dow, "Journal," May 31 (1850), p. 107/2.

Gross. Clumsy. A survival of rare occurrence.

1690 Some *gross* and confused Conceptions Men indeed . . . have.—Locke on the Human Understanding, III, X, § 22. (N. E. D.)

1874 Although it is a little *gross* perhaps to send the whole book [of Congressional debates], we are asked why can we not send a few pages, why not the little wise sayings that we get off.—Mr. Lot M. Morrill of Me., U. S. Senate, June 17: *C. R.*, p. 5089/2.

Grouchy. Ill-tempered, sulky. Slang.

1911 Even two *grouchy* brothers-in-law had a sneaking notion they would like to get together for the after-dinner smoke.—*N. Y. Evening Post*, Nov. 27, p. 6/2.

Ground and lofty tumbling. Acrobatic feats on the ground and on the rope. [1786-1854.]

1843 A strolling company of *"Ground and Lofty" Tumblers.*—Thurlow Weed, "Letters," p. 108. (1866.)

1868 General Sherman is suddenly honored with a brevet as general, and he is expected to put on the dress of a mountebank, and play for Mr. Johnson some feats of *ground and lofty tumbling* in the face of the nation; but the great flanker declines to be outflanked by an empty brevet, and goes off toward the sunset to look after the Indians.—Mr. John Coburn of Ind., H. R., Feb. 24: *C. G.*, p. 243/3, App.

Ground floor. To get in on the ground floor is to make a better bargain than other people: "to be allowed to share in a speculation on the same terms as the original promoters." (Farmer.)

1868 There must always be someone to stand between the seller and the company, else there could be no *"ground floor."*—Richd. B. Kimball, "Henry Powers," p. 157.

Ground, from the, up. Entirely.

1895 There never has been a time, until Grover Cleveland became President of the U. S., that a Democratic Administration has not been American *from the ground up*.—Mr. H. M. Teller of Colo., U. S. Senate, Feb. 6: *C. R.*, p. 207/1, App.

Ground hog. The woodchuck. [1789-1910.]

1894 If a jackal wants a shelter, he goes into a convenient cave. If a *ground hog* wants one, . . . he digs him a hole.—Mr. J. D. Warner of N. Y., H. R., July 18: *C. R.*, p. 6485/2.

Groundling. A plebeian. Obs. in England and rare in the U. S.

1622 We were born three stories high; no base ones. None of your *groundlings*, master.—John Fletcher, "Prophetess," I, iii. (N. E. D.)

1630 Here you shall see One unmeasurably haughtie, scorning to converse with these *groundlins* (for so it pleases him to tearme his inferiours). —R. Brathwait, "Eng. Gentleman" (1641), p. 31. (N. E. D.)

1896 I have been a *groundling* from childhood up. I had nobody to help me; not even to learn the alphabet of my native language.—Mr. W. V. Allen of Neb., U. S. Senate, Feb. 19: *C. R.*, p. 1932/2.

Grouty. Discontented. See Vol. I, **Grout.** [1836-1856.]

1898 I trust [Mr. Brucker] will not feel, to use an old-fashioned word, *"grouty"* toward the committee because we cannot do exact justice in every case.—Mr. Ray of N. Y., H. R., Feb. 4: *C. R.*, p. 1464/1.

Grub-prairie. Land that needs to be grubbed. Cf. **Grubs** and **Grubbing,** Vol. I.

1882 In *grub-prairies* in the Northwestern states, the soil is full of the roots of trees and bushes, often of the jack-oak, hazel, etc., that have been killed . . . by annual fires.—F. B. Hough, "Elements of Forestry," p. 52. (Century Dict.)

Grubstake. A bargain by which one person who is said to "grubstake" the other, furnishes him with supplies for a mining expedition, on the promise of sharing the proceeds. [1885-1900.] The usage has been extended to apply to other ventures, also.

1890 He is out of a job now and looking around for a *grubstake*.—Mr. J. B. Morgan of Miss., U. S. Senate, Apr. 15: *C. R.*, p. 3382/2.

1890 [When a prospector cannot work his claim], it is no more to him in value than the rock upon the mountain side; in fact it will not bring him intrinsically a single *"grub stake."*—Mr. G. C. Moody of S. D., U. S. Senate, Aug. 12: *Id.*, p. 8455/2.

1912 Colorado Springs, Col., Oct. 30.—Two million dollars' worth of the capital stock of the Grand Union Mining Company of New York and Mexico will be awarded to Dr. J. G. Hollingsworth, of Kansas City, in his suit against Edward Tufts, whom Hollingsworth claimed he *"grubstaked"* several years ago, if the recommendations of O. F. Collins, referee, made to the District Court here to-day, are approved by the court.

The suit has been tried in New York, Kansas City, and twice in Colorado.

Hollingsworth and Tufts were boyhood friends. Tufts, it is alleged, obtained $2,000 as a *"grubstake"* from Hollingsworth, and located a group of mines in Mexico.—*N. Y. Evening Post*, Oct. 31, p. 3/4.

Guano policy. A term applied to the policy of James G. Blaine, Secretary of State, with reference to his attitude in 1881, as to certain guano deposit claims in Peru. See Brown's "Dict. of Am. Politics," 1892, s. v. PERUVIAN GUANO TROUBLES.

Guard. See quotations.

1850 The other [door] leads out to the *guard*, as they call it, a long balcony or gallery, which passes round the whole boat.—Lyell, "Second Visit to the U. S.," II, 47. (N. E. D.)

1855 *Guards of a steamboat*, a widening of the deck by a frame-work of strong timbers, which curve out on each side to the paddle-wheels.—Ogilvie, Dict. Suppl.

1873 One of those mighty river steamers emerging from the canal, loaded down to the *guards* with iron, nails, and shovel-plows, &c.—Mr. O. J. Dodds of O., H. R., Feb. 22: *C. G.*, p. 136/2, App.

Gubernatorial. Belonging or related to a governor. [1734-1910.]

1862 There sits a Representative (Mr. Crittenden) who was for four years the Executive of Kentucky; and there sits his successor (Mr. Powell) in the *gubernatorial* chair.—Mr. Joseph A. Wright of Ind., U. S. Senate, Apr. 1: *C. G.*, p. 1470/3.

1864 See AT THAT.

1866 There is no *gubernatorial* or presidential election in California but what the State is scoured, every nook and corner searched, to find a voter and get him to the polls.—Mr. Wm. Higby of Calif., H. R., Jan. 25: *Id.*, p. 428/2.

Gudgeon. See quotation.

1894 An American cigar—a cigar that is American all through, wrapper, binder, filler—from stem to *gudgeon* an American cigar.—Mr. S. E. Payne of N. Y., H. R., Jan. 15: *C. R.*, p. 824/1.

Guess. A conjecture, a surmise. (Webster.)

1807 [This estimate] though it comes to us in the dignity of an official folio, is nothing more than what we Yankees call—a *guess*.—Mr. Quincy of Mass., H. R., Dec. 13: Norfolk (Va.) *Gazette*, Jan. 13, 1808, p. 2/1.

Guess, v. To conjecture or think. But see Vol. I. [1798-1888.]
1513   [Scho] Thocht scho had scharpit weill aneuch, *I 'ges,*
      The fyrst fury of sa dolorus rage.
      —Douglas "Eneados," ed. Small, 1874, Bk. VII, p. 110.
1513   [The dog star] is the sing [sign] Pretendand tyll all mortale folk,
      I ges, Contagyus . . . . seyknes.—*Id.,* X, p. 300.
1513   [Dido was] Of sik laubour ful besy tho, *I ges.*—*Id.,* XI, p. 15.
1513   Swyftar than the wynd he fled, *I ges.*—*Id.,* XII, p. 149.
1587   The picture was as neare as I can *gesse* in this maner.—Robert Greene,
      "Morando," part 2, I.
1589   Is this proportion to be obserued in love? I *gesse* no.—"Greene's
      Arcadia," E. (1616.)
1591   Sugar candie she is as I *gesse* fro the wast to the kneestead.—"Greene
      his Farewell to Follie," G 2.
1594   I doe not *gesse* the woman guiltie of this crime.—Robert Wilson, "The
      Coblers Prophesie," F 2.
1869   A man can speak of very much that he did not do himself, I *guess*
      there is no doubt about it.—Mr. Thos. A. Hendricks of Ind., U. S.
      Senate, March 2: *C. G.,* p. 1793/1.
Guideboard. A finger post.
1872   The guide went a little way to the one side, and there he found one
      of the *guide-boards,* which were in the shape of a cross.—W. S.
      Plumer, "Short Sermons," p. 38. (N. E. D.)
1880   We have undertaken to make an open pathway, and with *guide boards*
      to point the youngest member of Congress, so that if he has anything
      committed to his charge he can pursue his way to the end.—Mr. W. P.
      Frye of Me., H. R., Jan. 22: *C. R.,* p. 481/1.
Gulch. A small precipitous valley or gorge, especially one at the bot-
    tom of which lies the bed of a stream or torrent; a ravine. Prob-
    able origin, Dutch *Kolch.* [1832-1909.]
1863   In Colorado we had but little of these poor men's "diggings," these
      gulches and placers, where a miner, with his pick, pan, and shovel,
      and without other capital, could make his fortune.—Mr. H. P. Bennet
      of Colo., H. R., Feb. 28: *C. G.,* p. 139/2, App.
1900   The rule in Alaska [used to be] that the size of a placer claim should
      be 500 feet up and down the creek or *gulch.*—Mr. H. C. Hansbrough
      of N. D., U. S. Senate, Apr. 9: *C. R.,* p. 3931/1.
Gum. Humbug. [1843-1855.]
1815   I know what I du mean; and I won't hear nun of your *gum.*—David
      Humphreys, "The Yankey in England," p. 34.
Gumbo. A negro patois, spoken principally in Louisiana.
1886   English, German, French, and Spanish all were represented, to say
      nothing of Doric brogue and local *gumbo.*—*Century Mag.,* xxxi, 618.
1889   "Laroussel, you're the only Creole in this crowd," said the Captain;
      "talk to her! Talk *gumbo* to her."—*Harper's Mag.,* lxxvi, 749.
      (Century Dict.)
Gum-swamp. A swamp in which the black-gum or sour-gum, or any
    species of *Nyssa,* prevails. In the "Dismal Swamp" of North
    Carolina these areas are distinguished from the juniper-swamps.
    (Century Dict.)
Gun. A pickpocket, a member of the criminal class. [Thieves' cant.]
1859   *Guns* are briefly defined as pickpockets in Matsell's Vocabulum. In
      the Slang Dict., 1885, a *gun* is "a magsman or street thief."
1901   No one knows . . how many *guns* there are in New York; the Front
      Office itself could how not tell for a certainty the number of first-class
      thieves who are on the streets at this moment; but it is a generally
      accepted fact among the *guns* themselves that every day in the week
      there are enough grafters in the city to people a good-sized county-
      seat.—*McClure's Mag.,* xvi, 571-2. (Century Dict.)

Gun. A pistol or revolver. [1909.]
1900 The order was given to "keep your *guns* in your pockets."—*Courier-Journal* (Ind.), Dec. 17: cited in *C. R.,* p. 735/2.
Gundelo for **Gondola.**
1608 Run to the master of my *Gundelo* . . . . Madam, the *Gundelo* is ready. —John Day, "Humour out of Breath," E 4, and F.
Gunman. See quotations.
1913 Last evening one of the *gunmen* of the A. C. M. Co. came to the jail and tried to get a blacksmith out of here. . . . . The man's name is J. H. King, that of the *gunman* is Pink Nettles and is a member of the International Bartenders' Union of Missoula, according to some of the members of that body.—*Industrial Worker* (Spokane, Wash.), July 3.
1913 The Utah Construction Co., with the aid of the D. & R. G. Co., promptly filled the town of Tucker and the deep and narrow canyon in which the work is being done with a force of armed thugs, *gunmen,* scabherders and professional strike breakers.—The same, July 3.
Gunning. Hunting with a gun. [a.1622-1866.]
1875 [He] does desire that these men should quit their every-day chivalric sports of *gunning* upon negroes and republicans.—Mr. John A. Logan of Ill., U. S. Senate, Jan. 14: *C. R.,* p. 454/1.
1882 Some two or three weeks ago [Mr. Beck] went *gunning* after [Mr. Morrill] on account of some unguarded declarations he made in favor of a protective tariff.—Mr. Garland of Ark., U. S. Senate, Feb. 9: *Id.,* p. 1012/1.
1899 Men who were born and reared on adjoining farms, who had attended the same schools, played the same games, courted the same girls, belonged to the same lodges, and worshiped in the same churches, suddenly went *gunning* for each other as remorselessly as red Indians. —Mr. Champ Clark of Mo., H. R., Feb. 4: *Id.,* p. 1468/1.
Guttersnipe. A raker-up of offal; a person of the gutter, as a ragpicker or a street arab. Colloquial or slang.
1871 I am constrained to believe that some malicious wag, some *guttersnipe* of society, has [represented] himself as my colleague.—Mr. John C. Conner of Tex., H. R., March 3: *C. G.,* p. 1938/2.
1884 The *gutter-snipes* and Arabs of the streets of Gravesend.—*Century Mag.,* p. 557. (N. E. D.)
Gutter-snipe. See quotation.
1871 *Gutter-snipe,* a small and narrow bill or poster, which is usually pasted on curb-stones.—"Amer. Encycl. Printing." (N. E. D.)
Guy. v. To poke fun at. As a noun, a guy is a joke or a hoax. [1872-1904.]
1887 He testified that he swore in his former evidence that he was a demo-crat, as he says, for a "*guy.*"—Mr. S. E. Payne of N. Y., H. R., Jan. 25: *C. R.,* p. 1022/1.
1891 The Kearsarge officers are flaming mad, and the "*guying*" of naval officers on account of the Douglass affair has not the effect of sweeten-ing their temper.—Newspaper extract printed in the *C. R.,* Jan. 17: p. 100/1, App.
Guyascutus. For the story of this hoax, see Vol. I. [1849-1855.]
1899 Their next bugaboo will be more terrifying than Barnum's monstrous picture of the great American *gyascutus.* Next after Barnum, Bryan is the greatest humbug showman the world has ever produced.—Mr. H. R. Gibson of Tenn., H. R., Dec. 14: *C. R.,* p. 426/2.

H

Hack. A cab. Hence **Hackman,** etc. [1704-1869.]
b.1813 He sold [the horse] on the spot, and hired a *hack* from a Quaker.— "Journal of Peggy Dow," p. 225/2. (1851.)

1862 Anyone who will take the trouble to walk up Pennsylvania Avenue at this moment will see the white *hackman* and the negro standing side by side, waiting for a job.—Mr. James Harlan of Ia., U. S. Senate, March 25: *C. G.,* p. 1357/2.

1872 I am informed that every wheeled vehicle in Melbourne or Sydney, I think in Melbourne, every omnibus, every *hack,* every carriage, is of American manufacture.—Mr. Cornelius Cole of Calif., U. S. Senate, May 6: *Id.,* p. 3117/1.

Hail Columbia. The jocose use of the expression is illustrated. [1854-1869.]

1864 If [the negro] will not do this,—give him *Hail Columbia,* and never let his ugly face be seen among you again.—Edmund Kirke, "Down in Tennessee," p. 71. (N. Y.)

1894 The outraged farmer and wronged planter will . . . . proceed to give them *Hail Columbia* at the ballot box.—Mr. M. D. Harter of O., H. R., July 20: *C. R.,* p. 6606/1.

Haircut. See quotation.

1917 [In Paraguay] a *hair-cut* cost $5., and it was not a $5. *hair-cut.*—H. A. Franck, "Vagabonding down the Andes," p. 603. (Century Co.)

Hair-lifter. An Indian with his scalping-knife. Not in the dictionaries.

1876 Already the enterprising agents of the Government are penetrating the prairie fastnesses, the jungles and cañons of New Mexico, Colorado, Utah, and wherever else the best specimens of the American *hair-lifter* can be found, to snatch him from his happy hunting-grounds for centennial purposes.—Mr. John R. Goodin of Kan., H. R., Jan. 25: *C. R.,* p. 628/2.

Half-breed. A person of mixed race; usually the offspring of a white father and an Indian mother. [1775-1850.]

1869 Pierre Gavneaux is a *half-breed,* who, living among [the Indians], has been remarkably successful in teaching them to plant corn, to split rails, &c.—Mr. H. L. Dawes of Mass., H. R., March 19: *C. G.,* p. 169/3.

1876 The great body of the Indians and *half-breeds* are utterly unfit by reason of their ignorance to exercise intelligently the rights and privileges of citizens, though quite as intelligent as the average plantation negro.—Mr. G. W. Cate of Wisc., H. R., May 20: *C. R.,* p. 3236/1.

Half-breeds. A nickname for those Republicans who declined to go all lengths with the "Stalwarts" in 1881. [1881-1888.]

1881 N. K. McClure, the *Half-Breed* editor of the *Phila. Times,* is the father-confessor of Atty.-Genl. Wayne MacVeagh, the *Half-Breed* politician of Pennsylvania.—*Washington Republican,* June 24.

1881 The *Half-Breed* is a Republican who is dissatisfied with the . . . . Machine and acts against it.—*The Nation,* June 16, p. 415. (Century Dict.)

Half horse and half alligator. A ludicrous appellation of boatmen and backwoodsmen in former days. [1809-1860.]

1830 You must not understand that we [in South Carolina] are a set of *half horse and half alligator* gentry, although on the subject of the tariff we are not a little of the snapping turtle.—*Am. Beacon* (Norfolk, Va.), Aug. 28, p. 4/3. (From the *Am. Turf Register.*)

1880 We have heard of the Mississippi flatboatman who claimed to be *half horse and half alligator,* with a heavy cross of snapping-turtle; yet nobody ever regarded it as anything more than the boast of a braggadocio, inspired by bad whisky.—Mr. J. Proctor Knott of Ky., H. R., Feb. 17: *C. R.,* p. 954/1.

1892 See WHAT IS IT.

Halfway Covenant, The. An arrangement whereby all persons of upright and decorous lives were considered as church members and so entitled to the exercise of political privileges. The advocates of this movement, which was bitterly opposed, organized as a new society in Boston, in 1669. [1769-1856.]

1787   He stands in *half-way-covenant* sure,
      For five long years or more,
      One foot in church's pale secure,
      The other out of door. [Written in Connecticut.]
        —*Columbian Magazine* (Phila.), p. 445/1.

1878 [The New England Puritans] might rend the State itself in a contest over the covenant and the *half-way covenant,* the civil rights of communicants and non-communicants, but for the cause of free education as the foundation of self-government they joined hands.—Mr. John Goode of Va., H. R., Apr. 12: *C. R.,* p. 2486/2.

Halfway house, the. See quotation.

1841 Mr. Clay . . . became more close and pointed in his personal remarks upon Mr. Tyler's conduct, commencing with Mr. Rives's lodgment in the *"half-way house,"* i.e. the pet bank system, which was supposed to have been a camping-station in the transition from the democratic to the whig camp. He began thus:—"[Mr. Rives] stands in a peculiar position. I found him several years ago in the *half-way house,* where he seems afraid to remain, and from which he is yet unwilling to go." —T. H. Benton, "Thirty Years' View," II, 323/2. (1856.)

Halt, to call a. To stop and consider; to demand consideration of a problem.

1875 It ought to be enough to *"call a halt"* that entire States, once proud and majestic commonwealths, are in ruin.—Mr. C. A. Eldredge of Wisc., H. R., Feb. 4: *C. R.,* p. 982/2.

1875 I think we are going altogether beyond our jurisdiction, and it is time to *"call a halt."*—Mr. S. W. Kellogg of Conn., H. R., Feb. 17: *Id.,* p. 1428/1.

1880 Sir, it is time we had *called a halt.* It is time we looked on the other side of this picture.—Mr. Eli Saulsbury of Del., U. S. Senate, Apr. 26: *Id.,* p. 2734/2.

1884 The results . . . would be too far-reaching, and public opinion *calls a halt.*—Mr. J. R. Glascock of Calif., H. R., Dec. 11: *Id.,* p. 190/1.

1886 The Senator said it was time to *call a halt.* A halt about what? What does [he] mean by *calling a halt?*—Mr. John A. Logan of Ill., U. S. Senate, May 13: *Id.,* p. 4467. [See the rest of his speech.]

1886 It was thought best to serve notice on the whole thieving crowd that *a halt would be called.*—Mr. L. E. Payson of Ill., H. R., June 28: *Id.,* p. 6241/1.

1888 Is it not time to *call a halt,* and stop this reckless expenditure?—Mr. W. H. Sowden of Pa., H. R., May 7: *Id.,* p. 3793/1.

Hammer. To beat down the price of stocks or commodities.

1865 The chronic bears were amusing themselves by *"hammering"* i.e. pressing down the price of Hudsons.—*Harper's Mag.,* xxx, 619. (N. E. D.)

1890 Bears were induced to *hammer* the market on bad shipments reported from Glasgow.—*Daily News,* Jan. 28, p. 6/4. (N. E. D.)

1893 Instead of standing where the honest seller does, . . . [the speculator] stands there, in the language of the market, to *hammer* it, and *hammer* it he does until he has hammered the profit out of the pockets of the farmers.—Mr. Anthony Higgins of Del., U. S. Senate, Jan. 31: *C. R.,* p. 988/1.

Hammock. Southern U. S. A rounded elevation of land, usually wooded; an area characterized by hardwood vegetation. [1556-1855.]

1822 The Diego Plains'. . . . are bordered on the west by a Cabbage Swamp, or region of low *hammock,* which might be easily drained and reduced to cultivation. . . . . . The *hammocks* along the Musquitto, Tomoka, and other rivers and inlets further south, are thought to be peculiarly adapted to the cultivation of sugar. . . . The eastern banks of the St. John's, as far up as Bonavista, are generally high, and consist of narrow and insulated strips of *hammock,* well suited to the growth of cotton and provisions.—"Notices of E. Florida," pp. 6, 7. (Charleston, S. C.)

1837 The impervious swamps and *hammocks* that abound [in Florida].— Raleigh (N. C.) *Standard,* Apr. 5, p. 2/6.

1876 [In the Seminole war], the theater of operations was a wilderness, and every *hammock* and swamp a citadel for the enemy.—Mr. Felton of Ga., H. R., June 14: *C. R.,* p. 3790/1.

Hand-me-downs. Readymade clothes, otherwise called "reach-me-downs."

1894 Our friend from Ohio [has shown us] a ready-made suit of *"hand-me-downs,"* each, like Marc Antony, stirring up our frenzy.—Mr. J. C. Sibley of Pa., H. R., Jan. 18: *C. R.,* p. 1036/1.

1897 These cheap-johns, ready-made, *"hand-me-down"* statesmen, talk . . . . as though the farmer was not a laboring man.—Mr. Jerry Simpson of Kan., H. R., March 25: *Id.,* p. 274/1.

Handshake, American and English. See quotation.

1896 Why should [Mr. McKinley] be permitted to abandon the *American handshake?* Have any of you seen him in the last few years shaking hands; seen him raise his arm high in the air for his overhanded *English handshake?* Just think of how the American simplicity of a Jefferson or a Lincoln would be shocked by this effort to imitate the *English handshake!* We want an American President to shake hands right out from the shoulder—good old American style—none of this overhanded business.—Mr. John M. Allen of Miss., H. R., July 10: *C. R.,* p. 6402/2.

Handwrite. Handwriting. [1693-1856.]

1862 He said [the certificate] was so rumpled and such a poor *handwrite,* that it should be copied.—Mr. Samuel G. Daily of Neb., H. R., May 6: *C. G.,* p. 1978/3.

Hang up. To prevent from reaching a decision; to prevent from proceeding. [1854.]

1860 It is not many years since the nomination of Edward Everett [as minister to England] was *hung up,* and confirmation refused for weeks and weeks.—Mr. John P. Hale of N. H., U. S. Senate, Dec. 18: *C. G.,* p. 116/2.

1874 The first result of the passage of this bill will be to have it *hung up* in the Supreme Court for three years.—Mr. Thomas Whitehead of Va., H. R., March 23: *C. R.,* p. 2430/2.

1886 Mr. Henderson:—After [the bill] was agreed to be reported, it was *hung up* in air for some time, was it not? Mr. Matson:—No, sir; it is not *hung up.*—H. R., March 2: *Id.,* p. 1975/1.

1886 The Court of Claims said [these matters] did not fall within the provisions of the law and there they were *hung up* like Mohammed's coffin. —Mr. H. M. Teller of Colo., U. S. Senate, June 9: *Id.,* p. 5463/1.

1896 That act has been delayed, or *hung up* in the Supreme Court.—Mr. J. D. Richardson of Tenn., H. R., May 11: *Id.,* p. 5082/2.

1900 A canal treaty, *hung up* in the Senate, but approved by the President.— Mr. N. N. Cox of Tenn., H. R., March 26: *Id.,* p. 295/2, App.

Hard case. An incorrigible, a "tough customer." [1842-1857.]

1848 [He] might justly claim to be considered as *hard a case* as any of the mountaineers then present.—G. F. Ruxton, "Life in the Far West," p. 71. (Farmer.)

Hard money. Gold and silver, as distinguished from a paper currency. See Vol. I, **Hard Dollars.** [1706-1848.]

1862 The original intention of the framers of this Government, for a *hard-money,* constitutional currency, and against all paper money whatever. —Mr. J. R. Doolittle of Wisc., U. S. Senate, Feb. 13: *C. G.,* p. 56/3, App.

1867 In the pithy language of Nathaniel Macon, "our Government was a *hard-money* Government, founded by *hard-money* men, and its debts were *hard-money* debts."—Mr. James G. Blaine of Me., H. R., Nov. 26: *Id.,* p. 799/2.

Hard-money man. One who is for a gold and silver currency.

1874 [Mr. Morton of Ind.] said he was not so much of a *hard-money man* as he once was.—Mr. John B. Gordon of Ga., U. S. Senate, Jan. 20: *C. R.,* p. 14/2, App.

1874 I am, strictly speaking, a *hard-money man.* .....Well do I remember the time when Colonel Benton made this question the corner-stone of his party in my state.—Mr. Lewis V. Bogy of Mo., U. S. Senate, Feb. 19: *Id.,* p. 60/2, App.

Hardpan. Any earth, not popularly recognized as rock, which it is hard to dig into or excavate. (Webster.) [1821-1842.]

1870 I would have some time [set] when the Government should resume specie payments, when we should get somewhere near the reality of things, when we should approach what sensible business men sometimes call *"hard pan."*—Mr. Jacob Benton of N. H., H. R., June 29: *C. G.,* p. 4969/2.

1872 No democracy ever lasted long, no republic was ever built up strong from the foundation, no republic ever laid its foundations below the frosts, that did not dig down to the *hard pan,* to the rock, to the granite of universal public education.—Mr. G. F. Hoar of Mass., H. R., Jan. 25: *Id.,* p. 594/1.

1872 We ought to wait until we get to the *hard-pan* of real money, and to the *hard-pan* of fixed prices, before we undertake to re-adjust this question of salaries.—Mr. G. F. Edmunds of Vt., U. S. Senate, March 12: *Id.,* p. 1602/3.

1878 Inflated values in railroad stocks, in nearly all securities . . . . have got to, or are rapidly going, to use a common expression, to *"hard pan,"* and the quicker we get there the better.—Mr. W. W. Eaton of Conn., U. S. Senate, Feb. 5: *C. R.,* p. 754/1.

1878 It is said we are approaching *hard-pan* in the business of the country,— indeed have arrived there; if so, let us now take a new departure on the *hard-pan* principle. *Hard-pan* prices have been reached; let the Government then. . . . profit [by them].—Mr. Harry White of Pa., H. R., Apr. 23: *Id.,* p 2753/1.

1893 We are told we are getting down to *hardpan.* I want to know how much further towards Sheol we have got to go before we get there.— Mr. J. C. Sibley of Pa., H. R., Aug. 18: *Id.,* p. 465/2.

Hard row to hoe. A difficult job. [1839-1862.]

1896 That leaves me standing alone practically, and with *a hard row to hoe.* —Mr. U. S. Hall of Mo., H. R., Feb. 8: *C. R.,* p. 132/1, App.

1897 The country newspapers, at best, have *a hard row to hoe.*—Mr. J. P. Tracey of Mo., H. R., Jan. 6: *Id.,* p. 504/2.

Hard scrabble. Hard work; i. e., scrambling or scratching.

1888 For the farmer [under the tariff of 1846] there was mighty bad sledding on the road to *Hard Scrabble.* He was fleeced by middlemen, and frequently ruined by wildcat banks and depreciated currency.—Mr. M. A. Foran of O., H. R., May 1: *C. R.*, p. 3589/1.

Hartford Convention. A meeting of Federalists in Dec. 1814 and Jan. 1815. They were charged with planning secession and independence. See a letter of D. Webster to Hiram Ketchum, undated, but ab. 1844: "Private Corresp." (1857), II, 184-5.

1878 Participancy in the *Hartford Convention,* or any sympathy with its proceedings or its aims, was political death, and well-nigh social ostracism, to any man in Maine.—Remarks of Mr. Blaine on the presentation of the statue of Wm. King: *C. R.,* Jan. 22, p. 457/1.

Hashhouse. An eating-house. Slang.

1884 When it was charged by my colleague [Mr. Hatch] that some *hash-house* is at the bottom of this thing, I say we are not asking . . . for any hotel, or any court to support a hotel, in my district. There is something, perhaps, suggestive in this charge in the gentleman's own conscience. It may be the fact that he is desiring a *hash-house* or hotel in his own city [Hannibal].—Mr. A. M. Alexander of Mo., H. R., May 17: *C. R.,* p. 4260/2.

Hatchet, to take up the. To begin hostilities. See Vol. I, **Hatchet, bury the.** [1784-1848.]

1791 *"The hatchet is now buried,* and we smoke with our Indian neighbours the calumet of peace." Address of the Congregational Church of Midway to Geo. Washington, during his stay in Savannah.—*Augusta Chronicle,* June 4, p. 3/2.

1855 Shingis, sachem of the Delawares, . . . *took up the hatchet* at various times against the English.—W. Irving, "Life of Washington," I, 78. (Century Dict.)

Hat Indian. One who becomes civilized.

1898 See BLANKET INDIANS.

Haul. To convey by drawing. [1704-1812.]

1862 Sometimes [the flatboats] would strike the landing-place, sometimes they would hit the shore far below, and be *hauled* and poled back to the landing-place.—Mr. Roscoe Conkling of N. Y., H. R., Jan. 6: *C. G.,* p. 190/3.

1881 See SWAP.

1887 There is not one-tenth part of the risk in *hauling* dressed beef that there is in *hauling* live animals.—Mr. J. B. Beck of Ky., U. S. Senate, Jan. 10: *C. R.,* p. 484/1.

Hauls, long and short. Conveyance of goods or products, for long or short distances.

1884 The farmer has to pay for *short hauls* just about what they ask him. . . . . We must study the effect of one railroad upon another, of one system upon another, the influence of river, canal, lake, and sea upon land carriage, of *short hauls* and *long hauls,* &c.—Mr. James Wilson of Ia., H. R., June 18: *C. R.,* p. 5314/2.

1884 The relative advantage of position of the *short and long haul shipper* through natural causes.—Mr. Chas. Stewart of Vt., H. R., Dec. 10: *Id.,* p. 162/2.

1884 All that has been said about discrimination against *long hauls* [is] without foundation. It will be found that the discriminations, instead of being against the *long hauls,* are against the *short hauls.*—Mr. J. H. Reagan of Tex., H. R., Dec. 16: *Id.,* p. 294/1.

Have it in for. To be well primed and ready to attack.

1894 When I went out into my Congressional district, I found that nearly every labor agitator *had it in for* Harter, so to speak.—Mr. M. D. Harter of O., H. R., July 20: *C. R.,* p. 6602/1.

Hayseed. Rural. As a noun, a farmer.

[1874 I have oats in my pocket and *hay-seed* in my hair, and the western people generally are affected in the same way.—Mr. J. G. Cannon of Ill., H. R., Feb. 18: *C. R.,* p. 1609/2.]

1890 I live in that part of the State which is sometimes called the *"hay-seed"* part.—Mr. J. G. Sawyer of N. Y., H. R., Aug. 6: *Id.,* p. 8244/2.

1895 It has become fashionable to suppose that [a dissatisfied] feeling exists only with "greasy mechanics" and *"hayseed* socialists" and "men who never had a discount in their lives."—Mr. W. A. Harris of Kan., H. R., Jan. 31: *Id.,* p. 1592/1.

Haze. To bully, to persecute. [1840-1910.]

1882 That he might not be pursued by the police, *hazed* into prison, and robbed.—Mr. John A. Kasson of Ia., H. R., March 22: *C. R.,* p. 2172/1.

1885 His friends believe that he was fatally hurt in an encounter [at Annapolis] with the third class, by being put in a barrel and rolled around until "the *hazing* party" chose to let him out. Other instances of *hazing* have been brought to my attention.—Mr. S. S. Cox of N. Y., H. R., Jan. 7: *Id.,* p. 539/1.

1885 On Jan. 12, Hon. W. E. Chandler, Secretary of the Navy, wrote in reply:—There have been no "diabolical" cases of *hazing.* Every offense of *hazing* . . . that has come to the knowledge of the authorities during the past three years has been promptly punished.—*C. R.,* p. 665/1.

1901 [Young men at West Point] have been *hazed* to a degree that I think would have justified the *hazee* in killing the *hazer.*—Mr. H. D. Money of Miss., U. S. Senate, Jan. 16: *Id.,* p. 1075/1. [See the whole debate.]

Head, v. See quotation 1856. Cf. **Head off.**

1841 It was finally concluded that, instead of making war on Captain Tyler, they should resort to stratagem, and, in the elegant language of one of their number, . . . should endeavor to *"head"* him.—Mr. James Buchanan in the U. S. Senate: T. H. Benton, "Thirty Years' View," II, 330/1. (1856.)

1842 The act was passed to *"head"* the President, and [it] has proved unsuccessful.—Mr. John B. Weller of O., H. R., June 30: p. 5/2 of speech as separately published.

1856 This *"heading,"* applied to a person, signifies to check, or restrain; applied to animals (which is its common use in the South and the West) is, to turn one round which is running the wrong way.—T. H. Benton, "Thirty Years' View," II, 349/2.

Head-money cases. Three cases decided by the U. S. Supreme Court in 1884 (112 U. S. 580) which held that an Act of Congress (Aug. 3, 1882), imposing upon owners of vessels a duty for immigrants entering the U. S. was valid. (Century Dict.)

Head off. To turn back, as a deer or a fox is turned back by hunters.

1868 It is in my judgment of vital importance that this [scheme] be *headed off.*—Mr. Zach. Chandler of Mich., U. S. Senate, Dec. 19: *C. G.,* p. 159/1.

1882 [Mr. Beck] seems to have jumped into this controversy . . . . for the purpose of *heading off* the growing and budding prosperity of the South.—Mr. Justin S. Morrill of Vt., U. S. Senate, Jan. 10: *C. R.,* p. 319/2.

1891 To *head* my rival *off,* I indulged in a tremendous flirtation.—R. H. Savage, "My Official Wife." iii, 35. (N. E. D.)

Head of steam. An amount of pressure.

1862 I would get up a big *head of steam,* and . . . run over the Merrimac and sink her.—Mr. Daniel Clark of N. H., U. S. Senate, March 27: *C. G.,* p 1394/1.

1862 The "Merrimac" made direct for the "Cumberland" under a full *head of steam.*—*The Times,* March 27. (N. E. D.) [Note the coincidence of date in the two foregoing quotations.]

Head rights. Rights to property, accruing to a member of an Indian tribe. [1878.]

1888 One of the motives that induce a man to marry an Indian woman is that he may obtain certain rights under the tribe into which he marries, a *head-right* for instance.—Mr. S. R. Peters of Kan., H. R., July 26: *C. R.,* p. 6886/2.

Head-strings. See quotation. Not in the dictionaries.

1876 They struck her a blow on the head with such violence that it broke the iron axe just at the eye. They cut her *head strings* off.—Mr. D. M. Key of Tenn., U. S. Senate, Dec. 18: *C. R.,* p. 263/2.

Health, for one's (with the negative). "Not to be here for one's health" usually means having an ulterior purpose, like money-making. [1904-1911.] To do something "for one's health" means, also, that the action serves no useful purpose.

1900 I am not making this speech for fun, nor *for my health,* nor as an oratorical exercise.—Mr. Champ Clark of Mo., H. R., Feb. 5: *C. R.,* p. 1520/2.

Heaping. Piled more than even full.

1850 [The dog] will carry a *heaping* basket full of nuts in his mouth, and never spill one of them.—D. G. Mitchell, "Reveries of a Bachelor," p. 164. (Lond., 1852.)

Heated term. The hot season; the dog days. [1873-1878.]

1863 *Heated term.* There has been lately (August) much suffering here (in Washington).—Walt Whitman, "Specimen Days" (1887), p. 69.

1867 I think we could go on now during the *heated term,* and discuss all the great questions of the country better than we shall be able to do it during the cold season.—Mr. Simon Cameron of Pa., U. S. Senate, July 5: *C. G.,* p. 487/1.

Heathen Chinee. Peculiar.

1871, 1877 See CHINEE, THE HEATHEN.

1890 [It seems to me that this bill] has something of a *Heathen Chinee* flavor about it, and that it is framed with "intent to deceive."—Mr. W. Mutchler of Pa., H. R., June 7: *C. R.,* p. 5791/2.

Heel and pit. Probably Southern, with reference to cockfighting. [Has the phrase "well heeled" this origin?]

1814 [He] is fond of cockfighting (and of manfighting when drunk) and is said to *heel and pit* with much skill.—Norfolk (Va.) *Public Ledger,* Oct. 8, p. 3/4. (Advt.)

Heeler. A political follower ready to do dirty work. [1881-1909.]

1883 The cry proceeds from the friends of the Commerce Committee, from the *"heelers"* of that committee in this House.—Mr. John Van Voorhis of N. Y., H. R., Feb. 28: *C. R.,* p. 3433/1.

1893 If those laws [relating to elections] are to be repealed in the interest of the *"heeler,"* the statutes against mail robbing and counterfeiting should go next.—Mr. J. F. Lacey of Ia., H. R., Sept. 29: *Id.,* p. 1939/1.

1893 The thugs and *heelers,* outcasts and criminals, employed by Tammany, thronged the polling places.—Mr. G. W. Ray of N. Y., H. R., Oct. 6: *Id.,* p. 2231/1.

1896 [Mr. Tarsney] is the victim of the pluggers and *heelers* who set out to steal the election in Jackson County [Mo.] in 1894.—Newspaper, cited Feb. 26: *C. R.,* p. 2183/1.

1900 See THUGS.

Heft. Weight. [1558-1878.]

1640 Too many wives anchor all their hopes for outward matters on their husbands, and too many children lean all their weight on their fathers' shoulders; so that it is just with God to suffer these their wooden pillars to break, on whom they lay too much *heft.*—Thomas Fuller, Sermon on "Good from Bad Friends."

1849 Throwing the *heft* of the Pacific trade across the continent into the port of New York.—*N. Y. Herald,* Feb. 5. (Century Dict.)

Hefty. Heavy, bulky. [1871.]

1883 We do not want these great, *hefty*, big, lumbering people from Michigan to come in between us.—Mr. S. S. Cox of N. Y., H. R., Feb. 3: *C. R.*, p. 2049/1.

Hell-bent. Recklessly determined on a line of action. [Also **hell-bent for election.**]

1840
Maine went
Hell-bent
For Governor Kent.
—Political song. (Century Dict.)

Hellful. Diabolical. In this sense, not noticed in the N. E. D., and without doubt a "nonce-word."

1869 The healthful ministers of peace are guided by one code; the *hellful* agencies of war are controlled by another; but the State prescribes them both.—Mr. Timothy O. Howe of Wisc., U. S. Senate, Jan. 15: *C. G.*, p. 382/3.

Help. An assistant or servant. [1645-1909.]

1815 You are our principal *Help*. That is all. . . . . *Help* is not a discreditable name—not at all derogatory. There is nothing degrading in helping, is there?—David Humphreys, "The Yankey in England," p. 35.

Help, with the infinitive. See quotations. [1794-1888.]

1914 July 24, *The Times*, p. 12/2, reports the Marquess of Salisbury as saying that some tax should be put on heavy motor cars to *help pay* for the damage they caused.

Henchman. A politician who is strictly subservient to a politician of higher order, and engaged to execute commands without exercising his own judgment.

1880 Twenty-five years ago, if you spoke to an American of a *Henchman*, he would have understood that you were making an historical allusion . . . . At this moment, however, the term designates a very familiar figure in American politics. . . The *Henchman* is, in fact, a necessity of what is called machine politics, or, in plainer language, of the present mode of getting and keeping high office. . . It is the *Henchman* who corresponds with the Chief, and goes . . . . to see him when any emergency arises.—*The Nation*, xxx, 398. (Century Dict.)

1890 My own county falls under that head, and yet it was shown by the principal Republican *henchman* in that county that . . . . 1,300 qualified voters were . . . not allowed to vote.—Mr. John H. Rogers of Ark., H. R., Apr. 23: *C. R.*, p. 3744/2.

1890 [Mr. H. C. Lodge] can indulge in more lofty declamation on the beauties of civil-service reform, and at the same time secure more patronage for his political *henchmen* and retainers, than any member of the Massachusetts delegation.—Mr. H. G. Ewart of N. C., H. R., June 28: *Id.*, p. 6688/1.

1896 I give you my word I never appointed [a postmaster] because he was my political *henchman*; never.—Mr. J. R. Hawley of Conn., U. S. Senate, Apr. 2: *Id.*, p. 3488/2.

Henequen, Heniquen, Henequin. Sisal hemp. Spanish.

1880 The *henneguen* . . . from which is prepared Sisal hemp.—"Libr. Univ. Knowl." (N. Y.), ix, 777. (N. E. D.)

1884 The road passes through the *henequen* plantations.—F. A. Ober, "Trav. Mexico," p. 28. (Stanford Dict.)

1885 It is provided that we may take *henequen* bags, if made of Mexican *henequen* hemp, free from duty to Mexico.—Mr. Justin S. Morrill of Vt., U. S. Senate, Jan. 7: *C. R.*, p. 510/1.

Hens' teeth. An emblem of scarcity. [American?]

1863 [Horses are] *scarcer than hens' teeth* round here.—Edmund Kirke, "My Southern Friends," p. 250. (N. Y.)

1893 North of Mason and Dixon's line, colored county officials are *scarce as hens' teeth.*—Mr. Champ Clark of Mo., H. R., Oct. 2: *C. R.,* p. 2044/1.

Herd-header. The bull which heads a herd of cattle.

1901-2 The man who expects success as a breeder cannot look upon the selection of his *herd-header* as a light matter.—*Rep. Kas. State Bd. Agr.,* p. 50. (Century Dict.)

Herdic. A small carriage with the entrance at the back, supposed to have been invented by one Peter Herdic of Pennsylvania.

1882 Taking a *herdic* (small one-horse 'bus named after the inventor) we drove to the White House.—T. S. Hudson, "Scamper through Am.," p. 74. (N. E. D.)

1883 The *herdic-phætons,* or *herdics,* as they are universally called.— E. M. Bacon, "Dict. of Boston," p. 207. (N. E. D.)

1884 Inquiry among the *herdic drivers* of this city . . failed to elicit any information.—*Boston Herald,* Oct. 6, p. 1/6. (N. E. D.)

1888 There are two tracks on N. Y. Avenue, now . . . . You cannot go over them with a carriage or a *herdic.*—Mr. H. H. Riddleberger of Va., U. S. Senate, Feb. 20: *C. R.,* p. 1336/1.

1888 With the present lines of railroad, the *herdics,* and the carriages, [this is] the most crowded spot in the city of Washington.—Mr. A. P. Gorman of Md., U. S. Senate, Feb. 23: *Id.,* p. 1414/2.

Herring pond. The Atlantic Ocean. [1686-1815.]

1815 I guess you are a Yankey, who have been in perils on the great salt *herring-pond.*—David Humphreys, "The Yankey in England," p. 20.

Hickory-pole. A pole of hickory, used as a flagstaff.

1902 From 1828 to 1860 a pole of this kind, with a brush at the top, was the emblem of the Democratic party: in allusion to Andrew Jackson's popular name of "Old Hickory."—*Journal of Am. Folk-Lore,* p. 245. (Century Dict.)

Hicksites. Certain Quakers who seceded from the main body in 1827, under the leadership of Elias Hicks. They profess Unitarian principles. [1839.]

1871 A *Hicksite Quaker* says [so and so.] Now tell me what right he has to be called a Christian according to my belief. And yet . . . . if they can find a *Hicksite Quaker,* . . . . he is put in charge of Indians because he is a Christian of that kind.—Mr. Jas. W. Nye of Nev., U. S. Senate, Feb. 22: *C. G.,* p. 1492/3.

Highbinders. A set of organized villains in New York City; also, later, the term was applied to Chinese gangs on the Pacific Coast. [1806-a.1849.]

1876 Refined ladies could no longer submit to be jostled at the church door by the Mongolian *chiffonier* or *high-binder.*—*S. F. Call,* March 27: quoted in the *C. R.,* March 7, 1878, p. 1549/1.

1879 It is shown by the testimony that coolies attempting to evade their debt contracts are subjected to violence by a special class of Chinese known as *"High-binders,"* who not infrequently . . . . inflict the death penalty. . . . . Chinese agents, *"High-binders,"* and others are on the watch at the wharves, &c.—Mr. John P. Jones of Nev., U. S. Senate, Feb. 14: *C. R.,* p. 92/2, App.

1893 [The Chinamen in Calif.] refused to register, because they feared the iron bars and the pistols of the *"highbinders."*—Mr. J. G. Maguire of Calif., H. R., Oct. 13: *Id.,* p. 407/2, App.

1894 The fear of a *highbinder* outbreak in Chinatown grows, as the activity of the dreaded hatchetmen is observed.—*S. F. Chronicle,* Nov. 14.

Higher law. A supposed moral rule, excusing the citizen from obeying the law of the land. [1850-1861.]

1850 "There is a *higher law* than the Constitution." W. H. Seward in the U. S. Senate, on the admission of California into the Union.—C. L. Norton, "Political Americanisms."

1850   Mr. Pratt:—[I have heard Mr. Seward] say, that there was a *higher law*. Mr. Seward (in his seat):—I do not deny that. Mr. Pratt:— I call upon every Senator who hears me to say whether the Senator from New York did not say there was a *higher law*; a *higher law* than the Constitution, which he felt bound to obey when it came in conflict with the Constitution. Mr. Seward (in his seat):—I did not. —U. S. Senate, July 26, p. 7/2 of Mr. Seward's speech as separately reported.

1850   Let me give you a small sample of Sewardism. At a religious meeting convened at Poughkeepsie, N. Y., on the 8th inst., it was resolved, "That while we recognize the obligation to obey the laws of the land, we make an exception in the case of all such provisions as contravene the *'higher laws'* of God."—Wilmington (N. C.) *Commercial*, Oct. 22, p. 1/6.

1851   In these days of the *"higher law"* principle, we have let the Northern Whigs know we have a *"higher law"* than party law, when Southern rights are concerned.—*Id.*, Feb. 18, p. 2/4.

1851   The *higher law* that exists somewhere between us and the third heaven, I never knew exactly where. Our *higher law* is but the old doctrine of the fifth monarchy men revived.—Speech by Daniel Webster at Albany, N. Y., May 28, pp. 14, 18.

1861   Mr. Green:—This is a deficiency under a prior law. Mr. Douglas:— Under *the higher law*, did you say? Mr. Green:—No, sir; a prior law. I never resort to *the higher law* in the Senate; I do on my knees, privately.—Feb. 23: *C. G.,* p. 1143/3.

1861   The doctrine of a *higher law*, and of an irrepressible conflict, is assigned to [Mr. Seward], and [Senator Douglas] has called that a plagiarism.—Mr. Zach. Chandler of Mich., U. S. Senate, March 19: *Id.*, p. 1473/2.

1863   [The people of Kentucky know that Senator Wilson] has been hand in glove with the *higher-law* abolitionists; and censures from that description of men have no terror to them.—Mr. Jacob M. Howard of Mich., U. S. Senate, Feb. 23: *Id.*, p. 1189/2.

1864   [Massachusetts] set up her impudent and absurd *"higher law"* conceits, to break down the constitutional and legal guarantees with which [property in slaves] had been so long environed, and which she contributed so much to build up.—Mr. Garrett Davis of Ky., U. S. Senate, Feb. 16: *Id.*, p. 680/2.

1878   Over the popular delusion and political frenzy of the hour there reigns an inexorable *higher law*, waiting on the footsteps of all lawbreakers.—Mr. H. L. Dawes of Mass., U. S. Senate, Jan. 29: *C. R.,* p. 646/2.

High-falutin. Bombastic in talk or behavior. [1848-1909.] As a noun, bombast.

1872   *High-falutin,* as it is frequently written, is almost always addressed to educated or half-educated audiences who are supposed to appreciate bombast.—De Vere, "Americanisms," p. 271.

High grade. Of superior quality.

High-minded. Those Federalists who in 1815 did not join the Clintonians. They were much ridiculed in the campaign of 1820. But see Vol. I. [1824-1829.]

High-toned. Excellent, of superior rank or kind. [Usually of persons.]

1857   [The encounter between John Randolph and Henry Clay, in 1826] was about the last *high-toned* duel that I have witnessed.—T. H. Benton, "Thirty Years' View," I, 77.

1870   In my relations with the Committee on Foreign Affairs, it has been my good fortune to be thrown in contact not only with men of ability and national reputation, but with *high-toned* gentlemen.—Mr. Thomas Swann of Md., H. R., Feb. 15: *C. G.* p. 1297/2.

1873 Blanton Duncan, the leading Democratic spirit in Kentucky, a *high-toned* gentleman.—Mr. J. W. Flanagan of Tex., U. S. Senate, Feb. 27: *Id.*, p. 1889/2.

1890 You are asked . . . . to impeach the honesty and integrity and character of a *high-toned* and honorable people.—Mr. C. F. Crisp of Ga., H. R., June 3: *C. R.*, p. 5552/2.

1894 A man's business secrets are his source of profit, and no man, however *high-toned* or liberal he may be in the conduct of his business, wants it all exposed even to a revenue collector.—Mr. W. J. Coombs of N. Y., H. R., Jan. 30: *Id.*, p. 1662/2.

Hike, v. To walk vigorously. A college word. [a.1872-1909.]

1912 Prima Donna *Hikes* over Railroad Ties. Famous singer plods two miles to keep date. Mme. Norelli, delayed by wreck on Oregon electric, walks part of way to Chautauqua.—Headlines, *Sunday Oregonian,* July 14.

1913 *Hiking* to London Town. A propagandist pilgrimage in England. [Suffragettes.]—Headlines in *N. Y. Evening Post,* July 24, p. 5/4.

Hiker. An over-drawn bridle check. Southern and local. (Century Dict.)

Hindsights, to knock off. To beat, to demolish. [1834-1853.]

1892 The American producer, whether on the farm or in the shop, can knock the *hindsights* off the producer anywhere else on the face of the earth.—Mr. Thos. E. Watson of Ga., H. R., Apr. 1: *C. R.*, p. 2843/1.

Hippodrome. A fraudulent race or contest, in which it is arranged beforehand who shall win. (Century Dict.) Hence, as a verb, to fix matters up beforehand in such a case. Slang.

1898 I insist that I have the floor, and I will not be *hippodromed* from the floor.—Mr. J. H. Lewis of Wash., H. R., March 11: *C. R.,* p. 2736/1.

Hitch horses. To get along together. [a.1704-1872.]

[1608 Souldiers and Schollers could never set their horses together, especially in this kicking age.—John Day, "Law Tricks," B 4.]

Hitching post. One for fastening a horse. [1852-1884.]

1863 He shouted out in boyish glee, throwing his bridle over the *hitching post,* and springing to the ground.—Edmund Kirke, "My Southern Friends," p. 94. (N. Y.)

Hitch up. To get the harness on. [1857-1878.]

1870 He would *hitch up* at once and drive over to Elyria.—E. E. Hale, "Ten times One," ch. iv. (Century Dict.)

1872 I think that on the whole I would rather not *hitch up* a buggy when I can get somebody else to do it.—Mr. G. F. Edmunds of Vt., U. S. Senate, Apr. 11: *C. G.*, p. 2364/1.

Hobo. A tramp, not so formidable as a *yegg*. Also see quotation. [1891-1910.]

1913 As a result, we find the *hobo* on the average a shiftless, unreliable character, where persistence, system and revolutionary energy are required. . . . *Hobo* is a much misunderstood word. It should not be confused with tramp or vagrant. It means a casual, migratory worker, either unskilled or a jack-of-all-trades. One who works at seasonable occupations or on construction projects.—Corresp. of the *Industrial Worker,* May 1, p. 5/3. (Spokane, Wash.)

Hock. Prison. Also see quotations. [1902.]

1859 [Hock is] the last card in the box. Among thieves a man is *in hock* when he is in prison; but when one gambler is caught by another, smarter than himself, and is beat, then he is *in hock.* Men are only caught, or put *in hock,* on the race tracks, or on the steamboats down South.—G. W. Matsell, "Vocabulum; or, The Rogue's Lexicon," p. 113. (N. Y.)

1859 Matsell, in his "Vocabulum: or, The Rogue's Lexicon," defines "caught in *hock*" as caught by the heels, or caught in the act.

Hock, v.   To pawn or pledge. Slang.

1904 You can *hock* your overcoat before marriage to buy violets for a girl, but, &c.—G. H. Lorimer, "Gorgon Graham," p. 173.

Hog, v.   To appropriate greedily.   [1887-1896.]

1894 The Creator never meant that we should *"hog"* it all [all the commerce of the world], or we would have been made with snouts.— Mr. Champ Clark of Mo., H. R., Jan. 19: *C. R.,* p. 1077/1.

1897 Mr. Steele:—I understand that you justify that legislature in *hogging* the offices. . . . Mr. Bailey:—*"Hogging"* is a good word. I am glad to know that it is to have a place in the Record.—H. R., Feb. 23: *Id.,* p. 2158/2.

Hog and holiday. See quotation.

1878 He knows no more about Indian affairs *than a hog does about a holiday.*—Mr. J. K. Luttrell of Calif., H. R., Dec. 18: *C. R.,* p. 288/1. [Mr. Baker of Indiana objected to the use of "such coarse and vulgar terms."]

Hog and hominy. Pork and boiled maize: accounted poor fare. [1816-1885.]

1875 I think there is a great difference between *hog and hominy* in the log cabin and all the luxuries of life in the richly carpeted mansion.— Mr. R. H. Cain [a colored representative] of S. C., H. R., Feb. 3: *C. R.,* p. 956/2.

Hogtie, v.   To tie all four feet together.

1905 The sash, being of a soft, reluctant texture, and calculated to tie very tight into knots that would not slip, was of the precise best material with which to *hogtie* steers.—A. H. Lewis, "Sunset Trail," p. 3. (Century Dict.)

Hog wallow. A place in which hogs may wallow.

1829 It becomes a trespass to make a dam for a *hog wallow.*—Lorenzo Dow, "Omnifarious Law Exemplified," p. 51. (New London, Conn.)

1896 Within the past 20 years millions and millions have been wasted upon unknown duck ponds, remote *hog wallows,* utterly useless and irreparable no-thoroughfares.—*Washington Post,* cited *C. R.,* July 10, p. 6437/2.

Hog wallows. Prairies which have been turned into alternate mounds and hollows, sometimes symmetrically, by a succession of rains and droughts. [1840.]

1854 These *hog-wallows* are formations of pitfalls and elevations, hollows and hillocks of every variety, which succeed each other like cups and saucers turned topsy-turvy.—*Putnam's Mag.,* Feb. (Century Dict.)

Hold, or colloquially **Holt.** A thing to hold on to; an argument or proposition on which to rely firmly. See Vol. I, **Holt.** [1825-1888.]

1894 He drew a picture of the birds and the flowers [in Southern Illinois] and the beauties of the springtime there. That is his best *hold.*—Mr. C. H. Grosvenor of O., H. R., March 6: *C. R.,* p. 2639/2.

Hold-over. An officer who remains in office after the expiration of his term, until his successor takes his place.

1888 Assuming that these letters are written by Republican or *"hold-over* clerks," who were connected with the last administration, ... why all this "fuss and feathers" [about it]?—Mr. K. Nelson of Minn., H. R., June 1: *C. R.,* p. 4838/2.

Hold up. To promote for a candidacy.

1824 [Mr. Crawford's] friends begin to own that his death is now . . . . probable, and that in any event he can no longer be *held up* for the presidency.—Henry Clay to Francis Brooke, May 28: "Corresp.," p. 93. (1855.)

Home Guards. See quotation.

1896 Before Gen. Burnside came, the mountain men of East Tennessee organized themselves into companies called *"Home Guards."* . . . . These *"Home Guards"* piloted the Union refugees northward from the whole Southern country, from northern Georgia, from western North Carolina, from eastern Tennessee, up through the mountains into Kentucky, where they organized into regiments under the flag of the Union.—Mr. H. R. Gibson of Tenn., H. R., Apr. 25: *C. R.,* pp. 298-99, App.

Homespun. Cloth spun and woven at home. [1800-1880.]

1888 The dress of the girl was a well-worn but neat-checked *homespun,* and at the throat was a bit of faded ribbon.—*Century Mag.,* xxxvi, 896.

Homestead, v. To take up land as a homestead. Hence **Homesteader,** one who takes up land as a homestead.

1879 Many of our citizens have filed their naturalization papers in the land offices, to prove their right to pre-empt or *"homestead"* their lands.— Mr. Henry Poehler of Minn., H. R., Apr. 26: *C. R.,* p. 952/1.

1884, 1888 *Pall Mall Gazette.* (N. E. D.)

1887 Citizens of the U. S., who have by law a right to enter and *homestead* these lands.—Mr. Wilkinson Call of Fla., U. S. Senate, Jan. 21: *C. R.,* p. 874/2.

1888 The farmers who *homesteaded* on a Nebraska prairie twenty years ago.—*Chicago Advance,* Apr. 5, p. 216. (N. E. D.)

1888 As a *homesteader* myself, having proved up upon a homestead after five years of residence there, having settled in a new county in North-western Kansas, I know something about the conditions of developing that country.—Mr. E. J. Turner of Kan., H. R., June 26: *C. R.,* p. 5586/1.

1892 Any *homesteader* on 160 acres in [the Yellowstone National Park] would starve to death.—Mr. O. H. Platt of Conn., U. S. Senate, May 10: *Id.,* p. 4122/1.

Home stretch. The last part of a race.

1864 Already we see the slave States of Maryland and Missouri, Arkansas and Louisiana, and others, on the *home-stretch* to become free.—Mr. Hulburd of N. Y., H. R., March 12: *C. G.,* p. 1069/3.

1884 I travel very rapidly on the *home-stretch.*—Mr. R. T. Bennett of N. C., H. R., June 25: *C. R.,* p. 5598/2.

1897 The horses had . . . . wandered down the *home-stretch* with a [very close] finish.—*Boston Journal,* Jan. 6, p. 10/1. (N. E. D.)

Hommock. For definition, see **Hammock.**

1858 He advanced until he drove [the Indians] from the thick *hommock* into the open forest. . . . Every warrior was protected by a tree, and the thick foliage of the *hommock* shielded every movement from the scrutiny of our spies and officers.—Joshua R. Giddings, "The Exiles of Florida," pp. 117, 176. [See also pp. 278, 282; and Everglades.]

Hone, v. To yearn or long. Southern.

1600 Some of the Oxen . . . . missed their fellowes behind, and *honing* after them, bellowed as their nature is.—Holland's "Livy," I, vii, 6. (N. E. D.)

1754 She brought a servant up with her . . . . who *hones* after the country. —Samuel Richardson, "Sir Charles Grandison," ch. xxxv. (1812.) (N. E. D.)

1884 "I'm just *honin'* after food," is another example of the Tennessee patois.—*Harper's Mag.,* p. 800/1.

1893 [She announced] that she "des [just] natchelly *honed* arter one o' Aunt Em'lys tales."—Mary A. Owen, "Old Rabbit, the Voodoo," &c., p. 19.

Honey-cooler. A term of commendation. Western slang.

1868 Make [this Indian] your friend, for he is a good one. Do the square thing by him and he is a *honey-cooler*. Do anything mean to him, and he is a johan, and he will get even.—Letter of Indian agent from Idaho, July 4: see *C. R.*, July 19, 1894, p. 7692/2.

Honeyfugle. To cajole for selfish purposes. [Cf. the Southern to *sweet-talk* someone.]

1868 The design of that letter, to use a homely phrase, was to *"honey-fuggle"* Mr. Seward and Mr. Johnson.—Mr. W. T. Willey of W. Va., U. S. Senate, March 9: *C. G.*, p. 1747/1.

1890 What relief do you propose to give the negro? You propose to give him the force bill. You propose to put one arm around his neck and *"honey-fugle"* him, and get him to vote for the Republican ticket.—Mr. John H. Rogers of Ark., H. R., Aug. 23: *C. R.*, p. 9092/2.

Honk, Honking. The cry of the wild goose.

1854 The faint *honk* or quack of their leader. . . . . I was startled by the loud *honking* of a goose.—Thoreau, "Walden," pp. 247, 271. (N. E. D.)

Honk, v. To cry as wild geese cry.

a.1865 As the air grows colder, the long wedges of geese flying south, with their commodore in advance, and *honking* as they fly, are seen high up in the heavens.—O. W. Holmes, "An Old Volume of Life," p. 169. (Century Dict.)

Honker. A wild goose, so named from its cry.

1884 My first *Honker*. Well do I remember the morning on which he measured his length on the grass.—*Forest and Stream*, May 22. (Century Dict.)

1888 *Branta canadensis* . . . . [named] *Honker* or *Old Honker* in recognition of its hoarse notes or "honking."—Trumbull, "Bird Names." (N. E. D.)

Hooch. See **Kootchinoo.**

Hoodlum. A young rough, a rowdy. See Vol. I for probable origin of the word. [1872-1888.]

1872 Where were these vigilant guardians of the interests of San Francisco? Why were not crowds of *"hoodlums"* collected to burn my name and that of my colleagues?—Mr. A. A. Sargent of Calif., H. R., Apr. 23: *C. G.*, p. 2693/3.

1876 The term *"hoodlum"* has a terrible meaning with us in San Francisco. It means the wildest kind of boys, made such by absence of employment.—Mr. A. A. Sargent of Calif., U. S. Senate, May 1: *C. R.*, p. 2856/1.

1877 The conflict of the two races has always been apparent whenever they have come in contact, the Mongolian in his home persecuting the Caucasian with all the vehemence and vindictiveness with which the *hoodlum* in San Francisco pelts, beats, and, if opportunity offers, kills his Mongol neighbor.—Mr. E. R. Meade of N. Y., H. R., Feb. 28: *Id.*, p. 118/2.

1901 The only reason that the *hoodlums* run any town on the American continent is that the fine-haired people, the self-styled "better classes," think they are better than other people. They are unwilling to be jostled by a *hoodlum* on the day of election.—Mr. Champ Clark of Mo., H. R., Jan. 8: *Id.*, p. 744/2.

Hoodoo. Probably a corruption of *voodoo*. A charm like that of the "evil eye." Hence **Hoodoo,** v., to place under a charm. [1889-1909.] See two valuable papers on 'Voodoo Worship in Hayti,' by Mr. W. W. Newell, *Journal of Am. Folk-Lore*, I, 16-30 (1888) and II, 41-47 (1889) and subsequent notes. Mr. Newell traces the word, with considerable probability, to *Vaudois* or *Vaudoux*.

1889 The prospect of pleasing his party and at the same time escaping a *hoodoo* must be irresistibly attractive.—*N. Y. Sun*, March 20. (Century Dict.)

1896 If the McKinley bill of Republican fame was a *"hoodoo,"* your own Wilson bill has certainly been a "Jonah."—Mr. F. E. Warren of Wyo., U. S. Senate, Jan. 23: *C. R.*, p. 901/1.

Hoodoo. To make a great outcry or a great "to-do."

1900 I will tell you what [the Democrats] are *hoodooing* about.—Mr. J. G. Cannon of Ill., H. R., Feb. 27: *Id.*, p. 2336/2.

Hoof, on the. Alive; walking. [1830-1837.]

1879 [Formerly] cattle were made to transport themselves *"on the hoof,"* as the drovers say.—Mr. Hatch of Mo., H. R., June 5: *C. R.*, p. 1801/1.

1890 The State of Minnesota passed a law [providing] that all animals brought into the State and proposed to be slaughtered . . . . should be inspected *on the hoof.*—Mr. G. G. Vest of Mo., U. S. Senate, May 29: *Id.*, p. 5429/1.

Hook and ladder company. A company of firemen. [1902.]

1875 Two *hook and ladder companies,* with scaling apparatus, were among the appliances of legislation provided by these peaceably assembled and now indignant "representatives of a sovereign State."—Mr. Roscoe Conkling of N. Y., U. S. Senate, Jan. 28: *C. R.*, p. 842/2.

Hook, on one's own. On one's own account or responsibility, not as part of a general enterprise or venture. [1812-1866.]

1851 I stand *on my own hook,* and sail under my own flag.—Wilmington (N. C.) *Commercial,* March 1, p. 3/2.

1863 I vote here pretty much *on my own hook,* and I speak *on my own hook* too.—Mr. Samuel C. Fessenden of Me., U. S. Senate, Jan. 26: *C. G.*, p. 516/2.

1863 [I may] ask the Legislature of the State of Missouri to adopt a gradual system of emancipation *upon their own hook.*—Mr. John B. Henderson of Mo., U. S. Senate, Jan. 30: *Id.*, p. 613/2.

Hoosier. An inhabitant of Indiana. [1659-1861.]

1847 The victim happened to be an exceedingly mild *Hoosier.*—Ruxton, "Adventures in Mexico, &c.," p. 328.

1850 One Yankee traveller who saw the live *Hoosier* has again written.—Wilmington (N. C.) *Commercial,* Feb. 14, p. 4/3.

1874 A powerful old *Hoosier* was indicted for stealing hogs, and to avoid the danger of variance the pleader had charged that on a certain day, feloniously, &c., &c., the defendant took and carried away two hogs, two pigs, two boars, two sows, two barrows, and two of every kind of hog that he had ever heard of. When the indictment was read through to the *Hoosier,* he said, "Why, your honor, there never was such an evenly divided gang of hogs on earth; the indictment must be void."—Mr. Matt. H. Carpenter, U. S. Senate, Jan. 30: *C. R.*, p. 1042/1.

1876 We have a man from the *Hoosier State,* the old democratic warhorse.—Mr. Harrison of Ill., H. R., May 3: *Id.*, p. 3282/1.

1911 James Whitcomb Riley shares with Edward Eggleston the credit of having interpreted *Hoosier* life accurately, but the two writers have little in common, except their subject. Eggleston rather patronizes the people whom he depicts while all his personal tastes are literary and conventional. Riley loves his characters. He writes good poetry about the Indiana farmer because he could be a farmer himself without a pang of regret.—Sunday *Oregonian,* Dec. 3, p. 8/3.

Hopkinsians. The followers of Samuel Hopkins (1721-1803) who taught Calvinism in its most repulsive form. [1821-1850.]

1835 The late Rev. Dr. Hopkins was the founder of a theory of divinity, which may be fairly denominated American. Its grand doctrine . . . seems to be, that all virtue may be resolved into disinterested benevolence, and all vice into selfishness. One of its axioms is, that a Christian must possess a spirit willing to be damned, were he convinced it were necessary for the glory of God. This system, denominated *Hopkinsian*, has some other peculiar features and tenets. It was followed up by a succession of divines of respectable talent: as Emmons, Spring, Worcester, and the present Dr. Beecher.—Timothy Flint in the *Athenæum*, Sept. 19: p. 716.

Hopperdozers. See quotation.

1904 *Hopperdozers* are long shallow pans of any convenient dimensions, made of galvanized iron or other material, mounted upon runners about an inch thick. The pan is partly filled with water, a small quantity of kerosene is added to form a film, and a screen is placed upright on the back to prevent the locusts from jumping over the pan. As *hopperdozers* are drawn over the ground, ... the young locusts jump into the air, fall into the pan, and are wetted and killed by the kerosene.—*U. S. Dept. Agr., Circular 53,* p. 2. (Century Dict.; which gives a picture of this contrivance.)

Horizontal tariff. One which imposes a uniform rate of duty. [1842-1847.] Hence **horizontal,** uniform.

1844 A *horizontal tariff*! an absolute water level! In equal violation of the laws of hydrostatics and of the protective system!—Mr. McDuffie of S. C., U. S. Senate, May 30: p. 7/1 of speech as separately published.

1869 If you are going to strike down these new interests rising in the West and Northwest, rest assured we will not let you alone, but we will take a *horizontal tariff*.—Mr. Zach. Chandler of Mich., U. S. Senate, Jan. 18: *C. G.,* p. 418/1.

1872 The *horizontal reduction* of duties, such as the bill proposes, would do incalculable injury.—Mr. F. T. Frelinghuysen of N. J., U. S. Senate, March 28: *Id.,* p. 2016/2.

1872 When Robert J. Walker, in 1846, undertook to make a *horizontal tariff*, his scythe, sweeping across, struck tin at the rate of five per cent.—Mr. W. D. Kelley of Pa., H. R., May 1: *Id.,* p. 308/1, App.

1876 What principle may have been adopted in arriving at this 10 per cent idea, this *horizontal* figure of 10 per cent, I do not know. [A proposed reduction of salaries.]—Mr. S. B. Maxey of Tex., U. S. Senate, June 2: *C. R.,* p. 3490/2.

1884 A *horizontal reduction* of 20 per cent, as provided in the Morrison bill, is absurd; for it assumes that all products upon which there is now a duty can equally bear reduction. It is worse than Procrustes's iron bedstead.—Mr. S. L. Milliken of Mo., H. R., Apr. 30: *Id.,* p. 171/1, App.

1888 The late Hon. William R. Morrison, of *"horizontal"* memory.—Mr. N. P. Haugen of Wisc., H. R., May 12: *Id.,* p. 4040/2.

1890 The Democratic bill made a *horizontal cut* of 20 per cent, thereby reducing the revenue $12,000,000 annually.—Mr. J. H. Gear of Ia., H. R., May 9: *Id.,* p. 4392/2.

1894 [They have enabled] the unscrupulous manufacturer to make a *horizontal* cut in wages.—Mr. H. C. Snodgrass of Tenn., H. R., Jan. 10: *Id.,* p. 669/1.

Horn snake. "So called from a sharp horn it carries in its tail." [1705.] *Farancia abacura.*

1887 A blaze of lightning discovered the maimed form and black and red markings of a "bastard *horn-snake.*"—G. W. Cable, *Century Mag.,* xxxv, 733.

Horny-handed. An epithet sometimes applied to "workingmen," referring to the callouses caused by manual labor. Dr. John Brown used it (1859) in describing a man. (N. E. D.)

1879 Mr. Baker:—The *horny-handed* laborers of this country . . . . I yield to my friend from New York. Mr. Cox:—I will take the floor from my *"horny-handed"* friend, though I do not believe that the gentleman ever did a full old-fashioned day's work in his life. Mr. O'Neill:—I want to know who are the *horny-handed* men in [Mr. Baker's] district, who are crying out, "Down with taxation!" Mr. McCook:—I do not know that the State of Indiana has any exclusive privilege to *"horny-handed* sons of labor." Mr. Young:— I am speaking for the *horny-handed* yeomanry of the country, the down-trodden . . . taxpayers.—H. R., June 7: *C. R.*, pp. 1833-6.

1892 He must have employed indirectly tens of thousands of the *horny-handed.—Spectator*, Dec. 10, p. 847/2.

1900 The prejudice against the *horny-handed* toiler exists.—*Scientific American*, N. S., lv, 87. (Century Dict.)

Horseback opinion. One given hastily without consulting the authorities.

1879 I am not here as a judicial authority or oracle. I can only give a *horseback opinion* [on this question].—Mr. Chas. W. Jones of Fla., U. S. Senate, Apr. 23: *C. R.*, p. 728/1.

Horse case. One involving small pecuniary value.

1894 Mr. Boutelle to Mr. Outhwaite:—I do not want your judgment, and would not take it in a *horse case.*—H. R., Feb. 2: *C. R.*, p. 1811/1.

Horse doctor. A veterinary surgeon.

1672 I understand myself to be a great *horse-doctor.*—J. Lacy, "Dumb Lady" (1875), p. 25. (N. E. D.)

1723 Rope Dancers, *Horse Doctors*, Poppet Shewers.—*Lond. Gazette*, No. 6139/3. (N. E. D.)

1894 Mr. Frye:—We found . . . . that he was a veterinary surgeon, called in New England a *"horse doctor."* Mr. Gray:—*Horse doctors* are pretty good men in New England.—U. S. Senate, March 1: *C. R.*, p. 2500/1.

Horse lawyer. One of no great ability.

1890 Mr. Mansur:—He presented his authorities carefully, because he believed there were some legal principles governing even a horse trade. Mr. Tarsney:—He was a *horse lawyer*. Mr. Mansur:—Not exactly a *horse lawyer*, because if you speak of John McSweeney as a *horse lawyer*, God knows what will become of the State of Missouri.—H. R., July 1: *C. R.*, p. 6900/2.

Horse railroad, Horse car. Railroad cars and street cars drawn by a horse or horses. [1858-1859.]

1866 A *horse railroad* has been incorporated, and it is necessary that [it] should pass over a portion of [government] land—Mr. Henry Wilson of Mass., U. S. Senate, Jan. 29: *C. G.*, p. 472/2.

1866 I am compelled to patronize the *horse cars* that run on the avenue, particularly when they give me a free ticket.—Mr. Robert C. Schenck of O., H. R., June 5: *Id.*, p. 2978/3.

1870 The street railways, the *horse railways*, have taken advantage of this tax.—Mr. Simon Cameron of Pa., U. S. Senate, July 1: *Id.*, p. 5096/2.

Horse sense. Practical good sense. [1833-1893.]

[1868 This common perception is called by the old settlers *"wild-hog sense."*—Mr. H. P. H. Bromwell of Ill., H. R., March 18: *C. G.*, p. 286/2, App.]

1880 As the U. S. owned the . . . land, I did not, in my unsophisticated *horse-sense* view of things, see any difficulty in [leasing it].—Mr. James G. Blaine of Me., U. S. Senate, March 18: *C. R.*, p. 1670/1.

1890 [This bill] has good, hard, common, and what plain people call *horse sense* in it.—Mr. L. C. Houk of Tenn., H. R., Apr. 24: *Id.,* p. 3802/2.

1896 I do know something about harbors. I have common sense, I think; what they call in New England *"horse sense."* . . . . I am able to form a general judgment.—Mr. W. P. Frye of Me., U. S. Senate, May 11: *Id.,* p. 5056/1.

Horse-shed, v. See quotation.

1901 The witnesses were right there. There was no opportunity, as Mr. Lincoln used to say, to *"horse-shed"* them before they were brought in,—before their counsel or attorneys had had any opportunity to change their minds,—that is, to fix them up.—Mr. E. L. Hamilton of Mich., H. R., Feb. 4: *C. R.,* p. 1918/1.

Horse thief. A stealer of horses. [1768-1800.]

1730 A Proclamation. Whereas, the General Assembly of His Majesty's Province of New York, did on the Twenty-Eight Day of October last, represent to Me, That one Solomon Jennings hath been a notorious *Horse-Stealer* for many years past in several of the Counties of this Province, . . . [Gov. John Montgomerie of New York offers £20 reward for arrest of Jennings.]—*New York Gazette,* in D. T. Valentine's Manual of the Corporation of the City of New York, 1864, Nov. 9, p. 677.

1779 John Carr, a notorious *horse-thief.—New Jersey Gazette,* N. Jersey Archives, 2d Ser., III, 697, Oct. 20.

Hot cakes, like. With great rapidity. [1860-1861.]

1879 Four per cent bonds and ten-dollar certificates . . . . go off like *hot cakes.*—Mr. Deuster of Wisc., H. R., May 15: *C. R.,* p. 1368/1.

Hotel privilege.

1884 '86 See Water Privilege.

Hotfoot, n. In the quotation, this means expedition, and is a nonce-word. The N. E. D. gives examples of the word as an adverb, 1300-1893.

1869 The honorable Senator from Wisconsin (Mr. Howe) admonished us of the importance of *hot-foot* in this business, if I may say so, of allowing the testimony to be taken at once.—Mr. Jacob M. Howard of Mich., U. S. Senate, Jan. 15: *C. G.,* p. 389/3.

Hub, The. Boston, Mass. [1789-1858.]

1864 Boston . . . . is well called the *hub* of our universe, with her spokes now inserted in New York, Pennsylvania, Ohio, the great West, and the great Northwest.—Mr. Brooks of N. Y., in the H. R., Feb. 19: *C. G.,* p. 761/3.

1866 The honorable Senator from Pennsylvania is mistaken in supposing that this idea comes from what he calls, perhaps correctly, the *"hub of the universe,"* Massachusetts.—Mr. L. S. Foster of Conn., U. S. Senate, Dec. 13: *C. G.,* p. 98/3.

1870 This bill is antagonized by Boston and New England,—the *"Hub"* and its surroundings.—Mr. J. B. Howell of Ia., U. S. Senate, May 28: *Id.,* p. 3920/2.

1879 I found [these indications] center on *the hub* as the place where the job was intended to go.—Mr. Omar D. Conger of Mich., H. R., Apr. 10: *C. R.,* p. 366/1.

1882 A city editor, a cynical dyspeptic who runs a feeble daily near the world's *"Hub,"* says this measure is "bucolic buncombe."—Mr. John T. Updegraff of O., H. R., May 9: *Id.,* p. 313/2, App.

Hub, up to the. Thorough, sincere, thoroughly. [1800-1856.]

1815 I've been *up to the hub,* and didn't flinch.—David Humphreys, "The Yankey in England," p. 33. [Here possibly the original meaning of hub-deep in mud.]

1864　L. H. Chandler, like Anderson of Kentucky, is for the Administration *"up to the hub."*—*N. Y. Times,* cited in the *C. G.,* Feb. 29, p. 849/1.

Huffy. Easily offended, arrogant. [1800-1855.]

1871　He found C. and Co. rather *huffy,* and somewhat on the high-and-mighty order with him, and, being a democratic American, he didn't like it.—H. B. Stowe, "Oldtown Stories," p. 311. (Century Dict.)

Hugger-mugger. In the following citation the sense of this old word slides from secrecy to conspiracy and fraud.

1879　Mr. Blaine:—By some sort of an arrangement, ... by some sort of judicial *hugger-mugger,* all the prosecutions [in South Carolina] are abandoned. Mr. Voorhees:—[Mr. Blaine admits] that his own people were . . . . in a *hugger-mugger* to cheat justice. . . . I asked the question based on his own statement that a trade had been made, on that strange word which I do not know that I ever heard before, a *hugger-mugger* in court. . . . . . In the classic language of the Senator from Maine this *hugger-mugger* in fraud of justice.—U. S. Senate, Apr. 24: *C. R.,* p. 808/9.

Hull-gull. A guessing game for children. One player takes a number of beans, peas, or the like in his hand, saying "Hull gull." Another says "Hand full." Then the first says "Parcel how many?" The other player then guesses at the number, taking all if the guess is correct, otherwise making up the discrepancy. (Century Dict., 1911.)

1879　The honorable Senator means to get a fair jury by having what the boys used to call *"hull-gull a handful,"* a game of "odd and even."—Mr. James G. Blaine of Me., U. S. Senate, June 5: *C. R.,* p. 1791/2.

Hum, for home. [1787-1861.]

1815　*Hum* is *hum,* be it ever so *humbly.*—David Humphreys, "The Yankey in England," p. 19.

1815　I guess I belong to America, when I'm *at hum. Id.,* p. 39.

1815　How to git *hum* is the divil on't, as Jack the sailor says.—*Id.,* p. 40.

Human. A human being. [a.1611-1911.]

1628　Hee was not ought dependent or impure As wretched Humans are.—Austin's "Vrania," p. 8 (1629). Another instance on p. 33.

Hunk, Hunky. All right; in good condition. Slang. Sometimes given as *hunkydory.*

1856　Now he felt himself all *hunk,* and wanted to get this enormous sum out of the city.—Quoted in *N. Y. Tribune,* Dec. 30. (Century Dict.)

Hunkers. The conservative Democrats in the days of Tyler and Polk, the more radical members being the **Barn-burners,** q. v. [1844-1864.]

1848　It is well known that there is a division in the democratic party in the State of New York. The two divisions are distinguished by the names of "barn-burners" and "old *hunkers.*" We suppose the former name is applied to those who encouraged and excused the rioters who resisted the law in relation to the Van Ness estate.—Wilmington (N. C.) *Commercial,* Apr. 22, p. 2/3.

1849　The Old *Hunker* Convention, which has been in session [at Rome, N. Y.], adjourned, without being able to make any compromise with the Free Soilers.—Wilmington (N. C.) *Commercial,* Aug. 21, p. 2/5.

1849　It is shocking to think of the manner in which the Old *Hunkers* and Barnburners abuse each other.—*Id.,* Sept. 18, p. 4/2. (From the Washington *Republic.*)

1854　[It has been said] that in 1846 the "hards" or *hunkers* (for they are the same) defeated the election of Hon. Silas Wright.—Mr. F. B. Cutting of N. Y., H. R., Jan. 20: p. 14/1 of his speech as separately published.

1900　See Mossback.

Hunt up. To pursue eagerly, and to find what is pursued.

1791 They enter . . . with a view of chasing the roebuck, and *hunting up* the sturdy bear.—W. Bartram, "Carolina," p. 488. (N. E. D.)

1817 If he finds them within 3 or 4 miles of his house, he thinks himself fortunate; but it sometimes happens that he is two days in *"hunting them up,"* as they term it.—J. Bradbury, "Travels in America," p. 265. (N. E. D.)

1871 A gentleman was in Atlanta on that occasion. . . . He *hunted me up.* —Mr. Joshua Hill of Ga., U. S. Senate, Apr. 10: *C. G.*, p. 541/2.

Hurricane roof. Cf. **Hurricane Deck,** a light upper deck on a steamer. [1835-1882.]

1849 The after part [of the boiler] shot through the main cabin floor, cutting it all away, and passing obliquely through the *hurricane roof* immediately over the ladies' cabin.—Wilmington (N. C.) *Commercial,* Nov. 27, p. 1/6. (From the *N. O. Delta.*)

Hurry up. Be quick. [1849-1866.]

1879 You will lose your half minute if you do not *hurry up.*—Mr. S. S. Cox of N. Y., H. R., May 7: *C. R.*, p. 1136/1.

Husking. A social gathering for husking Indian corn. [1721-1851.]

1801 The owner of the violin was at a *husking.*—D. Webster to Jas. H. Bingham, Oct. 26: "Private Corresp." (1857), I, 96.

Husky. An Eskimo dog.

1886 The original *Husky* has always been an animal requiring firm treatment.—"Colonial and Indian Exhibns.," p. 75. (Century Dict.)

Hustler. An indefatigable and rapid worker; a vigorous, pushing fellow, not vexed by scruples of conscience. [1890-1909.]

1886 A strictly first-class stenographer and type-writer, young man, a *hustler* in every respect, wants a strictly first-class position.—*Publishers' Weekly.* Dec. 18. (Century Dict.)

1891 Suppose one of these political managers, called bosses and *hustlers,* who have got to be a separate and distinct profession, unfortunately, in the U. S., should conclude, &c.—Mr. G. G. Vest of Mo., U. S. Senate, Jan. 16: *C. R.*, p. 1458/2.

1893 This is not a body where some political boss or political *hustler* can crack his whip and compel the minority to conform to the wishes of a mere numerical majority.—Mr. M. C. Butler of S. C., U. S. Senate, Oct. 4: *Id.*, p. 2106/1.

1894 See ROUSTABOUT.

1894 [Mr. T.] is a *"hustler* from way back." He told the Democratic candidate for county clerk that, if he would agree to appoint him deputy, he would *hustle* for him, and he thought [he] would "get there."—Mr. R. R. Hitt of Ill., H. R., Apr. 17: *Id.*, p. 3804/2.

I

Ice-breaker. See quotation, 1875.

1875 An *ice-breaker* for harbors is a steam-vessel provided with means for . . . keeping open a channel for ships.—Knight, "Dict. Mech.," p. 1161/2. (N. E. D.)

1880 Such ice as forms in the Choptank is not strong enough at any time to resist the power of an ordinary *ice-breaker.*—Mr. Wm. Kimmel of Md., H. R., May 20: *C. R.*, p. 178/2, App.

1886 The Gothenburg *ice-breaker* keeps the channel open.—*The Times,* March 9, p. 11/6. (N. E. D.)

1904 See BREAKHEAD.

Ice cream. Sweetened cream or custard flavored, beaten, and frozen. [1688-1855.]

1861 The Deacon, not being in the habit of taking his nourishment in the congealed state, had treated the *ice-cream* as a pudding of a rare species.—O. W. Holmes, "Elsie Venner," ch. vii. (Century Dict.)

Ice gorge. An accumulation of ice in a river. [1862-1884.]

1896 The closing days of the session, when there is a perfect *ice gorge* of measures contending for precedence.—Mr. J. W. Daniel of Va., U. S. Senate, Feb. 5: *C. R.*, p. 1329/2.

Ice gush. A mass of ice and water at the bottom of a crevasse or glacier.

1904 Now and then a horse will lose his footing and slide down to the bottom with a rush, but never once did one of them refuse to climb out of an *ice-gush* when called upon to do so.—*Jour. Franklin Institute*, p. 304. (Century Dict.)

Ice harbor. See quotation. Not in the dictionaries.

1876 When the ice forms in the [Delaware] river, it is necessary that the shipping coming in from the ocean should have some place of refuge. Hence that *ice-harbor* [at New Castle] was established, not for the benefit of the State of Delaware, but for the general commerce of the whole country.—Mr. W. Saulsbury of Del., U. S. Senate, July 17: *C. R.*, p. 4655/1.

1880 An examination was made "of the mouth of the Little Kanawha River, West Va., to ascertain the adaptability of that locality for an *ice-harbor*."—*C. R.*, Feb. 16: p. 909/1.

1880 This appropriation is simply for the purpose of giving to the Mississippi River near the city of St. Louis an *ice-harbor* to protect private property and public property.—Mr. G. G. Vest of Mo., U. S. Senate, June 1: *Id.*, p. 4007/1.

1884 The fact that there is an *ice-harbor* at the mouth of the Muskingum River, at Marietta, does not dispense with the necessity of one at Bellaire.—Mr. J. D. Taylor of O., H. R., June 10: *Id.*, p. 4967/1.

Ice lobe. A forward-reaching part of an ice-sheet with a convex front, in shape resembling an ear lobe.

1903 The relation of the Michigan, Saginaw, and Huron-Erie *ice-lobes* in lower Michigan during the Wisconsin stage of glaciation.—*Science*, p. 224. (Century Dict.)

Ice-locked. Thoroughly impeded with ice. The N..E. D. gives no example. Much the same as *icebound*.

1866 The idea that this [from Montreal by the river] can become a rival route, *ice-locked* as it is nearly seven months in the year, ... is preposterous.—Mr. C. T. Hulburd of N. Y., H. R., Apr. 24: *C. G.*, p. 2147/2.

1866 The records show that in forty years the City of Philadelphia has never been *ice-locked*.—Mr. W. D. Kelley of Pa., H. R., June 7: *Id.*, p. 3017/3.

1867 The Philadelphia papers a few days ago expressed great hope that eighty vessels that were *ice-locked* at Newcastle would soon be able to reach Philadelphia.—Mr. James Dixon of Conn., U. S. Senate, Feb. 14: *Id.*, p. 1294/2.

If the court understands itself. A phrase picked up in some judicial proceeding, and used in the sense of "If I know what I am talking about," or "If we know, &c."

1875 Mr. Richard J. Oglesby of Ill.:—Would you have [this bounty bill] go back to the House under the present pressure of affairs, with the expectation of passing it? Never; not *if the court understands itself*, and it thinks it does. Mr. Hager:—"She thinks she do." [Laughter.] Mr. Oglesby:—"I think she do." [Laughter.]—U. S. Senate, March 2: *C. R.*, p. 2047/1.

1885 [Persons] who would not be admitted into any decent society in New York, if New York society *knows herself*, and "she thinks she do."—Mr. W. E. Robinson of N. Y., H. R., Jan. 10: *Id.*, p. 614/1.

Illy. Badly, ill. [1549-1904.]

1833 It *illy* becomes the chief magistrate to make this charge.—Mr. J. C. Calhoun, U. S. Senate, Feb. 15: "Works" (1856), II, 216.

1862 Those who control our armies will *illy* discharge their duty if they are guided by aught else than their own matured judgments.—Mr. C. H. Van Wyck of N. Y., H. R., Feb. 7: *C. G.*, p. 714/2.

1867 Some may say that it is dangerous to extend the suffrage to a race *illy* prepared to exercise it.—Mr. W. A. Newell of N. J., H. R., Jan. 4: *Id.*, p. 284/3.

1876 Where at times we have thought an office was *illy* paid, we have increased the salary.—Mr. Bayard of Del., U. S. Senate, June 2: *C. R.*, p. 3486/1.

1876 Just at the heel of the session we were compelled to pass a very *illy*-considered tax-bill.—Mr. John Sherman of O., U. S. Senate, *Id.*, p. 3490/1.

1876 The building was *illy* constructed even for the purposes for which it was originally employed.—Mr. Ingalls of Kan., U. S. Senate, June 5: *Id.*, p. 3583/1.

Immediatism, Immediatist. An immediatist was one who advocated the immediate abolition of slavery; an abolitionist of the extremest type.

1885 [Mr. H. G. Otis] was prepared to denounce the Society as a "dangerous association." Its *immediatism* makes it a revolutionary society. . . . . [He] denounced the "higher law"; denied that the Scriptures were anywhere opposed to Slavery; repeated that Christ was not an *immediatist*.—W. P. Garrison and F. J. Garrison, "Life of Wm. Lloyd Garrison," I, 499-500. (Century Dict.)

Imphee. The broom corn, or "planter's friend." The name appears to come from Natal, and is inserted here because of priority of date. See N. E. D.

1866 I suggest to the Senator that he may as well include the word *"imphee"* in his motion, and strike them both out. I believe *imphee* is but a species of sorghum.—Mr. Howard of Mich., U. S. Senate, June 21: *C. G.*, p. 3313/2.

1880 The *imphee* or Planter's Friend, is well adapted to the Queensland climate.—Silver's "Handbook to Australia," p. 273. (N. E. D.)

Improve. To clear, plant, or erect buildings on land. Hence *Improvement* and *improved*. See Vol. I, **Improvements.** [1684-1878.]

1743-5 [Gethsemane] was formerly covered with olive-trees, but it is now without any *improvement*.—Richard Pococke, "Description of the East," II, 24. (Century Dict.)

b.1799 My *improved lot* in the Town of Alexandria . . . . I give to [M. W.] and her heirs forever.—Will of Geo. Washington. (Century Dict.)

Indian. Maize, or Indian corn.

1651 To be paid . . halfe in Indian corne, the *Indian* when the said Daniell shall demannd.—Records of Dedham, Mass. (1892), III, 187. (N. E. D.)

1664 The barly att four shillings . . and the *Indian* att three shillings the bushell.—Plymouth Colony Records (1855), IV, 72. (N. E. D.)

1831 It is only to put a little more *indian*, or a few potatoes, into the bread.—*The Liberator*, May 7, p. 74/1.

Indian agent. An officer dealing on behalf of the U. S. government with an Indian tribe or tribes.

1869 Many years ago John Randolph of Virginia, with cutting sarcasm, said that to be an *Indian agent* would corrupt the angel Gabriel.—Mr. B. F. Butler of Mass., H. R., Feb. 4: *C. G.*, p. 883/2.

1869 An *Indian agent* cannot cheat and swindle without connivance on the part of some one else, generally of military officers.—Mr. John T. Deweese of N. C., H. R., Feb. 6: *Id.*, p. 950/1.

1879 An *Indian agent* is utterly powerless for good, and cannot even close a whisky-shop without calling on the military for assistance.—Mr. Thos. C. McCreery of Ky., U. S. Senate, Feb. 10: *C. R.*, p. 1154/1.

Indian corn. Maize. [a.1621-1788.]

1670 The Summers [in New England] are commonly hot and dry, . . . yet are the Harvests good, the *Indian Corn* requiring more heat than wet to ripen it.—S. Clarke, "Plantations in America," p. 29.—(Century Dict.)

1671 See MUSH.

Indian giving. See quotation.

1892 If an American child, who has made a small gift to a playmate, is indiscreet enough to ask that the gift be returned, he (or she) is immediately accused of being an *Indian-giver*, or, as it is commonly pronounced, Injun-giver.—Dr. H. C. Bolton in *Journal of Am. Folk-Lore*, V, 68.

Indian orchard. An old orchard of ungrafted trees, the time of whose planting is not known. (Bartlett.)

1902 The name is sometimes given to the neighboring village.—*Journal of Am. Folk-Lore*, p. 109. (Century Dict.)

Indian pudding, or hasty pudding. A mush made of Indian corn meal boiled in water.

1812 He was making his breakfast from a prodigious earthen dish, filled with milk and *Indian pudding*.—W. Irving, "The Knickerbockers," p. 152. (Century Dict.)

Indian summer. That season of genial weather which usually comes after the first autumnal frosts. [1794-1853.]

1830 For a week past we have had that mild and serene weather usually designated as the *Indian Summer*, with heavy dews at night, thick fogs in the morning, and smoky atmosphere the greater part of the day.—*Am. Beacon* (Norfolk, Va.), Nov. 4, p. 2/1.

Indispensable. A "bishop" [i.e. a bustle].

1819 A young gentleman in Philadelphia [tried] to pick up a lady's *indispensable*, which had dropped.—Norfolk (Va.) *Beacon*, Jan. 19, p. 4/1. (From the *Catskill Recorder*.)

Industrial. A share of stock in an industrial enterprise.

1903 Great bales and bundles of *"industrials"* have had to be thrown over . . . for protective purposes.—*N. Y. Times*, July 22. (Century Dict.)

Infant industries. A phrase much used by the advocates of a high tariff, and, in ridicule, by their opponents.

1870 But, argue our defenders of monopoly, let us protect our *infant industries*, and when they have grown to manhood, when their muscles are hardened, they will need no further protection. . . . . Before we listen further to this appeal, let us know how long infancy lasts in our country, and when these infants will be in a condition to be weaned.—Mr. S S. Marshall of Ill., H. R., March 29: *C. G.*, p. 240/3, App.

1882 He [Industry] may properly be called the *Great American Infant*. His inability to stand is in the inverse ratio to the amount of "protection" he receives to help him stand. . . . . The more he consumes the feebler he gets; the bigger he grows the weaker he becomes. . . . . My opinion is that he never will stand while the public will hold him up; that, so long as we feed him, he will lie on his back, hold on by the grass, and devour the food given him by the American people. —Mr. Vance of N. C., U. S. Senate, Feb. 14: *C. R.*, pp. 1122-3.

1883 This bill is full of *"infant industries."* These infants, being of royal birth, are to be born and bred millionaires. In a few years they will grow to lusty manhood, full grown millionaire cormorants.—Mr. R P. Bland of Mo., H. R., Jan. 27: *Id.*, p. 1678/2.

1884 The system [of protection] was first commended to the people on the ground that it was needed for the encouragement of *infant industries*, for the education of working men in arts unknown to them, and to persuade capital to enter enterprises which . . . would make us independent of the foreigner.—Mr. Wm. Dorsheimer of N. Y., H. R., May 1: *Id.*, p. 3660/2.

1884 It is time this *infant* stopped "puling (*sic*) in its nurse's arms." It will be an *infant* so long as Government pap is furnished it.—Mr. Jas. F. Clay of Ky., H. R., *Id.,* p. 3666/1.

1888 Are not these *infant industries* becoming rather aged? Ought they not to get along without the nursing-bottle?—Mr. M. H. Ford of Mich., H. R., Apr. 27: *Id.,* p. 3446/1.

1888 Mr. Clay, the great apostle of protection, in his debate with Mr. Calhoun, ... declared only for a temporary tariff for the protection of our *"infant industries."*—Mr. C. T. O'Ferrall of Va., H. R., May 1: *Id.,* p. 3597/1.

1894 Our Democratic friends have endeavored to ridicule protection out of existence by charging that it was only asked in the first instance on behalf of *"infant industries,"* and that the larger the infant has grown the more nourishment he requires.—Mr. A. J. Hopkins of Ill., H. R., Jan. 10: *Id.,* p. 637/2.

1894 [What Andrew Jackson said concerning a tariff] was said when the country was very young, when much was heard of the plea that our *"infant industries"* should be protected.—Mr. H. C. Snodgrass of Tenn., H. R., Jan. 10: *Id.,* p. 662/1.

1894 The Democratic party is about to follow the example of Herod, and commit infanticide by killing our *infant industries.*—Mr. T. W. Phillips of Pa., H. R., Jan. 26: *Id.,* p. 1511/1.

1894 Mr. Springer of Ill.:—Formerly the protectionists . . . came to Congress and asked protection for the [sake of] their *"infant" industries.* The industries are no longer infants, but are full grown, have boots on, wear whiskers and spurs. You cannot plead "the baby act" any longer. A member:—The babe has kicked the cradle all to pieces. Mr. Springer:—Yes, as my friend from Texas says, the babe has grown so big, it has kicked the cradle all to pieces.—H. R., Jan. 11: *C. R.,* p. 580/2, App.

1897 We have heard a great deal about *infant industries,* some of them one hundred and eight years old, which have held on to the public teat with the grim tenacity of snapping turtles, and waxed fat while three generations of people have been born, and lived, toiled, suffered, and passed off the stage of action,—while empires have sprung into birth, and kingdoms have crumbled into dust.—Mr. Champ Clark of Mo., H. R., March 26: *Id.,* p. 382/1.

Infare or **Infair.** See quotations. See N. E. D.

1878 There could be no wedding in a Hoosier village thirty or forty years ago without an *infare* on the following day. In those days the faring into the house of the bridegroom's parents was observed with great rejoicing.—E. Eggleston, "Roxy," ch. xxix. (Century Dict.)

1893 In Connecticut and in New York the bringing home of the bride was called a "Second-day Wedding"; in New Jersey, an *"Infair."*—Mrs. M. F. Hoagland in *Journal of Am. Folk-Lore,* vi, 301.

Infit. An allowance corresponding to an outfit. Hence **Infit, v.** To furnish (a sailor) with things needed after a voyage.

1841 [Foreign ministers] received an out-fit before they left home, and an *in-fit* to return upon. A year's salary was the *in-fit*; the out-fit was a year's salary, because it included the expense of setting up a house after the minister arrived at his post.—Mr. Benton in the U. S. Senate: Benton's "Thirty Years' View," II, p. 262/1. (1856.)

1887 The merchant is as anxious to *"infit"* as he was to "outfit" him, but the man must now bring an order from the agent or owner of the vessel.—"Fisheries of the U. S.," V, ii, 226. (N. E. D.)

Inflationist. An advocate of an exaggerated paper currency.

1874 Have we any *inflationists* on this floor? . . . There is a certain odious flavor about [the name].—Mr. Carl Schurz of Mo., U. S. Senate, Jan. 14: *C. R.,* p. 636/1.

1874   Did not the *inflationists* advocate an inflation of the currency pure and simple, inflation for its own sake?—The same, Apr. 6: *Id.,* p. 2827/2.

1876   The election of Tilden would spike the whole *inflationist* battery.— *N. Am. Rev.,* cxxiii, 451. (N. E. D.)

1878   The Wall Street stock-jobber was born of the French dealer in assignats, and the English *inflationist* of 1818, 1819, 1820, has his descendants on this side the water making corners in currency and coin—Mr. H. L. Dawes of Mass., U. S. Senate, Jan. 29: *C. R.,* p. 646/2.

1887   See SILVERITE.

Infract. To infringe on, to break. [1798-1859.]

1862   The reason of this clause would be more or less impugned and *infracted* by the Senator from Kansas [General Lane] being permitted to retain his seat.—Mr. Garrett Davis of Ky., U. S. Senate, Jan. 13: *C. G.,* p. 295/1.

1863   If an officer *infracts* the constitutional and legal right of the citizen, and thereby makes himself a trespasser, and liable to an action, &c.— Mr. Lazarus W. Powell of Ky., U. S. Senate, March 2: *Id.,* p. 1465/1.

1863   I believe it is my duty, not only as a citizen, but as a Senator, to preserve the Constitution, and to assault all who attempt to *infract* it.— The same, p. 1472/2.

1863   I use the word "criminal" to indicate those *infracting* the law.— The same, p. 1473/1.

1871   My friend from Massachusetts [Mr. Dawes] has *infracted* the rules of the house; but I hope no one will offer a resolution of censure.— Mr. S. S. Cox of N. Y., H. R., Apr. 15: *C. G.,* p. 721/3.

In it. "In the same class with"; to be considered worthy of attention.

1892   In the expressive saying of the day, the poor man is not *"in it."* His dollars are yet in the dim distance.—Mr. B. H. Clover of Kan., H. R., March 21: *C. R.,* p. 30/1, App.

1898   Jonah and his historic vine will retire in discomfiture, . . . for they are not *"in it"* with the great and marvelous growth of the sheep industry in Ohio.—Mr. R. E. Burke of Tex., H. R., Feb. 3: *Id.,* p. 1405/1.

Inlot. In Louisiana, &c., a village lot containing about half an arpent. (Century Dict.)

Innocuous desuetude. Harmless state of disuse. A phrase used by President Cleveland (see quotation) and often cited in ridicule.

1886   After an existence of nearly twenty years of an almost *innocuous desuetude*, these laws are brought forth [to hamper the Executive].— Message to the Senate, March 1.

1886   The explanation of the gentleman from Illinois goes into a state of *innocuous desuetude.* (Laughter.)—Mr. Hugh Buchanan of Ga., H. R., March 11: *C. R.,* p. 2308/2.

1886   The Senator from West Virginia gave utterance to a fit companion piece for this doctrine of *"innocuous desuetude,"* when he talked the other day about the "practical repeal" of the statute.—Mr. J. E. Brown of Ga., U. S. Senate, March 18: *Id.,* p. 2492/1.

1888   [The U. S.] arsenal at Liberty, Mo., continued in operation until the commencement of the Civil War, since which time it has fallen into a condition of *"innocuous desuetude."*—Mr. A. M. Dockery of Mo., H. R., Aug. 15: *Id.,* p. 7598/1.

1889   [We shall probably] allow our treaty rights to be disregarded, the lives of our citizens to be jeopardized, their property destroyed, the Monroe Doctrine to sink into *innocuous desuetude.*—Mr. J. N. Dolph of Ore., U. S. Senate, Jan. 30: *Id.,* p. 1332/2.

1890   In 1885 the nation was piling up the remonetized silver dollars in the Treasury, and President Cleveland was about to take office. He issued that famous letter to Congress, depicting the evils that would befall the country if the coinage of silver dollars was continued, ... desiring that the silver dollar go into *"innocuous desuetude."*—Mr. James O'Donnell of Mich., H. R., Sept. 27: *C. R.,* p. 10618/2.

1890   There was until recently a Republican paper in my town. It soon however went into *"innocuous desuetude."*—Mr. John H. Rogers of Ark., H. R., Apr. 23: *Id.,* p. 3744/1.

1892   See BACK NUMBER, A.

1896   See COFFEE-COOLER.

Inside. Acquainted with the inner working of the thing in question.

1870   Mr. Eldridge of Wisc.:—I ask the gentleman from Ohio to name the ships which he says have been sold for a song. The gentleman is *"inside"* on all these matters. Mr. Lawrence:—I am no more *"inside"* than [Mr. Eldridge].—H. R., Feb. 3: *C. G.,* p. 1022/1.

Institution. An established custom, practice, etc. Slavery was called the "peculiar institution" of the South. [1788-1908.]

1848   Gen. Cass . . . has declared himself opposed to the *institution* in all its bearings.—Wilmington (N. C.) *Commercial,* Sept. 21, p. 2/2.

1858   The camels form an *institution* of India . . . . and they must be respected accordingly.—*The Times,* April. (Century Dict.)

1863   I do not see why we cannot leave the people of [Arizona], as we have left others, organized of late years, to control that *institution* [slavery] as they please, without any interference of Congress.—Mr. Lazarus W. Powell of Ky., U. S. Senate, Feb. 20: *C. G.,* p. 1128/1.

1864   In the old States, ... staging is done away with, pretty much; but in the new States stage-coaches are quite an *institution.*—Mr. Pomeroy of Kan., U. S. Senate, June 2: *Id.,* p. 2658/2.

1877   See GOBBLE UP.

1881   [The South] surrendered; and with that was buried that "irrepressible conflict." Down with it, forever and for aye, went the *institution* of slavery; and I am glad of it. Down with it in a grave of blood and ruin and confusion went the *institution,* and there ended that "irrepressible conflict."—Mr. M. C. Butler of S. C., U. S. Senate, Apr. 28: *C. R.,* p. 418/2.

Instruct, Instruction. To instruct is to direct a representative how to vote. [1828-1862.]

1817   The ear of this House . . . is closed to truth and reason. What has produced this magic spell? *Instructions!*—John C. Calhoun, H. R., Jan. 17. ["Works" (1856), II, 177.]

1862   If I had any doubt on this subject, I am *instructed* by my people. They say that slavery ought to be abolished in this District [of Columbia].—Mr. William P. Fessenden of Me., U. S. Senate, Apr. 1: *C. G.,* p. 1473/1.

1863   Accursed, thrice accursed, be the man who would *"instruct"* Senators to vote against granting money to pay and feed and clothe our armies in the field.—Mr. Henry Wilson of Mass., U. S. Senate, Feb. 23: *Id.,* p. 1184/3.

Instructive ballots. See quotation.

1897   [The law of Illinois] provided that accompanying these ballots should be 8 *"instructive ballots"*—ballots prepared for the instruction of the voters, sample ballots.—Mr. L. W. Royse of Ind., H. R., Feb. 18: *C. R.,* p. 1970/1.

Insurge, v. To rise in revolt. Obs. Examples in N. E. D., 1532-1610.

1857   [Mr. Van Buren lost] much popular favor in the border States from his strenuous repression of aid to a neighboring people, *insurging* for liberty, and militarily crushed in the attempt.—Thos. H. Benton, "Thirty Years' View," II, 208.

Insurrectionist. An insurgent; one who promotes insurrection.

1845 The *insurrectionists* were speedily crushed.—J. G. Whittier, "Prose Works" (1889), II, 266. (N. E. D.)

1861 Missouri is comparatively quiet, and I believe cannot again be overrun by the *insurrectionists.*—President Lincoln's Message, Dec. 3: *C. G.,* p. 3/3, App.

Interindebtedness. Mutual indebtedness.

1892 Our coin alone amounts to 3.81 per cent on the *interindebtedness* of the country.—Mr. J. H. Walker of Mass., H. R., March 23: *C. R.,* p. 2468/2.

Interiorate. To occupy the interior of. A nonce-word.

1872 We have the Nashville and Northwestern line, which *interiorates* our own State, and delivers in our midst timbers from forests almost unbroken, and coal whose inexhaustible banks have not as yet been . . . . developed.—Mr. E. I. Golladay of Tenn., H. R., Apr. 13: *C. G.,* p. 2404/3.

Interval, Interval land. A tract of low ground between hills, or along the banks of a stream. (Webster.) [1653-1827.]

1867 League Island is a common low *interval land,* which probably has been formed in the course of the last six or seven hundred years by the confluence of the waters of the Schuylkill and the Delaware.—Mr. James W. Grimes of Ia., U. S. Senate, Feb. 13: *C. G.,* p. 1230/2.

Interview, v. To converse with, especially in order to get information for publishing.

1869 *"Interviewing"* is confined to American journalism.—*The Nation* (N. Y.), Jan. 28, p. 66. (N. E. D.)

1869 The *Sun interviews* Corbin, Fisk, . . . and whoever else has any story to tell or axe to grind.—*Daily News,* Dec. 17. (N. E. D.)

1869 A portion of the daily newspapers of New York are bringing the profession of journalism into contempt, so far as they can, by a kind of toadyism or flunkeyism, which they call *"interviewing."*—The same. (N. E. D.)

1890 In the night [Ulysses] was *interviewed* by the gods, who warned him of a certain dangerous island he was to pass, where the song of sweet sirens would allure him . . . ashore.—Mr. E. A. Morse of Mass., H. R., Feb. 21: *C. R.,* p. 1599/1.

In touch with. See Touch.

Inwardness. "The true inwardness" is the real character or purpose. [1877-1887.]

1877 I should not have performed my duty . . . without stating the *"true inwardness"* of this whole Petersburgh matter.—Mr. R. E. Withers of Va., U. S. Senate, Jan. 16: *C. R.,* p. 654/1.

1877 The *true inwardness* of the late Southern policy of the Republican party.—*N. Y. Tribune,* April. (Century Dict.)

1882 I highly appreciate [Mr. Burrows's] commanding ability; but . . . I cannot comprehend the *"true inwardness"* of his mathematical philosophy.—Mr. McClure of O., H. R., Feb. 13: *Id.,* p. 1107/1.

1888 [They] had learned by experience the *"true inwardness"* of the Chinese character and methods.—Mr. C. N. Felton of Calif., H. R., Aug. 18: *Id.,* p. 440/2, App.

1894 Just look at the *true inwardness* of the panic of 1893! How small a part [the farmer] has played in it!—Mr. H. C. Snodgrass of Tenn., H. R., Jan. 10: *Id.,* p. 662/1.

Ironclad oath, The. An oath required after the Civil War as a condition of holding certain offices. This oath was required by Act of Congress of July 2, 1862, and was meant to exclude from Federal offices those who had been secessionists.

1866   Give these [colored men of Mississippi] the ballot, and traitors never would be troubled with the *"iron-clad oath,"* for they never would have a chance to take it.—Mr. Daniel Clark of N. H., U. S. Senate, Feb. 14: *C. G.,* p. 835/1.

1866   It is easy for you today to admit these Representatives who are loyal, and can take "the *iron-clad oath,"* as you call it.—Mr. Samuel J. Randall of Pa., H. R., Feb. 27: *Id.,* p. 1057/2.

1866   If a State is simple enough to send a man here who cannot take the *iron-clad oath* that you and I and all of us had to take, Mr. Speaker, he shall not come in by my vote.—Mr. Dumont of Ind., H. R., March 17: *Id.,* p. 1476/2.

1867   [The] judges of election . . . . are required to be men who can take the *iron-clad oath,* as it is called, the oath prescribed by the Act of July 2, 1862.—Mr. John Sherman of O., U. S. Senate, March 16: *Id.,* p. 140/1.

1869   The *iron-clad oath* has long ago become but a spike upon which to impale conservatives.—Mr. B. M. Boyer of Pa., H. R., Jan. 8: *Id.,* p. 270/3.

1869   The offices of the State [of Virginia] were filled in large part by men who could not take what is known as the *iron-clad* or test oath. . . . The test oath hits everybody who has given any aid or comfort of any kind to any person engaged in hostility to the U. S. . . . Judge Rives says he cannot take the test oath.—Mr. John F. Farnsworth of Ill., H. R., March 18: *Id.,* p. 144/1-2. [See the whole discussion.]

1871   The *iron-clad oath* was iron-clad for obvious reasons. It was sweeping and searching; else it would not have been adapted to the purpose for which it was intended. It was passed early in the war, as a measure of immediate safety. It was not an organic provision, but a statute intended, not for all time, but for one time and one occasion. It works exclusion only from offices under the U. S. It does not extend to State offices.—Mr. Roscoe Conkling of N. Y., U. S. Senate, Feb. 13: *Id.,* p. 1168/1.

1885   [They may try] to follow the American precedent, and make "an *iron clad oath"* to preserve the union [of Great Britain and Ireland] a condition of election.—*Pall Mall Gazette,* June 6. (N. E. D.)

Iron horse. The locomotive engine. [1846-1874.]

1868   I should like the iron car to leap across the streams; . . . but, if that cannot be effected without breaking up the navigation of the river, the *iron horse* must stop there; and another *iron horse* must take up his onward career on the [farther] side.—Mr. Garrett Davis of Ky., U. S. Senate, July 21: *C. G.,* p. 4289/1.

1869   We have forty thousand miles of railroads, where the *iron horses* with nerves of steel and lungs of brass are competing in the race to transmit from the prairies of the West her millions of agricultural productions to your eastern metropolis.—Mr. Wm. Williams of Ind., H. R., Feb. 4: *Id.,* p. 889/3.

1870   When Leutz painted his "Westward the course of Empire takes its way" on the Capitol wall, he little thought the *iron horse* was so close behind his emigrant train.—Mr. John A. Logan of Ill., H. R., Jan. 22: *Id.,* p. 684/1.

1870   The locomotive, or in popular parlance the *"iron horse,"* no longer halts in its fiery course upon the eastern bank of the Mississippi, but starting on the eastern shore of the Atlantic is in full view of the Pacific by the time a week has intervened.—Mr. David Heaton of N. C., H. R., Jan. 25: *Id.,* p. 756/2.

1870   *The iron horse* has already borne a new revelation to the valleys of Utah.—Mr. W. A. Wheeler of N. Y., H. R., June 16: *Id.,* p. 4512/3.

1872   They kept on aiding [the Pacific railroad] until they saw the hoof
of the *iron horse* strike fire from the flinty summit of the Rocky
Mountains, and until they saw him breathing forth ·from his nostrils
fire and smoke as he plunged down, down toward the setting sun.—
Mr. Isaac C. Parker of Mo., H. R., Apr. 6: *Id.*, p. 2245/1.

Iron mountain. One yielding much iron.

1875   When the blaze of the iron furnaces in Pennsylvania could be seen
in almost every valley and at the foot of almost every *iron-mountain*
in that State, we beheld prosperity over the whole nation.—Mr. I. C.
Parker of Mo., H. R., Feb. 20: *C. R.*, p. 1549/1.

Irrepressible Conflict, The. A phrase apparently invented by Mr. William H. Seward (1801-1872), who said in a speech at Rochester,
N. Y., Oct. 25, 1858, that the antagonism existing between North
and South was "an *irrepressible conflict* between opposing and enduring forces." This expression came to be widely used, both in and
out of Congress.

1860   The South was again alarmed by the bold enunciation of the doctrine
of the *"irrepressible conflict,"*—"that all States must be free, or all
slave."—'Letter on the Crisis,' by Hon. Robt. McClelland of Detroit,
Dec. 31, p. 4.

1870   There is a new spirit and an old. The hope of the one is in the
future; the other clings to the past. ... The one is Rome, the other
is Carthage; ... the one is Washington, the other is George III;
... the one is Grant, the other is Lee; the one is the Republican
party, the other is modern Democracy. Here is the *"irrepressible
conflict."*—Mr. Jasper Packard of Ind., H. R., Feb. 5: *C. G.*,
p. 1055/2.

1877   We are now engaged in an *"irrepressible conflict"* between capital and
greenbacks.—Mr. S. B. Chittenden of N. Y., H. R., Nov. 23: *C. R.*,
p. 625/2.

1881   See INSTITUTION.

1898   The beginning of the war was the acme of that sectional hate which
had been ... increasing in bitterness for 30 years. The North had
no love for the South, and the South had no respect for the North.
The conflict was irrepressible.—Mr. E. E. Settle of Ky., H. R.,
June 1: *Id.*, p. 5409/1.

Irrigate. To drink. Slang. [1856-a.1880.]

1909   Sence the Country Life Commission called upon our rival town
There's a heap of old-time notions that'll nevermore go down;
We've cut out the type of rancher—and of all types he's the worst—
Who thinks that *irrigatin'* means a-quenchin' of his thirst.
          —Arthur Chapman in *Denver Republican*, Feb.

Issuance. The act of issuing.

1865   Whereas many persons who had so engaged in said rebellion have,
since the *issuance* of said proclamation, failed or neglected to take
the benefits offered thereby.—Andrew Johnson's Proclamation, May
29. (N. E. D.)

1872   What were the facts about the *issuance* of this certificate?—Mr.
Powell Clayton of Ark., U. S. Senate, May 21: *C. G.*, p. 3707/1.

1876   I am opposed to the *issuance* of scrip. .... We have already parted
with large areas of our public lands by the *issuance* of scrip.—Mr.
Dunnell of Minn., H. R., July 14: *C. R.*, p. 4600/1.

1885   Such allotment and *issuance* of individual patents.—*Century Mag.*,
p. 605. (N. E. D.)

1893   You must have the gold; you have but one way to get it, thrust this
nation ... into debt by the *issuance* of bonds.—Mr. N. Cox of Tenn.,
H. R., Aug. 21: *C. R.*, p. 68/2, App.

1895   The flexibility of *issuance* would be real, but [not that] of distribution.—*The Voice* (N. Y.), Feb. 7, p. 3/2. (N. E. D.)

Issue, a live. A controverted subject having a living interest.

1890 [The Democrats] did find *a live issue* the other day, and I want to congratulate them upon it. They found John I. Davenport of New York, and for two days they discussed his work, and I am willing to admit that they did find in him *a live issue.*—Mr. B. W. Perkins of Kan., H. R., Aug. 9: *C. R.,* p. 8384/2.

1900 The strenuous effort of the Republicans to resurrect the money question and make it *a live issue* is becoming ludicrous.—*The Speaker,* Sept. 8, p. 618/1. (N. E. D.)

Itemize. To enumerate by items. (Webster, 1864.) [1881-1888.]

1867 I wish to ask whether these estimates are not *itemized.* I think they are always *itemized.*—Mr. Conness of Calif., U. S. Senate, Feb. 18: *C. G.,* p. 1512/3.

1878 Postage stamps were too minute a kind of property to be *itemized.*— Mr. O. D. Conger of Mich., H. R., March 8: *C. R.,* p. 1596/1.

Itemizer. One who collects items for a newspaper.

1860 An itemizer of the "Adams Transcript."—*Congregationalist,* Sept. 21. (Century Dict.)

I. W. W. Industrial Workers of the World, corresponding to European (mainly French) "syndicalists."—Note from H. H. P. to R. G. T. on the *Industrial Worker,* the Spokane organ of the I. W. W. (July 3, 1913.)

J

Jacal. A native Mexican house or hut, of which the walls are constructed of rows of thin vertical poles, covered and chinked with mud. (Century Dict.)

1894 Sheep-herders, many of whom doubtless exist in *jacals,* men whose employment compels them to be out on the hills among the cacti.— Mr. W. H. Crain of Tex., H. R., Jan. 18: *C. R.,* p. 1011/1.

1894-5 This method is known to the Mexicans as *"jacal,"* and much used by them. It consists of a row of sticks or thin poles set vertically in the ground and heavily plastered with mud.—"Rep. Bureau Am. Ethnol.," p. 108. (Century Dict.)

Jacket. An envelope containing an official document or documents, and labelled accordingly.

1888 The P. O. officials must go to the files, hunt up that case, get the information from the *jacket,* &c. . . . . The information which can only be found upon the *jackets* of these cases.—Mr. S R. Peters of Kan., H. R., June 12: *C. R.,* p. 5174/1.

Jacklegged. A contemptuous term applied to an inferior lawyer and less commonly to members of other professions. [1839-1904.]

1892 He goes away, and a *jack-legged* officer could do nothing except to mark him as a deserter.—Mr. W. H. Enochs of O., H. R., May 27: *C. R.,* p. 4777/1.

Jack-Mormon. A "Gentile" more or less in league with the Mormons. [1850-1870.]

1886 I will bear testimony to their virtues and I will condemn their vice. I am not to be deterred because somebody says "You must be a *Jack Mormon."*—Mr. H. M. Teller of Colo., U. S. Senate, Jan. 7: *C. R.,* p. 514/1.

1890 In our country we have a *genus homo* called *"Jack-Mormon,"* an individual or class of individuals who do not belong to the Mormon church, who profess abhorrence of polygamy, yet who are even found doing the bidding of Mormon priests, and fighting with them to render futile the laws aimed at the destruction of their pernicious practices.—Mr. F. T. Dubois of Ida., H. R., Apr. 2: *Id.,* p. 2941/2.

1900 [Here we see] a *"Jack-Mormon"* county attorney overruling the supreme court of Utah.—Mr. C. B. Landis of Ind., H. R., Jan. 24: *Id.,* p. 1129/2.

Jack pot. A term in poker, meaning the pot or pool which cannot be opened until some player has a pair of jacks or better. (Webster.) [1902-1911.]

1880 I find that on another occasion the amount of money to be paid was by [Senator Edmunds] called a *"pot."* I do not know what that means up in Vermont or in the New England States, but I do know what it means in our country, and I suppose it means the same everywhere. It means money put in to be gambled for.—Mr. H. M. Teller of Colo., U. S. Senate, Feb. 27: *C. R.,* p. 1182/1.

1880 It has been spoken of as a grab, or as this fund being one that was *going into a common pot* to be divided.—Mr. P. B. Plumb of Kan., U. S. Senate, *Id.,* p. 1186/1.

Jack rabbit. The prairie hare. [1870-1882.]

1911 Garden City, Kan., Dec. 20.—Twelve hundred *jack rabbits* were shipped from this city to Topeka last night. There they will be distributed to the poor for Christmas. They were bagged in a big rabbit round-up of the sort now popular in western Kansas, where the *"jacks"* have been causing much trouble for farmers.—*N. Y. Evening Post,* Dec. 21, p. 7/2.

Jag cure. A cure for habitual drunkards.

1896 [Is it] the policy of the Board to run a saloon at one of the institutions and a *"jag cure"* at the other?—Mr. A. Milnes of Mich., H. R., Apr. 15: *C. R.,* p. 4024/1.

Jamboree. A carousal; a "good time." [1872.]

1888 [This meeting is intended] not for a picnic, not for a *"jamboree"* of any kind, but &c.—Mr. F. B. Spinola of N. Y., H. R., June 11: *C. R.,* p. 5131/1.

Jawsmith. A loquacious person. The term was first applied in 1886 by the St. Louis *Globe-Democrat* to an official "orator" or "instructor" of the Knights of Labor. (Century Dict.)

1891 One professional *jawsmith,* who came as the self-appointed messenger of American labor, wanted a Chinese-wall tariff, and subsidized ships to carry cargoes one way and ballast the other.—Mr. B. F. Shively of Ind., H. R., Jan. 16: *C. R.,* p. 1476/2.

Jay bird. A stupid or gullible person. Slang. (Webster.) Also used facetiously instead of "fellow" or "person."

1886   From the land of logs and peaches
            Came a callow *jay-bird* dressed
            In homespun coat and breeches
            And a gaudy velvet vest.

      —Eugene Field, in *Chicago Daily News,* July. (Century Dict.)

1892 The customs officer would say: "No, Joshua, that [kind of clothing] is not necessary and appropriate for an old *jay* like you."—Mr. G. W. Fithian of Ill., H. R., May 28: *C. R.,* p. 4795/1.

Jayhawker. A bandit. The nickname for a Kansan. [1861-1893.]

1862 The true commander-in-chief has not been intoxicated by the ranting schemes of the Kansas *"jayhawker."*—Mr. Nehemiah Perry of N. J., H. R., March 6: *C. G.,* p. 1105/1.

1862 I have understood that *jay-hawking* bands, a portion of them of Missouri and a portion of them of Kansas, have been engaged in depredations upon the people of Missouri.—Mr. John B. Henderson of Mo., U. S. Senate, June 20: *Id.,* p. 2839/1.

1867 It is said that boys ten years of age sit round on the street corners of Leavenworth City late in the night, smoking cigars and making plans for *jay hawking* in Missouri.—Mr. T. E. Noell of Mo., H. R., Feb. 12: *Id.,* p. 105/2, App.

Jeans. A coarse and cheap material used for clothing by countrymen. [1743-a.1870.]

1866 [Mr. Kasson] says very justly that formerly plantation labor cost the planters but a couple of suits of *Kentucky jeans* each year, and a scanty fare of cornbread and poor bacon; and that now the laborer requires . . . . good food, comfortable dwellings. education for his children, and broadcloth instead of *jeans* for his clothing.—Mr. N. P. Banks of Mass., H. R., June 27: *C. G.*, p. 3447/2.

Jeffersonian simplicity. A phrase sometimes used by those who would push economy to the verge of stinginess, and ridiculed by others.

1886 What would a man wedded to *"Jeffersonian simplicity"* do with $16,000 worth of new furniture? What can he possibly do [at the White House] with $13,000 worth of flowers? Just think of it, gentlemen,—you, who rode into power upon the idea of restoring *"Jeffersonian simplicity"* to the administration of public affairs! How many times during the campaign . . . . did the Democratic orators draw the picture of Mr. Jefferson riding alone, on a mud-besprinkled horse, along Pennsylvania Avenue to the Capitol, ... hitching his horse to a Virginia rail-fence, and going into the Senate Chamber to take the oath of office! This is the picture of *"Jeffersonian simplicity"* which enabled you gentlemen to elect [Mr. Cleveland] your President.—Mr. W. P. Hepburn of Ia., H. R., June 29: *C. R.*, p. 6302/2.

[1888 We were led to believe [that this] was to be a real drama of *"Jacksonian simplicity,"* and a true "business" administration.—Mr. C. H. Allen of Mass., H. R., March 29: *Id.*, p. 2493/1.]

Jesse, giving one. To beat him or to scold him violently. [1835-1863.]

1865 While I thought I was *giving you Jesse* on hearts, you were giving me fits on spades.—Alex. H. Stephens, "Diary," Sept. 29, p. 518. (1910).

Jew down. To beat down the price of anything in bargaining.

1870 This bill supposes that Congress, begrudging its former liberality, is ready to commence *jewing down* the pay of its General.—Mr. Matt. Carpenter of Wisc., U. S. Senate, July 7: *C. G.*, p. 5340/1.

1880 They might be able, living in New York, to *jew* the compositors *down* to a lower figure.—Mr. J. R. Hawley of Conn., H. R., March 16: *C. R.*, p. 1605/1.

Jigger. A drink of spirits. See quotation, 1892.

1882 I never saw an Irishman or a German who would not give up his dinner before he would his glass of beer, his *jigger*, or his pipe. It is a necessity. It is the solace of the poor man.—Mr. J. S. Williams of Ky., U. S. Senate, July 19: *C. R.*, p. 6195/2.

1889 After giving him two small *"jiggers,"* the civilities were brought to an end.—*Lisbon* (Dak.) *Star*, Feb. 15, p. 3/1. (N. E. D.)

1892 The *"jigger"* was a dram of less than a gill, taken [five times a day]. —A. E. Lee, "Hist. of Columbus, O.," I, 335.

Jigger. A term applied to several mechanical contrivances.

1890 After [the tin ore] is ground fine, it is sent into what is termed a *"jigger,"* and the process there is to drive off everything except the metallic tin.—Mr. G. C. Moody of S. D., U. S. Senate, Aug. 12: *C. R.*, p. 8454/1.

1901 A small street-railway car, drawn by one horse. (N. E. D.)

1901 A machine worked by electricity and indicating by means of a pointer dial the prices at which sales are made in 'change. (N. E. D.)

Jig (the) is up. All is over; the situation is hopeless, often used of a plot which has been discovered in time to make it impracticable. [1777-1869.]

1901 I called the claimant before me, and he admitted, to use his own language, that *the jig was up*.—Mr. John C. Spooner of Wisc., U. S. Senate, Jan. 23: *C. R.*, p. 1325/1.

Jim Crow Car. A car reserved for colored people. [1900-1910.]

1884 Colored men and women do have trouble in riding through the State of Georgia. They have a car called a second-class car; and notwithstanding a colored man may buy a first-class ticket here in Washington or anywhere else, to go perhaps to New Orleans, yet when he reaches the State of Georgia he is compelled to go into a *"Jim Crow car,"* which is placed next to the locomotive.—Mr. Robt. Smalls of S. C. [a colored man] in the H. R., Dec. 17: *C. R.,* p. 316/1.

1900 The accommodations of the [European] first-class cars are not equal to [those of] the ordinary *"Jim Crow"* car known in the South and used by the colored people.—Mr. T. H. Carter of Mont., U. S. Senate, May 18: *Id.,* p. 5695/2.

1911 If a respectable negro from Jamaica, being a British subject, were making a tour of the South and were ordered to go into a *"Jim Crow"* car, and then were to protest that this was a violation of his treaty rights, we should expect &c.—*N. Y. Evening Post,* Dec. 14, p. 4/2.

Jimmy. A coal car.

1887 [In a collision], the second car on the freight [train] was lifted from the rails and carried on top of two *jimmies* loaded with coal.—*N. Y.* (Semiweekly) *Tribune,* March 18. (Century Dict.)

Jimson weed. Originally *Jamestown weed.* A very poisonous weed (*Datura stramonium*) of the nightshade family. (Webster.)

1832 An eagle towering in his pride of height [*sic*] was not by a mousing owl, but by a pig under a *jimpson weed,*—not hawked and killed, but caught and whipt.—T. H. Benton in the U. S. Senate, July. Benton's "Thirty Years' View," I, 256.

Joe. See quotation. Cf. Vol. I. **Johannes** or **Joe.** [1762-1870.]

1787 Stolen, ... one *Half Joc,* and about eight dollars in round money. —*Georgia State Gazette,* May 26, p. 2/2. (Advt.)

1824 Being about to embark from Philadelphia for France, I observed an uncommonly large panther skin at the door of a hatter's shop. I bought it for *half a Jo* (sixteen dollars).—Thos. Jefferson. See "Private Corresp." of D. Webster (1857), I, 371.

Joggling-board. See quotation.

1904 A *"Joggling-board"* is the latest contrivance for exercise that has made its appearance in these parts, and it is liable to become the poor man's horse. . . . [It is] a hardwood board some twenty feet long, with solid supports at each end, that allow the board to move freely and yet keep it from becoming detached. One sits on the board, waves his arms up and down, and then "joggles," the board sending him up and down as on a horse.—*Kan. City Daily Star,* Aug. 18. (Century Dict.)

Johan. A term of opprobrium. Slang (Western).

1868 See Honey-cooler.

Johnny, John. A Chinaman. [1857-1878.]

1870 The presence of the Chinaman will never give us one additional mile of railroad. . . . *John* will never add another to our useful industries; he knows of nothing to add.—Mr. James A. Johnson of Calif., H. R., Jan. 25: *C. G.,* p. 753/3.

1875 A roaming vagabond Indian, *John Chinaman* in his wooden shoes [*sic*], an unnaturalized foreigner just landed on the dock in Boston, is a "person."—Mr. Matt. Carpenter of Wisc., U. S. Senate, Feb. 27: *C. R.,* p. 1863/1.

Johnnycake. Originally *Journey cake.* A kind of bread made of Indian corn meal, flour, eggs, milk, etc. [1775-1856.]

1739 New Iron Plates to cook *Johnny Cakes* or gridel bread on.—*South Car. Gazette,* Dec. 22, p. 4/2. (Advt.)

1867 See Pone.

Johnny-jump-up. A name given to certain flowers. In Aroostook, Maine, the pansy. (*Dialect Notes*, iii, 413.) [1858-1908.]

1888 She set a store by flowers, too, an' when the *johnny-jump-ups* and dandelions begun to come out . . . . she'd go up in the woods.—Boston *Sunday Budget*, n.d. (Century Dict.)

Johnny Newcome. A recent arrival. (Compare this with **Newcome** and **Johnny Raw** in the N. E. D.) [1865.]

1885 His Hawaiian Majesty,—a king with more alien *Johnny Newcomes* and coolies than subjects.—Mr. Justin S. Morrill of Vt., U. S. Senate, Jan. 7: *C. R.*, p. 512/1-2.

Johnny Reb. A Confederate soldier. See Vol. I, **Johnny.** [1867-1885.]

1866 What loyal heart did not rejoice when the *"Johnny Rebs"* were marched home by the boys in blue, keeping involuntary step to the music of the Union they had put forth such efforts to destroy?— Mr. John F. Benjamin of Mo., H. R., Apr. 7: *C. G.*, p. 1842/3.

1879 The two Union soldiers [seeing two crippled Confederate soldiers] immediately discoursed as follows: "See here, did you see them two *Johnnies* going up in the car?" The reply was "Yes."—Mr. Harry White of Pa., H. R., Apr. 2: *C. R.*, p. 182/2.

1890 In the thick of the fight he asked what he had better do. I said to him, "Rafe, if I were in your place I would go down the hill into that piece of pine woods. It is full of '*Johnnies.*' They will take you in." . . . He flew down the hill as though he had wings. The *Johnnies* captured him.—Mr. A. J. Cummings of N. Y., H. R., Apr. 21: *Id.*, p. 3635/1.

1890 You turned out a four-year Union veteran from my district, and put in a *"Johnny"* from the South right on the floor of this house.— Mr. J. W. Owens of O., H. R., Apr. 24: *Id.*, p. 3791/2.

1893 The Yanks and the *Johnnies* . . . . soon became trustful and considerate enemies, and no truce made for trade and barter between them was ever known to be violated.—Mr. A. R. Bushnell of Wisc., H. R., Feb. 17: *Id.*, p. 63/2, App.

1897 See You-uns.

Johnson grass. The *Andropogon Halepensis,* a species of sorghum. It is "a stout perennial much grown for hay in the Southern States. . . . When once established it is difficult to eradicate, and has become a very troublesome weed in some sections." (Century Dict.)

1894 [When the cocoa grass] once gets possession of a farm, the man has to abandon it. The *Johnson grass* is nearly as bad.—Mr. A. J. McLaurin of Miss., U. S. Senate, July 17: *C. R.*, p. 7587/1.

Johnsonize. To bring into agreement with Andrew Johnson. Apparently a nonce-word.

1867 There are few Democratic negroes, and they cannot be *Johnsonized.* —Mr. Henry Wilson of Mass., U. S. Senate, March 16: *C. G.*, p. 144/1.

1869 A portion of the Republican party are struggling here today to continue in force a law which will prevent President Grant from removing from office the *Johnsonized* political brigands who were floated upon the surface after his treachery.—Mr. John M. Thayer of Neb., U. S. Senate, March 20: *Id.*, p. 181/3.

Joint. An unlicensed drinking place; also an opium den. [1883-1909.]

1890 We have now four *joints,* and Jim Dougherty has come back and is to start, which will mean five.—Letter from Iowa, quoted July 19: *C. R.*, p. 498/1, App.

1901 See Rubber.

Joker, the little. A pea or small marble used in "thimble-rigging."

1858 The thimble-rigger's *"little joker."*—O. W. Holmes, "Autocrat," ch. 2. (N. E. D.)

1867 We have been playing political thimblerig with the South, and who can tell under which thimble the *little joker* which will secure restoration is to be found?—Mr. W. E. Robinson of N. Y., July 12: *C. G.,* p. 13/1, App.

1877 This is like a game of "thimble-rig," and Watts is the *"little joker"*; "now you see him and now you don't."—Remarks of Mr. Commissioner Abbott: 'Proceedings of the Electoral Commission,' p. 236/2.

1891 When the ballot box was opened, the secret was revealed. Several hundred of these *"little jokers"* bounced out, and were counted just as though they had been honestly voted.—John Wallace, "Carpet-Bag Rule in Fla.," cited in the *C. R.,* Jan. 16: p. 1415/2.

1894 [This bill] has changed its form, and like the *little joker* of the three-card monte dealer, "Now you see it, and now you don't see it."—Mr. C. F. Manderson of Neb., U. S. Senate, June 1: *Id.,* p. 5562/1.

Jolt-wagon. One that jolts.

1886 We may still go to church in a *jolt-wagon* instead of availing ourselves of the more modern phaeton.—Mr. B. Butterworth of O., H. R., May 14: *C. R.,* p. 4517/2.

Jonathan. The American people. [1816-1850.]

1829 John Bull and *brother Jonathan,* with all mankind, despise the traitor. —Lorenzo Dow, "Omnifarious Law Exemplified," p. 54. (New London, Conn.)

Jonathan. An individual American; particularly a "Down-Easter." [1827-1843.]

1837 One day last week, a *Jonathan* happened to be passing the State-House.—Raleigh (N. C.) *Standard,* Aug. 2, p. 3/4. (From the Concord *Statesman.*) .....

Josephites. See quotation.

1890 The Mormons are divided into two classes, known as *Josephites* and Brighamites. The *Josephites* to a man repudiate polygamy and bigamy; do not believe in them; say they never were embraced in the original revelations; and they live a sober life of monogamy, as much so as any class of people on this continent. It is the other class, the Brighamites alone, who believe in bigamy and in polygamy. —Mr. C. H. Mansur of Mo., H. R., Apr. 2: *C. R.,* p. 2933/1.

Josephus. A gold coin of Portugal(?) [1770.] See **Joe.**

Jounce. Also used in a reflexive sense. Cf. Vol. I, **Jounce,** to shake. [1833-1910.]

1904 He *jounced* into his buggy, and . . . . drove away.—W. D. Howells, "The Son of Royal Langbrith," p. 13.

Juba. A negro dance accompanied with patting or slapping. [1834-1890.]

1837 Your last potato is *"dancing Juba"* to the melancholy music of a tea-kettle.—Raleigh (N. C.) *Standard,* Oct. 25, p. 3/4.

Judgmatical. Judicious. [1774-1856.]

1826 A *judgmatical* rap over the head stiffened the lying impostor for a time.—J. F. Cooper, "Mohicans," ch. xxv. (Century Dict.)

Judicious tariff, a. See quotations.

1872 *A judicious tariff* is the idea. The word "judicious" in this connection, is what elected General Jackson President. . . . He was interrogated as to what his views were on the subject of the tariff, and he answered, "I am for *a judicious tariff.*" That suited every man North because a protective tariff was *"judicious"* for him; and the South was free and easy on the subject, and a squint at free trade was there considered *"judicious."*—Mr. J. W. Flanagan of Tex., U. S. Senate, May 30: *C. G.,* p. 4048/1.

1874 I have heard nothing like that since General Jackson's famous letter about a *"judicious tariff"* which captured Pennsylvania.—Mr. A. G. Thurman of O., U. S. Senate, Feb. 17: *C. R.,* p. 1558/1.

Jugful. A great deal. See Vol. II, **Not by a jugful.** [1835-a.1880.]
1893 Take the Republicans one at a time, and they are very clever sort of gentlemen; but take them *en masse,* and they will not do to tie to, *by a jugful.*—Mr. Champ Clark of Mo., H. R., Oct. 2: *C. R.,* p. 2048/2.

Jug-handled. One-sided; lacking in mutuality.
1881 English reciprocity in pleasure travel, like their often proposed commercial reciprocity, is comparatively *jug-handled.*—Mr. Justin S. Morrill of Vt., U. S. Senate, Dec. 8: *C. R.,* p. 60/2.
1886 Gentlemen of the South, this is no *"jug-handled"* question; you are receiving a reasonably fair share of our revenue and customs.—Mr. E. H. Conger of Ia., H. R., Apr. 2: *Id.,* p. 3053/2.
1888 The thing was . . like a *jug-handle,* all on one side.—Mr. C. T. O'Ferrall of Va., H. R., March 6: *Id.,* p. 1792/1.
1894 John Bull . . . said he would not have any of this *jug-handle* business, but would raise wheat for himself.—Mr. Champ Clark of Mo., H. R., Dec. 10: *Id.,* p. 185/2.
1896 [This amendment] is infinitely better than the one-sided, *jug-handled* proposition of the gentleman from Pennsylvania, which I thank God does not come from the "wild and woolly West."—Mr. D. B. Henderson of Ia., H. R., May 1: *Id.,* p. 4693/2.

Julep. A mixed drink flavored with mint. The word itself is about five hundred years old. N. E. D. [1760-1861.]
1592 [Eurinome] gave Philamis this *gillop* to coole his hot stomacke.—Thos. Lodge, "Euphues Shadow," H3.
1616 This drinke, or its cooling *Iulip,* of which three spoonefuls kils the Calenture, a pinte breeds the cold palsie.—Beaumont and Fletcher, "The Scornful Ladie," Sig. D.
1632 Her bloud Shall runne as cold as *Iulips* through her veynes.—Shakerly Marmion, "Hollands Leaguer," C2.
b.1678   Here something still like Eden looks;
    Honey in woods, *juleps* in brooks.
—Henry Vaughan, "Thalia Rediviva" ("The Bee"), ed. 1858, p. 236.

Jump. To take possession of what belongs to another. Especially to jump a [mining] claim. [1839-1856.]
1866 In these mining localities men are constantly *jumping each other's claims,* and devising every expedient to obtain the rights of each other.—Mr Geo. H. Williams of Ore., U. S. Senate, June 18: *C. G.,* p. 3234/1.
1870 See SQUATTER.
1900 Of all the contemptible creatures who ever saw the light of the sun [the worst] is the man who *jumps* another man's claim.—Mr. H. M. Teller of Colo., U. S. Senate, Apr. 9: *C. R.,* p. 3933/2.

Jump-gully. A rude cart.
1901 [The rural mail ought not to be] carried over this country, as it is now, in a *jump-gully,* with one wheel turned one way and another another, drawn by a Texas pony worth about a dollar and a half.—Mr. J. W. Maddox of Ga., H. R., Jan. 17: *C. R.,* p. 1147/1.

Junebug. A name applied to any insect that appears in June, especially large brown beetles. [1836-1862.]
1849 We would make a fire to burn *June-bugs* and save our plums [savs Mrs. Swisshelm].—Wilmington (N. C.) *Commercial,* July 10, p. 2/4.
1880 [The entomological division of the Agricultural Department] consists of one solitary, lone young man, who less than ten years ago was not reasonably expected to know a *June-bug* from a July-fly.—Mr. Henry Persons of Ga., H. R., May 10: *C. R.,* p. 3217/2.
1908 No *June bug* is more persistent in bumping into electric-light bulbs than were one and all in heading for our sacred flame.—*Atlantic Monthly,* Dec., p. 852/2.

Junk. Miscellaneous secondhand stuff. Hence **junk shop, junk dealer,** etc. [1842-1895.]

1867 The Government . . . . is reduced to a mere seller of the old blankets. blue overcoats, and *old junk* left by the war.—Mr. Justin S. Morrill of Vt., U. S. Senate, Dec. 11: *C. G.,* p. 124/1.

1869 Citizens of Philadelphia were outraged by seeing the navy-yard gorged like a *"junk-shop"* with old tools brought from different parts of the country.—Mr. W. D. Kelley of Pa., H. R., Jan. 5: *Id.,* p. 185/1.

1870 [Imported scrap iron is largely bought], not perhaps by the great rolling-mills, . . . but by the *junk-dealers* of the great cities.—Mr. H. L. Cake of Pa., H. R., Apr. 19: *Id.,* p. 2800/3.

1878 I fear disgrace more than defeat, and shall not consent to see our historic temples turned into *old junk-shops* where pinchbeck virtue is sold by mock auctioneers.—Mr. Timothy O. Howe of Wisc., U. S. Senate, March 25: *C. R.,* p. 2008/1.

1892 If the day of final settlement or redemption of paper and silver dollars was this day, of course the Government could sell its silver as *"junk"* at the rate of 70 cents [on the dollar].—Mr. J. H. Walker of Mass., H. R., March 23: *Id.,* p. 2470/2. [This assertion is economically doubtful.]

1894 [Silver] is not worth any more for any redemption purposes than it will sell for in the market as bullion. It is just the same as any old *junk.*—The same, Feb. 14: *Id.,* p. 2194/2.

1911 Since Massachusetts has sold the old voting machines for *junk,* there is a chance under the new law for voting-machine agents to besiege the State House and sell us some more, and there are hundreds of such agents.—*Worcester* (Mass.) *Telegram,* Dec.

Jury-fixer. One who "fixes" a jury, usually by bribing some of its members. [1882-1886.]

1890 The juries were at the mercy of the *jury-fixers,* then as now.— *N. Y. Tribune,* Aug. 8: see *C. R.,* p. 8242/1.

Just here, just what, &c. The word *just* in these phrases is equivalent to "precisely." [1884.]

1866 *Just here* was committed the fatal blunder which has led to all our present troubles.—Mr. Wm. Windom of Minn., H. R., June 14: *C. G.,* p. 3167/1.

1892 *Just what* should be done to arrest this process, ... *just how* in the midst of a multitude each one shall still be suffered to pursue his individual path, [I cannot now discuss].—Mr. Geo. W. Cooper of Ind., H. R., March 26: *C. R.,* p. 2593/2.

Just so. Precisely in a certain manner. [1794-1824.]

1862 I do not mean drill-sergeants or military old maids, who will not fight until everything is *just so.*—Mrs. Chestnut, "A Diary from Dixie," p. 175 (1905).

K

Kanaka. A native Sandwich Islander. [1840-1857.]

1876 The commission has found that a Sandwich Islander, for instance a *Kanaka,* puts in a claim &c.—Mr. G. F. Edmunds of Vt., U. S. Senate, July 15: *C. R.,* p. 4607/1.

1893 The Hawaiian Islands, with 90,000 inhabitants, but 4,000 of whom are whites, with *Kanakas,* Chinese, Japanese, Polynesians, the lineal descendants of cannibals.—Mr. G. G. Vest of Mo., U. S. Senate, Feb. 16: *Id.,* p. 1663/2.

1898 Does any Senator persuade himself that the *Kanaka* of Hawaii . . . can comprehend the parliamentary philosophy of the "Reed rules," or solve the problem of the previous question, or count a quorum, or fully realize a deliberative assembly where all deliberation is choked off by a Committee on Rules?—Mr. W. B. Bate of Tenn., U. S. Senate, June 30: *Id.,* p. 6525/2.

Katydid. An insect (*Cyrtophyllum concavum*) named from the shrill sound made by the males. [1800-1840.]

1876 The *Katydid*—how shall I describe its piquant utterances? One sings from a willow-tree just outside my open bedroom window, twenty yards distant: every clear night for a fortnight past has sooth'd me to sleep.—Walt Whitman, "Specimen Days" (1887), p. 138.

Kearneyism. The collective notions of a demagogue in California, named Kearney, who promoted the anti-Chinese agitation.

1879 *"Kearneyism,"* with all that the term implies, is not the cause of the discontent and clamor coming from the Pacific Coast. It is merely the product and effect of abnormal unwholesome conditions.—Mr. W. W. Corlett of Wyo., H. R., Jan. 28: *C. R.*, p. 51/1, App.

1879 I have no sympathy with agrarian notions; I believe in the rights of property; I believe in peace and order; I have no sympathy with *Kearneyism;* I am speaking in no such interest.—Mr. A. A. Sargent of Calif., U. S. Senate, Feb. 13: *Id.*, p. 1266/1.

Keep tab(s) on. To keep a record or memorandum of. [1888-1909.]

1897 We have *kept a tab* on all of the boys and girls who have been taught in the [Indian] school at Carlisle.—Mr. T. M. Mahon of Pa., H. R., Jan. 26: *C. R.*, p. 1189/2.

1898 It is shown by the evidence of one Elsie, who kept the Republican tally,—that is to say, he *kept tabs* on them, so to speak,—that 182 men voted for the contestant.—Mr. W. S. Mesick of Mich., H. R., Apr. 25: *Id.*, p. 344/1, App.

Keep your collar (or shirt) **on.** Don't get excited. Colloquial.

Kennebunker or **Kennebecker.** See quotation.

1902 A valise or small trunk which Maine lumbermen take with them "up the Kennebunk," or the Kennebec, or elsewhere into the woods.—*Jour. Am. Folk-Lore*, Oct.-Dec., p. 245.

Kentle. A quintal, a hundredweight. The N. E. D. furnishes examples of *Kyntawe, Kyntayl, Kyntall, Kentall, Kintal*, 1470-1842.

1861 *Kentles* of white-fleshed cod.—L. L. Noble, "Icebergs," p. 282. (N. E. D.)

1865 The chairman knows what the tax on salt is, and he knows, or ought to know, that it takes a bushel of salt to cure a *kentle* of fish.—Mr. Nathan A. Farwell of Me., U. S. Senate, March 1: *C. G.*, p. 1249/3.

Kentuck. A familiar designation of Kentucky, which in early days was spelled "Kentucke." [1784-1850.]

1786 You have certainly heard of the fertility of *Kentucke.*—*New Haven Gazette*, Feb. 16, p. 15/3. ["The district of Kentucky" is mentioned on p. 37/3.]

Kentucky pill, Kansas pill. A bullet. Hence a rebuke. [1861.]

1900 Champ Clark is here, and he will administer a *Kansas pill* to the King of Hog Ranch on Solomon River [Mr. Reeder]. Do you know what a *Kansas pill* is? Champ Clark knows, and so he will make the Kansas statesman swallow a Kansas grasshopper backward, and I will guarantee it will kick all of the intellectual stuffing out of him in two seconds.—Mr. P. J. Otey of Va., H. R., Feb. 28: *C. R.*, p. 2408/2.

Keystone State. Pennsylvania, as being the seventh among the thirteen original States. [1834-1861.]

1861 I speak for Pennsylvania, the great State, the *Keystone State*, which lies between these extremes [on the slavery question].—Mr. Edgar Cowan of Pa., U. S. Senate, Dec. 18: *C. G.*, p. 130/3.

1862 Born and bred on the soil of the State whose proudest title is to be "the *Keystone of the Federal arch*," I do not wish to see a new St. Domingo on her Southern border.—Mr. Charles J. Biddle of Pa., H. R., March 7, *Id.*, p. 1112/2.

1870 Pennsylvania sympathizes with this whole country. There is not an interest, there is not an industry which has not its counterpart in Pennsylvania. She is the *keystone* of this Union much more than in name.—Mr. R. J. Haldeman of Pa., H. R., Apr. 19: *Id.*, p. 2801/3.

1893 William Penn came to Pennsylvania and he dealt justly and honestly with the poor red man, and he still has his followers in that blessed *Keystone State* who are willing to deal honestly and justly with the poor white man.—Mr. J. C. Sibley of Pa., H. R., Aug. 18: *C. R.*, p. 466/1.

Kick. An objection, a complaint. [1839-1909.]

1893 The *kick* came from those who paid over their good money for a certificate in the deluded idea that it was exchangeable for a claim or a town lot.—Oklahoma City *Daily Press Gazette*, Sept. 18. See *C. R.*, p. 1824/2.

Kick. To object, to make a fuss. [1799-1888.]

1890 I made up my mind that . . . . I would do as fine a job of *kicking* as I was able to do. I have done my *kicking*; I accept the situation.—Mr. W. E. Mason of Ill., H. R., Aug. 28: *C. R.*, p. 9281/1.

1893 Men began to *kick* all over the country. . . .The good people everywhere . . . kept on *kicking*, and they *kicked* day after day and week after week. . . . I tell you I believe in *kicking*.—Mr. J. G. Cannon of Ill., H. R., Dec. 16: *Id.*, p. 282/2.

1894 If the property of the rich men of this country escapes the tariff taxes, and if we ask that it shall pay in some form, they grumble and *kick*, as we say out West, "like a bay steer."—Mr. John Davis of Kan., H. R., Jan. 30: *Id.*, p. 1664/2.

1894 For years the bill to improve rivers and harbors resolved itself into a great game of grab, in which every member, whether he lived on the arid plains or by the seashore, had to have his part of the appropriation, or he *kicked*.—Mr. Champ Clark of Mo., H. R., March 19: *Id.*, p. 3109/1.

1896 The matters of complaint from time to time among ourselves—and I do my full share of complaining and "*kicking*"—arise out of [this] system.—Mr. J. G. Cannon of Ill., H. R., May 20: *Id.*, p. 5468/1.

1897 Gentlemen may *kick* and grumble as much as they choose, but when the American people have declared for a policy, [their] *kicking* and grumbling . . . will be futile.—Mr. H. R. Gibson of Tenn., H. R., March 23: *Id.*, p. 175/1.

Kickable. Fit to be kicked.

1647 Fitter to be kickt, if shee were of a *kickable* substance.—Nathaniel Ward, "Simple Cobler of Agawam" (1843), p. 26. (N. E. D.)

1803 The Turks [are not] capable of bearing arms. They are so many tribute-paying *kickables*.—*Columbian Centinel*, Aug. 24: cited in *C. R.*, Feb. 1, 1900: p. 1411/1.

Kicker. A grumbler, an objector. [1888.]

1888 [Mr. Perkins of Kan.] seems to be a constitutional "*kicker*" against the administration of the Post-office Department.—Mr. B. A. Enloe of Tenn., H. R., May 24: *C. R.*, p. 4590/2.

1890 Mr. Springer:—How about the "*kickers*" in your own district? Mr. Boutelle:—If the gentleman has any familiarity with the operations of "*kickers*," I recommend him to tell the House about them some other time.—H. R., Aug. 5: *Id.*, p. 8170/2.

1899 The cheapest kind of statesman is a *kicker*, and the cheapest kind of laughter and applause is that which comes from the people sustaining the *kicker*.—Mr. D. B. Henderson of Ia., H. R., Jan. 27: *Id.*, p. 1164/1.

1912 If you are a *kicker* and see the shadows of failure in everything that is proposed to help the town, for heaven's sake go into some secluded cañon and kick your own shadow on the clay bank, and give the men who are working to build up the town a chance. One long-faced, hollow-eyed, whining, carping chronic *kicker* can do more to keep away business and capital from a town than all the droughts, short crops, chinch bugs, cyclones, and blizzards combined.—*White Hall* (Ill.) *Register*, Nov.

Kill. A tributary stream. Dutch.

1669 A Certain Island . . . lying and being in a *Kill* which runnes into the Scholekill.—"Penn. Archives," I, 29. (N. E. D.)

1796 A little pleasant stream, called *Eusopus Kill* or creek.—Morse, "Amer. Geog.," I, 494. (N. E. D.)

1886 These boats enter the *Kills* at Raritan Bay, and start upward when the tide begins to flow.—Mr. J. R. McPherson of N. J., U. S. Senate, May 19 : *C. R.*, p. 4665/2. [In this debate mention is made of Arthur Kill, the Kill von Kull, Reesh Kill, and Fresh Kills : Arthur Kill being about twelve miles long.]

Killie. A killifish; any of several small American cyprinodont fishes, usually marked with black, much used as bait. (Webster.)

1897 While you are feeding country *"Killies"* to great newspaper sharks, you ought . . to have regard for the great publishing interests.— Mr. A. J. Cummings of N. Y., H. R., Jan. 6 : *C. R.*, p. 518/1.

Kilter, out of. Out of order. [1643-1856.]

1693 I have read of a famous man, who having a *Clock-watch* long lying by him, *out of Kilture* in his Trunk, it unaccountably struck Eleven just before he died.—Cotton Mather, "Invisible World," p. 66. (Ed. 1862.)

Kind of. Rather; somewhat. [1830-1890.]

1864 Edwin M. Stanton and General Butler are making themselves *kind of* chief pontiffs, and are "running the churches," the one in the valley of the Mississippi, and the other in Norfolk and Portsmouth.—Mr. Powell of Ky., U. S. Senate, March 4 : *C. G.*, p. 68/3, App.

1866 [The Texans, when I knew them], were a set of free and easy, gay and festive boys, I confess; still, I *kind o'* liked them.—Mr. Dumont of Ind., H. R., March 17 : *Id.*, p. 1473/1-2.

King. Used much in apposition, to signify a man who has grown wealthy in some particular business or line of dealing.

1884 Here the *fur-kings* of the North-West . . spent their profits in generous hospitality.—S. E. Dawson, "Handbk. of the Dominion of Canada," p. 154. (N. E. D.)

1890 How is it that the rich men continuously come to the front out of the other classes, and that you do not hear of a plantation *cotton king*, or of a western *wheat king*, or of a western *corn king*, or of an *oat king*, or of a *tobacco king*, or of any other kind of a king who has won his kingship by toil?—Mr. J. W. Daniel of Va., U. S. Senate, Aug. 20 : *C. R.*, p. 8858/1.

1890 See Gold Bugs.

1892 The *silver kings* find a regular market for their product. Fortunes beyond the dreams of avarice have been piled up.—Mr. W. H. Brawley of S. C., H. R., March 23 : *Id.*, p. 2421/2.

1894 Relics of the palmy days of the old *sugar kings* of Jamaica.—*Outing*, xxiii, 380/2. (N. E. D.)

1897 The *ranch kings* get free pasturage on the vast plains.—Mr. D. Caffery of La., U. S. Senate, June 24 : *C. R.*, p. 1972/1.

1898 Annexation will make raw Hawaiian sugar come in free, and the *sugar kings* will pocket the tariff on the same.—Mr. Champ Clark of Mo., H. R., June 11 : *C. R.*, p. 5793/1.

King-pin. The principal or most important person in a group or in an undertaking. (Webster.) Figure from the game of bowling. [1895-1910.]

1888 It was a kind of mutual admiration society, Drew being the *king-pin* of the social coterie.—Henry Clews, "Twenty-Eight Years in Wall St." p. 119. (N. Y.)

Kink Calico. A nickname for King Kalakaua of Hawaii.

1876   It will not be twelve months before we shall have hogsheads of sugar by the thousand grown on the island of Cuba, tierces of rice by the myriads grown in China, entering our ports with the frank of *Kink Calico* upon them.—Mr. Gordon of Ga., U. S. Senate, Aug. 14: *C. R.*, p. 5572/1.

Kinks. Twists, knots; crotchets; devices; entanglements. Apparently of Sc. origin. [16—a.1894.]

1868   Shall we measure a man's rights in this free country by the *kinks* in his hair and the length of his heels?—Mr. Hamilton Ward of N. Y., H. R., Jan. 11: *C. G.*, p. 466/1.

1868   There would have been *kinks* in [the Arkansas bill], and somebody would have wanted to send it back.—Mr. James W. Nye of Nev., U. S. Senate, May 16: *Id.*, p. 2492/2.

Kinnikinnic(k). A mixture consisting of leaves and bark, used by the American Indians for smoking. [1799-1890.] See *Journal of Am. Folk-Lore*, xv, 246.

1872   The present is a time of profound peace. Domestic violence has ceased; the attitude of foreign powers toward our country is entirely pacific; and "Lo, the poor Indian" smokes his calumet filled with the *Kinikinick* of tranquillity.—Mr. B. F. Meyers of Pa., H. R., Apr. 6: *C. G.*, p. 2240/2.

Kissing bug. Any of several species of blood-sucking, venomous hemipterous insects that sometimes bite the lips, causing painful sores . . . (Webster).

1899   The Century Dict. states that the word originated in the newspapers in June, "many persons being bitten that summer, and often on the lip," by this "bug."

Kiss-joking. The use of "sugar-kiss" ballots. See quotation 1880.

1879   In many States . . . ballot-stuffing, *kiss-joking*, bulldozing, and murder have been . . unrestrained.—Mr. B. W. Harris of Mass., H. R., Apr. 24: *C. R.*, p. 843/1.

1879   Charleston, S. C., in 1878, cast for a democrat . . . . 22,707 votes. *kiss-jokers* and all, and for a republican 14,096.—The same, *Id.*, p. 844/1.

1880   There were in the box 135 *kiss-joke tickets*. . . .When they came to count the ballots there were 164 straight republican, 388 *kiss-jokes*, and 47 large democratic tickets.—Testimony from S. C., May 26: *Id.*, p. 3809/2.

1880   Then came in those *kiss-joke tickets*, printed on very thin tissue paper, which seem to have found their way into the ballots.—Mr. Rollins of N. H., U. S. Senate, May 26: *Id.*, p. 3809/1.

Kitchen cabinet. A term at first applied to certain friends of Andrew Jackson, "generally supposed to have more influence with him during his presidency (1829-37) than his official advisers." (Century Dict.) It was afterwards extended to similar juntos, real or imaginary.

1841   There is a rumor abroad that a cabal exists,—a new sort of *kitchen cabinet*.—Mr. Henry Clay in the U. S. Senate: T. H. Benton, "Thirty Years' View," II, 324/1. (1856.)

1886   Mr. Bayne:—The only ones that complain of these rules are the members of the *kitchen cabinet*. Mr. Adams:—Who are they? Mr. Bayne:—I do not know. But there is always a *kitchen cabinet*. There are always a certain number of politicians who devote themselves to securing appointments . . . . I can appreciate the power and force of the *kitchen cabinet*. It is an irrepressible cabinet.—H. R., June 9: *C. R.*, p. 5472/1.

Kite, v. To set going with a view to speculation.

Kiting. Purely speculative. See quotations.

1866 Every *kiting* [company] . . . that has not a rod of telegraph, that procures its charter for the mere purpose of selling out, with no intention to build.—Mr. James W. Nye of Nev., U. S. Senate, June 29: *C. G.*, p. 3482/1.

1872 They may hold the bonds, as has often been done in *kiting* corporations, and then take the property they have thus swindled the public out of.—Mr. G. F. Edmunds of Vt., U. S. Senate, Apr. 3: *Id.*, p. 2128/2.

1878 In the U. S. lightning was once drawn down from the skies with a kite; but single-handed most assuredly there is no "*kiting*" experiment by which the stable value of silver can now be uplifted and maintained. —Mr. J. S. Morrill of Vt., U. S. Senate, Jan. 28: *C. R.*, p. 610/1.

1878 This is a mere method for *kiting* an inflation of paper to take the place of silver.—Mr. G. F. Edmunds of Vt., U. S. Senate, Feb. 15: *C. R.*, p. 1104/2.

1878 This is to make the Government party to a *kiting* operation.—Mr. J. W. Johnston of Va., U. S. Senate, June 5: *Id.*, p. 4124/2.

Kiting. Flying heavenwards.

1874 Gold went up as soon as that law passed, *kiting, kiting*, almost out of sight.—Mr. Kellogg of Conn., H. R., Jan. 31: *C. R.*, p. 1085/1.

1894 Whenever a large mass seemed dangerously near the glass, they . . sent it *kiting* among its fellows.—J. J. Astor, "Journ. Other Worlds," II, 145. (N. E. D.)

Knife, v. To assail politically in an underhand way. [1888-1909.]

1890 You will be compelled to *knife* your own interests and your own friends when you strike down our whole section of country.—Mr. John H. Rogers of Ark., H. R., Aug. 23: *C. R.*, p. 9093/1.

Knights of the Golden Circle. See quotations 1863.

1862 This mild, equitable, just man [President Lincoln] is to be branded here as a *Knight of the Golden Circle*, with being a Grand Inquisitor! —Mr. B. F. Wade of O., U. S. Senate, Apr. 21: *C. G.*, p. 1736/2.

1863 The disloyal portion of the people of Kentucky has a secret military organization under the name and style of the "*Knights of the Golden Circle.*"—Mr. Garrett Davis of Ky., U. S. Senate, Jan. 5: *Id.*, p. 186/2.

1863 These factionists . . . plot in the dark secret councils of the *Knights of the Golden Circle*, and demand an armistice to negotiate an inglorious peace with rebels in arms.—Mr. Henry Wilson of Mass., U. S. Senate, Feb. 21: *Id.*, pp. 1162-3.

1863 This latter organization [the *Knights of the Golden Circle*], which was instituted by John C. Calhoun, William L. Porcher, and others, as far back as 1835, has for its sole object the dissolution of the Union, and the establishment of a Southern Empire.—Edmund Kirke, "Life in Dixie's Land," p. 76.

1864 These Northern Missouri men, under the name of Missouri state militia, ... did come over [into my district] and unite themselves with *Knights of the Golden Circle*, for the purpose of resisting the draft, and preventing Union men from filling up the quota of Iowa.— Mr. Grinnell of Ia., H. R., Feb. 27: *C. G.*, p. 49/3, App.

1864 The insidious work of that organization known as the "*Knights of the Golden Circle*" which was attempting to corrupt the army and destroy its efficiency.—Mr. James A. Garfield of O., U. S. Senate, Apr. 8: *Id.*, p. 1504/2.

1866 See PRECIPITATORS.

1870 General Price crossed the river with the avowed purpose of heading the *Knights of the Golden Circle* in the Northwest.—Mr. A. A. Sargent of Calif., H. R., Feb. 5: *C. G.*, p. 1053/1.

Knights of the White Camelia or **K. W. C.** A society formed in Louisiana, after the Civil War, to maintain the supremacy of whites over blacks.

1870   These *"Knights of the White Camelia"* were bound together by oaths and by-laws. . . . Their obligation compelled them, at the word of their superior officer, to take the field, if need be, against the colored race. . . . They could be brought to any given point by tapping on a bell.—Mr. Job E. Stevenson of O., H. R., Apr. 12: *C. G.*, p. 2620/3.

1870   [Mr. Stevenson] tells you that there were organized in the State of Louisiana, numerous societies called *"K. W. C.,"* or *"Knights of the White Camelia."* There was such an organization. . . . It contained perhaps less than one-fifth [of the Democratic party in that State].—Mr. M. C. Kerr of Ind., H. R., *Id.*, p. 2624/2.

1870   This order of the *Knights of the White Camelia* was not the Democratic party, because the form, the shell, did not belong to that order. But the Democratic party in [Louisiana] was just as full of *Knights of the White Camelia* as an egg is of meat.—Mr. Job E. Stevenson of O., H. R., Apr. 19: *Id.*, p. 2790/1.

1871   The principal part of the ritual of the order, relative to the admission of members, is to be found in the *C. G.*, Apr. 4, p. 297, App.

Knock. To keep on attacking until the party attacked gives in. N. Y. slang.

1901   There are several ways of getting into Tammany Hall. One is to be born there; and another is to work your way up in; a third is to lower yourself down in. The fourth, and a very successful way, is what the Tammany men call *"knockin'."* This is to fight Tammany Hall until the organization opens and receives you, paying in return almost anything within reason.—*N. Y. Comml. Advertiser*, May 11. (Century Dict.)

Knocker. A persistent grumbler. Slang.

1912   And though that question might be effectively answered a hundred times over for them, that class of *knockers* still, parrot-like, continue to sit in their little cages and croak out the same query.—*Grangeville* (Idaho) *Globe*, Dec. 26.

Knock the spots out of or **off of.** To beat soundly. The phrase may have originated in the practice of using cards as targets in pistol shooting. [1861.] Cf. such expressions as to "knock the tar out of."

1888   See WOODBINE.

Know-Nothings. A political party, 1853-1859, who called themselves "the American party," but usually said they knew nothing of its organization. [1854-1862.]

1863   The border State politicians are the remnant of the old Whig and *Know-Nothing* parties, who all their lives cherished an intense hatred of the Democracy.—Mr. M. F. Conway of Kan., H. R., Jan. 27: *C. G.*, p. 65/2, App.

1864   The doctrine and practice [which Mr. Davis of Maryland], brought forth into political life from a *Know-Nothing* lodge, arrayed rancorous partisans of native birth to drive naturalized citizens from the polls.—Mr. F. P. Blair of Mo., H. R., Feb. 27: *Id.*, p. 48/3, App.

1868   Is it not a fact that three-fourths of the alarms which convulse society are purely fanciful? The mind of the *Know-nothing* was kept in continual agitation by his fears of the Pope.—Mr. Thomas C. McCreery of Ky., U. S. Senate, May 28: *Id.*, p. 2632/3.

1869   A few years ago there was a political party in this country calling themselves the American or *Know-Nothing* party, which was prompted by a spirit that would, if it had possessed the power, have imposed upon the naturalized citizens of these U. S. political burdens and disabilities.—Mr. Geo. H. Williams of Ore., U. S. Senate, Feb. 5: *Id.*, p. 901/1.

1870 See the discussion in the H. R., May 23: *Id.*, pp. 3728-9, in which the term frequently occurs.

1893 In the name of the foreign-born element in America I entreat you, do not enact a law which will revive the memory of the dark *Know-nothing* time, a measure which is unjust to the foreigner and a discredit to the native-born.—Mr. J. Goldzier of Ill., H. R., Oct. 31: *C. R.*, p. 2997/2.

Know one from . . . . A humorous expression disclaiming acquaintance with a person or thing.

a.1860 She doesn't know me from *a side of sole-leather.*—G. W. Bagby, "Writings," I, 235. (1884.)

Know Ye. The allusion is uncertain. [1787-1789.]

1789 A *Know Ye* Rhode Islander, and a Pine Barren Carolinian.— *Savannah Republican*, May 2, p. 2/2.

Knucks. Pickpockets. Slang. The word is found in Matsell's "Vocabulum" (1859), pp. 22, 49, 80.

1893 See LEGPULLERS.

Kootchinoo. An intoxicating drink. Possibly this word (or **hoochinoo**) is the origin of the word "hooch."*

1871 When I first went to Alaska in 1871, the U. S. Government having but two or three years before taken possession by terms of sale with Russia, no liquor was allowed on the reservation except in the Medical Dept. of the Army.

The officers quickly discovered that the Indian chiefs had Martel brandy at the "Rancherie," which they had brought from Victoria in their canoes. At that very date the Indians were making *Hoochinoo* out of straight New Orleans molasses (no rum). If they had the rum, the use of the syrup would have been superfluous. It is a most vile liquor and deadly in effect, but drank nevertheless. The method of manufacture was as follows:

An empty 5 gal. kerosene [can] and piece of rubber hose, rolled in a coil and placed in a tub of cold water, one end attached to the can and the other free to drip.

The can was filled about one half full of molasses, and a fire did the rest. For a long while the authorities could not fathom the need of so much syrup at Sitka, so the illicit still flourished. I am perfectly familiar with the first spelling [*Hoochinoo*], which I am sure is correct.—[Extract from letter among R. H. T.'s notes, undated and unsigned.—Ed.]

1886 [These men in Alaska] join with the Indians in making with their rum and molasses their *Kootchinoo.*—Mr. O. D. Conger of Mich., U. S. Senate, Aug. 3: *C. R.*, p. 7913/2.

Kouse root. An umbelliferous plant, *Lomatium.*

1899 The Sioux Indians beat dried wild cherries with buffalo meat to form their winter stock of pemmican. In Oregon and Washington an immense amount of food was gathered from the camass root, and also from the *Kouse* root.—*Yearbook U. S. Dept. Agr.*, p. 308. (Century Dict.)

Ku Klux. The Ku Klux Klan was a powerful secret organization, formed in the Southern States after their reconstruction, to defeat the plans of the "carpetbaggers," and to keep the negroes from voting. [1879-1908.]

1868 I say that if this Congress adjourns without this Government appropriating arms to the Union men [in Tennessee &c.] to protect themselves, then the *Ku-Klux-Klan* will overrun those States.—Mr. Wm. B. Stokes of Tenn., H. R., July 23: *C. G.*, p. 4377/2.

---

* H. L. Mencken, "The American Language," p. 207, says "hooch" is from a northwestern Indian language, according to a recent writer in *Writers' Monthly*, March, 1921, p. 251.

1868   Were they *KuKlux*? Some of our citizens believe . . . that a club of *KuKluxes* has lately been established in this parish.—*Planters' Banner*, Oct. 24: see *C. G.*, July 2, 1870, p. 567/1, App.

1869   All over the State of Kentucky for the last two years we have had outrage upon outrage, murder upon murder, assassinations by night and by day by the *KuKlux Klan*, or Regulators, or whatever you may choose to call them.—Mr. John P. C. Shanks of Ind., H. R., Jan. 28: *Id.*, p. 695/3.

1869   [The Alaska seals] have not had to contend against such a savage, overbearing, cold-blooded, fiendish, and relentless foe as the Union-hating banditti commonly called the *KuKlux*.—Mr. Alex. H. Jones of N. C., H. R., Apr. 1: *Id.*, p. 436/2.

1869   There can be no doubt of the existence of numerous insurrectionary organizations known as the "*KuKlux Klan*," who, shielded by their disguise, by the secrecy of their movements, and by the terror which they inspire, perpetrate crimes with impunity.—Statement of Gen. Terry, Dec. 20: *Id.*, p. 260.

1870   See BOMB-PROOF; and refer to the debate in the Senate, *Id.*, pp. 2742/6.

1870   I confess there is one sight I should like to see on this earth before I die; I should like to see one of this *Ku Klux Klan*.—Mr. Willard Saulsbury of Del., U. S. Senate, Apr. 4: *Id.*, p. 2390/2. [See the rest of this debate.]

1870   The Senator from Delaware the other day said he hoped to live long enough . . . to see a living *KuKlux*. Well, Mr. President, I have here the ritual of *the Kuklux order*. . . . I will read the titles of the officers: . . . . "A grand wizard of the empire and his ten genii; a grand dragon of the realm and his eight hydras; a grand Titan of the dominion and his six furies; a grand giant of the province and his four goblins; a grand cyclops of the den and his two nighthawks; a grand magi (*sic*); a grand monk; a grand exchequer (*sic*); a grand Turk."—Mr. Oliver P. Morton of Ind., U. S. Senate, Apr. 14: *Id.*, p. 277/1, App. [See what follows.]

1870   Mississippi was unreconstructed, and in the hands of the *KuKlux*, and the KuKlux came down on these two parishes [of Louisiana]. At all events the Democrats of those parishes said that those KuKlux came from Mississippi. But they *Kukluxed* one poor man, a colored man, and found his ax which he had hidden under the floor of his house. He thought it a little strange that men who had come from a distance of 50 miles should know where his ax was. They *Kukluxed* this poor man. He escaped and fled to the swamps.—Mr. Job E. Stevenson of O., H. R., Apr. 19: *C. G.*, p. 2791/1. [See the rest of the debate.]

1870   See depositions &c. in the *C. G.*, July 2, pp. 552-5, 566-71, App.

1871   See the speech of Mr. A. E. Buck of Alabama, H. R., Feb. 14: *C. G.*, pp. 108-113, App. See also the speech of Mr. H. Maynard of Tenn., H. R., *Id.*, pp. 214-226, App.

1887   These men say that [he] was disguised as a *KuKlux*; was disguised so that his most intimate friend could not have known him or detected him on sight. He had a slouch-hat down over his eyes, a long loose coat extending from his chin to his heels, and his whole face except the eyes covered by a white cloth.—Mr. G. F. Hoar of Mass., U. S. Senate, Jan. 26: *C. R.*, p. 1033/1.

L

Lager beer. A light beer, so called in Germany because it is brewed to be laid by and kept.

1858   The German drinks his *lager* and drinks it . . . in indefinite quantities.— *N. Y. Express*, June. (Bartlett.)

1862   An amusing debate took place, March 20, in the H. R. Mr. Steele of N. Y. stated that someone had sworn to drinking seven gallons a day without being intoxicated. Mr. Philip Johnson of Pa. said it was a tonic, and the imposition of a tax of a dollar a barrel "would prevent its manufacture, and prevent its being kept during the whole winter to be used in the summer season." *Lager beer* was a much more sensible drink than "strong beer," and not so expansive in its effects. Mr. Samuel C. Fessenden of Me., on the contrary, said, "Our young men take their first lessons in intemperance in the strong beer, *lager beer*, and porter, which they get." Mr. Blair of Mo. replied that "the meaning of *lager beer* is laid beer. It is not strong beer at all"; and he had drunk a great deal of it. Mr. Pendleton* of Ohio :—"I have never known any beverage which is more healthful and deliciously refreshing than *lager beer*. Its praise ought to be sung by all good and generous men." He thought the name might have some connection with the *lager* or camp of Wallenstein, and the article itself might have "proved in those days a most efficient aid in carrying on military operations." Mr. Blair believed *"lager beer* did more to elect Mr. Lincoln than any other drink." Mr. Thaddeus Stevens of Pa. would "designate the effect of *lager beer* not as intoxicating but rather as exhilarating." A constituent of his came to see him on New Year's day. "How are you?" "Vare goot. I have trank my twenty-seven glasses lager." See *C. G.*, pp. 1312-13.

Lame ducks. See quotation. The phrase occurs in Horace Walpole's "Letters," 1761. See N. E. D. And it is familiar on the Stock Exchange. But the application here noted seems to belong to the U. S.

1863   [If the object of those who established the Court of Claims] was to provide for retired and broken down politicians—*"lame ducks,"* as the Senator from New Hampshire [Mr. Hale] very elegantly and very classically calls them—they did not succeed in what they set out to do. . . . . In no event could [that court] be justly obnoxious to the charge of being a receptacle of *"lame ducks."*—Mr. Lazarus W. Powell of Ky., U. S. Senate, Jan. 14: *C. G.*, pp. 306/7.

Land grabbing. Voraciously securing land, often by unfair or unlawful means. See Vol. I, **Land Grabber.**

1870   I expressed my fear that this was part of a grand scheme of *land-grabbing.*—Mr. Allen G. Thurman of O., U. S. Senate, Apr. 8 : *C. G.*, p. 2516/1-2.

Land jumper. One who takes possession of land belonging to another. See **Jump.**

1896   [Many men have had] to spend all they have in defending against fraudulent contests, or to purchase the claims of professional *land jumpers.*—Mr. T. C. McRae of Ark., H. R., March 16: *C. R.*, p. 2840/2.

Land lawyer. See quotation.

1894   This bill is in the interest of *land lawyers*, and no other class of citizens. No . . honest man can afford to support it.—Mr. A. J. Hopkins of Ill., H. R., July 11: *C. R.*, p. 7339/2.

Land poor. Having much land, but little money.

1889   He was not only *land-poor*, but he had no experience in the management of his plantation.—Joel C. Harris, "Ananias."

1892   [The Puyallup Indians] are not able to improve the property, and are simply *"land poor."*—Mr. John L. Wilson of Wash., H. R., March 1: *C. R.*, p. 27/2, App.

1894   To allow the Puyallup Indians to sell their lands would not be forcing. them to sell them. . . . As it stands, the lands are not doing themselves or anybody else any good. They are not able to improve the property, and are simply *"land poor."*—The same, July 13: *Id.*, p. 6250/2.

---

* One could have wished for Mr. Pendleton's sake, that the late C. S. Calverley had added a stanza or two to his well known verses on "Beer."

Land scrip. U. S. certificates representing land. [1862-1864.]
1869   I have introduced a bill to nullify the issue of the original *land scrip,* and providing for a new issue.—Mr. J. C. Abbott of N. C., U. S. Senate, Feb. 4: *C. G.,* p. 874/2.
1872   The *land scrip* given to the States for agricultural colleges has been generally sold for cash by the States, and in this manner immense areas of the public domain have passed into the hands of land speculators.—Mr. W. T. Clark of Tex., H. R., March 2: *Id.,* p. 1356/2.
Landslide (literal). A slipping down of a considerable mass of earth or rock on any steep slope; also, the mass which slips down. (Webster.) [1838-1862.]
1866   See TERRAPIN.
Landslide (political). An overwhelming defeat at the polls. [1895-1910.]
1912   See PLURALITY.
Lap, n. A state of overlapping.
1886   There is a *lap.* The two grants lap.—Mr. J. Hipple Mitchell of Ore., U. S. Senate, June 14: *C. R.,* p. 5654/1.
Lap robe. A fur robe or a blanket used to cover one's lap and feet when riding in a carriage or sleigh. (Century Dict.)
Lariat. A noosed rope or lasso. Spanish, *la reata.*
1835   *Lariats,* or noosed cords, used in catching the wild horse.—W. Irving, "Tour of the Prairies," p. 26. (N. E. D.)
1859   *Lariats* made of hemp are the best.—Marcy, "Prairie Travels," i, 41. (N. E. D.)
1870   See GOOD INDIAN.
1875   [Mr. Hamilton of Maryland] could say very glibly that one Southerner could come out with his *lariat,* and by breakfast bring in half a dozen green Yankees without any trouble.—Mr. J. W. Flanagan of Tex., U. S. Senate, Jan. 6: *C. R.,* p. 276/1.
Late land. That which is slow or backward in bearing crops.
1901   The superfluous water which tended to make the land cold, sour, and *"late,"* is removed, thus making the soil warmer and earlier.—*Yearbook U. S. Dept. Agr.,* p. 436. (Century Dict.)
Lateral. A side ditch or canal.
1901   If you had lived at the tail end of a *lateral* as long as I have, you would know something about this subject [of irrigation].—Mr. John C. Bell of Colo., H. R., Feb. 26: *C. R.,* p. 3078/2.
Law and order. The phrase is self explanatory. English (?)
1867   I am a *law-and-order* man myself.—Mr. Timothy O. Howe of Wisc., U. S. Senate, Apr. 12: *C. G.,* p. 834/2.
1881   To support the Lord Lieutenant [of Ireland] in maintaining *law and order.*—T. W. Reid, "Life of W. E. Forster" (1888), II, 371. (N. E. D.)
Lawful money. This term was used in the Act of Congress of June 30, 1864, which authorized the issue of compound interest Treasury notes. See the debate of Feb. 5, 1867, in the H. R., *C. G.,* p. 1021.
1879   The meaning of this phrase was discussed in the U. S. Senate, May 23: *C. R.,* pp. 1536-8.
Lay. Price; salary. [1712-1853.]
1890   I've a fair enough *lay,* thanks to your endorsement.—A. W. Tourgee, "Pactolus Prime," p. 63.
Lay off. To discontinue work. Hence a **Lay-off,** a holiday, usually enforced.
1886   The clerk who fails to pass a satisfactory examination, or who makes an unusual number of errors when out on his run, loses his position. The *"lay-off"* of the clerk then must largely be spent in studying the different schemes, &c.—Mr. S. R. Peters of Kan., H. R., March 25: *C. R.,* p. 2766/1.

1897   When the husbands come up, . . they don't want to go on a tramp
Sundays.   They want to *lay off* and rest.—W. D. Howells, "Landlord
at the Lion's Head," p. 65.   (N. E. D.)

Lay of the land.   The way in which the land lies.   "The lay of the
country" occurs in 1819.   (N. E. D.)

1864   I did not know the exact route myself, but steered by *the lay of the
land.*—Thoreau, "Maine Woods" (1869), iii, 163.   (N. E. D.)

1874   From *the lay of the land* it is quite obvious that there is no great need
of this property for a military reservation.—Mr. A. A. Sargent of
Calif., U. S. Senate, May 19: *C. R.*, p. 4003/1.

Layout.   The planning or disposition of land, streets, &c.

1888   Although the conception of its *lay-out* dates back nearly half a century,
the tree planting [in] Washington was begun only in 1872.—*Harper's
Mag.*, p. 285/1.   (N. E. D.)

1888   There is a story current in Boston that a Philadelphian visiting there
was very much annoyed by the crookedness of the streets, and
remarked rather petulantly to his Boston friend that he wished Boston
was "*laid out*" in the same manner as Philadelphia," to which the
Bostonian replied, "When Boston is as dead as Philadelphia, we will
have her '*laid out*' in the same way."—Mr. J. E. Russell of Mass.,
H. R., Apr. 28: *C. R.*, p. 3486/2.

1895   I never had [a constituent] to come here who did not take pride in the
beauty of these buildings, and all the *lay-out* of this city.—Mr. J. R.
Hawley of Conn., U. S. Senate, Jan. 3: *C. R.*, p. 583.

1895   In the *lay-out* and construction of a considerable part of the railway
service of this country.—*Forum* (N. Y.), p. 80.   (N. E. D.)

1898   A portion of the town is south of the original *lay-out.*—C. O. Par-
menter, "Hist. of Pelham, Mass.," p. 158.   (N. E. D.)

Lays.   See quotation.

1888   The fishing industry of New England is very largely carried on
by the system of "*lays*," as it is called, shares, co-operation.—Mr. G. F.
Hoar of Mass., U. S. Senate, Aug. 13: *C. R.*, p. 7491/2.

Lead-off road.   A lateral road.

1805   [To the camp ground] led a *lead-off road*, ending on this spot of
ground unoccupied.—Lorenzo Dow, "Journal," May 26 (1850), p.
107/2.

Leak out.   To become disclosed, known, or apparent.

1840   We had heard rumors of such a ship to follow us, which had *leaked
out* from the captain.—R. H. Dana, "Bef. the Mast," p. 33.   (N. E. D.)

1852   I can see it *leaking out* in fifty different ways—just that same strong,
overbearing, dominant spirit.—Mrs. H. B. Stowe, "Uncle Tom's
Cabin," xix.   (N. E. D.)

1877   It "*leaked out*" they were from Washington, ... and then the doors
were opened.—Mr. E. G. Lapham of N. Y., H. R., Feb. 28: *C. R.*,
p. 202/1, App.

Lean-to.   A building annexed to a larger one, and depending on it for
lateral support.   1461, 1618 (N. E. D.)   An awkward addition to a
dwelling house, very common in New England.

1638-9   Also the old house and *lean-toos*, yard and garden thereto belonging. . . .   [He] shall have . . . liberty to make a *leanto* unto the end
of the parlor—T. Lechford, "Note-Book" (1885), pp. 54, 217.
(N. E. D.)

1785   Hist! hist! ye mere Americans, attend:
Ope wide your mouths: your knees in homage bend:
While Curl discloses to the raptur'd view
What Peter, Paul, and Moses never knew;
The light of new-born wisdom sheds abroad,
And adds a *lean-to* to the word of God.
—Dr. Dwight to Col. Humphreys: "Misc. Works" of the latter
(1790), p. 105.

1854 On one side of the church-tower there was a little pent-house or *lean-to.*—Hawthorne, "Eng. Note-books" (1883), I, 509 (N. E. D.)

1861 A brown house of the kind that the natives call *"lean-to"* or *"linter."*— Mrs. Stowe, "Pearl of Orr's Island," p. 10. (N. E. D.)

Le Compton Constitution, the. A constitution adopted by the pro-slavery party in Kansas, in Sept. 1857, and recommended to Congress by President Buchanan, Feb. 2, 1858. It was resubmitted to the citizens of Kansas, and rejected. The name comes from the place where the convention of 1857 was held.

1866 There was an attempt made to make a constitution here in this District, and then force it upon the people of Kansas; that was called the *Lecompton constitution.* . . . I contended against it as well as I was able and as long as I could, and finally we defeated it.—Mr. B. F. Wade of O., U. S. Senate, Dec. 14: *C. G.,* p. 127/1.

1870 [After the Topeka constitution, we had] what was called the "Leavenworth convention" and "constitution," a form of government which perished like the Topeka constitution. In the third place came the *"Lecompton constitution."* This was somewhat national in its character, because it had a general ventilation, if I may so style it, all over the U. S. The conflict was brought to a focus in the *Lecompton constitution.* All civil law for a time was done away with, and we had martial law.—Mr. S. C. Pomeroy of Kan., U. S. Senate, March 18: *Id.,* p. 2055/3.

Left, to get. To be "out in the cold," or "in the lurch."

1888 To use the language of the irreverent, the [N. Y.] Times Editor *"got left"* that day, and he has been trying to "get even" ever since.— Mr. S. V. White of N. Y., H. R., June 1: *C. R.,* p. 4818/2.

1891 The man who does not sympathize with the Prohibition movement is afraid of *being left.*—*N. Y. Weekly Witness,* Nov. 11, p. 4/4. (N. E. D.)

1894 While our quarrel was going on, [she] went after him, and that's how I *got left.*—G. Moore, "Esther Waters," p. 84. (N. E. D.)

Leg-pullers. Swindlers. Slang. Scottish (?).

1893 [In New York the Republicans] employed knucks, bounty-jumpers, pocket-book droppers, plug-uglies, heelers, forgers, *leg-pullers,* pie-biters, and all other criminal vermin and riff-raff.—Mr. A. J. Cummings of N. Y., H. R., Oct. 6: *C. R.,* p. 2242/2.

Leg, to get one by the. To have the advantage of someone.

1894 President Cleveland is reported as saying, "The banks *have got the country by the leg.* They can drain the Treasury in 48 hours.—*C. R.,* Apr. 9, p. 3556/1.

1894 [The manufacturers] join hands with our enemies, the money changers, and form a solid wall around the speculators and bankers who, as the President says, *have the country by the leg.*—Mr. W. A. Peffer of Kan., U. S. Senate, Apr. 12: *Id.,* p. 669/1, App.

Lengthy. Long, and more or less tedious.

1799 *Lengthy* has been in use for half a century among writers, whose names would be disgraced to have a Cobbett's near them. [Cobbett had objected to the word.]—Mathew Carey, "A Plumb Pudding for Peter Porcupine," p. 13 *n.* (Phila.)

Let down the bars, to. To make exceptions to any restrictive rule; especially with reference to duties.

1869 Why should we thus *"let down the bars"* the first time a vacancy occurs, and revert to the system of having brigadier generals where before the war we had only colonels?—Mr. J. A. Garfield of O., H. R., March 22: *C. G.,* p. 199/1.

1890 [Mr. Mills of Texas says], "The Democratic party is going to *let down the bars*," and let these goods go to every people who want them, and take from those other people what they do not want. *"Let down the bars!"* What is to hinder the surplus now from going abroad? There is no export duty. But to *"let down the bars"* will swell our surplus at home, and incalculably aggravate our condition.—Mr. J. C. Burrows of Mich., H. R., May 8: *C. R.*, p. 4322/2. [See also the rest of his speech.]

Let out. To conclude. See Vol. I, **Let in, let out.** [1904.]

1888 [He said he] would meet her at the door of the Mount Zion tent when the meeting should *let out.*—E. Eggleston, "The Graysons," ch. x. (Century Dict.)

Let slide. Let the thing go without attention. [1847-1861.]

1861 [The Northerners] mean to *let freedom slide* a while until they subjugate us.—Mrs. Chestnut, "A Diary from Dixie," p. 119. (1905.)

1863 I will play the Yankee on you [Mr. Lovejoy], and ask you a question in return. If the Union is to be saved or the negroes freed, are you in favor of emancipating the slaves and *letting the Union slide?*—Mr. Charles A. Wickliffe of Ky., Jan. 29: *C. G.*, p. 603/1.

Letter carrier. A postman. [1552-1799.]

1863 [The proposed bill establishes] a free carrier system in all the cities in which *letter carriers* are now authorized by law.—Mr. Schuyler Colfax of Ind., H. R., Feb. 20: *C. G.*, p. 1149/3.

1868 The number of *letter-carriers* has been increased from 757 in 1865 to 1,198 in 1868.—Report of the Postmaster General, Dec. 3: *Id.*, p. 35/2, App.

1868 In public estimation the *letter-carriers* for cities are thought to be almost indispensable; but the system costs money.—The same, *Id.*, p. 36/3, App.

1870 Gentlemen who do not live in large commercial cities know nothing of the labor performed by *letter-carriers.*—Mr. Charles O'Neill of Pa., H. R., June 6: *Id.*, p. 4110. [And see the rest of the debate.]

1872 See SPRY.

Level best, one's. The best one can do. [1851-1869.]

1879 I am one of those who, in the slang phrase of the day, "did his *level best*" to fight out of the Union; but, since we have been restored to the Union, I have made an honest effort to maintain it.—Mr. A. M. Waddell of N. C., H. R., Feb. 28: *C. R.*, p. 2113/1.

Level head. One is said to have a level head when he is sensible and not flighty. See Vol. I, **Level, level headed.** [1869-1909.]

1892 See ARGONAUTS.

Levy. An elevenpenny bit; one-eighth of a dollar. [1832-1857.]

1851 See FIP.

Levy Court. See the last citation, kindly furnished by Mr. Henry Campbell Black of Washington, D. C.

1862 The Mayor of Washington . . . . or the Mayor of Georgetown may care for the child, or the *levy court* may care for it, until it is eighteen years of age.—Mr. Daniel Clark of N. H., U. S. Senate, Apr. 1: *C. G.*, p. 1477/1.

1864 [These citizens represent] that the *levy court* of the county, in whose hands is the power of taxation, is not chosen by them, not responsible to them.—Mr. James W. Grimes of Ia., U. S. Senate, Feb. 15: *Id.*, p. 643/1.

1879 This *levy court* and the corporations of Washington and Georgetown were abolished February 21, 1871.—Mr. John R. Eden of Ill., H. R., Jan. 20: *C. R.*, p. 585/2.

1911 *Levy Court.* A court formerly existing in the District of Columbia. It was a body charged with the administration of the ministerial and financial duties of Washington county. It was charged with the duty of laying out and repairing roads, building bridges, providing poor-houses, laying and collecting the taxes necessary to enable it to discharge these and other duties, and to pay the other expenses of the county. It had capacity to make contracts in reference to any of these matters, and to raise money to meet such contracts. It had perpetual succession, and its functions were those which, in the several states, are performed by "county commissioners," "overseers of the poor," "county supervisors," and similar bodies with other designations. *Levy Court* v. *Coroner,* 2 Wall. 507, 17 L. Ed. 851.

In Delaware, the "levy court" is an administrative board elected and organized in each county, composed of from five to thirteen "commissioners," who, in respect to taxation, perform the functions of a board of equalization and review and also of a board to supervise the assessors and collectors and audit and adjust their accounts, and who also have certain powers and special duties in respect to the administration of the poor laws, the system of public roads and the officers in charge of them, the care of insane paupers and convicts, the government and administration of jails, school districts, and various other matters of local concern. See Rev. St. Del. 1893, c. 8; *Mealey* v. *Buckingham,* 6 Del. Ch. 356, 22 Atl. 357.—Black's "Law Dictionary."

Lick-log. A block of salt for cattle to lick.

1840 I like a man to be up to the notch, and stand to his *lick-log.*—Haliburton, "The Clockmaker," ch. xii. (N. E. D.)

1887 He may catch him right then and there. It is not necessary to bait [the man] or to take him to a *lick-log.* He may catch him instantly and of a heap.—Mr. R. T. Bennett of N. C., H. R., Feb. 17. *C. R.,* p. 1880/1.

Licks, Big licks, Hard licks. Hard work.

1861 At length I went to mining, put in my *biggest licks.*—Daniel Bryant, "Songs from Dixie's Land," p. 26. (N. E. D.)

1894 Most of the money that is made in the section of the country from which I come is made by *hard licks* under the hottest sun of summer.—Mr. C. E. Hooker of Miss., H. R., Apr. 18: *C. R.,* p. 3830/1.

Lie around loose. See quotation. [1856-1857.]

1879 The cipher dispatches were suffered to "*lie around loose.*"—Mr. B. F. Butler of Mass., H. R., Jan. 21: *C. R.,* p. 609/2.

Lieu lands. Those given in lieu of other lands which had been erroneously granted.

1896 Mr. Lacey:—My colleague on yesterday explained that in Nebraska and in some other localities "*lieu lands*" had been patented in place of lands that the railroad companies had lost by reason of mistake. . . . . Mr. Tawney:—Why should we exempt *lieu lands,* and still let the "place" and "indemnity" lands sold to bona fide purchasers remain under the provisions of the act of 1887? Mr. Lacey:—We do nothing of the kind. The bill in express terms already protects the bona fide purchasers of all kinds of lands, "*lieu lands,*" "place lands," or any other kind of lands.—H. R., Feb. 19: *C. R.,* p. 1937/1.

Lift. To discharge, to pay off. [1846-1886.]

1862 It proposed to *lift* these bonds, by negotiation with the holders, at such rates as could be agreed on.—Mr. Thaddeus Stevens of Pa., H. R., Dec. 19: *C. G.,* p. 146/1.

1868 The greenback will be in demand; the greenback will be raised in value; it will be *lifted*; it will be nearly as good as gold.—Mr. Chas. Sumner of Mass., U. S. Senate, July 14: *Id.,* p. 4046/2.

1897 Have any of the farm mortgages in your district been *lifted* under the Wilson-Gorman bill?—Mr. J. A. Tawney of Minn., H. R., March 23: *C. R.*, p. 180/2.

Light-Horse Harry. General Henry Lee of Virginia. (1756-1818.) He was the father of General Robert E. Lee.

1870 There [Washington College] stands, the pride of Virginia. The son of *"Light-Horse Harry,"* penniless as a beggar, had completed a monument to Washington. It is not a shaft or an obelisk, ... but a monument replete with life and light and hope, radiant with intelligence, the home of the arts and the sciences.—Mr. T. C. McCreery of Ky., U. S. Senate, Dec. 13: *C. G.*, p. 74/2.

1872 If you will go with me to my estate, you will find that the adjoining estate is Wakefield, the birthplace of Washington; on the other side you will find Stratford, the residence of *"Light Horse Harry,"* of glorious revolutionary memory.—Mr. John Critcher of Va., H. R., Feb. 2: *Id.*, p. 800/3.

Lightning. A term applied to the Democratic policy in Alabama in 1880-1890.

1890 [This paper] was founded in May 1887 . . . . as an advocate of the *lightning Democratic creed* of 1880. . . . . Before we went into *lightning session*, Colonel G. withdrew. . . . What was it we proposed? The redemption of the county from the negro and Republican rule by *lightning*. . . . It was *lightning* in 1880; it was *lightning* in 1886.—*Wilcox* (Ala.) *Progress*, Apr. 2: See C. R., June 3, p. 5548/1.

1890 I have never until this day heard [Mr. M.] declare himself in favor of *lightning.*—Election address of S. D. Bloch of Ala., Apr. 9: See *C. R.*, June 3, p. 5548/1.

1890 No man can be appointed [in Ala.] to hold a precinct election unless he is known to be a *"lightning man,"* a ballot-box stuffer, a false counter.—Mr. J. H. Rowell of Ill., H. R., June 3: *Id.*, p. 5565/2.

Lightning. The lightning is said to strike, when a person or a place gains sudden and unexpected fame, notoriety, or good fortune. Not in the dictionaries.

1879 Mr. Sparks:—I wish to suggest to the gentleman from Iowa that in districts near his own *the lightning has been striking.* It may strike the gentleman's district. Mr. Price:—O no; that district *struck by lightning* is not near mine, it is much nearer sundown. No danger of that kind of lightning in my district.—H. R., Apr. 25: *C. R.*, p. 920/2.

1891 When the doctrine of practical reciprocity is applied, *the lightning will strike* next time somewhere about Arkansas.—Mr. John H. Rogers of Ark., H. R., Jan. 5: *Id.*, p. 925/1.

Lightweight. A person of small consequence. The N. E. D. cites an allusion (1809) to "light-weight princes." [1882.]

1882 I never took my friend from New Jersey [Mr. Geo. M. Robeson] to be a *light-weight* in any regard.—Mr. S. S. Cox of N. Y., H. R., May 22: *C. R.*, p. 4167/1.

Lightwood. Pine wood. [1705-1856.]

1822 It rained heavily, yet we were enabled to kindle a fire without difficulty, by the help of the *lightwood,* which lay in abundance around. This fuel is truly the traveller's friend, as it affords him a hearth in the wilderness in the worst weather, burning inextinguishably in the heaviest showers.—"Notices of East Florida, p. 35. (Charleston, S. C.)

Like as not. In all probability.

1867 He'll hev some upland plover *like as not.*—J. R. Lowell, "Fitz-Adam's Story."

1912 Western Indiana.—*Dialect Notes*, III, 581.

Likely. Able bodied, good looking, serviceable. [1454-1856.]

1732 A *Likely* Negro Fellow is to be sold, that has had the small-pox. —*So. Car. Gazette*, Dec. 9, p. 4/1. (Advt.)

1764 Just imported, Twenty very *likely* young Slaves.—*N. Car. Mag.*, Oct. 26, p. 167/1. (Advt.)

1787 A *likely* sorrel Gelding, about 14 hands high.—*Georgia State Gazette*, Jan. 27, p. 4/1. (Advt.)

1790 To be sold, Seven *likely* Virginia born Slaves.—*Augusta* (Ga.) *Chronicle*, Nov. 13, p. 3/2. (Advt.)

1831 Phillis is *likely*, of the middle stature of women, quite black, and about forty years of age.—*The Georgian* (Savannah), June 4, p. 3/2. (Advt.)

Limb. A leg. [1781-1873.]

1888 This claimant's right *limb* is much shorter than the other [and] the muscles are withered.—Mr. E. H. Funston of Kan., H. R., March 16: *C. R.*, p. 2178/1.

Limit, to go the. To go as far as is permissible.

1885 [The Alabama Legislature might] increase their salaries to $4,000, which I believe is *the limit that we have ever gone.*—Mr. John T. Morgan of Ala., U. S. Senate, Jan. 18: *C. R.*, p. 712/2.

Line, v. To follow the flight of bees.

1827 I had *lined* a beautiful swarm that very day into the hollow of a dead beech.—J. F. Cooper, "Prairie," I, 78. (N. E. D.)

1833 Girls . . . *lining* the wild bees to their haunt in the hollow tree. —Harriet Martineau, "Briery Creek," p. 32. (N. E. D.)

1879 A bee-hunter, when he *lines* a bee from this angle and a bee from that angle, finds where they meet.—Mr. Omar D. Conger of Mich., H. R., Apr. 10: *C. R.*, p. 366/1.

Liner. One who lives on the exact boundary line between two jurisdictions.

1866-7 That J. M. N., . . . a *liner* between the counties of Chambers and Lee, is declared to be a citizen of Lee County.—Laws of Alabama, p. 175. (Century Dict.)

Little Giant, The. Stephen A. Douglas, of Illinois. [1854-1860.]

1865 No two men were more unlike. Physically and mentally they were contrasts. Lincoln was the giant, Douglas was the *"little giant."* Small in person, a giant in intellect, Douglas was bold, denunciatory, impetuous, ardent, determined.—Mr. Isaac N. Arnold of Ill., H. R., Feb. 20: *C. G.*, p. 70/1, App.

1897 The *"Little Giant,"* Stephen A. Douglas, of Illinois, was an early convert to the proposition [of a Pacific railroad].—Mr. G. L. Johnson of Calif., H. R., Jan. 9: *C. R.*, p. 22/1, App.

Little Joker. See **Joker.**

Little Magician, The. Martin Van Buren.

1869 After *"the little magician,"* Martin Van Buren, had wormed himself into the confidence of "Old Hickory," and had produced a [permanent] hostility between Mr. Calhoun and General Jackson.—Mr. Garrett Davis of Ky., U. S. Senate, March 18: *C. G.*, p. 136/2.

Little-neck. A half-grown quahaug or round clam: so named from Little Neck, Rhode Island. (Century Dict.)

Little Rhody. Rhode Island. [1852-1862.]

1881 I think that, before I get through, *Little Rhody* will be taken care of.—Mr. R. G. Horr of Mich., H. R., Feb. 3: *C. R.*, p. 1193/2.

Live. Active, energetic, alert. [1857.]

1865 We want *live* men, who can follow a new fashion if the Government is determined on a new fashion.—Mr. Benjamin Wade of O., U. S. Senate, Feb. 16: *C. G.*, p. 825/1.

Living chance. A chance to make a living.

1894 Nobody pays more to ride than the farmer; let us at least give him a *living chance.* . . . Give the farmer a *living chance.* He provides the first necessities of life.—Mr. H. C. Snodgrass of Tenn., H. R., Jan. 10: *Id.,* p. 662/1.

Living price. A price at which one can earn a living. [1834-1892.]

1890 Things are at a "standstill." We have plenty to sell but no buyers at *"living" prices.*—Mr. John Lind of Minn., H. R., June 6: *C. R.,* p. 5692/1.

Lo. A word sometimes applied to an Indian, by a facetious misreading of Pope's well-known line.

1874 John Chinaman will soon be claiming this high prerogative of a freeman, and Mr. *Lo,* that elegant gentleman without a hat, will walk up to the polls with a ballot in one hand and a fresh scalp in the other.—Mr. L. V. Bogy of Mo., U. S. Senate, Apr. 20: *C. R.,* p. 3190/2.

1878 If I enumerated the stealings, there would be nothing left for the Indians. *"Lo"* would not have enough to buy himself a pair of moccasins or a belt of wampum.—Mr. Wright of Pa., H. R., Dec. 19: *Id.,* p. 316/2.

1879 Expressions of sympathy for *"Lo, the poor Indian,"* will not solve the difficulties of the situation.—Mr. W. M. Springer of Ill., H. R., Dec. 18: *Id.,* p. 178/2.

1888 When I happen to call up a bill for the benefit of a few poor men who want to construct a water-ditch, some one who knows that *"Lo"* has been imposed upon . . . rises and objects.—Mr. M. A. Smith of Ariz., H. R., July 10: *Id.,* p. 6100/2.

1890 Ardent admirers of that extinct tribe of Fenimore Cooper Indians that never did exist come on this floor, . . . and, with blazing indignation at fancied wrong perpetrated on "Poor *Lo,*" dare assert that we have been the heartless aggressor, and the Indian the meek victim of our cupidity, avarice, and crime.—Mr. M. A. Smith of Ariz., U. S. Senate, Feb. 18: *Id.,* p. 48/1, App.

1891 I went West desiring to see poor *"Lo."* I expected to find him all I had seen him painted. Instead, I found him a naked . . . vagabond, who will not work, whom you can not make work to save your life, who will not even hunt.—The same, Feb. 14: *Id.,* p. 179/2, App.

1891 [Mr. Blanchard's] great love for "Poor *Lo*" came from sleeping with all of Fenimore Cooper's Indian novels under his pillow.—The same, Feb. 16: *Id.,* p. 181/2, App.

1894 Has the Commissioner forgotten that New York itself is the home of *Lo,* the poor Indian? Has he forgotten the great Tammany tribe? —Mr. Julius Goldzier of Ill., H. R., June 7: *Id.,* p. 5945/1.

1894 There has been some diversity of opinion as to what we ought to do with *"poor Lo."*—Mr. H. U. Johnson of Ind., H. R., June 14: *Id.,* p. 6300/2.

1897 I believe that, when it comes down to a question between poor *"Lo,"* who has some rights, and the Standard Oil Company, this house will stay by the Indian.—Mr. J. S. Sherman of N. Y., H. R., Apr. 23: *Id.,* p. 837/1.

1898 While there may be some truth in the . . . . remark that all good Indians are dead,—

  "Lo, the poor Indian, whose untutor'd mind
   Sees God in clouds, and hears him in the wind"—

wakens the conviction that there may be worse people in life than *Lo Jo.*—Mr. W. C. Adamson of Ga., H. R., Jan. 22: *Id.,* p. 871/1.

Loaded. Ready to go off like a loaded gun.

1890 I was really toying and playing with the Senator, as a little boy
would play with a pocket-pistol, but I did not know he was *loaded*.—
Mr. J. T. Morgan of Ala., U. S. Senate, Aug. 12: *C. R.*, p. 8442/1.

Loafer. One who loafs about; an idler. [1835-1870.]

1848 [He was] contemplating a *loafer*, who was . . . . fishing from the
side of the boat.—Wilmington (N. C.) *Commercial*, Aug. 17, p. 1/6.

Loaning. Lending. See Vol. I, **Loan.** [1729-1909.]

1862 It is within my knowledge that the *loaning* of piano fortes is a very
considerable branch of business.—Mr. Thomas M. Edwards of N. H.,
H. R., March 31: *C. G.*, p. 1462/3.

1870 Private bankers do quite as well in the business of *loaning* to the
people as anybody.—Mr. John Coburn of Ind., H. R., Jan. 21: *Id.*,
p. 656/2.

Lobbying. The practice of bribing or persuading members of the
Legislature to pass bills which are to the interest of certain persons
or groups. Agents employed by public companies and private
individuals are in daily attendance in the lobby of the House.
[1832-1881.]

1866 Surely [Miss Vinnie Ream, the sculptor] has shown no lack of that
peculiar talent known commonly as *"lobbying,"* in pressing forward
her enterprise, and bringing it to the attention of Senators.—Mr.
Jacob M. Howard of Mich., U. S. Senate, July 27: *C. G.*, p. 4233/2.

1870 This city [Washington] has become a place for beggars, a place for
lobbiers, a place which, I might almost say, [is] a stench in the
nostrils of the community.—Mr. A. A. C. Rogers of Ark., H. R.,
June 25: *Id.*, p. 4848/1.

1884 I have been *lobbied* more this winter . . . . than I ever was before
in my life. It had no effect on me. I do not mean to say whether
lobbying does have an effect or not, but this at least had not.—Mr.
John A. Logan of Ill., U. S. Senate, May 27: *C. R.*, p. 4549/2.

1894 [The matter] has been *lobbied* in this House by one Butts, a man
who is interested, who is entitled to the privileges of the floor by
reason of being an ex-member, and who has used them for the purposes of *lobbying* for this measure.—Mr. C. S. Hartman of Mont.,
H. R., March 20: *Id.*, p. 3143/2.

Locate. To place, settle, establish. [1797-1852.]

1867 [In 1776] nearly the whole of the population of Maryland was *located*
on the borders of the Chesapeake.—Mr. Francis Thomas of Md.,
H. R. March 28: *C. G.*, p. 416/1.

1872 It was once said by a distinguished member from North Carolina,
Mr. Macon, a man of simple republican habits and thoughts, something of a Spartan in his nature, that it was a great mistake to *locate*
the capital where it was *located*.—Mr. Justin S. Morrill of Vt., U. S.
Senate, May 15: *Id.*, p. 3499/2.

1878 If Texas was willing to pay to *locate* the army in her midst, and
support and supply it, I would say, God bless Texas for taking that
elephant off our hands.—Mr. E. S. Bragg of Wisc., H. R., May 21:
C. R., p. 157/1, App.

Locate. To find the place of.

1888 We may *locate* this vessel, as in old fox-hunting times when I was a
boy we could *locate* a fox in the bottom of a narrow cave 100 feet in
the mountain, but the thing was, how were you going to get the
fox out.—Mr. G. F. Edmunds of Vt., U. S. Senate, Aug. 1: *Id.*,
p. 7112/2.

Loco. A plant of the genus *Astralagus*, which, when eaten by cattle,
horses, and sheep, produces loco-disease or locoism.

1883 The *loco*, or rattle-weed, met with also in California, drives [horses]
raving crazy.—*Harper's Mag.*, p. 503/1. (N. E. D.)

1886 A weed called *"loco"* has of late years largely increased in some of the cattle-ranges of Texas and the Indian Territory.—*Cornhill Mag.*, p. 297. (N. E. D.)

1889 A curious affection which exists among horses in north-western Texas, known as "grass-staggers," which is caused by eating the *loco weed,"* which gives rise to the saying that the horses are locoed.—*Science,* xiii, 176/1. (N. E. D.)

Locoism. See **Loco.**

1900 See CROTALISM.

Locofoco. A name at first applied to one section of the Democrats, but afterwards derisively applied to Democrats generally. See Vol. I. [1834-1862.]

1850 It is a *locofoco* party trick, and I can see through it.—Wilmington (N. C.) *Commercial,* July 2, p. 4/1.

1850 [Mr. Davis] said Polk was President of the party,—of course of the *Loco Foco* party.—Wilmington (N. C.) *Commercial,* Aug. 3, p. 1/4.

1868 They could scream louder, and were more *locofocoish* and locomotivish than any meeting I had ever before attempted to address.—Mr. W. E. Robinson of N. Y., H. R., May 13: *C. G.*, p. 2453/3.

Locust. A club or billy used by policemen: so called because commonly made of locust-wood. (Century Dict.)

Lodge. An Indian tent. See Vol. I, **Lodge-pole.** [1834-1855.]

1805 The report [of the guns] was heard at the Sioux *lodges.*—Pike, "Sources of the Miss." (1810), p. 14. (N. E. D.).

1807 Their *lodges* are about eighty in number, and contain about ten persons each.—P. Gass, "Journal," p. 45. (N. E. D.)

1839 Wandering among the Indian *Lodges* (wigwams is a term not used now-a-days) I heard a sort of flute.—Marryat, "Diary in Am.," I, 183. (N. E. D.)

1872 The Indians upon the north of the river stated the numbers of those still south of the river at seven hundred *lodges*, which would give an aggregate of 42 hundred to 4500 persons.—Commissioner F. A. Walker in *C. G.*, Dec. 11: p. 142/2.

Logical. Reasonable or to be expected under all circumstances. (Webster.) In accordance with the "logic of events."

1860 Having the sovereignty to dispose of, it seemed *logical* that the Estates might keep it, if so inclined.—J. L. Motley, "United Netherlands" (1868), I, 11. (N. E. D.)

1874 Stubbs, "Const. Hist." (N. E. D.)

1894 The statesman from Maine [Mr. T. B. Reed] who, to use a stock expression, will be the *"logical* candidate" of his party in 1896 for the Presidency.—Mr. O. A. Wells of Wisc., H. R., Jan. 24: *C. R.*, p. 1349/1.

Logic of events, The. Their convincing power.

1865 I have a firm conviction that there is such a thing as the *"logic of events."*—Mr. Rollins of Mo., H. R., Jan. 13: *C. G.*, p. 261/1.

1869 [That plea], more specious and delusive than any other, that the *"logic of events"* compels Congress now and then to step over the boundaries [set by the Constitution].—Mr. J. R. Doolittle of Wisc., U. S. Senate, Jan. 22: *Id.*, p. 121/1, App.

1880 The *"logic of events"* may prove too strong for them.—*Daily Telegraph*, Oct. 28. (N. E. D.)

Log rolling. Politically, mutual assistance in getting bills through the Legislature, especially for local objects. [1821-1869.]

1870 My friend from Vermont [Mr. Willard] says he would not feel that he was doing his duty, after having protected an interest in his own district, to refuse to vote for the protection of an industry outside of his own district. . . . . That is *"log-rolling."* (Laughter.) If you

vote for my interest I will vote for yours. That is the way these
tariffs are *"log-rolled"* through.—Mr. B. F. Butler of Mass., H. R.,
Apr. 14: *C. G.*, p. 2700/1-2.

1870 I would not allow [all these appropriations] to be grouped together,
. . . . in order to make what is called a regular *log-rolling bill*, in
which it is necessary that I should *help you to roll your log if I want
my log rolled*. . . .[Perhaps the Senator] fears that, if we get this
appropriation made, and *our log is rolled*, then we may not help him
to *roll his log*.—Mr. A. G. Thurman of O., U. S. Senate, May 23:
Id., p. 3719/2.

1890 There are more jobs and mutual-admiration societies run under [the
river and harbor bill] than any other legislative proposition in the
House—regular "you tickle me and I'll tickle you" society. Men get
together on both sides of the Chamber; they *log-roll* and say, "Now,
what bills will you have put through?" or, "How much will you take?"
"What bill will you have reported?" "What bills will you have called
up?"—Mr. W. H. H. Cowles of N. C., H. R., May 29: *C. R.*,
p. 5462/2.

Logy. Heavy, slow-moving, dull. See Vol. I, **Loggy, Logy.** [1888.]
1896 In the U. S. the word is applied to men or animals, as a *logy* preacher,
or a *logy* horse. In Newfoundland they will speak of a *logy* vessel,
a slow sailer.—Mr. Geo. Patterson in *Journal of Am. Folk-Lore*,
ix, 23.

Lone Star State, The. Texas. [1845-1860.]
1845 Texas, I infer from the ground taken by Senators Benton and Rives,
twinkles as a *"lone star"* for another year.—Thurlow Weed, "Letters,"
p. 386 (1866).

Long and short. See quotation 1859.
1859 *"Long"* means when a man has bought stock on time, which he can
call for at any day he chooses. He is also said to be *"long"* when
he holds a good deal. (Bartlett.)

1892 [The malevolence of this report] seems to be aimed at the *short*
seller. No censure is placed on the *long* buyer. The *short* seller,
who sells what he has not got and what he does not expect to deliver,
seems to be an imp of darkness; the *long* buyer, who buys what he
does not want and never expects to get, is presumably an angel of
light.—Mr. A. J. Cummings of N. Y., H. R., June 6: *C. R.*, p. 443/2,
App.

Longhorn. A shrewd old inhabitant. Cf. **Shorthorn.**
1905 There was a big chief on the range, an old *longhorn* called Abraham,
and his lil' ole squaw.—*N. Y. Times*, May 28. (Century Dict.)

Long Knives. Name applied by the Indians to the white men, especially
to the Virginians. [1784-1835.]
1832 [The Indians in 1755] often assured Smith that the *long knives* were
fools; that they . . . . stood still, as if to give their enemies the best
possible opportunity of shooting them down at their leisure.—John A.
McClung, "Sketches of Western Adventure" (Phila.), pp. 31-32.

1832 The cry ran through the village at once, that the *Long Knives* were
stealing their horses right before the doors of their wigwams.—*Id.*,
p. 104. [This was in 1773.]

Longs and shorts, the. See quotation.
1874 I imagine that we have in the country but two financial parties.
I am not sure that we ever had [more than two]. They are known
in the metropolis as the *"longs"* and the *"shorts."* In the country we
are in the habit of calling them the debtor and the creditor classes.—
Mr. Timothy O. Howe of Wisc., U. S. Senate, Jan. 15: *C. R.*, p. 671/1.

Long sauce and short sauce. Large and small vegetables. [1809-1860.] Applied humorously to any collection of miscellaneous articles.

1815   *Long sairse* and *short sairse*; consisting of a variety of leetle notions too tedious to mention, among which were inions, parsnips, butter, candles, soap, and ile.—David Humphreys, "The Yankey in England," p. 41.

Long sugar. See quotation.

1728   Their molasses comes from the same country, and has the name of *"Long Sugar"* in Carolina, I suppose from the Ropiness of it.— William Byrd, "Writings," p. 77 (1901).

Loony. Crazed, demented. Colloquial. [1872.]

1896   He was so *loony* and egotistic that he went on to say etc.—Affidavit by Jesse George of Kan., *C. R.*, Apr. 15: p. 4010/1.

Lope. A long, easy canter or gallop. [1825-1869.]

1904   [The horse] started with a long *lope*, and never changed his stride.— Lee's "Recollections of Gen. R. E. Lee," p. 107. (N. Y.)

Lope. To go at a long, easy canter or gallop. [1851-1910.] [The word is probably connected with Dutch *loopen*. "A Dutchy *lopeman*" is spoken of in "The Noble Gentleman" (1626), III, 4:—a play doubtfully attributed to John Fletcher.]

a.1577   I saw . . . The souldiour charge, the leader *lope* away.—George Gascoigne, "Fruites of Warre," V, 104 (1587).

1598   This whinyard has gard better men to *lope* than thou.—Robt. Greene, "James IV," Ind. (Century Dict.)

1826   The most confirmed gait he could establish was a Canterbury gallop with the hind legs, which those more forward assisted for doubtful moments, though generally content with a *loping* trot.—J. F. Cooper, "Last of the Mohicans," ch. ii. (Century Dict.)

1885   See Cayuse. See Singlefoot.

Lop-horn. An animal whose horns lop or droop. Cf. Vol. I, **Lop down.**

1850   I think your team a very good one; the old oxen, the starred steers, and the *lop-horns*.—D. Webster to John Taylor, Nov. 28: "Private Corresp." (1857), II, 405.

Lost Cause, The. The cause of the Confederacy.

1868   [The people have witnessed Andrew Johnson's] efforts to install the leaders of the *"lost cause"* in power.—Mr. Sidney Perham of Me., H. R., March 2: *C. G.*, p. 253/1, App.

1868   Such was the *"lost cause"* in its heyday, as it appeared to all but the deluded women and youth who decked its hideousness in the hues of their own gaudy imaginations. . . . Well is it called the "lost" cause, just as we speak of a "lost" woman, a "lost" spirit, a "lost" soul.—Mr. Horace Maynard of Tenn., H. R., July 16: *Id.*, p. 456/2, App.

1868   Governor Orr of South Carolina . . . is assailed today by every single sheet that I have set my eyes on, that still clings to the *"lost cause."*—Mr. John A. Bingham of O., H. R., March 17: *Id.*, p. 1929/2.

1870   It is now nearly six years since a confederate soldier fired a gun in defense of the *"lost cause."*—Mr. Edward Degener of Tex., H. R., Dec. 20: *Id.*, p. 201/2.

1875   When gentlemen went into what is now, or was last year, said to be *'the lost cause,"*—whether it was *the lost cause* or not the future will determine,—they went into it . . . . no doubt in the sincere belief that they ought to do so.—Mr. G. F. Edmunds of Vt., U. S. Senate, March 2: *C. R.*, p. 2043/1.

1876   See Chivalry.

1879   Even the judiciary . . . is challenged on the bench, and asked, as the price of life, to bow to the mandate of this ghost of the *lost cause.*— Mr. Moses A. McCoid of Ia., H. R., June 25: *Id.*, p. 119/1, App.

Low down. Degraded. [1850-1901.]

1894 [You shall compete with the bushmen] if you will persist in such *low-down* business as wool-growing.—Mr. W. W. Bowers of Calif., H. R., Jan. 8: *C. R.*, p. 560/1.

1896 I dissent *in toto* from the *low-down*, disreputable spoils system that is defended here.—Mr. J. H. Walker of Mass., H. R., Jan. 7: *Id.*, p. 512/2.

Low-grade. Of inferior quality. [Not in the Dictionaries.]

1876 *Low-grade* ores would be taken from the dump, mines producing *low-grade* ores would be brought into the market.—Mr. Patterson of Colo., H. R., July 29: *C. R.*, p. 4985/1.

Loyal Leaguers. An organization similar to the Ku Klux Klan but less violent in its methods.

1864 This last dirty move of the *Loyal Leaguers* to spite the Copperheads in view of the Chicago Convention.—G. A. Sala in the *Daily Telegraph*, Aug. 23. (N. E. D.)

1871 There has not been a Senator on this side, who has spoken on this subject, but has denounced these outrages perpetrated by the Ku Klux and by the *Loyal Leaguers*.—Mr. Willard Saulsbury of Del., U. S. Senate, Apr. 12: *C. G.*, p. 604/1.

Lugs. The worthless part of tobacco. (Bartlett, 1859.)

1872 It is the poorest quality of sweepings, clippings, and mere stems and *lugs*.—Mr. John A. Logan of Ill., U. S. Senate, May 30: *C. G.*, p. 4078/2.

1897 [The poor man] has to take cigars made out of what we called in Kentucky "*lugs*."—Mr. Samuel Pasco of Fla., U. S. Senate, June 25: *C. R.*, p. 2020/1.

Lump it. "Dislike it," in antithesis with "like it."

1833 Let 'em *lump it* if they don't like it.—John Neal, "The Down-Easters," I, 104. (N. E. D.)

1835-40 A man that would be guilty of such an action is no gentleman, that's flat, and if you don't like it you may *lump it*.—T. C. Haliburton, "Clockmaker," Preface. (N. E. D.)

1878 I'll buy clothes as I see fit, and if anybody don't like it, why they may *lump it*, that's all.—Mrs. H. B. Stowe, "Poganuc People," p. 94. (N. E. D.)

Lumpy jaw. A disease of cattle. See first quotation.

1890 Mr. Gray:—What is "*lumpy-jaw*"? Mr. Vest:—I will tell the Senator what that means. "*Lumpy-jawed cattle*" means cancerous cattle. . . . The "*lumpy-jaw*" is simply a cancer. It appears in lumps, and sores subsequently.—U. S. Senate, May 29: *C. R.*, p. 5428/1.

1891-2 The treatment of *Lumpy Jaw*.—U. S. Report, Title. (N. E. D.)

1895 Should an animal be suffering from *lumpy jaw* (*actinomycosis*) the inspector condemns it.—*The Times*, March 4, p. 3/3. (N. E. D.)

Lynch, Lynching. See quotations and **Lynch law**, Vol. I. [1817-1911.]

1829 In the "Whig and Tory" days of the South, when no man's person or property was safe, . . . a man by the name of *Col. Lynch* formed an association, to expel suspicious characters from the neighbourhood;— and chastising them at discretion—which practice is continued in some parts of the South and West to the present day—as exemplified on Lynch's Island, at the mouth of Cumberland River, in the Ohio. Dick and Bob understand it.—Lorenzo Dow, "Omnifarious Law Exemplified," p. 23.

1900 When they captured him they *lynched* him. They burned him at the stake.—Mr. J. M. Griggs of Ga., H. R., Feb. 1: *C. R.*, p. 1414/1.

1900 [Under certain circumstances] the oaks of Massachusetts' hills and dales would be desecrated with the bodies of the victims of "*lynching* bees."—Mr. J. M. Griggs of Ga., H. R., Feb. 1: *C. R.*, p. 1414/2.

M

Machine. A political organization. Usually in a bad sense. [1876-1911.] **Machine voting** is voting according to the wishes of the organization.

1866 By *machine voting* I mean that kind of voting they used to have in the City of Baltimore in Know-Nothing times,—votes given by Blood-Tubs, Black-Snakes, and Plug-Uglies.—Mr. Philip Johnson of Pa., Jan. 18: *C. G.*, p. 308/1.

1877 "No; we have got [say they] a new device; we have got what a Yankee would call a *"machine,"* that is going to work out all that the Constitution could work out, and is going to give us peace."—Mr. M. I. Townsend of N. Y., H. R., Feb. 26: *C. R.*, p. 1933/1.

1878 Those whom the citizens should most avoid, those who would be most familiar with the *"machine"* methods of seeking and obtaining control of your city politics.—Mr. Jacob D. Cox of O., H. R., March 28: *Id.*, p. 2116/2.

1879 The *"machine politicians"* in New York, as they are called, thought they knew better.—Mr. Roscoe Conkling of N. Y., U. S. Senate, June 25: *C. R.*, p. 2327/1.

1889 "The *machine system* not business-like." "The *machine system* fortified the spoils system." "The *machine system* injurious to all parties." "Why the *machine system* could not succeed." "How the *machine triumvirate* . . . disfranchised the people." "The *machine* gave opportunity to wrong-doing."—Sub-headings of speech by Mr. J. W. Daniel of Va., U. S. Senate, Feb. 6: *Id.*, pp. 1560-1.

Machinize. To turn into a machine.

1856 The traveller . . . reads quietly the Times newspaper, which, by its immense correspondence and reporting, seems to have *machinized* the rest of the world for his occasion.—R. W. Emerson, "Eng. Traits," iii, 41, (N. E. D.)

1901 The real purpose of these rules is to *machinize* this House; to create a one-man power; to magnify the machine and minify the member.—Mr. G. H. White of N. C., H. R., Jan. 8: *C. R.*, p. 738/1.

Mackerel. A school child.

1871 The free schools in Philadelphia are full to overflowing, and . . . . we see no necessity for running down and forcing into school-rooms the *"mackerels"* who will not receive an education.—Letter from Tennessee, Jan. 10: *C. G.*, p. 1040/2.

Mackinaw hat. A coarse straw hat. See *Journal of Am. Folk-Lore*, xv, 246.

McKinleyism. See quotation.

1869 That species of high protection of which Mr. Bayard spoke, called *McKinleyism*, is a false pretense and a fraud.—Mr. C. M. Cooper of Fla., H. R., March 19: *C. R.*, p. 2991/2.

Mad. Angry. [1847-1908.]

1576 Being more *mad* against them.—Geneva Bible, Acts XXVI, 11.

1591 I was . . . *mad* to behold this Scornefull pride.—Ab. Fraunce, "Yuy church," D4.

Mail. One's periodical supply of letters.

1874 See BACK AND FORTH.

1890 That official was opening his *mail*.—T. L. James, "Railways of Amer.," 319. (N. E. D.)

1896 I have had my *mail* packed with abusive and scurrilous articles against me.—Mr. G. F. Hoar of Mass., U. S. Senate, Feb. 26: *C. R.*, p. 2158/2.

1901 In his *mail* that day [he] found a despatch: "Unexpectedly called home."—*Harper's Mag.*, p. 784/1. (N. E. D.)

Mail-box, mail-bag, mail-carrier, mail-catcher, mail-messenger, mail-pouch, mail-rack, mail-rider, mail-sack. See quotations.

1799 The receipt and delivery of letters on the way, between post-offices, shall not be required of the *mail-carriers.*—"Statutes of the U. S." (1856) I, 736. (N. E. D.)

1874 From the last year the names of these two classes of officers was the same, but hitherto seven were known as *mail-boys* and the others as *mail-messengers.*—Mr. Garfield of O., H. R., Apr. 15: *C. R.*, p. 3099/1.

1874 When we make it an offense triable in the courts of the U. S. and punishable with death to strike a *mail-rider* from his mule and rob him, is it not a case of double punishment? . . . Suppose a *mail-carrier* in Oregon is struck from his horse, and injured or killed, does any man doubt that the assailant or slayer is indictable for assault or homicide in the State of Oregon, and punishable by . . . the laws of Oregon?— Mr. Roscoe Conkling of N. Y., U. S. Senate, Apr. 29: *C. R.*, p. 3457/1.

1890 The letter car is provided with a *"mail catcher,"* which is placed at a small door through which mail pouches are snatched from conveniently placed posts at wayside stations where stops are not made.— T. L. James, "Railways of Amer.," p. 326. (N. E. D.)

1896 Near one of the doors is the *mail-rack.*—*Cosmopolitan Mag.*, p. 406. (N. E. D.)

Make out. To manage, to contrive. [1609-1866.]

1865 Ewell said he was waiting before getting an artificial leg to see if the authorities were going to hang him; if he was going to be hung, he did not care to go to the expense; intended to wait and *make-out* on crutches until that matter was decided.—Alex. H. Stephens, "Diary," June 14, p. 220 (1910).

Man-fashion. Boldly, in manly fashion.

1874 [If Senator Morton] is entirely confident that his opinions are sound, why so timid? . . . Why not walk up to this *man-fashion?*—Mr. Lot M. Morrill of Me., U. S. Senate, Apr. 1: *C. R.*, p. 2682/2.

1881 I submit . . . that it would not be acting *man-fashion* to do that to Benjamin Holladay or to any other claimant.—Mr. Roscoe Conkling of N. Y., U. S. Senate, Jan. 17: *Id.*, p. 674/1.

Manhandling. Mauling, handling roughly. See Vol. II, **Manhandle.** [1886-1910.]

1911 Mr. Gompers is a law-abiding citizen. He would never counsel violence. He would not throw a brickbat at a "scab." If he saw some impetuous friends of his *manhandling* one of their fellows he would probably beg them not to nail his ears to the pump; and when, next day, he saw the ears nailed to the pump he would protest, "I am astounded beyond expression!" and then go away and weep.—*N. Y. Tribune*, Dec.

1911 Its dingy walls and ancient desks, its atmosphere surcharged with printer's ink, its maps and files and reference books worn with age and *manhandling*, have made the shop unlike that of any other newspaper in town.—*N. Y. Evening Post*, Dec. 25, p. 6/7. [The reference is to the editorial office of the *N. Y. Sun.*]

Manhattanese. Belonging to Manhattan Island, now covered by New York City.

1904 [This play] brings together a number of highly piquant *Manhattanese* types of to-day, sketched with captivating drollery.—*The Forum*, p. 410. (Century Dict.)

Man in the street, Man in the cars. The average man.

1841 *The man in the street*, finding no worth in himself which corresponds to the force which built a tower or sculptured a marble god, feels poor when he looks on these. . . . . A Greenwich nautical almanac he has, and so being sure of the information when he wants it, the *man in the street* does not know a star in the sky.—R. W. Emerson, "Essay on Self-Reliance," pp. 62, 85-86. (Century Dict.)

Man on horseback, The. General U. S. Grant.

1879 We want the statute-book purged from laws that make it possible . . .
for an army under President Hayes, or *"the man on horseback,"* if he
should come back into power, to interfere with the rights of the
people.—Mr. Eli Saulsbury of Del., U. S. Senate, June 25: *C. R.,*
p. 2324/2.

1880 *"The man on horseback"* is the battle-cry, and a stronger government,
the shibboleth, of the most dangerous element of the republican party.
—Mr. G. W. Geddes of O., H. R., May 10: *Id.,* p. 3200/1.

Manuel. A person of mixed descent, partly Spanish.

1884 Suppose a *manuel,* somebody or other in one of these cañons, having
been there a long time, considering his title to be absolutely secure,
does not [employ a lawyer &c.]—Mr. J. R. Hawley of Conn., U. S.
Senate, Feb. 4: *C. R.,* p. 853/2.

Margin. A surplus of profit.

1890 When an employer feels that his *margin* is slipping away from him,
the first thing done is to scale down the price of wages.—Mr. B. M..
Cutcheon of Mich., H. R., June 25: *C. R.,* p. 6499/2.

Marker. A "circumstance"; a thing worth mentioning. Slang.

1888 The waving of the bloody shirt would not have been a *marker.*—Mr.
A. J. Cummings of N. Y., H. R., Dec. 12: *C. R.,* p. 202/2.

1895 It ain't a *marker* to what's ahead.—H. P. Robinson, "Men Born Equal,"
p. 145. (N. E. D.)

Marm. Colloquial for Madam or Mrs.

1837 *Marm* Pugwash is as onsartin in her temper as a mornin in April.—
Haliburton, "The Clockmaker," Ch. x. (N. E. D.)

1872 See NIP AND TUCK.

Maroon. A fugitive negro. Probably from Sp. *Cimarron.* For early
examples see the N. E. D.

1858 The alternative title of Joshua R. Giddings's "Exiles of Florida" is:
The crimes committed by our Gov't against the *Maroons,* who fled
from South Carolina and other Slave States, seeking protection under
Spanish laws.

1858 A number of these people, said to have been led on by Spanish
maroons, crossed over to a small island called Indian Key.—*Id.,* p. 276.

Maroon. A pleasurable excursion. See Vol. II, **Marooning** [1834-1855.]

1785 On Monday we form a *maroon* party to visit some saw mills about
8 miles hence.—Timothy Ford's Diary.—*S. C. Hist. Mag.,* xii, 188
(1912).

Marooned. Cast ashore on an island; and, by analogy, blocked from
usual channels of transportation or communication. [1910.]

1912 Rescue parties found dazed families huddled in yards and *marooned*
on roofs. . . . Reaching the Union Station [at Denver], the torrent
rushed three feet deep through the yard, putting locomotive fires out,
marooning several hundred passengers, and closing the city to incom-
ing or outgoing traffic.—*N. Y. Evening Post,* July 15, p. 1/7.

1912 Hundreds of tourists were *marooned* in Colorado Springs because
the railroad tracks in both directions had been carried away.—*N. Y.
Evening Post,* Aug. 1, p. 8/1.

Martling men. The combination of "Lewisites" and "Burrites" which
supported Madison against Clinton for the Presidency in 1812.
They met in "Martlings Long Room," New York, and were also
known as "Bucktails." See Brown, "Dict. of Am. Politics" (1892)
s.v. "Clintonians."

Mash. A marsh.

1848 See STADDLE.

1876 One bright Dec. mid-day lately I spent down on the New Jersey
sea-shore. . . . Five or six miles at the last, our track entered a broad
region of saltgrass meadows, intersected by lagoons, and cut up everywhere by watery runs. The sedgy perfume . . . reminded me of the

"*mash*" and south bay of my native island [Long Island].—Walt Whitman, "Specimen Days" (1887), p. 146.

Mason and Dixon's line. A line run by two surveyors, Charles Mason and Jeremiah Dixon, in 1761-2, between Pennsylvania and Maryland. The term came to be used as signifying the northern limit of the slave states. [1824-1848.]

1860 I have never believed that actual disruption of the Union can occur without blood; and if, through the madness of northern abolitionists that dire calamity must come, the fighting will not be along *Mason and Dixon's line* merely.—Letter of Franklin Pierce to Jefferson Davis: see *C. G.*, Feb. 5, 1870, p. 1051/1.

1862 Can you prosecute a traitor south of *Mason and Dixon's line?* You might as well try the devil in hell, and summon as jurors his chief angels.—Mr. B. F. Wade of O., U. S. Senate, Apr. 21: *C. G.*, p. 1737/1.

1862 [If] you confiscate the real estate of the rebels, . . . you will have Robin Hoods in every Sherwood Forest from *Mason and Dixon's line* to Florida . . . before the feud is satisfied.—Mr. Edgar Cowan of Pa., U. S. Senate, Apr. 30: *Id.*, p. 1880/1.

1863 The slaveholders inhabit the country extending south from *Mason and Dixon's line* to the Rio Grande, and from the Atlantic Ocean west to the Rocky Mountains.—Mr. M. F. Conway of Kan., H. R., Jan. 27: *Id.*, p. 63/2, App.

1869 Does any one believe that for the next ten years at least there will be any fighting south of *Mason and Dixon's line?*—Mr. B. F. Butler of Mass., H. R., Feb. 17: *Id.*, p. 188/3, App.

1880 I say that the Democratic party for the last 30 years has not had an honest heart-beat north of *Mason and Dixon's line.*—Mr. Thos. B. Reed of Me., H. R., Apr. 23: *C. R.*, p. 2691/2.

1890 See Bloody Shirt.

Mass meetings. Large public meetings. [1847-1855.]

1865 The leading statesmen of all sections took the stump, and great crowds at "*mass meetings*" hung with rapt attention upon the stirring speeches of their orators.—Mr. Isaac N. Arnold of Ill., H. R., Feb. 20: *C. G.*, p. 70/3, App.

1880 [I know that Mr. Simonton] holds temperance *mass-meetings* in his district, every month.—Mr. Casey Young of Tenn., H. R., May 1: *C. R.*, p. 2938/1.

Masterly inactivity. This phrase appears to have been first used by Sir James Mackintosh in 1791 (N. E. D.) and became current during the Civil War.

1831 The highest wisdom of the State is a wise and *masterly inactivity.*—John C. Calhoun, "Works" (1874) iv, 143. (N. E. D.)

1863 See Contraband.

1865 *Masterly inactivity* is your wisest course now.—Mr. Robert Mallory of Ky., H. R., Feb. 22: *C. G.*, p. 998/3.

Matchcoat. An Indian mantle. [1642-1787.]

1763 [He had] a tomahawk wrapped up under his *matchcoat* out of sight.—John Woolman's Journal, p. 160. (Lond., 1824.)

Materialize. To appear in sight. To become a realized fact. [1888.]

1890 I think it will be conceded that the promised "mule" is not likely to *materialize.*—Mr. A. M. Dockery of Mo., H. R., July 31: *C. R.*, p. 7984/1.

Mattress house. A common lodging house.

1890 It will not do to talk here about *mattress houses* and lodging houses and all that practice or machinery for fraudulent elections which obtains in large cities.—Mr. Geo. Gray of Del., U. S. Senate, Dec. 6: *C. R.*, p. 174/1.

Maverick. An unbranded yearling. [1887.]

1883   Should there be any . . . unbranded *maverick*, feeding upon the pastures, . . . I should say &c.—Mr. Z. B. Vance of N. C., U. S. Senate, Jan. 11: *C. R.*, p. 1098/1.

1887   Unbranded animals are called *mavericks*, and when found on the round-up are either branded by the owner of the range on which they are, or else are sold for the benefit of the association.—Theodore Roosevelt, *Century Mag.*, xxxv, 507.

1893   [Mr. Raum's] successor in office finds this charge as a kind of *"Maverick"* wandering around, and he brands it and claims it as his own discovery.—Mr. J. F. Lacey of Ia., H. R., Dec. 16: *Id.*, p. 291/1.

Maximatically. In the shape of a maxim. Nonce-word.

1884   More axiomatically and *maximatically* expressed, the Federal Government is one of enumerated powers.—Mr. Luke Pryor of Ala., H. R., June 13: *C. R.*, p. 5097/2.

Mean. Shabby, contemptible. [1808-1891.]

1863   If [the southerners] should catch white men who are *mean* enough to command these negroes, the Lord knows what will be their fate.—Mr. Charles A. Wickliffe of Ky., H. R., *C. G.*, p. 602/1.

1869   I will say further, that the gas in [Washington] is the *meanest* that I know of in any city of the United States.—Mr. C. C. Washburn of Wisc., H. R., March 1: *Id.*, p. 1765/1.

1869   If ever there was a *mean* thing done on earth, it was for men to take the votes of negroes to get into the Georgia legislature, and then to vote the negroes out. It was meaner than stealing sheep. (Laughter.)—Mr. B. F. Butler of Mass., H. R., *Id.*, p. 1767/1.

1870   Of all the *mean-looking* men I ever saw on the face of the earth, even in the streets of Boston, these Nova Scotians whom I have seen on some of the coasters are the *meanest*.—Mr. John A. Peters of Me., H. R., May 13: *Id.*, p. 3471/3.

1871   Here is an army of civil as well as military officials, who are to settle down upon the land, covering it all over as thick as the locusts, and as *mean*, perhaps, as the lice of Egypt.—Mr. D. W. Voorhees of Ind., H. R., Feb. 15: *Id.*, p. 126/2, App.

1872   A few *mean* white men and a good deal of *mean* whisky soon make bad Indians.—Mr. J. W. Flanagan of Tex., U. S. Senate, March 7: *Id.*, p. 1492/1.

Meanness. Ill tempered malice.

1888   [He] has shot two or three white men in the past four years, and is known to be of desperate courage and *meanness*.—*Times-Democrat*, Aug. 17: See *C. R.*, Sept. 27, p. 8991/1.

Meat. One's prey or property.

1882   Come along—you're my *meat* now, my lad.—"Innocents at Home," ch. iii.

1898   I want to tell you . . . that so far as John Crocheron is concerned, he is not my *meat*. I am not called on to defend him.—Mr. A. F. Fox of Miss., H. R., Feb. 8: *C. R.*, p. 1553/2.

Medicine, to take one's. To accept defeat or ill luck in a philosophical manner.

1896   I fought for the views that I entertain . . ., and was licked out of my boots. *I took my medicine like a man.*—Mr. D. B. Henderson of Ia., H. R., Jan. 7: *C. R.*, p. 512/1.

1897   [General Grosvenor] might as well quit roaring. He will have to *take his medicine*, as we took ours in 1894.—Mr. Champ Clark of Mo., H. R., May 6: *Id.*, p. 937/1.

Melada. Spanish. See first quotation.

1875   *Melada* shall be . . . defined as an article made in the process of sugar-making, being the cane-juice boiled down to the sugar point, and containing all the sugar and molasses resulting from the boiling process, and without any process of purging or clarification.—U. S. Statutes, xviii, 340. (N. E. D.)

1878 [The Government has been swindled] by fraudulent coloring of sugar imported in the shape of *"melada"* at the lowest rate [of duty].—Mr. James B. Beck of Ky., U. S. Senate, March 5: *C. R.*, p. 1480/2.

Menhaden. A fish resembling a herring. [1792-1894.]

1870 On Peconic bay, an extensive and extending business has sprung up in connection with . . . the *Menhaden* fishery.—Mr. H. A. Reeves of N. Y., H. R., June 25: *C. G.*, p. 4855/3.

1887 Look at the *menhaden* fishery. Within a year or two we find that the *menhaden* have [been] very greatly reduced in numbers, &c.—Mr. J. R. McPherson of N. J.; U. S. Senate, Feb. 8: *C. R.*, p. 1484/1.

Mesa. A piece of table land. Spanish. [1775-1869.]

1890 There is no water running above them, and no possibility of ever bringing water over upon these *mesas*.—Mr. E. O. Wolcott of Colo., U. S. Senate, Sept. 25: *C. R.*, p. 10406/2.

1894 I would not have taken the land if I could have had [all] that is on the *mesa*.—Mr. J. C. Bell of Colo., H. R., Aug. 11: *Id.*, p. 8435/1.

Mescal. A variety of cactus; liquor made from any kind of agave; also any agave from which liquor is made. See *Journal of Am. Folk-Lore,* viii, 49-50 (1895).

Mescal-buttons. The dried tops of a succulent, spineless, turnip-shaped cactus growing in the arid regions of Texas and northern Mexico, known botanically as *Lophophora Williamsii,* and called by the natives in various localities *payote, hikuli,* and *wokowi.* . . . . These buttons have narcotic properties, and in Texas are sometimes called *dry whisky.* (Century Dict., which furnishes a picture.)

Mesquite. Sp. *mezquite* from Mex. A mimosaceous tree or shrub of the southwestern United States and Mexico, with fragrant flowers and pods rich in sugar. (Webster.) See Vol. II, **Mezquite bush.** [1833-1878.]

1865 The fruit of the *mesquite tree,* an acacia, has been the staff of life to the Indians of the Colorado. A prolific *mesquite* will yield ten bushels of beans in the hull; the beans are pounded in a mortar and made into cakes of bread for the winter season; and a kind of whisky is also made of the bean before it grows dry and hard.—Mr. Charles D. Poston of Ariz., H. R., March 2: *C. G.*, p. 1320/2.

1867 See PACK.

Mestee. The offspring of a white person and a quadroon. West Indies. (Webster.) See also **Mestizo,** Vol. II. [1582-1887.]

1732 Run away a *Mustee Negro* Woman.—*S. C. Gazette,* Oct. 21, 3/1. (Advt.)

1764 A Mulatto or *Mustee* Slave, called Tony.—*N. C. Magazine,* June 22, p. 32/1. (Advt.)

Meter, in short. Rapidly; "in short order."

1848 An' ef it worn't fer wakin' snakes, I'd home agin *short meter.*—*Biglow P.,* No. II.

1873 They could put them through *in short meter,* and you would hear nothing but Dixie played, and they play it most excellently.—Mr. J. W. Flanagan of Tex., U. S. Senate, Feb. 27: *C. G.*, p. 1888/3.

Metiff. An octoroon. [1808-1823.]

1863 At the sound of her master's voice the *metif* woman fell to the ground as if struck by a Minie-ball.—Edmund Kirke, "Life in Dixie's Land," p. 184. (Lond.)

Metis. (Fem. *metisse*). A person of mixed blood; a half breed. French.

1888 Louis Riel was a half-breed, and belongs to the class of inhabitants known as the *Metis* in Canada.—Mr. H. W. Blair of N. H., U. S. Senate, Oct. 9: *C. R.*, p. 9316/2.

Mexicanize. To reduce to the condition of Mexico or of a Mexican. Hence **Mexicanization.**

1887 The *Mexicanized* Spaniard is here, too proud to work.—C. F. Thwing, "Sermons," 8, 10. (N. E. D.)

1890 Gentlemen, do you know what a single silver standard means in this country? It means *Mexicanization.*—Mr. E. H. Conger of Ia., June 5: *C. R.*, p. 5655/1.

Michigander. A citizen of Michigan. [1848.]

1879 The House was tolerably disorderly to-day; but it was noticed that Mr. Conger, the eminent *Michigander*, was refreshingly quiet.—*N. Y. Herald*, Apr. 19, cited four days later in the *C. R.*, p. 738/1.

Middle-buster. A plow used to break out the middle of a cotton bed, and by genteel persons called a "middle-breaker." Colloquial, Southern.

1907 —Or by means of a *middle "buster,"* which is a double mold-board plow.—T. F. Hunt, "Forage &c in America," p. 352. (Century Dict.)

Middle of the road. See first quotation. Political slang.

1896 An epithet applied, especially in the presidential campaign of 1896, to those members of the Populist party who urged the nomination of a Populist by their party convention, and opposed the acceptance of the nominee of the Democratic party:—said to be derived from the habit, in some parts of the South-west, of keeping in the *middle of the road*, the better to protect oneself from enemies lying in ambush. (Century Dict.)

1896 The only honest Populist is the *"middle of the road"* Populist. The only men in the Populist party who have set principle above office are the *"middle of the road"* Populists.—Mr. D. T. Flynn of Okla., H. R., Dec. 10: *C. R.*, p. 80/2.

Mighty. In a great degree, very.

1869 I have been able to get but one bill before the Senate from the Committee on Claims this session, and I was *mighty* sorry I got that up.—Mr. Timothy O. Howe of Wisc., U. S. Senate, Feb. 13: *C. G.*, p. 1160/1.

1876 I am getting *mighty* tired answering questions, for I want to get through.—Mr. Caulfield of Ill., H. R., July 5: *C. R.*, p. 4406/1.

Mileage. An allowance for traveling. [1754-1862.]

See the debate in the Senate, Jan. 9, 1874: *C. R.*, pp. 516-20: in which Mr. Simon Cameron presented tables showing how the result was worked out individually under the Acts of 1856 and 1866.

Milk-and-water. Weak, devoid of energy, lacking courage. [1783-1810.]

1868 That class of *milk-and-water* men who were sort of for the Union and as much for the rebellion.—Mr. H. P. H. Bromwell of Ill., H. R., March 17: *C. G.*, p. 1932/3.

Milk in the cocoanut. The important or essential part of a matter. [1853.]

1870 This is the secret, this the *"milk in the cocoanut,"* this the "meat in the egg."—Mr. John A. Logan of Ill., H. R., June 15: *C. G.*, p. 500/2, App.

1879 I have long been looking for what sometimes has been called the *milk in the cocoanut*, and wondered why [Mr. Keifer] has been so anxious to support other [appropriation] bills.—Mr. E. S. Bragg of Wisc., H. R., Feb. 21: *C. R.*, p. 1734/1.

1882 I wish to state another reason . . . which to my mind is the real reason; it is *the milk in the cocoanut*; namely, &c.—Mr. J. H. Burrows of Mo., H. R., May 16: *Id.*, p. 4009/1.

1883 [Goods] must be produced more and more cheaply as inventive genius ...advances; everybody knows that. And here, sir, to use a vulgarism, is *"the milk in the cocoa-nut."*—Mr. W. A. J. Sparks of Ill., H. R., Feb. 8: *Id.*, p. 2294/2.

1888 Here is the *milk* of this political *cocoanut.*—Mr. G. G. Vest of Mo., U. S. Senate, Aug. 31: *Id.*, p. 8134/2.

1888 I was anxious to see certain specific articles manufactured in N. England—for that is *the milk in the cocoa-nut.*—The same, Oct. 15: *Id.*, p. 9458/1.

1893 Here is *the milk in the cocoanut*! A frank confession it is. The object of the proposed apportionment was to increase the Dem. delegation in Congress.—Mr. H. U. Johnson of Ind., H. R., Feb. 28: *Id.*, p. 2299/1.

1894 Our Republican friends want to postpone free wool and cheaper woolen goods until 1898. . . . Why do they want to make this postponement? I will tell you:—so that in 1896 they may again "fry the fat" out of the manufacturers, debauch the people, and elect a Republican President again. That is *the milk in the Republican cocoanut*. The gentleman from Vermont (Mr. Grout) says that, if the Wilson bill be passed, there will not be enough left of the Dem. party to make a grease spot. Do the Republicans believe that? Not a bit of it.— Mr. Champ Clark of Mo., H. R., Jan. 16: *Id.*, pp. 902, 903.

1899 See NIGGER IN THE WOODPILE.

Milk-shake. A beverage composed of milk and carbonated water, with the addition of a flavoring, mixed by being vigorously shaken up and down. (Century Dict.)

Milk train. See quotation.

1878 I see we are going to make a *milk train* of this, such as we have in N. England, that stops wherever an old lady with a basket of eggs or a can of milk wants to get on.—Mr. W. W. Eaton of Conn., U. S. Senate, June 5: *C. R.*, p. 4142.

1889 Away up 300 miles in the interior of New York the *milk trains* gather up the milk and cream and take it on to the city.—Mr. Frank Hiscock of N. Y., U. S. Senate, Jan. 15: *Id.*, p. 786/1.

Mill. The tenth part of a cent. [1791-1870.]

1862 The tax proposed may seem to be a small one—two *mills* per mile for each passenger. When we get down to talk about *mills*, it is difficult to make an impression on the judgment of anybody; but in the manufacturing business of the country a *mill* per yard is regarded . . . . as the difference between profit and loss.—Mr. Thomas M. Edwards of N. H., H. R., Apr. 1: *C. G.*, p. 1482/1.

Mill-Boy of the Slashes. Henry Clay, who was born in Hanover Co., Va., a low, swampy region.

1839 I was proud of [Henry Clay] as my fellow-countryman, and still prouder that the *Slashes of Hanover*, within the limits of my old District, gave him birth.—John Tyler in the Va. House of Delegates: see E. Sargent, "Life &c., of Henry Clay" (1844), p. 51n.

Millerites. The followers of William Miller of Massachusetts (1782-1849), who in 1831 began to teach that the end of all things would come in 1843. Now called Adventists. [1846-1857.]

1844 (Oct. 21.) Many of the *Millerites* believed that last week was appointed for the burning of the world. . . . Some of the *Millerites* have written glowing letters, intreating me to make haste to escape . . . Crowds are continually about the doors of the *Millerite* meetings. . . . Stones and brickbats are thrown in, and crackers and torpedoes explode under their feet.—Lydia M. Child, "Letters from New York," Second Ser., pp. 235-9. (Lond., 1845.)

1873 If my honorable friend from Vermont [Mr. Morrill] was about to be translated, if there was any danger of his becoming a political *Millerite*, putting on his ascension robes, &c.—Mr. Roscoe Conkling of N. Y., U. S. Senate, Feb. 24: *C. G.*, p. 1686/3.

Mill, go through the. To have practical experience of anything. [1837-1848.]

1888 The most successful men of Wall Street are those who came to the Street young, and have *"gone through the mill,"* so to speak.— Henry Clews, "Twenty-Eight Years in Wall St.," p. 36. (N. Y.)

Mill-seat. A site for a mill. [1784-1830.]

b.1813. He ran into debt for land that had a *mill-seat* upon it.—"Journal of Peggy Dow," p. 213/1. (1851.)

Mill-tail. A mill-race.
1804 The water, running like a *mill tail,* carried me down the stream two feet, whilst my mare could swim but one.—Lorenzo Dow, "Journal," Dec. 21 (1850), p. 100/2.

Mine-salter. One who "salts" a mine in order to sell it.
1890 [This is said to be] a bill to widen the market of the *mine-salter,* to remove the protection [now given] to the foreign capitalist by preventing him from being roped in by the gentlemen who "salt" the mines, or who have non-paying mines and want to unload on the . . . unsuspecting foreigner. . . . . I was at first rather captivated by the idea of extending the market of the *mine-salter* so as to take in the rich foreigner.—Mr. W. C. P. Breckinridge of Ky., H. R., Apr. 16: *C. R.,* p. 3443/1.

Mint-drops. Gold coins. [1837-1872.]
1870 I recollect that, before I was old enough to vote, the Democratic doctrine was that hard money, the gold shiners, were the only Dem. money. I remember when the Dem. stump speakers went about the country and carried the masses of the people by saying that they did not believe in this trash of a rag currency, that they wanted the gold, the *mint drops.*—Mr. Jacob Benton of N. H., H. R., June 29: *C. G.,* p. 4968/3.

Mint julep. A beverage of brandy or whisky with sugar, ice, and sprigs of mint. See Vol. II, **Mint-sling.** [1804-1826.]
1862 The art of composing what they call *mint juleps* and "slings" and "cocktails" and "punches," and the like artistic articles of luxury.—Mr. Elijah Babbitt of Pa., H. R., March 20: *C. G.,* p. 1311/1.

Minute-men. Men ready to turn out with their arms at a minute's warning. [1774-1860.]
1866 See PRECIPITATORS.

Miscegenation. An interbreeding of races. (Webster.) [1864.]
1864 [Do they] rely upon the new system, called by the transcendental abolitionists "*Miscegenation,*" to save the black? This is but another name for amalgamation; but it will not save the negro.—Mr. S. S. Cox of O., H. R., Feb. 17: *C. G.,* p. 709/3. [And he quotes from the *Anti-Slavery Standard,* Jan. 30, and the *Anglo-African,* a week earlier: p. 710/2.]
1864 That political drag-net set for partisan purposes at home, and drawn with the grimaces of buffoonery in dilating on the *miscegens.*—Mr. Grinnell of Ia., H. R., March 5: *Id.,* p. 954/3. [He is alluding to Mr. Cox's speech.]
1864 I desire those who thus argue to give a *miscegenatical* answer to these questions.—Mr. King of Mo., H. R., June 13: *Id.,* p. 2911/3.
1866 The Southern mulatto furnishes a conclusive answer to the argument on *miscegenation.*—Mr. W. T. Willey of W. Va., U. S. Senate, June 27: *Id.,* p. 3437/3.
1890 The bronze complexion of the races in the Congo Basin argues a former *miscegenation* of the negro with the Arab tribes.—Mr. J. T. Morgan of Ala., U. S. Senate, Jan. 7: *C. R.,* p. 420/2.

Mississippi Plan, the. The plan of asserting the rule of whites over blacks, by force if necessary.
1877 The three [Louisiana] parishes I have referred to are . . . near the boundary of Mississippi, and the plan of intimidation or bull-dozing is frequently spoken of as the "*Mississippi plan.*" . . . The "*Miss. plan*" was extended to Louisiana.—Mr. John Sherman of O., U. S. Senate, Jan. 9: *C. R.,* p. 501/1.
1878 This is not the first time that "*the Mississippi plan,*" as it is called, has been slandered, and I propose to defend it.—Mr. J. R. Chalmers of Miss., H. R., June 13: *Id.,* p. 478/2, App.
1880 The Edgefield policy or *Mississippi plan* was adopted as the democratic policy, and its first public demonstration was at Hamburgh [S. C.].—Mr. E. H. Rollins of N. H., U. S. Senate, May 26: *Id.,* p. 3808/2.

1881 "*The Mississippi plan,*" as it has been characterized, and as all the world understands it, furnishes the reason why the whole country has lately voted its want of confidence in the democratic party led by the southern end of it.—Mr. Eugene Hale of Me., U. S. Senate, Apr. 1: *C. R.*, p. 162/2.

1893 The *Mississippi plan* . . is acknowledged to be the most efficacious of all known methods for eliminating the "unwelcome voter."—Mr. H. M. Baker of N. H., H. R., Oct. 6: *Id.*, p. 2248/1.

Missouri compromise. This arrangement (1820) provided that Missouri should be admitted as a slave state, but that slavery should not be allowed in any new state lying north of 36° 30′.

1865 See SQUATTER SOVEREIGNTY.

1870 It was the Democratic party which broke faith with the nation in repealing the *Missouri compromise* which had been a sacred compact for thirty years between slavery and freedom. That great compact, which consecrated forever to human freedom all the territory north of the line of 36° 30′, the Dem. party violated or set aside . . . . in order to force slavery on the free soil of Kansas.—Mr. J. M. Thayer of Neb., H. R., Jan. 17: *C. G.*, p. 70/2, App.

1870 Mr. Clay may well have said that, when the *Missouri compromise* passed, the bells were rung, and the cannons were fired and every demonstration of joy was made throughout the Republic on account of its passage; and Mr. Douglas . . . may well have said that it was a sacred thing, akin to the Constitution of the United States.—Mr. Richard Yates of Ill., U. S. Senate, Feb. 16: *Id.*, p. 1327/3.

Misspeak oneself. To express one's meaning wrongly. Colloquial.

1894 I simply wanted to bring that matter out plainly, because I believe [Mr. Johnson] *misspoke himself.*—Mr. W. J. Coombs of N. Y., H. R., Jan. 19: *C. R.*, p. 1051/1.

Mixed or **Mixed up.** Confused, one with the other.

1886 Be sure that you do not get the gentlemen from Indiana *mixed.*—Mr. W. S. Holman of Ind., H. R., May 14: *C. R.*, p. 4515/1.

Molly Maguires. Members of a secret society in the coal district of the Lehigh Valley, Pa., which practised intimidation and murder. The name was taken from that of a society in Ireland, formed in 1843 to resist the payment of rent. (N. E. D.)

1867 The judge who tried this murderer was elected by the *Molly Maguires*; the jurors who assisted him were themselves *Molly Maguires.*—W. H. Dixon, "New America," II, 299. (N. E. D.)

1875 How many men have been slaughtered in cold blood by the *Molly Maguires* of Pennsylvania, and how many of those guilty wretches have been brought to justice?—Mr. T. C. McCreery of Ky., U. S. Senate, March 12: *C. R.*, p. 34/1.

1875 All violations of law and all combinations to violate the law are outrages, whether they are perpetrated by KuKlux, vigilance committees, or *Molly Maguires.*—The same, March 12.

Monitor. An ironclad vessel with revolving turrets.

1862 The iron-clad intruder will prove a severe monitor to those [secessionist] leaders. On these and [other] grounds I propose to name the new battery *Monitor.*—Ericsson, Letter 20; in Church's "Life" of him (1890) i, 255. (N. E. D.)

1864 The ability of a dozen *monitors* to take Charleston.—*Id.* ii, 49. (N. E. D.)

1865 Admiral Porter, ... indulging in some very high blowing about the merits of a certain *monitor*, states that she could cross the ocean, storm all the fortresses of England and France, and, after laying their cities under contribution, and playing havoc on a very large scale, could recross the ocean in perfect safety, *provided she could get coal*!—Mr. James G. Blaine of Me., H. R., Feb. 4: *C. G.*, p. 598/2.

1865   The speed of the *monitors* is not great (seven knots), but it is quite respectable with a clean bottom, and is fully equal to that of the *Ironsides.*—Report of Admiral Dahlgren, quoted by Mr. H. T. Blow of Mo., H. R., Feb. 6: *Id.,* p. 620/2. [And see this debate *passim.*]

1865   The original purpose for which these *monitors* were built is admitted on all hands to have failed. They cannot carry their turrets.— Mr. Benjamin Wade of O., U. S. Senate, Feb. 16: *Id.,* p. 824/3.

1865   That "queer looking cheese-box on a raft," which steamed into Hampton Roads in the gray dawn of that memorable morning, after an entire fleet of wooden ships had been sunk or driven ashore by a single rebel iron-clad, heralded the advent of a new epoch in naval warfare. . . . When the sun went down on that day's conflict, the age of wooden vessels for war purposes had passed into history. The London *Times* said that "the boasted fleet of England now consists of just four ships. . . . But the little *"Monitor,"* though an original creation of the genius of John Ericsson, was still not a perfect one. It is the first law of great ideas that they come forth rough hewn; and the *Monitor* was a great idea. . . . But she had many imperfections, and the test of battle showed them.—Mr. Brandegee of Conn., H. R., Feb. 28: *C. G.,* p. 1216/1. [See also the speech of Mr. H. W. Davis of Md., severely criticising the monitors:—*Id.,* pp. 36-40, App.]

1872   *Monitors* . . . . may be said to have saved the life of this nation; but they are of no earthly use now. . . . Who wants to buy a *monitor* any more than an elephant?—Mr. John P. Stockton of N. J., U. S. Senate, May 1: *Id.,* p. 2963/3.

Monkey, v. To interfere; to experiment, usually in a foolish way. [1886-1890.]

1889   I hope he'll fetch money. I've had enough o' *monkeying* 'long o' checks.—*Harper's Mag.,* lxxix, 465. (Century Dict.)

1889   This opens up the whole question, if any stockholder complains that there has been *"monkeying,"* so to speak.—Mr. Nelson Dingley of Me., H. R., Feb. 6: *C. R.,* p. 1569/1.

1891   I only stopped two Confederate bullets myself, and that was as many as I wanted to *monkey with.*—Mr. F. B. Spinola of N. Y., H. R., Jan. 27: *Id.,* p. 1885/1.

1893   If [Mr. Hendrix] thinks that he is the result of evolution, and that his forefathers were monkeys, I have no contention with him. But mine were not, and I am not here *monkeying* with this question either. —Mr. Edwd. Lane of Ill., H. R., Aug. 22: *Id.,* p. 84/1, App.

1894   A few rough-hewn lines of some doggrel rhymes feebly portray the clouds and darkness round about us:—

> From forges where no fires burn,
> From mills where wheels no longer turn,
> From looms o'er which no shuttles leap,
> From merchants' shops—which sheriffs keep,
> From banks gone up, from stocks gone down,
> From God-made country, man-made town,
> From Wall Street men, from sons of toil,
> From the bronzed tillers of the soil,
> From North, from South, from East, from West,
> Business is crying with a zest,
> "Don't *monkey with the tariff.*"

  —Mr. Marriott Brosius of Pa., H. R., Jan. 11: *Id.,* p. 745/2.

1894   It is always wise when you are dealing with figures—I will not use the slang phrase *"monkeying"* with figures—but when you are dealing with figures, to look out that you get at both ends of the calculation.— Mr. C. H. Grosvenor of O., H. R., March 7: *Id.,* p. 2698/1.

1897   [I have shown the actual receipts, so that gentlemen] can not *"monkey"* with the figures.—Mr. B. McMillin of Tenn., H. R., Feb. 13: *Id.,* p. 1806/1.

1897 If we had had an equal showing and a good cause, we would have . . . been a mighty "onproper" crowd to *"monkey"* with.—Mr. John M. Allen of Miss., H. R., Dec. 9: *Id.,* p. 66/1.

Monocrat. A Jeffersonian word applied to the Federalists; a promoter of autocracy. [1792-1793.]

1848 Mr. Jefferson styled those who contended for the veto power in the early days of the Republic, *Monocrats.*—Wilmington (N. C.) *Commercial,* Nov. 28, p. 2/2.

Monongahela. Whiskey distilled on the river of that name; thence American whiskey generally. [1834-1857.]

1850 Whiskey! Whiskey! 100 Bbls. "Old *Monongahela* Rectified" daily expected to arrive.—Wilmington (N. C.) *Commercial,* Feb. 28, p. 3/5. (Advt.)

1890 Mr. Cummings:—I assure the gentleman *"Monongahela"* does not trouble me. Mr. Cannon:—We all know that. (Laughter.)—H. R., Aug. 5: *C. R.,* p. 8170/1.

1897 [In a discusssion on bridging the Monongahela river]: Mr. Henderson:—I suggest that the gentleman from New York is not discussing the *"Monongahela"* that he is familiar with. Mr. Payne:—I should not presume to discuss that kind in the gentleman's presence.—H. R., Feb. 27: *C. R.,* p. 2466/1.

Monroe doctrine. The principle enunciated in Pres. Monroe's Message of Dec. 2, 1823, that "the American continents should no longer be subjects for any European settlement." [1848-1896.]

1865 The *Monroe doctrine* will be enforced by the people, perhaps even against the sanction of the Government.—Mr. Leonard Myers of Pa., H. R., Feb. 28: *C. G.,* p. 1218/2.

1870 Cuba belongs to this continent; she is an adjacent isle, and is a part of the American system, and is as fully included in what is called the *Monroe doctrine* as if she were a part of the mainland.—Mr. Oliver P. Morton of Ind., U. S. Senate, Feb. 9: *Id.,* p. 1130/2.

1870 The acquisition of San Domingo is an adherence to the *"Monroe doctrine"*; it is a measure of national protection; it is asserting our just claim to a controlling influence over the great commercial traffic soon to flow from west to east by way of the Isthmus of Darien.— President Grant's Message to Congress, Dec. 5: *Id.,* p. 14/1.

1871 There has been so much loose talk on the subject of the *"Monroe doctrine,"* socalled, that President Grant may have been justified in making an earnest experiment to find out its practical meaning. . . . It has by some been held to include much more than I think the simple declaration warranted. As read by me, it only declared "America no longer open to European colonization"; not that we wanted to colonize. . . . The doctrine was not that we were to seize all the land adjoining us, nor was it by any means susceptible of the selfish interpretation that European vultures were to be driven away in order that the American eagle might swoop down and clutch the prey.—Mr. Justin S. Morrill of Vt., U. S. Senate, Apr. 7: *C. G.,* p. 527/1.

1879 [This joint resolution concerning a ship-canal across the Isthmus of Darien] is simply a re-enunciation of what is known as the *Monroe doctrine,* a cardinal principle of American policy, which has for upward of half a century secured us from foreign interference in, or foreign control of, the affairs of the western continent. This doctrine was embodied in the annual message of President Monroe to the Eighteenth Congress, which first met in this city on the 1st day of December, 1823. At that time the Russians wanted to extend their dominions on the Pacific Coast of North America so far southward as to include California, and King Ferdinand of Spain . . . was endeavoring to form an alliance with other European powers, which would force back to their allegiance the revolted colonies of Spain in South America. Against this and similar demonstrations President Monroe formally protested declaring to the Old World that the United States would not tolerate the extension of their despotic machinations and intrigues to the New.—Mr. A. E. Burnside of R. I., U. S. Senate, Dec. 2: *C. R.*, p. 13/1.

1881 The *Monroe doctrine*, as I understand it, grew out of peculiar circumstances. In 1823 Russia, Prussia, France, and Austria were about to take steps to propagate upon this continent monarchical institutions by force. They contemplated restoring the authority and power of European monarchies over the colonies in South and Central America, which had established their independence and set up republican governments. When it was made known to our Government that such intentions were entertained, President Monroe sent in his famous message. Read by the light of surrounding circumstances, that message simply means this Government will resist any attempt on the parts of European monarchies to overturn republican governments on this continent.—Mr. H. A. Herbert of Ala., H. R., Feb. 26: *Id.*, p. 2154/2.

1884 We have outgrown the old *Monroe doctrine*. We are every day, and we have been for years, going further than the old *Monroe doctrine* went.—Mr. W. W. Eaton of Conn., H. R., July 5: *Id.*, p. 6130/1.

1891 When France was building the canal across the Isthmus, it looked as if we might be called upon to enforce the *"Monroe doctrine"* as we understand it, and protect that great artery of commerce.—Mr. Henry C. Lodge of Mass., H. R., Jan. 23: *Id.*, 1804/1.

1895 The principles of the *Monroe doctrine* are older than the special Executive message of Dec. 1823. They are as old as the Constitution itself. They were the logical sequence of the Declaration of Independence of 1776 and of the Treaty of Ghent which followed. They stand out in bold relief in the annals of President Washington's first administration and were reiterated with emphasis in his farewell address. They were subsequently reasserted by John Quincy Adams while Secretary of State. And they have been reasserted and upheld by every Executive of the United States who has ever had occasion to refer to them, from Washington to Cleveland.—Mr. L. F. Livingston of Ga., H. R., Feb. 6: *Id.*, p. 1833/1.

1896 See Senator Wolcott's discussion of the Monroe Doctrine, Jan. 22; and that of Senator Daniel, Jan. 23: *Id.*, pp. 856-60, 914-18.

Monumental City, The. Baltimore. See Vol. I, **City of Monuments.** [1834-1863.]

1827 The brave sons of Cincinnatus [sat] at the festal board in the *"monumental city."*—*Nat. Gazette* (Phila.), Nov. 20, p. 2/3. (From the Boston *Patriot.*)

1865 [The course of the Merrimac] in the Chesapeake [Bay] would have cut off the *Monumental city* from the world.—Mr. Henry T. Blow of Mo., H. R., Feb. 6: *C. G.*, p. 619/3.

Moonshine, -er, -ing. Moonshiners are those who secretly manufacture illicit whisky, which is called moonshine. These words are principally Southern; but see quotation 1884.

1884 It appears to be a Sussex provincialism. "At Piddinghoe they dig for *moonshine*; for smoke: for daylight."—*Notes & Queries*, 6 Ser., ix, 401. See also Gnose.

1888 This season . . . . might be made as romantic as vintage-time on the Rhine, or *moonshining* on the Southern mountains.—C. D. Warner, "Their Pilgrimage," p. 288. (Century Dict.)

1901 Georgia and Arkansas have the greatest number of *moonshine* stills.— *Munsey's Mag.*, xxv, 428/1. (N. E. D.)

Morgan. A fiction designed to serve a temporary use. See **Good enough Morgans**, pp. 166-167.

[1827 The general impression has been that Morgan was drowned in the neighbourhood of Fort Niagara.—*Nat. Gazette* (Phila.), Oct. 25, p. 1/4.]

1849 The *Standard* has got it up as a "very good *Morgan*" for political effect.—Wilmington (N. C.) *Commercial*, May 5, p. 2/2.

Mormon. The "hobomok skipper," a butterfly whose larvæ feed on grasses. (Century Dict.)

Mormon-weed. The velvet-leaf, *Abutilon Abutilon*. (Century Dict.)

Morrill tariff, the. The tariff framed by Mr. Justin S. Morrill of Vt., which became law in 1861. It was passed as a war measure, and embodied the principles of high protection.

Mortgage. A strong grasp.

1868 At the beginning of this war the devil had a *mortgage* upon all Maryland, or nearly all.—Mr. John Conness of Calif., U. S. Senate, Feb. 19: *C. G.*, p. 1268/1.

Mosey. To move along. Slang. [1836-1902.]

1864 He took the jug under his arm and "*moseyed* off" to the house.— Edmund Kirke's "Down in Tennessee," p. 89. See also pp. 110, 114, 155, 160, 161, &c.

Mossback. An unprogressive person; a fogy. [1850-1904.]

[1866 I do not want a system which will encourage men to be kept in places until they are *moss-grown*, until lichens are formed upon their legs and backs.—Mr. Robert C. Schenck of O., H. R., June 5: *C. G.*, p. 2979/2.]

1892 Mr. Watson:—The Ocala platform [was] repudiated by the regular rock-ribbed Democrats. Mr. Hopkins:—*Mossbacks*. Mr. Watson:— *Mossback* Democrats. If the other man can stand that, I can.—H. R., May 28: *Id.*, p. 4802/1.

1900 Primitive man lived in caverns, clothed himself with skins, and ate his meat raw, sitting on his haunches; and there has never occurred a change for the higher and better forms of life without arousing the hostility of some old *mossback*, conservative hunker[s], who will prate of those fairer and better days of old, when their grandfathers swung by their tails from the limbs of the trees.—Mr. J. C. Sibley of Pa., H. R., Feb. 1: *Id.*, p. 1408/1.

Mossbanker. See quotation. [1818.] See **Menhaden.**

1679 A sort of herring called the *marsbanckers.*—Dankers and Sluyter, "Voyage to New York," tr. in 1867, I, 100. (Century Dict.)

Mossy-backed rangers. See quotation.

1876 The balance of the male population [in the cotton states] besides the colored people was composed, first, of those too old for war; second, of those too cowardly to fight, who were known as "*mossy-backed rangers*" during the war, but came out fully fledged "Union men" after the war; &c.—Mr. Frank Morey of La., H. R., Jan. 13: *C. R.*, p. 411/1.

Most. For *almost*. This seems to be originally Scottish. See also **E'ena'most.** [1800-1878.]

1592 When I was *most* tyred with love, he expired at last.—Thos. Lodge, "Euphues Shadow," F. 3.

1610 "And in white lawn she went, *most* like an angel brave."—Giles Fletcher, "Christ's Triumph," Part II.

1671 Sharks are here in abundance, whose Back-bone looks *most* like a Japan.—Note(*r*) to John Hardie's "Last Voyage to Bermudas," pp. 15, 16.

a.1720 'Tis *most* dinner time. S'avvicina il tempo di desinare.—Henry Fleunus, Italian Grammar, p. 260. (Livorno.)

1736 He is a short thin visag'd Fellow, and looks *most* like a Saylor.— *S. C. Gazette*, Nov. 27, p. 4/4. (Advt.)

Mother of Commonwealths, The. Virginia.

1879   If it affords [Mr. Conger] any pleasure . . . to indulge in ill-natured flings and to pour out the vials of his impotent wrath upon the *"Mother of Commonwealths,"* let him enjoy it.—Mr. John Goode of Va., H. R., Jan. 10: *C. R.*, p. 413/2.

Mother of Presidents, The.   Virginia.   [1850.]

1868   [As Mr. Stevens] spoke of Virginia, the proud *mother of Presidents*, become a breeder of slaves for the southern market, the anger of her representatives could scarcely be restrained.—Mr. James K. Moorhead of Pa., H. R., Dec. 17: *C. G.*, p. 132/2.

Mother of States, The.   Virginia.

1879   When the *"mother of States"* comes, in the weeds of woe, asking [to be enabled to restore William and Mary College, &c.].—Mr. John Goode of Va., H. R., Jan. 10: *C. R.*, p. 414/1.

1896   That grand old Commonwealth of Virginia, the *mother of States* and statesmen, the *mother of Presidents.*—Mr. R. Z. Linney of N. C., H. R., June 9: *Id.*, p. 6342/2.

Mought for *might*.   Dialectic or vulgar.   [1821-1857.]

1558   Troy *mought* stil haue stand.—Phaer, "Eneidos," Bb. ii (1562).

1572   Ned Denny (fayre *mought* him befal.)—G. Gascoigne, "Herbes," p. 173 (1587).

1576   Where he him selfe, and no man better, *mought* Haue taught his brats to take a better waie.—The same, "Complaint," p. 350.

1594   And *mought* I live to see him sack rich Thebes.—Marlowe, "Dido," p. 264/1.   (Dyce.)

1597   Nor caroll out so pleasing liuely laies
        As *mought* the Grace moue my mirth to praise.
    —"Virgidemiarum," Book I, p. 2.

1597   What action *mought* be entred in the plea.—*Id.*, IV, 15.

Mound City, The.   St. Louis, Missouri: so named from the Indian mounds once occupying its site.

1866   Our rivers have no rivals as the great channels of trade, nor was there ever a plainer designation in nature (*sic*) that the opulent and now free *"Mound City,"* almost in the shadow of the mountains of minerals, shall be the home of ten thousand sons of Vulcan, &c.—Mr. Grinnell of Ia., H. R., March 6: *C. G.*, p. 1218/2.

Mounting side (of a horse).   The "near" or left side.

1732   A dark colour'd Horse, branded with M and a cross a top, on the *mounting* shoulder: . . . . also a bay Horse . . . branded with H on the *mounting* buttock.—*S. C. Gazette*, Feb. 5, p. 4/2,   (Advt.)

1737   [He is] branded on the *Mounting* shoulder with a Diamond, and has a Lock of white hair in his Withers.—*Id.*, Feb. 26, p. 3/1.   (Advt.)

1794   A black gelding, . . . branded on the *Mounting* buttock C.—*Id.*, July 29, p. 1/1.   (Advt.)

Mourned.   Draped with crape.

1834   Masters and Mates of Vessels and Seamen, with U. S. flag *mourned*. [Obsequies of Lafayette.]—*The Georgian* (Savannah), July 15, p. 2/5.

Mouth, to shoot or shoot off one's.   To talk.   Vulgar.

1883   I am the friend of the laboring man. . . . I shoot the way I vote and vote the way I shoot on that question; but some professed friends of the laboring man *shoot their mouths* in one way and vote the other. —Mr. R. Q. Mills of Tex., H. R., Jan. 26: *C. R.*, p. 1644/1.

Movie.   A moving picture or moving picture show.   (Webster.)

1913   At the out-door *movie*.   Some fun which a wheel-chair occupant may have.   The average healthy human being is not likely to realize the limitations and loneliness that fall to the lot of the occupant of the wheel-chair.   "At last I have found a place of amusement that I can get to, and where I don't have to be uncomfortably conscious that I am in some one's way"—the remark was intended only for the strong young nurse who was skilfully guiding the wheel-chair through the entrance gate of the outdoor *"movie,"* then along the cemented aisle, flanked by freshly painted green seats and two plots of real grass at one side of the fence.—*N. Y. Evening Post,* July 10, p. 5/7.

Muchly for *Much.* Examples 1621, 1647, (N. E. D.)

1888 [He is] a tolerably honest though a *muchly* misguided man.—Mr. John M. Allen of Miss., H. R., Dec. 11: *C. R.,* p. 162/1.

Mucilage. What in England is commonly called "gum." An aqueous solution used as an adhesive.

1879 [There was] a man in the days when the adhesive *mucilage* was not so good as it is now, [who] found great difficulty in making the stamp adhere to the letter, and . . . he wrote across it, "Paid if the picture sticks."—Mr. J. J. Davis of N. C., H. R., Apr. 23: *C. R.,* p. 793/1.

1894 The scissors and the *mucilage brush* had been busy.—Mr. J. W. Daniel of Va., U. S. Senate, Feb. 6: *C. R.,* p. 1939/1.

Mucker, Muckerish, Muckerism. A "mucker" (from the German) is a low, rough, coarse person. Slang.

1906 Both battalions were equally guilty, and we hope it does not mean an entrance of *muckerism* into our Army and Navy games.—*Outing,* p. 494. (Century Dict.)

Mudder. A horse which runs best on a muddy track. Racing slang.

1905 The second horse was King Pepper, . . .and the third horse, Athlone, is by Handsel, a *mudder* himself and the son of a *mudder.*—*N. Y. Evening Sun,* Aug. 17. (Century Dict.)

Mud-lumps. The earliest appearance of soft, spongy land at the mouth of the Mississippi. [1872.]

1874 The *mud-lump* must necessarily . . . rise in shallow water. Why? Because to make the *mud-lumps* there must be a sufficient amount of this tough deposit to hold the gases which come up from below, expanding into a sort of dome. And if you have not got that material you cannot have the *mud-lumps.*—Mr. S. A. Hurlbut of Ill., H. R., June 5: *C. R.,* p. 4623/2.

1901 Within this region lie a number of "mud volcanoes," apparently analogous to the *"mud lumps"* of the Lower Mississippi, which have attracted much attention by reason of their novelty.—*Smithsonian Report,* p. 71. (Century Dict.)

Mud scow. A scow used in dredging. [1766-1808.]

1882 [He] lived down on the raging Ohio, and was the gallant commander of a first-class *mud-scow.*—Mr. A. S. Willis of Ky., H. R., July 13: *C. R.,* p. 6015/1.

Mudsill. A word applied to the working classes by Senator J. H. Hammond, of South Carolina, in 1858. [1858-1863.]

1861 Senator Hammond is by no means alone in his conception of the dignity of labor. There are hundreds of thousands who concur in his estimate of laboring men as the mere *"mudsills"* of society, on which there should be erected an aristocracy.—Mr. W. T. Willey of Va., U. S. Senate, Dec. 20: *C. G.,* p. 37/1, App.

1864 It is a terrible fallacy that a stream cannot be purer than its fountain, that you cannot make a silken purse out of a sow's ear, or a gentleman and an aristocrat out of *mud-sill* material. Hammond himself, of *mud-sill* notoriety, was, it is said, the son of a butcher.—Mr. Dumont of Ind., H. R., March 12: *Id.,* p. 1072/2.

1868 Southern planters, who declared the negro incapable of citizenship, could not endure the *"mudsills"* of the North, and of course they deprecated impartial suffrage: but observe that they respected the *"mudsills"* no more than they did the slave. Their course was natural and logical.—Mr. F. C. Beaman of Mich., H. R., March 18: *C. G.,* p. 1971/1.

1868 According to my recollection, Governor Hammond has been dead about six years. I believe he was the author of the celebrated phrase about the *mudsills*; but I think it was his boast either that he was born in the North or that his father was a Massachusetts man.—Mr. Garrett Davis of Ky., U. S. Senate, July 10: *Id.*, p. 3910/2.

1878 New Jersey was not settled with cavaliers. New Jersey was settled with *mudsills*, and New Jersey went to work while Virginia went into politics.—Mr. M. I. Townsend of N. Y., H. R., Apr. 12: *C. R.*, p. 2492/1.

Muggin. A small mug. Probably a nonce-word.

1872 I, if I knew how to manufacture my little *"muggin"* of rum on Lake Michigan, had my drawback equally with the Yankees in New England. —Mr. Matt. Carpenter of Wisc., U. S. Senate, March 20: *C. G.*, p. 1824/2.

Mugwump. An Indian word meaning a chieftain. In the Blaine campaign of 1884, the *N. Y. Sun* styled the Independent Republicans by this name. [1835-1910.]

1886 We have been constantly embarrassed both by our Democratic brothers and by *Mugwumps* in trying to determine what are dead issues and what are live issues.—Mr. Butterworth of O., H. R., March 2: *C. R.*, p. 1977/2.

1886 There was not a Democrat within . . . half a mile of the town. They had to go away into the Pine Ridges on a by-road, and appoint a *Mugwump.*—Mr. L. C. Houk of Tenn., H. R., March 30: *Id.*, p. 2935/1.

1886 That maudlin political sentiment which we recognize, for want of a better, under the name of *"Mugwumpism,"* a kind of sickly, sentimental, Sunday-school, "Goody Two-shoes" party, which appears desirous of ruling the world, not as God has made it, but as they would have it.— Mr. R. B. Vance of N. C., H. R., March 31: *Id.*, p. 2946/1. [The speaker goes on using such phrases as "Pecksniffian snivel," "bibulous propensities," "the cheek of a town cow," &c., but his speech is hardly amusing enough to go into the Appendix.]

1888 Officials . . . . whose places were needed for hungry applicants, and whose removal it was feared would offend the *"Mugwumps."*—Mr. James Buchanan of N. J., H. R., May 24: *Id.*, p. 4596/2.

1888 You gentlemen, who came into power under the cry, "turn the rascals out," have deceived nobody but the dyspeptic *Mugwumps* who, believing first in free trade, bartered away for it civil-service reform.—Mr. L. E. McComas of Md., H. R., May 25: *Id.*, p. 4637/1.

1888 Four years ago a class of honorable and cultivated and able gentlemen attained the title of *Mugwumps*, otherwise *Big Indians.*—Mr. J. R. Hawley of Conn., U. S. Senate, Oct. 3: *Id.*, p. 9128/2.

1890 [These people] are always dissatisfied with every condition of things which may exist. They are what might be called *"Mugwumps"* in finance as much as the followers of Geo. Wm. Curtis are *"Mugwumps"* in politics.—Mr. M. S. Brewer of Mich., H. R., June 7: *Id.*, p. 5811/1.

1892 In 1884 I did myself the honor to stop voting the Republican ticket. I took a prominent, I may say a leading part in what was called the Independent campaign in Massachusetts, conducted for the purpose of electing a Democratic President. The men who took that course at that time now labor under the euphonious title of *"Mugwumps."* The true definition of *"Mugwump"* is, a man who left the Republican party in 1884, whatever he may have done since. . . . After that great movement, practically the whole body of the so-called *Mugwumps* did go over to the Democratic party.—Mr. Geo. F. Williams of Mass., H. R., March 18: *Id.*, p. 2195/1.

1892 My criticism is . . . . directed to the methods of the *"Mugwump"* party, and to the conduct of the *Mugwumps* as *Mugwumps.*—Mr. J. H. Walker of Mass., H. R., Apr. 23: *Id.*, p. 3590/2. [See the whole speech.]

1894 What is a *Mugwump*? My friend from Montana described a *Mugwump* here last August in poetic language. It is a cross between a Democratic cuckoo and a Republican cuckoo. If there were no cuckoos of one kind or the other, then there would be no *Mugwumps.*—Mr. Lafe Pence of Colo., H. R., Feb. 26: *Id.*, p. 2429/2.

1894 What with the grasping and inexorable avarice of gold mono-metalism on the one hand, and an overdose of *mugwumpery* on the other, I can not, as a Democrat, take a rose-colored view of the situation.—Mr. Robt. Neill of Ark., H. R., *Id.*, p. 2438/1.

Mule-train. A train of mules.

1876 Those expeditions are accompanied by immense wagon-trains and by *mule-trains* carrying provisions.—Mr. Martin Maginnis of Wyo., H. R., June 19: *C. R.*, p. 3885/2.

Muley. A hornless cow. Variant of *Mulley.*

1573 Leave milking and drie vp old *mulley* thy cow.—Thomas Jusser, "Husbandry" (1878), 135. (N. E. D.)

1838 Gives his Old *Mooley* a chance o'sneakin' into his neighbour's fields o'nights.—Haliburton, "Clockmaker," II, iv. (N. E. D.)

1879 I do not think this is a matter which depends on how many upper teeth a cow has got, or on the difference between a *muley* and a short-horn Durham.—Mr. J. R. Chalmers of Miss., H. R., Apr. 12: *C. R.*, p. 405/1.

1886 Every man in New Jersey who owns a *muley* or horned or other Jersey cow.—Mr. W. McAdoo of N. J., H. R., May 28: *Id.*, p. 5049/1.

Mull. To ruminate upon; to ponder thoughtfully.

1873 [Huxley] hopes I will add the chapter on 'Matter and Spirit,' which I have been *mulling* for a year back.—John Fiske to his wife: "Life of John Fiske," I, 488.

1917 [Herbert Spencer] was *mulling* over this profound subject in 1859.—J. S. Clark, "Life of John Fiske," II, 19. (Boston.)

Multimillionaire. A person who is worth many millions of dollars.

1894 The *multimillionaire* is a rare bird in this country. I do not think we need to be oppressing all the frugal and honest people in this country because there are said to be some *multimillionaires* in the city of New York.—Mr. G. F. Hoar of Mass., U. S. Senate, June 23: *C. R.*, p. 6778/2.

Murray Hill. The wealthy district of New York; hence a synonym for wealth. Cf. **Wall Street.**

1894 [Mr. Cockran] spoke of *Murray Hill* as a quarter of his city, where dwell the wealthy, who would feel some of the weight of an income tax; and of *Cherry Hill* as a humble section of the same great city, inhabited by the poor. . . . How much of fraternity and equality now exists between *Cherry Hill* and *Murray Hill*? . . . .How much of *Cherry Hill*, with its calloused hands and toil-stained garments, lounges, in the freedom of equality, in the parlors of *Murray Hill*?—Mr. D. A. DeArmond of Mo., H. R., Jan. 30: *C. R.*, p. 406/1, App. [See also Mr. Cockran's remarks, same day: *Id.*, p. 466/1, App.]

Muscle, on one's. By the use of physical strength.

1866 [He] knocked his earth-works all to pieces, pulled away the abattis, jumped over the ditch, got into the citadel, and went in generally *on his muscle.*—Mr. Ebenezer Dumont of Ind., H. R., June 4: *C. G.*, p. 2953/1.

Mush. Any kind of porridge. [1671-1854.]

1671   Here's Roots as well as Trees, Potatoes good
    For sustenance of man to make pure blood.
    And here Cassawder, to which, though its Juice
    Be Poyson, yet they now have a device
    To press and grate it, so in time of need

And sometimes else, they safely on it feed
Being bak'd in form of Bread; here's Indian-Corn
Whose weighty Eares on a long stalk is born:
In thickness like a Cane, it Nature roul'd
Close up in Leaves, to keep it from the cold:
Which being groun'd & boyl'd, *Mush* they make [*sic*]
Their hungry Servants Hunger for to slake.
—John Hardie, "Last Voyage to Bermudas," pp. 10, 11.

1866 The woman cooked me a breakfast of fried eggs, sweet potatoes, pumpkin-*mush*, and hot-cakes.—H. L. Estabrooks, "Adrift in Dixie," p. 149. (N. Y.)

1876 The landlady came in with a pan of corn-meal and commenced stirring it into the hot water, pouring it in with one hand and stirring it with the other until she got it to a proper consistency for what we call in the western part of the country *mush*.—Mr. James D. Williams of Ind. ["Blue-jeans Williams"], H. R., June 17: *C. R.*, p. 3870/1.

1877 I trust that we are not to be whistled down the wind . . . by any ridicule of corn-kitchens, or tilts at our time-honored dish of *mush and milk*, however brilliant or witty.—Mr. C. G. Williams of Wisc., H. R., Nov. 17: *C. R.*, p. 520/1.

Musher, mushing. See quotation.
Traveling by this means [by dog-sled] is known in the language of Alaska as "*mushing*," and the traveler is called a "*musher*." The "*musher*" does not ride on the sled, but follows . . . afoot, and urges the dogs forward.—*U. S. Geol. Survey*, Paper 20, p. 14. (Century Dict.)

Musical. Pleasant, agreeable, facetious. A New England expression. [1816-1835.]

1815 See FINE AS A FIDDLE.

Muss. An entanglement, a state of confusion; also a row or fight. [1840-1878.]

1844 You must know that "*muss*" is a favourite phrase with New-Yorkers, to express everything that is in a state of confusion.—Lydia M. Child, "Letters from New York," Second Ser., p. 129. (Lond., 1845.)

1869 In the excitement of the times I thought [Senator Conness] was in a "*muss*" last night, but he is here safe again.—Mr. Thomas A. Hendricks of Ind., U. S. Senate, Feb. 9: *C. G.*, p. 1032/2.

Mustee. See **Mestee.**

N

Nail City, The. Wheeling, W. Va.

1890 Down through the thriving city of Wheeling—*the Nail City* of the West—I could hear the rattling roll of machinery.—Mr. G. W. Atkinson of W. Va., H. R., May 9: *C. R.*, p. 4433/2.

Nail-sick. Leaky at the nail-holes. So a wooden ship, the bolts and spikes of which are corroded, is said to be iron-sick.

1865 Much smaller waves soon make a boat "*nail-sick*," as the phrase is.—H. D. Thoreau, "Cape Cod." p. 145. (N. E. D.)

1879 As the little craft was old and *nailsick*, she made a good deal of water.—T. Warden, "Crossford," II, 73. (N. E. D.)

Named for. Named after.

1890 The Capital city, . . . designated by Washington, planned by Washington, and *named for* Washington.—Mr. C. T. O'Ferrall of Va., H. R., Feb. 21: *C. R.*, p. 1602/1.

Nantucket sleigh-ride. The towing of a whale-boat by a whale. (Century Dict.)

Nary. A corruption of "ne'er a" or "never a." [1821-1909.] Here the reference is to a gambling game of cards.

1882   The Senator from North Carolina [Mr. Ransom] gets in here from the house with *nary a pair*, and he always goes out with a pile.—Mr. John T. Morgan of Ala., U. S. Senate, July 6: *C. R.*, p. 5672/2.

Nation.   Euphemism for *damnation*, used as adjective or adverb.   [1765-1853.]

1815   You were a *nation* wiser than brother Jonathan, brother Josiah, sister Deborah, sister Keziah, cousin Jemima, poor little Aminadab, and all the rest.—David Humphreys, "The Yankey in England," p. 19.

1815   When I got my body loose, I looked *nation* poorly for a lengthy time afterwards.—*Id.*, p. 42.

1879   A climate [that of Alaska] which I have heard described as nine months of winter and three months of *damnation* cold weather.—Mr. Vance of N. C., U. S. Senate, May 19: *C. R.*, p. 1460/2.

Nativism.   The doctrine of the Know-Nothing or self-styled "American" party.   See Vol. II, **Native American Party.**   [1845.]

1856   In a kind of feud now existing between American-born and foreign-born citizens, the former are said to profess *Nativism.*—*Notes & Queries*, 2nd Ser., I, 9.

1864   These necessities destroyed *nativism* and the political anti-Catholic party.—Nicols, "Forty Years of American Life," II, 90.   (N. E. D.)

1864   The baleful *Nativism* which had just broken out [1844] in the great cities, and had been made the occasion of riot, devastation, and bloodshed in Philadelphia, had alarmed the foreign-born population.—H. Greeley, "Amer. Conflict," I, 168.   (Century Dict.)

1867   The naturalized citizen, enjoying his rights largely through the opposition of Andrew Johnson to *Nativism* and Know-Nothingism.—Mr. W. E. Robinson of N. Y., H. R., July 12: *C. G.*, p. 12/2, App.

Navajo blanket.   See **Quarter.**

Navy Yard.   A Government dock-yard; now U. S.   (N. E. D.)

1771   Annual Register, p. 113/1, mentions Halifax *navy-yard*.   (N. E. D.)

1828   On the expediency of establishing a *navy yard*.—"Amer. State Papers" (1860), III, 275.

1876   The employes at the *navy-yard* with those from the custom house go hand in hand, . . and march down over the rights of the people of that district [in Boston.]   Custom-house and *navy-yard*, twin sisters on their mission of fraud and crime, join hands, that the work may be the more complete.—Mr. Poppleton of O., H. R., July 14: *C. R.*, p. 4597/1.

1876   See RING-MASTER.

Neck.   A peninsula.   [1555-1821.]

1710   Wee caused [the Negro] to be Conveyed into the Northern *Neck*, where he has Been and is Still Entertained.—Journal, House of Burgesses, Va., IV, 270.   (Richmond, 1912.)

1732   Run away of [off] the Town *Neck*, a Mustee Wench.—*S. C. Gazette*, Apr. 16, p. 4/2.   (Advt.)

Neckatee.   A neck-cloth.   Obsolete.

1894   Other colonists had speckled neck-cloths, lawn and silesia neck-cloths. Men and women both wore them.   They were also called neck-clothes, neckerchiefs, neckingers, and *neckatees*.—Alice M. Earle, "Costume of Colonial Times," p. 167.   (Century Dict.)

Neck-bang.   The short hair on a woman's neck, where the line of hair growth begins.

1905   She wore brown cotton gloves and a brown cotton veil to preserve her complexion.   Her *neck-bangs* . . . stood out like a bunch of tumbleweed.—*Century Mag.*, p. 602.

Neck of the woods.   A settlement in the forest; thence generally for any part of the country.   [1851-1874.]

1893   Ole Blue Jay, he say dat he am boss ob dis *neck ob de woods*.—Mary A. Owen, "Old Rabbit, the Voodoo, &c.," p. 60.

Neck, to get it in the.   To be figuratively beheaded.   Slang.

1892 Mr. Turner:—The gentleman says that the farmer gets it. Several Members:—*Gets it in the neck.* Mr. Turner:—In the language of current slang, the farmer is "not in it."—H. R., March 10: *C. R.,* p. 1946/1.

Negotiate. To surmount or traverse; deal with as desired;—used of an obstacle, etc. Colloquial. (Webster.)

1913 Cornish, N. H., July 11.—President Wilson went exploring in his automobile to-day. He took an unfrequented road and his big car picked its way slowly and cautiously over a mountainside. The machine *negotiated* the hills with little difficulty, but frequently in the descents the brakes were thrown on tight.—Press dispatch.

Negrophilist. A lover of the negro. See Vol. II, **Negrophilism.** [1846-1862.]

1842 When the *Eastern negrophilists* are prepared to pay a tax, they will &c. —S. Ward in Longfellow's Life (1891) I, 449. (N. E. D.)

1874 This sudden change from an old State-rights Democrat to what Caleb Cushing used to call a *negrophilist.*—Mr. S. S. Cox of N. Y., H. R., Jan. 13: *C. R.,* p. 616/2.

Negro regulators. Persons undertaking by violent measures to keep the negroes in order.

1866 Bands of "guerrillas" and *"negro regulators"* soon increased in numbers and audacity, and many lawless acts have been perpetrated by them.—Report of Major Gen. Jeff. C. Davis: *C. G.,* p. 33/1, App.

Neshannock. A species of potato. Name probably of Indian origin.

1902 *Neshannock.* A white-fleshed variety of potato. which has obtained its name from the [Neshannock] region of Pennsylvania [in Mercer County], where it first became noteworthy.—*Journal of Am. Folk-Lore,* xv, p. 251.

Nest, off one's. In error.

1894 [These gentlemen] are both—to adopt the expression of my friend from Kansas (Mr. Simpson) yesterday—*"off their nests"* right badly in regard to the Constitution.—Mr. C. B. Kilgore of Tex., H. R., Feb. 16: *C. R.,* p. 2254/1.

Netop, Netup. A crony, a chum. Natick Indian.

1900 Mr. Harum and I are great *"neetups,"* as he says.—E. N. Westcott, "David Harum," ch. xxxiii. (Century Dict.)

1902 *Netop.* A word once very commonly used in Massachusetts and some other parts of New England in the sense of "friend," and (later) "crony," "chum."—*Journal of Am. Folk-Lore,* xv, p. 251.

Newburgs, Newbergs. A preparation of delicate meat or shell-fish, stewed usually in cream, thickened with eggs and flavored with wine: frequently made in a chafing-dish. Apparently from Newburg, N. Y. (Century Dict.)

New Jersey mosquito. According to popular tradition, mosquitoes humorously supposed to be of superlative size, agility, cunning, and ferocity.

1897 I have never been in New Jersey, but I know the reputation of the *New Jersey mosquito*; and a *New Jersey mosquito* two seconds old out of the egg—if that is where he comes from—has more strength and more sense than [this resolution].—Mr. Geo. F. Hoar of Mass., U. S. Senate, May 18: *C. R.,* p. 1137/2.

Newness, The. A name given to New England transcendentalism at the time of its prevalence. (Century Dict.)

1889 Next to Brook Farm, Concord was the chief resort of the disciples of *the Newness.*—*Century Mag.,* xxxix, 129.

Newspaper man. A newspaper correspondent.

1870 A gentleman asks what I mean by a *newspaper man* in this connection. I answer that I mean a man who hangs about this city, and makes a precarious living by writing lies home to some newspaper.—Mr. B. F. Butler of Mass., U. S. Senate, Feb. 23: *C. G.,* p. 1527/2.

Newspaper train. One that takes the newspapers from the place of publication to the place of distribution.

1897 If I am correctly informed, that train is essentially a *newspaper train*. . . . . It does not take passengers, but takes the New York morning papers, so that they may be delivered early [in Washington.]—Mr. John Simpkins of Mass., H. R., Feb. 12: *C. R.*, p. 1770/1.

Newspaporial. A newspaper item. Also used adjectivally.

1787 English *Newspaporials.*—*Mass. Centinel*, July 18, p. 4/1. (N. E. D.)

1794 *Newspaporial* rule of three.—*Columbian Centinel* (Boston) May 14, p. 2/4. (N. E. D.)

1853 In this day of *newspaporial* dearth, anything above the mud level will create a sensation.—A. E. Lee, "Hist. of Columbus" [Ohio], (1892), I, 474. (N. E. D.)

N. G. No good. [1840.]

1898 The gentleman from Indiana amused the House . . . by reading the following memorandum:— "John F. Atkinson, discharged July 1, 1894. *N. G.*: lives in Indiana."—Mr. J. G. Maguire of Calif., H. R., Jan. 11: *C. R.*, p. 37/2, App.

Nicholites. See quotation.

1804 At night I lodged with one of the *Nicholites*, a kind of Quakers who do not feel free to wear colored clothes.—Lorenzo Dow, "Journal" (1850) I, 86/1.

Nickel. A five-cent piece. Formerly a one-cent piece. See N. E. D.

1883 Even *nickels* cannot be had without labor.—*Century Mag.*, p. 83/2. (N. E. D.)

1890 I can't go through Yale on nothing but a fifty-dollar note and two *nickels.*—A. C. Gunter, "Miss Nobody," ch. i. (N. E. D.)

1896 We are not asking for an appropriation and do not intend to ask for a *nickle* from this Government.—Mr. W. H. Doolittle of Wash., H. R., June 10: *C. R.*, p. 6407/1.

1898 When men are out of employment, and *nickels* are scarce, they walk rather than ride.—Mr. M. E. Olmsted of Pa., H. R., Feb. 7: *Id.*, p. 1507/1.

Nifty. Careful in dress and appearance. Slang.

Nigger. A negro. [1796-1862.]

1630 In most of those Provinces are many rich mines, but the *Negars* opposed the Portugalls for working in them.—Capt. John Smith, "True Travels," I, 49. (Century Dict.)

1863 [This] is the result of having had the command of negroes, or, to use the language of [Mr. Wickliffe], "*niggers,*"—a word I never use, because, in the first place, it is vulgar, and in the second place, the Secretary of State]Mr. Seward] is reported to have said that no one will ever be President who says "*nigger.*"—Mr. Owen Lovejoy of Ill., H. R., Jan. 29: *C. G.*, p. 603/2.

1863 [To make the negro effective in the army], surely you will not commence by placing the hateful badge "*nigger*" on his hatband.—Mr. Garrett Davis of Ky., U. S. Senate, Jan. 31: *Id.*, p. 655/2.

1864 It perhaps will be said, "Suppose somebody comes and claims this man as a chattel from the military officer?" The answer is obvious. He has a right to say, "I cannot tell whether this is your chattel or no"; or, as somebody put it, "I cannot tell whether you own the *nigger* or the *nigger* owns you."—Mr. Edgar Cowan of Pa., U. S. Senate, Feb. 13: *Id.*, p. 642/1.

1864 [Mr. Lincoln] was bringing the nation into contempt. A negro was to be *nigger* no longer, but an "American citizen of African descent." —Mr. Dumont of Ind., H. R., March 12: *Id.*, p. 1072/3.

1865 The Republican party of the present day—I mean no personal offence— has nothing except "*nigger* on the brain."—Mr. Willard Saulsbury of Del., U. S. Senate, Feb. 17: *Id.*, p. 858/3.

Nigger in the woodpile. A mode of accounting for the disappearance of fuel; an unsolved mystery; a hidden motive; in politics usually a provision for, or an intention to secure, special privilege. [1862.]

1864 He suspected, when this bill was introduced, that there was a *"nigger"* in it, and upon investigation he has found him.—Mr. Julian of Ind., May 12: *Id.,* p. 2250/1.

1876 I do not know how I would feel if someone should say . . . that there was some *"nigger in the wood-pile,"* some "cat in the bag," some motive to actuate me.—Mr. John Sherman of O., U. S. Senate, Aug. 4: *C. R.,* p. 5153/1.

1879 There is *a gigantic African* here [in the National Aquarium Bill.] . . . [Sandy Hook] is a splendid place for an Aquarium Company to put a shark in a tub, and to build a $500,000 hotel. . . . I want *the African* taken out of the bill.—Mr. Hawley of Conn., H. R., June 11: *Id.,* p. 1931/1.

1888 He accused me [in the *N. Y. Herald*] of deceiving the Senate. The article was headed *"A nigger in the wood pile,"* etc.—Mr. W. M. Stewart of Nev., U. S. Senate, Aug. 27: *Id.,* p. 7968/1.

1890 Just let it be understood that there is a negro in the case, *"a nigger in the woodpile,"* and each one of these gentlemen . . . bites and snaps at everything that has not the impress of the African on it.—Mr. C. T. O'Ferrall of Va., H. R., Apr. 11: *Id.,* p. 3304/2.

1892 It is indeed difficult to know *just how many Africans are hid away in this wood pile.* (The bill with reference to public printing.)—Mr. J. J. O'Neill of Mo., H. R., Jan. 19: *Id.,* p. 431/1.

1894 If the general were to look around, he would find a large-sized *colored man in his wood-pile.*—Mr. M. D. Harter of O., H. R., June 20: *Id.,* p. 6604/2.

1894 With all these facts before them, the Senate never would have voted to put a differential duty upon refined sugar . . . if there had not been *a colored gentleman in the wood pile.*—Mr. S. E. Payne of N. Y., H. R., Aug. 13: *Id.,* p. 1202/2, App.

1897 [This] reminds me of the old story of the negro who was charged with stealing wood. Some friend of his said, "Why, no, he would not steal wood; but when he sees a wood pile in the night, it is his wood pile."—Mr. W. H. Moody of Mass., H. R., Feb. 18: *Id.,* p. 1978/1.

1897 Like a great many others ignorant of facts, [Mr. Moody] finds *"a nigger in the wood pile"* where there is neither wood pile nor nigger.—Mr. N. T. Hopkins of Ky., H. R., Feb. 18: *Id.,* p. 61/1, App.

1899 The cat is out of the bag; the rat has escaped from the meal tub; *the Senegambian protrudes his head from the woodpile;* the milk in the cocoanut has been discovered.—Mr. Champ Clark of Mo., H. R., Jan. 30: *Id.,* p. 152/2, App.

Nigger-knocker. See quotation.

a. 1860 Another name for the *nigger-knocker* is hog-fish, and it is by far the ugliest tenant of the Virginia waters. Cat-fish are sweet and pretty compared to *nigger-knockers.*—G. W. Bagby, "Writings," I, 258. (1884.)

Night-riders. Lawless persons infesting some of the Middle States. [1909.]

1879 There was much said by [Mr. Conkling] of Ku Klux, white leagues, and *night-riders.* . . . There are no Ku Klux, there are no white leagues, there are no *night-riders* in the State of Louisiana.—Mr. Jonas of La., U. S. Senate, May 20: *C. R.,* p. 1480/1.

Nights. For *at nights.* [1786.]

1879 Supposing he could by traveling *nights,* and stealing food rather than begging, run the gauntlet &c.—Mr. E. H. Gillette of Ia., H. R., Apr. 23: *C. R.,* p. 795/1.

Nightstick. A club carried by a policeman at night.
1905 San Juan Hill and the Gut were under *nightstick* law until early this morning.—*N. Y. Times*, July 15. (Century Dict.)
Nimshi. In Eastern Massachusetts, a thorough blockhead; in Connecticut a foolish fellow. [1853.]
Nine-holes, in the. In straits or extremities.
1863 He owned [the slave] till he got *in the nineholes* one day, and sold har to the Gin'ral.—Edmund Kirke, "My Southern Friends," p. 76. (N. Y.)
1877 Mr. Conger:—Availing ourselves of our rights under the rules, we have put the gentleman in the *"nine-holes"*; and there we intend to keep him. Mr. Ewing:—I wish to say that the gentleman from Michigan put this bill in the *"nine-holes"* before one word was said about amendments. Mr. Willis:—I understand that this bill is now in the *"nine-holes,"* where I conscientiously believe it ought to be.—H. R., Nov. 3: *C. R.,* pp. 230-231.
1879 All committees have to report in the morning hour; and there is only one hour. It has been called *the "nine holes."*—Mr. Roger Q. Mills of Tex., H. R., June 25: *Id.,* p. 2330/2.
1910 I have been working all the Session for this bill. It has passed the Senate, and, to use a Western expression, it will put me "in the *nine hole"* if I do not get it through.—Mr. J. L. Wilson of Wash., H. R., June 12: *Id.,* p. 6002/1.
Nip and tuck. A neck-and-neck race. [1833-1888.]
1872 It will be seen that in the great [women's rights] race thus far the English and American marms are about *"nip and tuck,"* and the track ahead clearing for both.—Mr. S. Archer of Md., H. R., May 30: *Id.,* p. 632/3, App.
1886 To continue that policy is merely *nip and tuck* between the engineers and the tide—*nip* with the engineers and *tuck* with the tide.—Mr. J. G. Skinner of N. C., H. R., Apr. 20: *C. R.,* p. 3654/1.
Nippe. Among the voyageurs of the Northwest, a square piece cut from an old blanket, and used especially to protect the feet when snow shoes are worn, being wrapped in several thicknesses around the foot before the moccasin is put on. (Century Dict.)
Nixes. Postal matter which cannot be forwarded, because not properly addressed. (Century Dict.)
Nixie. Underpaid; receiving next to nothing.
1901 These poor *"nixie"* clerks in the post offices of this country.—Mr. W. A. Smith of Mich., H. R., Jan. 17: *C. R.,* pp. 1145/6.
No how. Not at all. [1833-1854.]
1845 See SHAW.
No man's land. This term was applied to a tract of land adjoining the Territory of Oklahoma. See **Cimarron.**
1890 Mr. Vest:—*No Man's Land* is not a portion of the Indian Territory; it is public land of the U. S. . . . *No Man's Land* today and the Yellowstone National Park stand alike, as dockyards, arsenals, and forts, where men can be punished . . . for the crimes that are provided for in the statutes of the United States, but where . . . the civil rights of property can not be protected. . . . *No Man's Land* being no portion of any State or of any Territory, the people there are absolutely without protection as to their civil rights. Mr. Plumb:—I say the condition of things existing in *No Man's Land* today is a scandal.—U. S. Senate, Feb. 13: *C. R.,* p. 1272.
1896 From the Sabine to the Rio Grande, and from *No Man's Land* to the Gulf of Mexico, [the late Wm. H. Crain] was known to all.—Mr. R. Q. Mills of Tex., U. S. Senate, May 16: *Id.,* p. 5338/2.
Non-concur. To defeat by not concurring. [1703-1820]

1862 I hope the House will *non-concur* in that amendment of the Senate.—
Mr. Henry L. Dawes of Mass., H. R., July 9: *C. G.*, p. 3214/1.

1862 I move that the amendments of the Senate be *non-concurred* in.—Mr.
W. S. Holman of Ind., H. R., July 9: *C. G.*, p. 3214/1.

1869 Now after we have concurred in a resolution, cannot we *non-concur*
and rescind it? And did we not *non-concur* and rescind that concurrent resolution when we voted that the vote of Georgia should not
be counted?—Mr. B. F. Butler of Mass., H. R., Feb. 10: *Id.*,
p. 1066/1.

None. Not any; not at all. See **Any.**

1769 [At dinner] I could eat *none*, nor speak a word.—Fanny Burney's
Diary, Jan. 7: I, 37. (1889.)

1879 I remember making . . . the first speech on the subject of admitting
Kansas, twenty-two years ago. Have we progressed *none* since that
time?—Mr. S. S. Cox of N. Y., H. R., Apr. 5: *C. R.*, p. 262/2.

None in mine. This phrase, originally meaning "no water (sometimes
no sugar) in my whisky," came to be applied by way of allusion.
Slang. "None of that for me."

1879 This is the entertainment [*i. e.*, the introduction of troops to keep
peace at the polls] to which we are invited. *"None in mine."*—Mr.
Eaton of Conn., U. S. Senate, May 16: *C. R.*, p. 1383/1.

1896 That is a sort of civil service that says "turkey" to every Democrat
and "buzzard" to every Republican. I want *no buzzard in mine.*—
Mr. H. R. Gibson of Tenn., H. R., Dec. 22: *Id.*, p. 409/2.

None too. *None* is here used for *not at all.*

1868 We have *none too many* friends in the South now. There are *none
too many* there who are willing, honestly and fairly, to accept the
situation—Mr. James A. Garfield of O., H. R., March 17: *C. G.*,
p. 1933/2.

1885 Their merits are *none too liberally* recognized.—*Law Times*, LXXIX,
169/2. (N. E. D.)

Noon-house. See quotation.

1892 There might have been seen a hundred years ago, by the side of many
an old meeting-house in New England, a long, low, mean, stable-like
building, with a rough stone chimney at one end. This was the
"noon-house," or "Sabbaday-house" or "horse-hows." . . . It was a
place of refuge in the winter time, at the noon interval between the
two services, for the half-frozen members of the pious congregation.
. . . They built in the rude stone fireplace a great fire of logs, and
in front of the blazing wood ate their noonday meal.—Alice M. Earle,
"Sabbath in Puritan N. Engd.," ch. ix. (Century Dict.)

No place, no time, no way. Not a suitable place, time, or way.

1862 This is *no time* to pass a resolution of this kind.—Mr. Daniel Clark
of N. H., U. S. Senate, July 17: *C. G.*, p. 3402/1.

1862 Cutting down pay is *no way* to maintain the Federal Treasury pending this war.—Mr. Henry Wilson of Mass., U. S. Senate, March 12:
C. G., p. 1190/1.

1865 See SWAP, Feb. 20.

1868 While there may have been abuse and carelessness, this is *no way* to
reach it.—Mr. W. P. Fessenden of Me., U. S. Senate, July 17: *Id.*,
p. 4152/2-3.

1872 I came to the conclusion that Utah was *no place* for me to stay.—
Mr. W. H. Clagett of Mont., H. R., Apr. 18: *C. G.*, p. 2545/2.

1882 Members "log-roll" in order to get their bills through. This is
no way to do business.—Mr. S. H. Miller of Pa., H. R., July 14:
C. R., p. 6064/1.

1885 It is *no time* for us . . . to be reducing this consular and diplomatic
appropriation.—Mr. Jonathan Chace of R. I., H. R., Jan. 10: *C. R.*
pp. 615-16.

1909   A boarding house is *no place* for a child.—Anna Fuller in the *Atl. Monthly*, p. 647/1. (Nov.)

Norther. A violent north wind. [1844-1888.]

1848   We succeeded . . . in reaching the point of attack in the midst of frightful *northers.*—Letter of Gen. Winfield Scott to Secretary W. L. Marcy, Feb. 24, p. 2/1.

1880   In a portion of Mexico, even in midsummer, the fierce *"norther"* sweeps down from the snow-clad mountains on its northern boundary, as cold as if it had been freshly born in the Arctic regions.—Mr. J. W. Caldwell of Ky., H. R., May 7: *C. R.*, p. 3135/1.

1883   A *norther* comes along; these cattle are feeding on the grass in the same great range, but by the *norther* they are scattered and get mixed.—Mr. S. B. Maxey of Tex., U. S. Senate, Jan. 29: *Id.*, p. 1703/2.

Northerner. One who lives north of Mason and Dixon's line. [1840.]

1865   The southerner is infatuated, who would fight for [slavery], especially with negro soldiers, and the *northerner* is crazy who would make a point (beyond the suppression of the rebellion) of fighting against slavery, especially at the price of the blood of white men.— Mr. Geo. H. Yeaman of Ky., H. R., Jan. 9: *C. G.*, p. 171/3.

No sir, no sir-ree. An emphatic negative. (Accent on the last syllable in each case.) [1847-1861.]

1900   Mr. Bartholdt:—Is it not a fact that the Election law . . . was passed by a Republican house in Missouri?—Mr. M. E. Benton:—*No, sir-ee, bob.* Mr. Bart.:—I know it is a fact.—H. R., Feb. 14: *C. R.*, p. 1801/1.

Note-shaving. Discounting bills. See Vol. II, **Note-shaver.** [1810-1856.]

1862   A man who . . . is pressed for money wants something as a circulating medium, and he must go into a *"shaving"* shop and have his certificates of indebtedness shaved.—Mr. Samuel Hooper of Mass., H. R., June 23: *C. G.*, p. 2884/1.

Not in it. Not in the "swim" or tide of success.

1892   See NECK, GET IT IN THE.

Notions. Ideas, inventions, contrivances; then miscellaneous articles carried round for sale. [1788-1894.]

1815   See LONG SAUCE.

1843   We have Two Thousand Wooden Clocks on board! These *"notions"* are of Massachusetts fabrication.—Thurlow Weed, "Letters," p. 7. (1866.)

1849   I will show you Boston *notions* of every kind, from pumpkins and smoked herrings down to wooden nutmegs.—Wilmington (N. C.) *Commercial*, Dec. 20, p. 1/5. (From Noah's *Sunday Times.*)

No two ways about it. No room for difference of opinion; no alternative. [1590-1861.]

1596   There is *no way* with thee but death.—Thos. Lodge, "A Margarite of America," D4.

No use for. To have no use for a man is to reckon him as a worthless man, or as an opponent.

1873   Go where you will in the South now, and you will find that if an individual of any distinction as a secessionist . . . comes forward as a candidate for office, all others are ignored. . . . They have *no use for* a Union Man—Mr. J. W. Flanagan of Tex., U. S. Senate, Feb. 27: *C. G.*, p. 1888/1.

Nub. The point or gist of a matter.

1859   The *nub* of a story is the point or gist of it. (Bartlett.)

1888   That was not the *nub* of the arrangement.—Mr. W. P. Frye of Me., U. S. Senate, May 29: *C. R.*, p. 4698/1.

1888 Let some one answer this question, and then he will have "touched the *nub*" of this issue.—Mr. Thomas Wilson of Minn., H. R., June 1: *Id.*, p. 4834/1.

1899 It's the *nub* of the whole matter.—*Scribner's Mag.*, XXV, 105/2. (N. E. D.)

Nubbin. An imperfect or spoiled ear of corn. [1850-1897.]

1867 It is a spectacle of great significance and moral sublimity, as you pass by a New England farm of a winter evening, to see the devoted husband with his head against the sides of old Brindle, squeezing the foaming milk into the pail, while his flaxen-haired first-born stands in front feeding her with "*nubbins.*"—Mr. T. E. Noell of Mo., H. R., Feb. 18: *C. G.*, p. 115/2, App.

1877 What can be expected from a body of political Jeremy Diddlers . . . who know not a full ear from a *nubbin*?—Mr. S. S. Cox of N. Y., H. R., Nov. 19: *C. R.*, p. 534/1.

1890 I presume that a Kentucky Democrat, if he had no other fuel, would go and look at a little pile of "*nubbins,*" and, while contemplating how much whisky he could get out of it, he would allow his family to freeze to death.—Mr. H. Kelley of Kan., H. R., May 12: *Id.*, p. 4590/1.

Nullification. The assertion of precedence of State rights over Federal laws. [1799-1839.]

1860 It is the same principle which first appeared in the celebrated resolutions of 1798, which was revived under the name of *nullification* by John C. Calhoun in 1830, and culminated in secession in 1861.— Mr. Thomas N. Stilwell of Ind., H. R., Feb. 5: *C. G.*, p. 669/2.

1869 Mr. Calhoun became ambitious; he became a *nullifier*; and we have thought that his sin of *nullification* tainted his whole politics in after life.—Mr. Garrett Davis of Ky., U. S. Senate, Mar. 18: *Id.*, p. 136/2.

1870 The doctrine of *nullification* was that, in case Congress passed an act the constitutionality of which was denied, although it had been maturely considered by Congress, and declared constitutional by the Supreme Court of the U. S., nevertheless a State which considered the act unconstitutional, might declare it void, and forbid and prevent its execution in such State.—Mr. Matt. Carpenter of Wisc., U. S. Senate, Feb. 16: *Id.*, p. 1323/2.

Nullifier. A State rights man. See Vol. II, **Nullification.** [1799-1839.]

1831 Is it possible that Mr. Calhoun is not only a *nullifier*, but at the head of the *nullifiers*?—*The Georgian* (Savannah), March 21, p. 2/2. (From the *Georgia Journal*.)

Nut-grass. A variety of sedge, so called from its tuberous roots.

1830 (West Indies.) See N. E. D.

1857 Tubers are produced, like those of the *Nut-grass* of the Southern States.—Asa Gray, "First Less. Bot." (1866) p. 43. (N. E. D.)

1860 *Cyperus phymatodes,* "*Nut-grass*" of Fla. *Hydra Cyperus,* "*Nut-grass*" of S. C.—W. Darlington, "Amer. Weeds, &c.," pp. 359-60. (N. E. D.)

1897˙ There is but one way to remove that *nut grass* from the land, and that is to go down and dig it up by the roots.—Mr. Marion Butler of N. C., U. S. Senate, July 6: *C. R.*, p. 2386/2.

Nutmeg State. See **Wooden Nutmegs.**

1894 My friend from the little "*Nutmeg State*" of Connecticut . . . wants protection . . . upon leaf tobacco.—Mr. B. F. Marsh of Ill., H. R., Jan. 15: *C. R.*, p. 824/2.

O

Obligated. Obliged. Under obligations. [1668-1857.]

1868 The company will be *obligated* to build the bridge at its own cost.— Mr. James Harlan of Ia., U. S. Senate, June 18: *C. G.*, p. 3253/1.

1886 A postmaster like Brady might . . . have expended the whole appropriation in half a year, and *obligated* the Government for as much more.—Mr. A. J. Warner of O., H. R., March 30: *C. R.*, p. 2934/1.

1897 If there is anything in the doctrine of obligation, the Republican party is *obligated* to this beet-sugar industry to assist it.—Mr. W. V. Allen of Nebr., U. S. Senate, July 6: *Id.*, p. 2393/1.

Ocala platform, the. A political credo adopted at Ocala.

1892 See MOSSBACK.

1897 Mr. B. McMillin of Tenn. styled Mr. Simpson of Kansas "the great apostle of the *Ocala platform.*"—H. R., March 26: *C. R.*, p. 357/1.

Occluded. Closed or shut up. See Vol. II, **Occlusion.** [1786-1806.]

1814 All Europe was still *occluded* to British commerce.—John C. Calhoun, H. R., Apr. 6. ["Works" (1856), II, 106.]

Ocean ferries. The trans-Atlantic steamers.

1892 The *ocean ferries* ply unceasingly . . . between this country and Europe.—Mr. A. P. Fitch of N. Y., H. R., Apr. 27: *C. R.*, p. 273/1, App.

Ocean greyhound. A swift ocean steamer.

1887 [These ships] are so swift of foot, as to have already become formidable rivals to the English *greyhounds.*—*Sci. Amer.*, Jan. 1, p. 2/2. (N. E. D.)

1891 An unarmoured cruiser, . . . capable of catching any of the great *ocean greyhounds.*—*Daily Chron.*, March 24. (Farmer.)

1895 [Will Mr. Eckels] sit on the deck of an *ocean greyhound* and believe, etc.—Mr. Jerry Simpson of Kan., H. R., Feb. 5: *C. R.*, p. 197/2, App.

Octopus. A grasping monopoly.

1893 The Electric *Octopus.* . . . Organization of the New England Street Railway Company.—*Boston Journal*, March 25, p. 2/1. (N. E. D.)

1900 At another time it may be proposed to add the disqualification of membership in a trust or an *octopus*, or the attorney of a trust or an *octopus.*—Mr. C. E. Littlefield of Me., H. R., Jan. 23: *C. R.*, p. 1084/1.

1900 New Jersey . . . is now the breeding-ground of trusts and *octopuses.* They are organizing corporations . . . based on air, and almighty thin air at that.—The same, p. 1097/1.

Odds, ask no. To desire no advantage or favor. [1806-1857.]

1890 [If the competition in tin-manufacturing were confined to Wales], this industry in South Dakota would *ask no odds* of Congress or otherwise.—Mr. G. C. Moody of S. Dak., U. S. Senate, Aug. 12: *C. R.*, p. 8455/1.

1894 Give us equitable laws and fair play, and South Dakota *asks no odds* of any State of the Union or any portion of the planet.—Mr. R. F. Pettigrew of S. Dak., U. S. Senate, May 29: *Id.*, p. 5447/1.

Off-color. Dubious; of doubtful propriety.

1907 Two or three things *off color*, as the phrase is here, told with anxious glances . . . to see if [the doors] are fast shut.—W. D. Howells, "Through the Eye of the Needle," p. 69.

Offensive partisanship. Disagreeable, aggressive expression of one's preference as to political party.

1886 Some gentleman on the other side of the House asked if [Mr. Dudley] was an "*offensive partisan.*" That is exactly the picture of "*offensive partisanship*" drawn by the present Democratic Executive [Mr. Cleveland], and drawn always by the Democratic party.—Mr. N. J. Hammond of Ga., H. R., March 2: *C. R.*, p. 1975/2.

1886 [A declaration was] made in a circular of one of the heads of departments, relating to "*offensive partisanship.*" . . . What is an *offensive partisan*? I have no doubt that the administration has had evidences and letters of what constitutes the offense.—Mr. A. H. Colquitt of Ga., U. S. Senate, March 22: *C. R.*, p. 2615/1-2.

Office-hunger. Anxiety to hold office.
1870   Bait is good, and especially for democratic *office-hunger.*—Letter from
Alabama, Oct. 20: *C. R.,* Feb. 27, 1875, p. 1891/1.
Offish. Distant and shy. [1842-1857.]
1882   As a general thing, the organs of the two old parties do not seem
to sympathize heartily with republicanism in Europe. They are rather
"*offish.*"—Mr. W. E. Robinson of N. Y., H. R., Jan. 26: *C. R.,* p.
11/1, App.
Off year. A year in which an election does not occur.
1882   An avalanche has swept over the country, and with it the strongest
condemnation of the practices of [the Republican] party. It is true
this was in the *off year,* and not the Presidential year.—Mr. J. E.
Brown of Ga., U. S. Senate, Dec. 14: *C. R.,* p. 277/2.
Ohioan. A native of Ohio; belonging to Ohio. [1835.]
1870   We always supposed that, if a Kentuckian's horse escaped into Ohio,
the Kentuckian could not take him back without a trial of his right
to property before the courts of Ohio and before a jury of *Ohioans.*—
Mr. Timothy O. Howe of Wisc., U. S. Senate, Apr. 12: *C. G.,*
p. 2614/3.
1876   The Senator from Ohio said the other day that Ohio had never asked
for one solitary dollar . . . for anything within its borders peculiarly
Ohioan.—Mr. Maxey of Tex., U. S. Senate, July 17: *C. R.,* p. 4655/2.
Ohio idea, the. See quotation.
1881   *The Ohio idea* is the absolute equality of all men before the law;
absolute and equal justice to all men by the law; and, in the administration of our State affairs, the administration of the few powers
committed to our State legislature by the Constitution in such wise
that every man may pursue his own avocations and his own scheme
of domestic life according to his tastes and his judgment and his
habits and his education to such extent, without interference by
sumptuary laws, as is consistent with the order of society and the
peace of the community. And in national affairs *the Ohio idea* is the
absolute performance of every act to which the plighted faith of the
nation is given. . . . This the democratic "*Ohio idea.*" It is the ideal
of Ohio democracy.—Mr. Geo. H. Pendleton of O., U. S. Senate,
Apr. 13: *C. R.,* p. 276/2.
Oil belt. A tract of land extending for a long distance, and abounding
in oil wells.
1894   The great *oil belt* in this country, commencing in New York, running
through Pennsylvania, West Virginia, Ohio, and Kentucky, has its
beginning in my district.—Mr. W. B. Hooker of N. Y., H. R., Jan.
31: *C. R.,* p. 1743/2.
O. K. Correct; to pronounce correct. Attributed to Andrew Jackson
as an abbreviation for "oll korrect." Another explanation is that
these letters represent a common Western mistake for O. R., *i. e.*
Ordered Recorded. [1828-1888.]
1864   He would not consent to come to [Mr. Long's] defense until he had
examined [his speech] carefully, and found it *O. K.*—Mr. Dumont of
Ind., H. R., Apr. 11: *C. G.,* p. 1555/1.
1891   [They] protested that their "occupation would be gone" if those who
were to go into the clerical service of the Government were to be
"*O. K'd*" by any one except the Civil Service Commission.—Mr.
C. H. Grosvenor of O., H. R., Feb. 13: *C. R.,* p. 2635/2.
1896   It was stated that under the old system of spies and informers the
deputy marshal, when he had spied out and worked up a case, would
send word to the prosecuting attorney asking for an "*O. K.,*" whereupon the district attorney, knowing that the prosecution would put
money in his pocket, would "*O. K.*" it, and the prosecution would be
instituted. But we have taken the teeth out of that dragon. Now

there is no inducement on [the part of] the district attorney to "*O. K.*" the prosecution, and none on the part of the marshal to father it.— Mr. C. G. Burton of Mo., H. R., March 5: *Id.*, p. 2507/1.

1896 [He] says he has helped try these cases, and knows they are *O. K.* —Mr. H. M. Baker of N. H., H. R., May 27: *Id.*, p. 5806/1.

[1898 Andrew Jackson spelled "God" with a small "g," and "Europe" "Urope"; but he was a great general, an incorruptible judge, and a capable President. He always believed the earth was flat instead of round, and insisted that the proper pronunciation of "development" was "devil-ope-ment," but he had great ruling qualities nevertheless.— Mr. W. P. Brownlow of Tenn., H. R., Jan. 11: *C. R.*, p. 29/2, App.]

Okra. See quotation.

1890 We also received small quantities of *okra*, a plant peculiar to the South, whose pods contained a mucilaginous matter that made a soup very grateful to those suffering from scurvy.—Statement of John McElroy, *C. R.*, Apr. 21: p. 3636/2.

Old Abe. Abraham Lincoln. [1860-1862.]

1864 It reminded me, as *old Abe* would say, of an anecdote.—Mr. Dumont of Ind., H. R., Apr. 11: *C. R.*, p. 1555/3.

1865 See Vol. II, Appendix XLII.

1880 Mr. Lincoln had performed professional services for a railroad company, and rendered his bill at $500. This the company refused to pay and he was compelled to bring suit, in which he recovered $5,000, and the money was paid. Thereupon Mr. Lincoln deducted his original bill as rendered, $500, and all expenses in the litigation, which left a balance of some $3,000 in favor of the company, which with his compliments he returned. In such ways he acquired the affectionate appellation of "*Honest Old Abe.*"—Mr. Matt. Carpenter of Wisc., U. S. Senate, Apr. 19: *C. R.*, p. 2516/2.

Old Boy, The. The devil. [1802-1858.]

1815 Perfectly at home! entirely at his ease! yet cunning (as he would say) as *the old Boy.*—David Humphries, "The Yankey in England," pp. 28, 29.

1815 For all your giggling and snickering, I know it was the *Old Boy.*— *Id.*, p. 79.

1878 My friend from Maine [Mr. Jas. G. Blaine] said that he was a boy in 1845. I doubt it. I doubt whether he ever was a boy in any political sense of the word. If he was, certainly in politics he is *the old boy* now.—Mr. W. P. Whyte of Md., U. S. Senate, Dec. 17: *C. R.*, p. 239/1.

Old Bullion. A nickname given to Thomas H. Benton of Missouri (1782-1858), who vigorously opposed a paper currency. [1876-1886.]

1850 *Old Bullion* [in a caricature] looks like an enraged Buffaloe Bull, tearing his hide open in front, daring a Camanche to fix an arrow deep in his panting breast.—Wilmington (N. C.) *Commercial*, May 30, p. 2/2.

1859 "*Old Bullion*" once said, "[Stephen A.] Douglas can never be President, sir! His coat tail is too near the ground, sir!—too near the ground, sir!"—*New York Herald*, Sept. 18, p. 5/2.

1878 Here is the argument of Mr. Thomas H. Benton, who was considered the father of the hard-money doctrine, and called "*Old Bullion.*"— Mr. John M. Bright of Tenn., H. R., Jan. 26: *C. R.*, p. 584/2.

1893 The gentleman lauds Thomas H. Benton, . . . and prays for some other man to rise up in the Mississippi Valley and make himself great by imitating the heroic example of "*Old Bullion.*"—Mr. Champ Clark of Mo., H. R., Aug. 19: *Id.*, p. 529/2.

1897 "*Old Bullion*" from Missouri, Thos. H. Benton, in season and out,

persistently advocated . . . the construction of a Pacific railroad.—
Mr. G. L. Johnson of Calif., H. R., Jan. 9: *Id.*, p. 22/1, App.

Old Dominion. Virginia. [1699-1861.]

1863   I do not believe that the *Old Dominion*, like a polypus, can be sepa-
rated into different segments, and each segment become a living,
constitutional organism.—Mr. Garrett Davis of Ky., U. S. Senate,
Dec. 15, objecting to the admission of senators from West Virginia:
C. G., p. 1/3.

1865   There are now standing upon the soil of the *Old Dominion* half a
million of armed men, testing the question whether that old commonwealth shall belong to the United States or [not.]—Mr. Jacob M.
Howard of Mich., U. S. Senate, Feb. 17: *Id.*, p. 847/2.

Old Glory. A term sometimes applied to the United States flag.

1893   *"Old Glory"* hauled down—Stars and Stripes no longer float over the
Hawaiians.—Headline, *Wash. Post*, Apr. 14.

1893   The flag was torn down,—*"Old Glory* desecrated," as some of the
press of the Provisional Government [in Hawaii] denominate it.—
Mr. G. G. Vest of Mo., U. S. Senate, Dec. 13: *C. R.*, p. 196/1.

1896   The chivalry and comradeship which inheres in every soldier, whether
he marched under *"Old Glory"* or the Stars and Bars.—Mr. W. S.
Kerr of O., H. R., Apr. 25: *Id.*, p. 4433/1.

1897   [After the first battle of Bull Run] the rebel flag could be seen from
the dome of the nation's Capitol, waving in defiance of *Old Glory.*—
Mr. G. L. Johnson of Calif., H. R., Jan. 9: *Id.*, p. 23/1, App.

1913   Side by side with *"Old Glory,"* the soldiers with Lee and Longstreet,
and the soldiers with Meade and Grant are marching together in
peace and good will at Gettysburg's semi-centennial.—*Living Church*,
July 5, p. 362/2.

Old Hickory. Andrew Jackson. [1813-1858.]

1867   I will refer to what tradition says occurred when Andrew Jackson
proposed to remove the deposits. Consulting with his Attorney General, he found that some doubts were entertained by that official as
to the existence of any law authorizing the Executive to do that act;
whereupon *Old Hickory* said to him, "Sir, you must find a law authorizing the act, or I will appoint an Attorney General who will."—Mr.
Geo. H. Williams of O., U. S. Senate, Jan. 14: *C. G.*, p. 439/2.

1882   When you undertook to nullify the laws, because they did not suit
you, you were taught better by a man who was an old-fashioned
Democrat—*"Old Hickory."* He told you that "by the Eternal" you
would obey the law, and for a little while you kept quiet.—Mr. R. G.
Horr of Mich., H. R., June 2: *C. R.*, p. 4485/1.

1896   The first veto of a river and harbor bill was made by Andrew
Jackson. . . . *Old Hickory* himself, on December 6, 1832, sent that
veto to the H. of R.—Mr. A. M. Dockery of Mo., H. R., July 10:
Id., p. 6432/2.

Old Hutch. Mr. Hutchinson of Chicago, a well-known speculator in
grain.

1890   See WHEAT PIT.

1892   Let us [assume] that *"Old Hutch"* had determined to place corn and
wheat on a parity of price. . . . As long as Mr. Hutchinson can back
up his proposition, it is perfectly plain he can control the price of
corn up to the wheat price.—Mr. T. L. Bunting of N. Y., H. R.,
March 23: *C. R.*, p. 2480/2.

Old Ironsides. See quotation.

1890   Like the famous frigate Constitution, [Admiral Charles] Stewart
received the appellation of *"Old Ironsides."*—Mr. A. J. Cummings of
N. Y., H. R., May 9: *C. R.*, p. 4383/1. [He was b. 1778, d. 1869,
and was a grandfather of Charles Stewart Parnell.]

Old-line Whig. One of a political party which grew up, in opposition to the Democratic party, out of the National Republican party. It was first called the Whig party in 1834. (Century Dict.) [1856-1860.] See also Vol. II, **Whig.**

1863 Mr. Lincoln is a politician of a past age. He belongs to the *old Whig* party, and will never belong to any other. He is anti-slavery, but of a genial southern type. His emancipation is that of Henry Clay.—Mr. M. F. Conway of Kan., H. R., Jan. 27: *C. G.*, p. 64/3, App.

1864 Even the *old-line Whigs* of the western shore portion of my district have forgotten their instincts.—Mr. Joseph Segar of Va., H. R., May 17: *Id.*, p. 2314/2.

1867 I was an *old Clay Whig* when the Democrats were in power. . . . I was an *old-line Whig* then, and I would be a recreant and a coward if I failed to denounce now enormities greater than those I then denounced.—Mr. W. E. Robinson of N. Y., H. R., July 12: *Id.*, p. 9/2, App.

1870 I was an advocate of Millard Fillmore for the Presidency as an *Old-line Whig*, and only as an *Old-line Whig.*—Mr. James Brooks of N. Y., H. R., May 23: *Id.*, p. 3729/1.

Old man. A term used to indicate the father of a family; or a husband. [1834-1878.]

1862 I sent a few lines to you by *old man* Jesse Price.—Letter of R. R. Butler of Tenn., Jan. 8: *C. G.*, March 4, 1868, p. 1664/1.

Old man Eloquent. John Quincy Adams (1767-1848). [1848-1861.]

1893 See GREAT EXPOUNDER, THE.

Old North State, The. North Carolina.

1849 I come from the *Old North State*, where people can't be bought.—Wilmington (N. C.) *Commercial*, Aug. 25, p. 2/5. (From the Boston *Atlas*.)

1871 Look at the *"Old North State,"* once so proud of her credit and of the conservative character of her people,—her financial standing dishonored, and her bonds a drug in Wall Street.—Mr. Thomas Kinsella of N. Y., H. R., Apr. 1: *C. G.*, p. 400/3.

1876 Once boasting the proud title of "the honest *old North State.*"—Mr. Freeman of N. C., H. R., May 19: *C. R.*, p. 3213/2.

1879 [William Gaston] was the author of that popular song called *"The Old North State,"* which so beautifully and graphically describes the character of the people and the State of North Carolina.—Mr. C. H. Brogden of N. C., H. R., Feb. 4: *Id.*, p. 45/2, App.

1880 See APPLE-JACK.

Old Probabilities. The Superintendent of the Weather Bureau, who is addicted to the word "probable." [1877-1888.]

1874 [It has been said] of a certain politician . . . that he seemed to have a political *"Old Probabilities"* who foretold for him the political atmosphere for the next 24 hours, and he cut his garb and wore his clothes according to that prognostication.—Mr. A. G. Thurman of O., U. S. Senate, Apr. 1: *C. R.*, p. 2679/1.

Old Public Functionary. A term applied to himself by James Buchanan in his message to Congress, 1857, and afterwards frequently used as a nickname for him.

Old Rosy. Gen. W. S. Rosecrans. (1819-1898.)

1884 In those days, if *"Old Rosy,"* as the boys loved to call him, gave us an order to march at once, or to move at one o'clock in the morning, we knew what it meant.—Mr. B. W. Perkins of Kan., H. R., Feb. 1: *C. R.*, p. 823/1.

Old Rough and Ready. Gen. Zachary Taylor. [1846-1849.]

1894 Hon. Richard Taylor, the son of *"Old Rough and Ready,"* and later a valiant general.—Mr. Adolph Meyer of La., H. R., June 2: *C. R.*, p. 5692/1.

Old Sledge. A card game. [1838-1856.]

1837 [This] threw a temporary stigma upon the game of *"old-sledge."*—W. Irving, "Capt Bonneville," I, 181. (N. E. D.)

1888 A fellow in my country was caught once with an extra jack in his sleeve when playing a game of *old sledge*, and in response to the fierce denunciation of his adversary he said, "Bill, you know we were six and six, and it was your deal; I was obliged to do something."—Mr. Z. B. Vance of N. C., U. S. Senate, Aug. 6: *C. R.*, p. 7263/2.

Old Spooney. A derisive nickname of Gen. B. F. Butler.

1871 [The President] has again unsealed . . . his lips, and spoken to Congress in behalf of *old Spooney's* designs upon the southern people.—*Rome Courier* (Ga.), March 25: quoted *C. G.*, May 30, 1872, p. 582/3, App.

Old Ti. Fort Ticonderoga.

1876 [Fort Ticonderoga] was instantly surrendered, and Ethan Allen and *Old Ti* were from that moment immortal.—Mr. Joyce of Vt., H. R., May 18: *C. R.*, p. 3182/2.

Old Tippecanoe. Gen. W. H. Harrison. Also called "Old Tip." [1840-1841.]

1844 The name of "Old Ironsides" would have been in itself a host, equal to that of *"Old Tippecanoe,"* and we cannot but think that the "Virgin Heifer" or the "Mill Boy of the Slashes," or the "boon of Ashland," itself would have faded into nothingness.—*Spirit of the Times*, Phila., Feb. 7.

Old Wythlacoochee. See quotation.

1868 General Duncan L. Clinch, a most gallant officer of the Army in years gone by, one whom we used to call upon this floor and throughout the country *"Old Wythlacoochee."*—Mr. Robert C. Schenck of O., H. R., March 16: *C. G.*, p. 1902/2.

Old Zach. Gen. Zachary Taylor. [1848-1850.]

1848   We've got *Old Zach* upon the track:
        He'll soon put Lewis on his back;
        In Mexico he whipped a nation;
        November next, he'll thrash creation.

—Wilmington (N. C.) *Commercial*, July 22, p. 1/4. (From the Harrisburg *Telegraph*.)

1848   *Old Zack's* the boy for Santa Anna,
          Ampudia or Arista;
        And long 'twill be ere they forget
          The field of Buena Vista;
        Though legions of the foemen swarm
          Against our brave defenders,
        Old Rough and Ready they will find
        The man who ne'er surrenders.

                      —*Id.*, Aug. 17, p. 1/4.

1848   The sov'reign people will it so;
        Old Zack must to the White House go.
        For that high station he was made;
        He never wore the black cockade.

        —*Id.*, Aug. 22, p. 1/4. (From the *N. J. State Gazette*.)

1848 There is no doubt that the blood of *Old Zach* was roused.—*Id.*, Aug. 24, 2/4.

1878 The names of General Scott and General Taylor, *"Old Zack"* and "Old Rough and Ready," as General Taylor was often familiarly called, are embalmed in the Pantheon of history.—Mr. C. H. Brogden of N. C., H. R., Feb. 27: *C. R.*, p. 85/2, App.

Old Zach. This name was also given to Senator Zachariah Chandler of Mich. (1873-1879.)

1880 The name of Zachariah Chandler, or *"Old Zach,"* as he was more commonly called, was familiar in every household.—Mr. Mark S. Brewer of Mich., H. R., Jan. 28: *C. R.,* p. 584/1.

Omnibus bill. One which combines different topics, thereby affording an opportunity for "log-rolling." [1842-1857.] This term was applied to the compromise bill introduced by Henry Clay in 1850.

1862 They produced a great bill which, from its character, for everything was involved in it, was called an *"omnibus bill."*—Mr. John P. Hale of N. H., U. S. Senate, Apr. 30: *C. G.,* p. 1881/2.

1868 [This appropriation bill] may be set down as an *omnibus* that a great many people can ride in.—Mr. Columbus Delano of O., H. R., June 16: *Id.,* p. 3205/2.

On age. In respect of age.

1870 Under the laws of Pa., if he was between 21 and 22 years of age, he had a right to vote *on age.*—Mr. Samuel J. Randall of Pa., H. R., Apr. 13: *C. G.,* p. 2655/2.

One-horse. Small, paltry, inferior. [1854-1890.]

1876 The question is . . . whether he was supplying the confederate army with [salt], or whether it was a little *one-horse* neighborhood affair, where he was making salt for the neighbors.—Mr. G. F. Edmunds of Vt., U. S. Senate, July 17: *C. R.,* p. 4650/1.

1877 I scarcely think that the gentleman from W. Va. [Senator H. G. Davis] would in seriousness get up here and urge the passage of a special bill to improve his little *one-horse* river in W. Va., and give the go-by to a great river like the Columbia.—Mr. John H. Mitchell of Ore., U. S. Senate, March 3: *Id.,* p. 2169/1.

1878 [The clause] means nothing else, and there is not a *one-horse* court in the U. S. anywhere that has ever taken any other view.—Mr. W. W. Eaton of Conn., U. S. Senate, Apr. 9: *Id.,* p. 2368/2.

1892 The one-horse universities and training schools so eager for Indian pupils are really hungering for the share of public money which goes with each Indian for his "support" while a member of the school.—Letter from an ex-Indian-agent, *Id.,* Feb. 22, 1893, p. 2024/1.

One man power. An autocracy. [1842.]

1842 The whole contest between the veto and the assembly . . . is a contest between "the *one-man power"* on both sides.—Mr. W. C. Preston of S. C., U. S. Senate, Apr. (p. 15 of speech as separately published).

1842 Well may Whigery [*sic*] exclaim: . . . O for a fiscal corporation, and utter destruction of the *one-man power*!—Mr. H. W. Beeson of Pa., H. R., July 9, (p. 9/1 of speech as separately published).

1849 We have no fears that this doctrine of the *"one man power"* will be tolerated by the American people.—Wilmington (N. C.) *Commercial,* July 3, p. 2/2.

1869 Andrew Johnson, the man of all others in this country . . . who has attempted to arrogate to himself the *one-man power.*—Mr. John Coburn of Ind., H. R., Dec. 20: *C. G.,* p. 259/1.

1878 If the *one-man power* is to hurl its veto at the heads of the representatives of the people, we can only say, "Let it come."—Mr. J. R. Chalmers of Miss., H. R., Feb. 21: *C. R.,* p. 40/1, App.

1890 There will go up a protest from the people . . . against the *one-man power,* the power of a usurping autocrat.—Mr. C. T. O'Ferrall of Va., H. R., Feb. 3: *Id.,* p. 1028/2.

1890 The plutocrat . . . demands new ways; . . . the ways of *one-man power* aimed to overthrow popular rights.—Mr. J. L. Chipman of Mich., H. R., June 30: *Id.,* p. 6785/1.

1892 I am opposed to *one-man power* on the floor or in the Speaker's chair.—Mr. J. B. McCreary of Ky., H. R., Jan. 27: *Id.,* p. 604/1.

Onion skin. A ballot on thin paper, used for purposes of fraud. The term, as describing a thin kind of paper generally, is in the Cent. Dict.

1879 If my friend takes position behind the literal term *"onion skin"* or "tissue ballots," I do not know whether they were used in Williamsburgh County or not. In fact I do not know just what the onion crop of South Carolina was in 1878, or whether there would have been enough to have gone around; but the term *"onion skin"* or "tissue ballots" has obtained a generic and well-defined meaning synonymous with the "stuffing" of ballot-boxes.—Mr. C. G. Williams of Wisc., H. R., June 23: *C. R.*, p. 120/1, App.

On shares. On a bargain to divide crop or produce. [1838-1857.]

1863 The cry goes up from the hardy miner to "bring us more mills to crush *on shares* the quartz we are digging out."—Mr. H. P. Bennet of Colo., H. R., Feb. 28: *C. G.*, p. 140/1, App.

On time. Punctual, punctually. [1848-1888.]

1905 See RAIL-SICKNESS.

Onto. On the top of; upon; on. (Webster) Also, appended to. [a. 1465-1890.]

1513 *Onto* his grandschir Priamus, the king. Bk. II, p. 95. (*Vntil*, Edition of 1553.)—Douglas, Eneados, ed. Small, 1874. [Many other examples in same work.]

1882 They should not be turned into the woods or *onto* the sands without any money or any provision.—Mr. O. D. Conger of Mich., U. S. Senate, March 20: *C. R.*, p. 2049/1.

1884 The amendment which the Senate voted *onto* the Atlantic and Pacific bill. . . . An amendment *onto* a bill of the character which I had the honor to offer at the last session.—Mr. John J. Morgan of Ala., U. S. Senate, Dec. 11: *Id.*, p. 181/2.

1885 I wish that [Mr. Bayne] could get the soot and the dust out of his eyes, and could climb up *onto* some high peak &c.—Mr. E. J. Ellis of La., H. R., March 3: *Id.*, p. 2539/1.

1886 This appendix does not inject [a stump speech] into the body, but it ties it *onto* the tail of the report.—Mr. A. H. Colquitt of Ga., U. S. Senate, March 22: *Id.*, p. 2619/2.

1888 Up went the waterpots *onto* each shoulder.—Mr. O. H. Platt of Conn., U. S. Senate, Feb. 6: *Id.*, p. 974/2.

1888 See UNLOAD.

1888 [The measure] wriggled its way out of the committee-room and *onto* this floor.—Mr. D. W. Voorhees of Ind., U. S. Senate, Dec. 19: *Id.*, p. 344/1.

1890 Where do [our boys] go? *Onto* another farm? No; by and by one of them gets down into a factory.—Mr. J. R. Hawley of Conn., U. S. Senate, Aug. 19: *Id.*, p. 8812/1.

1893 See SEVEN BY NINE.

1894 See BOILER-PLATE.*

Operative. See quotation.

1905 The word "detective" became so offensive . . . that it was dropped by some successful [detective] agencies. The word chosen by the Pinkertons to take its place was *"operative."* Don't telegraph to Bob to send you a detective; say, "send me an *operative."*—N. Y. Press, Oct. 23. (Century Dict.)

-Or, -our. Variant spellings. Dr. Chapman in his "Sermons" (Hartford, 1836) has *errour, favourite, horrour, inferiour, terrour.* [He was born in England, but emigrated at the age of nine, and received his education in the U. S.]

Order. Condition; "shape."

---

*Subsequent instances in the Congressional debates are numerous.

1743 The ships were all in prime *Order*, all lately rebuilt.—Bulkeley & Cummins, "Voyage," p. 1. (N. E. D.)

1832 The horses were in high *order*, but very wild.—John A. McClung, "Sketches of Western Adventure" (Phila.) p. 27.

1836 The ducks are in the finest *order* during the early part of the summer. —"Backwoods of Canada," p. 162. (N. E. D.)

Order, in short. Very quickly. At once. [1834-1876.]

1856 You'll get your walkin' ticket *on short order.*—"Widow Bedott Papers," No. XXV.

1872 I hope and trust that, whenever an attempt is made by scalawags to interfere with the elections of the people, they will read to them their death-warrant unless they leave the place *in short order.*—Mr. Willard Saulsbury of Del., U. S. Senate, May 14: *C. G.*, p. 3428/2.

Organic law. The Federal Constitution, and the Acts of Congress passed in pursuance to it. [1849-1883.]

1865 It is for Congress to say whether the people shall have an opportunity to change the *organic law* in this respect.—Mr. James G. Blaine of Me., H. R., March 2: *C. G.*, p. 1315/2.

Original package. This phrase has been much used with regard to sales, and is so used in a petition to the House of Commons, a. 1827. (N. E. D.)

1864 Mr. Collamer of Vermont:—"It was very fully decided in the Merriman case that, when goods were imported under an Act of Congress, the man importing the goods and paying the duties had the right to sell . . . those goods in spite of any law the State could make. Mr. Johnson:—In the *original package.* Mr. Collamer:—Well, that is the way negroes are generally sold. I think they are sold in the *original package*, if at all.—U. S. Senate, June 24: *C. G.*, p. 3237/2.

1869 The phrase was discussed in the U. S. Senate in its relation to goods furnished to Indians under treaties, March 31: *Id.*, pp. 393-4.

1890 An attempt was made . . . to introduce liquors [into Me.] in the *original package*, in half pint or pint bottles, I think it was. A man by the name of Burns set up establishments in two or three different cities, paraded his liquors on the shelves and announced that they were for sale, and could be sold under the law in the *original package.*—Mr. W. P. Frye of Me., U. S. Senate, May 9: *C. R.*, p. 4374/2.

1890 What the Supreme Court did decide [in the case of *Leisy* v. *Hardin*] was that the police power of the States did not attach to any article of interstate commerce; that until the *original package* was broken, and its contents mingled with the general property of the citizens of the State, the police power of the State did not attach.—Mr. G. G. Vest of Mo., U. S. Senate, May 20: *Id.*, p. 4957/1.

1890 [This decision of the Supreme Court] applies not only to prohibition, but to the taxing of what you might call *original package saloons.* The decision not only sets up these *original package saloons* in every State of the Union without taxation, . . . but without regulation of any sort. The *original package* men can import their liquor in pint bottles, half-pint bottles, and sell them without a tax and without regulation.—Mr. J. Z. George of Miss., U. S. Senate, May 27: *Id.*, p. 5330/1.

1890 Judge Foster [of Kansas] recently decided that liquor could only be sold in *original packages.*—*Daily News*, June 28, 6/2. (N. E. D.)

1890 See the debate on the *"Original Package Bill,"* H. R., July 19: *C. R.*, pp. 7487-7523.

Ornary. Mean, contemptible. A contraction for *ordinary*, which in this sense is nearly obsolete in England. [1785-1888.]

1911   But he's jest *ornery*. Plum *ornery*. Too *ornery* to do any work fer
himself, an' too *ornery* to hold a job with anybody else. Too *ornery*
to live, an' too *ornery* to die. He's jest pure *orneriness* itself.—*N. Y.
Evening Post*, Dec. 21, p. 6/5.

Orphant. An old form of *Orphan.*
1547-64 and 1632. See N. E. D.
b. 1613   [It] makes poore widdowes mourn, *Orphants* lame [n]t.—Sir John
Harrington, "Epigrams," III, 18. (1618.)
1615   If the Printer had not beene, I would have had [this worke] thrust out
as an *Orphant*, without any name to father it.—Robert Greene,
"Philomela," A 2.
1616   Alas poore widow; alas poore *orphants*! . . . How the vnkle is per-
plexed with thought of the poore *orphants* committed to his trust!—
Godfrey Goodman, "The Fall of Man," pp. 118, 127.
1676   The severell County Courts are answerable for all *orphants* estates.
—Petition from James City County, Virginia: *Journal of House of
Burgesses*, p. 108. (Richmond, 1914.)
1680   James Wilkinson, *Orphant* of James Wilkinson.—*Id.*, p. 124.
1912   Very common in Western Indiana.—*Dialect Notes*, III, 584.

Osage orange. An ornamental American tree closely allied to the mulberry; also its yellow, tubercled, apple-shaped fruit. The *Maclura
aurentiaca.*
1817   It bleeds an acrid milky juice when wounded, and is called by the
hunters the *Osage orange.*—J. Bradbury, "Travels," p. 160 n.
(N. E. D.)
1859   Wheels made of the bois d'arc, or *Osage-orange* wood, are the best.—
Marcy, "Prairie Travels," p. 26. (N. E. D.)
1890   The *osage orange* grows in great luxuriance in Southwest Missouri
and in Texas, and all the country intervening.—Mr. W. H. Wade of
Mo., H. R., June 12: *C. R.*, p. 5993/2.

Outage. This is defined in the Standard Dict. as "the difference
between the cubic extent of a measure of capacity, as a barrel,
and the amount of commodity . . . actually placed in it for transportation." The Century Dict., beside a definition relating to electric arc-lamps, says it is "a charge made by the State of Md. for
the labor of handling tobacco inspected for export." In the following citation it means the loss in bulk through the process of
repeated distilling.
1880   I can see no reason why we should tax the *outage* [on whisky] which
would not apply and require us to tax the *outage* of a bin of wheat
which had been run through a fanning mill by the farmer. You
might as well justify the taxing of tailings, because the remainder of
the wheat was so much better, as justify the tax of wastage because
the residue was of greater or more perfect value.—Mr. Barber, H. R.,
May 1: *C. R.*, p. 2934/2.
1884   The leakage clause of the Carlisle bill of 1880 . . . provided for an
outage of 7½ gallons for each barrel of 40 gallons.—Mr. J. D. White
of Ky., H. R., May 29: *Id.*, p. 4704/1.

Outfit. See quotations. [1869-1887.]
1870   The use of that word "*outfit*" is curiously broad upon the plains. It
means as many things as the Italian "roba" or the French "chose."
. . . It is rather amusing to hear a Durham bull referred to as having
rather a short *outfit* of horns; a mother threatening a refractory
child with the worst *outfit* he ever got in his life; or a stage driver
saying he has a big *outfit* of passengers.—F. W. Ludlow, "The Heart
of the Continent," p. 121.
1871   The Spanish *rancho* means a mess, and so the American herder speaks
of his companions collectively as the ranch or the "*outfit*."—L. Swin-
burne, *Scribner's Mag.*, II, 509.

1894 I am not going to abuse your great and good Cabinet as a whole. I am not going to abuse Grover Cleveland. If I dipped my tongue in gall, I could not say anything half so mean as the Democratic press is saying about the whole *"outfit."*—Mr. J. G. Cannon of Ill., H. R., Apr. 18: *C. R.*, p. 3835/1.

Outland, adv. The opposite of *inland.*

1879 Merchants who trade *outland* and inland.—Mr. S. S. Cox of N. Y., H. R., Apr. 17: *C. R.*, p. 80/2, App.

Outlaw. To bar a claim by lapse of time. [1850.]

1886 The last item of the charge would have been *outlawed* in the July following.—Mr. H. W. Blair of N. H., U. S. Senate, July 23: *C. R.*, p. 7346/2.

1890 [The offence] was *outlawed* now by lapse of time, and he was not afraid of prosecution by telling it.—Testimony of E. D. Morrill: *Id.*, June 3, p. 5547/2.

Outs, at. At variance.

1884 His church and the Unitarians [were] very much *at outs.*—Mr. T. A. Robertson of Ky., H. R., Apr. 23: *C. R.*, p. 3226/1.

Outsider. A person outside the society referred to. This is possibly American. [1833-1855.]

1848 With the *outsiders* of all descriptions, Barnburners, and everybody else with a spark of independent patriotism, the nomination of General Taylor is equally a source of delight.—*N. Y. Mirror,* June 10. (Bartlett.)

1866 If an *outsider,* a stranger, commits a violation of the rules of the House, you would punish him appropriately by fine or by imprisonment.—Mr. Aaron Harding of Ky., H. R., July 21: *C. G.*, p. 4011/1.

Outstart. A starting-point. Possibly American.

1866 To allow the country to be covered with war and desolation for months on account of . . . neglect at the *outstart.*—Mr. Edgar Cowan, of Pa., U. S. Senate, June 6: *C. G.*, p. 2990/2.

1866 Dora Greenwell, "Essays." (N. E. D.)

Overflow meeting, school, &c. One held or established to accommodate those who would otherwise be crowded out.

1880 Hengler's was filled to the brim, . . . and an *"overflow" meeting* was immediately organized at the Drill Shed.—*Daily News,* Feb. 4, p. 3/1. (N. E. D.)

1895 The building was overcrowded with applicants; . . . the number was so great that an *overflow school* was established . . . The *overflow school* was established for [instruction in business.]—Mr. J. H. Kyle of S. Dak., U. S. Senate, Feb. 2: *C. R.*, p. 1677/2.

Overly. Excessively; too. [1827-1878.]

1839 I never was *overly* ambitious.—Moris' "Mansie Wauch," ch. xxv.

1874 I have not been worried much under the prepayment of postage on public documents. I am not *overly* fond of that kind of enjoyment.— Mr. R. J. Oglesby of Ill., U. S. Senate, June 17: *C. R.*, p. 5091/1.

Over one's name or signature. An article or statement for which the author takes responsibility. [1806-1908.]

1803 We perceive the editor of the Evening Post is solicitous to correct an absurd mode of expression which has lately crept into considerable use,—it is that of the word *over* in place of *under.* It is said of an essayist, that he has written *over* such a signature. In this attempt we cordially join.—*Georgia Republican,* Dec. 16, p. 2/3.

1827 [June 5.] I always intended, should Mr. Clay come out *over his own name* and deny having any knowledge of the communication . . . that I would give him the name of the gentleman through whom that communication came.—Letter of Andrew Jackson to Carter Beverley. (B. M., 8177, g. 78.)

1837 A writer in the *Globe* over the signature of "Yeoman."—Raleigh (N. C.) *Standard*, Aug. 9, p. 2/2.

1850 A card *over the signature* of T. Ruffin, Jr. [and others.]—Wilmington (N.C.) *Commercial*, Aug. 29, p. 4/1. (From the Raleigh *Register.*)

1866 There are letters written *over assumed names*, involving an examination of the handwriting for the purpose of ascertaining the authors of them.—Mr. Geo. S. Boutwell of Mass., H. R., July 21: *C. G.*, 4018/3.

1866 The celebrated controversy between Mr. Madison and Mr. Hamilton in relation to the proclamation of neutrality, in letters written *over the signatures* of "Pacificus" and "Helvetius."—Mr. Reverdy Johnson of Md., U. S. Senate, May 1: *C. G.*, p. 2310/1.

1869 Mr. Conkling:—I beg to suggest to the Senator to change the phraseology, "*over his own signature.*" Mr. Hamlin:—"Under" is the proper word. Mr. Conkling.—"Under" would be better.—U. S. Senate, July 1: *Id.*, p. 410/2.

1881 [A certain newspaper writer said] that until Mr. Buchanan came out *over his own signature* and declared that there had not been any fight in the Cabinet, he would never [retract his statement that a fight had occurred].—Mr. H. L. Dawes of Mass., U. S. Senate, May 2: *C. R.*, p. 435/1.

1883 This is what Fitz-John Porter said *over his own signature.*—Mr. John A. Logan of Ill., U. S. Senate, Jan. 2: *Id.*, p. 732/2.

1914 We have received the following letter *over the signatures* of Lord Lichfield, Mr. Frank Morris, &c.—*The Times*, Nov. 21, p. 10/6.

Owl-line, owl-train. One running very late at night.

1866 He is expected to take the *owl-line*, the midnight line, as it passes his house.—Mr. John P. Stockton of N. J., March 26: *C. G.*, p. 1641/2.

1882 The Third avenue line runs its trains all night. . . . These are the *owl-trains.*—James D. McCabe, "New York," p. 190. (Farmer.)

Ox-work. Routine work.

1868 I do not see why we cannot . . . go forward with the regular *ox-work* (if I may be permitted to use a country term) of legislation.—Mr. Geo. F. Edmunds of Vt., U. S. Senate, May 16: *C. G.*, p. 2490/1.

P

Pacificator. One who pacifies; peacemaker. (Webster.)

1857 The friends of Mr. Clay believed that the title of *pacificator*, which he was to earn, would win for him a return of the glory of the Missouri Compromise.—T. H. Benton, "Thirty Years' View," I, 346.

Pacific Slope, the. A general term for the territory in the United States west of the Continental Divide.

1870 From Chicago, in Illinois, to the Sierra Nevada on *the Pacific slope*, there is not timber enough to house the human beings now there.— Mr. James Brooks of N. Y., H. R., March 3: *C. G.*, p. 162/2, App.

1870 The gentlemen from *the Pacific slope*,—I believe they are proud of calling it a "slope" although I do not know why they should; I do not think there is much more of a slope there than anywhere else (Laughter.)—have their prejudices in regard to those people from China.—Mr. Simon Cameron of Pa., U. S. Senate, July 9: *Id.*, p. 5390/1.

1882 I was on the *Pacific slope*, far away from these scenes of happiness which my fellow-members on the Eastern shore were permitted to enjoy.—Mr. W. M. Springer of Ill., H. R., June 6: *C. R.*, p. 4590/2.

1892 A vast number of Chinese [came] for the purpose of being engaged in opening up the *Pacific Slope*, in railway works, &c.—Mr. J. T. Morgan of Ala., U. S. Senate, Apr. 23: *Id.*, p. 3562/2.

1892   There has been no tremendous increase of Asiatics upon the *Pacific Slope.*—Mr. G. G. Vest of Mo., U. S. Senate, Apr. 25: *Id.*, p. 3626/2.

Pack.   To carry, to convey. [1844-1896.]

1832   Smith was loaded with a large piece of buffalo, which, after *packing* two or three miles, he found too heavy for him.—John A. McClung, "Sketches of Western Adventure" (Phila.), p. 26.

1867   Their only chance for fuel is to go out in the inclement weather and dig mesquite roots out of the ground and *pack* them in on their backs. —Mr. Lewis H. Ross of Ill., H. R., Jan. 31: *C. G.*, p. 895/3.

1868   [These Navajo Indians] have to *pack* wood upon their backs, and carry it for ten miles.—Mr. Conners of Calif., U. S. Senate, March 20: *Id.*, p. 2012/1.

1882   See BUCK.

Padding.   Ballot-box stuffing.

1898   When *padding* is done, where is it done? Why it is done at the end of the poll list. *Padding* is always done toward the close of the poll. The names that are added are the *padded* names.—Mr. E. E. Settle of Ky., H. R., Feb. 9: *C. R.*, p. 1590/1.

Paging.   The practice of securing seats in a legislative assembly through the intervention of boys known as pages.

1892   I offer that amendment to prevent the *"paging"* of seats while the drawing is going on.—Mr. John G. Otis of Kan., H. R., Feb. 4: *C. R.*, p. 857/1.

Palace car.   A railway-carriage sumptuously furnished.

1884   When you sleep in a *palace car*, you are liable to be jerked up on end by the sudden slowing up of the train.—*Pall-Mall Gaz.*, Dec. 9, p. 11/1. (N. E. D.)

1897   [Every free government ought to see] that the section hand, with his pick and shovel, be as free to cast his ballot as the director in the *palace car*.—Mr. David Turpie of Ind., U. S. Senate, March 23: *C. R.*, p. 172/1.

Paleface.   A white person;—so called, as alleged, by the American Indians. (Webster.) [1822-1826.]

1826   The hunting-grounds of the Lenape contained vales as pleasant, streams as pure, and flowers as sweet as the "heaven of the *pale-faces.*"—J. F. Cooper, "Last of the Mohicans," ch. xxxiii.

Palmetto State, the.   South Carolina. [1846.]

1858   The Secretary [of War] was from South Carolina, bred up in the chivalrous doctrines of the *Palmetto State.*—Joshua R. Giddings, "The Exiles of Florida," p. 226.

1871   Today a black man sits as judge in the highest court of the *Palmetto State.*—Mr. F. A. Sawyer of S. C., U. S. Senate, March 21: *C. G.*, p. 207/2.

Panhandle.   The handle of a pan; hence, any arm or projection of land suggesting the handle of a pan. (Webster.) [1862-1888.]

1872   That part of [the territory] north of the Red River, and between New Mexico and the Indian territory of the Choctaws, Creeks, and Cherokees, is generally designated in Texas as the *Pan-Handle*. This *Pan-Handle* is traversed east and west by the north and south forks of the Canadian and their tributaries. . . . This *Pan-Handle* country runs up to the parallel of 36° 30′, and nearly to the State of Kansas.— Mr. J. W. Flanagan of Tex., U. S. Senate, March 7: *C. G.*, p. 1492/1-2.

1880   There is [a postal] route from Vinita in the Indian Territory, in the Cherokee Nation, to Las Vegas in New Mexico, across the *pan-handle* of Texas.—Mr. S. B. Maxey of Tex., U. S. Senate, March 15: *C. R.*, p. 1551/1.

1885   They made some arrangement . . . for passing across that part of

Texas which is called the *Pan Handle*.—Mr. J. T. Morgan of Ala., U. S. Senate, Jan. 6: *Id.*, p. 474/2.

1892 A few years ago all that beautiful country west of my own State, to the *Panhandle* of Texas, was wild Indian country.—Mr. S. W. Peel of Ark., H. R., Feb. 18: *Id.*, p. 8/2, App.

Panhandler. The go-between of the shyster lawyer and the prisoner. Another name for a **Steerer**, q. v. in Vol. II, N. Y. slang.

1913 It advanced the prestige of the "*panhandler*," in the underworld, to be seen speaking with the prosecutor.—*N. Y. Evening Post*, June 30, p. 2/2.

Pan Handle State, the. West Virginia.

Panoche. Cane sugar. Spanish. [1848.]

1871 The Panoche valley [in Calif.] takes its name from a sweet cane used by the Indians, from which *panoche* or sugar is made.—Mr. A. A. Sargent of Calif., H. R., Feb. 20: *C. G.*, p. 1447/3.

Pan out. To turn out, to develop. A term adopted from the process of placer mining. [1881-1882.]

1875 That ingenious, inquiring, enterprising, industrious man wants to go and run into the bowels of the earth and see what he can *pan out* there.—Mr. J. L. Alcorn of Miss., U. S. Senate, March 2: *C. R.*, p. 2063/2.

1889 [These statements] amount to little, and when sifted down they *pan out* about upon the same average.—Mr. W. C. Cooper of Ohio, H. R., Feb. 12: *Id.*, p. 1796/2.

Pantaloons, Pants. The garments which preceded trousers. Then the word came to mean trousers. [1804-1860.]

1891 There are two or three words that have come into common use, which set a man's teeth on edge,—"ladies," "gents," and "*pants*."—Mr. W. McAdoo of N. J., H. R., Feb. 7: *C. R.*, p. 2358/2.

Pap. Political patronage, bestowal of offices, etc. [1841-1847.]

1866 I wish the line to be drawn between Democrats of the Democratic party and Democrats of the conservative Republican party who desire to live upon the *pap* and patronage of the Administration.—Mr. John W. Chanler of N. Y., H. R., Dec. 19: *C. G.*, p. 207/2.

1875 An adventurer who is willing to let his foot rest on any soil that will give him *pap* and emolument.—Mr. J. R. West of La., U. S. Senate, March 15: *C. R.*, p. 60/2.

1880 I would favor no process of juggling bills through by giving special *pap* to certain places.—Mr. S. S. Cox of N. Y., H. R., Jan 22: *Id.*, p. 486/1.

1884 It would be nearer the truth to say that the Government supports the rich on protection *pap*, and that the working men support both the Government and the rich.—Mr. G. L. Yaple of Mich., H. R., Apr. 23: *Id.*, p. 3308/2.

Papaw or **Pawpaw.** The papaya tree; also its fruit. The oblong yellowish fruit, with a sweetish, banana-like, many-seeded pulp, of a tree (*Asimina triloba*) of the central and southern United States; also the tree that bears it. [1613-1835.]

1671   Pomgranates, Gwavers, *Papawes*, Fig-trees too,
    Whereof a pleasant kinde of Drink they brew.
        —John Hardie, "Last Voyage to Bermudas," p. 10.

Paper. To supply or examine ship's papers.

1883 [All these men are] engaged either in the detection or prevention of smuggling, or in the *papering* of vessels and the care and control of the issuing of the papers.—Mr. Eugene Hale of Me., U. S. Senate, Feb. 1: *C. R.*, p. 1911/1.

Paper blockade. One proclaimed but not made effective. [1812-1863.]

1814 England must either keep up her present mere cruising or *paper blockade* of our sea coast . . . or modify her system in favor of all neutrals.—John C. Calhoun, H. R., Apr. 6. ["Works" (1856) II, 108.]

Papsuckers. Those persons who seek special privilege. See **Pap.**

1894 I am opposed to taking people's money away from them for the benefit of others, whether it is done by Dick Turpin, Robin Hood, Capt. Kidd, the bounty-grabber, or tariff *pap-suckers.*—Mr. Champ Clark of Mo., H. R., Jan. 24: *C. R.*, p. 190/2, App.

Paralyze. To stupefy with amazement. Humorous.

1838 The intelligence perfectly *paralysed* Mr. Bumble.—"Oliver Twist," ch. vii.

1890 You have placed a duty on Canadian eggs; you boast about what you have done for the American farmer, and you refer to it as a complete vindication of your "American policy." What audacity! It *paralyzes* me.—Mr. W. C. McClammy of N. C., H. R., May 19: *C. R.*, p. 4933/1.

Park, v. To arrange in a row, or in order; originally used with reference to artillery.

1864 (May 24.) The trains are *parked* along the edge of the river.—Memoir of Dr. John S. Billings, p. 95. (N. Y., 1915.)

Parking. Ground covered with turf, usually in the middle of a street.

1885 Spaces were left for a market-place, court-house green, and *parking* for the palace.—*Johns Hopkins Hist. Studies,* III, 109. (N. E. D.)

1893 Mr. Felton:—Is it proposed to use the *parking* for the purpose of erecting this building? Mr. Manderson:—I do not know whether it is proposed to use the *parking* or not. I submit that around the present Government Printing Office there is no *parking.* It is not a usual thing to find *parking* around manufacturing establishments in the heart of cities.—U. S. Senate, Feb. 20: *C. R.*, p. 1856/2.

Parole, v. To set free an ordinary prisoner on his own recognizances.

1888 The defendant was *paroled* on his own recognizance.—Troy (N. Y.) *Daily Times,* Feb. 7. (Farmer.)

1888 He was *paroled* until August 8.—*N. Y. Herald,* July 29. (*Id.*)

Parole camp. A camp of prisoners on parole.

1892 [Any man on this floor would] go to his home and help take care of [his family] under such circumstances, especially if he was simply resting in a *parole camp.*—Mr. J. A. T. Hull of Ia., H. R., March 18: *C. R.*, p. 2220/1.

Participance, Participancy. Participation.

1869 An Infinite Participance and Sympathy.—Mrs. A. D. T. Whitney, "Hitherto," p. 191. (N. E. D.)

1878 See HARTFORD CONVENTION.

Passivism. Passivity; inactivity.

1872 The Democratic party . . . is afflicted with the dry rot of "*passivism.*" It has no longer vitality.—Mr. A. A. Sargent of Calif., H. R., Apr. 18: *C. G.*, p. 2552/3.

Paster. See quotation 1888.

1870 The officer of the election swore there were ten tickets . . . which were scratched and had *pasters* with the name of Caleb N. Taylor.—Mr. John Cessna of Pa., H. R., Apr. 13: *C. G.*, p. 2659/3.

1888 Small slips of paper gummed at the back . . . are called "*pasters*" or "stickers," because the independent voter pastes them over [the names to which he objects.]—Bryce, "Am. Commonwealth," II, 494. (N. E. D.)

1892 He swears that the ticket he got from McArthur was a Noyes *paster*—that is, that a Noyes *paster* was put on a ticket over Rockwell's name, and this must have been a Democratic *paster.*—Mr. C. T. O'Ferrall of Va., H. R., Apr. 22: *C. R.*, p. 236/1, App.

1896 Tammany Hall had an official ballot, which was the Democratic ticket. The law also provided for what is known as a *"paster."* The voter could take any one of the official ballots and use a *paster* on it. He could place the *paster* over the name of any one candidate or over the entire face of any official ballot. . . . The *paster* might have but one name on it, or the names of all the candidates. . . . [This organization] had a *paster*, and it was known as the *Tammany paster.* [The modus operandi of the *Tammany paster* is then described.]— Mr. C. I. Long of Kan., H. R., June 2: *Id.*, p. 6013/1.

1896 This witness testifies that he does not know what the *paster* was, . . . that he recognized the ballot as a Democratic ballot, but did not know what the *paster* was.—Mr. J. G. Maguire of Calif., H. R., July 2: *Id.*, p. 405/1, App.

Pasture-man. A herder of cattle.

1621 Bootes, the heard or *pasture man.*—Anthony Caoè, "Sermons," p. 11. (N. E. D.)

1895 Mr. John S. Little of Ark. gives a list of the *"pasture men"* who have large holdings in the Indian Territory: H. R., Jan. 15: *C. R.*, p. 997/2.

Patent insides. Sheets printed on one side only, the other side being used for local news by country editors.

1888 [This item] even got into the *"patent insides"* copied from the metropolitan papers.—Mr. J. G. Cannon of Ill., H. R., March 15: *C. R.*, p. 2118/2.

1890 *Patent insides* are made up first from the American newspaper, of miscellaneous matter, political, literary and general. They are made up in the second place from stolen English stories.—Mr. O. C. Moore of N. H., H. R., May 2: *Id.*, p. 4144/2.

Paternalism, paternal government. That system by which the ruling power undertakes what are commonly regarded as private enterprises.

1881 There is nothing in the proposal that looks in the direction of *paternalism*, or the ownership and administration of industrial enterprises by the government.—*Chicago Times*, June 11. (N. E. D.)

1895 I suggest it is going a long way toward making this a *paternal government* when we expend public money in making experiments in the production of rice and sugar cane in various parts of the country.— Mr. N. W. Aldrich of R. I., U. S. Senate, Feb. 15: *C. R.*, p. 2225/1.

1897 The "bogy man" of the Government ownership of railroads has seemingly been conjured up . . . to frighten timid legislators, and every time it is mentioned there are loud cries of *"Paternalism!"*—Mr. Jas. McLachlan of Calif., U. S. Senate, Jan. 9: *Id.*, p. 623/1.

Pathfinder. One who spies and clears the way (here for burglars). Slang.

1905 The third prisoner described himself as Edward James, but Dougherty said he was James Casey, a thief of the "gay cat," or *"pathfinder"* class.—*N. Y. Times*, Jan. 2. (Century Dict.)

Pathfinder, the. John C. Fremont, American explorer and general (1813-1890).

Patroon. The master of a sailing vessel. See Vol. II, **Patron.** [1775-1850.]

1773 Alex^r. McKensie, *Patroon,* m. Sarah Whitle.—Hayne Records, Feb. 9: *So. Car. Hist. Mag.*, xi, 99. (1910.)

Paw-paw. See quotation.

1864 They accuse us radicals of speaking disparagingly of the militia of Missouri. It is false, utterly so, except so far as relates to what are called the *Paw-paws*, about whom I have no time to speak. The other militia contain the true men, the noble, the brave, the determined.—Mr. Joseph W. McClurg of Mo., H. R, March 9: *C. G.*, p. 1017/3.

Paxton Boys. See Vol. II [1818-1833] and Vol. III, **Augusta Boys.**

Pay dirt, Pay streak, &c. That which pays for working. [1857-1909.]

1867 [The miners] will go on struggling against [continued] loss in the hope of finding a "rich *pay*," as they call it, making a strike, and [thus] work on for years.—Mr. W. M. Stewart of Nev., U. S. Senate, Dec. 20: *C. G.*, p. 301/1.

1879 What miner or prospector will examine your geological reports to determine where he can find *pay-dirt*, or strike a mineral vein of the precious metals? I fear we are going to pay too dearly for our geological whistle.—Mr. J. H. Baker of Ind., H. R., Feb. 18: *C. R.*, p. 1564/1.

Pay school. One at which payment is charged.

1872 I do not think the West Point Academy is made to be a *pay school* for the education of foreign youths.—Mr. A. G. Thurman of O., U. S. Senate, Jan. 10: *C. G.*, p. 330/2.

Peace man. One who advocates peace.

1848 I'm a decided *peace-man*, tu, an' go agin the war.—"Biglow Papers."

1863 Patriotism . . . was conquered by selfish passion, prejudice, and private interest. There were *"peace men"* in those days.—Mr. James F. Wilson of Ia., H. R., Feb. 2: *C. G.*, p. 682/1.

Peaked. Thin and angular. [1835-1878.]

1844 While I kept my oyster-board, there was a thin, *peaked*-looking man, used to come and buy of me.—Lydia M. Child, "Letters from New York," Second Series, p. 51. (Lond., 1845.)

Peanut. A ground nut which grows profusely in Virginia and North Carolina. [1826-1835.]

1870 We have a tariff to study which affects all our interests, from the *peanut* of North Carolina, the luxury of my Bowery constituents, to the steamships of our people.—Mr. S. S. Cox of N. Y., H. R., March 8: *C. G.*, p. 1766/3.

Peanut, Peanut politics, &c. Small, mean, paltry. As a verb, *peanut* is to cause to be insignificant. [1854-1909.]

1884 [Mr. Randall] proposes to cut down, to cheese-pare, to *peanut* this whole business, so that if we should get into a war we will not be able to compete with any foreign nation.—Mr. J. B. Belford of Colo., H. R., Apr. 24: *C. R.*, p. 3356/1.

1892 This country is not a *peanut institution*; it is a great country.—Mr. W. W. Bowers of Calif., H. R., June 18: *C. R.*, p. 5394/2.

1894 It would be gross disrespect to a great commercial product of several States in this Union for me to denounce the course pursued by this Administration . . . as *"peanut politics."*—Mr. C. A. Boutelle of Me., H. R., Aug. 9: *Id.*, p. 8337/2.

Pea-time, the last of. The melancholy end of things. [1834-1861.]

1834 A month ago [Mr. Benton] had said it was *"the last of pea-time"* with these distress memorials.—T. H. Benton, "Thirty Years' View," I, 467. (1857.)

Peddle, Peddle out. To deal out in small quantities. Chiefly U. S. (N. E. D.)

1837 Going to *peddle out* a lot of huckleberries.—N. Hawthorne, "Twice-told Tales," (1851) I, 249. (N. E. D.)

1856 Many negroes were in town, *peddling* eggs, nuts, brooms, and fowls.—Olmsted, "Slave States," p. 630. (N. E. D.)

1870 I took the ground, that this house ought not to *peddle out* amnesty and pardon.—Mr. Jas. B. Beck of Ky., H. R., Feb. 21: *C. G.*, p. 1463/1.

1870 Gentlemen talk about these bills for the removal of political disabilities being *"peddled out"* for partisan reasons.—Mr. W. B. Stokes of Tenn., H. R., *Id.*, p. 1465/3.

1871 The advocates of universal amnesty call [the granting of individual amnesties] *"peddling"*; and, having given it a belittling name, continually repeat it as an argument. When a Governor pardons an offender for exceptional reasons, nobody calls it *peddling out* clemency.—Mr. G. W. Scofield of Pa., H. R., Jan. 28: *Id.*, p. 801/1.

Pedregal. An old lava-field. Spanish.

1856 An area more like the volcanic *pedragal* of the basin of Mexico than anything else.—Kane, "Arct. Expl." i, 197. (N. E. D.)

1881 [Santa Anna's] position was flanked on the west by a rugged field of broken lava, called the *Pedregal.*—Bryant & Gay, "Pop. Hist. U. S.," iv. 378. (N. E. D.)

1884 Between our army and the rear of Contreras there were great bodies of molten lava thrown out by volcanic eruptions of Popocatapetl and Iztaccihuatl, obstacles which appeared to render crossing impossible, and yet Scott's army did cross that *pedregal*, and reached the rear of the fortifications at Contreras.—Mr. S. B. Maxey of Tex., U. S. Senate, June 24: *C. R.*, p. 5517/1.

Peek. To peep, peer, or examine in a prying manner. [1789-1890.]

1576   That one eie winks as though it were but blinde,
      That other pries and *peekes* in everie place.
      —George Gascoigne, "The Steele Glas," fo. 301/2. (1587.)

1815 I'll *peak* a little furder. [Dodging and listening.]—David Humphreys, "The Yankey in England," p. 36.

1912 The Insurgents say that Mr. Smoot's recent tariff proposal is fair enough outside, but that a *peek* inside probably will show a fine colony of "jokers."—*N. Y. Evening Post*, Jan. 1, p. 3/1.

Peeled stick convention, The. See quotation.

1880 Did they not meet in Cleveland in the *"peeled stick"* convention, all armed and ready to resist the authority of the U. S.?—Mr. S. S. Cox of N. Y., H. R., March 19: *C. R.*, p. 1708/2.

Peelers. See quotation.

1881 How is it with the *peelers*? The *peelers*, I understand, are that part of the [Virginia] debt not yet funded. They are selling today at about 38 cents in the dollar.—Mr. H. G. Davis of W. Va., U. S. Senate, May 3: *C. R.*, p. 447/1.

Peeved. This word is used to mean *irritated, exasperated,* and *angry,* whether mildly or extremely so.

1912 President Roosevelt, it also appeared, was decidedly *peeved* because Secretary Hitchcock gave out to the press a personal letter written the President by Governor Higgins in regard to an Indian Territory land matter, referred to the Secretary by the White House for report.—*The Oregonian*, Sept. 29.

Pegging away. Proceeding in a steady, persistent way.

1837 *"Peg away,* Bob," said Mr. Allen to his companion.—"Pickwick Papers," xxx. (N. E. D.)

1862 Thackeray, "Philip," vii. (N. E. D.)

1864 [Lincoln, when asked what we should do if the war should last for years, replied:] "We'll keep *pegging away.*"—Leland, "Life," xi. 196. (N. E. D.)

1871 For more than ten years the Democratic party kept *pegging away* on that [Mexican War] debt, and then abdicated.—Mr. Jesse H. Moore of Ill., H. R., Apr. 6: *C. G.*, p. 2229/2.

Pemmican. Meat dried, pounded and made into cakes; frequently with a small mixture of dried cherries, currants, &c.

1801 The provision called *Pemican,* on which the Chepewyans and other savages in the North of America chiefly subsist on their journeys.— Sir A. MacKenzie, "Voy. St. Lawrence," Pref. 121. (N. E. D.)

1827   *Pannican*, a concentrated essence of meat dryed by a fire of oak and elm wood, so as to reduce 6 lb. of the best beef to 1 lb.—*Ann. Register*, p. 58/1. (N. E. D.)

1855   Then on *pemican* they feasted,
                    Pemican and buffalo marrow.
                            —Longfellow, "Hiawatha," xi. (N. E. D.)

1885   *Pemmican* is made from the round of beef cut in strips and dried, then shredded or mixed with beef tallow and currants.—Schley and Soley, "Rescue of Greely," p. 132. (Century Dict.)

1899   See KOUSE ROOT.

Pendency. Imminence.

1903   Some will be surprised to know that the evident *pendency* of the American Civil War was the immediate cccasion for the writing of this volume.—*Living Church*, Oct. 17, p. 850. (Century Dict.)

People's party. A party formed in 1891, advocating public ownership of railroads, telegraphs, etc. See Vol. 1I, **Populism.** [1892-1894.]

1896   It may be, sir, that this *People's Party* has "fanatics" in it; it may be that we are "wild-eyed lunatics."—Mr. M. W. Howard of Ala., H. R., May 15: *C. R.*, p. 5297/2.

Pepperpot soup. A stew of vegetables, meat or fish, and cassareep, common in the West Indies. A highly seasoned stew of tripe, meat dumplings, and vegetables, usually called *Philadelphia pepperpot*. [1794-1825.]

1801   [In Jamaica] they make a rare soup they call a *pepperpot*. It is an excellent breakfast for a Salamander.—*Baltimore Weekly Magazine*, Apr. 15, p. 257/2.

Per diem. An allowance per day. [1839-1855.]

1848   The *per diem* will hardly pay a gentleman for soiling his hands with it.—Wilmington (N. C.) *Commercial*, Aug. 24, p. 2/4.

1866   As the law originally stood, whether the members were present or not present, they received their *per diem*. As the law now is, their *per diem*, if it can be called a *per diem*, their proportion of the salary which the law gives, which would be due them if they stayed here, cannot be paid, unless they certify that they are absent on account of sickness.—Mr. Reverdy Johnson of Md., U. S. Senate, Dec. 14: *C. G.*, p. 132/3.

1869   We thought it wise, instead of allowing mileage and other constructive charges [to the census-takers], to pay a simple *per diem*, with no allowance for travel.—Mr. J. A. Garfield of O., H. R., Dec. 8: *Id.*, p. 37/2.

1870   See SUBSIST.

1882   For some considerable time before [L. S. Brumidi] died, he was employed by the Government at a *per diem*.—Mr. Justin S. Morrill of Vt., U. S. Senate, March 9: *C. R.*, p. 1734/1.

1885   The standing committees of this body . . . had only *per diem* clerks during the session.—Mr. C. H. Van Wyck of Nebr., U. S. Senate, March 21: *Id.*, p. 81/1.

Perique. A kind of strong-flavored tobacco produced in Louisiana, and cured in its own juices so as to be very dark-colored, usually black. (Webster.)

1882   And *perique* tobacco may be sold by the manufacturer or producer thereof, in the form of *carottes*, [cylindrical rolls] . . . without the payment of tax.—Bill to amend §3362 of the Revised Statutes of the U. S.: *C. R.*, p. 2642/2. [Apr. 6.]

Persimmon. The American date-plum. The fruit is highly astringent when unripe.

1866 I have not perhaps been trained in the same vinegar and *persimmon* school [as Senator Morrill.]—Mr. Edgar Cowan of Pa., U. S. Senate, Dec. 11: *C. G.,* p. 61/2.

1893 I would, in the language that is popular on the banks of the Mississippi River, where I reside, "let the longest pole knock the *persimmon.*"—Mr. B. F. Marsh of Ill., H. R., Aug. 25: *C. R.,* p. 904/1.

Personable. Comely in person. (Webster.)

1878 Parson Williams was a tall, straight, *personable* man, come of good family.—Harriet B. Stowe in the *Atl. Monthly,* Oct. p. 472/1.

Person, colored. A person with more or less negro blood. See Vol. II, **Person of colour.** [1796-1833.]

1864 Now, lo and behold, in the advancement of civilization and Christianity and refinement of which we hear so much, the negro has got to be a *"colored person."* And when you come to provide for calling them into the public service, there must be perfect equality.—Mr. Willard Saulsbury of Del., U. S. Senate, Feb. 13: *C. G.,* p. 642/2. [He also stated his impression that he was a man of full age before he ever heard the term *"colored person"* used; and he came of age in 1841.]

Peter-boat. A crate or box for fish, made with slats, and intended to be set in water to keep the fish alive.—Chesapeake Bay. (Century Dict.)

Peter Funk. A swindler. Bartlett says that at an auction "Peter Funk" is a puffer or a by-bidder. See Vol. II, **Peter Funk, Auction.** [1854-1858.]

1864 As to Onis and Tweed, auctioneers, they were not much better than *Peter Funks*—lived by acting as stool-pigeons and cheating generally.—"Was he successful?" by R. B. Kimball, p. 133. (N. Y.)

1867 [This lottery swindler] has an office in [Washington] where he claims to have the pictures exposed, as *Peter Funks* usually do.—Mr. Chas. H. Van Wyck of N. Y., H. R., July 19: *C. G.,* p. 737/3.

Peter out. To give out; to be exhausted. [1854-1888.]

1876 We may safely say that if our great bonanzas do not *"peter out,"* . . . we possess a power &c.—Mr. Chittenden of N. Y., H. R., Aug. 5: *C. R.,* p. 5224/1.

1892 We should find that this attempt at economy had *"petered out"* to a very small point.—Mr. Chas. A. Boutelle of Me., H. R., Jan. 6: *Id.,* p. 174/1.

1913 Paterson strike *petering out.* Dyers at work and plants full, weavers vote to-morrow.—*N. Y. Evening Post,* July 24, p. 2/2.

Petune. A liquid employed in petuning or spraying tobacco, which was itself called *Petun* or *Petum* by the Indians. See John Taylor (1630) and Tobie Venner (1660) in the Century Dict. (also N. E. D.) The *petunia* derives its name from the same source. The fillers only and not the wrappers [of cigars] are *petuned,* the intention being to give them a darker color, an improved flavor, and the appearance and character of a strong tobacco.—*U. S. Dept. Agr. Rep.* No. 59, p. 19.

At this stage the odor of the *petune* may be noticeable.—*Id.,* No. 62, p. 18.

Pewee. A species of fly-catcher, so-called from its cry. See Vol. II, **Phebe.** [1839-1854.]

1810 A *pewee* had fixed her nest on a projecting shelf of the rock.—A. Wilson, "Poems &c." (1876) I, 199. (N. E. D.)

1839-40 The Pe-wit or *Pewee* or Phoebe-bird; for he is called by each of these names, from a fancied resemblance to the sound of his monotonous note.—W. Irving, "Wolfert's Roost" (1855), p. 19. (N. E. D.)

1839-40 Another of our feathered visitors . . . is the Pe-wit, or *Pe-wee*, or *Phoebe-bird*. . . . They arrive early in the spring. . . . "The *Phoebe-birds have come!*" is heard on all sides.—W. Irving, "Wolfert's Roost" (1855), p. 19. (N. E. D.)

1870 The *pewee* is the first bird to pipe up in the morning.—J. R. Lowell, "My Study Windows" (1886), p. 19. (N. E. D.)

1890 Every man who has as much sense as a *pewee* knows &c.—Mr. G. W. Atkinson of W. Va., H. R., May 9: *C. R.*, p. 4432/1.

1893 Plain, dull-colored *pee-wee* or phoebe, . . . catching insects, or reiterating his own name, "*phoebe, phoebe.*"—*Scribner's Mag.*, p. 765/2. (N. E. D.)

Philadelphia lawyer. A person who, for some reason never as yet satisfactorily explained, is credited with superhuman sagacity. [1803-1866.]

1865 It is said that Philadelphia lawyers are very keen and cute and acute [*sic*], and it has been a by-word that "a man is as keen as a *Philadelphia lawyer,*" or "it would take a *Philadelphia lawyer* to do that." But, sir, smart as the Philadelphia lawyers were, keen as they were, and numerous as they were, there was not one of them keen enough for the purposes of this inquiry, and they sent to New Hampshire, and imported a lawyer from New Hampshire to Philadelphia, to investigate the frauds that were practised in the Philadelphia navy-yard upon the Navy Department. I think that hereafter the keenness of the Philadelphia lawyers will be at a discount.—Mr. John P. Hale of N. H., U. S. Senate, Jan. 28: *C. G.*, p. 468/3.

1866 It is very difficult to define the distinction between the meaning of the term "probable cause" and the meaning of the term "prima facie evidence." It would puzzle anybody except a *Philadelphia lawyer* to make any sensible and satisfactory distinction.—Mr. Reverdy Johnson of Md., U. S. Senate, May 14: *Id.*, p. 2566/3.

1866 It requires all the astuteness of a *Philadelphia lawyer* to find out what an officer's pay really is under the present law.—Mr. Robert C. Schenck of O., H. R., June 5: *Id.*, p. 2978/3.

1867 There is confusion, there is uncertainty, there is doubt, which even a *Philadelphia lawyer* could not unravel, as to the design of the bill reported by the Committee [on Reconstruction].—Mr. Fernando Wood of N. Y., H. R., July 12: *Id.*, p. 619/1.

1879 [These phrases] are so . . blended in the speech of [Mr. Windom] as to defy even a *Philadelphia lawyer* in his effort to understand what idea the Senator has of his own form of government.—Mr. Whyte of Md., U. S. Senate, May 20: *C. R.*, p. 1469/1.

1890 In my region, when anything is difficult to understand or to unravel, we say it would take *a Philadelphia lawyer* to unravel it.—Mr. J. H. Outhwaite of O., H. R., June 30: *Id.*, p. 6782/2.

Picayune. A small coin (*picaillon*), a mere trifle. The word is used as an adjective to signify small, mean, contemptible. [1819-1862.]

1841 See YORK SHILLING.

1881 It would be the part of higgling, a *picayune* kind of economy, for us to pretend that these [Rochambeau] papers ought to be further examined.—Mr. Justin S. Morrill of Vt., U. S. Senate, Oct. 25: *C. R.*, p. 533/1.

1882 Some men may object to a big House of Representatives on account of the expense of paying them, but such *picayune* patriots deserve both pity and contempt.—Mr. Tillman of S. C., H. R., Feb. 15: *Id.*, p. 1187/2.

1888 The responsibility . . . belongs on the back of the *picayune* Second Assistant Postmaster-General.—Mr. G. G. Symes of Colo., H. R., May 24: *Id.*, p. 4591/2.

1889 Any little *picayune* system of questions and answers about arithmetic or geography [is no test of trustworthiness].—Mr. J. W. Daniel of Va., U. S. Senate, Feb. 6: *Id.*, p. 1560/1.

1892 I do not care a *picayune* for either gold or silver—I mean I have no sense of favoritism between them.—Mr. M. D. Harter of O., H. R., Feb. 18: *Id.*, p. 1295/2.

1893 We do not care a *picayune* for your bill: it is a "back number."—Mr. John A. Pickler of S. Dak., H. R., Oct. 4: *Id.*, p. 210/1, App.

1912 The spirit of *picayune* economy that led the House to cut off the appropriation of $94,000 for the work of the State Department in extending our foreign trade, should be rebuked in the Senate by restoration of the items cancelled.—*N. Y. Evening Post*, May 20.

Pick. To select. [a. 1390-1911.]

1866 I can *pick* twenty men in this circle who are not inferior in intelligence or less earnest or honest in their convictions than the President of the U. S.—Mr. James W. Nye of Nev., U. S. Senate, May 9: *C. G.*, p. 2495/3.

1870 They soon *picked* their opportunity—Preamble to a bill, U. S. Senate, June 24: *Id.*, p. 4805/2.

1912 Women's Clubs *pick* Chicago. General Federation will hold next biennial meeting there.—*N. Y. Evening Post*, Sept. 12.

Pick up. To capture, to arrest. In its non-maritime use, this appears to be American.

1871 When they are *picked up* for taking horses or sheep or anything of that sort, they will call on [Mr. Edmunds] to defend that taking as a public calamity.—Mr. Garrett Davis of Ky., U. S. Senate, Jan. 5: *C. G.*, p. 317/2.

1885 He had . . . scattered the little army, so that the most of it could be *picked up* in detail.—U. S. Grant, "Personal Mem." I, 309. (N. E. D.)

Picnic. A pleasant, jovial time; a pleasure party.

1887 For that length of time the dogs had a *picnic.*—*The Voice* (N. Y.), Apr. 28, p. 3/2. (N. E. D.)

1894 Stockades were not pleasant places. They were not pleasant either for the besieged or the besiegers. That service was not a "*picnic.*"—Mr. C. H. Grosvenor of O., H. R., March 6: *C. R.*, p. 2640/1.

1896 The cattlemen and the officeholders have "had a *picnic*" out of this country about long enough.—*The Indian Chieftain*, Vinita, Feb. 13: quoted in *C. R.*, Feb. 20, p. 1990/2.

1899 Volunteers in the island of Cuba will feel that they are on a sort of *picnic.*—Mr. H. R. Gibson of Tenn., H. R., Jan. 25: *Id.*, p. 105/2, App.

Pictorial. An illustrated paper.

1872 Other *pictorials* might be published on paper a little smaller or a little larger—Mr. John Sherman of O., U. S. Senate, May 27: *C. G.*, p. 3909/1.

1880, 1904 N. E. D.

Pie. A prize or treat; especially a division of "spoils." Also anything which requires no effort. Slang.

1893 The gentleman complained yesterday of so many coming up to the "*pie counter*," and sustaining the views of the President. He had not reached the *pie counter* at that time. He was only taking crow. . . . He was willing to turn his back upon those grand old principles of Democracy that he had imbibed in his youth in Indiana, not for the purpose of getting *pie*, but for the purpose of getting an office.—Mr. W. D. Bynum of Ind., H. R., Aug. 25: *C. R.*, p. 932/1.

1894 As our slang phrase is, if *pie* is to be divided, [a man] is apt to wish that those who may be politically useful to him should have a slice of the pie.—Mr. T. L. Johnson of O., H. R., Aug. 13: *C. R.*, p. 1231/1, App.

1895 Green dogs are *pie* for [the racoon].—*Outing*, XXVI, 436/1. (N. E. D.)

1896 If you are going to make increases as to other districts, when we come to South Carolina I shall merely ask that we shall have some of the *pie* too.—Mr. B. R. Tillman of S. C., U. S. Senate, March 25: *Id.*, p. 3170/1.

1898 Just so that the President distributes "*pie*" in sufficient quantities, [his followers] care nothing for the dying women and starving babies in "the gem of the Antilles."—Mr. Champ Clark of Mo., H. R., Jan. 20: *Id.*, p. 795/1.

1898 When the election is over, the victory won, and the loaves and fishes, now vulgarly called "*pie*," are to be distributed, [the country editor] is generally forgotten.—The same, March 2: *Id.*, p. 2379/2.

Pie-biters. Persons on the look-out for plunder or "pie." Slang.
1893 See LEG-PULLERS.
1898 See CUCKOO.

Piece. A woman. [1866.]
a.1577 [I] have won by due desert a *peece* that hath no peere.—George Gascoigne, "Fable of Ieronimo," p. 232. (1857.)
1621 Ougly *peece*, For so I tearme thee. (Time is addressed.)—R. Brathwait, "Times Cvrtaine Drawne," A 5.

Piece. A person; an individual. Usually contemptuous.
1660 [Thersites was] The most deformed *peice* of all who came To th' Ilian Seige.—John Ogilby, "Homers Iliads," Book II: p. 39, I, 15.

Piece. A separate item of baggage or property in transit. (N. E. D.)
1809 The freight of a canoe . . consists in sixty *pieces*, or packages, of merchandize.—A. Henry, "Travels," p. 15. (N. E. D.)
1890 The cases in which *pieces* go astray are astonishingly rare.—Thos. M. Cooley, "Railways of America," p. 253. (N. E. D.)

Piker. A small speculator in stocks. Hence, anyone small or mean in his dealings. Slang.
1901 In the absence of complaisant lambs, the financial cannibals known as "room traders" and "*pikers*" tried to "scalp eighths" out of each other for weeks,—to take advantage of fractional fluctuations instead of waiting for big movements.—*McClure's Mag.*, p. 159. (Century Dict.)

Piker. A man armed with a pike, who guides the movement of cakes of ice into a storehouse.
1904 Forces of men known as "*pikers*," who stand beside the channels and force the cakes of ice, as fast as loosened, in the direction of the ice house.—*Sci. Amer.*, Supp., Jan. 2, p. 23408. (Century Dict.)

Pikery. A nauseous compound of gum and *Canella alba*, called *hiera picra*. [1878.]
1773 [She] would send him some *Higry Pigry*, which would stop it at once.—Graves, "Spiritual Quixote," VIII, xix. (N. E. D.)
1817 Scott has *hickery pickery* in "Old Mortality," ch. VIII. (N. E. D.)
1873 I once heard of a man in the State where I was raised, who was so fond of new rum that he drank up a bottle of his wife's *picra* in order to get it.—Mr. Timothy O. Howe of Wisc., U. S. Senate, Feb. 24: *Id.*, p. 1700/2.

Pile. A heap of money; a fortune. [1741-1870.]
1852 The old Californian principle of "*making a 'pile'* and vamosing the ranche."—F. Marryat, "Gold Quartz Mining," p. 8. (N. E. D.)
1882 See NARY.

Pimlico order. Precise order.
1864 We should have the expenses of the Government figured out to a copper in every particular, and everything placed in such minute, *Pimlico order*, that everybody could understand exactly what it was.—Mr. W. P. Fessenden of Me., U. S. Senate, Feb. 15: *C. G.*, p. 647/3.

Pinch. To arrest. Slang.

1913 On Wednesday night one of the A. C. M. Co.'s scabs was arrested and thrown in jail. (He met with a hot reception from the pickets. He was working at Camp 2 for the A. C. M. Co., as barn boss, when the strike was called and would not come out with the boys.) He was *pinched* for selling whiskey to Indians.—*Industrial Worker* (Spokane, Wash.), July 3.

Pinchbug or **Pinching-bug.** The dobson or hellgramite, a neuropterous insect.

Pindling. "Peaked"; delicate; unhealthy. (New England.)

1887 "Seems to me Leviny's lookin' kinder *pindlin*', ain't she?" said the fleshy old lady.—Mary E. Wilkins, "Humble Romance," p. 110. (Century Dict.)

Pine barrens. Open spaces of land with scattered pines. [1775-1827.]

1822 The timber of the *pine barrens* that abound in the country is not of a very good quality.—"Notices of East Florida," p. 8. (Charleston, S. C.)

1894 Sheep will thrive on what are called the "*pine barrens*," from which certain kinds of timber have been cut.—Mr. Jas. McMillan of Mich., U. S. Senate, July 12: *C. R.*, p. 6155/1.

Pine knots. Pieces of pine, so replete with turpentine that they can be used for illumination as well as for hot fires. [1778-1847.]

1866 I came upon two negro women gathering *pine-knots* for light-wood from the old planks of the road.—H. L. Estabrooks, "Adrift in Dixie," p. 157. (N. Y.)

Pine overcoat, a. A cheap coffin.

1896 The bill provides that the Committee shall immediately take possession of the remains, and . . . get as cheap a coffin as it can bargain for,—perhaps what they call in the army a *pine overcoat.*—Mr. J. R. Hawley of Conn., U. S. Senate, Jan. 20: *C. R.*, p. 796/2.

Pine-top. A low grade of whisky.

1883 See BUST-HEAD.

Pine-tree State, The. Maine.

1884 Maine is not big enough to control the vast scope of country lying west of the Allegheny Mountains. . . . What has the State of Maine—the little *Pine-tree State* on the Atlantic coast—to do with the great progress of the West?—Mr. J. B. Belford of Colo., H. R., Apr. 8: *C. R.*, p. 2775/2.

1888 The good old *Pine-tree State* is pretty well represented in this locality. —*Boston Transcript*, n. d. (Farmer.)

1896 All shall share equitably, whether the creditor lives at the Golden Gate or in the *Pine State* of Maine.—Mr. D. B. Henderson of Ia., H. R., May 1: *C. R.*, p. 4693/1.

Pinkertonism. Spying upon or watching.

1891 You can't make men moral by law and *Pinkertonism.*—*The Voice* (N. Y.), Feb. 26. (N. E. D.)

Pinkerton men. Armed private detectives, organized by one Allan Pinkerton in 1850, and hired out by his agency.

1888 Employed under the protection of *Pinkerton men* and special police-men.—Phila. *Inquirer*, Feb. 22. (Farmer.)

1892 I will not call it a military body, but . . . an armed mob; the *Pinkerton men* are nothing but an armed mob. . . . The *Pinkerton forces* are the merest mercenaries on the earth. They are worse than the Hessians. . . . We have two excellent penitentiaries in Indiana, one on the Ohio River and the other on Lake Michigan, and whenever a *Pinkerton man* is brought into our State . . . to make arrests, or in any way disturb our people, we have a cell for him in one of our penitentiaries.—Mr. D. W. Voorhees of Ind., U. S. Senate, July 7: *C. R.*, p. 5826/1-2. [The employment of these men by Mr. Andrew

Carnegie provoked this debate, in which Mr. Hale of Me. disclaimed on behalf of the Republican party all responsibility for Mr. Carnegie's conduct. See also pp. 5861-9.]

Pin Society, the. A secret society among the Indians, established about the year 1855, whose members at one time wore a pin as a badge of membership.

1873 Such is the history of the Cherokee Ku Klux, called *"the Pins,"* given to the world by a prominent member of the present Cherokee delegation. . . . I have it from the best authority that the power of this murderous *"Pin Society"* still dominates the Cherokee country: assassinations and arson go unwhipped of justice—Mr. John C. Conner of Tex., H. R., Jan. 15: *C. G.,* p. 618/1.

Pipe layers. Persons who introduced as voters, under various pretexts, those not entitled to vote. [1840-1888.]

1842 See SMALL POTATO.

1869 Where were the *pipe-layers* formed? Where were they cradled? What was their history? Where was this whole system of fraud and corruption born? Sir, it was born, cradled, and reared in the City of Philadelphia.—Mr. James Brooks of N. Y., H. R., Feb. 5: *C. G.,* p. 917/1.

1883 Among the Glentworth papers was a letter in which he said that the men sent from Philadelphia were to be employed in laying the pipes for the introduction of Croton water. The Whig leaders were immediately stigmatized as *pipe-layers.*—Thurlow Weed, "Autobiogr.," p. 493. (Century Dict.)

Pipe lines. Tubes or pipes for transporting liquids over long distances. [1860-1883.]

1894 The amendment provides that *pipe lines* may be laid across the public lands to connect these reservoirs [of water] with the railroads. —Mr. J. F. Lacey of Ia., H. R., July 24: *C. R.,* p. 7832/2.

Pishymew. A small white gull. (N. E. D.)

Pivotal. Constituting a pivot or turning point; that which controls the balance; the point on which all the rest hinges. [1888.]

1873 That is precisely the *pivotal* point of this case.—Mr. Smith of N. Y., H. R., Jan. 18: *C. G.,* p. 696/1.

1896 Why have the *pivotal* States made such tremendous gains in voting strength?—*Farm, Field, and Fireside* (Chicago), Dec. 5: see *C. R.,* Dec. 15, p. 161/1.

Pivot-bridge, Pivot-draw. One turning on pivot.

1872 The Act of Congress requires "that all bridges over the Ohio River, below the Covington and Cincinnati bridge, shall have, in addition to the high span prescribed above, a *pivot draw,* giving two clear openings &c."—Mr. Reagan of Tex., H. R., Jan. 9, 1877: *C. R.,* p. 522/2.

1875 A *pivot-bridge* of the New York Central Railway on the Linville principle.—Knight, "Dict. Mech.," p. 1721/2. (N. E. D.)

1877 There is not a *pivot-draw* in any bridge across the Ohio from Steubenville to the Cincinnati suspension bridge.—Mr. Reagan, as above: *C. R.,* p. 523/1. [See the rest of the debate.]

Placate. To appease. [1678-1910.]

1870 I gave [no] utterance to any sentiment with regard to *placating* rebels. —Mr. F. A. Sawyer of N. C., U. S. Senate, May 17: *C. G.,* p. 3521/2.

1911 The delusive plea that you can get a good man and at the same time "conciliate" or *"placate"* this or that political organization has had no part in Mr. Blankenburg's selections.—*N. Y. Evening Post,* Dec. 4, p. 4/2.

Placer. An area adapted to surface-mining. Spanish. [1846-1909.] For **Bench placer, Creek placer, Dry placer,** &c., see Century Dict.

1849 He received 60 lashes, had his head shaved, both ears cropped off close, and was ordered to leave the *placer.*—Wilmington (N. C.) *Commercial*, Dec. 22, p. 4/2. (From the *Pacific Weekly News.*)

1863 See GULCH.

1869 A new *placer* will be opened by the operation of this new [railroad subsidy] system, and the work of corruption and plunder will be complete.—Mr. C. Sitgreaves of N. J., H. R., Feb. 9: *C. G.*, p. 238/1, App.

1879 See BONANZA.

1900 See GULCH.

Planchment. Planking: especially that of a ceiling.

1891 *Planchment.*—Ceiling. Now seldom heard. An old woman said:—"The roof wets so, I'm afraid the *planchment*'ll fall." From planched, that is, boarded.—*Jour. Amer. Folk-lore*, p. 159. (Century Dict.)

Plank. One of the constituent parts of a political program or manifesto.

1894 I shall allude briefly to . . . the Neal *plank*, the Vilas *plank*, the letter of acceptance of Grover Cleveland, and the majority report of the Committee on Ways and Means.—Mr. Franklin Bartlett of N. Y., H. R., Jan. 30: *C. R.*, p. 1643/1.

1898 Mr. Vandiver of Mo.—Having abandoned the Cuban *plank* and the bimetallic *plank* and the civil-service *plank*, I want to ask you, What have you left to stand on? A Member:—Hanna.—H. R., Jan. 7: *Id.*, p. 449/2.

Planked. Cooked by being split and fastened on a thin board.

1877 One's ideas of *planked* Spanish mackerel.—W. D. Howells, "Out of the Question" (1882), p. 134. (N. E. D.)

1885 The principal dish was "*planked*" *shad.* . . . Four fish are fastened to a board and held towards a hot fire. Whilst cooking, the fish are continually basted.—*Science*, V, 426. (N. E. D.)

1896 [We lately adjourned] so as to allow members to go to a *planked shad* dinner down the Potomac.—Mr. G. L. Johnson of Calif., H. R., May 18: *C. R.*, p. 5382/2.

Plant. To bury. Western slang.

1876 I am not sure that I know the meaning of this term "*plant.*" I have heard of "*planting*" when you put a man under the ground.—Mr. Terry of Va., H. R., Apr. 19: *C. R.*, p. 2619/1.

Plantation manners. Rough, uncouth conduct.

1890 I was charged the other day with being "guilty of *plantation manners.*" —Mr. R. Q. Mills of Tex., H. R., May 14: *C. R.*, p. 4661/1.

1897 When I was a boy, . . . I used to read a great deal about what the early Republicans called "*plantation manners.*"—Mr. J. S. Williams of Miss., H. R., March 31: *Id.*, p. 548/2.

Planter. A sunken tree, deeply embedded and firmly fixed in a river. [1802-1835.]

1816 We struck a *planter*, and split and hung the boat.—Lorenzo Dow, "Journal" (1850), p. 157/1, §1010.

Plaster, v. To cover land with liens or charges.

1872 Those certificates will go into the hands of speculators, who will *plaster* the whole western country with more than two hundred thousand certificates for one hundred and sixty acres each.—Mr. Jas. R. McCormick of Mo., H. R., May 7: *C. G.*, p. 3170/3.

Plat. A ground-plan.

1598 To note all the Islands, and set them down in *plat.*—Hakluyt, "Voyages," I, 437. (N. E. D.)

1740 Every Surveyor shall return Two *Plats* upon every Survey to the Patent-Office.—"Hist. Jamaica," p. 227. (N. E. D.)

1866 After the *plat* is filed and the notice given, then the surveyor general makes his survey; but before a person is entitled to file his *plat*, he must make his claim in conformity with the usages and customs of the mining district where he resides.—Mr. Geo. H. Williams of O., U. S. Senate, June 18: *C. G.*, p. 3233/3.

Platform. A political program or manifesto. [1803-1910.] See **Plank.**

1844 The Whigs, whether on the Lexington *platform* or some other non-committal *platform*, will be . . . known as the party that opposed the country in her just and generous war.—Resolutions of Dem. Nat. Convention, May 30. (Century Dict.)

1870 There never was a grander plank in a political *platform* than that which was adopted at Philadelphia in 1856 [denouncing both slavery and Mormonism.]—Mr. Jasper Packard of Ind., H. R., Feb. 5: *C. G.*, p. 1056/3.

1882 The gentleman from Massachusetts [i.e. the speaker] stands with his feet on every plank of that *platform.*—Mr. W. W. Rice of Mass., H. R., March 15: *C. R.*, p. 1939/1.

1893 *Platforms* are said to be made to get in on and not to stand on; but it shall not be said of me that I rode in on a *platform* and deserted it as soon as I got in.—Mr. W. J. Talbert of S. C., H. R., Aug. 18: *Id.*, p. 499/1.

Platte purchase, the. See quotation.

1872 There [Joseph Roubideaux] beheld a country now called "*the Platte purchase,*" which thirty-five years ago was the home of the Indian and the buffalo, but which is now covered with beautiful farms, prosperous towns, thriving villages, and great and growing cities.—Mr. Isaac C. Parker of Mo., H. R., Apr. 6: *C. G.*, p. 2245/1.

Play. To make sport of; to trifle with; to produce a state of alternate freedom and restriction, as a fisherman playing a fish. Colloquial.

1891 Those who pass their lives in the bush . . . do love to *play* a new chum. —E. Kinglake, "Australian at Home," p. 117. (N. E. D.)

1892 The Government . . . invited a speculation which *played* Congress as fools and the consuming public as victims.—Mr. T. L. Bunting of N. Y., H. R., June 16: *C. R.*, p. 401/1, App.

Playa. A general name for the plain of silt or mud which marks the bottom of desiccated lake-basins in the Western States. Spanish. (Century Dict.)

Play Dick Smith, to. To sponge.

1876 Provide that out of that fund this House may receive that pittance which shall enable it to supply the necessary wants of its members, without either *playing "Dick Smith"* on the Senate or leaving so many of our members confined to their rooms by sickness resulting from drinking iced Potomac.—Mr. Conger of Mich., H. R., June 29: *C. R.*, p. 4260/2. [It had been the custom to provide lemonade and iced tea out of the contingent fund, during the hot weather; but "Blue-jean Williams" of Indiana managed to stop the practice, and members of the House used to run over to the Senate for cooling drinks.]

Played out. Exhausted. Used up. [1862-1902.]

1867 I know there is but little respect for [the Federal Constitution] here, and some on this floor have gone so far as to pronounce it "*played out.*" —Mr. James Brooks of N. Y., H. R., July 9: *C. G.*, p. 538/3.

1871 This business of taking some unreasonably high salary, and setting it up as a reason for increasing every other salary, is about "*played out.*" —Mr. J. B. Ela of N. H., H. R., Jan. 17: *Id.*, p. 559/2.

1875 This "outrage business" is about "*played out.*" The people have heard that song so often that it fails to be music to their ears.—Mr. Eli Saulsbury of Del., U. S. Senate, Jan. 8: *C. R.*, p. 343/1.

1877 Nowadays, . . . if any one makes an appeal for the soldier, you see a sneer or a kind of laugh on the faces of many. They say, "The soldier is *played out.*" Well, perhaps, he is.—Mr. John A. Logan, U. S. Senate, March 3: *Id.*, p. 2174/1.

1883　When England's coal beds and iron mines are *played out*, like her system of government, we shall still have our inexhaustible supply of both.—Mr. W. E. Robinson of N. Y., H. R., Jan. 12: *Id.*, p. 3/1, App.

1887　[The Chinese] are not an effete and *played-out* race, but merely one which by its isolation . . . presents a case of arrested development.—Mr. R. W. Townshend of Ill., H. R., Feb. 3: *Id.*, p. 82/2, App.

Play horse, to. To play the fool. Colloquial.

1894　I trust this discussion will result in something more than simply "*playing horse.*"—Mr. O. M. Kem of Nebr., H. R., Aug. 10: *C. R.*, p. 8395/2.

Play possum, to. To sham death or inability; to dissemble. [1824-1888.]

1822　After being severely wounded, they have been known to lie for several hours as if dead. . . . Hence the expression of "*playing possum*" is common among the inhabitants, being applied to those who act with cunning and duplicity.—"Notices of East Florida," p. 40. (Charleston, S. C.)

1872　[The Democratic party] are, to use a phrase that is now in the newspapers, "*playing possum*"; they are, to use a common phrase, "laying low."—Mr. Oliver P. Morton of Ind., U. S. Senate, Feb. 16: *C. G.*, p. 1073/1.

Plaza. A public square. Spanish.

1871　The lands which they claim have no more need of reclamation than the *plaza* of this city.—*Alta California*, Jan. See *C. G.*, March 3, p. 287/2, App.

Plead. This short preterite, pronounced *pled*, is very common in the U. S. It probably came in by way of Scotland. [1774-1907.]

a.1577　First he *pleaded* ignorance. . . . He came to his mistresse presence and there *pleaded* for himselfe.—George Gascoigne, "Fable of Ieronimo," pp. 201, 260. (1587.)

1866　The Senator from Ohio [Mr. Wade] has *plead* very strongly for what he calls justice to [the people of Nebraska].—Mr. B. G. Brown of Mo., U. S. Senate, Dec. 14: *C. G.*, p. 130/1.

1867　Can this be *plead* to extenuate or relieve you from your oath and duty?—Mr. L. S. Trimble of Ky., H. R., Jan. 21: *Id.*, p. 66/1, App.

[1870　I *pleaded* then for the colored race—Mr. Chas. Sumner of Mass., Jan. 21: *C. G.*, p. 640/1.]

1882　Just recall how the gentleman from Alabama whined last night and *plead* for more time.—Mr. R. G. Horr of Mich., H. R., June 2: *C. R.*, p. 4487/1.

1887　He *plead* his cause to twelve men as though he were talking to twelve thousand.—Mr. M. A. Haynes of N. H., H. R., Feb. 22: *Id.*, p. 2093/1.

Plebe. A newcomer at a naval or military academy.

1884　You could see a squad of "*plebes*" drilling.—Roe, "Nat. Ser. Story," ii. (N. E. D.)

1896　Although he was only a "*plebe*," as the newly entered cadet was termed, even the hazers respected the native dignity and modesty that marked his demeanor.—*Peterson's Mag.*, vi, 266/2. (N. E. D.)

1901　The first-class men never select their smallest man to go up and fight a six-footer who comes in as a "*plebe*," as the newcomers are called, but they select their biggest man.—Mr. H. D. Money of Miss., U. S. Senate, Jan. 17: *C. R.*, p. 1121/2.

Plebeskin. The dress in which a "plebe" enters the academy; civilian dress.

1888　The fourth class entered camp on Monday, but are still wearing their *plebeskins.*—*N. Y. World*, July 22. (Farmer.)

Plenty. Plentiful. Nearly obsolete in England. [1779-1869.]

1613   March out and shew your willing minds by twenty and by twenty.
To Hogsdon or to Newington, where Ale and cakes are *plenty*.
—Beaumont and Fletcher, "Knight of the Burning Pestle," I, 2.

1874   It makes money *plentier*, and that is what the people want.—Mr. O. P.
Morton of Ind., U. S. Senate, Feb. 17: *C. R.*, p. 1553/1.

"Pluck-me" system, The.   The system of requiring miners to purchase
their personal and domestic supplies at stores established by the
mine-owners.

1894   Mr. Tarsney asked this question: "Are you familiar with the political
nomenclature [in southwestern Missouri]? What is known as *the
'pluck me' system*? Are you aware that it was made a political
issue in that State?" . . . I am familiar with the legislation of Missouri,
and have never heard of legislative action in regard to *the "pluck me"*
system.—Mr. C. H. Morgan of Mo., H. R., Jan. 19: *C. R.*, p. 312/2,
App.

Plug hat.   A top or "stove-pipe" hat.   Slang.

1879   It reminds me of an Indian I once saw out in the far West, whose
entire toilet consisted of a red bandana around his neck and a *plug hat*;
and . . . he was perfectly unconscious of the ridiculous figure he
presented.—Mr. J. B. Weaver of Ia., H. R., Apr. 4: *C. R.*, p. 227/1.

1881   The *plug hat* is virtually a sort of social guarantee for the preserva-
tion of peace and order.—*Phila. Record*, No. 3455, p. 6.   (N. E. D.)

1886   [The Yellowstone Park] should be free to every American citizen
whether he wears a *plug hat* or the garb of a workman.—Mr. D. B.
Henderson of Ia., H. R., Aug. 2: *C. R.*, p. 7866/1.

1890   The ornamental gentlemen who wear diamond breastpins and kid
gloves and *plug hats.*—Mr. J. K. Jones of Ark., U. S. Senate, Aug. 7:
Id., p. 8269/2.

Plug-ugly.   A Baltimore rowdy; a rowdy in general.   [1857-1876.]

1864   The gentleman from the Baltimore district (Mr. Davis) . . . appeared
here as the Representative of the *Plug-Uglyism* of Baltimore.—Mr.
Harrington of Ind., H. R., Apr. 12: *C. G.*, p. 1592/1.

1864   The gentleman from Massachusetts is unfortunate in his sneer at the
loyal mechanics of Baltimore, whom he styles *"Plug Uglies."*—Mr.
Davis of Md., H. R., May 9: *Id.*, p. 2191/2.

1864   If I read the history of Baltimore aright, [Mr. Davis] did not come
to Congress until the laws of his State had been set at defiance by the
Plug Uglies, Black Snakes, and Blood Tubs of his district.—Mr.
Johnson of Pa., H. R., May 12: *Id.*, p. 2260/1.

1866   See MACHINE.

1879   Repeal these laws, and the "murderers" of New York, the *"plug uglies"*
of Baltimore, and the "repeaters" of Philadelphia and Cincinnati will
hold high carnival on election day.—Mr. Wm. Ward of Pa., H. R.,
June 11: C. R., p. 105/2, App.

1887   See THUG.

Plumb, plump.   Blunt, direct, downright, complete.   Also as adverb.
[1691-1893.]

1864   This is the *plump* sentence and sentiment of [Mr. Voorhees] on a war
which called for the sacrifice of hecatombs of men.—Mr. Grinnell of
Ia., H. R., March 5: *C. G.*, p. 954/2.

1866   "A full, solemn, *plump* disclaimer on the part of President Lincoln of
the exercise of that assumed power which I am now combatting, the
power asserted at present by President Johnson [as to reconstruction]."
—Mr. Jacob M. Howard of Michigan. "Has not the President quite
as distinctly, quite as *plumply*, disclaimed on his part any attempt to
influence Congress to admit members from the southern States upon
this floor?"—Mr. Edgar Cowan of Pa., U. S. Senate, May 11: *Id.*,
p. 2552/2.

1869 [He] has approximated very closely, if he has not struck *plumb*, the principles upon which this bill should be considered.—Mr. Garrett Davis of Ky., U. S. Senate, Jan. 6: *Id.*, p. 211/1.

1871 I am in the habit of meeting duties as I meet dangers, *"plump"*; and I will not avoid this one.—Mr. Joshua Hill of Ga., U. S. Senate, Apr. 10: *Id.*, p. 542/1.

1874 I will say *plumply* that . . . I shall vote to seat Mr. Gunter.—Mr. J. R. Hawley of Conn., H. R., Feb. 17: *C. R.*, p. 1569/2.

1879 [As the man said to his wife], "I am a man of few words, and now I am *plumb* done talking."—Mr. Vance of N. C., U. S. Senate, May 19: *C. R.*, p. 1461/1.

Plumed Knight. Robert Ingersoll applied this term to James G. Blaine in a political campaign. [1888-1908.]

1876 "Like an armed warrior, like a *plumed knight*, James G. Blaine marched down the halls of the American Congress, and threw his shining lance full and fair against the brazen forehead of every defamer of this country and maligner of its honor."—Col. Robt. G. Ingersoll, at the Republican Natl. Convention held in Cincinnati (June).

1879 The *"plumed knight"* from Maine [Mr. Blaine] and the distinguished parliamentary gladiator from Georgia [Mr. Hill] were the central figures in the discussion in [the 44th] Congress.—Mr. J. B. Weaver of Ia., H. R., Apr. 4: *C. R.*, p. 225/2.

1879 I said I had no right to give the name of the author of those sentiments which I have just read, but I may say he is the man whom the great Illinois humanitarian, after having captured the devil and knocked off his horns and cut off his tail, and found him an agreeable gentleman, and abolished hell and substituted in its stead green fields and pleasant places, once distinguished by calling him the *"plumed knight."*—Mr. E. S. Bragg of Wisc., H. R., Apr. 24: *Id.*, p. 853/1.

1881 I see my friend from Maine [Mr. Frye] whose forehead shines like a star in the sky. I call upon him first, because he represents the *plumed knight* of Maine.—Mr. S. S. Cox of N. Y., H. R., Jan. 27: *Id.*, p. 54/1, App.

1884 The Republican party of Pennsylvania and elsewhere, including, in newspaper phrase, *"the Plumed Knight of Maine,"* advocate the distribution of the surplus among the States.—Mr. W. C. Oates of Ala., H. R., May 5: *Id.*, p. 3849/1.

1893 I remember seeing the *Plumed Knight* sitting in this Chamber and declining to vote.—Mr. H. M. Teller of Colo., U. S. Senate, Oct. 18: *Id.*, p. 2644/1.

Plurality. A greater number, but less than half of the total (a majority being more than half of any total); also the excess of this greater number over the remainder. [1803-1860.]

1866 I do not deny that a *plurality* of a legislature, when the majority so determine, can elect a Senator. I concede that, but I say that [in the New Jersey case] nobody having competent authority undertook to prescribe that a *plurality* should elect.—Mr. Daniel Clark of N. H., U. S. Senate, March 22: *C. G.*, p. 1566/1.

1866 They had passed this rule in their joint convention, that a *plurality* should elect.—The same, March 23: *Id.*, p. 1594/3.

1882 It cannot be contended that either of the Republican candidates could have obtained a *plurality* over Mr. Shelley. Indeed it was as clear as the noonday sun that Mr. Shelley was bound to have a *plurality*, if not a majority.—Mr. F. E. Beltzhoover of Pa., U. S. Senate, July 20: *C. R.*, p. 524/2.

1890 Commencing with Lincoln in 1860, his *plurality* was 491,249, his minority 948,055 votes. In 1864 Mr. Lincoln's majority was 407,342. In 1868 Grant's majority was 305,458; in 1872 Grant's majority was

727,975; but in 1876 Tilden's majority was 157,020, while his *plurality* over Hayes was 250,918. . . . In 1880 Mr. Garfield's *plurality* was 3,834; his minority 314,253. In 1884 Cleveland's *plurality* was 26,584; his minority 403,773, but Blaine's minority was 430,357.—Mr. C. H. Mansur of Mo., U. S. Senate, July 1: *Id.*, p. 6899/2.

1896 It behooves the members of this House, before. they reverse a *plurality* of 40 votes and turn it into a [contrary] *plurality* of 30 votes, to [act carefully].—Mr. W. H. Moody of Mass., U. S. Senate, May 12: *Id.*, p. 5139/1.

1912 The figures of Douglas's *plurality* in the Republican landslide year of 1904 were 35,995, and hold the Massachusetts record for Democratic gubernatorial *pluralities.—N. Y. Evening Post*, May 30.

Pocket veto. When the Executive does not return a bill that has passed both houses, he is said to pocket it. [1848-1888.]

1866 The question of how much credit the Senator from Kansas [Mr. Lane] is entitled to for so advising the President, and urging him to *pocket that bill*, I leave for him and the Senate to determine.—Mr. B. G. Brown of Mo., U. S. Senate, Apr. 6: *C. G.*, p. 1804/2.

1866 [They] issued a protest charging Mr. Lincoln with being a usurper and a tyrant because he had *pocketed this bill* of theirs.—Mr. Edgar Cowan of Pa., U. S. Senate, May 11: *Id.*, p. 2558/1.

1869 The Thirty-Fifth Congress made an appropriation [for the Niagara ship-canal], but President Buchanan smothered the bill by a *pocket veto.*—Mr. H. E. Paine of Wisc., H. R., Jan. 14: *Id.*, p. 374/2.

1888 Passing at the end of a session of Congress, the President had not an opportunity to examine it. He retained the bill, and was greatly abused for what was denominated a *"pocket veto."*—Mr. C. R. Buckalew of Pa., H. R., Dec. 11: *C. R.*, p. 165/1.

Pocosin. From the Renape word *pakwesen*, a "dismal swamp," miry in summer and overflowed in winter.—W. R. Gerard, in "Handbook of Am. Indians," Wash., 1910. The name Pocosin (or Pocuosin) was applied to a small Virginia river as early as 1671. See Vol. II, **Poccoson lands.** [1709-1811.]

1728 This firm Land lasted not long before they came upon the dreadful *Pocoson* they had been threaten'd with.—William Byrd, "Writings," p. 42 (1901.)

Pod. A small herd of seals, whales, &c.; a small flock of birds. [1832-1840.]

1832 We saw several small *pods* of coots go by.—Daniel Webster, "Priv. Corresp." (1857) I, 526, (N. E. D.), [to Stephen White, Sept. 14].

1840 The Sperm Whale . . . usually occurs in parties, which are termed by whalers "schools" and *"pods."*—F. D. Bennett, "Whaling Voyage," II, 171. (N. E. D.)

1874 A *pod* of whales was seen in the offing.—C. M. Scammon, "Marine Mammals" (N. Y.), p. 36. (Century Dict.)

1897, 1898 N. E. D.

Pod augur. One of which the stem is straight, or slightly spiral. (Century Dict.)

1878 A law has been worked through,—and I say "worked through" in the highest *pod-augur* sense that you can express by it.—Mr. O. D. Conger of Mich., H. R., Feb. 15: *C. R.*, p. 1123/1.

Pointer. A bit of useful information; a suggestion. [1884-1902.]

1894 I expect [Mr. Walker of Mass.] will prove the fallacy of all my arguments. But I will just give him a *pointer.*—Mr. J. C. Sibley of Pa., H. R., July 19: *C. R.*, p. 936/1, App.

1899 Some of [the Kentuckians] could have given *pointers* to Fra Diavolo himself.—Mr. Champ Clark of Mo., H. R., Feb. 4: *Id.*, p. 1468/1.

1912 Yet, in spite of all this, the Boerse continues to watch nervously for adverse political *pointers*, and it is disposed to make the most of them as a justification either for selling stocks or for inactivity. Austria continues to be the centre of anxiety.—Corresp. *N. Y. Evening Post*, Dec. 26, p. 8/5.

Point-no-point. Having apparently a point, but really none; as, the address was point-no-point. (Standard Dict., 1909.)

1869 It may be that we decline to accept the *"point-no-point"* policy of the party whom [Mr. Fernando Wood] in part represents here.—Mr. Thos. Fitch of Nev., H. R., Apr. 1: *C. G.*, p. 432/3.

1878 This resolution is . . mere *brutum fulmen*. It sails for *point-no-point*, and it reaches no point.—Mr. Thomas F. Bayard of Del., U. S. Senate, Apr. 17: *C. R.*, p. 2606/1.

Pokerish. Dangerous, alarming; "eerie." [1827-1859.]

1831 She looked plaguy *pokerish* at me.—*The Georgian* (Savannah), Jan. 22, p. 2/5. (From the *Constellation*.)

Pole. To move a boat along with a pole. [1774-1814.]

1881 Streams that never would and never could float a steam vessel, or a sail-vessel, or anything more than a boat that was floated down with the current and *poled* up with poles.—Mr. Frank Kernan of N. Y., U. S. Senate, Feb. 26: *C. R.*, p. 2151/1.

Policy dealers, shops, tickets. "Policy" is a mode of gambling based on a lottery.

1876 Negroes and poor people all over this land have been swindled by *policy dealers*, whose swindling transactions are based upon the drawings of the lottery. . . It is a violation of the law in my State to sell a lottery ticket, or a ticket based upon a lottery, known as *"policy."*—Mr. Whyte of Md., U. S. Senate, June 30: *C. R.*, p. 4263/2.

1879 *Policy-shop*, an office opened for gambling in connection with lotteries. (Webster's Dict. Supp.)

1903 He has closed every gambling-den, pool-room, disorderly house and *policy shop*.—*Daily Chronicle*, Nov. 3, p. 5/3. (N. E. D.)

Politician. This word, especially in the United States, has acquired a sinister meaning. [1646-1879.]

1796 The mere *politician*, equally with the pious man, ought to respect and cherish [religion and morality.]—Farewell Address of Geo. Washington, Sept. 19.

1863 Smart hotel *politicians* with rakish moustache, infinitesimal shirt collars, and enormous breeches.—Mr. G. H. Yeaman of Ky., H. R., Feb. 26: *C. G.*, p. 133/1, App.

1866 I am but a poor *politician*, according to the meaning of that word in common parlance,—a word but the synonym for fraud, violence, and ignoble conduct.—Mr. B. G. Harris of Md., H. R., June 14: *Id.*, p. 3172/2.

Pollywog. A tadpole. The forms Polwygle, Porwigle, Polwig, etc. occur in the 15-17th centuries. [1835-1888.]

1871 Temperate drinking stands in the same relation to drunkenness that *porwiggles* do to frogs. Some *porwiggles* die before maturity; that is all the difference.—Mr. S. P. Morrill of Me., H. R., March 2: *C. G.*, p. 243/2, App.

Pompey. See quotation. The phrase, a local one, is also applied to ice when thawing. (Cent. Dict.)

1904 The floor is *"pompey,"* as the firemen say, when it bulges and sags. It is then time to get out. . . . It was thought time and again that firemen had been lost in the building.—*N. Y. World*, Jan. 3. (Century Dict.)

Pone. Corn meal bread; johnnycake.

1877 Is it possible that we can teach such a fastidious people [as the French] to eat mush and *pone*?—Mr. S. S. Cox of N. Y., H. R., Nov. 19: *C. R.*, p. 534/2.

1898 See COLLARDS.

Pool, pooling. A pool is "a common fund into or from which all gains or losses of the contributors are paid." (N. E. D.) [1879-1910.] To pool is to create and maintain such a fund; also to act in concert for common interests.

1872 I find myself charged by Mr. Gould . . . with being interested in a put or *pool* . . . with Mr. Drew and others.—W. R. Travers in *N. Y. Herald*, Nov. 25, p. 873. (N. E. D.)

1875 I do believe this claim is nothing but a "*pool*" and a plaything, that is knocked and kicked from one end of Pennsylvania Avenue to the other.—Mr. G. L. Fort of Ill., H. R., Feb. 9: *C. R.*, p. 1088/1.

1878 The bill by its express terms prohibits any such "*pooling*" arrangement hereafter. It . . . fosters competition between these lines, and prevents "*pooling*."—Mr. R. W. Townshend of Ill., H. R., Dec. 11: *Id.*, p. 100/1.

1878 Mr. Hewitt of New York:—[Mr. Townshend's] definition of the word "*pool*" does not correspond with that of the dictionary. These roads did combine to fix a rate, but they did not combine to "*pool*" their earnings. Mr. Townshend:—I understand the proper definition, and I say that, according to the newspapers they did in that instance combine to *pool* their earnings as well as to fix the rate.—H. R., Dec. 11: *Id.*, p. 101/2.

1881 What is *pooling*? An agreement or combination between different railroads to divide in a certain ratio their aggregate or net earnings; an agreement not to compete with one another for patronage; a combination or conspiracy to charge the maximum rates which traffic will bear, and divide the plunder between them. They "*pool their issues.*" It is a railroad union, by which they can effectively strike for higher wages, whenever spasms of prosperity appear in the country. It destroys all competition, and lays every industry and enterprise helpless at the feet of this vast money power.—Mr. W. J. Samford of Ala., H. R., Feb. 10: *Id.*, p. 120/2, App.

1881 The marine insurance men are still striving to form a *pool.*—*Chicago Times*, June 1. (N. E. D.)

1884 Stamford rich men have formed a *pool* to pay the fines imposed upon them for fast driving.—*Boston Journal*, Jan. 29, p. 4/4. (N. E. D.)

1884 This *pooling system* is the ligature that binds [the railroad companies] together like the Siamese twins, and, being corporations, [they] have no souls to damn or consciences to quicken.—Mr. J. H. Murphy of Ia., H. R., June 9: *C. R.*, p. 4927/2.

1884 Railroad wars occurred before the divine intricacies of the *pooling system* were evolved from the mental consciousness of the railroad expert. They have occurred since the *pool* has been in active operation, and the country still lives.—Mr. J. R. Glascock of Calif., H. R., Dec. 11: *Id.*, p. 189/2.

1884 Various accounts have been given of the *pool* by railroad people, and all lead to the one conclusion, that the object of the *pool* is to maintain rates.—Mr. P. Dunn of Ark., H. R., *Id.*, p. 195/1.

1884 *Pooling* contracts between divers competing lines of railroads are made to cut off all competition in the hauling of freight.—Mr. Wood of Ind., H. R., *Id.*, p. 201/1.

1887 The fact that "*pools*" are prohibited by the Constitutions of nine States,—Arkansas, Illinois, Colorado, Georgia, Ohio, Michigan, Missouri, Nebraska, and Pennsylvania,—ought to be strongly persuasive evidence that the principle is vicious in practice, while the fact that all the wrongs committed under the Standard Oil monopoly were perpetrated under the *pooling system* . . . ought to make Congress set its face against it.—Mr. J. B. Beck of Ky., U. S. Senate, Jan. 10: *Id.*, p. 483/2.

1888 The culminating point in the speculative history of Mr. [Henry] Villard . . . was the famous *blind pool* in Northern Pacific.—Henry Clews, "Twenty-Eight Years in Wall St.," p. 209. (N. Y.)

1890 The roads, being practically *pooled* under the worst form of a pool,—namely, quiet agreements between their agents,—are today charging not simply all that the traffic will bear, but more than the traffic will bear.—Mr. John A. Anderson of Kan., H. R., May 24: *C. R.*, p. 5254/1.

1893 A "*pool*" is an agreement among a coterie of operators to buy or sell, and manipulate the market. It may be a "bull" *pool* or a "bear" *pool*. A "*bobtailed pool*" is when a few men with little cash try to make a turn in the market. A "*blind pool*" is when the cash is supplied by different persons to be managed by one at his own pleasure.—Mr. Marriott Brosius of Pa., H. R., March 1: *Id.*, p. 72/1, App.

1894 Every interest seeking special privileges is taken into a *pool*, on the sole condition that it can furnish a vote in Congress for the common purpose.—Mr. J. G. Maguire of Calif., H. R., Jan. 11: *Id.*, p. 590/1, App.

Poor whites, Poor white trash. A class much despised in the South. [1836-1901.]

1865 The Senator from Wisconsin [Mr. Doolittle] goes off with a sickly sentimentality for the woolly-headed negro, and cares nothing for the "*poor white trash*" of Louisiana.—Mr. L. W. Powell of Ky., U. S. Senate, Feb. 3: *C. G.*, p. 582/1.

1866 What consideration have the southern oligarchy ever shown for the "*poor white trash*"?—Mr. Elijah Ward of N. Y., Jan. 25: *Id.*, p. 434/2.

1866 See DIPPING.

1876 In my own town I have heard of the declarations of colored people that they would not work for the *white trash*.—Mr. Saulsbury of Del., U. S. Senate, Aug. 5: *C. R.*, p. 5206/2.

1896 Mr. Walker:—[They] have gone back nearly to the ignorance of what were called "*poor white trash*" of the South before the war. . . . Mr. Williams:—I might say in response to the gentleman from Massachusetts that the phrase he uses, "*poor white trash*," is never used in the South, except by the negroes or novelists. . . . Mr. Walker:—Everybody knows that in the days of slavery there were a class of white people who were banished to the mountains and sand hills, who were called "crackers" and "*poor white trash*."—H. R., Dec. 22: *Id.*, pp. 439-441.

Poor-will. A bird of the genus *Phalænoptilus*.

1887 At nightfall the *poor-wills* begin to utter their boding call from the wooded ravines . . .; not "whip-poor-will," as in the East, but with two syllables only.—Theodore Roosevelt, *Century Mag.*, xxxv, 664.

Pop corn. Indian corn, the kernels of which may be burst open and puffed out by dry heat; also, the popped corn. (Webster.) [1854-1858.]

1877 [Mr. Hewitt] goes so far as to hint that the "*pop-corn*" fiend will be introduced upon the railways of France.—Mr. S. S. Cox of N. Y., H. R., Nov. 19: *C. R.*, p. 534/1.

1911 The women of Elgin have a suffrage *popcorn farm*, owned, cultivated, and generally managed by suffragists, but with no restriction as to political voting on the purchaser of the product. Dollars upon dollars have gone to the Illinois work through this revenue-producing enterprise, and incidentally recruits to the suffrage cause have been won, since it is said no man can till a suffrage *popcorn field* without almost immediately catching the spirit of the cause.—Decatur (Ill.) Correspondence of the *Chicago Tribune*, November.

Pope Night. The fifth of November. [1842-1903.[See extracts from N. H. newspapers, 1892: *Journal of American Folk-lore*, v, 335-6.

Popgun bills. A contemptuous term applied to bills which are assumed to be of small importance.

1894 I propose to speak generally of these 4 *"popgun" bills* which are . . to be fired from this House into the country to try to give some sugar-coating to the action of the House . . . on the general tariff bill.—Mr. S. E. Payne of N. Y., H. R., Aug. 13: *C. R.*, p. 1202/1, App.

1894 Bills which are shortly to come before the Senate, termed irreverently, as I submit, *"pop-gun bills."*—Mr. I. G. Harris of Tenn., U. S. Senate, Dec. 5: *Id.*, p. 47/1.

1895 [These men] run in here a *popgun*, horizontal, revenue-only *bill*.—Mr. H. G. Turner of Ga., H. R., Dec. 26: *Id.*, p. 322/2.

Popocrat. A nonce-word for Populist.

1898 A man is a very mean man who would try to steal a piece of five minutes, and none but a *Popocrat* would do it.—Mr. D. B. Henderson of Ia., H. R., Jan. 31: *C. R.*, p. 1308/2.

Poppycock. Nonsense, foolishness, bombast. Slang.

1890 I do not think their statement is worth a bawbee, and all their alleged wealth and respectability is *poppycock.*—Mr. John A. Anderson of Kan., H. R., June 9: *C. R.*, p. 5857/1.

1898 I suppose there is less superstition about me than any human being that ever lived, and less reverence for mere balderdash and *poppycock.*—Mr. J. S. Williams of Miss., H. R., Dec. 20: *Id.*, p. 344/2.

Populite. A Populist.

1898 Mr. Kolb, . . . who has been the head and shoulders of the *Populite* party of Alabama since its organization, . . . and perhaps has a warmer place in the hearts of the *Populites* of America than any other one man, . . . begged his *Populist* [*sic*] friends not to support Aldrich. . . . He said that if a *Populite* was nominated by a *Populite* convention for President he would support him.—Mr. A. F. Fox of Miss., H. R., Feb. 8: *C. R.*, p. 1553/1.

Porgy. A name applied to various species of fish. [1775-1857.]

1830 [He] was about discussing the tail of a *porgy* when the epidemic struck him.—*Am. Beacon* (Norfolk, Va.), Aug. 9, p. 4/2. [From the *N. Y. Courant.*)

1849 I caught some fish, namely, tautog and skippog, the same, I suppose, as are called *"Porgee"* in New York.—D. Webster to R. M. Blatchford, Aug. 12: "Private Corresp." (1857), II, 337.

Pork. Financial profit; "boodle." Slang.

1879 We know how *"pork"* makes men "holler." St. Louis is going to have some of the *"pork"* indirectly; but it will not do any good.—Mr. M. I. Townsend of N. Y., H. R., Feb. 28: *C. R.*, p. 2131/1.

1882 With this money in their pockets, with the *"pork"* in their possession, can it be hoped &c.?—Mr. A. S. Willis of Ky., H. R., July 8: *Id.*, p. 5814/1.

1883 [Mr. Burrows of Mich.] has antagonized this bill for the reason, I apprehend, that he did not get a large enough portion of the *"pork."*—Mr. R. W. Townsend of Ill., H. R., Feb. 28: *Id.*, p. 3434/2.

1884 [Mr. Calkins of Ind.] in his remarks on this bill evidently implied a belief on his part that there is *"pork* enough in the pot" to enable this bill to go through.—Mr. J. D. White of Ky., H. R., June 10: *Id.*, p. 4979/2.

1884 [Certain men] will not hesitate to vote millions of dollars out of the Treasury for any purpose whatever, almost, if they can only get a small "piece of the *pork"* for their own locality.—Mr. R. W. Townshend of Ill., H. R., June 14: *Id.*, p. 5154/1.

1886 I do not mean to say that they got any of the *pork*, but their neighbors have, and their constituents have, and they are simply standing by them.—Mr. J. R. Cobb of Ind., H. R., July 28: *Id.*, p. 7663/1.

1888 Has the *"pork"* been so cunningly divided amongst the members of the House in this bill [for rivers and harbors] that its final passage is assured?—Mr. W. H. Sowden of Pa., H. R., May 7: *Id.*, p. 3793/1.

1899 Mr. Maddox:—What have you got as your part of the *pork*? . . . For every dollar that the members from the South have obtained, gentlemen on the other side get about $10. . . . Mr. Talbert:—Buzzard-and-turkey business!—H. R., Feb. 28: *C. R.*, p. 2579/1. [See TURKEY, TO SAY.]

1901 [This river and harbor bill] has become known in the most remote corners of the U. S. . . . as the *pork* bill of Congress.—Mr. T. H. Carter of Mont., U. S. Senate, March 2: *Id.*, p. 3527/1.

Porkopolis. A name formerly applied to Cincinnati. [1844-1870.]

1871 Mr. Sherman:—If that gentleman was from Ohio, I should like to know his name. Mr. Hill:—He is big enough to come from Ohio, from *Porkopolis* or anywhere else. His name is Harris.—U. S. Senate, Apr. 10: *C. G.*, p. 541/1.

Portage. A place where canoes have to be carried across land. [1698-1821.]

1870 Interlacing railways for *portages* by land where navigable rivers are wanting.—Mr. O. D. Conger of Mich., H. R., June 13: *C. G.*, p. 477/2, App.

Porterhouse steak. A cut between the tenderloin and the sirloin. [1843-1909.]

1843 [In Dublin], a piece of boiled salmon or a *Porter-House steak* was placed upon my table.—Thurlow Weed, "Letters," p. 39. (1866.)

1895 [At the Congressional restaurant] an ordinary tenderloin steak costs from 90 cents to a dollar. . . . No; it goes higher than the sum I have stated. It goes up to $4 with truffles. I do not know what truffles are, but an ordinary *porterhouse beefsteak* with truffles costs $4.—Mr. W. V. Allen of Neb., U. S. Senate, Jan. 3: *C. R.*, p. 584/2.

Posted, Posted-up. Informed. [1850-1882.]

1850 While the several State conventions were deliberating on the proposed constitution, Russell kept the account of their progress *"posted up,"* in detail.—J. T. Buckingham, "Specimens of Newspaper Literature," II, 45.

1864 Virginia is somehow or somewhere a State, and to us, her loyal citizens, whose interest it is to keep *posted* about her, it is no difficult task to find her whereabouts.—Mr. Joseph Segar of Va., H. R., May 17: *C. G.*, p. 2316/1.

1866 I want you to *post* me in regard to [this alleged outrage]; to tell me in what its iniquity consists.—Mr. Ebenezer Dumont of Ind., H. R., June 4: *Id.*, p. 2953/2.

1869 The Chicago merchant is always *posted* on Mark Lane quotations.—Mr. F. A. Pike of Me., H. R., Feb. 13: *Id.*, p. 1187/2.

1870 I am willing at all times, on any question affecting the great mechanical or manufacturing interests of the country, to yield to those who I know are *posted* upon it.—Mr. H. C. Calkin of N. Y., H. R., Feb. 3: *Id.*, p. 1020/2.

1875 I do not profess to be thoroughly *posted* in parliamentary law.—Mr. J. B. Beck of Ky., H. R., Feb. 1: *C. R.*, p. 895/1.

1876 Unless Caldwell was *posted*, he might "blow" something that would ruin the whole kettle of fish.—Mr. J. Proctor Knott of Ky., H. R., Aug. 3: *Id.*, p. 5127/1.

1881 If my good friend from Illinois [Mr. Logan] would *post himself* a little better on the facts of this case, he would get along better.—Mr. Joseph E. Brown of Ga., U. S. Senate, March 24: *C. R.*, p. 52/1.

Poster. A bill or placard, often of a decorative character. (Webster.)

1871 The meeting was called through *posters* put up about town. One of these *posters* was instrumental in causing the streets of Meridian to run with blood.—Mr. C. H. Porter of Va., H. R., Apr. 4: *C. G.*, p. 279/1, App.

1873 Yesterday I found here this large paper (holding a large yellow-colored *poster* in his hand), which reminds one of the *posters* that may be seen at the cross-roads.—Mr. Chipman of the District of Columbia, H. R., Feb. 11: *Id.*, p. 1267/2.

Post-route. A fixed line of travel over which mail is to be carried. See Vol. II, **Route** [1850].

1879 The Second Assistant Postmaster-General is the one intrusted with the establishment of the additional *post-routes.*—Mr. Maxey of Tex., U. S. Senate, May 17: *C. R.*, p. 1418/2.

Post-trader. An authorized sutler at a military post.

1887 A ten gallon demijohn of *post-trader's* whisky.—*P. M. Gazette*, Aug. 10, p. 14/1. (N. E. D.)

1890 At some forts . . . the canteen is looked upon coldly by the officers, because it will decrease the revenue of the *post-trader*, who is a personal friend of theirs. In such a connection the canteen does not get established, for the reason that no officer will interest himself in it, and the result is that the *post-trader's* store booms on pay-day, the men get drunk, etc.—Statement of a soldier, cited in *C. R.*, May 9, p. 4376/1.

1894 The store and house of the *post-trader* where we bought our provisions.—*Outing*, xxiv, 85/2. (N. E. D.)

Pot. See **Jackpot**.

Potato bug. A black-and-yellow striped beetle *Leptinotarsa decemlineata*) which feeds on the leaves of the potato. (Webster.) [1801-1868.]

1880 When the *potato-bug* was invading the crops of this country, Professor Riley was called into the field.—Mr. John T. Morgan of Ala., U. S. Senate, June 9: *C. R.*, p. 4320/1.

Potato, to hold one's. To be quiet. Slang; uncommon.

1892 Now let me beg of the gentleman to *hold his potato.*—Mr. T. E. Watson of Ga., H. R., Jan. 27: *C. R.*, p. 600/1.

Potlatch. A gift, a distribution of gifts at a tribal feast. Chinook jargon.

1870 Let me say that I have been to distributions of annuities; they are called "*potlashes*" in my country; and I have seen blankets torn into quarters and distributed. I have seen bolts of red calico torn, and a yard given to every grown squaw, and half a yard to every papoose.—Mr. Garfielde of Wash., *H. R.*, March 2: *C. G.*, p. 1647/2.

1884 A *potlatch* is . . a sort of grand reunion and general gathering . . . an occasion for the exchanging of big presents.—*S. F. Chronicle*, Sept. (N. E. D.)

1890 On his return he again called the people together, and held a big *potlatch*, giving the Indians what appeared to them at that time great curiosities.—*Amer. Antiquarian*, p. 75. (N. E. D.)

Pow wow. A consultation or conference (of N. Am. Indians and thence extended to general use). A conjurer or medicine-man. [1659-1865.]

a.1645 A warr with the Narragansett is verie considerable to this plantation, for I doubt whither yt be not sinne in vs, hauing power in our hands, to suffer them to mayntevne the worship of the devill, which their *paw wawes* often doe.—Letter of Emanuel Downing from Massachusetts-Bay, cited in the *C. G.*, Feb. 16, 1864, p. 680/1.

1670 The Kings and great *Pawwoos* or Connirers [Coniurers] may have two or three Wives.—Samuel Clarke, "Acct. of the Plantations," p. 48.

1876   In their party *pow-wow* [Mr. Lamar and his friends] declared by formal resolution against the white-line policy.—*Meridian* (Miss.) *Mercury,* July 29: See *C. R.,* Aug. 4, p. 5183/2. [See WHITE LINE.]

Prairie dog. An American burrowing rodent, a kind of squirrel. [1805-1909.]

1805   See Appendix XXVI in Vol. II.
1810   See WISHTONWISH.
1870   See "The Heart of the Continent," by F. H. Ludlow, pp. 45-47, 164-5.

Prairie schooner. A long canvas-covered wagon used especially by emigrants crossing the prairies. (Webster.) [1858-1910.]

1870   Mr. Logan:—I would like to know if the gentleman ever saw a *"prairie schooner?"* Mr. Calkin of New York:—I never was on a prairie in my life.—H. R., Feb. 3: *C. G.,* p. 1020/3.

Praline, Prawleen. A sugared almond. Fr. A confection of nut kernels and sugar.

1727   Bradley, "Fam. Dict." (N. E. D.)
1809   [We were] provided with dried meat, frozen fish, and a small quantity of *praline,* made of roasted maize, rendered palatable with sugar.—A. Henry, "Travels in Canada," p. 265. (N. E. D.)
1893   She gave my two hands full of *prawleens,* and told me to eat them all.—Mary A. Owen, "Old Rabbit, The Voodoo, etc.," p. 36.

Preach a funeral. To preach a funeral sermon. [1851-1855.]

1641   The fiend . . . *preacht Sauls funerall,* as one calls it.—John Trapp, "Theol.," p. 193. (N. E. D.)
1655   In the absence of Doctor Humfreys designed for that service, Mr. Giles Laurence *preached his Funeralls.*—Thos. Fuller's "Ch. Hist.," ix, iii, 2. (N. E. D.)
a.1661   I could learn little from the Minister which *preached his funeral.*—Worthies, Hereford (1662), p. 41. (N. E. D.)
1890   [Among the mountain whites of the South] the *"funeral will be preached"* five, ten, or twenty years after the death, and will include in its scope all the members of the family who have died since the last funeral was celebrated.—Magazine article, quoted in the U. S. Senate, Feb. 10: *C. R.,* p. 1165/1.

Precipitators. Those who hurried on the Civil War.

1866   Here are Vigilance Committees and *Precipitators* and Knights of the Golden Circle, and it is hardly safe for a man to go out.—Mr. Edgar Cowan of Pa., U. S. Senate, June 6: *C. G.,* p. 2990/1.
1866   Where a man does owe direct, immediate allegiance, and where he acknowledges that he owes it, he has a corresponding and reciprocal right to demand from his Government, to whom he owes it, that it shall protect him, and that it shall not leave him to be overridden by a State organization, by a county organization, by an organization of Knights of the Golden Circle, by an organization of *precipitators,* by an organization of minute-men, or any other kind of men.—The same, Dec. 18: *Id.,* p. 166/3, App.

Preëmpt. To settle (on public land) with the right of purchasing before others. See Vol. II, **Pre-emptioner.** [1841-1850.]

1872   The man who desires to *pre-empt* land builds a shanty, scratches up a little bit of land, and gets two witnesses to swear that he has made an improvement.—Mr. John Coburn of Ind., H. R., Dec. 12: *C. G.,* p. 163/2.

Preposterosity. Preposterousness.

1876   Extravagance and *"preposterosity,"* as the late Mr. Sumner would say.—Mr. G. F. Edmunds of Vt., U. S. Senate, July 17: *C. R.,* p. 4653/2.

Present. To mention, to "remember" a person to another. [1808-1834.]

1843   [Jan. 24.] You will please *present* Mrs. Houston and myself to Col. and Madam Christy, also to Mr. Caruthers and family. Very truly, thy friend, Sam. Houston.—Letter to Col. Bryan: Reply of Gen. Thos. J. Green, p. 27. (1854.)

Pretzel. A small salted biscuit of twisted shape. [1888-1889.]
1886 See DUTCHMAN.

Previous, too. A jocose equivalent for *premature.* Needlessly prompt. [1885-1890.]
1890 Mr. Coleman:—I think [my colleague] was a little *"too previous."* Mr. Davidson:—I indorse the statement that the discussion of this question at this time was a little *"too previous."*—H. R., Apr. 9: *C. R.*, p. 3220/1.
1890 The grumbling . . . has been *too previous.*—Boston Journal, June 21, p. 2/3. (N. E. D.)
1895 Summer is *too previous.*—Boston Herald, May 11, p. 6/6. (N. E. D.)
1902 The Stock Exchange has been, in the language of the street, a little *"too previous."*—Westm. Gazette, July 16, p. 9/1. (N. E. D.)

Price level. See quotation.
1892 There is not a man present that does not know the meaning of a *"price level."* . . . *Price level* means what? It means that all the product to which you have given a price, the world over, is potentially present in the sample quart, or pint, or gallon, or pound, of the sample shown.—Mr. J. H. Walker of Mass., H. R., March 23: *C. R.*, p. 2467/2.

Priest. Name applied by early Quakers to the Congregational ministers of New England. Still locally applied to preachers who are not in holy orders. [1800-1878.]
1786 The *priest* [otherwise described as a "minister," with a wife] took the hint.—New Haven Gazette, Oct. 5, p. 267/2.
1787 Each Sunday, perch'd on bench of pew, To passing *priest* he bows. [Written in Connecticut.]—Columbian Magazine (Phila.), p. 445/1.

Privilege. Somewhat similar in meaning to a *concession.* A right, an immunity, or a site for a business, granted as a peculiar advantage or favor. See **Water privilege,** under which are given also examples of **Hotel privilege.**

Prize, v. To appraise.
1713 Owen took a Cow of Veisy *pris'd* at £4.—Sewall's Diary, June 2. (N. E. D.)
1746 A Bill, to oblige the Inspectors to *prize* Transfer Tobacco to Nine Hundred and Fifty Pounds Nett.—Journal of House of Burgesses of Va., March 25: Vol. VII, 201. (Richmond, 1909.)

Procession, behind the. Lagging in the rear of any general movement. Colloquial.
1900 When you turn the carpetbaggers loose on the Cubans, they will see an example of stealing as a fine art, and it will show that Spain is two hundred years *behind the procession.*—Mr. J. L. Slayden of Tex., H. R., May 15: *C. R.*, p. 5550/2.

Proclamation money. Coin valued according to a proclamation of Queen Anne, June 16, 1704, in which the Spanish dollar was valued at 6 s. [1735-1838.]
1733 [It would not] come to 50,000 l. *Proclamation Money.*—S. C. Gazette, Apr. 7. p. 2/1.

Propeller. A steamer propelled by a screw.
1860 Two *propellers* . . . might be sent out.—Capt. Maury, Merc. Marine Mag., vii, 233. (N. E. D.)
1869 If the experiments now in progress shall result in the utilization of petroleum for fuel, . . . there will be nothing to prevent American *propellers,* laden with wheat in Lake Michigan, from discharging their cargoes in Liverpool.—Mr. H. E. Paine of Wisc., H. R., Jan. 14: *C. G.*, p. 376/2.

1871   On the Welland Canal the ice is three inches thick, and eight *propellers* . . . are locked in.—*The Echo*, Dec. 15. (N. E. D.)

1873   The Princeton was the first *propeller* fully armed, with auxiliary sails, that ever was built as a war vessel, with all her machinery below the water-line incapable of being touched.—Mr. John P. Stockton of N. J., U. S. Senate, Jan. 20: *C. G.*, p. 710/2.

Proposition. A plan, a scheme, a thing contemplated. Latterly the word has been much abused, so as to become in many instances no better than slang.

1872   Outside of San Francisco, the people of California and the press, perhaps with one or two exceptions, are in favor of the Goat Island *proposition.*—Mr. A. A. Sargent of Calif., H. R., Apr. 27: *C. G.*, p. 2847/3.

1875   This is not the sheep-ranch *proposition*, but . . . another bill entirely.— Mr. A. A. Sargent of Calif., U. S. Senate, Feb. 20: *C. R.*, p. 1537/1.

1876   I think, before we rush a *proposition* of this kind through the Senate, . . . there should be at least a common understanding [as to the meaning of the words used.]—Mr. T. O. Howe of Wisc., U. S. Senate, July 6: *Id.*, p. 4420/2.

1890   What have you done in Kentucky? Talk about fairness. You send here under your gerrymandering *proposition* ten Democrats with 181,000 votes, while it takes 156,000 to send one Republican.—Mr. H. F. Finley of Ky., H. R., June 30: *Id.*, p. 6774/2. [See GERRYMANDER.]

1890   This *proposition* of robbing the farmers . . . is bearing its legitimate fruit.—Mr. J. K. Jones of Ark., U. S. Senate, Aug. 7: *Id.*, p. 8269/1.

1912   [Dr. Mitten] practiced medicine many years at Columbia City, Ind., came to Seattle in 1890, and became interested in streetcar and other *propositions.*—*The Oregonian*, June 1.

Pro rata. One's proportional share.

1896   Let each man come up, prove his debt, and receive his *pro rata* upon the debt that he has proven.—Mr. J. A. Connolly of Ill., H. R., Apr. 29: *C. R.*, p. 4583/2.

Prorate. To distribute or share pro rata; i.e. proportionally. [1860-1864.]

1878   This would amount to nothing, since both companies are bound to *prorate* with other roads.—Mr. J. K. Luttrell of Calif., H. R., June 8: *C. R.*, p. 424/2, App.

Pro-slavery. In favor of slavery. See Vol. II, **Pro-slave, Pro-slavery.** [1843-1863.]

1864   Horace Greeley stated our position correctly, when he said that "northern Democracy is not really *pro-slavery*, but anti-intervention: maintaining, not that slavery is right, but that we of the free States should mind our own business and let alone other people's."—Mr. S. S. Cox of O., H. R., Feb. 17: *C. G.*, p. 712/2.

1864   My four Jacobin colleagues were at that time *pro-slavery* to the backbone.—Mr. F. P. Blair of Mo., H. R., Feb. 27: *Id.*, p. 47/2, App.

1864   How stands the gentleman [Mr. S. S. Cox of O.], not now the "Buckeye Abroad," but here, with almost pontifical authority, declaring that slavery is not to go into the next political canvass—as well bind Æolus or stay the tide—and that his party is not *pro-slavery.*— Mr. Grinnell of Ia., H. R., March 5: *Id.*, p. 954/3.

1864   The American party in Missouri was only a subterfuge by which the *pro-slavery* men of the State attempted to overslaugh and defeat Colonel Benton, who was the only man who spoke against the institution of slavery.—Mr. Blair of Mo., H. R., March 7: *Id.*, p. 979/2.

Prospect, Prospecting. To prospect is to examine land, primarily with a view of locating a mining claim. A **prospector** is one who so examines land. [1845-1907.]

1863 A party of adventurers and *"prospectors,"* in the fall of 1860, found sure indications of gold in the San Juan and Silver Mountains.— Mr. H. P. Bennet of Colo., H. R., Feb. 28: *C. G.,* p. 140/2, App.

1870 I need not travel over the ground so fully *"prospected"* by the gentleman from California.—Mr. Edward Degener of Tex., H. R., Dec. 20: *Id.,* p. 200/2.

1871 Between the Rio Grande and the Pacific Coast, . . . gold and silver have been found in great abundance, but the roving bands of wild Apaches, who dwell in these mountain passes, have hitherto defied the *prospector.*—Mr. G. W. Whitmore of Tex., H. R., Feb. 21: *Id.,* p. 178/2, App.

1877 In order to prevent . . waste of money and time in *"prospecting,"* especial attention is given by the members of surveys to the mineral resources [of the Territories].—Mr. James B. Belford of Colo., H. R., Feb. 26: *C. R.,* p. 1951/2.

1879 Gangs of *prospectors,* insensible to heat and cold, and stimulated by avarice, were moving in every direction, delving, blasting, sweating, swearing, and praying [for gold].—Mr. Thos. C. McCreery of Ky., U. S. Senate, Feb. 10: *Id.,* p. 1152/2.

1879 See PAY DIRT.

1879 Next spring the teeming thousands who will pour into Colorado ... will *prospect* those mountains for rich mineral wealth.—Mr. J. B. Belford of Colo., H. R., Dec. 18: *Id.,* p. 179/2.

1890 See STRIKE IT RICH.

Provision State, The. Connecticut. See quotations.

1872 [Governor Trumbull] gave such counsel to the people that they produced flour, grain, and other commissary supplies [securing], to the State the honorable distinction of being called *"the provision State."* —Mr. W. A. Buckingham of Conn., U. S. Senate, March 8: *C. G.,* p. 1527/1. [On the presentation to the U. S. of Trumbull's statue.]

1872 Strange as it may seem at this day [Connecticut] was then called *"the provision State."* Often, very often, did Washington appeal to Brother Jonathan to furnish food and clothing for his suffering army, and never did he appeal in vain.—Mr. J. L. Strong of Conn., H. R., March 15: *Id.,* p. 1714/2.

Provost court. A military court intruding on civil jurisdiction.

1864 We have [in Virginia] a military governor to watch over our interests, who without regard to the civil authority has a *provost court* running, which imposes just such fines as it chooses.—Mr. Lewis McKenzie of Va., H. R., Feb. 26: *C. G.,* p. 848/1.

Pueblo. A small town. **Pueblo Indians,** those living in pueblos. Sp.

1818 There was in almost every valley a *pueblo* of peaceful and submissive Indians.—Am. State Papers (1834) IV, 307. (N. E. D.)

1869 The *pueblo* of Santa Aña . . . stands upon the same footing with the other *pueblos* that were confirmed in New Mexico by the act of December 22, 1858.—Mr. G. H. Williams of Ore., U. S. Senate, Feb. 4: *C. G.,* p. 864/3.

1870 [There are in New Mexico] some seven thousand semi-civilized people, *Pueblo Indians,* who, residing in permanent, well-built villages, supporting themselves by agricultural and manufacturing industry, are nearly equal in civilization to the lower order of the Mexican citizen. —Mr. Wm. F. Prosser of Tenn., H. R., Jan. 25: *C. G.,* p. 762/1.

1891 *Pueblos,* or small walled towns, that are scattered over this valley, are extremely picturesque.—C. Roberts, "Adrift in America," p. 86. (N. E. D.)

Pull. An advantage arising from influence, usually political. [1889-1910.]

1892 The maintenance of a horde of unworthy servants with a political *pull.*—Letter from an ex-Indian-agent, *C. R.,* Feb. 22, 1893, p. 2024/1.

1894   If a man has a *"pull,"* if he is chairman of some important committee that has something to do with the printing, he can get nine appointments where another man can get one.—Mr. R. E. DeForest of Conn., H. R., May 23: *Id.,* p. 5181/1.

1896   There is a certain kind of labor that has a very strong *pull,* to use a colloquialism.—Mr. B. R. Tillman of S. C., U. S. Senate, May 1: *Id.,* p. 4658/1.

1896   In the matter of removals, promotions, and reductions, the "spoils system" had a big *pull.*—Mr. M. Brosius of Pa., H. R., Dec. 22: *Id.,* p. 419/1.

Pull foot. To be off in haste. [1825-1837.]

1818   One of my ladies chose to *pull foot,* and did not return . . . till this morning.—M. G. Lewis, "Journal in the W. Indies" (1834), p. 109. (N. E. D.)

Pull up stakes. To change one's place of settlement. [1830-1866.]

1815   I will stur my stumps, and *pluck up stakes,* tu.—David Humphreys, "The Yankey in England," p. 33.

Pull wool (over one's eyes). To trick, to deceive. [1842-1862.]

1888   You have been *pulling wool* over the eyes of the American farmer for a good many years.—Mr. T. E. Tarsney of Mich., H. R., Apr. 28: *C. R.,* p. 3477/2.

1890   [They] *pulled the wool* over the eyes of the committee wonderfully.—Mr. H. L. Dawes of Mass., U. S. Senate, July 23: *Id.,* p. 7594/2.

Pulque. A fermented drink made in Mexico from the juice of the agave. (Webster.) [1693-1910.]

1893   My little three-year old boy . . . has come to know more about snakes and bugs than any gentleman who has not toyed too long with that seductive and bewildering beverage known as Mexican *pulque.*—Mr. Champ Clark of Mo., H. R., Oct. 18: *C. R.,* p. 2667/2.

Pummy. The pulp of ground apples. Dialectal.

1877   Drinking sweet cider, and eating apple *"pommels."*—G. W. Bagby, "Writings," I, 11. (1884.)

Puncture. To destroy as with a pin-prick. The figurative use appears to be originally American.

1896   When [Mr. Crain of Texas] felt it necessary to *puncture* a fallacy, he made his arrows laugh as they flew.—Mr. Roger Q. Mills of Tex., U. S. Senate, May 16: *C. R.,* p. 5339/1.

1896   A few of the fallacies . . . which Professor Nicholson *punctures.*—*The Nation* (N. Y.), June 25, p. 497/2. (N. E. D.)

1908   [He may satirize him] and even *puncture* him with epithet.—*Hibbert Journal* (Lond.), p. 633. (N. E. D.)

Pung. A kind of box sleigh; originally, a rude oblong box on runners. (Webster.) [1798-1907.]

1862   Mr. White of Ind. moved to add pleasure sleighs to the tax-roll. Mr. Stevens of Pa. said he ought to withdraw the motion, or else add *"pungs* and lumber boxes."—H. R., March 31: *C. G.,* p. 1463/2.

Pungle down or **pungle up.** To pay up. Slang.

1854   Gamblers *"pungling down"* their dust.—Wilmington (N. C.) *Journal,* Apr. 21, p. 2/3. (From a S. F. paper.)

a.1910 "Fuddleston," he said, "you can't make a sneak out of this game. *Pungle up,* or I'll throw you out of the window." It is recorded that Mr. Fuddleston at once *pungled up* to the extent of $5.—*Chicago Tribune,* n. d. (Century Dict.)

Punk, punky. Wood so decayed as to serve for tinder; touchwood. [a.1707-1876.]

1583   In *spunck* or tinder thee [the] quick fyre he kindly receaued.—Stanyhurst, "Æneis," p. 6.

Pure-blood. Full-blooded.

1889 The great body of [these Indians] are *pure-bloods*, and out of the *pure-bloods* I suppose it would be almost impossible to find a single man qualified . . to perform the duties of a juryman.—Mr. J. H. Reagan of Tex., U. S. Senate, Feb. 9: *C. R.*, p. 1714/1.

Push-boat. One propelled from the rear.

1881 They tell him that they want to have the stream made so that it can be navigable for boats so many feet in length, drawing so many inches, old-fashioned stern-wheel steamers, *push-boats*, or whatever they may desire.—Mr. J. R. Hawley of Conn., H. R., Feb. 15: *C. R.*, p. 1685/1.

1881 Cannot the commerce on the great national water highways be cared for and protected without squandering the people's money on a trade that can get over a series of "modified mill-dams" in "*push-boats*," or "pole-boats," or boats that float down stream to be hauled back in wagons?—Mr. T. Updegraff of Ia., H. R., Feb. 15: *Id.*, p. 128/1, App.

Pushful. Enterprising and aggressive.

1896 That *pushful* spirit which makes England's attempts to advance her lines and extend her Empire on this continent a subject of national sensitiveness.—Chief Justice Alvey. See *Westm. Gazette*, Jan. 21, p. 5/2. (N. E. D.)

Pusley. Purslane, a troublesome weed. [1854-1878.]

Among the annuals [annual weeds], especially in gardens, the purslane or *pusley* perhaps takes the lead.—*Amer. Naturalist*, xxii, 778. (Century Dict.)

Put out. To make tracks; to decamp. [1843-1849.]

1835 Apprehending Judge Lynch's law, he *put out* in a hurry.—*Niles's Register*, Aug. 22, p. 436. (N. E. D.)

1856 We "*put out*" in search of fire and a shelter.—G. D. Brewerton, "War in Kansas," p. 42. (N. E. D.)

1872 They told me to *put out*. I tried to run, and some threw rocks at me, and some said "Shoot him."—Testimony of Washington Eager, *C. G.*, May 30, p. 578/2, App.

Puts and calls. See first quotation.

1892 The future business comprehended in the words "*puts and calls*" is repudiated with great contempt by the high-heeled dealers who speculate in "futures," and the nomenclature of "bucket-shops" is applied as a term of opprobrium to the places where *puts and calls* are bought and sold. A "*put*" is an agreement on the part of one party . . that another party shall have the option of delivering a certain article at a specified time thereafter, at an agreed price to be paid when the delivery is made.

The party buying the "*put*" is not obligated to deliver the goods, but may do so or not when the time arrives, as he may elect; and [in fact] an actual delivery is not contemplated by either [party]. If the price advances, the seller makes what he has already received from the buyer of the "*put*," and if the price goes down the buyer realizes the difference in the price. . . . A "*call*" is the purchased privilege of demanding certain commodities at a given time and specified price. If the price goes down, the buyer of the *call* loses what he has paid; but if the price goes up, he receives the difference between the prices the day of purchase and the day he had the privilege of making the call.—Mr. Clarke Lewis of Miss., H. R., July 8: *Id.*, p. 541/2, App.

1892 Taken as a whole, members of Exchanges do not deal in "*puts and calls*"; and in most cities the fact of so dealing is a blot upon the business standing of the man who indulges in it.—Mr. J. D. Warner of N. Y., H. R., June 6: *C. R.*, p. 448/1, App.

Put through. To put anything through is to carry it to a successful issue. See Vol. II, **Put one through.** [1847-1862.]

1866 I have confidence [said Mr. Lincoln, that Mr. McCulloch] will *put our finances through*, and I am going to appoint him Secretary of the Treasury.—Mr. John B. Alley of Mass., H. R., March 23: *C. G.*, p. 1610/3.

1873 See METER, IN SHORT.

1897 You may pass such a law; you will *put it through*, in all human probability; but I warn you that you will hear from it inside of a year.—Mr. S. A. Northway of O., H. R., Feb. 27: *C. R.*, p. 2471/2.

Put up. To arrange beforehand; usually with a fraudulent purpose, as in a "put-up job."

1876 I called the sheriff before me, and . . . my suspicions were aroused that the case was one *put up* by him.—Mr. Alcorn in the U. S. Senate, Dec. 18: *C. R.*, p. 270/1.

1877 [Captain Rogers] says that Colonel Powers expressed the opinion it was a *"put-up job"* by Anderson himself.—Mr. J. D. New of Ind., H. R., Feb. 24: *Id.*, p. 162/1, App.

Put up. To pay up or deposit money. **Put up or shut up.** To "fish or cut bait"; to adopt a definite position.

1604 Ile be hangde if he ha not *put up* the money to cony-catch vs all.—Dekker, "The Honest Whore," D.

1884 A wealthy Bostonian yesterday wagered $1000, and *put-up* the money, that Mr. Blaine's majority in N. Y. State would exceed 40,000.—*Boston Journal*, Aug. 16. (N. E. D.)

1891 I will pick you up if you choose to *put up* a couple of dollars.—C. Roberts, "Adrift in America," p. 126. (N. E. D.)

1894 Let [these men] come here and do their duty, and either *"put up or shut up."*—Mr. W. J. Talbert of S. C., H. R., July 13: *C. R.*, p. 7464/1.

1897 Mr. Brucker:—Why pick out . . . these great corporations to receive this special privilege. Mr. Little:—They *"put up"* during the campaign. Mr. Brucker:—Yes, sir; they *"put up"* during the campaign.—H. R., March 22: *Id.*, p. 150/2.

Q

Quaker-Ladies. Bluets: the flowers of the *Houstonia cærulea*. (Century Dict.)

1900
    In their little grey-blue bonnets
      Chatting, brim to brim,
    Half a million *Quaker ladies*,
      Straight and small and slim.
—Sarah J. Day, "From Mayflowers to Mistletoe."

Quaker, Wet. One who is a dram-drinker "on the sly." *N. & Q.* 10 S. ii, 197.

A moderate Jew is a more confounding piece of anomaly than *a wet Quaker.*—Lamb, "Imperfect Sympathies."

Qualify. To take the necessary oath, provide sureties, etc., before assuming public office. [1857.]

1772 The said Dandridge has never yet *qualified* [as a Vestryman for St. John's Parish.] . . . Braxton [was] asked whether he did not desire Mr. William Aylett to meet at the next Court, in Order to *qualify* the said Dandridge before the meeting of the Vestry.—Journal, House of Burgesses of Virginia, March 10, p. 229. (Richmond, 1906.)

1867 [A man of small ability on receiving an appointment] went to the clerk of the court to file his bond and be sworn into office. He exhibited his commission, and said he had come to file his bond and be *qualified*. "Hold up your hand," responded the gruff old clerk, . . .

"I'll swear you in; all h--l can't *qualify* you."—Mr. Ebenezer Dumont of Ind., H. R., Feb. 16: *C. G.*, p. 165/3, App.

1868 The question arises, if Philip F. Thomas can be permitted to take the oath, or in other words to *"qualify"* as a Senator of the U. S.—Mr. Charles Sumner of Mass., U. S. Senate, Feb. 13: *Id.*, p. 1145/2.

1869 A man is familiarly said to *"qualify"* for an office.—The same, Feb. 5: *Id.*, p. 902/3.

Quarter. A quarter of a dollar.

1856 Here's a *quarter* for you.—Olmsted, "Slave States," p. 4. (N. E. D.)

1883 Twenty . . . oranges for a *quarter.*—*Harper's Mag.*, p. 950/2. (N. E. D.)

1895 Mr. Holman:—If the gentleman will come to my house, I will show him a [Navajo] blanket which I bought for a *quarter*, which has been used for ten years, and yet which will hold water. Mr. Bowers:—O, I have seen a great many Navajo blankets. A Member:—You bought that blanket pretty cheap, if you bought it for a *quarter.*—H. R., Jan. 17: *C. R.*, p. 1083/1.

Quarter race. A quarter of a mile race. [1792-1885.]

1866 If my horse was entered for a long race, I would not mind seeing a fast nag that was only good for a *quarter race* pass him.—Mr. McDougall of Calif., U. S. Senate, Jan. 24: *C. G.*, p. 400/3.

Quarter-section. A tract of 160 acres of land.

1879 Every man of fair character who comes to Canada has a right . . to obtain what is called a *quarter-section* of land.—Lord Beaconsfield, Speech, Sept. 18. (N. E. D.)

1894 A warm climate, free institutions, and civilization do not occur together; and a first-class man and a banana will not grow upon the same *quarter section.*—Mr. R. F. Pettigrew of S. D., U. S. Senate, May 29: *C. R.*, p. 5448/1.

Quattlebums. Boasters. **Quattlebummery,** nonsense; "tall talk."

1848 We do not wish to encumber our columns with the trash and fustian of the *"Quattlebums."*—Wilmington (N. C.) *Commercial*, Nov. 25, p. 2/3.

1850 The South gains nothing, and stands a chance of losing all, by the *quattlebumery* [*sic*] of Texas or any other section.—*Id.*, Aug. 31, p. 2/1.

Queen City. Cincinnati. [1861.]

1871 [Let us] enable the goodly *Queen City* to carry out her magnificent [railroad] scheme.—Mr. J. B. Donley of Pa., H. R., Feb. 28: *C. G.*, p. 251/3, App.

1894 We live under the shadow of the *Queen City of the West*, the strongest and most powerful city in Ohio.—Mr. A. S. Berry of Ky., H. R., Aug. 8: *C. R.*, p. 8314/2.

Queen City by the lakes. Chicago.

1880 [These words echoed from Senator Chandler's lips] on the midnight air of the *Queen City by the lakes.*—Mr. Henry W. Blair of N. H., U. S. Senate, Jan. 28: *C. R.*, p. 568/1.

Quiet as pigs in thunder. See quotation.

1894 Just as we had a bill well under way, . . . some member who had kept silent as a mouse, *quiet as "pigs in thunder,"* . . . would rise up.—Mr. G. W. Ray of N. Y., H. R., June 15: *C. R.*, p. 6384/2.

Quirt. A kind of riding whip. [1851-1853.]

1911 It was not until 1887 that the last of the cattle drivers laid aside his *quirt* and decided that he could save money by loading the stock on the new railroads being built into Texas. The Indian Territory was opened in 1889, and after that all the land between the Texas ranches and the northern shipping points was fenced with barbed wire.—*N. Y. Evening Post*, Nov. 30.

Quirt, v.   To strike with a quirt.
1887   A first-class rider will sit throughout it all without moving from the saddle, *quirting* his horse all the time, though his hat may be jarred off his head and his revolver out of its sheath.—Theodore Roosevelt, *Century Mag.,* xxxv, 854.

Quit.   To leave off doing anything.   [1863-1882.]
1869   I do not wish to dispute [with] the speaker, but when I *quit* speaking, he stated that I was entitled to nine minutes.—Mr. John A. Logan of Ill., H. R., Feb. 12: *C. G.,* p. 1147/3.
1890   We *quit* the fighting without [Great Britain's formal renunciation of the right of impressment.]—Mr. J. R. Hawley of Conn., U. S. Senate, May 26: *C. R.,* p. 5289/1.
1893   I promised to talk only half an hour, and I am going to *quit* right now.—Mr. W. W. Bowers of Calif., H. R., Oct. 3: *Id.,* p. 2098/1.

R

Race line.   Distinction between races.
1891   At Marion, Indiana, when the Democrats were attempting to have a rally, . . . they were attacked by the colored people, the *race line* being distinctly drawn by that race.—Mr. Jas. D. Richardson of Tenn., H. R., Jan. 17: *C. R.,* p. 100-101, App.

Race problem, The.   The aggregate of questions relating to the mutual relations of whites and blacks.
1891   If they would allow us to proceed, it would be but a short time until what is called *"the race problem,"* in my opinion, would settle itself. We have a great many doctrinaires who have been propounding theories for settling *the race problem.* The wisest theory upon that subject is for a man to attend to his own business and let *the race problem* alone.—Mr. John H. Reagan of Tex., U. S. Senate, Jan. 16: *C. R.,* p. 1431/1.
1898   Cf. SITTING ON A VOLCANO.

Rack, n. and v.   A gait which is half trot and half canter.   [1796-1888.]
1715   *Rack,* a Pace in which a Horse neither trots nor ambles, but is between both.—Kersey, "Dictionarium Anglo-Britannicum."

Rackabone.   A worn-out horse, reduced to skin and bone.
1900   A Western farmer had a college-bred son who went off preaching. He came back with an old *rackabone*—Mr. Martin H. Glynn of N. Y., H. R., March 6: C. R., p. 117/2, App.

Racket, stand the.   To endure stress or strain.   See **Stand the Racket.**

Racks.   See quotation.
1903   Another Americanism we miss under *Racks,* the technical name for the side plankings or buffers of our ferry slips.—*The Nation* (N. Y.), Aug. 6, p. 115.   (Century Dict.)

Racoon-bridge.   See quotation.
1791   We were obliged to carry every article of our effects, and this by no other bridge than a sapling felled across it, which is called a *racoon bridge,* and over this my Indian friend would trip as quick and light as that quadruped.—W. Bartram, "Travels through N. & S. Car. Etc.," p. 445.   (Century Dict.)

Raft.   An accidental accumulation of logs and driftwood.   [1802-1861.]
1878   The *raft* in the Red River is entirely outside of all our experience. . . . in the navigation of rivers. . . . I am told that trees have been found growing from the vegetable mold, which had formed upon that *raft.*—Mr. J. A. Garfield of O., H. R., Jan. 16: *C. R.,* p. 370/2.

Ragbaby, rags, rag money.   Terms applied opprobriously to a paper currency.
1816   This paper was emphatically called "trash" or *"rags."*—John C. Calhoun, H. R., Feb. 26.   ["Works" (1856), II, 158.]

1875 The *Rag-baby* was introduced into the field of caricature by Thomas Nast, Sept. 4.

1876 I am astonished that a hard-money man like the gentleman from Pennsylvania [Mr. Townsend] should offer [to convert] silver coin into greenbacks. He has paid a compliment to what they call the "*rag baby.*"—Mr. W. A. Phillips of Kan., H. R., March 29: *C. R.*, p. 2046/1

1876 The chief end and purpose of the eastern moneyed power is to enlarge and perpetuate the national banks, and to secure the uninterrupted reign of "*rag money*" and the "*rag baby.*"—Mr. A. H. Buckner of Mo., H. R., Apr. 8: *Id.*, p. 2317/2.

1876 Who distrusts these Treasury notes? Where is the skeptic? With his shriveled lips of scorn crying out *rag money* to the democratic party, when he is advocating and pandering to the only *rag-money* institutions in this country, the *rag currency*, not money, in this country, the national banks.—Mr. Bright of Tenn., H. R., June 14: *Id.*, p. 3796/1.

1877 It was the "*rag baby*" that saved this Union; that enabled you, Mr. Speaker [Mr. Rice of Ohio] to go forth at the head of your column to lay one of your limbs upon a distant field. Gold, the coward, had fled the country. The "*rag baby*" stepped forward and gave you and your men arms, ammunition, food, medical care, and transportation.— Mr. W. D. Kelley of Pa., H. R., Nov. 15: *Id.*, p. 435/2.

1887 The "specie basis" of the national banks is now chiefly paper—the "*rag baby*"—346 millions of greenbacks.—*N. Am. Rev.* cxli, 207. (Century Dict.)

Ragocrat. An advocate of paper money. (Nonce-word.)

1842 "Pauper labor" indeed—and we have now, thanks to the *ragocrats*, got some of that blessing here.—Mr. H. W. Beeson of Pa., H. R., July 9: p. 12/2 of speech as separately published.

Rag-time music. A music in syncopated time. [1901-1911.] [A name applied to an odious kind of jerky music, originating with the lowest class of Southern "darkies."—R. H. T.]
The sound of *ragtime music* came from the two music halls across the way.—Molly E. Seawell, "Papa Bouchard," Ch. 1. (Century Dict.)

1906 An Italian band played Chinese *ragtime* with German thoroughness and a French finish as the guests of the State piled into carriages.— *N. Y. Press*, Feb. 2. (Century Dict.)

1913 The early plantation songs were at one time thought to be folk-songs brought from Africa, but the generally accepted theory is that they were picked up by the negroes from the revival preachers. But the curiously marked rhythm of the melodies—*rag-time*—is of undoubted African origin.—*London Chronicle*, Aug.

Rag, to chew the. To lament over some real or supposed grievance. To talk interminably. Slang.

1901 "There are a few soreheads," one man remarked to me, "who *chew the rag* about corruption an' the way the town's run, but they don't represent you an' me an' the citizens. They're sore 'cause they aint got any offices, that's what's troubling them."—*McClure's Mag.*, p. 576. (Century Dict.)

Rail-bird. One who, having no reserved seat, sits on the rail or fence at a race or at a fair. Slang.

1901-2 Pity the poor judges when thirty bull calves romp out before them: pity the "*railbirds*" who pass judgment on them.—*Rep. Kan. State Board Agr.*, p. 203. (Century Dict.)

1902 Along the fence where in the forenoon the "*rail birds*" had perched, muffled and humped, talking sagely of "Himyar hoses," "St. Blaise hocks," "iron legs," and "selling skates."—*Munsey's Mag.*, p. 916. (Century Dict.)

Rail-car. A car running on rails.
1843 Steamboats and *rail-cars.*—Whittier, "Prose Works" (1889) I, 352. (N. E. D.)
1871 [The genius of the American people] seeks you in your hotel, and embarks with you in your steamboats and *rail-cars.*—Mr. Joseph S. Fowler of Tenn., U. S. Senate, Feb. 20: *C. G.,* p. 1425/2.

Rail fence. One made out of split rails. See Vol. II, **Post-and-rail fence** [1806-1823].
a.1864 Simple and rustic as the gap in a *rail fence.*—N. Hawthorne, "Grimshawe" (1891), p. 142. (N. E. D.)
1870 One of the male birds accompanies me, flitting from post to post of the *rail-fence.*—J. R. Lowell, "Study Windows," p. 18. (N. E. D.)

Railroad, v. To expedite; to hurry along. [1888-1909.]
1888 A N. Y. daily some time ago reported that a common thief was *railroaded* through court in a few days.—*Pop. Sci. Monthly,* xxxii, 758. (Century Dict.)
1892 I say it seems strange that this bill has to be *railroaded* through in an hour.—Mr. J. J. Seerley of Ia., H. R., Feb. 8: *C. R.,* p. 933/1.
1893 We know that a good many claims have been sought to be *"railroaded"* through Congress, which had been paid by the Confederate government.—Mr. J. D. Sayers of Tex., H. R., Oct. 4: *Id.,* p. 2136/2.
1897 Why this emergency legislation, and why should this bill be *railroaded* through at breakneck speed?—Mr. T. W. Sims of Tenn., H. R., March 24: *Id.,* p. 218/2.
1904 The Alien act, that was *railroaded* through at the close of the last session.—*Scientific Amer.,* N. S., lvii, 37. (Century Dict.)

Railroad, v. To travel by rail.
1855 A quiet Sunday after a week's *railroading.*—James R. Lowell, "Letters," I, 251. (N. E. D.)
1889 Now steaming along the coast, now *railroading* along the shore.— *Lit. World,* Boston, June 8, p. 190/3. (N. E. D.)

Railroad, v. To work on a railroad.
1887 *Railroading* is considered by all who do not follow it as a "low-down job."—Morley Roberts, "Western Avenues," p. 203.
1893 I was born in Chicago, . . . and *railroaded* ever since I was corn-high. —A. C. Gunter, "Miss Dividends," p. 52. (N. E. D.)

Railroader. A worker on a railroad, a "railroad man."
1881 Experienced *railroaders* . . . soon placed them again upon the rails.— *Lewisburg Chronicle,* No. 1938. (N. E. D.)
1895 We had a most vigilant brakeman on the train. . . . I called the attention of this *railroader.* . . .—*Outing,* xxvi, 369/2. (N. E. D.)

Railroadphobia. A horror of railroads.
1890 I have never been one of those men who has [*sic*] what may properly be called *"railroadphobia,"* and who are as ready to fight a railroad at any time as a mad bull is a red cloth shaken in his face.—Mr. S. L. Milliken of Me., H. R., June 23: *C. R.,* p. 6392/1.

Rail-sickness. A disturbance similar to seasickness, though less severe, which troubles some nervous persons on the railroad cars.
1905 In running over its mountain division, the . . . flyer, if it is to be on time, will have to negotiate the curves at a speed for which no amount of super-elevation of the outer rail can fully compensate, and *"rail-sickness"* may claim its victims.—*Scientific Amer.,* p. 478. (Century Dict.)

Rail-splitter. A man who makes logs into fence-rails.
1865 [He] earned his life as *rail-splitter,* deck hand, farm-labourer, clerk. *Macmillan's Mag.,* Nov. 7. (N. E. D.)
1871 The predecessor of Mr. [Andrew] Johnson was was a laboring man, a boatman and a *rail-splitter.*—Mr. H. W. Slocum of N. Y., H. R., Dec. 19: *C. G.,* p. 223/1.

Rain belt. A tract of land subject to rain.
1894 In the *rain belts* of the East the vegetation comes up in the spring. In July and August it withers.—Mr. J. C. Bell of Colo., H. R., Aug. 11: *C. R.*, p. 8434/1.

Rainbelter. See quotation.
1902 Just now there is a fever of speculation in farm lands in the Northwest, and the tide of immigration has set in strongly toward a region heretofore considered valuable only for grazing. There is again an influx of the *"rain belters,"* a venturesome . . . class of settlers, who, disregarding or without knowing of the experience of the pioneers . . ., are crossing the meridian beyond which the rainfall is scanty and uncertain.—*N. Y. Tribune*, Sept. 30. (Century Dict.)

Raise. To rear children or animals; to grow plants, crops, or vegetables. [1601-1850.]
1734 The Trustees for establishing the Colony of Georgia in America, being greatly desirous to encourage the *raising* of silk in the Province of Carolina·and Georgia, etc.—*S. C. Gazette*, Apr. 6, p. 4/4.
1870 I was *raised* in the Democratic party, on the pot-metal basis, not on the greenback, lamp-black, rag paper currency basis.—Mr. S. S. Cox of N. Y., H. R., July 1: *C. G.*, p. 5066/2.
1878 See BRANCH.
1879 See FLYER.
1880 Sir, I was *raised* in the West, where it is permissive to go a little fast. I may admit I was *raised* a little fast myself. . . . Out West we call it progressive.—Mr. G. F. Rothwell of Mo., H. R., Feb. 26: *C. R.*, p. 1164/1.
1880 I never learned that a rattlesnake *raised* in one's own garden is any less poisonous than one *raised* in the mountains of Virginia or Pennsylvania.—Mr. Hiram Price of Ia., H. R., May 1: *Id.*, p. 2933/1.

Raise Cain. To make trouble generally. The phrase admits of variation. [1803-1901.]
1705 Sir, give me an Account of my Necklace, or I'll make such a Noise in your House I'll *raise the Devil* in't.—Sir J. Vanbrugh, "The Confederacy," v, ii. (N. E. D.)
1890 At the other end of the Capitol there is being discussed a bill intended to raise—I will not say hell, because that would not be proper language here, but to *"raise Cain"* throughout the country.—Mr. John H. Rogers of Ark., H. R., Dec. 20: *C. R.*, p. 749/1.

Rake in the shekels. To gather in the money. Slang.
[1583 By which kind of theft . . . they *rake in great somes of mony.*——Stubbes, "Anat. Abuses" (1882), II, 54. (N. E. D.)]
1896 He *rakes in the shekels* at a per capita profit of about $15. per victim.—Mr. R. W. Blue of Kan., H. R., Apr. 15: *C. R.*, p. 4008/2.

Rally, n. A mass-meeting, usually for some political object.
1904 At the last Presidential Election, at a great Republican *rally*, there were two [notable] speeches made.—*N. Y. Tribune*, Dec. 21. (Century Dict.)

Ramskin. See quotation.
1828 What must be [his] feelings, when he goes to jail, to "swear out," and so pay with a *ramskin?*—Lorenzo Dow, "Journal" (1850), p. 179/1.

Ranch. A farm, of any size, in Western U. S.; an establishment and farm for grazing and rearing horses, cattle, or sheep. See Vol. II,
Ranche. [1808-1855.]
1867 I was pointed to a *ranche* which, two days before, was stampeded by a party of Indians, and the stock driven off.—Mr. John B. Henderson of Mo., U. S. Senate, July 5: *C. G.*, p. 491/1.

1870   [The man] had a *ranch* with some stock on the Humboldt river ; . . .
      there was only one man living on a line of 500 miles, and he was
      simply *ranching* some stock.—Mr. W. M. Stewart of Nev., U. S.
      Senate, Feb. 19: *Id.*, p. 1425/2.

1871   See OUTFIT.

1883   The grazing lands of Western Texas are rapidly passing into the
      hands of those who open up cattle and sheep *ranches.*—Mr. S. B.
      Maxey of Tex., U. S. Senate, Jan. 29: *C. R.*, p. 1703/2.

Ranchero.   The owner of a ranch. Sp.

1840   A law was passed, . . . declaring all the Indians free and independent
      Rancheros.—R. H. Dana, "Before the Mast" (1854), p. 118.
      (N. E. D.)

1846   The *Rancheros,* part of the material of the Mexican army, are half
      Indian and half Spanish.—*The Times,* June 16, p. 8/2. (N. E. D.)

1871   Over this extended plain herds of countless cattle and horses have
      roamed . . . for more than half a century, the pride of the patriarchal
      ranchero and "princely padre."—Mr. G. W. Whitmore of Tex., H. R.,
      Feb. 21: *Id.*, p. 178/1, App.

Ranger.   See **County Ranger.**

Ranger.   A steer or horse raised on a cattle-range.

1901-2   The best *rangers* I ever saw on the Chicago market were high-
      grade short-horns from Montana.—*Rept. Kan. Bd. of Agr.*, p. 15.
      (Century Dict.)

Rangers, Ranger regiments.   Those employed to scour the frontier.
      [Chiefly U. S.—N. E. D.]

1742   For the defense of the Colony, it is necessary to have . . . *rangers*
      who can ride the woods.—"State Prov. Georgia" (1897), p. 15.
      (N. E. D.)

1796   The *rangers* in Virginia, who were sent out against the Cherokee
      Indians.—Stedman, "Suisnam," I, 81. (N. E.D.)

1835   We learnt that a company of mounted *rangers,* or riflemen, had de-
      parted but three days previous.—W. Irving, "Crayon Misc." (1863),
      p. 22. (N. E. D.)

1870   Our Legislature [in Texas] passed, a few days ago, a *ranger* bill,
      involving an expense of $1,200,000 for a single year. . . . Gentlemen
      acquainted with the frontier know precisely what is meant by calling
      a *ranger regiment* into the field. It means war; nothing else. It
      means aggressive war, not mere frontier defense. The Texas boys,
      when they get upon a trail, are accustomed to "tree their game."
      They will tree those Indians, whether they be in the Santa Rosa moun-
      tains of Mexico, or upon your reservation between Arkansas and
      Texas.—Mr. Edward Degener of Tex., H. R., June 30: *C. G.*, p.
      5010/1-2.

Rangy.   Disposed to wander; long-limbed and slender; also, large,
      spacious, and commodious.

1885   The ponies . . . used for the circle-riding in the morning have need
      rather to be strong and *rangy.*—Theodore Roosevelt, "Hunting Trips,"
      ch. i. (Century Dict.)
      A large *rangy* shed for the horses.—"Sportsman's Gazetteer," p. 452.
      (Century Dict.)

Rank.   To outrank; to take precedence of. [1842-1901.]

1862   It is claimed by some that General Frémont *ranks* General McClellan.
      Their commissions bear date the same day.—Mr. Abraham B. Olin of
      N. Y., H. R., Apr. 2: *C. G.*, p. 1505/3.

1862   [Has not the President] the power, when the occasion occurs, to
      assign to a given command one general who is *ranked* by another
      in the same department?—Mr. Roscoe Conkling of N. Y., H. R.,
      Apr. 2: *Id.*, p. 1505/3. [On the next page Mr. Conkling uses the
      word *outrank.* So does Mr. Olin, p. 1507/1.]

1869 Young, inexperienced, and comparatively unfledged officers of the Army . . . . have frequently got brevet rank that gave them the right to control and the right to *rank* men of much more age, much greater talent, and much more solid merit than themselves.—Mr. Garrett Davis of Ky., U. S. Senate, Feb. 25: *Id.*, p. 1586/1.

Rare. Imperfectly cooked; underdone. [1655-1859.]

a.1540 Yolkes of *rere* egges.—Dr. Lynacre's "Compendyous Regyment of Health," Sig. D ii. (Library of Surgeon-General, at Washington.) This is perhaps the earliest example.

1717 New-laid eggs, which Baucis' busy care Turned by a gentle fire, and roasted *rare.*—Dryden's "Ovid," viii, 98. (Century Dict.)

Rat. A printer who works at lower rates than the usual ones. [1824-1892.]

1891 Mr. Cummings:—Are you willing that the Government shall employ *"rat"* printers if it can get them? And are you willing that it shall employ *"rat"* printers even if it has to get them under false pretences? Mr. Grosvenor:—Well, I do not know great deal about the *"rat"* printer business. Several members:—What is a *"rat"* printer?— H. R., Jan. 28: *C. R.*, p. 1937/1.

Rat. A rat-like hair-pad.

1867 If you attempt to caress a girl by stroking her front hair, she will cry out, "Take care of my *rats!*"—Mr. T. E. Noell of Mo., H. R., Feb. 11: *C. G.*, p. 111/1, App.

1869 She can't buy coils and braids and two-dollar *rats.*—Mrs. Whitney, "We Girls" (1874), p. 98. (N. E. D.)

1888 The crescent shaped pillows on which [hair] was put up, the startling names of which were *"rats"* and "mice."—*Century Mag.*, Sept., p. 769/1. (N. E. D.)

Rat-fall. A trap into which rats fall. Cf. **Deadfall.**

1896 A most excellent *"rat-fall"* may be made of a strong barrel, about half full of water. The cover should be placed on a pivot and well baited.—*Yearbook U. S. Dept. Agr.*, p. 164. (Century Dict.)

Ratification meeting. A public meeting held to signify approval of the result of an election. [1848.]

1868 On the 20th of December 1860 the South Carolina convention passed an ordinance of secession. On the same day a grand *ratification meeting* in honor of the . . . . proceeding was held at Memphis.—Mr. Jacob M. Howard of Mich., U. S. Senate, Feb. 14: *C. G.*, p. 1169/3.

Rattage. Loss by rats.

1878 How much can there be left after deducting cost of sacks, storage, wharfage, *"rattage,"* and waste, to pay the up-river freights?— *Palouse* (Wash.) *Gazette*, May 7: cited in *C. R.*, May 29, p. 3888/1.

Rattled. Flurried; confused. [1869-1910.]

1892 Do you suppose that the Republican party is going to allow a standing committee of scared and *rattled* politicians . . . to drive it from its position with a battery of worn and dilapidated phrases?—Mr. J. P. Dolliver of Ia., H. R., March 29: *C. R.*, p. 2667/1.

1896 Mr. Talbert:—I asked the question for information, and not to *"rattle"* the gentleman at all. Mr. Hall:—It does not *"rattle"* me.— H. R., Feb. 8: *C. R.*, p. 131/2, App.

Rattlings. A variant of *radlings* or *raddlings*, as to which see the N. E. D. Wood cut into strips about 4 feet long, for kindling, and tied up in bundles. Prov., U. S. (Century Dict.)

Rattoons. See quotation.

1890 Your attention is called to the fact that sugar-cane is "propagated from cuts called *'rattoons,'* as the plant rarely ripens its seed in the most favored localities."—So says . . . . Professor Chandler of Columbia College.—Mr. J. H. Gear of Ia., H. R., May 9: *C. R.*, p. 4387/1.

Ravison. An inferior kind of rapeseed.
1903 Sunflower seed, rapeseed, colza, poppy seed, sesamum, *ravison*, mustard seed, and many other exclusively oil-yielding seeds.—*Yearbook U. S. Dept. Agr.*, p. 412. (Century Dict.)

Raw, n. An untrained mustang or cow-pony. Western slang.
1895 The animals are mostly from the Texan and New Mexican mustang herds. They pay for a "*raw*" on an average fifty dollars.—*Outing*, p. 389. (Century Dict.)

Razor-back. A thin-bodied, long-legged, half-wild hog, somewhat common in the South.
1867 Rev. R. S. Hawker alludes to "the old Cornish *razor-back*." (N.E. D.)
1890 The *razor-backs* which roam the canebrakes of northwestern Mississippi do not take to fat kindly.—Mr. John F. Lacey of Ia., H. R., Aug. 21: *C. R.*, p. 8983/1.
1894 [Mr. Sperry] said that the people of the Southern States were not interested in the tariff discussion, because they were not consumers, or did not consume anything but hominy and *razor-back hogs.*—Mr. W. J. Talbert of S. C., H. R., Jan. 20: *Id.*, p. 1146/1.
1894 See Appendix.
1901 In the vernacular of the South, they were *razor backs* .... Nevertheless, these two hogs had a value.—*Munsey's Mag.*, xxiv, 494/1. (N. E. D.)

Read out. To turn out of a political party—apparently derived from some kind of sectarian excommunication. [1841-1860.]
1870 See SNAP JUDGMENT.
1872 See SOREHEAD.
1874 In the good old times of Andrew Jackson, . . . if any democratic Senator failed "to come to time," "to go it through thick and thin," right or wrong, he was "*read out of the party.*"—Mr. G. F. Edmunds of Vt., U. S. Senate, Apr. 28: *C. R.*, p. 3431/2.
1875 *The Tribune*, the *Times*, the *Nation*, the *Sun*, ... and hundreds of [other papers], . . . have been *read out of* the republican party because they will not sanction the acts of the [Grant] Administration.—Mr. J. K. Luttrell of Calif., H. R., Feb. 27: *Id.*, p. 1897/1.
1882 See BOURBON.
1892 Mr. Hatch:— When you want a Democratic platform, you will get it from Democrats, and not from men whose swaddling clothes have not been on them a week, or a month, or a year. The gentleman gets up here— Mr. Williams:—You want to *read me out*, do you? Mr. Hatch:—No, sir; I do not want to *read you out;* I am simply repelling your endeavor to *read me out.*—H. R., March 24: *C. R.*, p. 2518/2.

Readjuster. A member of a political party (formed in 1877-8) in Virginia, which advocated a legislative readjustment of the State debt. (N. E. D.)
1879 Further news from Va. indicates that the Repudiators, or *Readjusters*, as they call themselves, have elected a majority of the General Assembly.—*The Nation* (N. Y.), Nov. 13, p. 317/2. (N. E. D.)
1883 The *readjuster* reminds the negro that he was a slave when this debt was formed.—M. D. Conway in *Glasgow Weekly Herald*, Sept. 1, p. 3/2. (N. E. D.)
1892 [On Apr. 3, 1882, upon Mr. Crapo's motion], the nays were no Republicans, 69 Democrats, and 9 Greenbackers and *Readjusters*. . . . On April 17, the nays were no Republicans, 78 Democrats, and 11 Greenbackers and *Readjusters.*—Mr. J. K. Jones of Ark., U. S. Senate, June 9: *C. R.*, p. 5175/1.

1898 In the year 1879 there sprang up in the State of Virginia a party
known to history as the *"Readjuster"* party. That party rode into
power upon one simple issue,—the scaling down, or repudiation, of
the public debt of Virginia.—Mr. W. A. Jones of Va., H. R., Apr.
26: *Id.*, p. 368/2, App.

Real. Really. [1718-1908.]

b.1729 It is still true, even in the present state of things, bad as it is,
that a *real good* man had rather be deceived, than be suspicious.—
Joseph Butler (afterwards Bishop of Durham), "Fifteen Sermons"
(1845), p. 139.

1891 A bright mulatto girl, when she was at the point of death, insisted
that the pall-bearers at her funeral should be *"real* light people," that
is to say, mulattoes.—Mr. James D. Richardson of Tenn., Jan. 17:
C. R., p. 103/1, App.

Realizing sense. An appreciation of the true character of a person or
thing. The phrase was used in a canting way by the Methodists
in the U. S., forty or fifty years ago.

1898 Since he had no *"realizing sense"* of men, how could he hold men?—
Henry Harland, "Comedies and Errors," p. 87. (Century Dict.)

Rebeldom. The area or system of rebellion.

1862 As to *Rebeldom*, there is now hardly any State that we have not got
some foothold in.—Asa Gray, "Letters" (1893), 480. (N. E. D.)

1872 When a bill comes here, which lets all *rebeldom* into your treasury,
etc.—Mr. Timothy O. Howe of Wisc., U. S. Senate, Apr. 30: *C. G.*,
p. 2908/7.

1872 [I might get] such an "inside view" of *Rebeldom* as might not be
agreeable.—Edmund Kirke, "Down in Tennessee," p. 10.

Rebelism. Rebellion.

1867 [President Johnson's conduct] can have no other effect than . . . to
feed the spirit of *rebelism*, and incite insubordination.—Mr. Chas. D.
Drake of Mo., U. S. Senate, Dec. 10: *C. G.*, p. 103/3.

Reckon. To think, to "guess." Now dialectal in England; more used
in the South than in other parts of the U. S. [b.1811-1908.]

1878 Mr. Eaton:—I beg to say to my honorable friend that, while he is
fully entitled to his opinion, he has not quite as good a right as I
to "guess," coming from Virginia, as I might have, coming from
[Conn.]. Mr. Withers:—But I can *"reckon."* Mr. Eaton:—Yes,
you can *"reckon."*—U. S. Senate, Feb. 8: *C. R.*, p. 853/2.

Recommend, n. A written recommendation. [1827-1907.]

1623 Intreat from you a private *recommends* . . . . To a friend in Malta.—
Webster, "Devil's Law-Case," D.

1894 I think he would give it an autograph *recommend.—Harper's Mag.*,
p. 351/2. (N. E. D.)

Reconstruct, Reconstruction, etc. These terms were much used with
reference to the readmission of the Seceding States into the Union,
under President Johnson's administration.

1865 As to what is commonly termed *"reconstruction,"* it is . . . . the
whole organism of Southern society that must be reconstructed.—
Carl Schurz in Hart's *Am. Hist.* (1901) iv, 454. (N. E. D.)

1866 The *"reconstructed"* adjutant general of Mississippi . . . . issued an
order. . . . . The *"reconstructed"* State authorities of Mississippi were
allowed to rob and disarm our veteran soldiers. . . . . [The gentlemen
from N. Y. and N. J.], invoking the aid of the *"reconstructed"*
rebels, chant anew the requiem of copperhead Democracy and antiquated conservatism.—Mr. Sidney Clarke of Kan., H. R., Apr. 7:
C. G., pp. 1838-9.

1866 As a sample of one of these *reconstructed* States comes this lean,
lank, cadaverous Cassius-looking Stephens [Mr. Alexander H.
Stephens of Ga.], who has got treason in every lineament of his

face, and never laughs.—Mr. James W. Nye of Nev., U. S. Senate, May 9: *Id.*, p. 2496/3.

1868 [Senator Garrett Davis] was the great inventor of the term, now become historic, *"Reconstruction."*—Mr. Lot M. Morrill of Me., U. S. Senate, Feb. 5: *Id.*, p. 112/2, App.

1868 There have been a whiskey insurrection, a Hartford convention, a South Carolina nullification, and a Dorr rebellion. But neither Washington nor Madison nor Jackson nor Tyler thought of inflicting the pains and penalties, the confiscations and disfranchisements which follow in the train of modern *reconstruction.*—Mr. Thos. C. McCreery, of Ky., U. S. Senate, May 28: *Id.*, p. 2631/3.

1869 A bill having been introduced "in relation to the appointment of midshipmen from the lately *reconstructed* States," Mr. S. C. Pomeroy of Kan. said, "What States are *reconstructed?* It may be a proper title, but it is something new."—U. S. Senate, Jan. 28: *Id.*, p. 664/1.

1869 [Colonel Christie] is now as much a *reconstructed* rebel as any rebel who has been *reconstructed.*—Mr. James Brooks of N. Y., H. R., March 1: *Id.*, p. 1767/2.

1892 We are all *reconstructed.* I was a rebel, and I am not ashamed of it; but I was the first man to take the oath of allegiance in my county. . . . I believe to-day I am a *reconstructed* rebel.—Mr. Robt. Bullock of Fla., H. R., Dec. 17: *C. R.*, p. 204/2, App.

Record, travel out of the. To go outside the alleged facts of the case. [1770-1848.]

1864 The committee even *travel out of the record* to find objects for assault.—Mr. Powell of Ky., U. S. Senate, Mar. 3: *C. G.*, p. 57/3, App.

Record-breaking. Surpassing prior exploits. See Vol. II, **Record, to break the.** [1909.]

1901 Additional furnaces are getting ready to blow in, and there is a prospect of a *record-breaking* production [of Bessemer Steel] in April and May.—*N. Y. Commercial Advertiser*, Apr. 11. (Century Dict.)

Red or Redd up. To set to rights; to clean up. Scot. [1842-1896.]

1513 The rowtis *red* hym plane rovm on the bent (i.e. they cleared a space for him on the field).—Douglas, "Eneados," ed. Small, 1874. Book XII, p. 121.

Red or Red cent. The smallest copper coin. Used contemptuously. [1848-1878.]

1866 [The manufacturers say] We haven't made a *red*,—not a dollar; we have not been making a dime for the last ten years; we have been patriotically running large mills . . . . solely for the benefit of the country.—Mr. John Hogan of Mo., H. R., Mar. 7: *C. G.*, p. 1249/2.

Red dog. The most worthless of the private banks, about 1837-1860, were styled *"red dog."* See Vol. II.

1842 The *red-dog* dying in its turn, our currency consists now of Stockton, wild cat, and Good Intent stage-plasters.—Mr. H. W. Beesom of Pa., H. R., July 9: p. 13/1 of the speech as separately published.

1874 They gave some sort of security, but the security was not quite as good as that which purported to be furnished by the Michigan wildcats, for that was coin. They gave some sort of security in Indiana, and they furnished money known familiarly all over the West as *"red-dog."*—Mr. Zach. Chandler of Mich., U. S. Senate, Feb. 18: *C. R.*, p. 1584/2.

1879 See Stump-tail.

1881 Anyone at all familiar with the old days of State banks, of fluctuating paper, of *"red-dog,"* *"wild-cat,"* and *"shin-plaster"* notes, will fully concede the incomparable superiority of the present system.—Mr. John A. Anderson of Kan., H. R., Jan. 18: *Id.*, p. 35/1, App.

1881 See Shyster.

Red dog. A very low grade of flour.

1893 Some of the very lowest grades of flour, the flour which is called . . . *"red dog,"* which is very little better than offal. . . . [is] not generally branded.—Mr. W. D. Washburn of Minn., U. S. Senate, Jan. 4: *C. R.,* p. 313/1, App.

Redemptioner. An immigrant who had to work out his passage money after landing. [1784-1812.]

1871 Garrett Covode, a native of Holland, was when a child kidnapped in the streets of Amsterdam by a sea-captain, who brought him to Philadelphia, and under then existing laws sold him into bondage as a *"redemptioner,"* in which condition he was held for some years after coming to manhood, and was subsequently employed as a domestic servant in the household of General Washington.—Remarks of Mr. W. D. Kelley of Pa. on the decease of Hon. John Covode, a grandson of Garrett Covode, in the H. R., Feb. 9: *C. G.,* p. 1094/3.

Red-eye. Strong cheap whiskey. [1837-1888.]

1867 See TANGLE-FOOT.

1872 Take what we call in Kentucky *red-eye* whisky, and the best Bourbon, ... and the tax is the same on each.—Mr. J. W. Stevenson of Ky., H. R., May 28: *C. G.,* p. 3969/3.

Redheaded. Impetuous. Colloquial.

1894 His motto is: "A *red-headed* man never squeals."—*Outing,* xxiv, 123/2. (N. E. D.)

1900 We are dealing with a question which merits the most careful consideration; but you are *"red-headed,"* and nothing that we do, or fail to do, suits you.—Mr. J. G. Cannon of Ill., H. R., Feb. 27: *C. R.,* p. 2336/1.

1900 I asked [Mr. Cannon a question] and the only answer that I could get, which was hardly satisfactory, was that I had become *"red-headed."*—Mr. J. J. Fitzgerald of N. Y., H. R., Feb. 28: *Id.,* p. 2416/1.

Red-hearted. Having the heart (of a tree) red by reason of the fungus *Trametes Pini.*

1900 The wood at first turns dark red-brown, and trees in this stage are known to the lumberman as *"red-hearted"* timber.—*Yearbook U. S. Dept. Agr.,* p. 206. (Century Dict.)

Red-hill. See quotation.

1888 You may take the oldest *red-hill* in South Carolina or Georgia, and fertilize it, ... and you can make more cotton to the acre upon it than you could when it was virgin soil.—Mr. J. T. Morgan of Ala., U. S. Senate, Dec. 12: *C. R.,* p. 182/2.

Red horse. A Kentuckian. [1833.]

1835 The spokesman was evidently a *"red-horse"* from Kentucky.—C. F. Hoffman, "Winter in the West," I, 210. (N. E. D.)

1835-40 These last have all nicknames. There's the hoosiers of Indiana, ... the *red horses* of Kentucky.—Haliburton, "The Clockmaker" (1862), p. 318. (N. E. D.)

Red-horse. A name applied to certain kinds of suckers.

The short-headed *red horse, Moxostoma breviceps,* abounds in the Great Lakes and the Ohio Valley. *Texas red-horse.* A sucker, *M. congestum,* which inhabits the streams of Texas. (Century Dict.)

Redistrict. To arrange in new districts.

1850 A committee to *redistrict* the town.—"Hist. of Pelham, Mass.," (1898), p. 198. (N. E. D.)

1888 When Mass. was being *re-districted.*—Bryce, "Am. Commonwealth," I, 1. (N. E. D.)

1890 The President divides the U. S. into [pension] districts and defines the geographical limits of each pension agency. . . . . He can *redistrict* them any day he desires.—Mr. F. M. Cockrell of Mo., U. S. Senate, May 9: *C. R.,* p. 4367/1.

Reedbird, Ricebird. A small bird, the American ortolan; the bobo-link. [1747-1862.]
1877 The fat bullionist . . . . pats his rounded vest, locks his box, and with a gentle "tra-la-la" saunters off to Delmonico's to dine on terrapin and *reed-birds.*—Mr. Carter H. Harrison of Ill., H. R., Nov. 7: *C. R.*, p. 280/2.

Register. A registrar. [1804-1816.]
1864 The press had been muzzled; Congress had become the mere *register* of [the President's] will.—Mr. W. J. Allen of Ill., H. R., Jan. 27: *C. G.*, p. 383/1.
1865 It now appears that the *Assistant Register* is afflicted with paralysis. . . . . We have a *Register* who is an able-bodied man, who is able to write.—Mr. James F. Wilson of Ia., H. R., Mar. 2: *Id.*, p. 1323/2.

Regrassing. The operation of reconverting land now barren into grass land.
1901 In order to obtain some information as to the possibility of restoring these . . . . lands, experiments in *regrassing* were undertaken at Tucson, Arizona.—*Yearbook U. S. Dept. Agr.*, p. 30. (Century Dict.)

Reject, n. A thing cast off or rejected.
1890 [These objects], which have hitherto been assumed to be palaeolithic, and to represent the rude implements of primitive man, are in fact nothing but the *"rejects"* of much more recent times.—*Smithsonian Rep.*, p. 42. (Century Dict.)

Relinquishment. A tract of abandoned land.
1886 *"Relinquishments* for sale." *"Relinquishments* always on hand." "We have deeded land and *relinquishments*, so cheap it will make you smile." *"Relinquishments* bought and sold."—Extracts from Kansas advertisements, quoted by Mr. L. E. Payson of Ill., H. R., June 28: *C. R.*, p. 6238/1.
1897 He had come late in the previous summer, bought a *relinquishment* up the river, etc.—*Outing*, xxix, 570/2. (N. E. D.)

Re-locate. To make a new settlement on land.
1864 In [many] cases these persons, having taken homesteads, and again desiring to sell and *relocate*, ... have paid for the lands.—Mr. Thaddeus Stevens of Pa., H. R., Mar. 9: *C. G.*, p. 1018/2.
1894 The congregation is preparing to *re-locate* in the north part of the city.—*Chicago Advance*, May 31. (N. E. D.)

Rendition. Rendering; surrendering. Used in various senses, 1601-1716, N. E. D. [1859-1865.]
1854 "The *Rendition* of A. Burns,"—Sermon by Jas. F. Clarke, Boston.
1870 What is the position of the gentlemen who advocate this *rendition* [interpretation] of this clause?—Mr. Garrett Davis of Ky., U. S. Senate, Feb. 23: *C. G.*, p. 1511/2.
1885 [The money was] paid within four days after the *rendition* of the judgment.—Mr. O. D. Conger of Mich., U. S. Senate, Jan. 16: *C. R.*, p. 748/1.

Rendrock. An explosive powder.
1880 The explosives were dynamite, *rendrock*, and vulcan powder.—"Libr. Univ. Knowl." II, 628. (N. E. D.)
1881 All kinds of gun-cotton and *rend-rock*, which are to be carried up among the rain-clouds and there touched off by some bold and dashing navigator of the air.—Mr. S. S. Cox of N. Y., H. R., Feb. 7: *C. R.*, p. 1329/1.

Renig. To back out. [1853-1903.]
1917 Hays *renigged* at the last moment, but I accepted the invitation.—H. A. Franck, "Vagabonding down the Andes," p. 32. (Century Co.)

Repeater. One who votes, or tries to vote, more than once.

1870 [Frauds will surely] be perpetrated, where a stake of such vast magnitude as the entire electoral vote of a large state is made to turn on the voting of a few aliens, the importation of a few non-residents, the passing of a few *"repeaters,"* or a slight miscount.—*Chicago Tribune,* Jan.—See *C. G.,* Feb. 23, 1871: p. 196/1, App.

1870 Michael McDermott was arrested on the charge of *repeating* . . . ., but it being found that a *repeater* had previously voted on his name, thus causing a misapprehension, [he] was discharged.—*Commercial Advertiser,* Nov. 8. See *C. G.,* Feb. 15, 1871, p. 131/2, App.

1879 See FALSE COUNTERS. See PLUG-UGLY. See SHOULDER-HITTER. See STIFFS.

1888 [Troy] is full of fellows who go to serve as *"repeaters"* at Albany elections.—Bryce, "Am. Comm.," II, 474. (N. E. D.)

Repetitious. Marked by "damnable iteration."

1815 The observation which you have quoted from the Abbé Raynal, which has been written off in a succession not much less *repetitious,* or protracted, than that in which schoolboys of former times wrote.—Quoted by Pickering from the *Quarterly Review,* Boston. (Century Dict.)

1883 The whole passage . . . . is diffuse, involved, and *repetitious.*—*Proc. Am. Philol. Assn.,* p. xxii. (Century Dict.)

1887 An irrelevant or *repetitious* speaker.—*Harper's Mag.,* lxxv, 515. (Century Dict.)

Reportorial. Belonging to or characteristic of a reporter.

1888 The great newspapers of New York have capital, editorial talent, *reportorial* enterprise, and competent business management.—*Harper's Mag.,* lxxvii, 687. (Century Dict.)

1890 You would call it the *"reportorial"* conscience," I suppose?—A. W. Tourgée, "Pactolus Prime," p. 217.

Reportorially. After the manner or by the use of reporters.

1901 But, unfortunately, the weather will not let the newspaper alone, and so . . . . the newspaper must keep pegging away at it, editorially and *"reportorially,"* until the present anomalous state of things is developed.—*Pop. Sci. Mo.,* p. 382. (Century Dict.)

Repudiation, Repudiator, etc. Terms used especially with reference to national and other indebtednesses.

1843 I am accused of applying the epithet *repudiation* to States which have not repudiated.—Sydney Smith, "Works" (1859) II, 331/2. (N. E. D.)

1867 The *repudiationists* are undoubtedly strong.—*The Nation* (N. Y.), p. 446/1. (N. E. D.)

1868 I do not consent to the idea that the President [Andrew Johnson] has made a proposition of *repudiation,* or that he is himself a *repudiator.*—Mr. James Dixon of Conn., U. S. Senate, Dec. 17: *C. G.,* p. 44/3, App.

Request envelopes. See **Special request envelopes.**

Resolute. To pass resolutions. Cf. **Evolute.**

1860 When you have done *resoluting,* you will only have lost your time.—De Vere, "Americanisms" (1871), p. 655.

1888 [They] flocked every Sunday afternoon to cheer denunciations of corporations and monopolists, and to *"resolute"* against the rich generally.—Bryce, "Am. Comm.," III, 233. (N. E. D.)

1900 [This combination] assembles here in the House, it runs over to New York, it journeys about with Bryan, it goes out to Chicago with Altgeld and Weaver and Mrs. Gougar, and they *resolute,* you know.—Mr. J. G. Cannon of Ill., H. R., Feb. 17: *C. R.,* p. 1901/2.

Resumptionists. The advocates of a speedy return to specie payments.

1878 We are *resumptionists.* We deny that there is [in the West] one particle of repudiation.—Mr. H. L. Humphrey of Wisc., H. R., Jan. 26: *C. R.,* p. 598/1.

Resurrect. To revive. [1852-1909.] See N. E. D. for citation in 1772.

1869 [The bill] proposes to exhume, ... to recreate the old constitutional convention of Mississippi, and, having *resurrected* this body, to strip from it the shrouds and habiliments of death, clothe it with new powers and privileges, etc.—Mr. Thomas Fitch of Nev., H. R., Apr. 1: *C. G.*, p. 432/2.

1870 Here is a piece of land apparently open for settlement; a man goes upon it; he pre-empts it, pays for it, obtains his patent, and the first thing he knows an order is *resurrected* from some pigeon-hole in the War Department showing that it is a military reservation.— Mr. G. H. Williams of Ore., U. S. Senate, Jan. 26: *Id.*, p. 776/2.

1870 When the physician goes to eradicate disease, he expects to go before death ensues, to prevent death, not to go after death to *resurrect* the body.—Mr. Oliver P. Morton of Ind., U. S. Senate, Feb. 16: *Id.*, p. 1324/2.

1870 *Resurrect* your Taney; *resurrect* your Wayne; *resurrect* your whole court; and in this blaze of light and constitutional reform they would never dare utter the sentiments they uttered under the old *régime*.— Mr. Jas. W. Nye of Nev., U. S. Senate, Feb. 23: *Id.*, p. 1514/1.

1872 It occurs to me that when anyone . . . . has been permitted to live sixty years, particularly when he had [has] been a bad man, as I think the Democratic party has been, and it is now being understood that the party is dead, I propose not to come to the rescue and *resurrect* it.—Mr. J. W. Flanagan of Tex., U. S. Senate, Apr. 29: *Id.*, p. 2880/1.

1874 [France's] first thought was to get out of the financial clutches of her German conqueror. . . . . Her call for the loan was like a *resurrecting* trump.—Mr. John M. Bright of Tenn., H. R., June 13: *C. R.*, p. 456/1, App.

1879 The people of this country . . . . would bury [the democrats] so deep that the horn of Gabriel would not *resurrect* them.—Mr. Marsh, H. R., May 17: *Id.*, p. 1443/2.

1890 Your workingman whom you so love goes clothed in the *resurrected* and rejuvenated tatters of beggary, or the discarded garments of disdainful luxury.—Mr. W. McAdoo of N. J., H. R., May 10: *Id.*, p. 4472/2.

1890 That brings up the very serious question whether Congress can revive, *resurrect*, and restore . . . . a void statute of Iowa.—Mr. J. T. Morgan of Ala., U. S. Senate, May 29: *Id.*, p. 5434/1.

1900 See ISSUE, A LIVE.

Revelant. Perfectly explanatory.

1905 Why not avoid, if we can, those loose habits of reasoning, those looser habits of expression, which so easily beset us? Let us learn *revelant*, clear-cut, and well-ordered expression.—*N. Y. Times*, July 15. (Century Dict.)

Revelator. A revealer; one who has a revelation. [1801-1866.]

1882 Brigham [Young] set up in business as a first-class seer and *revelator* after he got charge of things.—Mr. G. W. Cassidy of Nev., H. R., Mar. 13: *C. R.*, p. 1863/2.

Ricebird. The bobolink. See **Reedbird.**

1886 Your favor of Feb. 24, asking for information concerning the devastations of the bobolink or *rice-bird* in the Southern States, has been duly received. The bobolinks make their appearance here during the latter part of April. At that season their plumage is white and black and they sing merrily when at rest. Their flight is always at night. . . . . In the morning their appearance is heralded by the popping of whips and firing of musketry by the bird-minders in their efforts to keep the birds from pulling up the young rice. This warfare is kept up incessantly until about the 25th of May . . . . . Their next appearance is in a dark yellow plumage, as the *rice-bird*. There is no song at this time, but instead a chirp, which means ruin to any rice found in milk. My plantation record will show that tor the past ten years, except when prevented by stormy south or southwest winds, the *rice-birds* have come punctually on the night of the 21st of August, apparently coming from seaward. . . . . Curious to say, we have never seen this flight during the day; but always during the nights of August 21, 22, 23, and 24, millions of these birds settle in the rice-fields.—Letter of Capt. William Miles Hazzard, of Annandale, S. C. See *C. R.*, June 10, p. 5497/1. [He calculates the annual loss, including the cost of fighting the rice-birds for 35 days, on a plantation of about 1200 acres, at $8,250, or $6.87 per acre.]

Ride herd, to. To guard cattle by keeping on the edge of the herd.

1902 I'm romancin' leisurely along the street when I encounters a party who's *ridin' herd* on one of these yere telescopes.—A. H. Lewis, "Wolfville Nights," Ch. xviii. (Century Dict.)
Blacknell was *riding herd* on a small bunch of calves who with heels mostly in the air were making life a burden to him and to his wiry cow-pony.—J. Bronson, "The Lost River," ch. i. (Century Dict.)

Ride (a man) on a rail. A mode of expulsion in accordance with lynch law. [1854-1866.]

1866 Assuming the restraints of the General Government are all to be removed from Tennessee, you ask me if northern school teachers would be allowed to educate negroes. I answer no, not in Middle and West Tennessee. In two cases out of every three the schoolhouses would be burned, and the teachers *rode upon a rail*.—Letter of Gov. W. G. Brownlow of Tenn., Jan. 1: *C. G.*, p. 465/3.

1866 If a citizen of a free State, visiting a slave State, expressed his opinion in reference to slavery, he was treated without much ceremony to a coat of tar and feathers and a *ride upon a rail*.—Mr. Hiram Price of Ia., H. R., Feb. 27: *Id.*, p. 1066/2.

1891 On Tuesday night an attempt was made to *ride* a negro barber out of this town [Winchester, Ill.] *on a rail*.—Newspaper citation, Feb. 13: *C. R.*, p. 99/1, App.

Rift. To gape open, to split. The N. E. D. quotes Cursor Mundi (a.1300). Palsgrave, Shakespeare, Bacon, etc., and questions "obsolete."

1879 I understand [Mr. Wallace] to admit that one very large rock has been struck on, and that the thing would have *rifted* and been wrecked on that particular point.—Mr. James G. Blaine of Me., U. S. Senate, June 16: *C. R.*, p. 2042/1.

Right away. Immediately. A phrase possibly imported from the S.W. of Ireland. [1818-1889.]

1895 Mr. Loud:—When is that to be? Mr. Simpson:—*Right away.* Mr. Loud:— Well, we have heard the same thing for many years, and it has not come yet.—H. R., Feb. 15: *C. R.*, p. 2241/1.

Right here. Just at this point. Similarly, **Right at this time, Right there**, etc.

1640 *Right at this time* there raged and reigned in the Church of Corinth an epidemical disease.—Thomas Fuller, comment on 1 Cor. xi. 30.

1863 Let me say to the Senator *right here* that I do not like this croaking about civil war. It certainly has not pinched the toes of the northern people much yet.—Mr. B. F. Wade of O., U. S. Senate, Feb. 20: *C. G.*, p. 1127/2.

1864 Will the Senator permit me to say a word *right there*?—Mr. John Conness of Calif., U. S. Senate. Jan. 14: *Id.*, p. 202/1.

1864 *And right here*, Mr. Chairman, let me say etc.—Mr. John R. McBride of Ore., H. R., Feb. 17: *Id.*, p. 718/3.

1865 Will my friend allow me to interrupt him *right there?*—Mr. Charles Sumner of Mass., U. S. Senate, Feb. 3: *Id.,* p. 578/2.

1868 *Right here* I wish to say that I have heard [remarks] which I did not expect to hear in the Senate.—Mr. Thos. A. Hendricks of Ind., U. S. Senate, Feb. 17: *Id.,* p. 1208/1.

1873 *Right here* it was that commerce decided again to locate the seat of her marvelous power.—Mr. Taffe of Neb., H. R., Jan. 21: *Id.,* p. 749/3.

1900 Will the gentleman *right in that connection* allow me to make a suggestion?—Mr. H. H. Bingham of Pa., H. R., Jan. 16: *Id.,* p. 870/1.

Right smart. Very considerable. Rather large in amount, extent, etc.

1870 [A gentleman visiting North Carolina asked a rustic] how far it was to such a place. The country fellow answered, "It is three screeches and a *right smart* go-by."—Mr. C. D. Drake of Mo., U. S. Senate, May 17: *C. G.,* p. 3521/2. [Similar expressions are "two steps and a straddle," "two hoots and a holler," etc.]

Ring. A combination in jobbing or in politics. [1869-1881.]

1864 There is what is known in the City of New York as the *"gold ring,"* . . . . a set of men who are all the while speculating in gold.— Mr. Chandler of Mich., U. S. Senate, Apr. 15: *C. G.,* p. 1644/1.

1864 This *gold ring,* if you call it so—I do not know what the name of it is—this set of gamblers in New York cannot control the relative price of gold and currency.—Mr. Collamer of Vt., U. S. Senate, Apr. 16: *Id.,* p. 1667/1.

1869 The commercial community has a right to be protected against whims, caprices, and cabals,—*"rings,"* in the phrase of the day.—Mr. Roscoe Conkling of N. Y., U. S. Senate, Feb. 11: *Id.,* p. 1075/1.

1872 A national debt furnishes the occasion . . . . for the formation of tariff *rings,* bond *rings,* bank *rings,* railroad *rings,* and other *rings,* which enter the political arena and aspire to make Presidents and control the legislation of the country.—Mr. J. M. Bright of Tenn., H. R., May 3: *Id.,* p. 351/2, App.

1878 It is said there is a *"wood ring,"* and that no objection has been made to the taking of wood for domestic purposes by settlers.—Mr. Henry M. Teller of Colo., U. S. Senate, Mar. 13: *C. R.,* p. 1723/1.

1878 There has [have] been years since I have lived in Colorado when no man could burn a stick of wood, when not a house nor a church nor a school-house could be built, unless the timber was taken from the public land. There are no *"wood rings"* there, the Secretary of the Interior notwithstanding. I say there is no such thing in the western country as a *"wood ring."*—The same. Mar. 19: *Id.,* p. 1862/2.

1891 Samuel J. Tilden said . . . . that the proper definition of a *ring* was "an organization with sufficient influence in both parties to control both."—Mr. Daniel Kerr of Ia., H. R., Feb. 5: *Id.,* p. 2211/1.

Ringer. A supplementary cheer; an ultimate "tiger."

1901-2 When the result had been announced, the air was rent with cheers. Auctioneer Judy called for a tiger for Mr. Joseph, and then a *ringer* for . . . . who had sold the highest priced beef steer in the world.— *Rep. Kan. State Bd. Agr.,* p. 360. (Century Dict.)

Ringing out. A brokers' arrangement, operating in the manner of an offset of "puts" against "calls." See quotation. See **Puts and Calls.**

1892 The process of *ringing out* is not a substitute for actually fulfilling a contract, but simply an expedient to avoid extra expense and trouble in fulfilling it. The buyer or seller has no part in this *"ringing out,"* and it does not prevent him from receiving or excuse him from delivering the precise produce he has bought or sold. The *"ringing out"* is exclusively an arrangement by which brokers in providing for their numerous customers, do so at the least expense to themselves. . . . . In other words, *"ringing out"* is simply an adjustment between brokers, to save the cost of transferring back and forth.— Mr. J. D. Warner of N. Y., H. R., June 6: *C. R.*, p. 449/2, App.

1894 See *Id.*, June 18, pp. 6484-5.

Ringmaster. The controller of a "ring."

1876 The *ringmasters* would not give up the speech of the court on the subject of fraud in elections. *That* was the valuable part of the memorial; *it* they regarded as a great political "bonanza," an "eye-opener," so to speak, something that would electrify the people.—Mr. G. W. Cate of Wisc., H. R., May 20: *C. R.*, p. 3235/2.

1876 The impression that Mr. Platt was the grand mogul that controlled the whole thing, that he was the *ring-master* of that [Norfolk] navy-yard.—Mr. Goode of Va., H. R., July 26: *Id.*, p. 4891/2.

Ring-shake. A defect in timber, usually originated by frost. See quotation.

1905 The defect known as cupshake, *ringshake*, ... is frequently met with in many kinds of wood. It consists in a partial or entire separation of two consecutive annual rings, and appears on a cross section as one or more splits running concentrically around the log.—*Scientific Amer.*, Mar. 25. (Century Dict.)

Ringsider. One who watches the judging of animals, leaning over the fence or railing of the ring or enclosure. Colloquial.

1901-2 In a large ring there are sure to be several different types of cattle. Sometimes it is not a hard matter to place them right; other times there may be a "topper" of each type in the class, each having many friends among the *ringsiders* for premier honors.—*Rep. Kan. State Board Agr.*, p. 173. (Century Dict.)

Ringster. A member of a ring. See above and also Vol. II, **Ring.** [1869-1881.]

1878 As the honest contractor will not go into a business where he has to evade the law, the *ringster* has it all his own way.—Mr. J. G. Cannon of Ill., H. R., Mar. 20: *C. R.*, p. 1915/1.

Rinse. The **Scottish pronunciation** *rench* is still observed among persons of Scottish descent.

[Compare with this the use of *clenge* for *cleanse*:
1513 Of sum the cryme committit *clengit* be
Vndir the wattir or deip hiddeous see;
And in the fyre the gilt of other sum
Is pvrifeit and *clengit* all and sum.
—Bishop Douglas, "Eneados," ed. Small (1874), Bk. VI, p. 60.]

Riprap. A term from masonry, meaning a foundation or sustaining wall of stones thrown together without order, as in deep water or on a soft bottom; also stones so used. (Webster.) **Riprapping,** strengthening or supporting with a riprap.

1805 The transition from the stream to the eddy is sometimes very visible, by causing what those pilots (off the Florida coast) call *Rip-Raps* — *Georgia Republican*, Feb. 4, p. 2/3.

1868 There is not water enough on those *rip-raps* . . . . for anything to pass over their top until there is fifteen feet of water in the river.— Mr. P. G. Van Winkle of W. Va., U. S. Senate, July 21: *C. G.*, 4284/2.

1874 The trouble with Fort Sumter was that it was built on *ripraps* in the water, where an earthwork would be impossible.—Mr. B. F. Butler of Mass., H. R., Feb. 11: *C. R.*, p. 1411/1.

1882 The bridge . . . . shall be built with the piers parallel to the current, leaving the water-way unobstructed by *rip-rap* or piling, or other obstructions.—Bill for a bridge over the Saint Croix River: *Id.*, Aug. 7, p. 7006/1.

1886 Mr. Hepburn:—What was the improvement? Mr. Blanchard:—It is stated there in the report. Mr. Hepburn:—It was the *riprapping* of the levees of the river.—H. R., Apr. 15: *Id.*, p. 3527/1.

1897 [Money was voted] for the purpose of building a *riprap* wall to stop up a breach which the ocean has made across the sand spit which connects Sandy Hook with the mainland.—Mr. M. Pitney of N. J., H. R., July 7: *Id.*, p. 2448/2.

1899 [The banks of the Missouri] can be made stationary by what is called *riprapping.*—Mr. S. Maxwell of Neb., H. R., Feb. 2: *Id.*, p. 1401/1.

Rising. "More than." **The rise** is the excess. [1775-1861.]

1789 A small Bay Horse, *raising* [*sic*] four years.—*Augusta* (Ga.) *Chronicle*, June 27, p. 4/2. (Advt.)

1876 See STAR ROUTE.

Rising-seat. In a Friends' meetinghouse, one of a series of ascending seats, facing the congregation. Also called *facing-seat* or *high seat.* (Century Dict.)

1809 In the sing-song drawl once peculiar to the tuneful exhortations of the *rising seat*, he thus held forth.—M. C. Lee, "A Quaker Girl of Nantucket," p. 28.

River-driver. A man who conducts logs down running streams. (Bartlett, 1859.)

1864 A famous *river-driver*, who was to have fifty men under him next winter.—Lowell, "Fireside Travels," p. 141. (N. E. D.)

1893 Every *river driver* wore a long red sash.—*Scribner's Mag.*, p. 714/1. (N. E. D.)

Roach, Roach up. To trim a horse's mane, or a man's hair, to within an inch or two of the skin. [1776-1889.]

1790 A Bay Horse, *roached* mane and a small switched tail.—*Augusta* (Ga.) *Chronicle*, Mar. 13, p. 3/1. (Advt.)

1887 I *roached* his mane and docked his tail, and put him in a warm stall.— *Century Mag.*, xxxvii, 335.*

Road agent. A highwayman; a robber. [1866-1890.]

1866 During the four years of rebellion, a good many of our "Southern brethren" in California took upon themselves the occupation of what is there technically called *"road agents."* . . . . They turned out upon the public highways, and became robbers, highway robbers.—Mr. John Conness of Calif., U. S. Senate, May 30: *C. G.*, p. 2892/2.

1879 That quite differs from an attack of *"road agents,"* who pull up the rails, etc.—Mr. J. R. Hawley of Conn., H. R., Apr. 4: *C. R.*, p. 234/2.

1879 On the prairies and west of the Rocky Mountains the highwaymen and the robbers are called *road agents.*—Mr. E. S. Bragg of Wisc., H. R., Apr. 15: *Id.*, p. 458/1.

1894 [I shall not] call anybody robbers. There is a term which is not quite as objectionable as that in sound,—*"road agents."*—Mr. O. H. Platt of Conn., U. S. Senate, May 22: *Id.*, p. 5060/1.

Road house. A wayside inn.

1901 The revival of road coaching as a popular amusement, ... the habit of well-known persons to make use of the better class of *road houses*, ... seem to point to the revival of a spring season.—*N. Y. Commercial Advertiser*, May 11. (Century Dict.)

Roanoke. An inferior kind of wampum.

1624 *Rawranoke* or white beads that occasion . . . . dissention among the Salvages.—Capt. Smith's "Virginia," III, 418. (N. E. D.)

1656 *Roanoke* and Wompompeeke to keep their wonted value.—Statutes of Virginia (1823) I, 397. (N. E. D.) See *Journal of Am. Folk-Lore*, xv, 256.

Robber tariff. A phrase sometimes applied to a tariff which is not "for revenue only."

* Item given incorrectly in Vol. II.

1890 [The burning of Indian corn as fuel] is heralded as an evidence of the poverty and distress under which [the farmer] is laboring, and of the operation of this *"robber tariff."*—Mr. G. C. Moody of S. D., U. S. Senate, Aug. 12: *C. R.*, p. 8452/2.

1890 Republicans say that "the farmer lives until he dies," but the laborer under this *robber tariff* dies even while living.—Mr. W. B. Bate of Tenn., U. S. Senate, Aug. 14: *Id.*, p. 8559/2.

1892 Some of the crimes I have adverted to were local; some were gross and monstrous; but they are as nothing when compared with the *robber tariff* of to-day.—Mr. J. D. Richardson of Tenn., H. R., Apr. 6: *Id.*, p. 3020/1.

1892 I have sat here and have seen the advocates of the *"robber tariff"* skulk behind a pretended protection to labor.—Mr. J. R. Whiting of Mich., H. R., July 8: *Id.*, p. 5908/1.

1894 Under our *robber-tariff* system there was a license granted . . . . to rob the farmers and laborers of the country, and from such robbery there was no chance to appeal to the courts.—Mr. Edw. Lane of Ill., H. R., Jan. 31: p. 1755/2.

Robe. A dressed skin used for a carriage-rug.

1887 Under the head of *robes* [were] included all [buffalo] cow skins taken during the proper season, from one year old upward, and all bull skins from one to three years old. Bull skins over three years of age were classed as hides, and while the best of them were finally tanned and used as *robes*, the really poor ones were converted into leather.—W. T. Hornaday, *Smithsonian Report*, ii, 443. (Century Dict.)

Rock. A stone. Hence to rock a person is to stone him. [1712-1901.] [In early days in New England, it was the custom to do a great deal of "rocking." For example, in Marblehead, the usual treatment for a stranger was to "rock him 'round the corner." The boys of neighboring and rival towns "rocked" each other frequently, when not engaged in "rocking a funeral."]

1513 [Turnus] dyd aspy quhar that a gret *rok* lay, Ane ald crag stane huge, gret, and gray.
          —Douglas, "Eneados," ed. Small, 1874, Book XII, p. 162.

1851 [He] struck him with all his force with a *rock* which he held in his hand.—Wilmington (N. C.) *Commercial*, Mar. 1, p. 4/1.

1872 See PUT OUT.

1888 I am glad I have thrown a *rock* which has hit somewhere, and to judge from the effect it has produced it struck all round.—Mr. B. A. Enloe of Tenn., H. R., June 2: *C. R.*, p. 4852/2.

1892 In the language of a grandiloquent orator who was once in this body, "gentlemen who reside in houses constructed of diaphanous materials should not throw projectiles." In other words, people who live in glass houses ought not to throw *rocks*.—Mr. G. G. Vest of Mo., U. S. Senate, Jan. 19: *C. R.*, p. 402/2.

1894 Three rioters shot—Bullets and *rocks* in a riot at the Silver Brook Colliery in Pa.—Heading of item in *N. Y. Herald*, June 10.

1900 When . . . . a boy went to mill with grain in one side of his sack and a *rock* in the other to balance it, some one said, "Why do you carry the *rock*?" The boy said, "To balance the grain."—Mr. G. L. Wellington of Md., U. S. Senate, May 18: *C. R.*, p. 5695/1.

Rock and rye. Whiskey with rock candy.

1880 [These heroes] were the bright consummate flower, the cream, or, to use a metaphor more suitable to the subject, the combined sweetness and strength, the very *"rock and rye"* of the democracy.—Mr. Thos. B. Reed, H. R., Apr. 23: *C. R.*, p. 2692/1.

1884 I had heard . . . . that the breechless sons of the Lothians were not averse to a wee drop of *"rock and rye,"* and not over particular if the *rock* was left out.—Mr. W. J. Green of N. C., H. R., Apr. 21: *Id.*, p. 145/1, App.

Rock-pile. A stone-heap.
1888 If this were a police court, the Senator from Indiana (Mr. Voorhees) would be sent to the *rock-pile* for being drunk and disorderly.—Mr. J. J. Ingalls of Kan., U. S. Senate, May 1: *C. R.*, p. 3571/1.

Rock-rooted. Immovably fixed, unshakable.
1890 Every *rock-rooted* advocate of the gold standard is in favor of [this provision]; every bi-metallist is opposed to it.—Mr. H. F. Bartine of Nev., H. R., June 7: *C. R.*, p. 5802/1.

Rocky. Difficult to deal with. Slang.
1875 A colored man goes into a railroad car, and one of the officers of the road says, "You cannot go into that car; it is a ladies' car." . . . . Are you going to have the case brought up in the U. S. court, trying to prove that he is a lady? You might have a *"rocky"* time if you tried to prove that.—Mr. Thomas Whitehead of Va., H. R., Feb. 3: *C. R.*, p. 953/1.

Rocky. Intoxicated.
1737 "The Drinker's Dictionary."—*S. C. Gazette*, May 7, p. 1/2.

Rocky. Infirm. Slang.
1901 Old Mosey? He's pretty *rocky*. I'm afraid he won't pull through.—*Century Mag.*, p. 227.

Rodeo. A gathering of cattle to be branded or marked; a round-up. Sp. (Century Dict.)
1890 The ranch owner who gives the *rodeo* takes his own cattle, ... and drives them in with the ones to be branded, leaving in the *rodeo*-ground the cattle bearing the brands of all other ranchers.—Kate D. Wiggin, "A Summer in a Cañon," p. 255. (Century Dict.)

Roil. To disturb (the temper); ruffle; vex. To render turbid by stirring up sediment. (Webster.) See Vol. II, **Rile.** [a.1734-1872.]
1815 Here's some of the old family licker scalding hot in my vains, when I'm a leetle *roiled* and put out.—David Humphreys, "The Yankey in England," p. 34.
1863 The stream . . . . was so *roiled* by the recent rain that we could not distinguish the foot prints of the horse beneath the surface.—Edmund Kirke, "Life in Dixie's Land," p. 197. (Lond.)
1867 The fable of the poor lamb which was killed by the wolf for *riling* the water, etc.—Mr. W. E. Robinson of N. Y., H. R., July 12: *C. G.*, p. 9/3, App.
1879 The Potomac River . . . . is liable to be *roiled*, and to have the fluctuant lighter material which lies at the bottom stirred up by rains.—Mr. Roscoe Conkling of N. Y., U. S. Senate, June 3: *C. R.*, p. 1738/1.

Roll up. To accumulate. The N. E. D. gives examples (1887, 1890) of the same expression in an intransitive sense, noting its Australian origin as thus used.
1877 At the October election the democratic party of Georgia *rolled up* an astonishing . . . . majority of 75,000 votes.—Mr. Robert Smalls of S. C., H. R., Feb. 24: *C. R.*, p. 123/2, App.
1898 In the election of 1896 [the people of N. J.] *rolled up* a majority for William McKinley, for Garrett A. Hobart, and for honest money.—Mr. M. Pitney of N. J., H. R., Feb. 1: *Id.*, p. 1336/1.

Romal. A braided thong of leather, rawhide, or horsehair, with a divided end, looped to the bridle or the ends of the reins, and used as a whip. Western. (Century Dict.)
1887 He rode ahead on his blue-roan Indian pony, twirling his *romal*, a long leathern strap attached to the bridle, the end divided like a double whip-lash.—Mary H. Foote, *St. Nicholas*, xiv, 33.

Roommate. A fellow lodger.
1838 With a Frenchman and a Greek for my *roommates.*—J. L. Stephens, "Travels," I, 251. (N. E. D.)

1849   My interesting *roommates* were . . . . able to take the air upon deck.—W. S. Mayo, "Kaloolah," p. 107. (N. E. D.)

1869   Mr. [W. P.] Fessenden was my friend, associate, *roommate*, and bed fellow in my early boyhood.—Mr. James Brooks of N. Y., H. R., Dec. 14: *C. G.*, p. 132/2.

Room traders. See PIKERS.

Rooster. Cock; chanticleer. [1806-1866.] In the picturesque campaign of 1840, an editor named Chapman conducted the democratic newspaper in Indianapolis. Some partisans thought that he was not sufficiently energetic, and the word went round, "Tell Chapman to crow." The vote of Indiana remained for some time in doubt, but it finally turned out that the Whigs were triumphant, and Chapman's crowing had been premature. The crowing fowl became, however, an emblem of democratic victories in succeeding years.

1874   [Mr. Morrill] thinks there is no word but "regent" that will suit . . . . ; that our language is so poor that it furnishes no other designation for these three "*roosters*" who are to preside over this people [of D. C.].—Mr. A. G. Thurman of O., U. S. Senate, Dec. 16: *C. R.*, p 103/1.

1890   Of course the New England *roosters* will refuse to crow when the Democratic party comes into power in 1892.—Mr. J. R. Williams of Ill., H. R., May 19: *Id.*, p. 4941/2.

1894   Mr. Meredith:—What has become of the *roosters* that were crowing so lively? Mr. Ray:—O, the Democrats wore them all in their hats, rejoicing over the election in 1892, and now the Democratic laboring men, deprived of all other means of sustenance, are engaged in eating them up.—H. R., Jan. 29: *Id.*, p. 1600/2.

1897   He goes out of the way to suggest that I am not a very good Republican, and refers to me as a vanquished rural *rooster* smarting under defeat.—Mr. N. T. Hopkins of Ky., H. R., Feb. 18: *Id.*, p. 57/2, App.

Root. To shout for, or otherwise noisily applaud or encourage, a contestant, as in sports. (Webster.) [1907-1909.]

1911   See BLEACHERS.

Root. To make one's way slowly and with difficulty, as a hog does. To work hard. Hence the phrase "Root hog, or die." [1833-1870.]

1867   The soil of the manufacturing districts is sterile, and it is "*root hog or die*" with the inhabitants. This produces thrifty people. It is said that a Yankee baby once lay in his cradle and rolled his eyes around till he invented a new back-action rocker, for which he took out a patent as soon as he was old enough to talk.—Mr. T. E. Noell of Mo., H. R., Feb. 12: *C. G.*, p. 105/2, App.

1886   To pick out [these Indians] and say to them, "*root, hog, or die*," with the certainty that it will be "die," seems to be a refinement of cruelty.—Mr. P. B. Plumb of Kan., U. S. Senate, Feb. 17: *C. R.*, p. 1559/1.

Root beer. A drink containing the extracted juices of various roots, as of dock, dandelion, sarsparilla, and sassafras. (Century Dict.)

1851   No less than five persons, during the forenoon, inquired for ginger-beer, or *root-beer*, or any drink of a similar brewage.—N. Hawthorne, "House of the Seven Gables," ch. iii.

Root doctor. An empiric who sells decoctions of roots as medicine.

1890   Carmier was what people call down here a *root doctor*. He possessed ordinary intelligence, and was very successful in his practice.—N. Y. *Age*, Apr. 19: quoted in *C. R.*, Dec. 17, p. 559/1.

Rope funeral. A hanging.

1895 The judge feels that he has sent enough men to the penitentiary and attended enough *rope funerals* of the outlaws of the [Indian] country to make it a very paradise of peace.—Mr. John S. Little of Ark., H. R., Jan. 15: *C. R.*, p. 1003/2.

Rope in. To gather in collectively. (Bartlett, 1848, 1859.)

1872 The object and intent [of this bill] simply is to *rope in* the State election of La., and place it under . . . . military machinery.—Mr. T. F. Bayard of Del., U. S. Senate, May 8: *C. G.*, p. 3176/1.

1872 The Senator from Indiana [Mr. Morton] a day or two ago found fault with a careless phrase of mine, in which I spoke of the disposition of Congress to "*rope in*" the State elections, and put them under Federal control. Well, sir, it was not a very elegant phrase, perhaps not very senatorial; but it was true, and it was good English.—The same, May 10: *Id.*, p. 3278/3.

1890 See MINE-SALTER.

Roper. A lassoer.

1808 Taking the wild horses, in that manner, is scarcely ever attempted, even with the fleetest horses and most expert *ropers.*—Z. M. Pike, "Sources of the Miss." (1810), p. 160. (N. E. D.)

1888 A really first-class *roper* can command his own price.—*Century Mag.*, p. 506. (N. E. D.)

Roper, Roper-in. A gambling-house decoy; a "tout."

1859 A young man at his hotel, who turned out to be a *roper-in* of a gambling house. (Bartlett.)

1875 The *ropers* for gambling houses . . . . haunt each conspicuous corner.— E. King, "Southern States," p. 61. (N. E. D.)

1877 He proposed as a matter of proof, that this man once kept a snake-show, or was a *roper-in* for a snake-show, as he called him.—Mr. Hurlbut of Ill. before the Electoral Commission, Feb. 9: *Proceedings*, p. 68/1.

1894 Dealing in futures is gambling. . . . The professional gambler stakes his own money; these men stake other people's money and property, and the [fact] that they make money out of sanguine gentlemen brands them as "*ropers-in.*"—Mr. T. R. Stockdale of Miss., H. R., June 21: *C. R.*, p. 1088/2, App.

Ropes, to know the. To know the "modus operandi" of any thing. A nautical phrase originally. [1840-1866.]

1871 This gentleman, who is familiar with *all the ropes* [in the P. O. Department] can show him how to "whip the devil round the stump." —Mr. G. F. Edmunds of Vt., U. S. Senate, Feb. 16: *C. G.*, p. 1311/2.

1890 The gold monometallists . . . . know the wires; they *know the ropes.*—Mr. F. M. Cockrell of Mo., U. S. Senate, July 9: *C. R.*, p. 7052/2.

Rosebud Senator, The. Henry B. Anthony of R. I. (1815-1884).

1885 Within an irreverent but limited circle of acquaintants he was called "*the rosebud Senator,*" which sobriquet might have been bestowed as a tribute to the healthful glow which mantled his cheek, or from the fact that . . . . he constantly wore a bud or other flower.—Mr. W. D. Kelley of Pa., H. R., Jan. 21: *C. R.*, p. 908/1.

Rotten, To rot. The N. E. D. gives a single example, from Speed (1611), of the word used in a transitive sense.

1869 The grapes and peaches and apples now *rottening* annually.—Mr. Jas. R. McCormick of Mo., H. R., Feb. 12: *C. G.*, p. 1154/1.

1889 [These ships] will be used in the coast-wise trade, or lie at the ports *rottening* and useless.—Mr. W. M. Stewart of Nev., U. S. Senate, Jan. 14: *C. R.*, p. 730/1.

Rough and Ready. Zachary Taylor. See **Old Rough and Ready.**

1848 The name of old *Rough and Ready* resounded from almost every tongue.—Wilmington (N. C.) *Commercial*, July 8, p. 1/6.

1848   Come fall in, boys, eyes right and steady,
    And raise the shout for *Rough and Ready*.
    He licked old Peg-leg with his Pass,
    And now he'll use up Lewis Cass.
        —*Id.*, July 20, p. 1/4 (From the Richmond *Republican*).
1848   Aug. 17.   See OLD ZACH.

Roughneck.   A slang term for a tough or a rowdy, such as a member
of one of those gangs that at one time terrorized the people of the
slums of New York or Chicago.   The term is also used to denote
a person who lacks manners or refinement, in contrast to one who
has a good address and the appearance of culture, as "Oh! he's a
rough-neck!"   [1836.]

1903   His [Sam Parks] stated income amounts to union wages from his
union of *rough-necks*, as the iron-workers call themselves, as walking-
delegate.—*N. Y. Evening Post*, Aug. 17.

Rounder.   One who makes the round of the prisons; a habitual criminal; a tough.   [1881-1891.]

1866   The *"rounders"* and ruffians who instigate mobs against harmless
and peaceable people . . . . are not the most fit men in the world
for the ballot.—Mr. George W. Julian of Ind., H. R., Jan. 16: *C. G.*,
p. 257/1.

1884   A *rounder*, bruiser, and shoulder-hitter.—*Fortnightly Review*, p. 389,
March.   (N. E. D.)

1887   See THUG.

1890   A class of repeaters or *rounders*, as they are° termed, some . . . .
recommitted more than a hundred times to the same prison.—*Chicago
Advance*, Dec. 4.   (N. E. D.)

1891   The regular *rounders* who are beginning to receive long sentences
under the new drunkenness law.—*Boston Journal*, July 7, p. 2/4.
(N. E. D.)

Roundsman.   A police-officer usually in charge of a patrol.

1883   A *roundsman* and five patrolmen were present to preserve order.—
Daily News, Oct. 18, p. 3/2.   (N. E. D.)

1896   I distinguish between a person who performs the function of a sneak
and one who performs that of a superintendent.   I have designated
the latter as a *"roundsman."*   He patrols his beat examining as to
the efficiency of the [postal] service within that territory.—Mr. L. E.
Quigg of N. Y., H. R., Mar. 11: *C. R.*, p. 2696/2.

Round trip.   Round voyage.   One which includes going and returning.

1866   *Provided*, That in addition to the twelve *round voyages* now required,
one additional *round voyage* shall be required.—Amendment offered
by Mr. Sumner of Mass. to the resolution on mail service to China.
U. S. Senate, July 17: *C. G.*, p. 3861/2.

1870   [The farmer would have] a very small dividend, or rather none at
all, at the end of the *round trip*.—Mr. E. G. Ross of Kan., U. S.
Senate, May 5: *Id.*, p. 3244/1.

1872   The English Government pays the Cunard line and the Inman line
$3,500 gold for each *round trip*.—Mr. Alex. Mitchell of Wisc., H. R.,
Apr. 6: *Id.*, p. 2243/1.

1892   A stated fare will be charged for the *round trip*.—*Pall Mall Gazette*,
July 4, p. 7/2.   (N. E. D.)

1897   When railroads establish *round-trip* rates which are less than double
the one-way rate, the public right inures to any person to make the
round-trip journey for the *round-trip* price.   But there is no public
right by which one person can go in one direction on a *round-trip
ticket*, and another person make the return journey on the same
ticket.—Mr. James S. Sherman of N. Y., H. R., Feb. 27: *C. R.*,
p. 64/1, App.

[End of Part X.]

Round-up, n. Act or process of collecting cattle by riding around them and driving them in. (Webster.)

Round up, v. [1878-1886.]

1876 [The Mexican raiders] *"round up"* a herd of cattle, and start with them at a full run for the Rio Grande.—Mr. Schleicher of Tex., H. R., June 30: *C. R.*, p. 4309/2.

1886 [The Indians] were ranging through the country where the cowboys were proceeding to make their *"round-up."*—Mr. G. G. Symes of Colo., H. R., May 15: *Id.*, p. 4556/2.

1900 I would have *rounded up* with the Senator on that proposition.— Mr. B. R. Tillman of S. C., U. S. Senate, May 18: *Id.*, p. 5692/1.

Roustabout. A wharf laborer or deck hand, especially on a river steamboat; also, a vagrant who lives by chance jobs. (Webster.) [1746-1911.]

1883 [He was] one of the kind called *"roustabouts"* . . . . , people who live in a happy-go-lucky sort of way, dependent from day to day on stray jobs or stray thefts.—Sherwood Bonner, "Dialect Tales," p. 121.

1890 In the middle of the group was an old Mississippi *roustabout,* singing the famous old river song called "Limber Jim."—*N. Y. Sun,* Mar. 23. (Century Dict.)

1890 From a carefully made statement before me in a Galena paper, the Gazette, it appears that "exclusive of *roustabouts,* there are three times as many steamboat men live in Galena as in Dubuque."—Mr. R. R. Hitt of Ill., H. R., Apr. 1: *C. R.*, p. 2882/2.

1894 I found [in a "remonstrance" emanating from San Angelo, Texas] the names of men who wrote their occupations down as hustlers and *roustabouts* and grangers No. 2, whatever that means.—Mr. W. H. Crain of Tex., H. R., Jan. 18: *Id.*, p. 1011/2.

1894 See EXPRESS, v.

Route, v. To direct on a line of travel.

1832 Each man selected the time, manner, and route of his retreat for himself. . . . . The Indians, astonished at seeing men *route themselves* in this manner, sallied out of their redoubts and pursued the stragglers. —John A. McClung, "Sketches of Western Adventure," p. 132. (Phila.)

Route agent. The manager of a postal route.

1878 I myself have the appointment of 7 or 8 *route-agents* upon those postal cars.—Mr. O. D. Conger of Mich., H. R., Dec. 17: *C. R.*, p. 262/2.

Roving commission. A commission of search, with vaguely defined powers; authority without specified limitations.

1867 I think it would be safer to leave this matter [of certain State claims] to the direct inspection of the War Department, than to send out a *roving commission.* We have had enough of these *roving commissions.*—Mr. Oliver P. Morton of Ind., U. S. Senate, Mar. 22: *C. G.*, p. 273/2.

1882 If that is to be the mission that Congress is to enter upon by these *roving commissions,* taking testimony and printing whatever any set of gentlemen may give as their own views, ... I for one shall oppose it.—Mr. J. B. Beck of Ky., U. S. Senate, Mar. 9: *C. R.*, p. 1737/2.

1890 I do not think Congress would want to give to a board of this kind a *roving commission* to go anywhere in the city and establish a Government Printing Office.—Mr. P. B. Plumb of Kan., U. S. Senate, July 19: *Id.*, p. 7469/1.

1894 Is it a legitimate expenditure of the public money to send out consuls with *roving commissions* to hunt up commerce for a certain class of our people?—Mr. T. R. Stockdale of Miss., H. R., Apr. 25: *Id.*, p. 4098/1.

Row, to hoe a. To perform a task. Cf. Vol. II, **Row to hoe.** [1835-1846.]

1900 Any man who can serve in Congress twenty-five years, *hoe as big a row* as Bland did, and grow all the time, is big enough for any position.—Mr. Champ Clark of Mo., H. R., Apr. 7: *C. R.*, p. 3899/1.

Rowdy. One who engages in rows, or in rough behavior. (Webster.) A ruffian. [1819-1864.]

1822 The bargemen, who bring cotton down the rivers, are a most dissolute set, and are known by the significant name of *Rowdies*. This is their general term; but they are divided into classes, such as *Tuscaloosa Roarers, Alabama Screamers, Cahawba Scrougers,* and the like gentle names. These fellows, whose meat and drink it is to fight, challenge each other, by crowing like a cock, or neighing like an ass, from their respective boats.—*Am. Beacon* (Norfolk, Va.), Sept. 6, p. 4/1: from the *Georgia Advertiser*. [Cf. HALF HORSE AND HALF ALLIGATOR.]

Rubber. To gaze about. See **Rubber-neck.** Slang.

1901 [If Police Commissioners are] any good they probably *rubber* around on their own hook, an' they must see these joints. . . . Everybody *rubbers* in [Boston].—Josiah Flynt in *McClure's Mag.*, p. 117. (Century Dict.)

Rubber-neck. One who turns his head to see every new thing, as if his neck were made of rubber. Slang.

1901 In the West we have long used the term "*rubberneck,*" just now so popular with you in the East. Its meaning there differs slightly from the interpretation you put on it. A "*rubberneck*" West is one who snoops around and tries to get into business deals and like things. Now the term is countrywide and attracts but little attention; but formerly, when confined to the West, it always caused inquiry from the Eastern Visitor.—*N. Y. Tribune*, Apr. 14. (Century Dict.)

Ruin, To scratch for dead. To make a violent effort.

1882 We have gone to work like a lot of boys playing goal, where each chap *scratches for dead ruin* to get to some place first.—Mr. R. G. Horr of Mich., H. R., Jan. 18: *C. R.*, p. 498/2.

Rulable. According to rule; permissible.

1874 It is not *rulable* to recognize two gentlemen on the same side of the question for an hour each.—The Speaker of the H. R. [Mr. James G. Blaine], Feb. 18: *C. R.*, p. 1608/1.

1888-9 It shall be *rulable* to reject any . . . packages varying widely . . . from the bulk of the lot.—*N. Y. Produce Exchange Report*, p. 305. (Century Dict.)

Rum. Any intoxicating liquor. **Rum Shop,** a place where such liquor is sold. [1858-1872.]

1872 Judge Allison in a speech delivered in Phila. in 1872, says: "In our criminal courts we can trace four-fifths of the crimes that are committed to the influence of *rum*. .There is not one case in twenty, where a man is tried for his life, in which *rum* is not the direct or indirect cause of the murder."—*C. R.*, 1876-7, p. 10/1. App.

1880 Twenty-two *rum* shops . . . were discovered in the city of New York peddling out blank naturalization certificates.—Mr. W. P. Frye of Me., H. R., Apr. 10: *Id.*, p. 2297/2.

1890 The hell-holes and *rum-shops* of the villages near which these Army posts are situated.—Mr. E. S. Williams of O., H. R., March 29: *Id.*, p. 2821/1.

1890 You may travel 150 miles in that State without being able to get a single glass of whisky—*rum*, as it is called in Maine. It is all *rum* there.—Mr. Mark H. Dunnell of Minn., H. R., July 19: *Id.*, p. 492/2, App.

1896 The sign over every *rum shop* ought to be in fire, and there ought to be a skull and crossbones over the door for a trademark.—Mr. E. A. Morse of Mass., H. R., May 18: *Id.*, p. 5379/2.

Run. To conduct; to manage. [1789-1890.]

1867 [The Secretary of the Treasury, Mr. Hugh McCulloch] does not know enough about finance to *run* a dry goods store in Detroit.—Mr. Zachariah Chandler of Mich., U. S. Senate, Feb. 27: *C. G.*, p. 1887/3.

1877 The people want (to use an expression peculiar to one portion of the country) to *"run"* this Government on as economical principles as possible.—Mr. A. M. Waddell of N. C., H. R., Feb. 2: *C. R.*, p. 1216/2.

1880 The great State of New York is *run* by the rascals and deadbeats in New York City.—Mr. Philip C. Hayes of Ill., H. R., March 10: *Id.*, p. 1449/1.

1888 Mr. Ryan:—That [appropriation] is not for establishing the plant; it is for *running* it. Mr. Clements:—It is for establishing and *running*.—H. R., March 15: *Id.*, p. 2119/2.

1888 Governor William Allen, of Ohio, used to say that it was "as hard to *run* a powder-house in hell as an honest government with a plethoric treasury."—Mr. S. S. Cox of N. Y., H. R., May 17: *Id.*, p. 4331/1.

1890 I have reduced my opinion to poetry, and this is it:

> John Wanny *runs* the Sunday-school,
> Levi *runs* the bar,
> The baby *runs* the White House,
> And, damn it, here we are.

—Mr. J. M. Allen of Miss., H. R., Apr. 22: *Id.*, p. 3685/1.

1901 See HOODLUM.

Running mate. A companion; especially, a fellow candidate.

1912 Concerning the nomination for the Vice-Presidency, Gov. Wilson said to-day: "Gov. Marshall bears the highest reputation both as an executive and as a Democrat, and I feel honored by having him as a *running mate*. He is, I am happy to say, a valued personal friend of mine as well as a fellow Democrat."—*N. Y. Evening Post*, July 4, p. 1/5.

1912 In a headline, Sept. 30, p. 2/4, the *N. Y. Evening Post* calls Mr. J. W. Wadsworth, Jr., of N. Y., *"Hedges's Running Mate."*

Rupert of debate, The. This phrase, applied in England to the fourteenth Earl of Derby, has been applied in the U. S. to Mr. James G. Blaine of Maine. (1830-1893.)

1879 My friend from Maine has been called with great propriety by an enthusiastic friend of his *"the Rupert of debate."* That had a meaning. Well, the Rupert of Charles the First never challenged his adversary in this way.—Mr. Eaton of Conn., U. S. Senate, May 16: *C. R.*, p. 1383/1.

"THE RUPERT OF DEBATE."

A few weeks ago Sir William Hutt, in a speech to his constituents, credited Mr. Disraeli with this oft-quoted phrase. It was of course easy to show, as was done at the time, that its author was Lord Lytton, who used it in his satire, *The New Timon,* to describe Lord Stanley (the present Earl of Derby). I am not so sure, however, that Sir William Hutt was not substantially right, and that the germ of Lord Lytton's felicitous phrase is not to be found in a speech made by Mr. Disraeli in the House of Commons in April, 1844 (nearly two years before the publication of *The New Timon*), during one of the angry discussions which arose at that time out of Mr. Ferrand's gross attack on Sir James Hogg and the late Sir James Graham in regard to the Nottingham election. On the occasion referred to, Mr. Disraeli is reported to have said that "the noble Lord (Stanley) was the Prince Rupert to the Parliamentary army—his valour did not always serve his own cause."—N. & Q. 4 S, i, p. 410.

Rural free delivery. Free delivery of mail in the country districts.

1892 [Mr. Watson of Ga.] is perfectly consistent in advocating a *rural free delivery* system which would mount carriers on horseback and send them to every habitation in the land to deliver and collect the mails.— Mr. B. A. Enloe of Tenn., H. R., May 28: *C. R.*, p. 4815/1.

1900 There has not been established within my recollection a more popular branch of the public service than the *rural free mail delivery* for the farmers of the country.—Mr. W. A. Smith of Mich., H. R., Jan. 16: Id., p. 864/1.

Rush the growler. To go or send often for beer to be brought in a "growler" (a pitcher or pail). Slang. (Century Dict.)

Rustler. An alert, energetic, driving person; a hustler. (Webster.)

1891 Bernard was a determined partisan. He was what is called a *"rustler"* of the first class.—Mr. G. G. Vest of Mo., U. S. Senate, Jan. 16: C. R., p. 1453/1.

Sabbaday. A corruption of Sabbath day, erroneously used for Sunday.

1815 See Go-to-meeting clothes.

Sabbath-day houses, Sunday houses. These were small two-roomed houses, built not far from a meeting house, in order to afford shelter and warmth and opportunity for a meal during the interval between morning and afternoon services. They were locked up during the week. Two families often united in building a house. Mr. H. E. Scudder thinks that these houses were peculiar to Connecticut. See Dr. Fowler's "History of Durham, Conn.," pp. 97, 98: cited in Scudder's "Life of Noah Webster," end of Ch. 1. [They are found outside Connecticut, also; for example, in Fredericksburg, Texas.—Ed.]

Sachem. Originally meaning an Indian chief, this word came to be applied to political leaders, especially in connection with Tammany. [1773-1819.]

1803   [Let our wine sparkle high while we gratefully give
         The health of our *Sachem*, and long may he live.]
This song was sung at the London Tavern, March 4, 1803, the anniversary of Jefferson's inauguration.—*Georgia Republican*, May 12, p. 3/4. [For additional lines of this song, see Vol. II, quotation dated 1805.]

Sail in. To pitch in; to go ahead. [1889.]

1868 I fancy the gentleman [Mr. E. B. Washburne] haranguing the assembled hosts of heaven. . . . How he would *sail into* them! How he would rout them!—Mr. Ignatius Donnelly of Minn., H. R., May 2: C. G., p. 2353/2.

Saloonist. A saloonkeeper. Rare.

1885 The *Saloonist* would be in constant trouble if he could not sell beverage spirits from the medicinal spirits bottle, or medicinal spirits from the beverage spirits bottle. Two bottles for the same article is one too many.—Mr. G. E. Seney, H. R., Jan. 5: *C. R.*, p. 11/2, App.

1887 My persistent effort to enforce the Sunday laws against the Saloon is met by the saloonist with the counter-effort to enforce the laws against legitimate business.—*Pop. Science Monthly*, xxx, 16. (Century Dict.)

Salted down. Reduced to a compact and available shape. Term derived from the laying by of meat for winter use.

1890 He said he had all the proofs of his wounds and sufferings *"salted down."*—Mr. J. R. Hawley of Conn., U. S. Senate, June 23: *C. R.*, p. 6384/1.

Salt licks. See quotation.
1786   Deers, buffaloes, etc., are fond of salt, and frequently resort [to places]
        where that mineral abounds, from which circumstances they are called
        salt licks.—Columbian Mag. (Phila.), p. 107/1.
Salt River. An imaginary river up which defeated political parties or
        candidates retire to oblivion.   (Webster.)   [1833-1860.]
1848   Farewell, my friends, your labor's vain;
                        The people are up in their might;
                    From lake and river and mountain and plain
                        They shout for freedom and right;
                    And old Zack Taylor in the field
                        The victor evermore!
                    My visions of the White House yield
                        To old *Salt River's* shore.
        —'Cass' Lament,' Wilmington (N. C.) *Commercial,* Oct. 3, p. 1/5.
1848   Here is a Locofoco who desires to take passage in the Ocean Monarch
        for *Salt River.—Id.,* Nov. 18, p. 2/3.
1868   By way of ridicule, Mr. John F. Benjamin of Mo. moved, as an
        amendment to an amendment of the River and Harbor bill,—"for the
        improvement of the navigation of *Salt River,* that the dreary passage
        up the rapid and turbulent waters of this great national highway may
        be rendered less grievous to the motley crowd of involuntary exiles
        who, about November next, will be seeking 'some sequestered spot'
        where a 'white man's government' may be maintained in its purity,
        etc."—H. R., June 29: *C. G.,* p. 3593/1.
1884   [Mr. White of Ky.] offered an amendment to the bill appropriating
        the sum of $40,000 for the improvement of Salt River, Kentucky. It
        is an old but a good joke. . . . He said he wanted to improve that
        river for the benefit of the Democratic party. Well, we have not *gone
        up Salt River*—not far or much. The magnetic statesmen from Maine
        and his co-ordinates and companions have *gone up Salt River* with all
        the meanders thereof.—Mr. S. S. Cox of N. Y., H. R., Dec. 12:
        C. R., p. 216/1.
Sam.   A term used in connection with the Know-nothings, who pro-
        fessed extraordinary patriotism and zeal for "Uncle Sam." [1855-
        1860.]
1866   I never had anything to do with the Know-nothings except in 1854.
        I was a candidate for the Legislature, and just at the close of the
        polls I looked back over my shoulder, and saw *"Sam"* a short distance
        behind.—Mr. Philip Johnson of Pa., H. R., Jan. 18: *C. G.,* p. 308/1.
Sam Patch.   A famous jumper.   [1827-1854.]
1891   *Sam Patch* said, when about to jump the falls of Niagara, that "some
        things could be done as well as others," but he found that jump was
        not one of them.—Mr. Justin S. Morrill of Vt., U. S. Senate, Jan. 6:
        C. R., p. 947/1.
Sand.   Force of character; stamina; grit.   (Cent. Dict.)   Colloquial.
1889   A man like that . . . has got plenty of *sand.—Century Mag.,* xxxix,
        74.
Sandbag.   To hit or stun with a sandbag, usually in order to rob the
        victim.   See Vol. II, **Sandbagger.**   [1884-1888.]
1901   [In reference to appropriations], this District is lying in wait, as it
        were, from one year's end to the other, awaiting an opportunity to
        sandbag the public.—Mr. W. W. Rucker of Mo., H. R., Jan. 23:
        C. R., p. 1345/1.
Sandhiller.   A type of "poor white."   [1841-1901.]
1865   She was a perfect specimen of the Sandhill "tackey" race, sometimes
        called "country crackers." . . . She was stumpy, strong, and lean,
        hard-featured, horny-fisted.   Never were people so aided in every

way as these *Sandhillers.* Why do they remain *Sandhillers* from generation to generation?—Mrs. Chestnut, "A Diary from Dixie," p. 401. (1905.)

1865 Whether the North Carolina "dirt-eater," or the South Carolina *"sand-hiller,"* or the Georgia "cracker," is lowest in the scale of human existence, would be difficult to say.—Letter in the *Boston Daily Advertiser,* dated from Fort Valley, Ga., Nov. 15: *C. G.,* Jan. 1866, p. 552/1.

1866 See CLAY-EATER.

1875 See TARHEEL.

Sand-hog. A man who works in caisson or foundation-work, in the sand-bottoms of rivers or harbors. Slang. (Century Dict.)

Sandia. A mountain or ridge, which. when seen in profile, resembles half a watermelon. Sp., and used in Southwestern States. (Century Dict.)

Sand-lot orators. Men of the type of Dennis Kearney, who in 1878 "orated" on the S. F. sand-lots against Chinese immigration.

1893 Mr. Morse:—The *"sand-lot orators,"* the Dennis Kearney type, who has been, and I think ought to be in the house of correction now. Mr. Geary:—I understand the gentleman from Mass. to say that it is only people of the *"sand-lot"* type of orators who favor the treatment of the Chinese proposed by the legislation now in force. . . . . Are we to understand the gentleman from Mass. that the entire State of California are [*sic*] to be classed with the type of people whom he denominates *"sand-lot orators"*?—H. R., Oct. 13: *C. R.,* p. 2495/2.

Sang hoe. See quotation.

1888 The *"sang hoe"* is a small hoe of domestic manufacture, with which the people dig ginseng root, which is the only agricultural staple of a portion of the mountain district in southeastern Kentucky.—Mr. W. D. Kelley of Pa., H. R., May 1: *C. R.,* p. 3587/2.

Saphead. A blockhead. [1843-1852.]

1899 I said, "I shall oppose any organization of the Army composed of tessellated military satraps on the one hand and gilded society *sapheads* on the other."—Mr. J. H. Lewis of Wash., H. R., Jan. 31: *C. R.,* p. 123/1, App.

Sardine. A stupid fellow, a muff, a "little fish." Slang. [1856-1857.]

1870 The name for a spindling little fellow, whom the plainsman does not wish to compliment, is "You *Sardine.*"—F. H. Ludlow, "The Heart of the Continent," p. 118.

Saskatoon. A name applied to the service-berry and to other berries. See quotation.

1902 *Saskatoon.* The name in the Canadian Northwest for a species of berry and the bush on which it grows. The word is of Blackfoot origin.—*Journal of Am. Folk Lore,* p. 257. (Century Dict.)

Savagerous. Strong and savage; fierce. [1832-1866.]

1850 Of all the untiring, unaccountable, and unspeakable *"Savagerous"* rumpuses ever kicked up Cape Horn takes the banner.—Wilmington (N. C.) *Commercial,* March 7, p. 1/6. (From the *Yankee Blade.*)

Savanna. A treeless plain; a meadow. [1705-1854.]

1673 A *sevanoe* with the land about it for three or four miles.—Records of the Grand Council, March 4: *S. C. Hist. Mag.,* xi. 80. (1910.)

1674 Hickery land wth divers spatious *Savanas.*—*Id.,* p. 83.

1822 Dr. Turnbull, the founder of New Smyrna, upwards of 40 years ago, dispatched an expedition over land to the head of the [St. John's]. He employed his relation, Mr. Andrew T., who . . . pursued the Eastern bank of the river, until he reached the great *Savanna,* mentioned by Captain Leconte.—"Notices of East Florida," pp. 23, 24. (Charleston, S. C.)

1822　The *savanna*, in many parts, had the appearance of a beautiful lake, whose purple expanse, bordered by lofty groves or level fields of reeds, afforded a novel and pleasing prospect. Though 2 or 3 feet deep in water, in many places, I was told that it is often quite dry in summer.—*Id.*, p. 48.

Saw gourds. To snore.

1870　In five minutes, we were all "*sawing gourds*" together in the land of Nod.—F. H. Ludlow, "The Heart of the Continent," p. 91.

Saw-grass. A marsh-plant with culms from 4 to 8 ft. high, and long slender saw-toothed leaves. Southern. (Century Dict.)

1822　They were obliged to defend their horses' feet with wrappings of cow-hide, in order to prevent their being injured by the sharp *saw grass*, a species of triangular reed, with which this watery desart is thickly overgrown.—"Notices of East Florida," p. 24. (Charleston, S. C.)

1858　The *saw-grass* was so high as partially to protect the bodies of our men from view.—Joshua R. Giddings, "The Exiles of Florida," p. 176.

Saw wood. To attend to one's own affairs. The phrase is sometimes worded "saw wood and say nothing." [1909.]

1894　Is it possible that the framers of the bill hold a grudge against the voters who "*sawed wood*" last November?—Mr. J. F. Lacey of Ia., H. R., Jan. 24: *C. R.*, p. 1347/2.

Sawyer. See quotation. [1801-1857.]

1816　There are many *sawyers* in [the Mississippi], i.e. trees fastened by the branches or roots to the bottom of the river, which saw up and down by virtue of the pressing of the water.—Lorenzo Dow, "Journal," §1010 (1850), p. 157/1.

Saybrook platform. A series of propositions affirmed by a Congregational Synod which met in Saybrook, Conn., Sept. 9, 1708. [1863.]

1879　Over all this life religion, as understood in that day, maintained a strict and sleepless watch; and all the people squared their daily walk and conversation by its teachings. The "*Saybrook platform*" was the formula into which the really liberal . . . principles of their religion had been cramped and crowded.—Mr. Henry L. Dawes of Mass., U. S. Senate, Feb. 21: *C. R.*, p. 1715/1. [Speech on the decease of Gen. Alpheus S. Williams, of Conn.]

Say-so. A bare assertion; an "ipse dixit." [1804-1862.]

1637　They are only *say-soes*, and no proofs at all.—Heylin, "Antid. Lincoln," I, 49. (N. E. D.)

1676, 1757. (Foote) etc.—N. E. D.

1866　See Go it blind.

1876　When you rely on another, then we will come back to his *say-so*.—Mr. S. J. Randall of Pa., H. R., May 19: *C. R.*, p. 3199/2.

1890　We need not depend on anybody's *say-so* for proof of all this.—Mr. G. W. Atkinson of W. Va., H. R., May 9: *Id.*, p. 4432/1.

Say, to have one's. To have one's will carried out.

1891　If I *had my say,* I would stop the immigration of Mormons, Communists, anarchists, nihilists, bomb throwers, paupers, lunatics, and idiots.—Mr. E. A. Morse of Mass., H. R., March 2: *C. R.*, p. 3777/1.

Scab. A workman who works for lower wages than, or under conditions contrary to, those prescribed by the trade union; also, one who takes the place of a striker. (Webster.)

1913　See Pinched.

Scalawag. A worthless fellow. Probably from Old Sc. **scurryvaig.** See quotations 1869, 1870, 1871, for political significance. [1851-1854.]

1513　Bishop Douglas classes together "Swingeouris and *Scurrevagis*, swankers and swanis."—"Eneados," ed. Small, 1874, Prologue to Book VIII, p. 144.

1867 [I heard Mr. Blaine say]: "There will be no impeachment by this Congress; we would rather have the President [Johnson] than the shallywags [*sic*] of Ben Wade."—Mr. Thaddeus Stevens of Pa., H. R., March 23: *C. G.*, p. 317/1. [Mr. Blaine replied that Mr. Stevens had heard only a part of the conversation.]

1868 They were either freedmen, or loyal men, or "*scallawags*," or "carpet-baggers," or officers of the bureau or of the army.—Mr. Henry Wilson of Mass., U. S. Senate, Dec. 15: *Id.*, p. 84/3.

1868 The stranger, the minority, the untutored negro with no capacity for self-government, the *scalawag*, and the carpet-bagger,—I would not have used these phrases if the honorable Senator from Mass. himself had not introduced them, . . . have usurped those State governments. —Mr. Garrett Davis of Ky., U. S. Senate, Dec. 15: *Id.*, p. 85/2.

1869 In my state I am called a "*scalawag*"; and why? Because I support the Government and its laws. A "*scalawag*" there means a citizen carpet-bagger. . . . My ancestry, I guess, were carpet-baggers. It was a lot of "carpet-baggers" that landed on Plymouth Rock. William Penn and Henry Clay were "carpet-baggers." Daniel Boone was a "carpet-bagger." . . . The truly loyal people of Arkansas extend a hearty welcome to all loyal "carpet-baggers" who may come among them. "*Scalawags*" are on the increase there.—Mr. J. T. Elliott of Ark., H. R., Feb. 2: *Id.*, p. 126/2, App.

1870 The men who stood by this country in the hour of danger . . . are denounced every day and every hour as "carpet-baggers" because they were born in the North, or as "*scallawags*" if they were born in the South.—Mr. Chas. H. Porter of Va., H. R., Dec. 22: *Id.*, p. 284/2.

1871 Those who were born in the South and remained faithful to the Government, or have since joined the Republican party, are stigmatized as the "*scalawags*," as low persons of the baser sort.—Mr. Oliver P. Morton of Ind., U. S. Senate, Apr. 4: *Id.*, p. 253/3, App.

1872 See ORDER, IN SHORT.

1874 Every man who sustains a *scalawag* individually contributes to building up radicalism.—*Opelika Times* (Ala.), Sept. 30. See *C. R.*, Feb. 27, 1875, p. 1901/2.

1876 See FREEDMEN'S BUREAU.

Scalp, to have or take one's. To obtain a signal victory over an opponent; to oust him from office. [1850.]

1872 [This Hall is not], as the honorable Senator from Mass. of today would have it, an arena for the exhibition of political *scalps*.—Mr. J. W. Tipton of Neb., Feb. 16: *C. R.*, p. 1076/3.

1880 [Mr. Calkins yesterday] reminded the democrats on this side of the House how Governor Curtin used to *take their scalps*.—Mr. Emory Speer of Ga., H. R., May 11: *C. R.*, p. 3249/1.

1890 The force was run in season and out of season for the purpose of taking off *Democratic Scalps*. Now I am willing to have the victor gather the *scalps* if he wants to, but let him go like a man, etc.— Mr. B. McMillin of Tenn., H. R., March 17: *Id.*, p. 2323/1.

Scalping tickets. See **Ticket-scalper.**

Scattering. Scattered. The votes at the tail-end of the returns are said to be *scattering*. [1798-1869.]

1867 Is not the President of the U. S. bound to respect the great mass of this Senate, those in favor of him hardly numbering enough to count as "*scattering*?"—Mr. James W. Nye of Nev., U. S. Senate, Apr. 12: *C. G.*, p. 837/3.

1879 The fifty-eight persons who voted against me were, I think, *scattering* democrats.—Mr. Alex. H. Stephens of Ga., H. R., June 10: *C. R.*, p. 1904/2.

Schoolma'am. A schoolmistress. [1840-1906.]
1871 Only a short time since, a Yankee *school-marm* [in Mass.] was stoned and murdered by her own pupils.—Mr. A. E. Garrett of Tenn., H. R., Apr. 5: *C. G.*, p. 205/3.
1888 You can not teach Indian children how to make shoes with a *school-marm* in a log school-house, . . . merely with a *school-marm* at $600 a year.—Mr. H. L. Dawes of Mass., U. S. Senate, June 1: *C. R.*, p. 4810/2.

Schooner. A tall glass used for liquor, especially lager-beer, and supposed to hold more than an ordinary beer-glass. Colloquial. (Century Dict.) [1886.]

Scissorbill. A localized slang term. In this article it refers to the "home-guard" worker who is filled with bourgeois ideas and ethics. It ordinarily describes a worker who has some source of income other than wages—a patch of land or money from parents—and is thus enabled to work for less than the "going" wages or to refuse to make common cause with the genuine proletarian. (*Industr. Worker.*)
1913 [The hobo] encounters among his many enemies his pet aversion, the *Scissorbill*. He repays the slurs of this gentry of the borrowed brains upon his hobo character, with deep cutting sarcasm and withering satire. —Corresp. of the *Industrial Worker*, May 1, p. 5/3. (Spokane, Wash.)

Scoop. The securing and publishing by a newspaper of a piece of news in advance of its rivals. Slang. (Century Dict.) Also used as verb, "to get ahead of" one's opponents.
1876 [It may have been] necessary to pop down upon that identical reservation, and, as they say out West, *scoop* it.—Mr. G. F. Edmunds of Vt., U. S. Senate, July 19: *C. R.*, p. 4718/2.
1878 [It was understood that these railroad directors and others] had, as they say out West, "scooped the whole concern."—The same, Apr. 9: *Id.*, p. 2365/1.

Scooter. An oblong narrow shovel, used chiefly to break up furrows in fields or cotton-beds. Southern.
1902 As soon as the tobacco plants are firmly set, a *"scooter"* is run between the rows, which throws up a flat bottom furrow through which the water is directed from the troughs.—U. S. Census Bureau, *Bulletin 16*, p. 24. (Century Dict.)
1907 A *scooter*, which is merely a flat shovel four to five inches wide, and about twelve inches long.—T. F. Hunt, "Forage, etc.," p. 352. (Century Dict.)

Scrap. A rough encounter; a "muss." [1812-1904.]
1900 The gentleman refers to a little *"scrap,"* so to speak, that Mr. Robbins and Mr. Aldrich had in a hotel.—Mr. Martin H. Glynn of N. Y., H. R., March 6: *C. R.*, p. 115/2. App.

Scrape. See quotation. A Carolina word.
1863 Your trees are old, and now yield little of anything but *scrape*. (Note) *"Scrape"* is the turpentine gathered from the face of the pine. On old trees, the yearly incision is made high above the boxes, and the sap, in flowing down, passes over and adheres to the scarified surface. It is thus exposed to the sun, which evaporates the more volatile and valuable portion, and leaves only the hard. . . . *"Scrape"* turpentine is only about half as valuable as "dip."—Edmund Kirke, "My Southern Friends," p. 131. (N. Y.)

Scrapper. A fighter. Slang.
1897 Instead of the mighty man from Maine occupying the Speaker's Chair will be the young statesman from Texas, or one of the gifted sons of old Tennessee, or possibly Simpson, our own Jerry, the *"scrapper"* from Kansas.—Mr. M. S. Peters of Kan., H. R., July 19: *C. R.*, p. 292/1, App.

Scrapple. A "Pennsylvania Dutch" term. A kind of sausage meat, usually made into cakes, then sliced and fried; scraps of meat boiled together with chopped herbs and flour or Indian meal. [1890.]

Scratch a ticket. To strike out some names, thereby voting only for a part of the ticket. [1847-1861.]

1870 See PASTER.

1870 It is the habit of the American voter as a rule to *scratch his ticket*, to take from it such names as do not please him.—Mr. Eugene Casserly of Calif., U. S. Senate, May 24: *C. G.*, p. 3761/1.

Screed. A long speech or dissertation. [1855-1881.]

1837 Derwent Coleridge . . . launched out into a Coleridgean *screed* on education.—Caroline Fox, "Journal," p. 46. (Century Dict.)

1875 I have no doubt the people of Vermont have heard in every parish [*sic*] and corner of that State this same *screed* of hatred preached by [Senator Edmunds].—Mr. A. G. Thurman of O., U. S. Senate, Jan. 5: *C. R.*, p. 249/2.

1888 The newspapers [complained] about the misuse of money in junketing expeditions, and all sorts of *screeds* of that kind.—Mr. G. F. Edmunds of Vt., U. S. Senate, July 31: *Id.*, ·p. 7075/1.

1897 [Senator Allen] has indulged himself in this long *screed* as to my personal relations.—Mr. Geo. Gray of Del., U. S. Senate, Jan. 27: *Id.*, p. 1201/2.

Scrip. Any of various documents used as evidence that the holder or bearer is entitled to receive something . . .; also such documents collectively. (Webster.)

1884 [The lumbermen] have long been in the habit of getting [pine land] under different forms of *scrip*, under the soldiers' additional *scrip*, under the Sioux half-breed *scrip*, under the Cherokee *scrip*, and every other damnable kind of *scrip* that could be had.—Mr. K. Nelson of Minn., H. R., June 10: *C. R.*, p. 4994/2.

Scrouge. To squeeze oneself forward. (American?) [1798-1830.]

1715 To *Scruse*, to crowd, to press, or thrust hard.—Kersey, "Dictionarium Anglo-Britannicum."

Scrub, Scrubhorse. One of poor quality.

1894 It has been said that the best way to make a thoroughbred out of a *scrub horse* is to get him killed by a railroad train.—Mr. Champ Clark of Mo., H. R., July 13: *C. R.*, p. 7431/1.

1900 Observation . . . convinces me that raising *scrubs* can be set down against the East rather than against the middle section, or even the West.—*Scientific Amer.*, N. S., lv, 373. (Century Dict.)

Sculpin, Sculpion. Any of numerous spiny, large-headed, broad-mouthed sea fishes. . . . The flesh is usually scanty and bony. (Webster.) The word seems to connect itself with *Scolpin, Scolpion.* 15 & 16 c: See N. E. D. [1769-1873.]

Scuppernong. A variety of the muscadel grape.

Seat, v. To settle on land.

1710 If persons can be allowed to claim more land than they are able to occupy, they keep out others who might *seat* the same.—Journals of House of Burgesses, Virginia, Dec. 5, Vol. IV, 293. (Richmond, Va., 1912.)

1738 Certain Foreign Protestants who are daily expected in order to *seat* upon Roanoke River.—*Id.*, Nov. 14, Vol. VI, 339. [In the subsequent proceedings the word is *settle*.]

Seater. A settler on land.

1653 Provided that such *seaters* settle advantageously for security.—Journals of House of Burgesses, Virginia, I, 374. (Richmond, 1915.)

1822 Mr. Clay quoted several laws of the colony of Virginia, passed near two centuries ago, providing that the true owner should compensate the *seater* of land.—*Am. Beacon* (Norfolk, Va.), Feb. 19, p. 2/2.

Secesh. Secessionist. [1862.]
1864 The secessionists got hold of the meeting, and, with the wildest excitement I ever saw, passed the most violent *secesh* resolutions.—Mr. McHenry of Ky., H. R., May 27: *C. G.*, p. 2529/1.
1867 Mr. Butler voted against the Union members of the Legislature of Tenn., and with the leading *"Secesh"* members of that body.—Mr. James Brooks of N. Y., H. R., Nov. 21: *Id.*, p. 769/1. [See the rest of his speech.]
Secesher. One who seceded from the Union. [1862.]
1862 See Vol. I, HOOTER.
Secessia. The region of secession. [1862-1863.]
1864. I have thought sometimes the Republican members of this House have doubted the loyalty of Kentucky, and looked upon the majority of the members from that State as merely "locum tenens," holding their positions here as a half-way house between *"secessia"* and the "Union States."—Mr. Law of Ind., H. R., July 1: *Id.*, p. 3475/3.
Seckel. A variety of pear, named after the first grower of it.
1872 The finest pear tree in the world is the *seckel*, the pear discovered in Pennsylvania about 90 years ago.—Mr. Simon Cameron of Pa., U. S. Senate, May 27: *C. G.*, p. 3900/2.
Section. One thirty-sixth part of a township; one square mile of land.
1879 See TOWNSHIP.
Sectional, Sectionalism. Terms used principally with reference to the antagonism between North and South. [1836-1861.]
1854 I do not wish to be *sectional*. I do not wish to be regarded as for the South alone.—Mr. Sam Houston of Tex., U. S. Senate, Feb. 15. [Speech, as separately printed, p. 14/1.]
1872 *Sectional* hatreds have packed our horizon with thick clouds, and I see yet no bow in the heavens which gives token that they are passing away—Mr. Timothy O. Howe of Wisc., U. S. Senate, March 8: *C. G.*, p. 1532/3.
Sectionalize. To render sectional.
1871 The South regarded the Government as *sectionalized* in the election of President Lincoln.—Mr. John M. Bright of Tenn., H. R., Apr. 3: *C. G.*, p. 420/2.
Section-hand. A laborer on a section, or division, of a railroad.
1897 See PALACE CAR.
Selectmen. Officers in New England corresponding to aldermen. [1685-1857.]
1804 The *select men* of the Church and society of Midway will receive proposals etc.—*Georgia Republican*: May 15, p. 4/2.
1890 Here is a list of the abandoned farms reported by the *selectmen* of the various towns [of N. H.].—Mr. John R. McPherson of N. J., U. S. Senate, Aug. 11: *C. R.*, p. 8404/2.
Semi-occasionally. Infrequently. [1854-1876.]
1864 [Mr. Fernando Wood has had repentant moments] at long intervals and *semi-occasionally.*—Mr. Dumont of Ind., H. R., Apr. 11: *C. G.*, p. 1557/3.
1878 There is a sporadic kind of mail service between this country and Brazil. A *semi-occasional* ship carries the mails, but there is no contract made.—Mr. A. M. Waddell of N. C., H. R., June 14: *C. R.*, p. 4612/1.
Sequi. See quotation.
1870 I found a number of *"Sequis,"* or distributing ditches, already run, connecting with a small rivulet which came from Camp Creek Cañon [Colo.].—F. H. Ludlow, "The Heart of the Continent," p. 183.
Sequin. A large basket of the Californian and Southwestern Indians, used for storing seeds.

1903 The art sense of the western basket makers extends to other objects made of grass or plants, and is . . conspicuous in their so-called "*sequin*," or granary, which, while crude, is essentially artistic.— *Scientific Amer.*, p. 263. (Century Dict.)

Set-down. A full meal. Slang.

1901 He would hardly speak to me, he felt so important, but his main notion of style now is a sumptuous "*set-down*" and a well-filled pipe of "snipe" after it. Even if you should find him dressed in newspapers and a blue necktie he would not mind . . provided you caught him tucking away the *set-down*.—Josiah Flynt, in *McClure's Mag.*, p. 117. (Century Dict.)

Set out. To undertake, to commence a thing.

1862 　　　　　[We] kerry a hollerday, ef we *set out*,
　　　　　Ez stiddily ez though 't wuz a redoubt.
　—"Biglow Papers," 2nd. S., vi.

Settling-clerk. The New York name for the "in-clearer," i.e. the bank clerk whose duty it is to represent his bank in the clearing-house, and receive through it all the bills of exchange, checks, etc., payable by his bank. (Century Dict.)

Set-up. Preconcerted. Cf. **Put-up.**

1870 I think there is a "*set-up*" arrangement to make money out of the whisky; if the tax on it can be increased.—Mr. Simon Cameron of Pa., U. S. Senate, June 24: *C. G.*, p. 4813/2.

Seven by nine. Inferior, third-rate. The phrase probably originated from the size of common window-glass. [1794-1862.] Other dimensions are occasionally used with the same meaning.

1890 The *Boston Herald* says: "You can buy a New Hampshire farm for just about what you have to pay for a 7 by 9 room for a single season at a fashionable summer hotel."—*C. R.*, Aug. 14: p. 8559/2.

1892 Mr. Little talked the other day as though the Exposition was a Chicago Fair (an 8 by 10 show, the ordinary size of any institution in the eyes of a New Yorker outside of his State).—Mr. R. E. Doan of O., H. R., July 16: *C. R.*, p. 605/2, App.

1893 These Indians . . . are now penned up in little *seven-by-nine* Indian reservations up there in the northern part of Wisconsin.—Mr. A. R. Bushnell of Wisc., H. R., Feb. 2: *Id.*, p. 1107/1.

1893 You see my friend from Arizona expects his 6 by 7 Territory to come in next. . . . He shows us that, after the Mormon of Utah, we are to have the Gila monsters of Arizona for fellow-citizens and lawmakers.—Mr. M. D. Harter of O., H. R., Dec. 12: *Id.*, p. 185/1.

1893 Men call him a crank, and all the little *two by seven* newspapers and all the little *two by nine* politicians in the country jump onto him.— Mr. Jerry Simpson of Kan., H. R., Dec. 13: *Id.*, p. 211/1.

1894 Those little two penny, *seven-by-nine* protection furnaces were replaced by the magnificent Democratic furnaces erected under the low-tariff period between 1846 and 1860.—Mr. M. D. Harter of O., H. R., Jan. 11: *Id.*, p. 743/2.

Seven-shooter. A firearm with seven chambers.

1877 They were armed with breech-loading rifles, *seven-shooters*, and had also their belts and revolvers.—Mr. E. G. Lapham of N. Y., H. R., Feb. 28: *C. R.*, p. 202/2, App.

Seven-up. A card game, otherwise called "all-fours." [1856.]

1863 A few were whittling, a few pitching quoits, or playing leap-frog, and quite a number were having a quiet game of whist, euchre, or "*seven-up*."—Edmund Kirke, "Life in Dixie's Land," p. 219. (Lond.)

1864 See CHUCK-A-LUCK.

Shack. A wooden cabin. [1907-1909.] See *N. & Q.*, 10 S, xii, 306.

Shack. A miscellaneous catch of fish. (New England coast.)

1904 Such fish, tumbled in together, without effort at classification, are known as *shack.—Rep. Mass. Comm. Fisheries,* p. 78. (Century Dict.)

Shade tree. One planted to give shade. [1806-1847.]

1871 Wherever we appropriate money to set up a *shade-tree,* there comes along a cow, or a horse, or a goat, and tears it down the next day.— Mr. G. F. Edmunds of Vt., U. S. Senate, Jan. 24: *C. G.,* p. 687/2.

1878 See BLAZE.

Shadow, v. To watch closely. [1877-1910.]

1877 [Two policemen] were told to meet Mr. Dana at the depot, and, as they express it, to *"shadow"* him while he was in Washington.— Report of a committee: *C. R.,* March 3, p. 2242/2.

1886 [The agents of the railroad ring] have *shadowed* this Hall and the Senate Chamber from the beginning of this session.—Mr. J. M. Glover, of Mo., H. R., Aug. 2: *Id.,* p. 7866/1.

1888 The President [Grant] was carefully *shadowed* by the detectives of the clique.—Henry Clews, "Twenty-Eight Years in Wall St.," p. 193. (N. Y.)

Shady. Disreputable. Colloquial. (American? See N. E. D.)

1886 The public might be misled into subscribing to a *shady* undertaking.— *D. Telegraph,* Sept. 11. (Encyclopædic Dict.)

1888 Nonsuited plaintiffs and defendants of *shady* record.—W. D. Howells, "Annie Kilburn," ch. xxv. (Century Dict.)

1893 His principal business seems to have been [that of a] billiard-marker, which he combined with much *shadier* ways of getting money.— *Century Mag.,* xxxv, 558. (Century Dict.)

1894 The assessor of income taxes, a man who subsequently was proved to be *shady* in other transactions, but who was thought to be one of the best men in the Community.—Mr. Walker, H. R., Jan. 30: *C. R.,* p. 1651/1.

Shake. To shake hands.

1601 First, Marcus Brutus, will I *shake* with you.—"Julius Cæsar," III. i.

1891 *Shake.* That's right.—J. Newman, "Scamping tricks," vii, 59. (N. E. D.)

Shake. To get rid of, to dismiss.

1873 Thet she should just *shake* you—that is what gits me.—Bret Harte, "Fiddletown," 24. (N. E. D.)

Shake, a fair. A fair deal, possibly a term from the games in which ⁕dice are used. [1839-1847.]

Shake a stick at. A comical expression used in describing a large quantity of anything. [1818-1866.]

1891 There are more chief justices here tonight, . . . who have not yet taken the oath of office, than you can *shake a stick at.*—Mr. J. G. Cannon of Ill., H. R., Feb. 26: *C. R.,* p. 3400/2.

Shaking Quakers. The Shakers, ". . a religious celibate sect popularly so named from movements in dancing, which forms a part of their worship." (Webster.) [1784-1787.]

1815 Like *dancing Quakers, shaking.*—David Humphreys, "The Yankey in England," p. 87.

Shanty. A small wooden house or room. [1820-1855.]

1842 The line of tumbling wooden *shantees.*—Lydia M. Child, "Letters from New York," p. 171. (Lond., 1843.)

Shape. Form, state, or condition. (Usually, **in good shape** or **in bad shape,** etc.)

1876 [This amendment is bad,] because it makes patchwork of a bill which is already in better *shape.*—Mr. Hurlbut of Ill., H. R., Apr. 20: *C. R.,* p. 2664/2.

1877 He had more than vouchers enough, . . . but they were in an irregular *shape,* and could not be allowed.—Mr. A. E. Burnside of R. I., U. S. Senate, March 3: *Id.,* p. 2213/2.

1892 I think the bill now is *in good shape.*—Mr. John Sherman of O., U. S. Senate, Feb. 19: *Id.,* p. 1325/2.

1892 The Democratic party arrived in [Portland, Me.] yesterday *in great shape* with a majority.—Mr. Benton McMillin of Tenn., H. R., March 9: *Id.,* p. 1884/2.

1895 Mr. Talbert:—Did [the old gentleman] get back all right? Mr. Harris:—He came back in good *shape.*—H. R., Jan. 31: *Id.,* p. 1591/1.

Shares, on. On a bargain of sharing the crop. [1817-1822.]

1733 We came to the Plantation of Joshua Nicholson, where Daniel Taylor lives *for Halves.*—William Byrd, "Journey to Eden," p. 322. (1901.)

Sharpshin. A small and worthless hawk. [1804-1829.]

See *N. & Q.,* 11 S., vii, 206, 273.

Sharpshooter. The Mexican cotton-boll weevil.

1901 Early cotton . . . avoids to a great extent damage to the plant by the boll-worm, cotton worm, and *sharp-shooter,* as well as by a large number of fungous diseases.—*Yearbook U. S. Dept. Agr.,* p. 377. (Century Dict.)

Shaw, Pshaw! An expression of impatience or contempt, nearly obs. in England. [1825-1862.]

1864 Some one with less sense than sensibility may cry out, "Oh! you are the defender of the slave trade." There is only one answer to this: the monosyllabic answer, *"Pshaw!"*—Mr. S. S. Cox of O., H. R., June 13: C. G., p. 2916/2.

Shays' Rebellion. One of the insurrections in Massachusetts, 1786-87. The leaders of it were Daniel Shays, Luke Day, Adam Wheeler, and Eli Parsons: all of Massachusetts. See Vol. II, **Shayites, Shaysites.** [1786-1813.]

1884 The words "odious," "inquisitorial," "detestable," and "infernal," which are repeated day after day on this floor have a old and familiar sound. They come to us from the days of *Shays' rebellion* against the whisky tax.—Mr. Burr W. Jones of Wisc., H. R., March 27: C. R., p. 66/2, App.

Shebang. A common shanty or tent. [1867-1871.] "Depreciative, often jocose." (Webster.)

1863 (Jan.) The soldiers . . . came out from their tents or *shebangs* of bushes with rumpled hair and half-awake look.—Walt Whitman, "Specimen Days" (1887), p. 43.

1865 In a visit to Spanish Fort . . . we stopped at the *"shebang"* of one of [the poor whites.]—Letter of B. C. Truman to the *N. Y. Times,* dated Montgomery, Ala., Oct. 23: C. G., Jan. 1866, p. 552/1.

Sheep, v. To use as a sheep-range. **Sheeped,** grazed bare by sheep. The township has little value for pasturage, as it was long ago thoroughly *"sheeped."* . . . The lands, wherever accessible, have been *"sheeped"* so long that the grass has been exterminated. . . . Most of the township has been closely *"sheeped,"* and its grazing value is exceedingly low.—U. S. Geol. Survey, Paper xxii, pp. 36, 38, 54.

1901 The country was all *sheeped off,* not a young tree growing.—Mr. Chas. Newhall in *The Forum,* Feb.: Cited in C. R., March 1, p. 3284/1.

Sheep ranch. A Western farm on which sheep are reared.

1875 See PROPOSITION.

Sheepskin. A college diploma. [1843-1862.]

1804 Feeling some anxiety about your *"sheep-skin,"* I wrote to Merrill, and begged him to put his finger on the President's pulse.—D. Webster to Ezekiel W., June 10: "Private Corresp." (1857) I, 173.

1866 Men who come out of these colleges with their *sheepskin rolls* and high-sounding degrees.—Mr. Andrew J. Rogers of N. J., H. R., June 5: C. G., p. 2969/3.

1875   I wonder what [Mr. Thurman] sitting upon the bench . . . would have thought of any man with a *sheepskin* in his pocket who had risen before him to demonstrate a point upon authority, and had cited cases in which the question was never raised.—Mr. Roscoe Conkling of N. Y., U. S. Senate, Jan. 5: *C. R.*, p. 243/2.

Sheer. Very thin; gauzy, clear, pure. [1799-1902.] The N. E. D. has *"sheir* lawn," 1641, and *"shear* muslins," 1706.

1513   [Mercury vanished] in the *schyre* air. (Lat., *in tenuem auram.*)— Douglas, "Eneados," ed. Small, 1874. Bk. IV. p. 192.

1590   Spenser: "a fountain *shere,"* "Faerie Qu.," III, ii, 44.

Sheer-boom. A boom with a sheer or curve.

1882   [The clause] for the protection of Rock Island bridge by *sheer-booms.* —Mr. A. H. Buckner of Mo., H. R., July 8: *C. R.*, p. 5817/1.

1884   I would like to have [Mr. Washburn] explain the provisions of the bill, as touching the question of providing *sheer-booms* for guarding rafts and boats.—Mr. L. H. Weller of Ia., H. R., June 9: *Id.,* p. 4911/1.

1908   Ide had installed a system of *sheer-booms.* They spanned the current diagonally, and were to be the silent herders that would edge the log-flocks away from the banks, and keep them running free.—Holman Day, "King Spruce," p. 334. (Century Dict.)

Shell game. Thimblerig: walnut shells being used. Cf. **Joker, the little.**

1899   I never believed in this *shell game;* for one time in my life I ran up against a *shell game.* I was a young man then. . . . It is that old game in which now you see it and now you don't see it; and you cannot guess what shell the ball is under.—Mr. W. L. Greene of Neb., H. R., Jan. 24: *C. R.*, p. 1009/2.

Shenanigan, Shenaniging. Nonsense, tomfoolery. Slang.

1872   How long have you been playing this *shenaniging?*—Examination of Theodore Jacques by Mr. Carpenter: C. G., March 3, 1873; p. 2107/2.

1912   Used on Long Island, but not common in Ill., Pa., Mo., or Vt.— *Dialect Notes,* III, 568.

Sherrivallies (or **Sherrivalleys**). Coarse trousers worn by farmers. [1802-1833.]

1825   An advertisement of a tailor in a Springfield paper (says Alice Morse Earle) reads thus:

> *Shorrevals* and overalls
> And Pantaloons he'll make,
> Cutting, too, he'll always do,
> And will no cabbage take.

—*Journal of Am. Folk Lore,* 1891, iv, 354.

Shiftless. Lacking in expedients . . . inefficient. (Webster.)

1630-   The court held him worthy of death, in undertaking the care of a
1649   *shiftless* maid and leaving her . . . [where] he knew she must perish. —John Winthrop, "Hist. of New England," I, 290. (Century Dict.)

Shilling. Usually 12½ cents or 16 cents, but differing in value in different states. [1791.]

1881   I am reminded of a family council held in reference to the purchase of a dog. The proposition was first made to pay fifty cents for him, and if he could not be bought for fifty cents to pay a dollar; if the dollar was not enough, then twelve *shillings* should be offered for him. —Mr. L. A. Brigham of N. J., H. R., Jan. 13: *C. R.*, p. 613/1.

Shiners. Gold coins. [1810-1827.]

1870   See MINT-DROPS.

Shingle. A signboard, particularly one put out by a lawyer. [1842-1857.]

1852   Hiram Powers, whose *"shingle,"* as we express it, hangs out [in Florence] to indicate his studio.—Thurlow Weed, "Letters," p. 508. (1866.)

1890   My friend [Mr. Carter] had better go down into that section and stick out his *shingle* as a practicing lawyer.—Mr. W. Vandever of Calif., H. R., July 30: *C. R.*, p. 7934/2.

1911   "If," said Wendell Phillips to a friend, soon after he had hung out his lawyer's *shingle*; "if clients do not come, I will throw myself heart and soul into some good cause and devote my life to it."—*N. Y. Evening Post*, Nov. 27, p. 6/4.

Shingled.   Covered as with shingles; "roofed over" with over-lapping mortgages.

1869   Where else [than in the U. S.] are great cities built upon a soil *shingled* with mortgages drawing enormous rates of interest? Where before ever did the world behold so much financial success founded upon so much financial ruin?—Mr. John Coburn of Ind., H. R., Jan. 7: *C. G.*, p. 239/1.

1871   [General Butler] swears that he advanced $12,000 in 1864 to purchase an interest in a property *shingled* over with all sorts of liens.—Mr. John F. Farnsworth of Ill., H. R., March 3: *Id.*, p. 284/2. App.

Shinnery.   A dense growth of shrubby timber, mainly of dwarf oaks, one of which (*Quercus undulata*) is called scrub-oak or shin-oak. Southwestern.

A great deal of the *shinnery* country . . . represents a recent gain of timber on prairie divides.—*U. S. Forestry Bulletin* 49, p. 23. (Century Dict.)

Shinning around.   "Riding shank's mare"; going about. Depreciatory or jocose.

1890   They have bitten off more than they can chew, to use a vulgar expression, and they find a difficulty in *shinning around* to borrow money.—Mr. John Sherman of O., U. S. Senate, Sept. 18: *C. R.*, p. 10188/2.

1897   Our choice and select gentry [are] disporting themselves in German, English, and French clothes, and the rest of us *shinning around* in overcoats purchased during Harrison's administration.—Mr. J. P. Dolliver of Ia., H. R., March 23: *Id.*, p. 195/2.

Shinplasters.   Paper currency. [1824-1867.]

[1780   The rubs and jostlings of that night
                   Were more by half than I shall write;
                   Can things like these in rhime be written?
                   How by a dog my friend was bitten;
                   How Bradley tore a piece of skin,
                   Like *paper dollar*, from his shin; . . . . .
—Col. David Humphreys, Letter to a young Lady: "Misc. Works," 1790, p. 94 (N. Y.)]

1864   The printer of the public money [is] coining paper, coining Treasury notes, coining *shin plasters*, or sticking plasters as they used to be called.—Mr. James Brooks of N. Y., H. R., Jan. 25: *C. G.*, p. 335/1.

1874   No man can say we had a sufficiency of good currency before the war. A sufficiency of currency never existed in the West or South. . . . We had a lot of the most miserable *shin-plasters* that human ingenuity, and I might almost say devilish ingenuity, could invent. . . . . . We had an enormous amount of discredited stuff, composed of individual *shin-plasters*, plank-road notes, private bankers' promises, insurance-company notes, free-bank notes, and State-bank notes.—Mr. John Coburn of Ind., H. R., Apr. 8: *C. R.*, p. 2914/1.

Ship.   To send by rail.

1885   See DEPOT.

Ship's lawyer.   A lawyer of no great skill; a "horse lawyer."

1894   You remember [how Judge Turner of Ga.] examined me . . . . publicly here in this House, and decided that I might pass as "*ship's lawyer*" to practice in this court. . . . I think that a "*ship's lawyer*" is perfectly competent to practice [here.]—Mr. J. H. Walker of Mass., H. R., May 31: *C. R.*, p. 5547/2. [See also p. 5551/1.]

Shipwreck. A shipwrecked person. Rare.

1896 American labor cherishes its constitutional rights of "life, liberty, and the pursuit of happiness," and will never deny them to others. It will never kick *shipwrecks*, while attempting to board our well-supplied craft, back into the roaring sea.—Mr. Richard Bartholdt of Mo., H. R., May 19: *C. R.*, p. 5423/2.

Shirk. See quotation.

1879 The meaning of this word was discussed in the U. S. Senate, May 7. Mr. Blaine:—Down in Maine, in the way we speak the English language, *"shirk"* means "to depart from; to quit; to shift off." That is what Noah Webster and Worcester say it is. Mr. Voorhees:—*"Shirk"* in the western sense means to run away and skulk and hide like a coward.—*C. R.*, p. 1116/1. [It is curious that neither speaker definitely recognizes shirking as evading a duty or a responsibility.]

Shirk (for oneself). To manage; to bestir oneself. To "shift" for oneself. See Vol. II, **Shirk.** [1843-1850.]

1863 [I let you go] down ter Newbern, an' *shirk* fur you'seff.—Edmund Kirke, "My Southern Friends," p. 116. (N. Y.)

1864 "How do you get on *shirking* for yourself?" I asked: "you are very old."—Edmund Kirke, "Down in Tennessee," p. 126. (N. Y.)

Shoat. A half-grown pig. [1699-1889.] Also a person of no account.

1576 Thomas Poulter of Broughton bequeaths, *inter alia*, two bacon hoggs, one sowe, and two *shotes*.—Wills, *Hunts., Register* No. 2, Somerset House.

1596 Hee hath no more sense then a *shoat* in pickle.—Thos. Lodge, "Wits Miserie," p. 81.

1608 Yong *shoates* or yong hogs.—Withals' Dict., p. 72. (Nares.)

1756 To Mary Snider, for one Hog and one *Shoat*, 45 lb. Tob. (Apr. 20). —Journal of House of Burgesses, Virginia, VIII, 378. (Richmond, Va., 1909.)

Shoe-string District, The. The Sixth Congressional District in Miss., constructed irregularly for political purposes in 1874. Cf. **Dumbbell District** and **Gerrymander.**

1878 I will promise to meet [Mr. Lapham] on the northern border of *"the shoe-string district,"* and to escort him safely to its southern extremity.—Mr. J. R. Chalmers of Miss., H. R., June 13: *C. R.*, p. 478/2. App.

1882 The *Shoe-string district* in Mississippi is bad enough, but it is only the work of an apprentice; it is child's play to the skillful carving of our Pennsylvania artists in fraud.—Mr. Beltzhoover of Pa., H. R., Feb. 13: *Id.*, p. 1105/1.

1882 The map which I have sent up to the Clerk's desk represents the State of Miss. as laid off in Congressional districts. And the strip on the western side of Miss., which is colored black, represents what is known as the *"shoestring district."* It is about four or five hundred miles long, as I am informed, and about forty to fifty miles wide on an average. . . . [The district] is confessedly so made because it eliminates from the rest of the districts of the State a large black vote.—Mr. W. H. Calkins of Ind., H. R., Apr. 29: *Id.*, p. 3442/1.

Shoo-fly. The wild indigo, *Baptisia tinctoria*: so called in allusion to the belief that the presence of the plant [near] the harness will keep away horse-flies. (Century Dict.) To *shooe*, i.e. to scare away fowls, is found in Florio, 1611. "Shoo-fly" came to be used as an interjection of annoyance, and even as a verb.

1888 When Ben Butler *"shooflied"* into silence the bantam of the Democracy [Mr. S. S. Cox], people had reason to believe that he would forever cease to pose as a funny man.—Mr. W. Woodburn of Nev., H. R., June 11: *C. R.*, p. 5114/2.

Shoo-fly. A man employed is some cities to spy upon police patrolmen.
1909 [Let us now consider] the employment of spies, who are usually
called *"shoo-flies."* These spies may be patrolmen in citizen's clothes,
uniformed roundsmen sent out from headquarters, superior officers in
citizen's clothes, or private citizens.—Leonhard F. Fuld. "Police
Administration," p. 456. (Putnams.)

Shook. A set of staves and headings sufficient for one hogshead,
barrel, or box.
1888-9 All Empty Barrels must have six hoops, and be delivered in form,
shooks or staves not being a good delivery.—*N. Y. Produce Exchange
Rept.*, p. 280. (Century Dict.)
1894 We exported in 1893 of . . . . . box *shooks*, $238,605; barrel *shooks*,
$702,403.—Mr. G. G. Vest of Mo., U. S. Senate, May 28: *C. R.*, p.
5377/2.
1897 Any ordinary person of fair ability can look into a car loaded with
box *shooks* and easily determine about how many thousand feet of
lumber it contains.—Mr. R. O. Crump of Mich., H. R., March 31:
Id., p. 12/2. App.

Shooting iron. A gun or a pistol. [1833-1853.]
1887 Timothy . . . . drew his *shooting-iron* from his boot-leg and [cocked]
it with a metallic click.—*Harper's Mag.*, lxxvi, 78. (Century Dict.)

Shop, v. To imprison. [1678-1844.]
1601 Others were crying, *Nay, but shoppe them up, keep them as pledges.*
—"Declaration of Treasons," F 2. (Anon.)

Short. One who sells stock which he does not possess and does not
expect to deliver.
1892 See LONG AND SHORT.

Shortage. A deficiency.
1884 There is a *shortage* in these States and Territories [in the post office
account.]—Mr. R. G. Horr of Mich., H. R., March 8: *C. R.,* p.
1726/2.
1888-9 [On all such grain] *shortage* in excess of one bushel per thousand
bushels will not be guaranteed.—*N. Y. Produce Exchange Report,*
p. 236. (Century Dict.)

Short boys. A gang of ruffians which infested New York about 1855-
1860.
1880 See DEAD RABBITS.

Shorthorn. A new arrival; a "tenderfoot." Western slang.
1906 Don't let no *shorthorn* have my room, I may need it myself; an' in
case I do, I don't want to be obleeged to bootcher no harmless
stranger.—A. H. Lewis. "Sunset Trail," ch. 2. (Century Dict.)

Shotgun. A smoothbore gun for firing shot at short range. (Webster.)
[1820-1862.]
1865 Their temper became like that of the farmer who blew the vane
from his barn with a *shot-gun* because it would obstinately and persistently point northeast.—Mr. J. M. Broomall of Pa., H. R., Feb. 7:
C. G., p. 52/2. App.
1871 Exchange the whisky-shop for the school-room, the bowie-knife for
the pen, the pistol and *shot-gun* for the slate and pencil, and you will
find this policy more effective than whole armies of troops.—Mr.
W. T. Clark of Tex., H. R., Feb. 8: *Id.*, p. 1073/1.
1876 By means of *shot-guns* [they] intimidated the men who were the supposed rightful owners of the soil and drove them from it.—Mr. A. A.
Sargent of Calif., U. S. Senate, May 31: *C. R.*, p. 3406/1.
1876 A condition of society in which men have been in the habit of carrying revolvers and bowie-knives, and of resorting to the *shot-gun* to
settle their personal difficulties.—Mr. Hoge of S. C., H. R., July 18:
Id., p. 4715/1.

1882 At that [Fort Christmas] poll, ten . . . valiant Democrats appeared with their *shot-guns* and muskets.—Mr. A. A. Ranney of Mass., H. R., June 1: *Id.*, p. 4424/1.

1891 If we are compelled to resort to desperate or doubtful means, I for one should far prefer to take a *shot-gun* and say to the negro "You can not vote," rather than to stuff the ballot box.—Mr. James H. Berry of Ark., U. S. Senate, Jan. 16: *Id.*, p. 1402/1.

1894 [These men] threw themselves into the service without uniforms, armed with their *shotguns* and squirrel rifles.—Mr. J. F. Lacey of Ia., H. R., Apr. 6: *Id.*, p. 3534/2.

Shotgun policy, system, etc. In U. S. political slang, a name used by partisan extremists in the North to denote the alleged political control of negro votes in the South by violence and intimidation. (Century Dict.)

1880 The *shot-gun policy*, which worked so well in 1876, and secured such grand results for the democracy, has been continued up to the present time.—Mr. Philip C. Hayes of Ill., H. R., March 10: *C. R.*, p. 1450/1.

1893 You were not able to produce a single instance of intimidation or violence in that district [in Miss.] that had such an overwhelming majority of colored people, in the period in which you say the elections were conducted under the *"old shot-gun system."* . . . . Gentlemen talk about the *"shot-gun period."* . . . . They say that under the old *shot-gun system* which prevailed in 1888 the Republican vote was 30,096.—Mr. H. D. Money of Miss., H. R., Oct. 5: *Id.*, p. 2171/2.

Shotted. Equipped with artillery; scarred with shot.

1894 [North Carolina] left 764 dead soldiers scattered over those *shotted* hills [of Gettysburg.]—Mr. M. W. Ransom of N. C., U. S. Senate, Aug. 8: *C. R.*, p. 8294/1.

Shoulder-hitter. A bully. Hence, **Shoulder-hitting,** bullying. [1858.]

1867 Are we so used to Presidential *shoulder-hitting*, that we will neither fend off nor strike back?—Mr. Chas. D. Drake of Mo., U. S. Senate, Dec. 10: *C. G.*, p. 102/1.

1869 [The system of examinations in the Civil service] will exclude the *shoulder-hitter*, the garroter, the repeater, the pipe-layer, the ballot-box smasher, the false oath taker, the ward-room bully, the primary meeting manager, the ballot changer, the smuggler, the rioter, the peculator, the gambler, the thief.—Mr. Thos. A. Jenckes of R. I., Apr. 5: *Id.*, p. 521/1.

1879 [Mr. Conkling's] argument was that we required the Federal Army to protect the citizens of a portion of our State from "the thugs and *shoulder-hitters* and repeaters, all the carriers of slung-shots, dirks, and bludgeons, all the fraternity of bucket-shops, the rat-pits," and the products of what he chose to call the "slums" of New York.—Mr. Kernan of N. Y., U. S. Senate, May 14: *C. R.*, p. 1320/2.

1879 The statute requires that the juryman shall be intelligent, of good moral character; but the man who selects him may be a *shoulder-hitter* in the purlieus of the streets of New York.—Mr. H. L. Dawes of Mass., U. S. Senate, June 16: *Id.*, p. 2026/1.

1879 I will say nothing about *shoulder-hitters*, or the graduates of rat-pits or of any of the nurseries of modern democracy.—Mr. Roscoe Conkling of N. Y., U. S. Senate, June 20: *Id.*, p. 2236/2

1879 Those fellows in Jersey City and Newark, only a few miles from New York, could not bear to see these bummers and thugs and *shoulder-hitters* flourishing in the State of New York as deputy marshals, receiving a large sum per diem, and employed ever so long, and they get nothing.—Mr. A. G. Thurman of O., U. S. Senate, May 15: *Id.*, p. 96/2, App.

1884 See ROUNDER.

1893   There are other people in this country besides the repeaters, the *shoulder-strikers,* and the tigers of N. Y. City.—Mr. W. W. Bowers of Calif., H. R., Oct. 3: *Id.,* p. 2096/2.

Show.   A chance, an opportunity. A term derived from card-playing.

1888   Tom may be innocent; and he ought to have a fair *show,* anyhow.— Edwd. Eggleston, "The Graysons," ch. xi. (Century Dict.)

1890   The gentleman from Tennessee in the fullness of his kind heart, wishing to give every man a *show,* has allowed himself, etc.—Mr. H. D. Coleman of Ia., H. R., May 27: *C. R.,* p. 5349/1.

1894   We trust that some Congress will be wise enough, magnanimous enough, to give the arid lands of the country an equal *show* with rivers and harbors.—Mr. D. H. Mercer of Neb., H. R., Aug. 10: *Id.,* p. 8393/1.

1897   [Mr Lincoln], driving along one day, saw a struggling bug upon its back, and got out of the carriage, and with his cane turned the insect to its feet, and . . . said, "Well, I have given him a *show,* an equal *show* with all other bugs."—Mr. W. E. Mason of Ill., U. S. Senate, May 18: *Id.,* p. 1133/2.

Shuck-bottom, Shuck-bottomed.   Having a seat filled with the husks of corn. See Vol. II, **Shuck, Shucking,** and **Shucks.** [1811-1909.]

1888   She sank down on a *shuck-bottom* chair by the door of the tent. . . . He drew up another *shuck-bottomed* chair.—E. Eggleston, "The Graysons," ch. x, xxxi. (Century Dict.)

Shuck-pen.   See quotation.

1848   [They] put me in a *shuck-pen* to keep the hogs from eatin me.— Wilmington (N. C.), *Commercial,* May 25, p. 1/5.

Shunpike.   A side road. [1862.]

1853   Some of this very loan is to be applied to the Oswego Canal, which has been called a *"shun pike."*—Mr. Wm. McMurray in the N. Y. Senate, March 28: p. 17/1 of speech as separately published.

1903   There was a road which branched off from the turnpike, about a mile from the town, and which, after some windings, entered the pike again beyond the toll-gate, and, although this road was not always in very good condition, it had seen a good deal of travel, which in time gave it the name of the *shunpike.*—F. R. Stockton, "The Captain's Toll-gate," p. 6. (Century Dict.)

Shut-down.   The closing for a time of a mill, factory, or other working-place; a "lock-out."

1890   There has . . . been a *shut-down* of a large number of wells, to check a wasteful overproduction.—*Science,* xix, 283. (Century Dict.)

Shyster.   A pettifogging lawyer; a contemptible rascal. [1856-1910.]

1867   I have never alluded to any members of this House, or to anybody else, as *"shysters"* and "sharks" and "strikers" and "suckers."—Mr. William Windom of Minn., H. R., Dec. 5: *C. G.,* p. 54/2.

1868   The galleries were packed . . . by lobbyites, male and female, and by *shysters* and adventurers.—Mr. E. B. Washburne of Ill., H. R., March 26: *Id.,* p. 2135/3.

1869   It will be next to impossible to legislate in this body comfortably and intelligently, if we invite this multiplication of claim agents and *shysters.*—Mr. Jacob M. Howard of Mich., U. S. Senate, Jan. 7: *Id.,* p. 229/3.

1870   Only sharks and *shysters* will lend [the pensioners] any money.— Mr. B. F. Butler of Mass., H. R., Jan. 19: Id., p. 583/1.

1878   Our commissioners [in N. Y. City] have been selected from the very best men in the city, and they have stood between the *shysters* and the immigrants.—Mr. M. I. Townsend of N. Y., H. R., June 10: *C. R.,* p. 4402/2.

1881   Under this law *shysters* cannot establish a bank. It is a necessary prerequisite before you can establish a bank under the national banking act [that] you must have some money. And that does not suit some gentlemen who would like to afflict this country, as they did twenty-five years ago, with the wild-cat, red-dog, and stump-tail currency, so that when you went to bed at night with a few dollars in your pocket you did not know whether you would find good money there in the morning or not.—Mr. Hiram Price of Ia., H. R., March 1: *Id.*, p. 2323/2.

1886 I do not know that there exists a creature who is to politics what the pettifogger is to the law; and I do know that the pettifogger is not more loathed by the lawyer than the political *shyster* by the politician.—Mr. R. LaFollette of Wisc., H. R., March 25: *Id.*, p. 2780/1.

1888 I have practised law some, Mr. Chairman. I always found that, when the lawyer had a very bad case on the merits, his scheme was to befog and becloud the issue, and to side-track the jury. I have known some lawyers, *shysters*, who had one particular branch of the law in which they thought they were perfect, and every case they had they attempted to run in that line. For instance, I know a *shyster* who won a case once on the doctrine of estoppel; he never had a case since but he attempted to draw it into estoppel. I know an old gentleman in Mississippi who won a case on a demurrer. He was not a lawyer. But he was sued again, and he wrote to his lawyer, "Please send me a couple more of those demurrers; these fellows have sued me in two more cases." His great idea was that a demurrer was the thing that knocked every case out of court.—Mr. E. P. Allen of Miss., H. R., May 12: *Id.*, p. 4066/2.

1890 It was the deliberate purpose of the *shysters* employed to take the testimony to . . . prevent a disclosure of the facts.—Mr. J. H. Rowell of Ill., H. R., June 3: *Id.*, p. 5566/1.

Side-bars. Elastic wooden bars placed one on each side of the body of some forms of light wagon or buggy, to connect it with the gearing, and to serve both as a support and as a spring. (Century Dict.) An American invention.

a.1897 Light vehicles of the *side-bar* description.—*Scientific Amer.*, N. S., lviii. 91.

Side issue. A collateral question; a less important question than the main issue.

Any consideration of this aspect of the matter . . . is likely to be complicated by *side-issues*.—*N. Y. Medical Journal*, xl. 17. (Century Dict.)

Side meat. See quotation.

1882 *Side-meat*, in the South and West, is the thin flank of a porker, salted and smoked after the fashion of hams.—*St. Nicholas*, xviii, 39. (Century Dict.)

Side, on the. Surreptitiously.

1893 He will have no pension attorney for a silent partner, no relative doing business "*on the side*" with that bureau.—Mr. M. R. Baldwin of Minn., H. R., Dec. 18: *C. R.*, p. 360/1.

Side partner. An equal coadjutor, esp. in the police. (Century Dict.)

1890 The arrest was made by the witness's *side partner*, it being his night off.—*N. Y. Evening Post*, May 23.

Side-show. A small exhibition (sometimes of a low type) annexed to a fair or a circus, with a separate entrance-fee.

1876 Mr. Banks:—Why should we undertake . . . to set up a celebration of our own . . . ? Mr. Conger:—A mere *side-show*. Mr. Banks:—Yes; as the gentleman from Michigan well suggests, a "*side-show*."—H. R., June 30: *C. R.*, p. 4304/2.

1890 The gilded dome of the State House . . . came into view . . . , and I knew that this *side-show* was over.—*Atl. Mag.*, lxv, 268. (Century Dict.)

1891 It was a six weeks' fête, . . . with rifle galleries, swings, and all sorts of *side-shows.—Century Mag.*, xl., 176.

Sideswipe. To strike a glancing blow on the side.

1912 Portland Express Cars Derailed—Then *Sideswiped* by Freight. Milford, Conn., November 16.—The Portland Express, which runs to New York, by the way of Springfield, Mass., was derailed here this morning, probably by a spreading switch.—*N. Y. Evening Post*, Nov. 18, p. 3/5.

1913 Engine *Side-swipes* Sleepers. Car Damaged but Passengers Escape Unhurt.—*Id.*, Aug. 4, p. 3/2.

1913 One Dead in Train Accident. Freight Train *Sideswipes* Passenger Car on Vandalia Line.—*Id.*, Aug. 28, p. 1/7.

1917 Here and there the jungle crowded so close that it *side-swiped* the car.—H. A. Franck, "Vagabonding Down the Andes," p. 179. (Century Co.)

Sidetrack, v. To set on one side; to shunt onto a sidetrack while the train passes over the main track; hence, to involve in "side issues." [1888-1910.]

1888 See SHYSTER.

1893 They well understood the intention of the bill to be to *side-track* the free-coinage bill.—Mr. Jas. L. Pugh of Ala., U. S. Senate, Sept. 11: *C. R.*, p. 1383/1.

1901 I do not propose to be *side tracked* by any Senator from the other side of the Chamber. I myself will decide when I will go on the side track.—Mr. Marcus A. Hanna of O., U. S. Senate, Feb. 15: *C. R.*, p. 2476/1.

Sidewalk. A walk by the side of a street or road, whether simply trodden down, or boarded, or paved. [1817-1864.]

1851 He loved . . . to look out of the arched window, and see a little girl, driving her hoop along the *sidewalk.*—N. Hawthorne, "House of the Seven Gables," ch. xi. (Century Dict.)

1872 See COAST.

1874 If a man . . . should commit murder on the *sidewalk* of the post-office, he would be hung under the laws of Congress.—Mr. Matt. H. Carpenter of Wisc., U. S. Senate, Apr. 21: *C. R.*, p. 3233/1.

Sidewheeler. A steamboat with drive wheels on the sides.

1889 The *Miami*, a powerful and very fast *side-wheeler*, succeeded in eluding the *Albemarle.—Century Mag.*, xxxvi, 425. (Century Dict.)

Sidewinder or **Sidewiper.** The small horned rattlesnake, *crotalus cerastes*, common in Arizona. (Century Dict.)

Sidewinder. A heavy swinging blow from the side, which disables an adversary. (Webster.)

Siege, hard siege. A period of sickness or trouble. [1862-1908.]

1878 The man has gone through a tremendous *siege*, almost as bad as General Moreau had in his retreat through the Black Forest.—Mr. H. B. Wright of Pa., H. R., Feb. 1: *C. R.*, p. 713/1.

Sign. A trail-track; a trace of trail. [1855-1860.]

1870 Here and there a broad grizzly *"sign"* intersected our trail.—F. H. Ludlow, "The Heart of the Continent," p. 425.

Silent man, the. An epithet applied to General Grant.

1879 The distinguished friend of *"the silent man"* of 1868 and 1872.—Mr. E S. Bragg of Wisc., H. R., Apr. 24: *C. R.*, p. 854/1.

1880 Had it not been for *the silent man* who occupied the presidential chair, the leaders of the democratic host might have plunged the country into another war.—Mr. Philip C. Hayes of Ill., H. R., March 10: *Id.*, p. 1451/2.

Silver Dick. A nickname of Richard P. Bland of Mo. (1835-1899.)

1900 See his eulogy by Mr. Champ Clark of Mo., H. R., Apr. 7: *C. R.*, p. 3898/2.

Silver Grays. A term applied to the N. Y. Whigs, otherwise called Cotton Whigs (see **Conscience Whigs**) who rallied to the support of Millard Fillmore in 1850.

1855 Mr. Erastus Brooks:—I might allude to a public meeting called in the city of Albany in the summer of 1848. Mr. Dickinson:—It was a meeting of *Silver Grays.* Mr. Brooks:—No, sir.—U. S. Senate, Feb. 7. [Mr. Brooks's speech as separately printed, p. 6/2.]

Silverite. An advocate of free coinage.

1887 The attempt is made to cast a slur upon the *Silverites* by calling them inflationists, as if to be an inflationist were the greatest of monetary sins.—*Science*, vii., 267. (Century Dict.)

1892 [St. Paul] found his way to Ephesus, and persuaded many people that the silver gods were not worth worshiping. The *Silverites* rose in arms against the new doctrines. Like the *Silverites* of our day, they had a craft to save.—Mr. Marriott Brosius of Pa., H. R., March 23: *C. R.,* p. 2466/1.

Singlefoot. The same as **Rack.**

1885 Most of the time the horse kept on a steady *single-foot,* but this was varied by a sharp lope every now and then.—Theodore Roosevelt, "Hunting Trips," p. 210. (Century Dict.)

Sir Richard Rum. A nickname for intoxicating liquor. [1750-1827.]

1737 *Sir Richard* has taken off [the man's] Considering Cap. . . . [He has] been too free with *Sir Richard.*—"The Drinker's Dictionary," *S. C. Gazette,* May 7, pp. 1/2, 2/1.

Sitting on a volcano. In a very precarious situation, usually foolishly unaware of danger.

1898 We are [*sitting*] today *on a* race *volcano,* now apparently extinct, now eruptive.—Mr. J. S. Williams of Miss., H. R., Dec. 20: *C. R.,* p. 343/1.

Sit up nights. An expression indicating zeal and perseverance. [1855-1910.]

1890 I find I have incurred the adverse criticism of [Mr. Candler], although I *sit up of nights* trying to work out how I can obtain his approval.—Mr. J. M. Allen of Miss., H. R., Apr. 26: *C. R.,* p. 3873/1.

Siwash. An Indian of the N. Pacific Coast. Chinook jargon. [1852-1857.]

Size one up. To take one's measure. [1890-1909.]

1885 We had to *size up* our fellow legislators, to find out their past history and present character and associates.—*Century Mag.,* xxix, 821.

Skedaddle. To scatter; to flee from an enemy. [1861-1885.] **Skedaddler,** a coward.

1866 The traitors, semi-traitors, bounty jumpers, *skedaddlers* from drafts, cowardly soldiers, . . will all look and act so much like traitors that the future ethnologist will be compelled to classify them all as rebels.—Mr. H. S. Bundy of O., H. R., May 5: *C. G.,* p. 208/2, App.

Skeery. Terrifying. Rustic.

1583 The poore Dido, this sight so *skearye* beholding.—Stanyhurst, "Æneis," p. 73.

Skin game. A cheating or "confidence" game, in which the victims are "skinned." Hence **Skinhouse,** a house where such games are played. Slang.

1890 This is the real *skin-game* annex to the Louisiana State Lottery, and poor servant girls, children, bootblacks, draymen, hackmen, in fact men of high and low degree by the thousands, patronize this scheme.— Mr. H. C. Evans of Tenn., H. R., Aug. 16: *C. R.,* p. 8714/1.

1892 Already the *skin games* of 1890 have been pulled by the police.— Mr. J. P. Dolliver of Ia., H. R., March 29: *Id.,* p. 2670/2.

1894 ['[We are not] proposing any Pacific Railroad "confidence" or subsidy *"skin games"* of any sort to fleece the people of millions.—Mr. O. M. Kem of Neb., H. R., Aug. 10: *Id.,* p. 8397/2.

Skippog (or **Scippaug**). A fish.
1849 See PORGY.

Skunkcabbage. A broad-leaved plant of the arum family, which in the spring sends out a disgusting odor. [1816.]
1892 See APPENDIX LXVII.

Skunk's paradise, Skunk's purgatory. An expression used humorously in complaint of unpleasant odors.
1824 See Vol. I, GOTHAM and HORSE-HEAVEN.

Sky pilot. A clergyman or preacher. Slang.
1891 [Mr. Morse] no sooner took the floor than he took an appeal to high Heaven, a court in which I knew he had no right to practice. Being something of a *sky pilot,* I could but feel that he had taken an advantage of me.—Mr. Marcus A. Smith of Ariz., Feb. 16: *C. R.,* p. 181/2, App.

Skyscrapers. Very tall buildings, usually built for offices.
1899 We are told . . . that *"sky-scrapers"* are preventers of conflagrations and that a law should be passed requiring the erection of a double row of them, the length of Broadway.—*Scientific Amer.,* Jan. 21, p. 39. (Century Dict.)

Slabsided. Having long, lank sides. [1809-1867.]
1863 [The Carolina swine are] a long, lean, *slab-sided* race, with legs and shoulders like deer, and bearing no sort of resemblance to the ordinary hog, except in the snout.—Edmund Kirke, "Life in Dixie's Land," p. 191. (Lond.)
1884 I know all about these Texas cattle. A Texas steer is a great, tall, long, thin, *slab-sided* brute, with wide-extended horns.—Mr. John S. Williams of Ky., U. S. Senate, Apr. 23: *C. R.,* p. 3291/2.

Slang. Careless, foolish talk. Also, the vocabulary or cant peculiar to a locality, a college, a political party, etc. [1806-1861.]
1841 I hope that Virginia will no longer be affected by the *slang* of the "Enquirer."—Henry Clay to Francis Brooke, Jan. 7: "Corresp.," p. 448. (1855.)
1850 I will tell you if [the letter] be studied or real; if it be the merest *lip-slang* put into words, or heart-talk blazing on the paper.—Donald G. Mitchell, "Reveries of a Bachelor," p. 54. (Lond., 1852.)
1864 Why this everlasting partyism and party *slang?*—Wilmington (N. C.) *Journal,* May 31, p. 2/2.
1866 Is there any language that can be found in Billingsgate or Hudibras, any low term of political reproach, any indecent *slang,* any hateful anathema, that is not made use of toward the [Democratic] minority here day after day, and put upon the wings of the press and carried to every quarter of this country?—Mr. John W. Chanler of N. Y., H. R., May 14: *C. G.,* p. 2574/1.
1874 [He is] the object of all the attacks, of all the *slang,* which malignity and genius combined can invent to throw at his devoted head.—Mr. A. A. Sargent of Calif., U. S. Senate, Jan. 9: *C. R.,* p. 510/1.
1878 I am not sensitive about the word *"demagogue."* What do I care about the *slang,* "demagogue?" God bless me, I stand here past middle life.—Mr. H. B. Wright of Pa., H. R., Feb. 1: *C. R.,* p. 713/1.
1894 Short-lived partisans, fertile in the invention and swift in the repetition of derogatory *slang.*—Mr. J. S. Morrill of Vt., U. S. Senate, Dec. 11: *Id.,* p. 197/1.

Slang-whanger. A careless, foolish talker or writer. [1809-1862.]

1811 It embraces alike all manner of concerns, from the organization of a divan . . . to the appointment of a constable, the personal disputes of two miserable *slang-whangers,* etc.—W. Irving, "Salmagundi," No. 14. (Century Dict.)

Slavite. An advocate of slavery. Obsolete.

1831 The most abominable . . . spectacle which the wickedness of war presents in the sight of Heaven is a reverend *slavite.*—W. Lloyd Garrison, *The Liberator,* I, 115. (Century Dict.)

1831 To say that a clerical *slavite* is bound to follow his own precepts, is preposterous.—*The Liberator,* Jan. 8, p. 1/2.

Sleazy. Flimsy; wanting firmness in texture. [1820-1894.]

a.1618 I cannot well away with such *sleazy* Stuff, with such Cobweb-compositions.—James Howell, "Letters," i, 1. (Century Dict.)

1715 *Sleazy,* slight, or ill wrought, as some sorts of Linnen-Cloth are.—Kersey, "Dictionarium Anglo-Britannicum."

1728 For want of Fulling, that kind of Manufacture is Open and *Sleazy.*—William Byrd, "Writings," p. 56. (1901.)

1870 There are certain mean, *sleazy* goods, made under the system of pauper labor in Europe, and imported into [the U. S.].—Mr. Robert C. Schenck of O., H. R., Apr. 13: *C. G.,* p. 2663/3.

Sleeper. A railway sleeping car.

1879 The car itself, the *sleeper,* with curtains drawn and lights turn'd down.—Walt Whitman, "Specimen Days" (1887), p. 216.

1893 [On my way hither] I met on the train at Cincinnati a banker; we were in the *sleeper* together.—Mr. Edward Lane of Ill., H. R., Aug. 22: *C. R.,* p. 83/2, App.

1913 See BIG FOUR.

Sleepy coot, Sleepy duck. The ruddy duck, *Erismatura rubida,* Atlantic coast. (Century Dict.)

Slick. A variant form of *sleek,* meaning smooth, neat, easy; also smoothly, quickly. [1604-1909.] Often used with a comparison; e.g. **Slick as a whistle.**

1513 To feding and to dant their *sleik* swaill stedis. (Lat., *Nitentes pasceri equos.—Swaill-*plump.)—Bishop Douglas, "Eneados," ed. Small (1874), Bk. vi, p. 53.

1595   Fat, *slicke,* faire and full.
        Is better lik't then leane, lancke, spare, and dull.
                            —Thos. Lodge "A Fig for Momus," sig. H.

1864 Birch carried [the depositions] in his pocket without being sealed up, till they were worn *sleek.*—Mr. King, of Mo., H. R., June 1: *C. G.,* p. 2647/3.

1867 See AT THAT.

1881 Get [Mr. Hoar of Mass.] in a close place, and he can come out *slicker* and better than any man I ever saw.—Mr. B. H. Hill of Ga., U. S. Senate, March 30: *C. R.,* p. 123/2.

Slick, n. A smooth place in the sea.

1849 You have seen on the surface of the sea those smooth places which fishermen and sailors call *slicks.* . . . Our boatman said they were caused by the bluefish chopping up their prey, . . . and that the oil from this butchery, rising to the surface, makes the *slick.* Whatever the cause may be, we invariably found fish plenty whenever we came to a *slick.*—Daniel Webster to Mr. Blatchford, Aug. 8: "Private Corresp." (1857) II, 333.

Slicker. See quotation.

1888 He had on what was called a *"slicker,"* or yellow oil-proof coat.—Mr. J. C. Spooner of Wisc., U. S. Senate, Sept. 27: *C. R.,* p. 9005/2.

1888 Nothing is more common in the South than for one of these *slickers,* as they are called,—they are wet-weather overcoats, that is all,—to be worn by people.—Mr. Richard Coke of Tex., U. S. Senate, Sept. 27: *Id.,* p. 9008/2.

1888 We had turned the horses loose, and in our oilskin *slickers* cowered, soaked and comfortless, under the lee of the wagon.—Theodore Roosevelt, *Century Mag.,* xxxv, 864.

Slide rock. See quotation.

1900 In the mountains we often find the hillside slopes covered with broken stone of various sizes. This we call *slide rock.* This *slide rock* may be very coarse, and the surface extremely ragged, when it is called "heavy slide." . . . It may be fine and dry, and run just like sand when one attempts to walk on it; . . . this is called "fine slide rock." —*Yearbook U. S. Dept. Agr.,* p. 195. (Century Dict.)

Slim. Poor, meagre; low in spirits. [1809-1869.]

1815 I guess I be [home-sick], for I feel pritty *slim.*—David Humphreys, "The Yankey in England," p. 40.

Slimsy. Flimsy, thin.

1851 The building is old and *slimsy.*—S. Judd, "Margaret," II, 8.

Sling. A drink concocted with spirits. [1788-1839.]

1800 The cordial drop, the morning dram,·I sing,
The mid day toddy, and the evening *sling.*
—*Baltimore Weekly Magazine,* Aug. 30, p. 152/1.
[Same as quotation from *Mass. Spy,* 1806, in Vol. II.]

Slip. A narrow pew in church. [1838-1854.]

1864 The . . . young lady in the next *slip.*—R. B. Kimball, "Was he successful?" p. 296 (N. Y.).

Slip. A place for a vessel beside a wharf. [1796-1832.]

1828 He strolled to Peck *slip,* and deliberately threw himself into the dock. —*Nat. Gazette* (Phila.), June 14, p. 1/4.

Slippery elm. The red-elm or moose-elm, *Ulmus fulva:* so called because the inner bark (which is used in making a demulcent) is mucilaginous. (Century Dict.)

Slip up. To make a mistake; to miscalculate; to come to grief. [1854-1904.]

1873 He said [the returns] were all more or less corrupt, and that is how Governor Warmoth *"slipped up."*—Mr. J. H. Sypher of La., H. R., March 3: *C. G.,* p. 2107/1.

1888 *Slip up* in my vernacular! How could I? I talked it when I was a boy with the other boys.—*Century Mag.,* xxxvi, 279.

1912 That is where . . . business government *slips up.*—Charles Marriott, "The Dewpond," p. 99.

Sliver, v., tr. and intr. To split into shreds.

a.1606 Slips of yew *Sliver'd* in the moon's eclipse.—"Macbeth," iv, 1.

1879 The planks being cut across the grain to prevent *slivering.*—*Century Mag.,* xx, 79.

1880 The operation of *slivering* [fish] is shown.—G. B. Goode, "History of the Menhaden," p. 147.—(Century Dict.)

Slop over. To be unduly sentimental and "gushing." [1910.]

1872 To me universal amnesty seems like sickly sentimentalism; it is magnanimity *slopping over*; it is spurious generosity.—Mr. Oliver P. Morton of Ind., U. S. Senate, Jan. 23: *C. G.,* p. 524/2.

1884 A word in regard to all this *slopping over* about the soldiers.—Mr. G. W. Steele of Ind., H. R., Apr. 4: *C. R.,* p. 2613/2.

1889 As Artemus Ward says, "[Geo. Washington] never *slopped over.*" —*Harper's Mag.,* lxxviii, 818. (Century Dict.)

1894 Mr. Harter:—I will devote a little attention to you after awhile. Mr. Reed:—I thought you would probably *slop over* somewhere.—H. R., June 20: *C. R.,* p. 6603/2.

Sloshing around. Wallowing, or going about indiscriminately, usually colliding with everything and everybody else. [a. 1854-1862.]

1886 I will try to locate [Senator Ingalls]; but he has a method according to what they call out West *"sloshing around,"* so that sometimes we can hardly locate [him].—Mr. H. M. Teller of Colo., U. S. Senate, May 26: *C. R.,* p. 4961/2.

1892 I suppose it is the proud prerogative of the gentleman from Kansas [Mr. Simpson] . . . like Paddy at the fair, to *"slosh around,"* and strike a head wherever he may see it.—Mr. C. L. Moses of Ga., H. R., May 17: *Id.,* p. 4333/1.

Slough or Slue. A low ravine; an inlet or lateral branch of a river. [1845-1855.]

1870 On my meadow land the water was four or five inches deep, which had all dried up in *sloughs.*—Affidavit of a Calif. rancher, Oct. 31. See *C. G.,* March 3, 1871, p. 289/3, App.

1888 Comanche *Slough* has never been considered a navigable channel of the river, its use in connection with through navigation only being practicable at high [water]. The main use of the *slough* appears to be as a storage-ground for logs and harbor for tow-boats.—Report of Major A. Mackenzie, Dec. 5: *C. R.,* May 27, 1890, p. 5354/1.

Slug. A fifty-dollar gold piece. [1853-1862.]

1890 An interesting reminder of early days in California in the shape of a round fifty-dollar *slug.* . . . But 50 of these round pieces were issued when orders came from the East prohibiting private coinage.—*S. F. Bulletin,* May 10. (Century Dict.)

Slump. A heavy fall in the price of stocks. [1804-1850.]

1900 The bonds of the . . . company suffered a *slump* in the market.—Mr. G. G. Vest of Mo., U. S. Senate, Jan. 16: *C. R.,* p. 858/1.

Slung shot. A small mass of metal or stone fixed on a flexible handle or strap, . . . for use as a weapon. (Webster.) [1842-1876.]

1849 [One of them] struck him a violent blow on the head with a *slung-shot,* which knocked him down.—*N. Y. Courier,* Oct. 16.

1879 [Was there any one to protect the Indian], when he held his life at the mercy of any ruffian who could fire a pistol or throw a *slung-shot?*—Mr. Thos. C. McCreery of Ky., U. S. Senate, Feb. 10: *C. R.,* p. 1152/2.

1879 See SHOULDER-HITTER.

1879 I do not care to be knocked down with a *slung-shot* or stabbed with a dirk-knife.—Mr. Roscoe Conkling, U. S. Senate, June 20: *Id.,* p. 2236/2.

Slush fund. An opprobious term applied to the annual appropriation of $5,000,000 at one time administered by the Secretary of the U. S. Treasury, and afterwards used more widely.

1874 It was a matter of economy and good judgment . . . to consolidate all these offices into one bill, and dispense with what has been received out of . . . the *"slush fund."* . . . We have had this *"slush-fund"* since 1866. It is the fund which my friend from Indiana (Mr. Holman) and my friend from Kentucky (Mr. Beck) talk so much about, although during Andrew Johnson's administration that *"slush-fund"* was five or six times larger than it ever has been since.—Mr. S. W. Kellogg of Conn., H. R., Apr. 17: *C. R.,* p. 3166/1.

1892 My friend knows that the greater part of the money appropriated for building ships is a *"slush fund,"* and he knows what that means.— Mr. W. S. Holman of Ind., H. R., Apr. 16: *Id.,* p. 413/2, App.

1892 [The Republican party] under its new leaders has treated the public Treasury as a *"slush fund,"* and it has taxed the people with an utter disregard of their welfare.—The same. Aug. 5: *Id.,* p. 547/2, App.

1894 [Mr. Cleveland] was not elected in 1888 because you had got the "fat fried" out of your manufacturers; because of pious John Wanamaker and his $400,000 of campaign *slush funds*, and because of men like to him; because of Dudley and his blocks of five in Indiana; because you debauched the people of two States; because you used a good deal of "diplomacy and soap," as Mr. Chester A. Arthur declared at the Delmonico banquet.—Mr. Champ Clark of Mo., H. R., Jan. 16: *Id.*, p. 904/1.

1894 This is properly known in the P. O. Department, Mr. Chairman, as the "*slush fund.*"—Mr. E. F. Loud of Calif., H. R., Apr. 10: *Id.*, p. 3640/2.

Smacked. Crushed or ground. Southern. *Smacked* (ground—as *smacked* corn.)—*Trans. Am. Philol. Ass'n.*, xvii, 46.

Small, by the. By retail.

1869 Whether a man sold "*by the small,*" as we say in the West, or whether he sold in large quantities by wholesale.—Mr. R. C. Schenck of O., H. R., Feb. 12: *C. G.*, p. 1152/1.

1870 A man who sells by the drink, "*by the small,*" to be drank at the place where sold, ought to be considered a retail dealer, [irrespective of the amount of his sales].—Mr. Robt. C. Schenck of O., H. R., July 9: *C. G.*, p. 5416/2.

Small potatoes. Persons or things of no account. [In New England the expression is made still more derogatory by wording it "small potatoes and few in the hill."—Ed.] Hence the adj. use, meaning worthless, mean, cheap. [1836-1880.]

1864 We want no "*small potato business*" here. We want our men well paid. We want them paid in coin.—Mr. Strouse of Pa., H. R., June 7: *C. G.*, p. 2793/1.

Smart. Clever, tricky. [1823-1890.]

1869 Mr. Nye:—Will the Senator allow him to ask him a question? Mr. Cameron:—I would rather not yield to a question from my friend, because I am afraid I should not be able to answer it, he is so *smart*.— U. S. Senate, Jan. 13: *C. G.*, p. 329/3.

1884 Our New England friends have the word "sharp," somewhat analogous to our Southern one of "*smart,*" to qualify the possessor of "ways that are dark" and means that are doubtful.—Mr. W. J. Green of N. C., H. R., Apr. 21: *C. R.*, p. 145/1.

Smarty. A pretentious fellow; a "show-off"; a cheap wit. Colloquial.

1874 I said the colored people of my district were content with their condition. I should have stated with a few exceptions, and I am sorry to say that these are what is known as "*smarties,*" or "would-be" leaders. —Mr. R. R. Butler of Tenn., H. R., June 4: *C. R.*, p. 4592/2.

1880 "Did you make [catch] the train?" . . . "No," said *smarty*, "it was made in the car-shop."—*Boston Transcript*, March 6. (Century Dict.)

Smile. To drink in company. Slang. [1850-1890.]

1858 Some [are] devoted . . . to horses, some to *smiling*, and some to "the tiger."—*Balt. Sun*, Aug. 23. (Bartlett.)

Smoker. A smoking car or compartment. (Webster.)

1894 Last summer I was going home on the train, and when I got tired of having nobody to talk to I went into the *smoker* and [talked] with a man I found there.—Mr. Champ Clark of Mo., H. R., Dec. 11: *C. R.*, p. 5/1, App.

Smokestack. A chimney. [1844-1884.]

1871 I have always been under the impression that in the region around Lake Superior it was cold enough for at least nine months in the year to freeze the *smoke-stack* off a locomotive.—Mr. J. Proctor Knott of Ky., H. R., Jan. 27: *C. G.*, p. 67/3, **App.**

1888 Every *smoke-stack* that marks the presence of a manufacturing house is a guaranty to the farmer that his market is getting surer and better. —Mr. D. B. Henderson of Ia., H. R., Apr. 30: *C. R.*, p. 3532/1.

1892 I saw our villages and our cities, I saw the *smokestacks* with their vapor floating toward the skies.—Mr. S. E. Payne of N. Y., H. R., March 17: *Id.*, p. 2163/1.

Smouch. To crib; to pilfer. Colloquial.

1888 The rest of it was *smouched* from House's Atlantic paper.—*New Princeton Review*, v, 49. (Century Dict.)

Snag. A submerged tree obstructing navigation; any obstruction to the course of events. [1819-1875.]

1715 *Snag*, a Knot, Knob, or Bunch.—Kersey, "Dictionarium Anglo-Britannicum."

1829, 1833, 1847. See SAWYER.

1869 In the navigation of the Mississippi route five great obstacles were encountered: the *snags* and sawyers, the sand-bars in low water, the ice blockade of the Upper Mississippi, the rapids at Keokuk, and the rapids at Rock Island.—Mr. H. E. Paine of Wisc.; H. R., Jan. 14: *C. G.*, p. 373/2.

1876 This matter . . . is an old *snag* in the Committee on Appropriations in both Houses.—Mr. A. A. Sargent of Calif., U. S. Senate, July 1: *C. R.*, p. 4324/2.

1890 The creek bed was full of roots and *snags* and briars, and vines trailed across it.—Statement of John McElroy, *C. R.*, Apr. 21: p. 3638/1.

Snag, v. To clear of snags.

1889 [These men] are engaged in *snagging* the waterways, which will be dredged out to form the canal.—*N. Y. Times*, July 21. (Century Dict.)

Snag-boats. Those engaged in removing snags from rivers. [1843-1911.]

1844 [We are] keeping afloat, and in active operation, the *snag-boats* upon the Mississippi River and her tributaries.—Speech of Mr. Bowlin of Mo., H. R., Jan. 16: p. 3 of the same as separately published.

1869 The National Government, soon after the enactment of the law of 1824 for the improvement of the Ohio and Mississippi rivers, undertook to remove the snags from the rivers by means of *snag-boats.*— Mr. H. E. Paine of Wisc., H. R., Jan. 14: *C. G.*, p. 374/3.

Snag-scow. One used in pulling snags out of a river.

1907 The white *snag-scow* that likes to hang round St. Louis considerable did keep the snags pulled out of the mouth of the Missouri anyway.— C. D. Stewart, "Partners of Providence," ch. xiii. (Century Dict.)

Snake, v. To drag or draw; to sneak or move stealthily. [1829-1868.]

1880 That earlier day when I *snaked* saw-logs and caught sunfish in the . . . thundering surf of the magnificent Muskingum.—Mr. S. S. Cox of N. Y., H. R., Jan. 22: *C. R.*, p. 490/2.

1883 Unless some legal loophole can be found, through which an evasion or extension can be successfully *snaked.*—Phila. *Press*, No. 2810, p. 4. (Century Dict.)

1892 A bill was . . . surreptitiously *snaked* through Congress by the same crowd in 1873, by which silver was destroyed as a circulating medium. —Mr. J. C. Kyle of Miss., H. R., March 31: *Id.*, p. 84/1, App.

1896 Mr. Elkins:—It is a serious charge that [this provision] was *sneaked* into the bill. Let the Senator confine himself to the word "*sneaked.*" Mr. Hill:—I mean it was put in in violation of the rules of the House. Mr. Elkins:—He again lays emphasis on the word "*sneaked.*" Mr. Hill:—This provision did not get in here by accident. . . . [The question comes in here, gets in, crawls into this appropriation bill.]—U. S. Senate, March 27: *C. R.*, p. 3267/2. [See also pp. 3268/2, 3272/2.]

Snake doctor or **Snake feeder.** 1. The hellgrammite. (Pa.) 2. The dragon-fly, horse-stinger, or mosquito-hawk. Local. (Century Dict.)

Snap. Vivacious energy.

1872   When the curtain rose on the second act, there was an enormous amount of applause, and that act went with the most perfect *snap.*—Lester Wallack in *Scribner's,* iv, 722. (Century Dict.)

1892   What the people want in Kansas is *snap,* backbone, industry, and economy.—Mr. Joseph D. Taylor of O., H. R., May 16: *C. R.,* p. 4292/2.

Snap, Snapper. A snap is a glass-maker's tool for holding goblets etc. while being finished. A snapper is one who thus works.

1903   Eighteen *"snappers"* of the Kansas window-glass factory returned to work today.—*Kan. City Star,* Dec. 12.

Snap, Soft Snap. An easy job; a lucrative bargain. [1845-1909.]

1886   [The discharge of unnecessary clerks] would disturb the *"soft snaps"* of some "political workers," but it would save [money.]—Mr. James Buchanan of N. J., H. R., Apr. 10: *C. R.,* p. 403/1, App.

1892   They regard it as a private *snap* that does not require any [extra] work.—Mr. G. W. Fithian of Ill., H. R., March 16: *Id.,* p. 2118/2.

1893   The Government agents had worked up a fine *snap.*—Oklahoma City *Daily Press Gazette,* Sept. 18. See *C. R.,* p. 1824/2.

1895   So far as I have been able to ascertain, these [Revenue-Cutter officers] have a decidedly *"soft snap"* in this life. [It is said] that one of them is 94 years old. Mr. Speaker, it appears that some of these men in these soft berths will live so long that they will have to be taken out on the day of judgment and shot to get rid of them.—Mr. Champ Clark of Mo., H. R., Feb. 18: *Id.,* p. 2350/2.

Snap-bean. A string-bean.

1865   The first *snap-beans* I have seen this season.—Alex. H. Stephens, "Diary," June 19, p. 236 (1910).

Snap convention. See quotation.

1896   Mr. Vest:—[The Senator from Ill. said] that the silver Democrats had made some progress through *snap conventions.* Will [he] explain to what conventions he alludes? Mr. Palmer:—If the term *"snap conventions"* shall be at all offensive, I will withdraw it, but I will say that I know of no better term by which to describe it.... It was a convention called for the deliberate purpose of committing the Democratic party of Missouri, in advance of any actual necessity, to the free-silver dogma.—U. S. Senate, May 7: *C. R.,* p. 4928/2.

1896   I take but little stock in the clamors which are raised against so-called *"snap conventions."* They are usually simply the clamors of the defeated minority.—Mr. David B. Hill of N. Y., U. S. Senate, May 7: *Id.,* p. 4931/2.

Snap judgment. One delivered hurriedly and without consideration. [1841-1888.]

1865   The amendment which I am advocating is not a *snap judgment* against the interests of the Southern States.—Mr. James G. Blaine of Me., H. R., March 2: *C. G.,* p. 1315/2.

1866   I propose that [the bill] do not lie on the Speaker's table, where any member can get up here (*sic*) some afternoon, and take a *snap judgment* on the House.—Mr. John Wentworth of Ill., H. R., June 25: *Id.,* p. 3399/2.

1870   I have never threatened to read [Mr. Bingham] out of the Republican party. Nobody can ever do that but himself: and whether he has done that in passing a bill through this house by a *snap-judgment....* the country will judge.—Mr. B. F. Butler of Mass., H. R., Jan. 24: *Id.,* p. 717/2.

Snap objection. One captiously and suddenly raised.
1879 The decisions of all courts favor proceedings to admit aliens against technical and *snap objections.*—Mr. S. S. Cox of N. Y., H. R., Apr. 17: *C. R.*, p. 82/1, App.
Snap tally. One taken without full and regular notice.
1896 When the *snap tally* was taken, he went to the clerk, made affidavit, etc.—Mr. J. G. Maguire of Calif., H. R., Feb. 27: *C. R.*, p. 2214/2.
Snare drum. A small drum with rawhide strings across one end, a "side-drum"; a villainous instrument of discord.
1888 The man who plays "The girl I left behind me" on a *snare-drum* with a "double drag."—Mr. S. S. Cox of N. Y., H. R., Oct. 17: *C. R.*, p. 592/2, App.
1893 I rose up from my seat in my office in Hartford, hearing a little *snare drum.*—Mr. J. R. Hawley of Conn., U. S. Senate, Feb. 21: *Id.*, p. 1914/1.
Snarl, n. An entanglement. [1825-1862.]
1846 [Sir James Harvey] has been transferred from Nova Scotia to New-foundland, where Lord Falkland had got into a *snarl.*—*N. Y. Comml. Advertiser*, Apr. 1. (Bartlett.)
1866 I found a perfect *snarl* of roads on the farther side of the river.—H. L. Estabrooks, "Adrift in Dixie," p. 155. (N. Y.)
1866 There were several rotten logs, one immense overturned stump, and a perfect *snarl* of briers and underbrush.—*Id.*, p. 196.
1869 Have you no greater object than to sting one another to death like a *snarl* of snakes?—Mr. John W. Chanler of N. Y., H. R., Feb. 26: *C. G.*, p. 1606/2.
1909 Who would not prefer it to the kind [of hair] that got into horrid *snarls,* and had to be combed and tweaked into order?—Anna Fuller in the *Atl. Monthly*, p. 647/1, Nov.
Snarl, v. To entangle. [1814-1861.]
1594 [Snakes shall] *ensnarle* their teeth amongst thy braines, as an Angler *ensnarleth* his hooke amongst weedes.—Thos. Nashe, "Christs Teares," fo. 72.
1604 I think Vulcans Net, that *snarled* Mars himselfe, were not able to hold them.—Barnaby Rich, "Fruites of Experience," p. 55.
1692 The whole business is become . . so *Snarled,* and the determination of the Question . . . so dismal, that etc.—Cotton Mather, "Invisible World," p. 84. (ed. 1862.)
1715 *Snarl,* to be intangled, as a Skain of Thread or Silk may be —Kersey, "Dictionarium Anglo-Britannicum."
1890 Perhaps we may in the future get hold of the right thread of the *snarled* skein that links capital with labor.—Mr. James O'Donnell of Mich., H. R., Aug. 28: *C. R.*, p. 9292/2.
Snide. Mean, low, contemptible. [1888.] Used also as a noun.
1887 The same thing has happened to several other corporations, ... namely, that it becomes a "*snide.*"—Mr. Anderson of Kan., H. R., Feb. 14: *C. R.*, p. 1751/1.
1898 Much of this advertising of these "*snide*" papers is the advertising of patent medicines, the advertising of all sorts of "*snide*" schemes.—Mr. J. H. Walker of Mass., H. R., March 3: *Id.*, p. 2432/2.
Snook. See quotation. Cf. **Snoop.** It suggests also the word *sneak.*
1715 To *Snook,* to lie lurking for a thing.—Kersey, "Dictionarium Anglo-Britannicum."
1879 The partisan detectives . . . are called investigating agents, who are sent to *snook around* among the carpet-baggers etc.—Mr. E. S. Bragg of Wisc., H. R., Apr. 15: *C. R.*, p. 458/1.
1912 Mr. James "*snooked*" around the shop. He ran his nose over the tables, and inch by inch (he must be very shortsighted) along the

walls, stood on tiptoe and pulled down volumes from high places, rummaged in dark corners, was apparently oblivious of the presence of anything but the books.—*N. Y. Evening Post*, Oct. 28, p. 7/1.

Snoop. To prowl about; to pry into affairs not one's own. Dutch, *Snoepen*. [1834-a. 1899.]

1864 They don't come *snooping* around to find out whether you sometimes go to the theatre.—R. B. Kimball, "Was he successful?" p. 183. (N. Y.)

1891 I have heard the word in Worcester [Mass.] where there are no resident families of Dutch descent. There it would be said: "They caught him *snooping* at the door," that is, peeping and listening.—Alice Morse Earle in *Journal of Am. Folk-Lore*, iv, 160.

1901 See RUBBERNECK.

Snowplow. Any of various contrivances used to clear away snow from roads. [1792.]

1878 See Appendix LVI.

Snowsheds. Structures erected to protect railroads from the sliding down of snow.

1869 The company coming from the Pacific side have built very stout *snow-sheds* over their roads to the extent of twenty-five or thirty miles.—Mr. Cornelius Cole of Calif., U. S. Senate, Apr. 5: *C. G.*, p. 502/2.

1878 See Appendix LVI.

Snub line. In lumbering, a hawser used to control the movement of a load of logs down a steep slope. [Maine.]

1908 It was well into February before they began to haul their logs to the landing-place on Blunder Stream. But . . . time was ample, for the *snub-line* down the steep quarter-mile of Enchanted's shoulder made a cut-off that doubled the efficiency of the teams.—Holman Day, "King Spruce," ch. xxvi. (Century Dict.)

Snub post, Snubbing post. A post around which a line is thrown to stop movement suddenly. See Vol. II, **Snub, Snubber.** [1846-1853.]

1868 My gallant friend from Kentucky [Mr. Davis] will have to seek affiliation with another party before he gets in a majority. He will have to join the party of progress and freedom, hitching to no *snub-post* of the past.—Mr. James W. Nye of Nev., U. S. Senate, July 10: *C. G.*, p. 3910/2.

1871 That old class of "gentlemen" who hitch to the *snubbing-post* of the past, and ride all the storms and gales with security.—The same, Feb. 17: *Id.*, p. 1343/2.

1888 Near the middle of the glade stands the high, circular horse-corral, with a *snubbing-post* in the center.—Theodore Roosevelt, *Century Mag.*, xxxv, 655.

Soap. Originally used by the Republican managers during the campaign of 1880, as the cipher for "money" in their telegraphic despatches. In 1884 it was revived as a derisive war-cry on the part of the Democrats.—*Mag. of Am. Hist.*, xiii, 394.

1889 They paid for this lease of power with political influence, political "fat," political "*soap*," as political corruption is called by a slick and vulgar euphonism in our political slang.—Mr. J. T. Morgan of Ala., U. S. Senate, Jan. 16: *C. R.*, p. 841/1.

1894 See SLUSH FUND.

1894 A distinguished ex-President, now dead, said that *soap* was needed in a great campaign, and had done great good; but I do not care about introducing partisan allusions. I know our friends on the other side feel kindly to *soap*.—Mr. G. G. Vest of Mo., U. S. Senate, May 18: *Id.*, p. 4920/1.

Sobby. Wet. Sometimes used of land. [1878.]

1894 [The sugar was of] that old yellow *sobby* sort so rank that if you put a cup under it over night you would have a mess of molasses in the morning.—Mr. Benton McMillin of Tenn., H. R., Aug. 13: *C. R.,* p. 1241/2, App.

Sobrante. See quotation.

1871 On the making of the survey [in Calif.] there was found to be what was known in the Mexican law as a *sobrante,* that is a surplus of land lying between the exterior boundaries of the original grant and the inner boundaries of the survey ascertained by our own authorities. [These people] claim to have rights upon that *sobrante* or surplus as settlers.—Mr. Eugene Casserly of Calif., U. S. Senate, March 13: *C. G.,* p. 66/1.

"Social status" colonizers. Persons not legally resident in the ward in which they attempt to vote, but having a status in the community.

1870 [G. S. Repplier] was a *"Social Status" colonizer.* He was but a temporary sojourner in the division. . . . [S. S. White] was another *"social status" colonizer,* and clearly [as] illegal as Repplier.—Mr. S. J. Randall of Pa., H. R., Apr. 13: *C. G.,* p. 2655/1.

Sod crop. See quotation.

1888 Flaxseed or flax in this country is very largely . . . . what we call a *sod crop.* It is the crop of a new country. . . . . They can raise a crop of flax on the new sod, sowing it after the land is broken for the first time.—Mr. Thomas Wilson of Minn., H. R., June 9: *C. R.,* p. 5078/2.

Soft thing. A "snap"; an easy living with very little work or none at all.

1892 I have in my district two communities, and one-half of all the people in them want to be Indian agents, and the other half want to be physicians to the Indians. . . . . Why, to be an agent is to have gotten *a soft thing,*—he has struck it rich.—Mr. W. W. Bowers of Calif., H. R., Feb. 18: *C. R.,* p. 1302/2.

Solar plexus blow (or **hit on the solar plexus**). A blow which ends the fight; a knockdown blow. [1910.]

1912 Mr. Roosevelt dealt a body blow to contingency when he announced last winter that he would be a candidate at Chicago, *if* the people wanted him. He hit contingency on the *solar plexus* when he declared at Chicago that there would be a third party, *if* the people wanted it, and that he would lead the third party, *if* no one else was chosen.— *N. Y. Evening Post,* July 4, p. 4/1.

1912 Socialists and Industrial Workers received a *solar plexus blow* in attempting recall of Oakland officials.—*Oregonian,* Aug. 7, p. 10/4.

Solid. A solid man is a man of property and position. [1799-1888.] To get solid with anyone is to have influence with him.

1890 Are the bridges of Boston *solid?* The men of Boston are *solid,* but the bridges are not.—Mr. W. M. Evarts of N. Y., U. S. Senate, Aug. 16: *Id.,* p. 8668/1.

Solid South. The Southern states voting solidly together as a political unit against the North.

1878 In my heart I regret that the necessity has ever existed in this country for what is termed *"a solid South."*—Mr. John T. Morgan of Ala., U. S. Senate, Dec. 17: *C. R.,* p. 242/1.

1879 The gentleman from South Carolina [Mr. Aiken] glories in a *solid South.* What does a *solid South* mean, sir? What will result from a *solid South?* . . . A *solid South* means a solid North. And what does that signify? Unrest, national disquietude, and constant alarm and disturbance of the public mind.—Mr. C. C. Ellsworth of Mich., H. R., Feb. 25: *Id.,* p. 126/1, App.

1879   Fling your political banner to the breeze, and inscribe in golden letters on its waving folds your chivalric motto, *"A Solid South."*—Mr. J. M. Bailey of N. Y., H. R., Apr. 22: *Id.*, p. 682/2.

1880   See TISSUE-BALLOT.

1881   The cry of a *"solid South,"* that was sounded so loudly and fiercely in the recent political campaign by the "stalwarts" of the republican party, to frighten the timid and harmonize the discordant elements of that party . . . . has lost its terrors, and possesses no charms.—Mr. W. G. Colerick of Ind., H. R., Feb. 5: *Id.*, p. 117/2, App.

1881   We have heard something of *"the solid South"* in this debate. At the last election, from Maine to New Jersey we had a solid New England; from New Jersey to Missouri we had a solid central belt; from Missouri to the lakes we had a solid Northwest; and not one of these solid sections of the country had the justification or the apology which *"the solid South"* presents to us. The South is confronted with a great domestic problem, truly said by the Senator from Connecticut [Mr. Joseph R. Hawley] to be one of the painful problems of government.—Mr. Geo. H. Pendleton of O., U. S. Senate, Apr. 13: *C. R.*, p. 277/2.

Solid, to vote a ticket. To vote as one, exactly alike.

1890   It undoubtedly is true that the polygamous wives of the Mormon hierarchy in Utah did *vote the ticket* of the hierarchy *solid.*—Mr. G. F. Edmunds of Vt., U. S. Senate, July 19: *C. R.*, p. 7462/1.

Some. Somewhat, to some extent; often used in the sense of greatly, considerably. [1785-1907.]

1834   [The woman is] large, and well set, and likely *some* marked with the whip.—*The Georgian* (Savannah), Dec. 29, p. 3/2. (Advt.)

1888   See SHYSTER.

1894   The address I delivered in Chicago shook up the country *some* on this question.—Mr. J. H. Walker of Mass., H. R., Dec. 18: *C. R.*, p. 414/1.

Some pumpkins. A person or thing of consequence; the opposite of **Small Potato.** [1846-1909.]

1849   [We came] to the conclusion that Harmanson himself [candidate for Congress from La.] was *"some pumpkins,"* and an all-fired smart talker.—Wilmington (N. C.) *Commercial*, July 21, p. 4/1.

1864   Arriving in the Territory [of Washington, the Federal appointees] very frequently imagine themselves, if not "monarch[s] of all they survey," at least decidedly *"some pumpkins."*—Mr. Cole of Wash., H. R., June 7: *C. G.*, pp. 2794-5.

Soo, the. The Sault St. Marie Canal.

1894   The freight tonnage passing the *"Soo"* Canal in 1890 was 8,554,434, or 1,664,341 [tons] more than the Suez Canal.—Mr. John Patton of Mich., U. S. Senate, June 22: *C. R.*, p. 6697/2.

1897   Our great lakes contain one-half the fresh water of the world, and the *Soo* Straits do more business than the Suez Canal.—A Fourth of July oration, quoted July 7 in the *C. R.*, p. 2444/1.

Sooner. One who arrived on the ground early, especially when Oklahoma was thrown open for settlement in 1885, in order to secure a good location. [1893.]

1890   Mr. McRae:—Certain facts relative to the class of persons known as *"Sooners"* in Oklahoma. Mr. Perkins:—We have recognized the fact that there are *"Sooners"* there. . . . . Mr. Pickler:—Entering into the duties of these commissions must necessarily be what is known as the *"sooner question"*; that is, the question whether a man who obeyed the law . . . . . shall be put at a disadvantage by about from 200 to 500 persons who went into the town of Guthrie before they had a right to go in under the law, and whether such persons shall be allowed to locate and establish claims contrary to law.—H. R., Jan. 17: *C. R.*, pp. 657 and 660.

1890   Mr. Pendleton:—We are not familiar in my part of the country with the vocabulary which prevails so far West, and some of us would like to know just what is meant by a *"sooner."* Mr. Mansur:—A *"sooner"* is a man who went into the Territory [of Oklahoma] before the hour of 12 o'clock noon on April 22, the time designated by the proclamation of the President for entrance.—H. R., Jan. 18. *Id.*, p. 680/1.

1893   An army of *"sooners"* [in the Cherokee Strip] disguised as soldiers, deputy marshals, and railway trainmen.—Oklahoma City *Daily Press Gazette*, Sept. 18.

1893   Mr. Wilson:—Will the gentleman explain to the House what a *"Sooner"* is? Mr. Flynn:—A *"sooner"* is a man who goes into the territory before the time specified in the President's proclamation. Mr. Wilson:—The men who go in first are *"sooners"*? Mr. Flynn:— Yes, Sir.—H. R., Sept. 26: *C. R.*, p. 1826/2.

1894   If these provisions are adopted, the land jumpers and *"Sooners"* will take every valuable piece of land that you open to settlement.—Mr. T. C. McRae of Ark., H. R., June 16: *Id.*, p. 6427/1.

Sophomore.   A college student in his second year. [1726-1888.]

1774   The Presdt. may give Leave for the *Sophimores* to take out some particular Books.—Laws of Yale Coll., p. 23. (Hall, "College Words.")

Sophomoric, Sophomorical.   Crude and superficial. [1847-1873.]

1879   [They were] speculating upon the nature of things in an easy, bold, *sophomoric* way.—G. W. Cable, "Old Creole Days," p. 13. (Century Dict.)

1890   [He was] sustained only by the *sophomoric* eloquence of Mr. Benjamin.—*Century Mag.*, xxxix, 563.

1896   In some of those speeches . . the language has been well chosen and the words have been well delivered, although somewhat *sophomoric* in style, and fallacious as a rule in argument.—Mr. Franklin Bartlett of N. Y., H. R., Jan. 16: *C. R.*, p. 748/2.

Sorehead.   A discontented person who has a real or fancied grievance. [1862.]

1866   A small number of *sore-heads*, and those whose acute nasal organs snuff presidential patronage on the breeze.—Mr. H. S. Bundy of O., H. R., May 5: *C. G.*, p. 208/1, App.

1872   If I have joined the party of *soreheads*, I submit that it is not [Mr. Trumbull's] business to read me out of that party. I can tell him that I am just as good a *sorehead* as if I lived in Illinois.—Mr. G. F. Edmunds of Vt., U. S. Senate, Apr. 29: *Id.*, p. 2882/1.

1872   I suppose that persons who are out of office, *"sore-heads,"* can get together without [special] authority.—Mr. Lyman Trumbull of Ill., U. S. Senate, May 30: *Id.*, p. 4041/1.

1882   This report . . . . is not made to give consolation to any complainer, or to spread a plaster over the wounds of any *"sorehead."*—Mr. W. H. Calkins of Ind., H. R., Jan. 19: *C. R.*, p. 528/2.

1882   I differ with [Wm. C. Goodloe] in politics, for he is a *sorehead* and I am not.—Mr. John D. White of Ky., H. R., June 22: *Id.*, p. 5231/2.

1888   There was a secret movement engineered by *"sore-head"* politicians, . . . to thwart patriotic purposes.—Henry Clews, "Twenty-Eight Years in Wall St.," p. 314. [N. Y.]

1890   There are many decent Republicans in Arkansas who will not lend themselves to the election of every bolting *sore-head* Democrat who happens to run for office.—Mr. T. C. McRae of Ark., H. R., June 30: *C. R.*, p. 6803/1.

1901   See RAG, TO CHEW THE.

Sort of.   In a manner; "kind of." [1833-1866.]

1868   See MILK AND WATER.

Soul-driver. An opprobrious name applied by the abolitionists to the overseers of slaves. [1818-1849.]

1888 Today every old *soul-driver* of the South is a free-trader.—Mr. L. E. McComas of Md., H. R., May 2: *C. R.*, p. 3647/1.

Soulful. Full of soul or emotion. Hence **soulfully, soulfulness.**

1872 There wasn't a sounding-line on board that would have gone to the bottom of her *soulful* eyes.—Chas. D. Warner, "Backlog Studies," p. 58. (Century Dict.)

Sound on the goose. Sound from a Southern point of view, on the slavery question. See Vol. II, **Right on the goose.** [1855-1866.]

1880 Mr. McMahon:—Not the idea of the gentleman from Iowa to kill the goose which lays the golden egg, but to foster the goose which lays the golden egg. Mr. Price:—That is a slander on the goose. Mr. McMahon:—The gentleman from Iowa is not *sound on the goose*, and I do not take his opinion on that question. Mr. Price:—Not that sort of a goose, I am not.—H. R., May 1: *C. R.*, p. 2933/2. [Here the phrase loses its original allusion.]

Souphouse Bill, the. See quotation.

1882 [Is not this] the bill introduced by [Mr. Bayne], commonly called the *Soup-house bill*? I refer to the bill for the establishment of soldiers' homes throughout the country.—Mr. P. B. Thompson of Ky., H. R., Dec. 5: *C. R.*, p. 31/1.

Soup, in the. Almost equivalent to "in the lurch." Slang.

1890 [This answer] left me *in the* "*soup*," so to speak, because the inference might be drawn that I am in favor of this class of legislation.—Mr. E. P. Allen of Mich., H. R., Aug. 7: *C. R.*, p. 8292/2.

Sourdough. A "prospector"; a miner who lives alone or with a partner, and eats bread of his own making.

1905 Strange as it may seem, the closing in of winter [in Alaska] opens up the country to the "*sourdough*," for dogs can pull where horses fail, and the prospector with his team and "grubstake" roams at will.—*Nat. Geog. Mag.*, p. 107. (Century Dict.)

1907 Mr. Robert W. Service published "Songs of a *Sourdough*." (T. Fisher Unwin.)

1913 The Rev. C. H. H. Bloor, the pioneer clergyman of Cape Nome and Council City, Alaska, who went to the North in the last years of the last century, and is well known to all the old-timers and *sourdoughs* of Seward Peninsula, is now located in Portland.—*Oregon Churchman*, May, p. 10/1.

Souse. Head cheese; pickle made with salt; something steeped in pickle, as fish or pigs' feet. [1801-1883.]

1573 And he that can rear up a pig in his house
Hath cheaper his bacon, and sweeter his *souse*.
—Tusser, "January's Husbandry," st. 2. (Century Dict.)

1575 Their teeth were farre too fine, to feed on porke and *souse*.—G. Gascoigne, "Flowers," p. 40. (1587.)

1596 The host, *souced* in *souce* like a pickled herring, ran away.—Thos. Lodge, "Wits Miserie," p. 81.

1599 There is some good will betwixt Madge the *Sousewife* and I.—"The Pinner of Wakefield," C 1.

a. 1606 I have brought him vp hardly, with browne Bread, fat Bacon, Puddings, and *Souce*.—"Wily Begvilde," B 4.

1720 *Sousce* (Fr.), in Cookery, a Jelly, made of Hogs-Ears and Feet boil'd in Water, and afterwards cut into small Pieces, to be stew'd in Vinegar and Sugar.—Phillips's "New World of Words," 7th ed.

Southerner. An inhabitant or native of the Southern United States.

1862 The fiery *southerner* had learned [in Missouri] to abate his prejudices against what he once termed the pharisaical Yankee.—Mr. John B. Henderson of Mo., U. S. Senate, Apr. 8: *C. G.*, p. 1569/1.

1865 See NORTHERNER.
1875 See LARIAT.
1875 The *Southerners* had every guaranty they could desire that they
should not be interfered with at home.—James F. Clarke, *N. Am. Rev.*
cxx, 65. (Century Dict.)

Sozzle. A state of sloppy disorder. [1854-1878.]
1867 In despite of poverty and every discouragement, [she] had always
hated . . . anything like what she called a *sozzle.*—Adeline T. Whitney,
"Leslie Goldthwaite," ch. vii. (Century Dict.)

Span. A pair of horses driven together. [1769-1859.]
1828 A *"span"* of horses (a pair) is a fashionable expression through all
the states, from New York even into Upper Canada. That this origi-
nates from their Dutch ancestors I had an opportunity of proving, by
finding the same term in use at the Cape.—*Nat. Gazette* (Phila.)
March 11, p. 2/2. (From "Letters on New South Wales.")
1870 See STOVE-PIPE HAT.
1878 [Mr. Francis Walker, in his work on Money] illustrates his view of
the double standard by taking the case of two horses driven in *span.*—
Mr. W. A. Phillips of Kan., H. R., Feb. 21: *C. R.*, p. 1245/2.
1894 See BRONCHO.

Spang. A harsh, quick, ringing sound, as of a plucked bowstring.
[Noun and verb, the same as **twang**.] Sc.
1513 The flayne [arrow] flaw fast wyth ane *spang* fra the string.—Bishop
Douglas, "Eneados," ed. Small (1874). Bk. vii, p. 116.
1513 The arrowis flaw *spangand* fra every string.—*Id.*, x, p. 288.

Spat. A brief quarrel. Colloquial. [1804-1850.]
1806 He had a *spat* with the Doctor, about keeping his hat on in the
meeting at prayer time.—Lorenzo Dow, "Journal," §820 (1850), p.
122/2.
1850 The bull-dogs settled private *spats,*
All chased imaginary cats, etc.
—J. R., Lowell, "Unhappy Lot," Part 1.
1869 They was pretty apt to have *spats.*—H. B. Stowe, "Oldtown Folks,"
p. 33. (Century Dict.)

Speakeasy. An unlicensed drinking-shop. Vol. II says "The word
seems to belong to Philadelphia." Later used generally.
1901 If the internal-revenue receipt does not appear in one of the *"speak-
easies"* or underground places which are said to be conducted in
[Maine], the internal-revenue officers . . . would make an arrest.—
Mr. T. H. Carter of Mont., U. S. Senate, Jan. 18: *C. R.*, p. 1164/2.

Speak one's piece, to. To express one's opinion. Metaphor taken from
a schoolboy's recitation.
1875 My friend from Kentucky [Mr. McCreery] *has spoken his piece,* and
I suppose feels better.—Mr. O. P. Morton of Ind., U. S. Senate,
March 12: *C. R.*, p. 34/1.
1879 I expect to read tomorrow [in the papers] that I *spoke a piece,* that
is the way they print it sometimes, in favor of slavery.—Mr. Eaton of
Conn., U. S. Senate, May 16: *Id.*, p. 1380/2.

Special-request envelopes. See quotation.
1893 You have allowed . . . the right of the Postmaster-General to have
printed upon the *request envelope,* "if not called for" within any number of days fixed, "return to ————." To that extent your law
allows *special-request envelopes* to indicate in print to return. The
paragraph in the appropriation bill allows simply to print the name
and address, for instance: "If not called for within ten days, return
to John Jones, Philadelphia, Pa."—Mr. H. H. Bingham of Pa., H. R.,
Feb. 18: *C. R.*, p. 1802/1.
1893 The issue of *special-request envelopes* has been going on ever since
1865, increasing from three-quarters of a million in that year to nearly

314,000,000 in 1892.—Letter of the Postmaster-General, Feb. 3: *Id.*, p. 1802/2.

Speck (frequently pronounced *Schpeck*) is the hybrid offspring of English pronunciation and a German word: the generic term applied in Southern Pennsylvania to all kinds of fat meat, but especially pork. See *Trans. Am. Philol. Assoc.*, xvii, App., p. 12. (Century Dict.) [1809.]

1633 Adue good Cheese and Onyons, stuffe thy guts
With *Specke* and Barley-pudding for digestion.
      —Thos. Heywood, "English Traveller," i, 2.

Speed, v. To drive rapidly.

1888 Perhaps it was a note of Western independence that a woman was here and there seen *speeding* a fast horse, in a cutter, alone.—*Harper's Mag.*, lxxvi, 876. (Century Dict.)

1899 [The engineer] rose to the emergency and *speeded* the battleship "Oregon" far in excess of her rating.—Mr. Low of N. Y., H. R., Jan. 13: *C. R.*, p. 663/1.

Spell. A period, with reference to the continuance of weather, cold, hot, dry, or wet.

1775 Nothing new has happened in this quarter since my last, except the setting in of a severe *spell* of cold weather and a considerable fall of snow.—G. Washington to J. Reed, Dec. 25. (Century Dict.)

Spell. A period of ailment or ill feeling; a fit of illness; a "turn."

1869 Wal, after all, we sot out, and Hepsy she got clear beat out; and when Hepsy does get beat out she has *spells*, and she goes on awful.—Harriet B. Stowe, "Oldtown Folks," p. 171. (Century Dict.)

Spell. A short while. Colloquial.

1888 No, I hain't got a girl now. I had one a *spell*, but I'd rather do my own work.—C. D. Warner, "Their Pilgrimage," p. 145. (Century Dict.)

1889 Why don't ye come and rest a *spell* with me, and tomorrow ye kin go on ef ye like?—*Harper's Mag.*, lxxx, 349. (Century Dict.)

Spell baker, to. To do something difficult: supposed to refer to *baker* as one of the first words met by children in passing from the "easy" monosyllables to the "hard" dissyllables in the old spelling-books. Old and colloquial. (Century Dict.)

1868 If an old man will marry a young wife,
Why then—why then—why then—he must *spell* Baker.
      —Longfellow, "Giles Corey," ii, 1. (Century Dict.)

Spellbinder. An orator; a political speaker who "holds his audience spellbound." [1888-1910.]

1888 *Spellbinders.* The word occurs in a headline of the N. Y. *Tribune*, Nov. 15.—C. L. Norton, "Political Americanisms."

1891 An intelligent people, once humbugged, now only laugh at ranting "*spell-binders*," the fake conjurers of international spooks, etc.—Mr. W. McAdoo of N. J., H. R., Feb. 27: *C. R.*, p. 3488/1.

Spieler. A "barker" for side shows. Also anyone who "makes a spiel," i.e. gives a talk.

1899 In front of the entrance a "*spieler*" stood on a starch box and beat upon a piece of tin with a stick, and we weakly succumbed to his frenzied appeals.—*N. Y. Times*, June 12. (Century Dict.)

Spike, v. To mix, with deleterious effect.

1897 They use these plants for the purpose of making corn flour, which is "*spiked*" into the wheat flour.—*Atlanta Constitution*, Nov. 21: cited in the *C. R.*, Feb. 22, 1898: p. 221/2, App.

1898 Your speech .. relative to the *spiking* of corn flour into wheat flour . . . A bill which is intended to remedy the evil of *spiking* wheat flour with corn flour.—Letters from Tennessee, *Id.*, p. 222, App.

Spiketailed coat. A clawhammer.

1880 Who loses a wink of sleep in this country because one minister fails to attend the Queen's levee in a *spiked-tailed coat*, . . . or another minister fails to shiver in the antechamber of the ice palace of the Czar.—Mr. S. S. Cox of N. Y., H. R., Jan. 22: *C. R.*, p. 485/2.

1884 This committee . . . is a mere ornament. Its only occupation is to go in *spike-tail coats* and dine with diplomates.—Mr. G. D. Wise of Va., H. R., May 28: *Id.*, p. 4634/1.

1894 See Appendix LXXII.

Spile. A large stake driven into the ground as a support; a pile. (Webster.) Also, a spigot. [1824-1866.]

1850 The spiles [were forced] out laterally, or into the mud vertically.— Wilmington (N. C.) *Commercial*, Oct. 15, p. 2/3.

1886 One of the oldest [oyster-boat] captains said: "We have only just learned that the sound was to be blocked by driven *spiles.*"—*N. Y. Herald*, Feb. 8: cited in the *C. R.*, May 19, p. 4665/2.

Spirit-duck. The bufflehead, *Clangula albeola*: so called from its expertness in diving, and its sudden appearances and disappearances. (Century Dict.)

Split tickets. Those on which the voter has marked out the names of some of the candidates. See **Scratch a ticket**; Vol. II, **Split the ticket.** [1842.]

1864 The *split* or scratched *tickets* they tied up, ... putting on the back of the package some mark indicating that they were not whole tickets. —Mr. Dawes of Mass., H. R., March 4: *C. G.*, pp. 943-4.

Spoils system, the. The system of distributing offices among the adherents of a victorious party. The maxim, "To the victor belong the spoils," appears to have been formulated by William L. Marcy of N. Y. (1786-1857.)

1832 They see nothing wrong in the rule that *to the victor belong the spoils* of the enemy.—W. L. Marcy in the U. S. Senate debate on the nomination of Martin Van Buren by Andrew Jackson as minister to England.

1835 Now the dismissal of thousands, when it is openly avowed that the public offices are *"the spoils of the victors,"* produces scarcely a sensation.—John C. Calhoun, U. S. Senate, Feb. ["Works" (1856), II, 440.]

1870 I think that, as we have got on very well with it for a great number of years, certainly since the accession of General Jackson to power, and as the country has flourished tolerably well under this system, called as it is by the Senator from Missouri [Mr. Carl Schurz] *"the spoils system,"* we had better . . . . go on in the old way.—Mr. Jacob M. Howard of Mich., U. S. Senate, Jan. 27: *C. G.*, p. 781/3.

1872 It was the *"spoils"* of party and the *"spoils"* of commerce that held the North back for years in the war on slavery. . . . . [The Democratic party's] crimes against liberty would never have been possible, had it not debased itself and debauched the people through Mr. Marcy's infamous doctrine.—Mr. C. W. Willard of Vt., H. R., Apr. 7: *Id.*, pp. 2513/4.

1872 Whoever declared, if any Democrat ever did, that *"to the victors belong the spoils,"* put forward no new proposition, but only expressed what was well known and existing at the time.—Mr. C. N. Potter of N. Y., H. R., Apr. 18: *Id.*, p. 2551/1.

1878 During the administration of Andrew Jackson one of the great political parties . . . promulgated the doctrine that *"to the victors belong the spoils,"* and since that time it has been practically adopted and carried into effect by both parties.—Mr. C. H. Joyce of Vt., H. R., Feb. 9: *C. R.*, p. 876/2.

1879   Mr. Kernan:—William L. Marcy was elected Governor three times. Mr. Morrill:—Will the Senator from New York inform me whether that is the same name that is often credited with the epigrammatic sentence, *"To the victors belong the spoils"*? Mr. Kernan:—I have heard it said that Mr. Marcy used that language, but . . it was not a doctrine that he had to preach to [the republican] party, for . . they never failed to take advantage of the spoils.—U. S. Senate, May 14: *Id.,* p. 1323/1.

1880   The corrupting doctrine, that *"to the victors belong the spoils,"* is inseparable from congressional patronage as the established rule and practice of parties in power.—Annual message of Pres. R. B. Hayes, Dec. 6: *Id.,* p. 3/1.

1881   The system of appointments and removals . . . has made Guiteau a possible aspirant for office, and assassination a possible vengeance for his disappointment. These are the fruits of *the spoils system.*—Mr. Geo. H. Pendleton of O., U. S., Senate, Dec. 13: *Id.,* p. 80/2.

1881   See the Speech of Mr. Geo. Wm. Curtis before the American Social Science Association, at Saratoga, Sept. 8, in which he reviewed the history of this system.

1882   I do not laud the sentiment mentioned by the Hon. Senator from Mass., which he attributes to Mr. Marcy, that *"to the victors belong the spoils."* He said it was rather coarse. Probably it was; but yet to a very great extent it has been the system practiced from the first day of the inauguration of this Government, and whatever you may put upon the statute-book it will be the system practiced until its funeral knell is sounded.—Mr. J. E. Brown of Ga., U. S. Senate, Dec 14: *Id.,* p. 278/1.

1882   *The system of spoils* was not born with Jefferson, . . . nor with Andrew Jackson when he was President. The first constitution of the State of New York . . . in 1777 put this system into full operation.— Mr. Warner Miller of N. Y., U. S. Senate, Dec. 14: *Id.,* p. 282/1. [See the rest of his speech.]

1889   Nearly all the old employes of the Government had been selected under what the doctrinaires generally call the *"spoils system."*—Mr. J. W. Daniel of Va., U. S. Senate, Feb. 6: *Id.,* p. 1560/1.

1890   Sir, Thomas Jefferson was the author of the doctrine that *to the victors belong the spoils.* [Cries of "Jackson!" "Jackson!"] No, sir: Jefferson was the author of [that] doctrine, ... but Gen. Jackson and Governor Marcy gave it a more defined and a wider application.—Mr. Marion Briggs of Calif., H. R., Apr. 24: *Id.,* p. 3794/1.

1893   We still agree with the sentiment of that grand old patriot, Andrew Jackson, in that he said long ago, *"To the victor belongs (sic) the spoils."* That was the rallying slogan of victory announced by an American who was always the implacable enemy of monopoly.—Mr. H. C. Snodgrass of Tenn., H. R., Dec. 15: *Id.,* p. 261/1.

1896   The idea underlying the *spoils system* was clearly expressed by Senator Marcy in that famous utterance in the U. S. Senate, that "There is nothing wrong in the rule that *to the victor belongs the spoils* of the enemy."—Mr. Marriott Brosius of Pa., H. R., Dec. 22: *Id.,* p. 417/1.

1898   Mr. Marcy of New York, a Democrat, afflicted the country with that catchy phrase, *"To the victors belong the spoils of the Enemy,"* which . . means, "Grab all you can get."—Mr. W. H. Fleming of Ga., H. R., Jan. 11: *Id.,* p. 25/2, App.

Spook. A ghost; a hobgoblin. Dutch. [1801-1909.]

1583 That night in forrest to vs *pouke bugs* gastly be tendred. [Probably *spouke bugs* is meant. The *immania monstra* of Virgil.]—Stanyhurst, "Œneis," p. 58.

1815 [She has] spirits in her closet.—Sperits! *Spooks*! I spose.—David Humphreys, "The Yankey in England," p. 30. [*Spoons* in the text, corrected in the *errata*.]

1870 Are we children to be frightened by such *spooks*; or knaves to be moved by such petty influences? A settler who objects to railroads! There is no such settler.—Mr. Thos. Fitch of Nev., H. R., Apr. 29: C. G., p. 3107/1.

1884 There are men who . . shudder at the very name "corporation," and a chill goes over them as it does over a child when it hears of "ghosts" and "*spooks*."—Mr. B. M. Cutcheon of Mich., H. R., Dec. 16: C. R., p. 47/2, App

Spool. A reel; a cylinder on which thread or yarn is wound. [1816-1878.]

1615 Winding of *spooles*, or such like easie paine. — R. Brathwait, "Strappado for the Deuill," p. 193.

1842 The portraits of Victoria on our cotton-*spools*.—Lydia M. Child, "Letters from New York," p. 180. (Lond., 1843.)

1862 How much would a soldier have to pay for a *spool* of cotton in Richmond? If we were to take possession, ... [he] would have to pay twenty-five cents a *spool*.—Mr. Francis P. Blair of Mo., H. R., March 10: C. G., p. 1146/3.

1865 [The new tariff bill] is prohibitory in the simple article of *spool-cotton*.—Mr. James Brooks of N. Y., H. R., Feb. 16: Id., p. 842/1.

1870 There are two kinds of *spool cotton* made. There is a three-corded *spool cotton* and a six-corded *spool cotton*.—Mr. S. S. Cox of N. Y., H. R., Apr. 7: Id., p. 2512/1.

1883 [To place soldiers] in a position where the enemy could roll them up like a string upon a *spool*.—Mr. E. S. Bragg of Wisc., H. R., Feb. 15: C. R., p. 244/1, App.

Sport, Sportsman. One who pursues sports, especially of the field; one interested in sports, now especially for gambling; hence: a gambler; also, a flashy, cheap person. [1802-1878.]

1878 The other two were no doubt clever men, but comparatively ignorant, acting under the adroit and sleight-of-hand Stebbins, who could handle a ticket as a *sportsman* would a playing-card.—Mr. John T. Harris of Va., H. R., March 27: C R., p. 2093/1.

1892 "The *sports*," by which is meant those who like fast living.—*Contemporary Review*, liii, 228. (Century Dict.)

Spot cash, Spot cotton, etc. That which is to be paid or delivered at once. Thus **spot freight** is that which is to be "shipped" immediately, and **spot rate** is charged thereon.

1893 Mr. White:—I should like to ask what was the relative parity in price between *spot cotton* and future cotton. Mr. George:—In the New York market, without a single exception upon any one day, futures were sold lower than *spots*. Mr. White:—My question did not address itself to the relative price of *spots* and futures in the same month. . . . This year the *spot* market was depressed because of the controversy as to the size of the crop. . . . Speculators forced the *spot cotton* up, and forced the spinner to buy. Mr. George:— . . . . It is said that the sale of futures keeps up the price of *spots*. . . . [In fact, however,] futures are uniformly sold lower than *spots*.—U. S. Senate, Jan. 23: C. R., pp. 777-778.

1894 This bill would put the factories under the thumb of the men who will corner the *spot cotton*.—Mr. J. D. Warner of N. Y., H. R.,

June 18: *Id.*, p. 6488/1. [On pp. 6492-3 are the sales of "*Spot No. 2 red winter wheat*," from Jan. 1890 to May 1894.]

1900 Admiral Dewey found George Washington Aguinaldo a contented lounger at Hongkong, living in clover as the result of the transfer of his patriotism to Spain for *spot cash*.—Washington *Evening Star*, June 1: Cited in *C. R.*, p. 6499/1. [Aguinaldo's real first name was Emilio.]

1901 At the beginning of the season, *spot rates* on grain shipped to the United Kingdom were about $9 per ton.—*Yearbook U. S. Dept. of Agric.*, p. 579. (Century Dict.)

Spots, in. Partially.

1894 No man deserves the sacred name of Democrat who is only in favor of tariff reform *in spots*.—Mr. O. A. Wells of Wisc., H. R., Jan. 24: *C. R.*, p. 1348/2.

1894 I said a few minutes since that on this side we are tariff reformers *in spots*. On the other side they are free traders *in spots*.—Mr. Champ Clark of Mo., H. R., Jan. 24: *Id.*, p. 191/2, App.

Spreadeagle. A term applied to extravagant "high-falutin" oratory, especially patriotic or political speeches. [1858-1861.]

1876 John Adams was not ashamed to make Fourth-of-July orations,—orations which, if uttered today, would be sneered at as *spread-eagle* speeches.—Mr. C. H. Harrison of Ill., H. R., Jan. 19: *C. R.*, p. 503/2.

1877 Star-spangled banner and *spread-eagle speeches* do not . . . satisfy a suffering people.—Mr. H. P. Bell of Ga., H. R., Nov. 14: *Id.*, p. 401/1.

Spree. A frolic, a carousal, usually associated with drinking. Hence *going on a spree* or *spreeing* means "going on a drunk." [1834-1902.]

1850 He was a dissolute character, and had been *on a spree* for a week.—Wilmington (N. C.) *Commercial*, Sept. 10, p. 1/6.

1873 [The man] would go off and *spree it* for a week or two at a time.—Mr. J. W. Flanagan of Tex., U. S. Senate, March 3: *C. R.*, p. 2182/1.

1873 He was sent to the poor-house of Pulaski County, after a long drunken *spree*.—Mr. Powell Clayton of Ark., U. S. Senate, March 25: *Id.*, p. 192/1.

1882 He is accused . . . of being under the influence of drink, of being intoxicated, *on a spree*.—Mr. Sparks, H. R., Feb. 10: *Id.*, p. 1065/1.

1884 After he came home that night he told [his mother] that he had met a lot of boys, had *got on a spree* with them, and had voted the Democratic ticket.—Mr. J. F. Follett of O., H. R., May 27: *Id.*, p. 4584/1.

1896 There is no reason to doubt that [the man] got on "a bit of a *spree*," and was taken to the hospital.—Mr. B. Wood of Ill., H. R., May 14: *Id.*, p. 5268/1.

Spring-back tickets. Fraudulent voting-papers. See quotation.

1884 The committee were of opinion that these *spring-back tickets* . . . were as distinctly marked as if there were photographs of one or the other of the candidates on the ticket itself. . . . The Republican ticket [in Ind.] was printed upon a heavy material, called by many of the witnesses "card-board," but by persons engaged in the manufacture and sale of such material as "plate" or "Western plate," and by some of contestee's witnesses as heavy "book." Because of the extraordinary character of the material, and the tendency of the ticket to spring open when folded, thus facilitating double voting, the tickets became known as "cardboard" or "*spring-back*" tickets.—Mr. G. L. Converse of O., H. R., May 20: *C. R.*, pp. 410/2, 413/1, App.

Springhouse. A small building constructed over a spring or brook, where milk, fresh meat, etc., are placed in order to be kept cool. (Century Dict.)

1860　As I was a settin' in the *spring-house* . . . a-workin' my butter, I says to Dinah, "I'm goin' to carry a pot of this down to Miss Scudder."— Harriet B. Stowe, "The Minister's Wooing," ch. iv. (Century Dict.)

Spry. Lively, alert, active. [1789-1856.]

1872　Many young men like to become letter-carriers. While the labor is hard, it is performed by young men who are nimble and *spry*, and can run up and down stairs.—Mr. John F. Farnsworth of Ill., H. R., March 8 : *C. G.*, p. 1553/2.

Spunk. Courage, audacity, "grit." [1794-1860.]

1815　You have convinced me of your *spunk*.—David Humphreys, "The Yankey in England," p. 34.

Squantum. An annual festival observed near Boston is called the *Feast of Squantum*. [1812-1832.] In Vol. II, the quotation for 1832 gives a full description of this feast.

1879　We will take [the investigating committee] down to *Squantum* and treat them to a clam-bake.—Mr. Burnside of R. I., U. S. Senate, May 27 : *C. R.*, p. 1623/1.

Square. A city block, bounded by four streets. [1784-1859.]

1787　After . . . destroying a *square* of the principal houses and stores, [the fire at Richmond, Va.] abated.—"American News" in the *Gentleman's Magazine*, p. 266/2.

1862　These horse railroads carry passengers only a few *squares* as a general thing.—Mr.Thaddeus Stevens of Pa., H. R., Apr. 1 : *C. G.*, p. 1483/2.

Square. Used colloquially for *Squire*.

b.1600　The confusion of *squire* with *square* is more than 300 years old. "Do you know my lady's foot by the *squire*?"—"Love's Labour's Lost," II. v.

Square. Full, fair, complete. Often "fair and square." See Vol. II, **Square meal**, etc. [1854-1909.]

1596　While they continued *square* play, he was no looser.—"Greenes Groatsworth of Wit," D4 (1617).

1864　The Senate has declined upon a *square* vote to raise the salaries of the Assistant Secretaries.—Mr. T. A. Hendricks of Ind., U. S. Senate, June 27 : *C. G.*, p. 3301-2.

1869　An honest, *square* proceeding by men at the head of these two great railroads would have linked their names with immortality.—Mr. James W. Nye of Nev., U. S. Senate, Apr. 6 : *Id.*, p. 549/3.

1874　I do not think there is much in the phrase that we have heard here as coming from the people, that they demand *a square repeal*.—Mr. A. I. Boreman of W. Va., U. S. Senate, Jan. 9 : *C. R.*, p. 516/1.

1875　Make it till half past five : that will make *square hours*.—Mr. G. F. Edmunds of Vt., U. S. Senate, March 20 : *Id.*, p. 107/1.

1876　If [Mr. Edmunds] does not like to vote *square* against [this bill or for it], this is the right way to defeat it. . . . I would rather see it defeated in a *square fight*.—Mr. John A. Logan of Ill., U. S. Senate, July 5 : *Id.*, p. 4397/1.

1877　Give me a *square* answer. Say what salary was reduced.—Mr. C. Foster of O., H. R., Feb. 2 : *Id.*, p. 1217/1.

1880　I believe I could do some *square work* but for this chasing for spoils.— Mr. Edwin Willits of Mich., H. R., June 15 : *Id.*, p. 258/1, App.

1892　[We are here to compose difficulties], if not by compromise, then by the *square* defeat of somebody and the honorable submission of the other side.—Mr. J. R. Hawley of Conn., U. S. Senate, June 30 : *Id.*, p. 5658/2.

Squarely. Fully, plainly, honestly. To *meet squarely* is to meet "face-to-face," without dodging or evasion. [1860.]

1865　I do not think we shall ever get rid of [the question] until we repeal fishing bounties *squarely*.—Mr. Lyman Trumbull of Ill., U. S. Senate, March 1 : *C. G.*, p. 1252/2.

1872 The late rebellion was nominally a defense of liberty, but really a defense of slavery; and, until this truth was recognized, the issue was not *squarely* made, or the battles *squarely* fought.—Mr. C. W. Willard of Vt., H. R., Apr. 17: *Id.*, p. 2512/1.

1879 He [was] sitting at a point from which the clock is not very *squarely* visible.—Mr. Roscoe Conkling of N. Y., U. S. Senate, May 20: *C. R.*, p. 1482/2.

Squash. The fruit of any of several vines (genus *Cucurbita*) of the cucumber family. (Webster.) [1683-1821.]

1715 *Squash,* a little Creature in *America,* somewhat resembling an *Ichneumon*: Also a Fruit growing in those parts, much like a Pumpion.— Kersey, "Dictionarium Anglo-Britannicum."

Squatter. A person settling on land without a legal title. Under acts of Congress, bona fide squatters on Western lands became **Preëmptors,** q.v. [1809-1857.]

1829 The place where we made fast was a wooding station, owned by what is called a *Squatter,* a person who, without any title to the land, or leave asked or granted, squats himself down and declares himself the lord and master of the soil for the time being.—Basil Hall, "Travels in N. America," II, 297. (Century Dict.)

1870 If there is one term more than another which is opprobrious to our people, one term that would be distasteful to the Western settler, whether pre-emptioner, homestead settler, or miner, it is the term "*squatter*." It is a term which we use to express our contempt for those men who encroach upon the property of their neighbors, who refuse to work for themselves, but, in mining parlance, "jump" the lands which others have improved.—Mr. A. A. Sargent of Calif., H. R., March 23: *C. G.*, p. 2173/3.

1875 Mr. Edmunds:—I understand [that these men] were *squatters* in the very strongest sense of the term. Mr. Sargent:—The Senator will allow me to say that I do not know the distinction in my State between a settler and a *squatter*. . . . As far as my State is concerned, we have nothing applying to that class of people which would make an opprobrious term proper in reference to them. Mr. Edmunds:—I do not know that "*squatter*" is an opprobrious term. If it is, I withdraw it.—U. S. Senate, Feb. 20: *C. R.*, p. 1536/1.

Squatter sovereignty. A term applied to the doctrine advocated by Stephen A. Douglas, that the territories shall settle the slavery question for themselves; but sometimes used more widely. The term originated with John C. Calhoun. [1855-1884.]

1865 After voting to apply the Missouri line to Texas, [Mr. Douglas] finally adopted the position of popular sovereignty, or *Squatter Sovereignty* as it was called, leaving the people of each Territory to settle the question of slavery for themselves. In accordance with this principle, he caused the repeal of the Missouri Compromise.—Mr. Isaac N. Arnold of Ill., H. R., Feb. 20: *C. G.*, p. 70/1, App.

Squaw man. A white man who has married a squaw.

1878 When you have deducted the pay of agents, interpreters, *squaw-men*. and other expenses, there will be but a small balance left. . . . I would not let your agents and interpreters and *squaw-men* go on as they have gone. . . . There is an army of interpreters, *squaw-men*. speculators.—Mr. H. B. Wright of Pa., H. R., Dec. 19: *C. R.*, pp. 316-17.

1888 Nowadays those who live among and intermarry with the Indians are looked down upon by the other frontiersmen, who contemptuously term them *squawmen*.—Theodore Roosevelt in the *Century Mag.*, xxxvi, 832.

1895 That class consists . . . of the Indians in whose veins the white blood largely predominates, and of the "*squaw men*," as they are commonly called.—Mr. John S. Little of Ark,. H. R., Jan. 15: *C. R.*, p. 997/1.

Squaw winter. A short period of cold weather preceding the Indian summer, or else occurring after the spring has set in.

1901   *Squaw winter* is giving us a good long visit.—*Seneca County Courier*, Nov. 21. (Dial. Notes, II, vi.) .

1903   We have had *squaw winter*; now we look for Indian summer.—*Ithaca* (N. Y.) *Journal*, Nov. 16. (*Id.*)

1907   Kingston, Ont., April 8. This morning people awoke to find themselves in the midst of *squaw winter*, some 3 inches of soft snow having fallen during the night.—Toronto *Daily Star*.

Squeteague. ˝The Narraganset name for the weakfish or sea-trout.

Squire. A magistrate or justice. The term is often used loosely. See also **Square.** [1784-1854.]

1699   A Piscattaway Indian known by the name of *Esqre Tom.*—Journal of House of Burgesses, Va., May 10: Vol. IV, 158. (Richmond, 1913.)

Squirm. To twist about with contortions like an eel or a worm; wriggle; writhe. (Webster.) [1804-1867.]

1870   [I. think that Senators] were rather inclined to *squirm* and equivocate in their answers [on the Georgia question].—Mr. Carl Schurz of Mo., U. S. Senate, March 18: *C. G.*, p. 2064/1.

1874   I have noticed a peculiar sort of *squirming* on the part of the Republicans in this House. They dodge responsibility.—Mr. S. S. Cox of N. Y., H. R., May 20: *C. R.*, p. 4107/1.

1897   Whenever any attempt is made to abolish trusts, you Republicans *squirm* like skinned eels in a hot skillet.—Mr. Champ Clark of Mo., U. S. Senate, March 31: *Id.*, p. 551/2.

Squirrel hunters. See quotation.

1873   [Late in 1862] Ohio sent out several thousands of what they called "*squirrel hunters*" along the shores of the Ohio River, to protect Cincinnati and the State from invasion.—Mr. James A. Garfield of O., H. R., Jan. 18: *C. G.*, p. 695/1.

Stake and rider fence. A fence made with crossed stakes and rails laid on them, the highest of which is the "rider." [1829-1839.]

1877   *Staked and ridered fences*, tangled underwood, gullies, etc.—G. W. Bagby, "Writings," I, 12. (1884.)

Stake out. To mark the boundaries of land by driving stakes into the ground. Cf. Vol. II, **Stakes, to pull up.** [1841.]

1888   The modest Northerners who have got hold of [Fla.] and *staked* it all *out* into city lots, seem to want to keep it all to themselves.—Chas. D. Warner, "Their Pilgrimage," p. 49. (Century Dict.)

1889   When [he] disbanded his men, he had not only found a large number of . . . monuments, . . . but he left the ground chronologically *staked out.*—*Century Mag.*, xxxix, 333.

Stakes, to drive. To settle down; the converse of "to pull up stakes."

1906   Well, after drifting about several years I finally *drove stakes* on the Spokane River. I carried people across and kept a general store.— G. Morris, in *Outing*, p. 605. (Century Dict.)

Stalwarts. The followers of Roscoe Conkling in the political campaign of 1878-1879; uncompromising Republicans generally. [1881-1888.]

1879   [Mr. Garfield] was not a *stalwart* last session, but [he] is a sword-and-buckler *stalwart* now.—Mr. Thomas Ewing of O., H. R., Apr. 27: *C. R.*, p. 75/1, App.

1879   See COWBOY.

1879   It is but a little while ago since a confederate brigadier first took part in the control of public affairs. He was invited to do so by the candidate of the *stalwarts* for the next presidency, General Grant. Grant appointed Brigadier-General Amos T. Akerman, of Ga., to a seat in his cabinet.—Mr. D. W. Voorhees of Ind., U. S., Senate, June 18: *Id.*, p. 2118/2.

1879 I saw a great company of *stalwarts* approaching. And the big *stalwarts* from Ohio, New York, and Maine, cried out, "Revolution, treason, rebel conspiracy, and starvation of the Government." And all the little *stalwarts* clapped their hands with joy.—Mr. J. W. Caldwell of Ky., H. R., Apr. 26: *Id.*, p. 89/2, App.

1881 See SOLID SOUTH.

1881 All I ask is to pair my colleague with a republican, with one of the *stalwarts* in front of you, either of the three, the Senator from Illinois (Mr. Logan), the Senator from Iowa (Mr. Allison), or the Senator from Kansas (Mr. Ingalls).—Mr. Jas. B. Beck of Ky., U. S. Senate, Apr. 13: *C. R.*, p. 282/1.

Stampede. A rush of panic-stricken cattle; hence, of persons. [1846-1861.]

1850 A general *stampede* occurred [among the guests].—Wilmington (N. C.) *Commercial*, Aug. 17, p. 4/2. (From the N. O. *Delta.*)

1863 At the first ring of the bell a general *stampede* took place; some twenty hungry souls rushed to the dining-room.—Louisa M. Alcott, "Hospital Sketches," p. 63. (Century Dict.)

1868 Something scared [the cattle], and they began going round and round, and piling in, as cattle will, making a perfect *stampede.*—Mr. P. G. Van Winkle of W. Va., U. S. Senate, July 21: *C. G.*, p. 4284/3.

1876 See CORRAL.

1882 See BUCK.

1893 A successful draw in the Louisiana lottery throws from their poise a hundred men, and *stampedes* a community.—Mr. Marriott Brosius of Pa., H. R., March 1: *C. R.*, p. 70/2, App.

Stamping ground. The place of man's exploits. [1839-1853.]

1887 The District of Columbia ... is a sort of national *"stamping ground."* —Mr. Barbour, H. R., Feb. 12: *C. R.*, p. 1749/1.

Stand in with. To have influence with; to associate with powerful men, more or less secretly, for the sake of profit. Slang.

1894 [He] ought to be a Republican under a Republican administration, so as to *"stand in"* with the authorities.—Mr. B. A. Enloe of Tenn., H. R., July 13: *C. R.*, 7439/1.

Stand pat. Standpatter. To stand pat, in politics, is to adhere unflinchingly to a high tariff; hence, to adhere firmly to any opinion. [1908.]

1896 Mr. J. G. Cannon:—That proposition was fought bitterly in the House; but the Senate *stood*, if the gentlemen will allow me the expression, *pat*; ... and they had their own way, because no bill can pass without an agreement between the two houses. Mr. G. L. Johnson of Calif.:—I understand the explanation made by the gentleman from Illinois, with the single exception of some technical, abstruse term which he used, but which I suppose is well understood in Illinois, though unfamiliar in California. I will ask the gentleman however why should not the House *"stand pat,"* as the Senate did? Mr. Cannon:—O ·no: It was invented in California and put into the dictionary there.—H. R., Feb. 28: *Id.*, p. 2268/1-2.

1911 It is surely the oddest of paradoxes that dubs as *"standpatters"* party leaders who are apparently suspected of disloyalty to the old-time, third-party candidate, and confers the name of insurgent upon those who stand unwaveringly by the party traditions.—*Id.*, Dec. 14, p. 4/1.

1912 "Gov. Harmon is either a *standpatter* or a progressive. He cannot be both," says Mr. Bryan. Yet that is just what the overwhelming majority of American citizens actually are. Whole-hog *standpatters* are about as scarce as whole-hog progressives. Most of us are *standpatters* on some things, and progressives on others. This is true even of distinguished progressive leaders. Gov. Wilson, for example, is a *standpatter* on the tenure of judges, a progressive on workmen's compensation and kindred subjects, and a mitigated progressive on the initiative and referendum. Mr. Bryan himself, who was once a mighty progressive on government ownership of railroads, looks now wonderfully like a *standpatter* on that subject, seeing that even "ultimate" ownership has apparently ceased to interest him.—*Id.*, Jan. 1, p. 4/2.

Standing round. Great activity; or conversely, excessive inactivity. See Vol. II, **Stand around.** [1840-1853.]

1878 As one witness in the eighteenth ward [of the city of Boston] said, "they [the supervisors] did the heavy *standing round*."—Mr. M. A. Candler of Ga., H. R., March 15: *C. R.*, p. 1792/2. [I.e. they only looked on.]

Stand the racket. To endure stress or strain; also, to withstand investigation. [1830-1834.]

1882 He is as ready as myself to *stand the racket* of subsequent proceedings. —*Daily Tel.*, Sept. 8. (Encycl. Dict.)

1895 Your national banks throughout the country failed to the number of 150, while only one bank in the State of Mississippi failed, and that was a national bank. All the other banks in that state "*stood the racket*" and maintained their credit during that terrible panic [of 1893].—Mr. C. E. Hooker of Miss., H. R., Feb. 7: *C. R.*, p. 1909/2.

Star bid, Star route, Star service. An agreement to carry the whole mail on a certain route for a stated sum of money. The Star Route prosecutions for conspiracy furnished large material for the newspapers in 1881-1882. [1854-1882.]

1876 The increase in steamboat service will be $21,974, while the decrease in what is known as the *star-route* service will be $41,745, making a reduction on the expenditures of last year for steamboat and *star-route* service of a little rising $19,000.—Mr. Holman of Ind., H. R., May 12: *C. R.*, p. 3050/2.

1877 Most of us are interested in the *star service*. It is a service that does not yield much, and is a very expensive service to the Government, while the revenues of the Department are principally yielded by those sections of the country through which the trunk lines run.—Mr. Joseph G. Cannon of Ill., H. R., March 3: *Id.*, p. 2224/1.

1877 [The purpose of this amendment] is to appropriate $700,000 for the *star service*, by which is understood post-routes outside of steamboats and railroad lines. In other words, to carry the mail on horseback or by stage.—Mr. A. H. Smith of Pa., H. R., Nov. 21: *Id.*, p. 590/2.

1880 The *star service* is the poor man's mail; it penetrates the most remote sections; and . . . I shall resist any attempt to cripple it.—Mr. Emory Speer of Ga., H. R., Jan. 27: *Id.*, p. 548/2.

Stars and bars, the. The flag of the Confederate States.

1870 [After the battle of Bull Run in 1861] it was a question of doubt in many minds whether the stars and stripes might not be torn from their place above the Speaker's chair, and Jefferson Davis occupy that chair with the "*stars and bars*" above him.—Mr. W. Townsend of Pa., H. R., June 8: *C. G.*, p. 4231/2.

1871 I am willing to bury the [Confederate] gray and the *stars and bars*, and that their friends shall drop their tears on their graves.—Mr. W. Warner of Ala., U. S. Senate, March 3: *Id.*, p. 276/3, App.

1876 A new generation has sprung up, and at a not far distant day there will be "*stars and bars*" floating proudly over our sunny South.—Address attributed to Rev. Taylor Martin, of Charlotte, N. C., May 5: See *C. R.*, Aug. 4, 5183/1.

1877 The bravest men that ever I saw under the "*stars and bars*" were Union men until after the battles of the war began.—Mr. Francis M. Cockrell of Mo., U. S. Senate. March 3: *Id.*, p. 2200/2.

1894 No man who fought under the *"stars and bars"* and failed has a word to say against giving deserved pensions to those brave men who succeeded under the Stars and Stripes.—Mr. B. E. Russell of Ga., H. R., March 7: *Id.*, p. 2689/2.

1896 See OLD GLORY.

Stars and Stripes. The flag of the United States.

1884 I wish to see the men who carried our flag into a foreign land, who planted the *Stars and Stripes* upon the Halls of the Montezumas, . . . I wish to see them pensioned.—Mr. F. L. Wolford of Ky., H. R., June 27: *C. R.*, p. 5711/2.

Star Spangled Banner, The. The United States flag.

1894 Whenever an old soldier of the Confederacy comes up loyally to the support of the *Star Spangled Banner,* he will find the hand of fellowship extended to him.—Mr. G. W. Ray of N. Y., H. R., June 15: *C. R.*, p. 6385/2.

Starter. A beginning; an entering wedge.

1895 [Mr. Bowers] says that this bill will not cost over $40,000 a year. That is only a *starter.* It will grow as the years go by.—Mr. Champ Clark of Mo., H. R., Feb. 18: *C. R.*, p. 2350/2.

1898 I suggest this reduction of one cent per pound as a *starter*, and I ask the friends of economy to support it.—Mr. J. C. McRae of Ark., H. R., Feb. 5: *Id.*, p. 1476/1.

Statehood. Condition or character of being a State. (Webster.)

1885 This question is one not of breaking into or breaking out of the Union, but breaking into *Statehood* without the consent of Congress.—Mr. G. G. Vest of Mo., U. S. Senate, Dec. 18: *C. R.*, p. 303/1.

1888 You are not capable of self-government, unworthy of *Statehood.*—Mr. C. S. Baker of N. Y., H. R., May 24: *Id.*, p. 4598/2.

States, The. A term at one time much used in the Far West, distinguishing the organized States from the territories. [1826-1890.]

1872 The only defensible policy . . . upon which the building of a railroad from *"the States,"* as they call it, to the Pacific coast . . . must rest.—Mr. W. E. Niblack of Ind., H. R., March 7: *C. G.*, p. 1519/3.

Stave, v. To proceed rapidly. [1825.]

1872 I should run as hard as I could *stave.*—G. W. Bagby, "Writings," II, 244. (1885.)

Stay-at-homes. The Century Dict. refers to Mrs. Gaskell's "Sylvia's Lovers," 1863, ch. ix. The word was used as a term of reproach for those who did not personally engage in the Civil War.

1867 This is simply a question whether the *stay-at-homes*, political sluggards, sullen rebels, men who never take any interest in an election, and never go to an election, can defeat the work of reconstruction.—Mr. Oliver P. Morton of Ind., U. S. Senate, March 16: *C. G.*, p. 147/3.

1868 Those who have been in arms against the Government, or given aid and comfort to the enemy, and all those who sympathized with such enemies, being what we call the *"stay-at-home"* or "do-nothing" rebels, are disfranchised.—Mr. John F. Benjamin of Mo., H. R., July 16: *Id.*, p 4125/2.

Stay law. A law stopping, or more usually suspending procedure or execution.

1874 I believe it was once held that a *stay-law* passed after a note was given could not affect that debt . . .; but where the law is passed before the debt is created, a *stay-law* is good in every State.—Mr. Oliver P. Morton of Ind., U. S. Senate. Feb. 5: *C. R.*, p. 1226/1.

1894 Were it not for the *stay law* of Dakota, she would be moved down, body, soul, and breeches, sheep and all and turned over to the manufacturers of Connecticut and Massachusetts under foreclosure of contract of mortgage.—Mr. O. A. Wells of Wisc., H. R., Jan. 24: *Id.*, p. 1349/1.

Steady habits. "The land of steady habits" is New England, and especially Connecticut. [1781-1853.]

1864 Connecticut, the *"land of steady habits,"* where I was born, reared, and educated, a capital State to be reared and educated in, if, as Douglas said of Vermont, "one emigrated early," was not free from the "sin of slavery." She turned many an "honest penny" in the traffic.—Mr. Law of Ind., H. R., July 1: *C. G.,* p. 3477/3.

Steal, n. A theft or robbery.

1872 I speak irrespective of party, and to those gentlemen who [call this appropriation] a swindle or a *steal.*—Mr. Dwight Townsend of N. Y., H. R., May 21: *C. G.,* p. 3677/2.

1878 [They have been] endeavoring to get me not to resist this *steal* from Mexico . . . The air is full of the cries of men who are laboring for this *steal.*—Mr. J. R. Chalmers of Miss., H. R., June 4: *C. R.,* p. 4112/1.

1883 Individual members [were abused] as "jobbers" and participants in a *"steal."*—Mr. H. S. Harris of N. J., H. R., Feb. 28: *Id.,* p. 305/1, App.

1883 How many "little *steals*," if I may be pardoned for using that expression, may be found hereafter lurking in the new [tariff] classifications, no one can now predict.—Mr. W. M. Springer of Ill., H. R., March 3: *Id.,* p. 3731/1.

1885 [Mr. Hancock] says that I have found a *"steal"* in this pending bill. In the remarks that I made I said nothing about a *steal.*—Mr. J. R. Thomas of Ill., H. R., Feb. 28: *Id.,* p. 2314/2.

1893 A regular *steal* it was, the most colossal in all history. [The seating of President Hayes.]—Mr. B. E. Russell of Ga., H. R., Oct. 5: *Id.,* p. 2163/1.

1895 [Senator Chandler] did make that statement about my being concerned in a *"steal"* or "robbery." He did it in a polite sort of way. He charges men with crimes, and says he meant no offense; he charges men with being engaged in a *steal,* and then wonders why they should be at all disturbed.—Mr. David B. Hills of N. Y., U. S. Senate, Feb. 28: *Id.,* p. 2928/1.

1912 [President Gomez] has been openly charged with corruption by a large section of the Havana press, and there is no question that *"steals"* of a kind to make Tammany's mouth water have been easily slipped through Congress [in Cuba.]—*N. Y. Evening Post,* June 10, p. 4/6.

Steep. Extravagant in price or amount. [1856-a.1872.]

1865 They replied, three dollars the hog. He rejoined, "That is rather *steep,"* to which they said, "That is the best we can do," and the matter was dropped.—Mr. Garrett Davis of Ky., U. S. Senate, Feb. 27: *C. G.,* p. 1131/3.

Stepmother State, The. Massachusetts. See quotation.

1878 These events greatly increased the bitterness between the District [of Maine] and the *"Stepmother State,"* as Massachusetts came to be humorously termed; and after the peace of 1815 the agitation for independence proceeded with increased force.—Remarks of Mr. Blaine on the presentation of the statue of Wm. King: *C. R.,* Jan. 22, p. 457/1.

Stick, a good. A fast rate of speed.

1830 "He whirls [the coach] away at *a pretty good stick,"* said another.—*Am. Beacon,* Sept. 11, p. 4/3. (From the N. Y. *Constellation.*)

Stick a pin there. Make a note of that; "nota bene." [1836-1861.]

1821 *Sticking a pin there,* it is a fact that such a petition was presented.—Cobbett's *Weekly Register,* Sept. 15, col. 586.

1848 [The editor of the *Journal*] *"sticks a pin"* upon the assertion. This is a favorite expression of the *Journal,* and if he continues to *stick a pin* into all his political fibs, he will not have a pin left to stick into the truth.—Wilmington (N. C.) *Commercial*, Aug. 31, p. 2/1.

1850 Yesterday every one of Benton's annoying resolutions [was] voted down by the Senate. ☞ *Stick a pin there.*—Wilmington (N. C.) *Commercial*, Apr. 25, p. 2/1.

Stickers. The same as **Pasters**, q.v.

1878 Reference is made to what are called "*stickers*" or "pasters" in the ballot-boxes, these being . . . blank pieces of paper, or pieces of paper with names on them, which have been pasted or stuck over the names of candidates upon the ticket in order to change a vote. . . They argue . . . that "*stickers*" or "pasters" must have fallen off the ballots after the first count. . . In this case . . . there were no loose "*stickers*" or "pasters" found.—Mr. Jacob D. Cox of O., H. R., March 27: *C. R.*, pp. 2082-3. [See the rest of the debate.]

1890 Where was that "*sticker*" stuck? Was it not upon the words "For Congress?"—Mr. B. H. Compton of Md., H. R., March 19: *Id.*, p. 2394/1.

Stiff. A corpse. Slang.

1879 Over 8,000 of those on the Philadelphia list were myths, "*stiffs*," men of the grave-yard, whose names were used by repeaters and person-ators.—Mr. S. S. Cox of N. Y., H. R., Apr. 17: *C. R.*, p. 79/2, App.

Still hunt. One conducted with secrecy.

1897 This bill . . . has been defeated twice. It seems now that somebody is on a "*still hunt*," and is endeavoring to triumph through such methods. But the people are awake.—Mr. A. J. Cummings of N. Y., H. R., Jan. 5: *C. R.*, p. 480/1.

Stillhunt, v. To hunt quietly and cautiously.

1885 The only way to get [a grizzly bear] is to put on moccasins and *still-hunt* it in its own haunts.—Theodore Roosevelt, "Hunting Trips," p. 327. (Century Dict.)

Stived up. Choked up, crowded together; confused. [1851-1853.]

1851 "Things are a good deal *stived up*," answered the Deacon: "People's minds are sour, and I don't know what we can do."—S. Judd, "Margaret," ii, 8. (Century Dict.)

Stocking feet. Feet with stockings, but without shoes. [1829-1902.]

1863 The neighboring patients must move in their *stocking feet.*—Walt Whitman, "Specimen Days" (1887), p. 72.

1894 [Before I would cut down the appropriation for schoolhouses,] I would wear a farmer's frock, and linsey-woolsey and moccasins, or go in my *stocking feet.*—Mr. J. H. Walker of Mass., H. R., March 9: *C. R.*, p. 2791/2.

Stoga, Stogy. An abbreviation of Conestoga; rough farmers' shoes. [1847-1853.]

1884 He went down to the store, got a pair of *stoga boots*, put on overalls, and went out among farmers as a common cow-doctor.—Mr. E. K. Valentine of Neb., H. R., Feb. 26: *C. R.*, p. 1407/1.

Stogy. A cigar of low quality.

1917 [In Paraguay] brown maidens . . . sat with a half-smoked *stogy* in a corner of their mouths, and now and then spat through their teeth like New York toughs.—H. A. Franck, "Vagabonding Down the Andes," p. 604. (Century Co.)

Stoop. A porch, properly one with benches on each side. Dutch. [1749-1908.]

1842 Neighbours went to each others' "*stoops*," to spend a social evening.—Lydia M. Child, "Letters from New York," p. 182. (Lond., 1843.)

Stop. A weir.

What they called *stops* . . . were in effect wears or Kidels.—Hawkins, in Walton's "Compleat Angler." (Century Dict.)

1772 The erecting Mill Dams, and setting Fish Hedges and *Stops* across the said Rivers.—Journal, House of Burgesses of Virginia, March 21, p. 262. (Richmond, 1906.)

Stop-off, Stop-over. The breaking of a railroad journey, with the privilege of proceeding by a later train.

1904 If a sufficient number join the station and desire the organization of a party to make the trip together, such organization will be undertaken, and the trip will be made by one of the . . . routes with the usual *stop-offs* in the mountains.—*Science*, Apr. 22, p. 676. (Century Dict.)

Store clothes. Those purchased at a store, not homespun. [1818-1890.]

1896 Accustomed to see men clad exclusively in *store clothes*, and judging men entirely by their garb, himself arrayed in a dude costume, . . . the average pension examiner . . . writes down all these homespun people as frauds.—Mr. H. R. Gibson of Tenn., H. R., Feb. 29: *C. R.*, p. 2310/1.

Stovepipe hat. One of the conventional type, so called from its resemblance to a short section of a stovepipe. [1855-1890.]

1869 What a beautiful sight it would be to see an Indian walking about, wearing a *stove-pipe hat* before he has got on his breeches, the *stove-pipe hat* having been furnished to him by this Gentleman from Dakota! —Mr. John A. Logan of Ill., H. R., Feb. 27: *C. G.*, p. 1708/1.

1870 Some gentleman high in authority sweeps by in his splendid phaeton, behind a spanking span of thoroughbreds, driven by a flunky dressed in a drab overcoat and a *stove-pipe hat* with a silver buckle in front of it almost as big as a garden gate.—Mr. J. P. Knott of Ky., H. R., May 20: *Id.*, p. 363/3, App.

1880 See CLAWHAMMER.

Stove up. Broken to pieces; ruined. See Vol. II, **Stove.** [1819-1837.]

1894 I want to tell you how [John] Morgan traded horses. . . He took the Kentucky thoroughbreds and rode them until they got *stove up*, and then he dropped them.—Mr. Champ Clark of Mo., H. R., Dec. 11: *C. R.*, p. 3/2, App.

Straddle. To occupy the fence with regard to a disputed matter.

1884 The platform [of the Ohio Democrats] contains the well-known plank, *straddling* the tariff question, which has appeared in previous Democratic platforms.—*The Nation* (N. Y.) July 3, p. 4. (Century Dict.)

Straddlebug. A species of tumblebug. [1853-1862.]

1879 Out in the woods for a good time. Cloth spread on the greensward, crickets and *straddlebugs* hopping and crawling over sandwiches and everything else.—*St. Nicholas*, xvii, 12, advt. (Century Dict.)

Straight ticket. The regular ticket as issued. See **Scratch a ticket** and **Split tickets.** [1862.]

1870 I do not suppose that ten per cent of the members of this body have voted what is called a *straight ticket* for a great number of years.— Mr. Eugene Casserly of Calif., U. S. Senate, May 24: *C. G.*, p. 3761/1.

Straight whisky. Unmixed, unqualified; unadulterated. "Table whiskies," Bourbon and rye are called "straight."

1864 From the impassioned tone of the gentleman from Illinois [Mr. Washburne] one would suppose that he had been investing in whisky *straight*, but such is not the fact, I am happy to state.—Mr. Morrill of Vt., H. R., Apr. 21: *C. G.*, p. 1786/2.

1867 Old drinkers, I believe, do not indulge in grog, but take whisky *straight*.—Mr. Samuel McKee of Ky., H. R., Jan. 21: *Id.*, p. 60/1, App.

1880 Why should this artificial process be more favored than the natural process through which *straight whisky* is made marketable?—Mr. A. S. Willis of Ky., H. R., Apr. 28: *C. R.*, p. 2843/1.

1894 They can blend with 3 or 4 barrels of neutral` spirits a barrel of *straight whisky*, . . . give it somewhat the taste of *straight whisky*, and impose it upon the public as *straight whisky.*—Mr. Wm. Lindsay of Ky., U. S. Senate, June 28: *Id.*, p. 6948/1. ℭ

1896 You can not now go into a saloon . . . and purchase a bottle of whisky, and drink it feeling assured that it is *straight* whisky.—Mr. D. G. Colson of Ky., H. R., May 18: *Id.*, p. 5379/1.

Streaked. Disconcerted, frightened, annoyed; probably "hot and cold." [1834-1878.]

1815 The good, gracious Suzz! how *streaked* I feel all over!—David Humphreys, "The Yankey in England," p. 57.

1878 The doctor felt sort o' *streaked* at fust when they told the story on him.—Mrs. Harriet B. Stowe in the *Atlantic Monthly*, Oct., p. 474/2.

Street, The. Wall Street, New York. [1870.]

1888 Mr. Cisco apprised *"the Street"* of the instructions he had received from Washington concerning the empty condition of the Treasury.— Henry Clews, "Twenty-Eight Years in Wall Street," p. 39. (N. Y.)

Strict constructionist. One who seeks by construction to narrow the operation of the Federal Constitution as it affects States' rights. [1841-1865.]

1866 [President Andrew Johnson] is a Democrat, a *strict constructionist*, a State-rights man in the just and reasonable interpretation of that term.—Mr. Dumont of Ind., H. R., March 17: *C. G.*, p. 1475/2.

1866 [The late Senator Wright of N. J.] believed that a *strict* as distinguished from what was termed a liberal construction of the Constitution of the United States, and a liberal as distinguished from a *strict construction* of the rights reserved to the States and the people by that Constitution, was not only conducive to the harmonious operation of both Governments, but absolutely necessary to their continuing existence.—Mr. A. G. Cattell of N. J., U. S. Senate, Dec. 17: *Id.*, p. 149/2.

1874 Jefferson, a *strict constructionist*, could find no power in the Constitution for the purchase of Louisiana. But he took it, and let others hunt for the "power." They have not found it yet.—Mr. J. R. Hawley of Conn., H. R., May 7: *C. R.*, p. 257/2, App.

1888 Among all the great statesmen of the past, Jefferson was regarded as the strictest of the *strict constructionists* of our Constitution.—Mr. A. P. Hovey of Ind., H. R., Apr. 20: *Id.*, p. 3172/1.

Strike a place, or a man. To reach, to arrive at; to meet, to encounter. [1798-1910.]

b. 1813 We . . *struck* the Ohio River at Wheeling.—"Journal of Peggy Dow," p. 214/2 (1851).

1865 Coming down Four-and-a-half street, . . . I *struck* the Sergeant-at-Arms, or rather the Sergeant-at-Arms *struck* me.—Mr. A. Myers of Pa., H. R., Feb. 9: *C. G.*, p. 703/2-3.

1877 When General Gibbon *struck* the Nez Perces, if he [had] only had a hundred more men, he could have ended that war then and there.— Mr. Martin Maginnis of Mont., H. R., Nov. 9: *C. R.*, p. 323/2.

1878 He said they would *strike* the Gulf Stream and cross it, before they got abreast of Norfolk, [Va.]—Mr. M. C. Butler of S. C., U. S. Senate, June 5: *Id.*, p. 4142/1.

1881 John Smith in the early days of Virginia history took a row-boat and went up the Chickahominy, expecting to *strike* the Pacific Ocean. He never *struck* it. He *struck* Pocahontas, who took him back to Jamestown.—Mr. S. S. Cox of N. Y., H. R., Feb. 15: *Id.*, p. 1658/1.

1886 He discovers in conversation with him, that he "knew more about levees than any man he ever *struck*."—Mr. J. M. Browne of Ind., H. R., June 4: *Id.*, p. 5253/1.

1890   The gentleman from Texas [Mr. Mills] reached the climax when he *struck* rye.—Mr. S. E. Payne of N. Y., H. R., May 9: *Id.*, p. 4400/1.

1890   We understand that the water comes rapidly down [the Potomac] until it *strikes* tide water here at Georgetown.—Mr. J. H. Reagan of Tex., U. S. Senate, Aug. 8: *Id.*, p. 8317/2.

1893   If [Mr. Morse] would come to Utah and meet some of the men born, educated, and brought up there, he would feel that he had *struck* a country in which he was in reality a tenderfoot, and had something to learn.—Mr. J. L. Rawlins of Utah, H. R., Dec. 12: *Id.*, p. 179/1.

1895   See FIREWATER.

1914   "A returned exile," writing to *The Times*, July 3, about country inns, mentions one which he found excellent. "But [he says] I *struck* one drawback."

Strike breakers. Men hired to take the place of strikers, with a view to defeating the strike. **Strike,** to quit work in order to obtain or resist a change in conditions of employment. (Webster.)

1913   [The Company] promptly filled the town of Tucker and the deep and narrow canyon in which the work is being done with a force of armed thugs, gunmen, scabherders and professional *strike breakers.—Industrial Worker* (Spokane, Wash.), July 3.

Strike it rich To find a rich vein or deposit of ore; hence, to meet with any great financial good fortune. (Webster.)

1890   Men will take the most desperate chances, travel hundreds of miles into the wilderness on the strength of a mere rumor, incur great expense and labor for years in prospecting barren ground, vainly hoping sooner or later to *"strike it rich."*—Mr. H. F. Bartine of Nev., H. R., June 7: *C. R.*, p. 5797/1.

Strike oil. To find petroleum when boring for it; also, the same as "strike it rich." [1867-1909.]

1892   See SOFT THING.

String, without a. Without qualification, modification, or drawback.

1897   In principle and practice . . . I am a free trader *without any string to it.*—Mr. Jerry Simpson of Kan., H. R., March 25: *C. R.*, p. 274/2.

Stripe. Sort, kind, type. [1853-1862.]

1866   The *Memphis Avalanche* and the *Richmond Enquirer* [and other papers] are *all of a stripe,* and seek the same end.—Mr. E. C. Ingersoll of Ill., H. R., May 5: *C. G.*, p. 2406/2.

1867   The President [Andrew Johnson] will send men here only of a particular political *stripe.*—Mr. Timothy O. Howe of Wisc., U. S. Senate, Apr. 11: *Id.*, p. 830/1.

1872   If we open the civil service to examination, men of all *stripes* and hues of party may come in for examination.—Mr. Seth Wakeman of N. Y., H. R., Feb. 3: *Id.*, p. 808/2.

1874   Our anterevolutionist fathers were republicans of the right *stripe.* They fought eight years, not so much against oppression as for an idea.—Mr. L. V. Bogy of Mo., U. S. Senate, Apr. 20: *C. R.*, p. 3190/1.

1892   See CALAMITY HOWLER.

1893   I do not quite agree with the parties on either side of the House. I do not agree with the unometallists of the gold *stripe,* nor with the unometallists of the silver *stripe;* for I am a bimetallist.—Mr. T. D. English of N. J., H. R., Aug. 18: *Id.*, p. 480/2.

1900   [The writer of the editorial seems to be] a Republican of the Hanna *stripe.*—Mr. W. Sulzer of N. Y., H. R., Jan. 17: *Id.*, p. 925/1.

Stuff, v.   To fill with lies, to deceive. Slang.

1894   [Mr. Cobb of Mo.] is mistaken in his assumption, and indeed he must have been *"stuffed"* by wicked men with intent to lead him astray.—Mr. J. D. Warner of N. Y., H. R., June 18: *C. R.*, p. 6482/2.

Stuffed prophet, the. An opprobrious term applied to President Cleveland. Slang.

1897 The adoption of a monetary commission . . . is only putting on the raiment of Clevelandism. This plan was proposed during the reign of the "*stuffed prophet*."—Mr. C. F. Cochran of Mo., H. R., May 3: *C. R.*, p. 870/1.

Stuffing out of one, to knock the. To demolish one's adversary like a doll stuffed with sawdust. Slang.

1892 Instead of repulsing their enemies, they simply *knock the stuffing out of each other*.—Mr. John Davis of Kan., H. R., July 1: *C. R.*, p. 5731/2.

Stump, v. To nonplus; foil. Colloquial.

1889 Uncle Sam himself confesses that he can do everything but enjoy himself. That, he admits, *stumps* him.—*Harper's Mag.*, lxxviii, 977. (Century Dict.)

Stump, v. To dare, to challenge, to "banter."

1889 In some games . . . younger children are commanded, or older ones *stumped* or dared, to do dangerous things, like walking a picket fence or a high roof.—*Amer. Jour. of Psychol.*, III, 66.

Stump, Stump speech, on the Stump. Early in the nineteenth century, a tree stump was the common pulpit of political speakers in the country. Hence, the speaker was "on the stump." [1835-1869.]

1865 The friends of Lincoln were not without anxiety when the challenge was given, and accepted, for a campaign *on the stump* [with Stephen A. Douglas against him.]—Mr. Isaac N. Arnold of Ill., H. R., Feb. 20: *C. G.*, p. 70/2, App.

1875 [This] is a thing that will come back to plague us on every *stump* in every State in this Union.—Mr. Oliver P. Morton of Ind., U. S. Senate, Feb. 10: *C. R.*, p. 1104/1.

1879 Possibly it may be a part of the duty of Congress to furnish *stump material* of that kind [i.e. a tabulated statement by States of claims growing out of the war], but I did not know it.—Mr. G. F. Edmunds of Vt., U. S. Senate, Dec. 9: *Id.*, p. 35/2.

Stumpage. The charge for cutting timber. [1846.]

1866 [He] says that *stumpage* is five dollars in Michigan, and that in Canada *stumpage* is only worth fifty cents a thousand.—Mr. John Hogan of Mo., H. R., March 7: *C. G.*, p. 1248/2.

1870 The American lumberman pays about $2. per 1000 feet for *stumpage*, so called, upon the quantity he cuts. The proprietor is reasonably entitled to it.—Mr. John A. Peters of Me., H. R., March 21: *Id.*, p. 2104/2.

Stumptail currency. See quotation.

1879 Some day . . . this nation will be destroyed, and the country will go back to the wild-cat and the red-dog and *stump-tail currency* that we had before we established the national banks.—Mr. Hiram Price of Ia., H. R., Feb. 22: *C. R.*, p. 1788/1.

1881 See SHYSTER.

Stunt, Stent, Stint. A task or feat. College slang.

1851 Margaret had a new *stint* at quilling.—S. Judd, "Margaret," I, 2. (Century Dict.)

1888 If you are weak, and can't finish your *stent*, you are given twenty blows with the cat.—*Century Mag.*, xxxvii, 36.

1903 Boys did some great *stunts* on and under water.—*N. Y. Herald*, Aug. 15. (Century Dict.)

Submissionists. Those opposed to nullifying the tariff (1832), in Charleston, S. C. Federal rights men. See Vol. II, **Nullification.** [1799-1839.]

1834 The Nullifiers call us *Submissionists*.—*The Georgian* (Savannah), July 8, p. 2/6.

1850   [*Submissionists.*] We find this is getting to be a word quite in common use among the Southern ultras.—Wilmington (N. C.) *Commercial*, Oct. 22, p. 2/1.

Subsist. To maintain.

b. 1799   I will raise one thousand men, *subsist* them at my own expense, and march myself at their head for the relief of Boston.—Geo. Washington, quoted in Adams's Works, II, 360. (Century Dict.)

1870   The testimony is very clear that she did *subsist* these troops; that she did it . . . under compulsion: and the bill allows her a per diem subsistence less than the amount the State gave for the keeping of prisoners.—Mr. Willey of W. Va., U. S. Senate, Feb. 4: *C. G.*, p. 1035/3.

1872   In large districts of country . . . families *were being subsisted* upon boiled barley.—Mr. A. A. Sargent of Calif., H. R., Feb. 16: *Id.*, p. 1078/2.

1874   That they will safely keep, *subsist*, clothe, and furnish the necessary medical attendance . . . for such prisoners as may be sent.—Letter of Mr. Geo. H. Williams, Attorney-General of the U. S., Nov. 12: See *C. R.*, July 14, 1888, p. 6320/2.

1878   A bill was introduced into the H. of R. for "collecting and *subsisting* Apaches and other Indians of Arizona and New Mexico."—*C. R.*, Dec. 19, p. 314/1.

Substitute broker. One who procured substitutes in the Civil War. [1863.]   Cf. **Bounty Broker.**

1865   Take a *substitute broker*, if you please, the vilest of mankind, still he is a citizen, and he is entitled to a fair trial.—Mr. Edgar Cowan of Pa., U. S. Senate, Feb. 6: *Id.*, p. 612/2.

1865   I understand that these *substitute brokers* in the city of New York have a brokers' board, and have regular meetings.—Mr. Henry Wilson of Mass., U. S. Senate, Feb. 6: *Id.*, p. 614/3.

1865   Every one who knows anything about the practices of this most unmitigated scoundrels on the face of the earth, the *substitute brokers*, knows that in nine cases out of ten the broker pockets nearly if not quite all the money given for bounty, and the man enlisted gets none of it.—Mr. Robert C. Schenck of O., H. R., Feb. 23: *Id.*, p. 1036/1.

1865   There never has been . . . a more corrupt and detestable organization of men than those who center around the recruiting offices under the name of *substitute brokers*.—Mr. John W. Chanler of N. Y., H. R., Feb. 23: *Id.*, p. 1036/2.

1865   What is a *substitute broker*? A man who establishes an office, and offers to furnish substitutes for different localities. He pays bounties, and gathers men in gangs for sale; and when the committees of any town are hard pressed to fill up their quotas, they send to the *substitute broker*, and buy his wares at exorbitant rates.—Mr. James A. Garfield of O., H. R., Feb. 24: *Id.*, p. 1075/1.

Sucker. A native of Illinois. [1833-1862.]

1867   Members from Illinois said [the rebel States were] dead, and the *Suckers* of that State wiggled their tails with joy at the discovery.—Mr. T. E. Noell of Mo., H. R., Feb. 12: *C. G.*, p. 105/1, App.

Sucker. A greenhorn. Slang. [1857-1863.] [Name of a fish closely related to the carps.—Ed.]

1888   I do not believe this hook is baited right to catch "*prairie suckers*" successfully.—Mr. O. S. Gifford of Dakota, H. R., June 9: *C. R.*, p. 211/1, App.

1898   The gentlemen who form the platform[s] are always adroit enough to frame them so as to catch the "*suckers*" on Election day.—Mr. Jerry Simpson of Kan., H. R., Jan. 20: *Id.*, p. 804/1.

Sugar bush. A grove of sugar maple trees. [1839.]

1883 [The pension agents] seem to be acting on the principle of the English-man who bought a *sugar-bush* and said he was going to make sugar, and if he found the thing profitable he was going to keep it running all summer.—Mr. E. S. Bragg of Wisc., H. R., Feb. 19: *C. R.*, p. 2946/1.

Sugar in one's spade. Smooth and polite conduct on the part of one who seeks to gain something. [Sugar by the spadeful—Ed.]

1894 I am inclined to think that [Attorney General] Taft did say to Mr. Bernard, *"You bring a good deal of sugar in your spade,"* in order to get the voucher signed, and before Mr. Taft signed the voucher. . . . When persons go to the departments to get vouchers signed, they are too apt to be impatient and petulant and to scold and find fault, instead of which they ought to be courteous, and to bring *"sugar in their spades."* . . . If I were to advise any one now seeking to get a voucher allowed, . . . I would say by all means, notwithstanding the Senator from Missouri [Mr. G. G. Vest] considers it an alarming transaction, . . . *"Bring sugar in your spade,* and nothing else."—Mr. W. E. Chandler of N. H., U. S. Senate, Jan. 25: *C. R.*, p. 1383/1.

Sugar-kiss tickets. Tickets of the thinnest material.

1876 The Conservatives of Portsmouth, [Va.], had printed tickets of the smallest possible size, on the thinnest paper, and by folding several in a large ticket and presenting it as their vote they succeeded in filling the ballot-boxes with over 1000 of these small tickets—*sugar-kiss tickets* as they are called. . . . The same thing was done in Petersburgh, and I hold in my hand one of the *sugar-kiss tickets* used [there], just one inch long and three-quarters wide.—Mr. Brown of Kan., H. R., July 25: *C. R.*, p. 4873/2.

Sugar party. One assembled to prepare maple sugar.

1907 I once went to a *sugar party* up in New Hampshire when I was a girl, and I never enjoyed myself so much in my life.—W. D. Howells, "Through the Eye of the Needle," p. 65.

Suicide, v. To commit suicide. [1871-1887.]

1881 He wanted to *suicide.* A mysterious and respectable stranger fished out of the river.—Headlines in the *Louisville Courier-Journal,* June 13.

1886 The wrong partner *suicided.*—Mr. Van Wyck of Neb., U. S. Senate, Apr. 26: *C. R.*, p. 3826/1.

Suit. A set, a supply. [1704-1858.]

1851 The face of this gentleman was strikingly marked by a *suit* of enor-mous black whiskers that flowed together and united under his chin.— S. Judd, "Margaret," ii, 3.

1893 [The young lady] wound her rich *suit of hair* into a knot, and wore it as a topknot.—Mr. D. B. Hill of N. Y., U. S. Senate, Sept. 19: *C. R.*, p. 1582/1.

Suitcase. A flat valise, made to hold a dress suit.

1905 Two *suit-cases* filled to their limit with nearly 2000 bright silver Mexican half dollars.—*N. Y. Times,* Dec. 24. (Century Dict.)

Sulky. A light two-wheeled carriage for one person. (Webster.)

1834 The contract for running the Mail once a week in *sulkies* from Darien to St. Mary's is $1050.—*The Georgian* (Savannah), July 9, p. 2/4.

Sultan of Bath, The. Gov. Wm. King of Maine. (1768-1852.)

1878 Engaging in commerce and navigation . . . in a few years he became known as *"the Sultan of Bath,"* was one of the greatest ship-builders in the United States, and the owner of more ships engaged in the foreign trades than any other man in New England.—Remarks of Mr. Wm. P. Frye of Me., on the presentation of Wm. King's statue: *C. R.*, Jan. 22: p. 469/2.

[End of Part XIII.]

Sundown. A wide-brimmed straw hat.

1888 Young faces of those days seemed as sweet and winning under wide-brimmed *sundowns* or old-time "pokes" as ever did those that have laughed beneath a "love of a bonnet" of a more *de rigueur* mode.— *Century Mag.*, xxxvi, 769.

Sundown, Sunup. Sunset, sunrise. [1796-1878.]

1826 Such a horse as that might get over a good deal of ground atwixt *sun-up* and *sun-down*.—J. F. Cooper, "Last of the Mohicans," ch. iv. (Century Dict.)

1870 Go out to the Government buildings beyond Judiciary Square any morning from *sun up* to ten o'clock.—Mr. J. Proctor Knott of Ky., H. R., Feb. 2: *C. G.*, p. 983/3.

1879 See LIGHTNING.

1892 I do not have to get up at *sunup* to meet the gentleman from Georgia for anything. I am not a *sunup* man in that way. I am not brave enough for that.—Mr. B. McMillin of Tenn., H. R., June 22: *C. R.*, p. 5456/1

Sunfish, v. See quotation.

1893 Sometimes [the bronco] is a "plunging" bucker, who runs forward all the time while bucking: or he may buck steadily in one place, or *sunfish*—that is, bring first one shoulder almost down to the ground, and then the other.—Theodore Roosevelt, *Century Mag.*, xxxv, 854.

1903 See TWISTER.

Sunflower State, The. Kansas. [1891-1909.]

1893 [Kansas] is a great State; the *Sunflower State*; a State with great and fertile prairies; but somehow or other the people there have always managed to keep up an excitement and to focus the eyes of the country upon them.—Mr. H. D. Money of Miss., H. R., Oct. 5: *C. R.*, p. 2174/1.

Sure-enough. Real, genuine. Colloquial.

1888 It was at once agreed that he "wasn't the *sure-enough* bronco-buster he thought himself."—Theodore Roosevelt, *Century Mag.*, xxxvi, 837.

1896 Bills for the pensioning of actual, *sure-enough* soldiers, men who carried sword and musket.—Mr. J. A. Connolly of Ill., H. R., March 27: *C. R.*, p. 3301/1.

1896 I believe [this bill] is in the interest of the old soldier,—in the language of the gentleman from Illinois of the "*sure-enough*" soldier.—Mr. F. C. Layton of O., H. R., Apr. 24: *Id.*, p. 4371/1.

1896 A brave and true and really good and "*sure-enough*" Union soldier is entitled to the benefit of liberal pension legislation.—Mr. J. W. Miles of Md., H. R., Apr. 25: *Id.*, p. 4434/2.

1896 I will suggest a better method to save the money for the old *sure-enough* soldier, and that is to keep off the pension rolls the deserters and bounty-jumpers.—Mr. J. W. Miles of Md., H. R., May 8: *Id.*, p. 5007/1.

Surfer. The surf-duck. (Massachusetts.)

1876 F. C. Browne.—(Century Dict.).

Surprise party. Sometimes called a donation party. [1859.] Also, generally for any unexpected event.

1859 "*Surprise Party* at East Medford."—*Boston Transcript*, March 26, p. 2/4. [Heading of item.]

1859 "Was he never at a husking, . . . a bee, a *surprise party*, a '*social*' . . . ?" —J. Redpath, "Roving Editor," p. 86.

1894 I am enjoying something of a "*surprise party*," for I had not intended to address you.—Speech by Senator Warren at Omaha. See *C. R.*, Aug. 10, p. 8393/2.

Surrogate. A judge of a probate court. (N. Y.)
1889 In Georgia the court is called the court of the "Ordinary," in New York, the *Surrogate's court.*—Thos. Woodrow Wilson, "The State," §958. (Century Dict.)

Surround, n. A mode of hunting large animals by driving them as it were into a corner.
1887 The plan of attack [in hunting buffalo], which in this country is familiarly called a *surround*, was . . . agreed upon.—W. T. Hornaday, *Smithsonian Report*, II, 481. (Century Dict.)

Suspenders. Braces. [1810-1858.]
1841 Correspondences are like small-clothes before the invention of *suspenders*; it is impossible to keep them up.—Sydney Smith, "Letters." (Century Dict.)
1862 The soldier is well fed. He wants nothing, unless it may be a [little] tobacco, and now and then a pair of *suspenders*, and such like.—Mr. James H. Campbell of Pa., H. R., March 10: *C. G.*, p. 1145/2.
1893 [They] are already turning up the bottoms of their trousers, and taking an extra reef in their *suspenders*.—Mr. W. W. Bowers of Calif., H. R., Oct. 3: *C. R.*, p. 2096/2.

Suspicion, v. To suspect. [1834-1890.]
1884 He *suspicioned* him when he gave him the ticket.—Mr. R. Q. Mills of Tex., H. R., May 27: *C. R.*, p. 4587/2.

Swamp Angel. The term was applied to a Parrot gun used in the siege of Charleston, S. C., 1863-64. The gun fired shot and shell weighing 150 to 200 lbs.
1876 The *Swamp Angel* that hurled its ponderous shells into Charleston.—Mr. W. D. Kelley of Pa., H. R., May 19: *C. R.*, p. 3215/2.
1882 I was quite startled at that assertion [made by Mr. Burrows]; it was a sort of "*swamp angel*" shot from his mathematical battery.—Mr. McClure of O., H. R., Feb. 13: *Id.*, p. 1106/2.

Swamp angel. A dweller in the swamps. [1857.]
1876 If I am to credit what I hear, [J. M. W.] was once known as a "*swamp angel.*"—Mr. W. B. Spencer of La., H. R., Dec. 27: *C. R.*, p. 384/1.
1890 "Jim" Liddell was there with his crowd of "*Swamp Angels*" (for this badge was worn by them all—a green silk ribbon with "*Swamp Angel*" on it).—A letter quoted in the U. S. Senate, Jan. 23: *C. R.*, p. 804/2.

Swampoodle. A name sometimes applied to the low-lying and poor section of a town or city.
1871 Until we compel [the railroads] to bring their passenger trains where they can receive and discharge their passengers to their convenience, they will be left out here at this part of the city that is known as *Swampoodle.*—Mr. Horace Maynard of Tenn., H. R., Apr. 15: *C. G.*, p. 718/1.
1894 There is a part of that city which was at one time the suburbs of old Kansas City, Missouri. It was made up of what you would call here "*swampoodle.*" It was made up of cabins, and little houses in ruins, and of tents and other makeshifts.—Mr. E. H. Funston of Kan., H. R., Aug. 1: *C. R.*, p. 1117/2, App.

Swap. To exchange. [1742-1870.]
1592 By the helpe of Coridon [she] *swapt* a bargaine with his Landslord.—Thos. Lodge, "Euphues Golden Legacie," F2.
1715 To *swap*, or *swop*, to exchange one thing for another.—Kersey, "Dictionarium Anglo-Britannicum."
1790 He never sold, *swapp'd*, or traded [the Tobacco Note] for any consideration whatever.—*Augusta* (Ga.) *Chronicle*, March 13, p. 3/1. (Advt.)
1862 If we were to *swap* positions, we should undoubtedly *swap* opinions.—Mr. Garrett Davis of Ky., U. S. Senate, March 13: *C. G.*, p. 126/2.

1862 Our juveniles *swap* knives at precocious ages, and *swap* horses before they are out of their teens.—Mr. Lot M. Morrill of Me., U. S. Senate, March 31: *Id.*, p. 1457/3.

1865 The President [Lincoln] is not across the stream yet, and you know he said on a memorable occasion that it was not well to *swap horses* while crossing a stream.—Mr. Powell of Ky., U. S. Senate, Jan. 9: *Id.*, p. 166/3. [See *N. & Q.*, II S, iii. 269, 358, 433.]

1865 In my judgment the country would make a poor exchange to *swap off* a monitor for a dispatch.—Mr. F. A. Pike of Me., U. S. Senate, Feb. 4: *Id.*, p. 49/1, App.

1865 If two men . . . are taxed when they buy horses, will they be taxed when they *swop horses?*—Mr. Justin S. Morrill of Vt., H. R., Feb. 17: *Id.*, p. 878/2.

1865 "It is no time to *swap horses* while crossing a stream" is more appropriate in this connection [the topic of reconstruction] than the one in which the author used it.—Mr. Le Blond of O., U. S. Senate, Feb. 20: *Id.*, p. 940/2.

1866 Can we not *swap* our cultivated men who cannot perform menial offices for uncultivated men who cannot do anything else?—Mr. T. O. Howe of Wisc., U. S. Senate, Jan. 26: *Id.*, p. 438/3.

1867 I have heard of two Yankees that got rich in prison by *swapping* jack-knives.—Mr. B. F. Wade of O., U. S. Senate, Jan. 24: *Id.*, p. 704/2.

1873 I have come to that condition of mind where I will always *swap* a recital for an enactment.—Mr. Matt. H. Carpenter of Wisc., U. S. Senate, Feb. 27: *Id.*, p. 1892/3.

1881 The New Hampshire man carries his potatoes to Cuba and *swaps* them for oranges; both parties are benefited, and the greatest profit is with the party that did the hauling.—Mr. J. B. Beck of Ky., U. S. Senate, Jan. 27: *C. R.*, p. 960/2.

1881 An Indian out West, desiring to get rid of his wife, refused to sell her out and out to another for money, fearing a rescission; but he *swapped* her off for a dog, and then he killed the dog, which prevented her return.—Mr. John T. Morgan of Ala., U. S. Senate, Apr. 14: *Id.*, p. 290/2.

1884 It is idle to sit here *swapping* two shirt-buttons for a coat-button in the calculation as to which office pays and which does not pay.—Mr John S. Wise of Va., H. R., March 13: *Id.*, p. 1873/1.

1892 Value is commercial equivalence. It is the second term in a *swap*. You can not find the value of a dollar till you *swap* it for something that is not money.—Mr. W. A. McKeighgan of Neb., H. R., March 23: *Id.*, p. 2434/2.

Swartwout. To swindle and abscond. See quotations. [1839-1844.] [Vol. II has a fuller note on Samuel Swartwout.]

1857 Samuel Swartwout is dead. He is best known as having at one time filled the situation of Collector of the Port of New York. In this perilous post, he so conducted himself as to add a new verb to the English language. To *swartwout* means to abscond with public money—I *swartwout*, Thou swartwoutest, He swartwouts,—We swartwout, Ye or You swartwout, They swartwout. He probably died rich, for some of the newspapers of a sister city are quite eulogistic in regard to him.—*American Notes & Queries*, I, 21.

1876 Swartwout . . . was accused of unparalleled dishonesty in office. And his supposed dishonesty has given a new word to our language. "*Swartwouting*" is equivalent to embezzlement and official peculation.—Mr. Black, Apr. 27: Trial of W. W. Belknap, p. 14/1.

Swat. To strike with a heavy blow. Slang.

1913 You see an evil, and you *swat* it with a bill; you ask no questions as to remote or collateral effects.—*N. Y. Evening Post*, June 5, p. 4/3.

Swath, cut a wide. To cut a wide path with a scythe; hence, to "cut a dash."

1898 Mr. Ray of N. Y.:—[The bondholders] wear their broadcloth, they give their dinners, they drink their wine, but they . . . have no interest in our commerce. Mr. Brucker:—Not ostensibly; but as a matter of fact they *cut a pretty wide swath.*—H. R., Feb. 18: *C. R.*, p. 1915/2.

Swear or **vow,** euphemistic expressions for. These oaths were invented by the youth of New England. See Vol. I, **I swan, I swow, I snore; I van, I vum, I vow.** [1785-1878.]

1633 [*I swan to man.*] The euphemism involved in the use of the word *man* finds a parallel in Ben Jonson's "Tale of a Tub," II, 1: "For the passion of *man,* hold!"

1815 I shood never have swimmed to shore, dead or alive, to all atarnity, *I swamp it.*—David Humphreys, "The Yankey in England," p. 19.

1815 The distemper . . . was a flea-bite to it: *I swouch it.*—*Id.,* p. 56.

1815 [I came across in] a vessel, *I vum.*—*Id.,* p. 40.

1815 I don't care a cent for you and all your close, I *vumpers.*—*Id.,* p. 70.

1815 I can hardly hold my hair on, *I van;* nor my heels down, *I vags* on't.—*Id.,* p. 97.

1827
　　　Once in our Bay, I *vum* by chowder
　　　The Tea was made of good Gunpowder.
—*Nat. Gazette* (Phila.), Oct. 13, p. 4/1. [Boston Bay.]

Sweeny, the. Hard punishment; euphemism for "the devil."

1883 It gives a poor man's pocket-book the *swinney* to buy [a thrashing-machine].—Sherwood Bonner, "Dialect Tales," p. 48.

1894 We could, no doubt, raise oranges in Maine, or upon Jay Cooke's banana belt along the Northern Pacific Railroad; but a barrel of them would give Wm. Waldorf Astor's pocket-book *the sweeny.*—Mr. Champ Clark of Mo., H. R., Jan. 19: *C. R.*, p. 1077/1.

Swelled heads. Self-conceit.

1858 See SPREAD-EAGLE, Vol. II.

Swill-milk. Milk produced by cows fed on swill, especially on slops from distilleries. (Century Dict.)

1888 Parties who produce *swill-milk* for sale in large cities find swill to be the cheapest food for the production of milk, and consequently use it to success.—*Science,* x, 72. (Century Dict.)

Swim, in the. In the current of affairs. One who is not in the swim is antiquated. Colloquial.

1889 His neighborhood is getting *into the swim* of the real-estate movement.—*Harper's Mag.,* lxxviii, 313. (Century Dict.)

1889 A girl *in the swim* hasn't time to paint or to draw.—*Century Mag.,* xl, 275.

Swipe. A strong blow given with a sweeping motion. (Webster.) A vulgar expression in the South for a severe beating is "He *swiped up* the very earth with him," or "He *swiped* the whole thing out,"—in these cases meaning about the same as *sweep.*—*Trans. Amer. Philol. Assn.,* xvii, 44. (Century Dict.) ["*Wipe* up the earth with someone" is probably more common in the North.]

Switch. A spur or sidetrack on which cars may be shunted or "switched." [1862-1910.] [A *switch-engine* is in New England (Vt.) also called a "shifter."—Ed.]

1890 There are scores of these *switches* in New York. You find them in . . . Buffalo, Cleveland, New Haven, Providence, and in every manufacturing city. Chicago is gridironed with them. Why, it is such railroad facilities that really develop the life of a city. In one street in Philadelphia there are over seventy such *switches.* The more manufactories the more work for the people, and the more *switches* the more manufactories.—Mr. A. J. Cummings of N. Y., H. R., June 23: *C. R.*, p. 6404/2.

Switch off. To divert from the main issue; to "sidetrack."

1876 The resolution . . . was *switched off* so handsomely that I [must] say something in regard to it.—Mr. O. P. Morton of Ind., U. S. Senate, Aug. 5: *C. R.*, p. 5200/1.

1890 I am simply directing myself—and I do not propose to be *switched off* from it,—to one single assertion.—Mr. G. G. Vest of Mo., U. S. Senate, Aug. 20: *Id.*, p. 8873/2.

1892 I do not believe the gentleman from Georgia ought to ask us to *switch off* from this fight and go into a star-route service fight.—Mr. J. M. Pattison of O., H. R., June 2: *Id.*, p. 4956/1.

Sycamore of the Wabash. See **Tall Sycamore of the Wabash.**

Symmes's hole. A hole supposed to pass through the earth from pole to pole. A theory propounded by Capt. John Cleves Symmes, in 1818, relating to concentric spheres and the hollowness of the earth. [1824-1835.]

1818 About a year since, [I] decided on the geometrical necessity of all the planets being hollow, and consisting of separate concentric spheres involved in each other.—John Cleves Symmes in the *Missouri Gazette*, July 3.

1822 Mr. R. M. Johnson (of Kentucky) presented a petition from John Cleves Symmes, of Cincinnati, in Ohio, stating his belief of the existence of an inhabited concave to this Globe, etc.—*Am. Beacon* (Norfolk, Va.), March 11, p. 1/2.

1844 [Barnum] would mount Phaeton's car to catch the comet with seven tails, plunge into *Symmes's Hole* for a dog with two heads, and go down the Maelstrom for a sea-serpent.—Lydia M. Child, "Letters from New York," Second S., p. 174. (Lond., 1845.)

1870 When it was proposed to [Gov. Reynolds of Illinois] to recommend to Congress an exploration of the north pole, or to find what was then called *Symmes's Hole*,—"Why," said he, "if there had been any *Symmes's Hole*, the Yankees would have had a wagon-road through it before now."—Mr. Richard Yates of Ill., U. S. Senate, May 27: *C. G.*, p. 3898/2.

1878 In this year (Apr. 29) Mr. McCreery of Ky. presented a petition praying that Americus Symmes might be assigned to an official position in Captain Howgate's expedition to the north pole. It appeared that many persons yet had faith in his father's theory. See *C. R.*, p. 2909/1.

1878 I am very much delighted to see my friend from Maine [Mr. Eugene Hale]. I was afraid he had gone so far north that he had dropped into *Simm's Hole*, or some other place.—Mr. S. S. Cox of N. Y., H. R., Dec. 2: *Id.*, p. 11/1.

1882 I understand that a Mr. Symmes, some 50 years ago, tried to prove that the earth was a hollow sphere, and that at the north pole there was a great opening, into which an entrance might be made, and I remember it being called "*Symmes's Hole.*"—Mr. W. E. Robinson of N. Y., H. R., Jan. 26: *Id.*, p. 14/1, App.

T

Tabby or **Tappy.** A material consisting of oyster shells embedded in a matrix of burnt shell lime.

1775 Fort Lyttelton, S. C., was repaired with *tappy.*—*S. C. Hist. Mag.*, vi, 90-1. (1905.)

Tackeys. A type of "poor white," called also "country crackers."

1861 They were sandhill *tackeys*, . . . not very anxious to fight with anything, or in any way.—Mrs. Chestnut, "A Diary from Dixie," p. 58. (1905.)

1865 See SANDHILLER.

Tacky. A small pony. [1835-1896.]

1813 Having procured me a *tackey*, . . . I started for the West..—Lorenzo Dow, "Journal," §919 (1850), p. 143/2.

Taffy. Fulsome compliment. Slang. "To feed one taffy" means, also, deliberately to mislead or deceive him.

1879 [I wish to prevent them] from issuing campaign documents, and calling us Confederates, ... and denouncing me as the coadjutor of the South, distributing *"taffy"* to the South.—Mr. E. S. Bragg of Wisc., H. R., Apr. 15: *C. R.*, p. 462/1.

1879 There will be a reaction, and the whole party will unite in an offering of *"taffy."*—*N. Y. Tribune*, Sept. 16. (Century Dict.)

1884 The speech which [Mr. S. S. Cox] made on the census is equal to the speech that Demosthenes made on the crown. Now, that is not *taffy* at all.—Mr. Jas. B. Belford of Colo., H. R., March 6: *C. R.*, p. 1658/2.

1890 Flattery, as [Mr. Cummings] suggests, means *"taffy,"* and sometimes it means a little more than that.—Mr. B. A. Enloe of Tenn., H. R., Aug. 1: *Id.*, p. 8041/1.

1890 Is this *taffy* he's giving me, or are you really a bloated bondholder?—A. W. Tourgée, "Pactolus Prime," p. 49.

Tailgate. The movable tail board of a wagon.

1888 The two were picking near together, and throwing corn over the *tailgate* of the wagon.—E. Eggleston, "The Graysons," ch. xxxiii. (Century Dict.)

Tailings (of wheat). The refuse or residue in threshing.

1880 See OUTAGE.

1885 The lowest grade [of flour] comes from the *tailings* of the middlings-purifying machines.—*Century Mag.*, xxxii, 46.

1893 See USING-GROUNDS.

Tail out. To wind up a sale with prices tapering down.

1901 Every intelligent feeder knows the value of uniformity; it enables him to sell his product without *tailing out* a lot at inferior price.—*Report Kan. State Bd. Agr.*, p. 177. (Century Dict.)

Take back. To retract a statement. [1775-1860.]

1870 The Speaker:—The gentleman from Tennessee calls the gentleman to order for using unparliamentary language. The Chair is bound to sustain that point. Mr. Fernando Wood of N. Y.:—Then I will not repeat it: but I will *take nothing back.*—H. R., July 1: *C. G.*, p. 5068/3.

Take stock in. To put faith in.

1896 See SNAP CONVENTION.

Take the cake, Take the rag. To carry off the palm. [1833-1854.]

[The former refers to winning the prize at a "cakewalk," a negro dance.—Ed.]

1810 This *"takes the rag off the bush"* so completely, that we suppose we shall hear no more. . . . . about the Chesapeake business.—Norfolk (Va.) *Gazette*, Sept. 19, p. 2/3. (From the *Federal Rep.*)

1850 See SAVAGEROUS.

Talk through one's hat. To talk rubbish. Slang.

1894 Whenever I hear a person predicting absolute free trade, if he is a Democrat, I think, to use a slang expression, he is *"talking through his hat,"* and if he is a Republican he is "talking through two hats."—Mr. W. H. Bower of N. C., H. R., Jan. 17: *C. R.*, p. 966/2.

1896 The gentleman is only *talking through his hat.* I favored no such amendment. . . . . . [He] persists in *talking through his hat,* although it is in the cloakroom.—Mr. W. J. Talbert of S. C., H. R., Apr. 10: *Id.*, p. 3860/1.

1898 The remarks of my friend from Kansas [Mr. Simpson] would seem to indicate that he is *"talking through his hat"* as usual.—Mr. Nelson Dingley of Me., H. R., Feb. 3: *Id.*, p. 1421/2.

Tall. Remarkable, prodigious. [1840-1880.]

1891   There always has been some kind of a *tall* yarn about the Jews wanting to buy the Vatican copy of the Hebrew Bible.—*N. Y. Times,*
Jan. 26. (Century Dict.)

Tall Sycamore of the Wabash. A nickname applied to Mr. Daniel W.
Voorhees of Indiana (1827-1897) on account of his commanding
figure.

1870   The only apprehension I have is that when [Mr. V.] goes to . . . the
Piegans, and tells them he is a chief, and his name is "*Tall Sycamore
of the Wabash,*" he may lose his broad-brim and come home with a
wig.—Mr. Job E. Stevenson of O., H. R., Feb. 28: *C. G.,* p. 1602/3.

1878   It matters not that the proposition may be clothed in gorgeous rhetoric,
like the autumnal leaves shaken from the "*Tall Sycamore of the
Wabash.*"—Mr. W. P. Whyte of Md., U. S. Senate, Jan. 29: *C. R.,*
p. 647/1.

1879   The murmurs of disapproval of this style of argument were not so
loud nor so emphatic as to show that the practical politics of the *Tall
Sycamore of the Wabash* was wholly unpopular among his hearers.—
National Republican, Washington, May 1: cited in *C. R.,* p. 1006/1.

1881   Thos. Nast drew a picture of the "Tall Sycamore" handling the
British Lion.

Tammany. A political association in New York, organized to support
the policy of Thomas Jefferson, and continued under Democratic
auspices. The Indian chief for whom it was named was jocularly
or ignorantly called "Saint Tammany" or "King Tammany"; and
a festival was kept in his honour on old May-day. [1788-1842.]

1791   The celebration of *St. Tammany* occurred at Augusta, Ga., May 2.
A dinner was served in an adjacent grove, and fifteen toasts were
drunk, the first three being:
> The memory of St. Tammany.
> Our great and beloved Warrior.
> The Half King of our Nation.
>   —*Augusta Chronicle,* May 7, p. 2/3.

1876   It is said that *Tammanund,* after whom a very belligerent society has
been named, was a chief of many days because he was a wise and
merciful sachem.—Mr. S. S. Cox of N. Y., H. R., Apr. 5: *C. R.,*
p. 2233/2.

1879   [Tammany Hall] dates back as far as the year 1789, when it was
first established. In 1805 it was incorporated as a charitable organization, but it was soon perverted from its original purposes into a
political machine, unscrupulous, powerful, and dangerous beyond
example in history. The celebrated Aaron Burr was one of its
original members, and De Witt Clinton was one of its most relentless
enemies. . . . . While it has an outside organization that is public, it
has an internal one that rules it absolutely and despotically. It is
secret; it has its "sachems" and its "sagamores"; it practically
registers the decrees and obeys the behests of one man; and it is
essentially anti-democratic in all of its ways and tendencies.—Mr.
A. G. McCook of N. Y., H. R., Apr. 24; *Id.,* p. 924/1-2.

1890   *Tammany* is as clean as a hound's tooth, and we defy all the criticism
and investigation that can be made on the subject.—Mr. F. B. Spinola
of N. Y., H. R., Apr. 22: *Id.,* p. 3691/2.

1893   Today *Tammany* is in full control in New York City. . . . From the
inner chambers of the wigwam are issued the edicts that are to control
the party. . . . These *Tammany Chiefs* fear neither God, man, nor
the devil. . . . The *Tammany tiger,* sleek and fat with the political
spoils it has stolen, basks in the sun, content and secure, except when
John I. Davenport is gunning, . . . and then it lashes its tail in fury.—
Mr. G. W. Ray of N. Y., H. R., Oct. 6: *Id.,* p. 2231/2.

1900   See COMMONER, THE GREAT.

1901   See KNOCK.

Tanglefoot. A slang term for whisky; especially an inferior kind. [1871.]

1864 Take about a gallon of first-rate whisky,—not any of the *tanglefoot* article.—Mr. Amos Myers of Pa., H. R., Dec. 20: *C. G.*, p. 85/2.

1867 I need not tell you how much "red-eye," "*tangle-foot*," and "bust-head" it took to roll up four thousand Radical majority in the St. Joseph district.—Mr. T. E. Noell, H. R., Feb. 18: *Id.*, p. 114/3, App.

1892 [This proposed measure] is like giving an Apache a bottle of *tangle-foot whisky* to fit him for a race.—Mr. A. J. Cummings of N. Y., H. R., June 6: *Id.*, p. 444/2, App.

Tap. To draw from, in a way analogous to drawing off a fluid. See quotations. As applied to a railroad, this use seems new.

1878 His purpose is . . . . to *tap* the Texas and Pacific and draw the trade across the steel bridge at Saint Louis.—Mr. Herbert of Ala., H. R., June 6: *C. R.*, p. 4212/2.

1884 What was desired was to bring a branch road up from the Union Pacific line and *tap* it by a line from the Northern Pacific road.—Mr. John A. Logan of Ill., U. S. Senate, May 27: *Id.*, p. 4549/1.

Tapeworm ticket. See quotations.

1875 I exhibit a ticket prepared in the City of Washington and sent to Mare Island in my own district, known in California as the "*tape-worm*" *ticket*, which is three inches in length, one-16th of an inch in width, and with the State, county, and township ticket printed upon it in letters so small that it required a microscope to read them. . . . . This ticket was gotten up by the party of progress, etc.—Mr. J. K. Luttrell of Calif., H. R., Feb. 27: *C. R.*, p. 1890/2.

1878 Gentlemen will remember those tickets which were exhibited here some time ago, called "*tape-worm tickets*." They were printed upon a small piece of paper four or five inches long, and only a half-inch wide. These small tickets were given to a certain class of voters, and as they were put into the ballot-box the employers of the voters could easily tell whether such tickets were voted or not.—Mr. W. M. Springer of Ill., H. R., Feb. 6: *Id.*, p. 804/2.

1882 Here is another specimen of Republican tickets. Here is what they call in California the "*tape-worm*." It is about 3 inches long, and less than one-fourth of an inch wide. . . . . This is the ticket that the workmen at the Mare Island navy-yard were required to vote by their Government bosses.—Mr. R. Q. Mills of Tex., H. R., June 2: *Id.*, p. 4460/1.

Tarburner. See quotation.

1808 [This], according to the arithmetick of the ignorant "*Tarburners*," would amount to eleven hundred and fifty dollars.—Letter from "A Nansemond Tarburner." *Norfolk* (Va.) *Gazette*, March 16, p. 2/4.

Tarheel. A North Carolinian; a "poor white" of that State. [1864-1889.]

1875 It is the class of men thrown up by the war, ... the "*tar-heels*" and the "sandhillers" and the "dirt-eaters" of the South,—it is with that class we have all our trouble.—Mr. R. H. Cain of S. C. [a mulatto], H. R., Feb. 10: *C. R.*, p. 1152/2.

1878 The man has waited a long time for his money. He is an honest man; he is a "*tar-heel*."—Mr. Robert B. Vance of N. C., H. R., June 7: *Id.*, p. 4271/2.

1899 [This] amendment we *Tar Heels*, or a large majority of us, do most heartily commend.—Letter from Raleigh, N. C., Jan. 20: *C. R.*, Jan. 26, p. 1078/1.

1912 Josephus Daniels and Thomas J. Pence, two *Tarheels* from North Carolina, hold important positions in the Wilson campaign. The one is at the head of the publicity bureau; the other is righthand man to the chairman of the National Committee.—*N. Y. Evening Post*, Aug. 26, p. 7/1.

Tariff of abominations, the. A name given to the tariff of 1828, which aroused opposition in the South, and gave rise to the doctrine of Nullification, q.v.

1833 The act of 1828, that *"bill of abominations,"* as it has been so often and properly termed.—John C. · Calhoun, U. S. Senate, Feb. 15. ["Works" (1856), II, 217.]

Tar-knots. Pine knots abounding in tar.

1890 Burn some North Carolina *tar-knots.* That will destroy your malaria. —Mr. C. W. McClammy of N. C., H. R., June 23: *C. R.*, p. 6393/2.

Tautaug or **Tautog.** The blackfish. [1765-1843.]

1844 See PORGY.

Tax-dodger. One who evades the tax-collector.

1876 The *tax-dodger* is one who, finding that the rate of taxation in Boston is too high for his means, flies with his wife and children to some rural town.—*The Nation* (N. Y.) March 30, p. 202. (Century Dict.)

1894 There are *tax dodgers* under any system which may be inaugurated; and there always will be.—Mr. H. A. Dinsmore of Ark., H. R., Jan. 29: *C. R.*, p. 277/1, App.

Team, a. "A host in himself." [1833-1865.]

1878 [A man] is a whole *team* when he is smart; when he is very smart, he is a whole *team* and a horse to spare; and when [he is] smartest, a whole *team* and a horse to spare and a pair of coach dogs under the wagon.—*N. Y. Mercury,* March 2.

Teddy bear. A doll in the form of a brown bear. Named with allusion to Mr. Theodore (Teddy) Roosevelt.

Teeter, v. See quotation.

1846 *Teeter.* To see-saw on a balanced plank, as children [do]. (Worcester's Dict.)

Teeter, Teeter-board. A see-saw.

1867 An' I tell you you've gut to larn thet War ain't one long *teeter*
Betwixt *I wan' to* an' *'T wun't du,* debatin' like a skeetur
Afore he lights—all is, to give the other side a millin'.—"Biglow Papers," 2nd S., No. 3.

1894 The scheme would ruin the very men whom it is [meant to help], while the moneyed men could work the financial *"teeter" board* to suit their pleasure.—Mr. E. J. Hainer of Neb., H. R., June 6: *C. R.*, p. 915/1, App.

1902 A quorum of the committee is away *teeterin'* about in their own affairs.—A. H. Lewis, "Wolfville Nights," ch. xvii. (Century Dict.)

Teetotally, Teetoaciously. Completely, utterly. [1833-1878.]

1832 These Mingoes . . . ought to be essentially, and particularly, and *tee-totally* obflisticated off of the face of the whole yearth.—Hall, "Legends of W. Phila.," p. 38. (N. E. D.)

1894 The second class is that of paying large pensions to men simply because they held rank above that of a private soldier. I am *teetotally* opposed to pensions of that kind.—Mr. Champ Clark of Mo., H. R., June 15: *C. R.*, p. 6380/2.

1900 I am *teetotally* opposed to me or my people helping pay a part of the salary of the keeper of anybody's harem.—The same, Feb. 5: *Id.*, p. 1524/2. [The allusion is to the Sultan of Sulu.]

Tempest, v. To agitate.

1866 The time is now to put a hook in the jaws of this leviathan [President Andrew Johnson] that has *tempested* the waters, and moor him to his proper place under the Constitution.—Mr. Thos. Williams of Pa., H. R., Dec. 5: *C. G.*, p. 23/1.

Ten-cent. Sometimes used contemptuously. See the following phrase. [An expression similarly used is "two for a cent."]

1890 A *ten-cent* supervisor takes the place of the President of the United States.—Mr. J. J. Clunie of Calif., H. R., July 2: *C. R.*, p. 6932/1.

Ten-cent Jimmy. A nickname applied to President James Buchanan. See quotation, 1874. [1856.]

1842 "Can't go *ten cents a day*"; "Can't go this Buchanan and Van Buren," were phrases extensively taught.—Mr. H. W. Beeson of Pa., H. R., July 9: p. 12/2 of speech as separately published.

1864 Why, Mr. Speaker, I had no idea there were so many "*ten-cent Jimmys*" on the intensely loyal side of the house.—Mr. Johnson of Pa., H. R., May 12: *C. G.*, p. 2260/1.

1874 A distinguished statesman [once] said that it would be just as well to have wages ten cents a day, provided the purchasing power of ten cents was equal to what a dollar was then, as to have wages at a dollar a day, and I believe that he obtained by that remark the *sobriquet* of "*Ten-cent Jimmy.*"—Mr. O. P. Morton of Ind., U. S. Senate, Jan. 15: *C. R.*, p. 667/2.

Tend. To attend, wait on, look after. [1767-1869.]

1764 A Person that understands *tending* a Saw-Mill.—*N. C. Magazine,* Aug. 3, p. 72/2.

1815 See Chore.

Tenderfoot. A newcomer in the West; also a "greenhorn" generally. [1861-1902.]

1885 Hunters .... who bedizen themselves in all the traditional finery of the craft, in the hope of getting a job at guiding some *tenderfoot.*— Theodore Roosevelt, "Hunting trips," p. 32. (Century Dict.)

1892 [The scientific geologists] are called in that [Western] country, *tenderfeet.* They are laughed at. They are scientific *tenderfeet,* and nobody would think of acting on their advice about mines.—Mr. W. M. Stewart of Nev., U. S. Senate, July 8: *C. R.*, p. 5888/2.

1893 See Strike.

1894 Everybody except a *tenderfoot* will realize that nobody would call a real-estate man in the West reliable when he is giving information to a *tenderfoot.*—Mr. Jerry Simpson of Kan., H. R., Jan. 26: *Id.*, p. 1475/2.

1894 It is only the *tenderfoot* in the protection camp who now asks for a tariff on the ground his father held. It is only the *tenderfoot* in the Republican camp who now prates of the infant industry, while a tariff is levied to protect the forest primeval and to stimulate the flow of salt wells.—Mr. J. J. McDannold of Ill., H. R., Jan. 29: *Id.*, p. 1615/2.

Tenderloin. A choice cut next to the "Porterhouse." [1832-1883.]

1895 See Porterhouse.

Tenderloin. The "fast" and disreputable district in a city. [1909-1910.]

1898 If laws generally suitable to a city do not suit some Slavic, Polish, or other quarter, or some "*tenderloin*" district, the local police must pass upon those laws.—*N. Y. Voice,* Jan. 6: p. 413. (N. É. D.)

1913 [This church] was located perilously near to the City's *tenderloin.*— *Living Church,* Aug. 23, p. 587/2.

Tenement house. See first quotation.

1881 What is a *tenement-house?* The law defines it as a "house occupied by more than three families living independently and doing their cooking on the premises." ... In some of these houses .... there are often crowded together from ninety to one hundred and eighty souls. ... From four to nine persons occupy each apartment.—Bp. Henry C. Potter, "Sermons of the City," 4th S., p. 51. (Standard Dict.)

1891 See Down-town.

Tenspot. A ten dollar bill. [1848.]

1888 The point was seen at once, and the "*ten-spot*" was forthcoming.— Boston *Journal,* Nov. 6, p. 2/3. (N. E. D.)

Tenter. The occupant of a tent.

1888 The pretty girl of our civilization, who pushes into the canvas home of the *tenters.*—*Harper's Mag.*, lxxvii, 801. (Century Dict.)

Tepee. An Indian tent. [1876.]
1872 One has to travel far before the smoke of your wigwam or of your *tepie* blurs the evening air.—W. F. Butler, "Great Lone Land," p. 125. (N. E. D.)
1881 You go to an Indian village, and you find there little *tepes* strung about at the most convenient places along the side of a watercourse, the little tents in which they live. . . . This bill provides that the surveyor shall meander a provisional line between those various *tepes,* etc.—Mr. John T. Morgan of Ala., U. S. Senate, Jan. 29: *C. R.,* p. 1034/2.
1886 See BLANKET INDIAN.
1892 See TRACKS, IN ONE'S.
1900 When the girls and boys went back to the *tepee* at night, all the work of the day by the Jesuits was obliterated.—Mr. G. G. Vest of Mo., U. S. Senate, Apr. 7: *C. R.,* p. 3885/1.

Terrapin. A small kind of tidewater turtle.
1613 The *torope* or little turtle.—Whitaker, "Good News from Virginia," 42. (N. E. D.)
1728 We catcht a large *Tarapin* in the River, which is one kind of Turtle. The flesh of it is wholesome, and good for Consumptive People.— William Byrd, "Writings," p. 215. (1901)
1849 His mouth was shut as fast as a highland *tarrapin.*—Wilmington (N. C.) *Commercial,* June 21, p. 4/2.
1866 The soil of South Carolina was within the exterior lines of the Union before the war, and as there has been no land-slide down in that region, and a State cannot pick itself up and walk off like a land *terrapin,* nor be located like a land-warrant on the best vacant land that can be found, I presume, etc.—Mr. Dumont of Ind., H. R., March 17: *C. G.,* p. 1473/3.
1894 See TORUP.

Territorialize. To convert into a territory.
1869 Mr. Boutwell asked me . . . whether we intended to oppose that bill. I asked, "What bill? The bill to *territorialize* the State of Mississippi?"—Mr. Chas. A. Eldridge of Wisc., H. R., Apr. 1: *C. G.,* p. 437/2.

Territory. An organized division of the country, not yet admitted to the complete rights of statehood. (Century Dict.)
1886 The nation has never regretted delay in erecting a *territory* into a state.—*The Nation* (N. Y.), Jan. 28.

Test-oath. The "ironclad" oath required after the Civil War as a condition of holding certain offices.
1869 See IRONCLAD OATH.
1870 Mr. John F. Farnsworth of Ill.:—I am opposed to these multiplications of *test-oaths. Test-oaths* are always distasteful. . . . I say that *test-oaths* are not required by any exigency now existing. Mr. Wm. Lawrence of Ohio:—This bill does not require any *test-oath.* It is not what is commonly known as the *iron-clad test-oath* of 1862.— H. R., Jan. 12: *C. G.,* p. 401/2.

Texas. A structure on the hurricane-deck of a steamboat, containing the cabins for the officers. The pilot-house is on top of it. Western. (Century Dict.) See Vol. II, **Texas-deck.** [1875.]

Texas fever. A splenetic fever affecting cattle. See **Tick fever.**
1890 Texas cattle are charged with . . . communicating to other cattle what is known as *Texas fever,* a splenetic disease. . . . . We provided that splenetic fever, known as *Texas fever,* should not go into this bill.—Mr. Sayers and Mr. Funston, H. R., Aug. 20: *C. R.,* pp. 8893-4.

Texas northwester. A violent wind. See quotation.
1879 You could not haul [a large vessel] into the harbor of Galveston with all the steam engines that are in the United States today, unless

you tore her keel off. She has got to go there and lie out in the roadstead, and when one of these *Texas northwesters* comes this ship has to sail without unloading.—Mr. John T. Morgan of Ala., U. S. Senate, Feb. 20: *C. R.*, p. 1653/2.

Thank-you-ma'am. A hollow or ridge in a road, which causes persons passing over it in a vehicle to nod the head involuntarily. (N. E. D.) A New England expression.

1849 We went like the wind over the hollows in the snow;—the driver called them *"thank-you-ma'ams,"* because they made everybody bow.— H. W. L., "Kavanagh," xi. (N. E. D.)

1867 Life's a road that's got a good many *thank-you-ma'ams* to go bumpin' over, says he.—O. W. Holmes, "The Gdn. Angel," xiv. (N. E. D.)

1874 We jogged along very comfortable and very happy, down steep hills crossed by abrupt and jerky *thank-you-mams.—Scribner's Mag.*, viii, 565.

1897 At one of the *thank-you-marms* in the road, the sick man stopped, like a weary horse, to breathe.—W. D. Howells, "The Landld. of the Lion's Head," p. 192. (N. E. D.)

That's so. Something accomplished—positive.

1857 A sentence recently adopted by the vulgar, and seems likely to be generally used.—*Am. Notes and Queries*, No. 2.

1867 Mr. Henderson:—I believe that the motion pending is to go into executive session. The President *pro tempore*:—*That is so.*—U. S. Senate, Apr. 12: *C. G.*, p. 843/2.

1876 *That is so.* That is what the Chair has ruled.—Mr. Clymer, Speaker *pro tempore.*—H. R., Aug. 3: *C. R.*, p. 5134/1.

Thereaway. In that region. [1848.]

c.1670 "Among Carnal and Historical Christians *there-away.*"—Penn. "Works" (1726) I, 156. (N. E. D.)

Third party. A name applied to the "People's Party," organized in Cincinnati in May, 1891. Among its leaders were Gen. Jas. B. Weaver of Iowa and Senator W. A. Peffer of Kansas.

1894 Not only has the Republican party legislated against the farmer, but they have been aided in inflicting this great wrong by the Green-backers, Populists, or *Third-party* men.—Mr. Joseph Wheeler of Ala., H. R., June 21: *C. R.*, p. 6668/2.

Thirty cents, to feel like, look like, etc. To feel or look small. Slang.

1902 "I say old chap, what does that mean? Make [a man] *look like thirty cents.* It's awfully queer you know." In his most sepulchral tone the actor volunteered: ". . . . That is merely a colloquial expression indicative of the acme of mediocrity."—*N. Y. Times*, Dec. 28. (Century Dict.)

Thlack. A quartillo, a copper coin. Texas. [1892.]

1886 [The prisoner] is allowed six Mexican *tclacos* per day upon which to subsist, equal to 8½ cents American money.—Affidavit, July 1: See *C. R.*, p. 7922/1.

Thousand of brick, like a. With terrific force.

1884 If I came down upon [Senator Williams] as he says . . . . *like a thousand of brick*, he will find when that bill comes up that I will come down upon him like a five-story edifice.—Mr. J. J. Ingalls of Kan., U. S. Senate, March 14: *C. R.*, p. 1900/2.

Thrip. A coin between a nickel and a dime. [1834-1848.]

1889 I've seen folks that had to rub the silver off a *thrip* to tell whether it was passable or not. I might be fooled about the silver in a *thrip*, but you can't fool me about a grown man.—Joel C. Harris, "The Old Bascom Place."

Throater. A knife used to cut the throats of fish; also, one who uses the throater. New Brunswick. (Century Dict.)

Through. To be *through* is to have done, to have finished.

1880 Mr. Wright:—Am I defeated in the effort to explain how a wrong has been inflicted? . . . *Am I through*, against my will? The Speaker:—The Chair is unable to know whether the gentleman *is through* with his remarks or not. Mr. Wright:—But *I am not through*.—H. R., Jan. 27: *C. R.*, p. 545/2.

1894 If you are *through* with your comments on my question, I am *through* with my comments on your criticisms.—Mr. M. A. Smith of Ariz., H. R., Feb. 14: *Id.*, p. 2191/2.

Through train, through travel. That which goes all the way.

1871 A large portion of the *"through travel,"* as it is called, to the South, instead of coming through [Washington] will either go by the way of Norfolk and the sea-board, or else by Richmond and the lower Potomac.—Mr. Horace Maynard of Tenn., H. R., Apr. 15: *C. G.*, p. 718/1.

Thug. A murderous ruffian.

1887 During our civil war, the regiments which were composed of plug-uglies, *thugs*, and midnight rounders, with noses laid over to one side as evidence of their prowess in bar-room mills and paving-stone riots, were generally cringing cowards in battle.—*Century Mag.*, xxxvi, 249.

1900 I have been driven off the stump, time and time again, from 1866 to 1874, by Democratic *thugs* and Democratic heelers.—Mr. C. E. Pearce of Mo., H. R., Feb. 14: *C. R.*, p. 1806/1.

1913 Considering . . . . we have put up a gallant and strenuous fight that has taught this labor skinning company a severe lesson by inflicting upon them a loss of thousands of dollars through the cessation of work and the cost of maintaining their armed *thugs* and hired assassins. —*Industrial Worker* (Spokane, Wash.), July 3. [See, also, Strike-breakers.]

Thumb-papers. See quotation. [Probably papers merely to count or "thumb over."]

1880 Tell me what [these certificates were] given for. Was it to make *thumb-papers* out of by those who held them? Was it to make paper to plaster their walls with?—Mr. A. H. Garland of Ark., U. S. Senate, March 18: *C. R.*, p. 1671/1.

Thunderbird. A bird famous in Indian legend, art, etc.

1898 For the Tillamook legend (Pacific Coast) see *Journal of Am. Folk-Lore*, xi, 23-27; also p. 140.

Thusly, Thusness. Comical expressions invented by "Artemus Ward."

1876 I whispered to myself that every dog has his day, and I asked myself, "Shall this ever be *thusly*?"—Mr. Harrison of Ill., H. R., May 23: *C. R.*, p. 3282/1.

1883 Expound me this *thusness*, I pray.—W. Hamilton, "Parodies" (1886), III, 159. (N. E. D.)

1888 In the language of a distinguished American philosopher and man of letters,—a man of more letters than proper spelling requires, "Why this *thusness*?". Why this patriotic indignation?—Mr. Z. B. Vance of N. C., U. S. Senate, Aug. 6: *C. R.*, p. 7263/2.

1889 On his way home George mused *thusly*.—*Boston Journal*, Jan. 17, p. 2/3. (N. E. D.)

Ticket, The. The list of nominees for office. [1789-1862.]

1711 Chester (Pa.) carried their *ticket* entire.—Isaac Norris in *Penn-Logan Corr.*, II, 438. (N. E. D.)

1810 The Democratick *Ticket* has succeeded in Southwark (Philadelphia) by a majority of only 167.—Norfolk (Va.) *Gazette*, Oct. 3, p. 3/1.

1822 A rumor is in circulation, that you and D. Clinton are playing in concert, and that you and he will run on the same *ticket*.—Peter B. Porter to Henry Clay, Jan. 29: "Corresp.," p. 63. (1855.)

1828 The Virginia *ticket* is open to one exception, viz.: that the names of Mr. Madison and Mr. Monroe have been placed at the head of it.— *Nat. Gazette* (Phila.), Jan. 19, p. 1/2.

1834　How stands it with the *ticket* of the Nullifiers?—*The Georgian* (Savannah), July 2, p. 2/2.

1854　In Oneida, where Mr. Seymour lived, it was asserted that Mr. [Silas] Wright ran several thousand *behind his ticket.*—Mr. F. B. Cutting of N. Y., H. R., Jan. 20: p. 14/1 of his speech, as separately published.

Ticket-scalper.　A dealer in unused or partly used railroad tickets.

1880　Thomas P. Mills, a *ticket-scalper* of Indianapolis, . . . swore that he would be glad to see "20,000 bucks" come into the State for political purposes.—Mr. Wm. Windom of Minn., U. S. Senate, June 14: *C. R.,* p. 4521/1.

1882　With the eternal quarrel between railroads and *scalpers,* passengers have nothing to do.—*The Nation,* Oct. 5. (Century Dict.)

1897　The railroads themselves have created the conditions out of which the *scalper* makes his money. If the railroads did not discriminate against noncompetitive points, the business of the *scalper* would go.—Mr. Patterson of Tenn., H. R., Feb. 27: *C. R.,* p. 2470/1.

1897　See the speech of Mr. James S. Sherman of N. Y., Feb. 27: *Id.,* pp. 61-66, App.

Tick fever.　The Texas fever. See quotation.

1897　A disease which was causing much heavier direct losses . . . . was known by the local name of Texas, or Spanish fever. [It] has more recently been called . . . . . splenetic fever, Southern fever, and *tick fever.*—*Yearbook U. S. Dept. Agr.,* p. 240. (Century Dict.)

Tickler.　A dram of spirits. Colloquial.

1888　Whiskey was sold and drunk without screens or scruples. It was not usually bought by the drink, but by the *tickler.*—*Harper's Mag.,* lxxix, 388. (Century Dict.)

Tickler.　A memorandum book used as a reminder in banking and other business. Colloquial.

1889　The *ticklers,* showing in detail debts receivable in the future, those past due, and also the overdrafts, require explanation.—*Harper's Mag.,* lxxx, 464. (Century Dict.)

Ties.　Railroad "sleepers." See quotation, 1891. [1802-1862.]

1868　The higher embankments are not brought up to the proper standard, and in some instances the width of the top is less than the length of the *ties.*—Report of the Secretary of the Interior, Nov. 30: *C. G.,* p. 40/2, App.

1869　The road-bed, wherever there is an embankment, is in many places so narrow that the *ties* overlap the earthwork.—Letter to *Chicago Tribune,* March 10: *Id.,* p. 536/1.

1872　The company had purchased and carried on to the track every rail, spike, splice, and *tie* needed.—Mr. M. H. Dunnell of Minn., H. R., Dec. 16: *Id.,* p. 224/2.

1876　[Mr. C. P. Huntington] knew the rails for the Southern Pacific were bought by the Central Pacific. He could tell whether they were steel or iron, the name of the wood, out of which the *ties* were hewn, etc.— Mr. Wm. Woodburn of Nev., H. R., Apr. 8: *C. R.,* p. 2334/1.

1891　A *tie* is "one of a series of beams, commonly of wood, laid on a permanent way and bedded in the ballast, on which are laid the rails to form the track." (Century Dict.)

Tie up.　Remain at a wharf or dock, tied to a "snubbing post," to prevent drifting.

1868　An ordinary fleet of boats loaded with coal cannot pass at night through the spaces afforded by these bridges, but must *tie up* till daylight.—Mr. R. W. Clarke of O., H. R., Dec. 10: *C. G.,* p. 52/2.

Tie-up.　A suspension of traffic or business, as by a strike of employees, a breakdown of machinery, etc. (Webster).

1913　The call to strike was answered by a general walkout of thirteen hundred men along the grade, and for several weeks a complete *tie-up* of the work ensued.—*Industrial Worker* (Spokane, Wash.), July 3.

Tiger, the. A term derisively applied to the Democratic party. The "Tammany Tiger" was invented in 1871, by Thos. Nast, who took the idea from a tiger's head on the engine of the "Big Six," the fire company of which the notorious William Tweed was **chief.** See "Thomas Nast, His Period, etc." by Albert B Paine, p. 11. (N. Y., 1904.)

1871 I am sorry to see that the gentleman from Kentucky [Mr. Beck] is disposed to lash up *the party tiger* on this matter of appropriations.— Mr. J. A. Garfield of O., H. R., Feb. 27: *C. G.*, p. 1252/2.

Timber. Material for candidates of any kind.

1612 They are the fittest *timber* to make great politics of.—Sir Francis Bacon, "Essay on Goodness." (Century Dict.)

1894 I do not want to see all the presidential *timber* in the Democratic party destroyed.—Mr. M. D. Harter of O., H. R., June 20: *C. R.*, p. 6604/1.

Timbered. Wood, planted with trees. [1776-1826.]

1701 Piggott's Farm, . . . being well *Timbred.—Lond. Gazette*, No. 3724/4. (N. E. D.)

Time and again. Repeatedly. [1841-1896.]

1865 The Secretary of the Navy has *time and again* urged upon us the duty of providing [ship-yards, dry-docks, etc.]—Mr. H. T. Blow of Mo., H. R., Feb. 6: *C. G.*, p. 622/2.

1872 Any man may write a slander upon the back of an envelope, and deposit it in the post office. It has been done *time and again.*—Mr. James N. Tyner of Ind., H. R., Apr. 9: *Id.*, p. 2302/3.

1884 See DUMP.

1890 *Time and again* I have heard men declare that they would die before they would submit to capture.—Mr. M. M. Boothman of O., H. R., Apr. 21: *C. R.*, p. 3635/2.

1892 We have heard it here *time and again* . . . that we are here as a protest against the czarism of Mr. [Thomas B.] Reed, of the last Congress.—Mr. T. E. Watson of Ga., H. R., Jan. 27: *Id.*, p. 600/1.

1893 *Time and again* [the Democratic party] has carried doubtful States.— Mr. H. U. Johnson of Ind., H. R., Sept. 28: *Id.*, p. 197/1, App.

1894 *Time and again* we have passed bills in cases of this kind.—Mr. B. H. Bunn of N. C., H. R., Aug. 9: *Id.*, p. 8350/2.

Time, like. With great rapidity; "like everything."

1864 It was fully 300 yards wide, and the current was running *"like time."* —Edmund Kirke, "Down in Tennessee," p. 118. (N. Y.)

Tin-bucket parade. A term applied to the class of day-laborers who carry their lunch in tin pails or buckets.

1890 Fancy brings before me now that long line, the *"tin-bucket brigade"* of railroad laborers, extending from the Atlantic seaboard to the Pacific Ocean, and from the perpetual summers of the South to the endless winters of the North.—Mr. S. L. Milliken of Me., H. R., May 12: *C. R.*, p. 4576/1.

1892 There is no class of our people who are so . . vitally interested in the passage of this [pure food] bill as the poor, the men who compose what are termed the *"tin-pail brigades,"* . . . . who construct our railroads, build our cities, work in our factories.—Mr. A. S. Paddock of Neb., U. S. Senate, March 4: *Id.*, p. 1721/1.

Tinclad. A gunboat protected by very light plating, used on the Western rivers [during the war]. Colloquial. (Century Dict.) [Capt. Eads] converted . . . . . seven transports into what were called *tinclads.* or musket-proof gunboats.—*Scientific Amer.*, N. S., lvi, 263. (Century Dict.)

Tippy, adj. Dressed in the highest fashion, modish. (Jamieson's Sc. Dict.) Cf. Vol. II, **Tippies.** [1804-1805.]

Tip-up, or Teeter-tail. The spotted sand piper.

1900 The killdee and plover flew over the hills, and the kingfishes and the little *tip-up* were seen upon the shores of the river.—Mr. A. J. Cummings of N. Y., H. R., Apr. 30 : *C. R.*, p. 4872/2.

Tired, to make one. To exhaust his patience; to exasperate.

1895 Who builds your Western and Southern railroads? Who laid the iron rails across the continent? Why, these same "robber barons" that we hear denounced on this floor. Why, this talk *makes me tired.*—Mr. E. A. Morse of Mass., H. R., Jan. 8: *C. R.*, p. 739/1.

1911 It makes the court feel a little *tired* to think that the men most guilty are those who are false to their trust and cannot be punished.—Judge Martin of N. Y. in the Duveen case: *N. Y. Evening Post*, May 25, p. 2/6.

Tissue ballots. Ballots printed on thin paper, for the purpose of ballot-stuffing.

1879 See ONION SKIN.

1880 If you could take from the President the power to use troops at the polls to preserve peace, you could carry a Solid South by your *tissue-ballots*, bulldozing, and murder.—Mr. Philip C. Hayes of Ill., H. R., March 10: *C. R.*, p. 1452/2.

Tobacco seconds. An inferior sort of tobacco; a second crop springing from the old stalks. The word is still used.

1769 The Acts . . . prohibiting the tending of *Tobacco-seconds.*—Journal of House of Burgesses of Va., May 1, p. 205. (Richmond, 1906.)

Toe the mark, Toe the scratch. To abide strictly by the rules or laws.

1868 My colleague is afraid to *"toe the scratch"* and take a vote directly on the question.—Mr. Sam. J. Randall of Pa., H. R., March 19: *C. G.*, p. 1974/1.

Toggle, v. To fasten harness together with bits of rope, etc., in a makeshift way. [1854.] [1775, Ash has *Toggel.* Webster, 1828, has the same.]

1853 Each man has a canvas strap . . . fastened to the tow-line, or, nautically, *toggled* to the warp.—Hare, "Grinnell Exped." (1856), xi, 83. (N. E. D.)

Toll, v. To carry, to take to lead, to entice. See Vol. II, **Tole.** [1835-1867.]

1577 If they did but let them stand, they should but *toll* beggars to the towne.—Holinshed, "Descr. of England," II, xiii.

1594 She . . . with sweet sighes them on doth *toule.*—Carew's "Tasso" (1881), 117. (N. E. D.)

1596 This is an only fellow to traine a man to an arrest. . . . . or to *toale* a yoncker to an harlot.—Thos. Lodge, "Wits Miserie," p. 33.

1604 The sensitive appetite often . . . . . *toaleth* and haleth the will to consent and follow her pleasures and delights.—Thomas Wright, "Passions of the Minde," i, 8. (Century Dict.)

1791 A reward is offered for the recovery of a horse, "if strayed and not *tolled.*"—*Augusta* (Ga.) *Chronicle*, Oct. 1, p. 4/2.

1801 To *toll* us back to the times when we burnt witches.—Thos. Jefferson, "Writings" (1830), III, 467.

1894 O, you can not *toll* me back now to the time when Christopher Columbus landed.—Mr. Champ Clark of Mo., H. R., Feb. 17: *C. R.*, p. 2262/2.

1897 Used in Newfoundland, in the sense of alluring with bait.—*Journal of Am. Folk-Lore*, x, 212.

Toll, v. To pay a tax; to establish proof of ownership. [The following are Justices' notices.]

1739 Every person which . . . . shall buy or exchange any Horse . . . . without avouching or *tolling* the same before a Justice of the Peace, etc.—*S. C. Gazette*, July 14, p. 1/2.

[End of Part XIV.]

1789   Archibald Smith has *tolled* before me a yellow bay gelding.—*Augusta* (Ga.) *Chronicle*, Apr. 11, p. 4/3.

1789   Absalom Rhodes had *tolled* before me a bald eagle horse.—*Id.*, May 9, p. 3/2.

1789   David Harris *tolls* before me a white and red pied cow.—*Id.*, July 11, p. 3/1.

1794   Mr. David Liston *tolls* a brindled steer. . . . . Mr. William West *tolls* a brown cow.—*S. C. State-Gazette*, Aug. 15, p. 3/5.

Toll gin.   A public cotton gin, maintained by a toll or charge.

1896   With the subdivision of farms an almost new industry was developed in the way of *toll gins*. The old plantations had each its own gin-house, but the small farms could not bear the expense, and public gins became a necessity.—*U. S. Agr. Bulletin*, p. 357. (Century Dict.)

Tomato.   The pulpy, edible fruit of *Lycopersicum*; the love-apple. [1822-1840.]

1604   *Tomatoes*, which is a great sappy and savourie graine.—D'Acosta's "Hist. Indies," VII, ix, 519. (N. E. D.)

Tombs lawyers.   A class of men in New York, resembling the "Old Bailey practitioners," but, if possible, more unscrupulous.

1864   A man as corrupt as sin, as venal as a *Tombs lawyer*, and as ignorant as a darkey.—Edmund Kirke, "Down in Tennessee," p. 67. (N. Y.)

Tom-toe.   The great toe. Colloquial. (Century Dict.)

Tonging.   Catching oysters with tongs. **Tongers.** Men employed in this industry.

1886   A few years ago, the old method of catching oysters in Chesapeake Bay . . . . . was "*tonging*." Then the dredge system was introduced. . . . . I have it from the *tongers* as well as from the dredgers that the effect has simply been to spread the oyster-beds over the bottom of the bay.—Mr. C. B. Lore of Del., H. R., May 21: *C. R.*, p. 4784/2.

Tongue-fish.   *Symphuras plagiusa*, a small flat fish found along the coast from Virginia to Texas. (Century Dict.)

Tonguey.   Loquacious, talkative. [1835-1862.]

1382   Strive thou not with a *tungy man*.—Wiclif, "Ecclus," viii, 4.

Tony.   Genteel. Slang.

1890   Such as himself and his wife . . . . didn't expect any of her society, but Mrs. Branner ought to be *tony* enough for her—*Atlantic Mo.*, lxvii, 240. (Century Dict.)

Toot.   A lazy person. Slang.

1888   Marsh Yates, the "shif'less *toot*," and his beautiful, energetic wife.—*Harper's Mag.*, lxxvii, 801. (Century Dict.)

Toothache-grass.   The *campulosus aromaticus* of the Southern States. The culm is 3 or 4 ft. high, and bears a curious, dense, and much-awned one-sided spike with a flat rachis, which is strongly curved backward. This grass has a very pungent taste. (Century Dict.) [1837.]

Too thin.   Any disguise or pretense "easily seen through" is said to be *too thin*. [1861.] [This amounts to much the same as when one is said to "lay it on *too thick*."]

1870   When a State attempts to repudiate as against a corporation, or to impair the obligation of contracts, it does not escape from the Constitution of the United States because it does it under a pretense of amending the charter of a corporation. That disguise is *too thin.*—Mr. Roscoe Conkling of N. Y., U. S. Senate, March 10, *C. G.*, p. 1828/2.

1872   The allegation of any public necessity is too transparent: to use a common phrase, "it is *too thin*."—Mr. Eugene Casserly of Calif., U. S. Senate, May 29: *Id.*, p. 4012/2.

1879   That [objection] is t. t.—*too thin,* in the ordinary vulgar phrase.—
Mr. J. G. Cannon of Ill., H. R., Feb. 28: *C. R.,* p. 2130/2.

Top-buggy.   One with a cover.
[He] had brought his *top-buggy* along, so's he could fly high and have
a big time with the girls.—Fursman, "A Sanctified Town," p. 212.
(Century Dict.)

Top-loader.   A man who works on the top of a load of logs.
1904   But the *top-loader* is the man who runs the greatest risks, for he has
little room in which to work, and he is liable at any time to be
caught and crushed between the logs.—*Amer. Inventor,* Apr. 15.
(Century Dict.)

Top-notcher.   A first-class specimen of its kind.   Colloquial.
1902   As a matter of course there are not a sufficient number of *"top-
notchers"* to go around, the result being . . . . the use of many inferior
specimens [of cattle].—*Rep. Kan. State Board Agr.,* p. 64.   (Century
Dict.)

Tortillas.   See quotation.
1912   In the markets of Mexico the women are always in evidence with a
handful of dough and a little portable charcoal stove on which to cook
tortillas and hot tamales.   The *tortillas* are a kind of cake made from
parboiled Indian corn.   A rolling pin, made of stone, and a small
stone table serve as the implements with which to crush the corn and
a paste is formed of the meal by the addition of a little water.   The
cake is baked on a plate of iron or earthen ware and served hot.   The
Mexicans of San Antonio, Tex., have a well-established *tortilla* habit
there, too.   In the old days, eighteen years or so ago, the *tortilla* was
always to be found on the "plaza tables," those long, rough, makeshift
tables of planks, set up in Alamo, Main, and Military Plazas on
Saturday nights, and lighted by flaring torches.—*N. Y. Evening Post,*
Sept. 5, p. 5/2.

Torup.   The snapping-turtle.   Southern.
1894   The small edible tortoise has a name and a fame; it is the terrapin.
But whence that name?   Not from *terra,* earth.   Farmers and sailors
call the big "snapper" the *torup* or *torop.* . . . There can be no doubt
that it is an Indian name originally.—*The Critic,* p. 268.   (Century
Dict.)

Totalize.   To reduce to a sum total.
1879   They sent the probable results, and when those results were *totalized*
the managers knew etc.—Mr. Roscoe Conkling of N. Y., U. S. Senate,
May 16: *C. R.,* p. 1389/2.

Tote, v.   To carry, usually in the hand or on the back or shoulders.
[1677-1868.]
1781   *Tot* is used for "carry" in some of the southern states.—J. Wither-
spoon, "Works" (1802) IV, 470.   (N. E. D.)
1803   (Dec.)   I came to a camp where some negroes were *toting* tobacco to
market.—Lorenzo Dow's "Journal," Vol. I, p. 82/1.   (1850)
1863   [He sold the drinks] at the rate of a "bit" a glass, and of four bits
for "as much as a man could *tote.*"—Edmund Kirke, "My Southern
Friends," p. 49.   (N. Y.)
1868   I cannot believe that [Gen. Grant] will ever degenerate into a kind of
hand-organ to be *toted around* on the back of the gentleman from
Illinois [Mr. E. B. Washburne], while his whole family sit on top of
the machine grinning and catching pennies like a troop of monkeys.—
Mr. Ignatius Donnelly of Minn., H. R., May 2: *C. G.,* p. 2353/1.
[His speech, uttered under strong irritation, several times passed the
bounds of parliamentary etiquette.]
1874   Is it not time to call a halt in this wild negro-*toting* legislation?—Mr.
W. M. Robbins of N. C., H. R., Jan. 24: *C. R.,* p. 900/1.
1893   I will stay here till the ants *tote* me out of the keyhole before I will
give up this fight.—Mr. T. E. Watson of Ga., H. R., Feb. 21: *Id.,*
p. 1972/2.

Tote, n. A pack or burden. Uncommon. [1831.]
1771-2 That this was the whole *tote* of his case is notoriously known.—Ess.
Batchelor (1773) II, 40. (N. E. D.)

Totem. The emblem of a clan or family among the Indians, especially
on the Pacific Coast; usually the figure of an animal, carved in wood
and rudely colored. The people of Seattle have secured great
totem-posts, and set them up.

Tottle. A combination of *toddle* and *totter*. [1838.]
1872 It is simply an iron and unyielding shoe, into which, like that of the
Chinese woman, the foot of this growing country is to be pressed, so
that all the rest of its life it will *tottle* impotently among the nations
of the earth.—Mr. H. L. Dawes of Mass., H. R., March 13: *C. G.*,
p. 1658/3.

Touch. Sympathy or close relation. American?
1889 The European in Morocco feels that when he is in company with a
Barbary Jew he is *in touch with* Europe.—*The Academy*, Lond., June
1, p. 371. (N. E. D.)
1890 I do not want a large force of officials . . . whose avowed duty . . .
will be to go around among the people and come *"in touch"* with
them.—Mr. A. P. Gorman of Md., U. S. Senate, June 24: *C. R.*, p.
6417/2.

Towhead. The hooded merganser, *Lophodytes cucullatus.* Southern.

Towhead. A shoal or other obstruction in a stream-bed, perceptible
through a ripple caused by it on the surface. (Century Dict.)

Towhee, Towhee Bunting. The chewink, ground-robin, or marsh-
robin of the U. S., *Pipilo erythrophthalmus*, or any other species of
the genus *Pipilo.* (Century Dict.)

Towney. A townsman. Slang.
1905 He wa'n't no outlandish man neither: he was a born and bred *towney*
of ourn.—G. S. Wasson, "The Green Shay," ch. vii. (Century Dict.)

Town Meeting. In New England, New York, Wisconsin, Michigan,
Minnesota, and Illinois, a primary meeting of the voters of a town
or township, legally summoned for the consideration of matters of
local administration. The functions of the town meeting are most
extensive in New England. (Century Dict.)
18.. In a *town-meeting* the great secret of political science was uncovered,
and the problem solved how to give every individual his fair weight
in the government, without any disorder from numbers.—R. W.
Emerson, "Historical Discourse at Concord."

Township. In surveys of United States public lands, a division of territory six miles square containing 36 sections. (Webster.) Also, a
primary unit of local government, varying in different localities; in
New England it is called the **town.**
1639 Plymouth Colony Records, I, 113.
1643 Records of Plymouth, Mass. (1889) I, 14.
1649 Boston Record Commissioners' Reports II, 96.
1870 The Senator from Vermont told me the other day that people were
moving from his State in [by] *townships.*—Mr. S. C. Pomeroy of Kan.,
U. S. Senate, Apr. 7: *C. G.*, p. 2484/1.
1879 There is in Colorado a desert which, if laid off in sections and *townships*, a worm could not live on.—Mr. L. C. Gause of Ark., H. R.,
Feb. 18: *C. R.*, p. 1563/1.

Trace. A track or trail. [1829-1854.]
1667 These as a line their long dimension drew,
Streaking the ground with sinuous *trace.*—"Paradise Lost," vii, 481.
1807 We . . . took the large Spanish *trace* of the Arkansas river.—Pike,
"Sources of the Mississippi" (1810) II, App. 24. (N. E. D.)

Track. A railway line.
1865 There is now between Washington and Baltimore a *double track* amply
sufficient to answer all [necessary] purposes.—Mr. Reverdy Johnson
of Md., U. S. Senate, Feb. 21: *C. G.*, p. 941/3.

1866 The laborer who constructs the *track* and keeps it in repair.—**Mr. Wm. A. Newell** of N. J., H. R., May 19: *Id.*, p. 2701/2.

1877 He said that the railroad *tracks* were torn up. He was asked what length of *track* was torn up. . . . He was asked how many men it would take to tear up those *tracks* during one night.—Mr. Carter H. Harrison of Ill., H. R., Nov. 9: *C. R.*, p. 325/1.

Track, v. To make footmarks upon.

1869 "Stand still there!" she called to me as I approached the door, "and don't come in to *track* my floor."—Mrs. H. B. Stowe, "Oldtown Stories," p. 21. (Century Dict.)

Tracker. One who tracks or tows a boat or raft.

1890 A hundred naked, shouting, and arm-swinging *trackers* dragged each one [a junk] slowly along, now straining every muscle at the long tow-line now slacking up, as the man seated at the bow of the boat directed them.—*Century Mag.*, xli, 729.

Track layer. A plate-layer; one who lays down rails for a railway, and does other work incidental thereto.

Trackman. One who looks after the track of a railroad.

1871 The *trackmen*, in their red overstockings, their many-colored blouses, and their brilliant toques, look like gnomes.—*Scribner's Mag.*, iv, 646. (Century Dict.)

Tracks, to die in one's. To die where one stands, without retreating. [1843-1864.]

1866 [These people] would *die in their tracks* rather than falter.—Mr. Edgar Cowan of Pa., U. S. Senate, Dec. 18: *C. G.*, p. 166/3.

1882 See BUCK.

1889 He was in for stealing horses, but I think the real thief swore it off on him. . . . . He had better have shot the boy *in his tracks.—Century Mag.*, xl, 224.

1891 The whites swore by all that was holy that they would *die in their tracks* before the negroes should take charge of the high school.—Newsp. extract. *C. R.*, Jan. 17: p. 101/2, App.

1892 A Friday afternoon recess would be given, when a certain number of [Indian children] would be furloughed for four days, perhaps, to visit their parents in tepees. The little creatures would go out of the doors, and you might speak to them in English, and they would *die in their tracks* before they would speak a word of English to you.—Mr. J. T. Morgan of Ala., U. S. Senate, March 23: *Id.*, p. 2403/2.

Track walker. A trackman who inspects a certain section of railway-track, especially before the passage of very fast trains, to look for breaks or other defects, and to tighten up wedges and nuts. (Century Dict.)

1872 The chapters give a logical account of the origin and development of Railways in America, and describe the work of the railroad man from president to *tract-walker.—Scribner's Mag.*, vi, p. 29 of advts. (Century Dict.)

Trade, n. A bargain, an exchange.

1879 See HUGGER-MUGGER.

1884 If anybody ever found [a Yankee], even if he was considered intellectually a very inferior man in a New England town, who could not get the best of any other human being outside of New England in any *trade*, from a jack-knife up to a $350,000 ship, I should like to hire him and loan him out to Barnum.—Mr. G. G. Vest of Mo., U. S. Senate, May 1: *C. R.*, p. 3658/1.

Trade, or Trade off. To exchange. [1806-1888.]

1865 Most prisoners [at Salisbury, N. C.] *traded* the buttons from their blouses for food.—Deposition of Thomas E. Wolfe, Jan. 30: *C. G.*, Jan. 30, p. 491/3.

Trade Dollar. A coin containing 378 troy grains of silver and 42 grains of alloy, and intended to be used in trade with Asiatic countries.

1873 The *"trade dollar"* has been adopted mainly for the benefit of the people of California, and others engaged in trade with China. That is the only coin measured by the grain instead of by the gram.—Mr. John Sherman of O., U. S. Senate, Jan. 17: *C. G.*, p. 672/3.

1876 The most striking change made by the Act of 1873 was the introduction of a new dollar called the *trade-dollar*. . . . There was a great demand for silver in China; and the Mexican pillar dollar . . . had gotten into the markets of China, and was the most desirable coin, because it was worth a little more than the dollar of the United States, and more than the dollar of any other country. . . . . . In order to induce the Chinese to take our dollar instead of the Mexican dollar, ... we ·authorized the holders of bullion to present their bullion at the mints of the United States, to be coined into trade dollars containing four hundred and twenty grains of standard silver.— The same, Apr. 10: *C. R.*, p. 2343/2.

Trail. A rude path made by the repeated going upon it of men or animals, or both. [1883.]

1807 The rocks were in some places breast high, and no path or *trail* of any kind.—P. Gass, "Journal," 125. (N. E. D.)

1886 A large part of the country of the Pacific Coast has scarcely been penetrated outside of the roads or *trails* which lead from the seaports to the interior.—*Pop. Sci. Mo.* xxviii, 722. (Century Dict.)

Trailer, Trailer Car. A rear car, drawn by a forward car.

1897 Mr. Bingham:—What does the gentleman mean by *"a trailer car"*? Mr. Loud:—I mean such as are used in the [postal] service in the city of Washington. Mr. Bingham:—I merely wanted the gentleman's definition of a *"trailer."* Mr. Loud:—I think the House understands that a *trailer* car is one which does not require either a conductor or a motorman.—H. R., Feb. 12: *C. R.*, p. 1779/1.

Train shed. A station consisting merely of a platform with a roof supported by posts.

1904 "Now don't over-eat," [said she] as she said good-bye to her husband in the *train-shed* at Chicago.—*The Reader*, p. 646. (Century Dict.)

Tramp. An idler who goes from place to place, doing as little work as possible; often a begging, thieving vagrant. Contracted form of **Tramper.**

1878 We pass'd quite a number of *tramps*, singly or in couples,—one squad, a family in a rickety one-horse wagon, with some baskets evidently their work and trade,—the man seated on a low board, driving.— Walt Whitman, "Specimen Days" (1887), pp. 178-9.

1881 The "sturdy beggars" who infested England two or three centuries ago reappear in our midst under the name of *tramps*.—James F. Clarke, "Self-Culture," p. 280. (Century Dict.)

1883 Under your protective-tariff system, ... millionaires can be counted by the thousands, and on every hand are counted the *"tramps,"* a name that was never heard of until this high protective system brought into existence the class which it describes.—Mr. R. P. Bland of Mo., H. R., Jan. 27: *C. R.*, p. 1678/2.

1884 The [Mormon] people are an industrious, laborious people. No beggars or *tramps* are found in the streets.—Mr. Joseph E. Brown of Ga., U. S. Senate, May 27: *Id.*, p. 4555/2.

1888 For a number of the years since 1870, the country has been filled with *"tramps."*—Mr. G. D. Wise of Va., H. R., May 9: *Id.*, p. 153/1, App.

1890 It was under a high protective tariff that the word *"tramp"* was invented to express the actual condition of . . . . that homeless, thriftless, wandering, gypsy population which from year to year lead the life of beggary and destitution.—Mr. W. B. Bate of Tenn., U. S. Senate, Aug. 14: *Id.*, p. 8564/2.

1894 See COMBINE.

Tramp steamer, Ocean Tramp. A vessel carrying freight as occasion serves, not plying regularly between certain ports.
1897 The larger proportion of steamships now belongs to regular lines, not *"tramps"* as formerly.—Mr. Adolph Meyer of La., H. R., Feb. 23: *C. R.*, p. 80/2, App.

Travail, Travois, Travoise. A primitive vehicle of the North American Indians, usually two trailing poles serving as shafts and bearing a platform or net for a load. (Webster.) See the Century Dict., which gives a picture of this contrivance. Fr.
1892 On the plains they will have horses dragging *travoises*, dogs with *travoises*, women and children loaded with impedimenta, a colt or two running loose.—*Harper's Mag.*, p. 508. (Century Dict.)
1904 In a month "Richard's himself again," ready to fly over the grassy sward with his savage master, or to drag the *travaux* and pack the buxom squaw.—*Century Mag.*, xxxvii, 339. (Century Dict.)

Traveler, Traveling. For the discussion of one *l* or two, see Vol. II. [1824-1869.] A similar simplification of spelling is observed in *worshiper, worshiping.* For an example of the latter, see **Silverite**, 1892.
1850 See HOOSIER.
1880 See WATER-BAR.
1912 A "hostile manifestation," in the eyes of a railroad, might seem to shipper or *traveller* the best of actions in their behalf.—*N. Y. Evening Post*, Jan. 1, p. 4/5.

Treaty Indians. Those living under a treaty with the United States.
1876 The gentleman must not confound the hostile with the *treaty Sioux.*—Mr. Martin Maginnis of Wyo., H. R., June 19: *C. R.*, p. 3885/2.

Tree, v. To drive up a tree, or "into a corner." [1818-1882.]
a.1700 *Tree the Martern*, Dislodge him.—Dict. Canting Crew. (N. E. D.)
1870 See RANGERS.

Tree nail. A large wooden peg. [1800-1817.]
1295 Exchequer Accounts. (N. E. D.)

Tribune of the People, The. Henry Clay. (1777-1852.)
1872 A great man, Henry Clay, who in his day was called *"the tribune of the people."*—Mr. James Brooks of N. Y., H. R., Apr. 2: *C. G.*, p. 2110/1.

Trig, n. An obstacle or brake; hence, gravel or other stuff laid on a slippery downhill road. **Trig,** v., to act as a brake or check. [1830.]
1647 Nor is his suit in danger to be stopt Or with the *trigges* of long demurrers propt.—Stapylton "Juvenal," xvi, 62. (N. E. D.)
1720 Phillips's "New World of Words" has: To *trig*, to skid, scratch, or stop a Wheel. *Trigger*, an Iron to *trig*, or stay a Wheel.
1908 Put the swale hay to the rest of the pitches. It will *trig* better than gravel.—Holman F. Day, "King Spruce," ch. xxv. (Century Dict.)
1908 Twenty rods further they struck the hay, spread thickly for the *trig*,—the checking of the runners. And the sled-runners, biting it, jerked and halted.—The same, ch. xxvi.

Trimmings. Accessories, furnishings, facings, adornments. Used colloquially in a wide sense. [1840-1851.]
1612 Shelues, deskes, seates, and other needful *trimmings.*—Will of T. Bodley. (N. E. D.)
1894 We ask only a plain brick building, with limestone *trimmings.*—Mr. A. S. Berry of Ky., H. R., Aug. 8: *C. R.*, p. 8314/1.
1896 Mr. Cannon:—[The Chicago building] may have some additions. Mr. Crisp:—Some *trimmings.* (Laughter.)—H. R., Jan. 22: *Id.*, p. 887/1.

Trip and twitch. A catch in wrestling.
1876 In this body . . . . there is none of that *trip and twitch* by which legislation is jerked through so quickly that you cannot see it go.—Mr. Roscoe Conkling of N. Y., U. S. Senate, Aug. 8: *C. R.*, p. 5302/2.

Trotting horse. A fine horse used in trotting-races.

1869 I would like to know whether this man might not possibly raise the money he is required to pay by mortgaging his *trotting-horse* Hero.—Mr. W. D. Kelley of Pa., H. R., Feb. 5: *C. G.*, p. 917/1.

Trowsaloons. A humorous combination of *trousers* and *pantaloons.*

1827 [One shot] glanced and passed through the *trowsaloons* of the Jackson man.—Norfolk (Va.) *Beacon*, Oct. 13, p. 2/2.

Truck, Garden truck. Market-garden produce. [1784-1902.]

1894 The Canadians were willing to offer almost anything to secure a market for their surplus "garden *truck*."—Mr. W. D. Washburn of Minn., U. S. Senate, Apr. 23: *C. R.*, p. 3990/1.

Trunk railroad, Trunk line. A main line with branches. [The Grand Trunk Railway of Canada, for example.]

1884 Here are eight or ten—I think eight—great *trunk railroads* running eastward from Chicago to the New York market.—Mr. Stewart of Vt., H. R., Dec. 10: *C. R.*, p. 163/1.

Trusts. Combinations which aim at monopolies.

1888 Take the Standard Oil *trust*, the whisky *trust*, the cotton-seed-oil *trust*, the sugar *trust*, and various coal *trusts*; take the whole list from A to Z, and not one of them stands upon or is supported by the authority of national law.—Speech of Mr. James G. Blaine at Dover, Me., Aug. 31. See *C. R.*, May 10, 1890, p. 4526/1.

1888 I want to say a word about *trusts.* We are constantly told that high tariff produces *trusts.* Let us see about this. The most gigantic and merciless "*trust*" today is the *coal-oil trust.* There is no duty upon coal-oil; because the tariff does not protect the *trust.* But it is proposed . . . to aid this *trust* by the tariff. . . . The next largest trust in the world is the "*sugar trust*," and it is proposed to continue this. . . . . . . The "*coffee trust*," which raised the price of coffee . . . a short time ago, had no duty to aid or protect it. The richest grain and pork "*trusts*" are purely speculative.—Mr. O. S. Gifford of Dakota, H. R., June 9: *Id.*, pp. 211-12, App.

1890 Those combinations which have so frequently and so arbitrarily limited production, and increased the prices of the prime commodities of life, and which in commercial circles are classified as "*trusts*."—Mr. A. M. Dockery of Mo., H. R., May 8: *Id.*, p. 4314/1.

1890 Almost all of them [are] English *trusts*,—the iron *trust*, the tin *trust*, the china and earthenware *trust*, the plate-glass *trust*, the foreign sugar *trust*, the coffee *trust*, the undertakers' *trust*, the carriage, cart, and wagon *trust*, the sheet-iron *trust*, the wooden-screw *trust*; and the gentleman from Maryland [Mr. McComas] told my friend Mr. Wilson the other day that he certainly could name twelve *trusts* that he knew of in England. . . . I care not whether they are called "*trusts*" or "combinations."—Mr. D. B. Henderson of Ia., H. R., May 10: *Id.*, p. 4525/2.

1892 As to the various kinds, see *C. R.*, 1892, July 26: pp. 6759-75, 6780-3.

1892 The oil *trust*, the whisky *trust*, the sugar *trust*, and the cotton-seed oil *trust*, were all formed for the . . purpose avowed by the supporters of the subtreasury.—Mr. C. J. Boatner of La., H. R., Aug. 4: *Id.*, p. 7046/2.

1898 A cracker *trust*, a tobacco *trust*, and a new coal *trust*, all within a short month.—Mr. Jerry Simpson of Kan., H. R., Feb. 3: *Id.*, p. 1407/2.

Tumbleweed. A name given to several kinds of plants, the tops of which separate and are rolled about by the wind, scattering their seed. Also called **rolling-weed.**

1877 The list of plants having the habit of rounding up their stems and branches so as to form a nearly spherical plant body, which at the end of the season breaks away at the root, thus forming a *tumble-weed*, must be increased by adding the winged pig-weed.—*Amer. Naturalist* (Phila.) xxi, 929. (Century Dict.)

1894 As soon as [the Russian thistle] becomes ripe, it loosens from the ground and goes traveling over the prairies for a distance of 20 miles, like the ordinary *tumbleweed*. It will roll from county to county.— Mr. J. H. Kyle of S. Dak., U. S. Senate, July 17: *C. R.*, p. 7580/2. [See also the report, pp. 8046-8.]

Tump-line. A strap by which a pack is carried across a portage or through the woods. It crosses the forehead, [leaving] the hands free for clearing the way with an ax or otherwise; [but] is frequently shifted so as to cross the breast, for temporary relief. Maine. (Century Dict.)

Tum-tum. The heart. Chinook jargon. [1856.]

1888   (24.) Tawun güd naika tlatowa
          Naika nanitch naika sister.
          Naika tlōs *tumtum.*
          (I went to town.
          I saw my sister.
          My heart was glad.)
          —"Chinook Songs," *Journal of Am. Folk-Lore,* I, 223.

Tunker. A Dunker or Dunkard. [Ger. *tunken*, to dip.] One of a religious denomination originating in Germany, which still flourishes in the south of Pennsylvania. The official name is *German Baptist Brethren.* [1800-1833.]

1874 I knew of one case in my country where an honest old *Tunker*, one of the people known as Mennonites, . . . left the [tobacco] stamp on his boxes.—Mr. Thomas Whitehead of Va., H. R., Jan. 10: *C. R.*, p. 558/2.

Tunket. A meaningless term used for "devil," "hell," etc. (Century Dict.) [1847.]

1905 "Who in *tunket* is it backs up the old creetur, anyways?" asked Master Fairway.—G. S. Wasson, "The Green Shay," ch. iii. (Century Dict.)

1908 "Hey? Did you speak to me?" asked the widow sweetly. "Did I speak? No, I screeched! what in *tunket* . . . ."—J. C. Lincoln, "Cy Whittaker's Place," ch. xiv. (Id.)

Turkey, to say. To "say turkey" to someone is to give him the advantage in a bargain. See quotations. [This differs from "talking turkey" to him, which means talking seriously, or telling him "what's what."] [1851-1909.]

1866 The advantage is all on one side. It is like the Indian and the white man dividing the possum and the turkey. The white man said to the Indian, "Now you take the possum and I take the turkey, or, if you do not like that, I will take the turkey and you take the possum." "Why," said the Indian, "*you have not said turkey to me once.*"— Mr. Edgar Cowan of Pa., U. S. Senate, June 6: *C. G.*, pp. 2987-8.

1876 It seems to me that the Turkish officials have never *said* "turkey" to us once.—Mr. W. M. Springer of Ill., H. R., Feb. 9: *C. R.*, p. 976/1.

1876 We do not *say turkey* to the minority once.—Mr. Brown of Kan., H. R., Apr. 29: *Id.*, p. 2838/2.

1883 [Turkey, to say.] The story about the Indian is told also by Mr. R. Q. Mills of Tex., H. R., Jan. 26: *Id.*, p. 1643/2.

1884 [This bill] proposes to raise the pension of the widow of the Union soldier, but "*turkey*" *is not once said* to the widow of a Mexican soldier.—Mr. John S. Williams of Ky., U. S. Senate, June 24: *Id.*, p. 5519/1.

1896 That is a sort of civil service that *says* "turkey" to every Democrat and "buzzard" to every Republican. I want no buzzard in mine.— Mr. H. R. Gibson of Tenn., H. R., Dec. 22: *Id.*, p. 409/2.

1899 Why do these professed champions of liberty insist on *saying "turkey"* to the Filipinos and "buzzard" to the negroes? The same, Jan. 25: p. 108/1, App.

1899 See PORK.

Turn down. To disregard and repudiate. Colloquial.

1894 As soon as anyone of these parties or societies . . . . has shown signs of anarchy, communism, or oppression, . . . such parties have been *"turned down"* and relegated to their proper place.—Speech by Senator Warren at Omaha. See *C. R.*, Aug. 10, p. 8393/2.

1896 The House did not assent to that Senate amendment. . . I was not sorry . . that it was *turned down.*—Mr. J. G. Cannon of Ill., H. R., May 27: *Id.*, p. 5807/1.

1896 [This man] is a helpless paralytic. He cannot sit up without being propped. . . . . . Yet in spite of these reports the Pension Office has *turned him down.*—Mr. E. J. Hainer of Neb., H. R., June 11: *Id.*, p. 6453/2.

1898 Mr. Clay . . . . wrote his celebrated Raleigh letter against the annexation of Texas, and was *turned down* by the popular voice.—Mr. W. B. Bate of Tenn., U. S. Senate, June 30: *Id.*, p. 6524/1.

Turnout. A railway siding, where one train turns out to let another pass along the track. [1846-1853.] The word occurs in an Act of Geo. IV, 1826, but is now disused in England, "siding" having taken its place. (N. E. D.)

1879 The railroad companies require additional switches, *turnouts*, tracks, yards, chutes, etc., for the purpose of distribution.—Mr. McPherson of N. J., U. S. Senate, May 26: *C. R.*, p. 1615/2.

Turtlers. A turtle-catcher. [1769-1778.]

1697 The Jamaica *turtlers* have such [nets].—Dampier, "Voyages" (1729), I, 395. (N. E. D.)

Twister. A local whirlwind. Colloquial.

1902 [These] whirling winds are strong enough to blow down trees and overturn buildings. Violent local storms of this kind are often called cyclones, or *prairie twisters*, in the Mississippi Valley.—W. M. Davis, "Elem. Phys. Geog." (Century Dict.)

Twister. A twisting movement on the part of a horse.

1903 It was a broncho named "E. A." (who used a combination of "sunfish" and *"twister"*) that proved the hardest to ride.—*Wide World Mag.*, p. 548. (Century Dict.)

Twistical. Not "straight"; dark and devious.

1815 In his dealings with t'other sex, he is a leetle *twistical*, according to their tell.—David Humphreys, "The Yankey in England," p. 43. [The vocabulary, p. 109, says: tortuous, not above-board, not quite moral.]

Twitter. The refuse of blubber.

1904 See DECK-POT.

U

Ugly. Ill-natured, vicious. [1809-1864.]

1869 He was jest the crossest, *ugliest* critter that ever ye see, and he was ugly jest for the sake o' *ugliness.*—Mrs. H. B. Stowe, "Old-Town Stories," p. 196. (Century Dict.)

1870 You will sometimes see one active, *ugly* man in a community make the whole community more or less [vicious]. He will control a great many others by his bad influence.—Mr. John F. Farnsworth of Ill., H. R., Jan. 12: *C. G.*, p. 402/3.

Ultraism. The holding of extreme opinions. [1850-1862.]

1836 *Ultraism* is another evil, growing out of the division of churches. . . . . One church sufficed for the apostles. Three hundred will not content the *ultraists* of our age.—Dr. G. T. Chapman, "Sermons," pp. 357-8. (Hartford, Conn.)

1844 [These men] went over to General Jackson, and with them a spirit of *ultraism.*—Epes Sargent, "Life etc. of H. Clay," p. 44/1.

1850 We find in the South none of the *ultraisms* in politics and religion [which exist] in Northern Communities.—Wilmington (N. C.) *Commercial,* Oct. 29, p. 2/3.

Ultraist. A person who carries things to extremes; of extreme opinions and views. [1850-1862.]

1844 In Broadway there walks here and there an *ultraist* of fashion.— Lydia M. Child, "Letters from New York," Second S., p. 108. (Lond., 1845.)

Ultra measures. Extreme procedures; measures embodying the views of **Ultra's,** q.v.

1863 See CAP THE CLIMAX, TO.

Ultras. Extremists; especially of Northern or Southern leanings. [The word also has a general use meaning the *"creme de la creme"*; for example, the ultra fashionable, the highest of society; the most radical of radicals, etc.]

Uncle. A term frequently used in the South in addressing or speaking of an old "darkey." [1835-1861.]

1879 The majority of [the arrivals in Kansas City] are either old *uncles* and *aunties* or pickaninnies; never saw so many people with no middle-aged among them.—Letter, Apr. 25. See *C. R.,* p. 2351/2.

Uncle Sam. The United States Government. [1813-1864.]

1869 Thrice happy quadrupeds! [The furred animals of Alaska.] But yesterday added to the household of *Uncle Sam,* and known to us only by tradition, and already you are subjects of particular solicitude.— Mr. Alex. H. Jones of N. C., H. R., Apr. 1: *C. G.,* p. 436/1.

Uncle Sam's Webfoot. See quotation.

1896 I doubt if you will find more encomiums . . . . of what the immortal Lincoln called *"Uncle Sam's webfoot"*—the Navy—than have been spoken during the present debate.—Mr. J. B. Robinson of Pa., H. R., March 26; *C. R.,* p. 3248/2.

Underbilling. Charging at less than the true measure or weight.

1889 Two cases of *underbilling* have been investigated during the present month. In one of them a shipper at a small country station procured the station agent to bill 44,100 pounds of grain as 30,000 pounds, a fraud which, if not detected, would have saved him $27.67 in freight. In the other a car-load shipper obtained a series of short weights from a weigh-master in charge of the company's scales; the loss to the line upon two car-loads only would have been $45.99.—*Report of the Interstate Commerce Commission,* Feb. 23: See *C. R.,* p. 2667/1.

Under ditch. Irrigated land. Local.

1888 [The] land thus improved was *"under-ditch,"* to use the parlance of the country, . . water had been conducted from the mountain sides to the barren alkali land, and made it blossom like the rose.—Mr. C. F. Manderson of Neb., U. S. Senate, July 30: *C. R.,* p. 7020/1.

Underpinning. The foundation of a building, or a part of it; hence, the figurative use, meaning the foundation upon which anything rests. [1804-1860.]

1774 The treacherous *underpinning* and clumsy buttresses of arbitrary power.—Edmund Burke, on American Taxation. (Century Dict.)

1872 We found the *underpinning* of the [Executive Mansion], if I may so call it, all its underwork, in a state of extreme rottenness.—Mr. A. A. Sargent of Calif., H. R., May 22: *C. G.,* p. 3759/2.

1895 A fisherman hysterically floundering on a quagmire, with his feet unsteady on the quivering *underpinning* of the marsh, may not have so clear a conception of the proper method of his release . . . . . as some one standing on firm ground above the mire.—Mr. C. A. Russell of Conn., H. R., Dec. 28: *C. R.*, p. 396/2.

Unionize. To bring under the influence of a trade-union.

1900 New England papers [report] that nearly every *"unionized"* town in that section has now the eight-hour day for building trades workmen.—*Review of Reviews*, xxi, 651. (Century Dict.)

1903 The shadow of the coal heap lies dark upon these *"unionized"* little ones as they grow up. . . . Within a few years the breaker boy will be a miner.—*McClure's Mag.*, p. 444.

Union Leagues. Associations formed to maintain the Federal authority.

1871 Immediately after the close of the war, *Union leagues* were organized, I believe, all over the South, at all events in North Carolina.—Mr. A. I. Boreman of W. Va., U. S. Senate, Apr. 13: *C. G.*, p. 227/2, App.

Unit Rule, the. The rule adopted in Democratic National Conventions, of counting the vote of each' State as a unit, disregarding in each case the minority. The Republican National Convention of 1880 refused to adopt a similar rule.

United States. Plural, not singular.

1894 Up to within a very recent period the nomenclature of the Constitution has been universally followed by our public men. I know of no State paper, though there may have been, prior to the message of Pres. Cleveland upon the subject of Hawaii, which departs from the language of the Constitution on that subject. Mr. Calhoun universally used United States in the plural, and so did his great antagonist Mr. Webster.—Mr. J. Z. George of Miss., U. S. Senate, Apr. 6: *C. R.*, p. 3492/2.

Unload. To dispose of property the holding of which is risky or undesirable to some one who is probably unwilling to receive it. To transfer, generally. To get rid of [an incubus]. [1881-1890.]

1876 Mr. S. S. Cox:—Why did your party at Cincinnati *unload* [Mr. Blaine]? Why are you all the time *unloading?* You *unloaded* a candidate for governor in Indiana the other day. What for? What had he done? Why did you *unload* Ex-Secretary Bristow? Mr. Robinson:—We *unloaded* one, and you *unloaded* four. Your men stole $67,000, and your party admitted it, and *unloaded* them. We *unloaded* one, and are now 10,000 votes ahead.—H. R., Aug. 8: *C. R.*, p. 5332/2.

1888 Mr. Peters:—We know that you *unloaded* your Indians onto us. Mr. Cobb:—*Unloaded* them on the gentleman from Kansas! Who was there first, he or the Indians? Mr. Peters:—Who was in your country first, you or the Indians? Mr. Cobb:—Did we *unload* the Indians on the gentleman, or did he *unload* himself on the Indians?—H. R., July 26: *Id.*, p. 6878/2.

1890 See MINE-SALTER.

1897 He was . . . anxious to *unload* an old speech which he had carried in his pockets for several months.—Mr. N. T. Hopkins of Ky., H. R., Feb. 18: *Id.*, p. 57, App.

1900 You *unload* a lot of embryo and unbaked college graduates upon us.—Mr. E. O. Wolcott of Colo., U. S. Senate, June 5: *Id.*, p. 6668/2.

Unpleasantness, the late unpleasantness. The Civil War; any disturbance of the peace.

1868 Leaving out of view *"the late unpleasantness."*—Mr. W. M. Stewart of Nev., U. S. Senate, Feb. 14: *C. G.*, p. 1174/1.

1868 Perhaps the ovation which the rebel generals received in New York has inspired them with new hope, and they think the *"little unpleasantness"* did not amount to much, after all.—The same, July 9: *Id.*, p. 3880/2.

1868 In the riot of St. Landry, while the carpet-baggers were fleeing for their lives at the close of the *"unpleasantness,"* the negroes . . . were flocking to Opelousas.—*Planters' Banner,* Oct. 17. See *C. G.,* July 2, 1870: p. 565/3, App.

1869 [If war is to be conducted without injury to private property], it is no war, but, in the cant language of the day, a "slight *onpleasantness*" for the moment.—Mr. Jacob M. Howard of Mich., U. S. Senate, Jan. 7: *Id.,* p. 229/3.

1870 There seems to be a desire to take away from the rebellion every criminal feature, to make [it] what it has been called by some, a mere *unpleasantness.*—Mr. O. P. Morton of Ind., U. S. Senate, May 16: *Id.,* p. 3489/2.

1871 [This] is a claim upon the United States for certain property in the city of Charleston . . . destroyed in a bombardment of that city which took place during what my friend from South Carolina, I suppose, would call the *"late unpleasantness."*—Mr. G. F. Edmunds of Vt., U. S. Senate, March 3: *Id.,* p. 2008/2.

1872 During *"the late unpleasantness"* it became the duty of the Government to do several things that it had never done before.—Mr. Timothy O. Howe of Wisc., U. S. Senate, Apr. 30: *Id.,* p. 2911/3.

1882 We know the history of the recent *"unpleasantness,"* as I will call it,—well, "war," gentlemen say.—Mr. John A. Logan of Ill., U. S. Senate, June 1: *Id.,* p. 4418/1.

1887 A Democratic House of Representatives, in which very naturally those who had the fortune or misfortune to wear clothing of a certain color during the *"late unpleasantness"* found ourselves seated at the foot of the table.—Mr. C. A. Boutelle of Me., H. R., Jan. 6: *Id.,* p. 412/2.

1891 I always deplore the recalling on the floor of Congress of the history of the past *"unpleasantness."* I do not think it ever conduces to the benefit of legislation or the country.—Mr. E. S. Williams of O., H. R., Jan. 29: *Id.,* p. 1981/2.

Unterrified. An adjective derisively applied to the Democratic party, and sometimes coupled with "unwashed." [1832-1863.]

1848 The *"unterrified democracy"* are very hard [pushed] to understand the character of the Oregon Bill.—Wilmington (N. C.) *Commercial,* Sept. 2, p. 2/1.

1866 [Andrew Johnson's] traducers charge that he actually suffered *unterrified Democrats* to stand around him, listening to his speech; and that too without invoking the aid of provost marshals to hunt them down and incarcerate them in the military bastile on Capitol Hill.—Mr. James W. Patterson of N. H., H. R., May 19: *C. G.,* p. 2699/1.

1870 In those days we were called the "barefooted" Democracy, the *"great unwashed,"* and other like significant names. I wondered at it then, but I do not now. . . . We were not to blame for our appearance. The fact was, we did not even possess enough of their jingling sixpences to buy shoes for our feet or soap for our ablutions.—Mr. E. C. Ingersoll of Ill., H. R., June 9: *Id.,* p. 528/1, App.

1882 If that shirt has been on that fellow these whole twelve years, I think he would be a good representative of the *unwashed Democracy.*—Mr. R. G. Horn of Mich., H. R., March 9: *C. R.,* p. 1759/1.

1890 The Democracy has always . . . stood rockribbed and *unterrified* for . . . the eternal principles of truth and justice.—Mr. Edward Lane of Ill., H. R., Feb. 12: *Id.,* p. 1253/1.

1901 The Democratic party . . . have been long known as the *"great unwashed."*—Mr. W. W. Grout of Vt., H. R., Jan. 23: *C. R.,* p. 1345/2.

Up-to-date. Abreast of the times in style, manners, information, etc. (Webster.)

1897 [Mr. Stone of Pa.] is an *up-to-date* man.—Mr. R. Pearson of N. C., H. R., Feb. 12: *C. R.,* p. 1769/1.

Using-grounds. Places where grouse or quail gather.
1893 The *"using-grounds"* of the coveys are generally known or suspected by the farmer who is fond of shooting, and . . . he scatters "tailings"— a poor quality of wheat—where the starving quail can find them.— C. D. Lanier in *Harper's Mag.*, p. 681. (Century Dict.)

V

V. A five-dollar bill. [1837-1857.]
1912 "I tell you, advertising pays." "Well, what is on your mind?" "Some time ago I advertised for a lost five-dollar bill, and a stranger who had picked one up on the street restored it to me. This morning while looking through an old suit I found the *V* I thought I'd lost."— *Boston Transcript*, April.
Vagarious. Given to vagaries.
1866 Massachusetts is supposed, on the part of the Teutonic tribes who inhabit the State from which I come, to be somewhat *vagarious*—her political notions, somewhat visionary.—Mr. Edgar Cowan of Pa., U. S. Senate, May 9: *C. G.*, p. 2489/3.
1872 A. De Morgan, "Budget of Paradoxes," p. 153. (Century Dict.) [Earlier also in the *Athenæum*.]
Vamose. To depart quickly; to "absquatulate." From Sp. *vamos*, let us go (but pronounced "vamoose"). [1848-1888.]
1852 See PILE.
Vaquero. A herdsman; cowboy. [1846.] Spanish.
1888 The American cowboys of a certain range, after a brisk fight, drove out the Mexican *vaqueros*.—Theodore Roosevelt, *Century Mag.*, xxxvi, 836.
Variety store. One in which miscellaneous small articles are sold. [1824-1842.]
1822 Joseph T. Allyn's *"Variety Store"* is advertised: *Am. Beacon* (Norfolk, Va.), Jan. 19, p. 2/5.
Vegas. Meadows. Sp. Also, see quotation. [1855.]
1873 The best properties known as *vegas,* or tobacco farms, are comprised in a narrow area to the southwest part of the island.—S. Hazard, "Cuba with Pen and Pencil," p. 329. (Century Dict.)
Vendue master. One who presides at a public sale; an auctioneer. See Vol. II for **Vendue.** [1762-1862.]
1787 Robert Montfort announces that he has been appointed a *Vendue-Master* for the town of Savannah.—*Georgia State Gazette*, Feb. 10, p. 3/2.
Venge, n. Vengeance.
1620 What there is of *venge* [*sic*] in a Lyon chaft amongst dogs.—Beaumont and Fletcher, "Phylaster," p. 56.
1864 With the tiger's *venge* [he] would follow up a victory and reap its fruits.—Mr. Dumont of Ind., H. R., Apr. 11: *C. G.*, p. 1555/3.
Vermin. Any noxious or disgusting animal; especially such animals collectively, when of small size, of common occurrence and difficult to control. (Webster.) Certain insects, birds, rodents, and persons are classed as vermin.
1676 Destruccion of wolves and other *vermin.*—Journal of House of Burgesses, Va., II, 108. (Richmond, 1914.)
Vestibule train. A passenger train, of which each car is provided with enclosable end platforms, so that a passenger can walk from car to car.
1889 You might as well compare the stage-coach and the *vestibule express train.*—Mr. W. McAdoo of N. J., H. R., Feb. 28: *C. R.*, p. 2467/2.

1893   In the *vestibule trains* it would be impossible to go between the cars, because a *vestibule train* is a solid train. It has only a front end and a rear end to the entire train.—Mr. John R. McPherson of N. J., U. S. Senate, Feb. 10: *Id.*, p. 1420/2.

1894   [The present building] bears no more relation to the building that should succeed it than a freight caboose bears to a *vestibuled* palace car.—Memorial concerning the Federal Bldg. at Chicago, Jan. 17: *C. R.*, Aug. 8, p. 8326/2.

Village, the largest.   It is a standing joke, that Philadelphia is the largest village in the U. S.

1876   Mr. Piper of Calif.:—[Mr. Randall] ought not to compare the empire city of the Pacific coast with an old overpopulated manufacturing country *village* on a mud creek. Mr. O'Neill:—[Mr. Piper] speaks of this *village* on the Delaware River. Now I want to tell him and the members of this House what that *village* is . . . In the first place it is a village that contains about 143,000 or 144,000 dwelling-houses. Mr. Piper:—Only a *village*, nevertheless.—H. R., Apr. 25: *C. R.*, p. 2739/2.

Villify for Vilify.   [1766.]

1870   [Georgia] is ruled, *villified*, and plundered by a set of worthless adventurers.—Mr. J. B. Beck of Ky., H. R., June 24: *C. G.*, p. 4789/1.

1871   When General George H. Thomas died, they *villified* and abused him.—Mr. W. J. Smith of Tenn., H. R., Jan. 7: *C. G.*, p. 361/1.

1875   Why is it that [Horace Greeley] in his lifetime was so pursued and *villified* by the Administration now in power?—Mr. T. T. Crittenden of Mo., H. R., Feb. 27: *C. R.*, p. 29/2, App.

1881   The brutality of our politics, which traduces character and *villifies* motives.—Mr. Geo. H. Pendleton of O., U. S. Senate, Dec. 13: *C. R.*, p. 80/1.

1893   No State in the American Union has been so slandered, so lied about, and *villified* as the great Commonwealth of Missouri.—Mr. Champ Clark of Mo., H. R., Oct. 2: *Id.*, p. 2045/1.

Vim.   Energy.   [1850-1888.]

1864   Drunk or sober, the enemy's forces have charged up to our lines with *vim*.—Wilmington (N. C.) *Journal*, June 7, p. 2/1.

1866   I am indebted to [my journey across the plains] for the *vim* with which I am now enabled to nail [these] charges to the floor.—Mr. John A. Kasson of Ia., H. R., Jan. 15: *C. G.*, p. 241/3.

Violative of.   In violation of.   [1861-1862.]

1868   [The policy of admitting sparsely populated districts as States] is *violative* of the democratic idea and the representative principle.—Mr. James M. Ashley of O., H. R., July 22: *C. G.*, p. 4345/1.

Virginia fence.   A drunken man, by reason of his devious movement, is said to make a "Virginia fence."   [1745-1889.]   [A Virginia fence is one "made of split rails laid zigzag, with the ends resting on each other, and often supported by rough posts in pairs driven slantingly into the ground.   Also called **Stake-and-rider fence, Virginia rail fence, worm fence.**"   (Century Dict.)   It is also called **Snake fence.** —Ed.]

1737   He makes *Virginia fence.*—"The Drinker's Dictionary," *S. C. Gazette*, May 7, p. 2/1.

1831   I saw lots of fellers [in New York] walking *Virginia fence*, and some at the corners holdin up a post.—*The Georgian* (Savannah), Jan. 22, p. 2/5.   (From the *Constellation*.)

1850   See Vol. II, SLIVER.

Visible admixture law, the.   A law of the State of Ohio, requiring certain questions to be proposed to persons offering to vote, "having a distinct and *visible admixture* of African blood."

1868 Viewing the whole question of the *"visible admixture"* law, the soldiers' asylum law, etc., it is one of the most . . . characteristic chapters in modern Democratic history.—Mr. James A. Garfield of O., H. R., May 13: *C. G.*, p. 2452/2.

1870 [Recently, in Ohio] the Democratic party endeavored to exclude what are called *"visible admixture"* persons,—persons who had a visible admixture of black blood.—Mr. John Sherman of O., U. S. Senate, Feb. 23: *Id.*, p. 1510/2.

Volunteer State, The. Tennessee. [1861.]

1898 Tennessee was once called the *Volunteer State*, and that is the general name it goes by in our country today.—Mr. E. W. Pettus of Ala., U. S. Senate, July 1: *C. R.*, p. 6575/1.

Vum, vumpers, etc. See **Swear** or **vow**, euphemistic expressions for.

W

Waffle. A batter-cake baked in **waffle-irons**. German. [a.1750-1846.] [Citations from the Century Dict., which furnishes a cut of two waffle-irons.]

1794 Florian Charles Mey advertises *"Woffle irons."*—*S. C. State-Gazette*, Aug. 30, p. 1/2.

1804 One Matt *waffle* and wafer irons.—*Georgia Republican*, June 1, p. 1/3. (Advt.)

1812 *Waffle Irons*, Oil Cloths, etc.—Norfolk (Va.) *Herald*, Feb. 17, p. 1/4. (Advt.)

1882 We sat at tea in Armstrong's family dining-room; . . . the waitress passed out and in, bringing plates of *waffles.*—*Century Mag.*, xxvi, 283.

1888 She took down the long-handled *waffle-irons*, and made a plate of those delicious cakes.—E. Eggleston, "The Graysons," ch. xxxi.

Wagon. To convey by wagon. [1841.]

1871 [We say: "You have only] to *wagon* your goods and families 150 miles to Dallas, and get on a car behind a swift locomotive." We shall only have to *wagon* 150 miles to get to the Texas Pacific! It is not far.—Mr. B. F. Rice of Ark., U. S. Senate, March 3: *C. G.*, p. 1957/3.

Walk a track. Walk in approximately a straight line. Cf. **Virginia fence.**

1865 Some persons judge a man to be intoxicated the moment he takes a single glass of alcoholic drink, and others hold that he is not intoxicated as long as he can *walk a track*, or very nearly a track.—Mr. John P. Hale of N. H., U. S. Senate, Feb. 6: *C. G.*, p. 611/2.

Walker tariff, the. The tariff framed upon the suggestions of Mr. Robert J. Walker, Secretary of the Treasury, which became law in 1846. It classified all articles under eight heads, and modified the rates charged by the Act of 1842.

Walk-out. A workingmen's strike. Colloquial.

Wall Street. The moneyed interest of the country.

1879 If *Wall Street* scowls, it is a sure indication that the policy is right . . . *Wall Street* takes snuff, and the central powers of the Government and large numbers of the two Houses of Congress sneeze. *Wall Street* says, let us have the bloody shirt for a flag, and up it goes to the masthead. *Wall Street* would put the hounds on a false scent. *Wall Street* would encourage a fight on a dead issue.—Mr. H. B. Wright of Pa., H. R., Apr. 4: *C. R.*, pp. 230-231.

1879 Mr. McMahon:—I supposed [Mr. Garfield] owed an allegiance to [the U. S. soldiers] far superior to the allegiance he might owe to *Wall street* or the capitalists. . . Mr. Garfield:—When my colleague said that I appeared to act as though I owed my chief allegiance to *Wall street*, he said what he had no right to say . . . I do not know but I have cast as many votes as any man on this floor against *Wall street*.—H. R., Apr. 10: *Id.*, pp. 360/1, 363/1.

1890 *"Wall street"* is a term supposed to suggest conscienceless greed for and criminal methods to obtain money, and has been applied to the investors and creditor class of our people indiscriminately.—Mr. Frank Hiscock of N. Y., U. S. Senate, June 5: *Id.*, p. 5608/1.

1892 See CONTRACTIONIST.

1893 *Wall Street* and *Broad Street* continue to flood the Senate and the country with misstatements of facts.—Mr. G. L. Shoup of Idaho, U. S. Senate, Oct. 28: *Id.*, p. 2914/1.

Wamblecropped. Ill; thin; pale; in poor health; dejected.

1737 *Wamble Crop'd* = intoxicated. "The Drinker's Dictionary," *S. C. Gazette*, May 7, p. 1/2.

Want. To desire (that). See Vol. I, **I want** [1833-1891] and Vol. II, **Want** [1852-1853].

1866 *I want* every officer who served his country well shall be liberally compensated.—Mr. Thomas T. Davis of N. Y., H. R., June 5: *C. G.*, p. 2972/2.

Want out. Cf. **I will** *home.* 1605, "Volpone," II, i.

War Democrats. See quotations.

1869 I desire to say that I did not refer to *War Democrats* in using the term "Copperheads."—Mr. John M. Thayer of Neb., U. S. Senate, March 20: *C. G.*, p. 183/2.

1896 As a *War Democrat* I voted for the Union ticket. As a *War Democrat* I voted for General Grant, the nominee for the Presidency in 1868.—Mr. N. J. Cummings of N. Y., H. R., March 24: *C. R.*, p. 3159/1.

War Governor. The governor of a State during the Civil War. The term is specially applied to those governors who, like John A. Andrews of Mass. (1818-1867) and A. G. Curtin of Pa. (1817-1894), were particularly zealous in raising troops.

1888 It was the judgment of the Republican party of Iowa that the old *war governor*, old Sam Kirkwood, should be nominated.—Mr. J. B. Weaver of Ia, H. R., July 11: *C. R.*, p. 6147/2.

1892 To rekindle the camp fires and fight anew the battles was a favorite subject whenever the distinguished *war governor* of Pennsylvania came in their midst.—Mr. J. A. Geissenhainer of N. J., H. R., March 26: *Id.*, p. 2590/2.

Warhawks. Persons violently in favor of war; agitators of war. [1798-1847.]

1812 [They exclaimed] "Here goes the fellow that voted for war; here is the *war hawk*."—Statement of Joseph Bartlett and others, Selectmen of Plymouth, Mass. Norfolk (Va.) *Herald*, Aug. 24, p. 2/2.

1846 With the *war-hawks*, the catch-word is *honor*, but the meaning is *fight*.—Luther Baker, Letter to J. Q. Adams on the Oregon Question, p. 7.

War-paint. The paint put on by American Indians when ready to make a hostile expedition. [Hence, anyone is said to have his war-paint on when he shows belligerent tendencies.—Ed.]

Warpath, on the. To be or go on the warpath is to begin hostilities.

1826 His nation would not go *on the war-path*, because they did not think it well.—J. F. Cooper, "Last of the Mohicans," ch. xxviii. (Century Dict.)

1868 The Indian will make a treaty in the fall, and in the spring he is again *"upon the war-path."*—Mr. J. M. Cavanaugh of Mont., H. R., May 28: *C. G.*, p. 2638/3.

Wash. A gravelly slope of debris, the result of heavy rains, which sometimes make the "wash" a gully.

[End of Part XV.]

1902 Boulder channels or *washes* which extend . . . across the valley.—
F. H. Newell, "Irrigation in the U. S.," p. 237. (Century Dict.)

1904 As we entered the valley (called by the Mormons a *"wash"*) we were
struck with its weird and desolate appearance, stretching as it does as
far as the eye can see, naked of all vegetation except stunted sage-
brush and greasewood, hemmed in on the east by high precipitous
cliffs of red sandstone, with curious knobs and needles jutting upward
and weathered into fantastic shapes.—"American Inventor," p. 82.

Watap, Watapeh. The long, slender roots of the white spruce, *Picea
alba*, which are used by canoe-makers in the Great Lake region
for binding together the strips of birch-bark. (Century Dict.)

Watchdog of the Treasury. A nickname applied to W. S. Holman of
Indiana in the H. R., from the year 1859, who was also known as
"the great objector" [to appropriations]. Also used for other advocates of governmental economy. [1853-1862.]

1869 I admire the ambition which seems to inspire [Mr. E. B. Washburne
of Ill.] to be the *"watchdog of the Treasury,"* and my desire to see
such a spirit raised to its highest usefulness leaves [leads] me to
regret that it should hurl its thunders blindly against every expenditure, whether it be a measure of dishonest or unnecessary appropriation, or an expenditure necessary for the highest interests of the
nation.—Mr. Sidney Clarke of Kan., H. R., Jan. 22: *C. G.,* p. 532/1.

1873 Mr. Washburne while here was always a rigid economist. . . The
gentleman from Massachusetts [Mr. Hoar] should not defame him,
for nearly all his history was earned as *"the watchdog of the Treasury."*—Mr. S. S. Cox of N. Y., H. R., Feb. 18: *Id.,* p. 1459/2.

1874 The gentleman from Indiana [Mr. Holman] is a very excellent *"watchdog of the Treasury"* except when any of the family passes by, and
at such times he forgets to bark.—Mr. W. R. Roberts of N. Y., H. R.,
Feb. 11: *C. R.,* p. 1413/1.

1876 Here you behold him who was called *the watch-dog of the Treasury*
when in this Hall [Mr. E. B. Washburne], but as soon as he gets
abroad he begins to waste the people's money in every conceivable
manner.—Mr. W. M. Springer of Ill., H. R., Feb. 9: *Id.,* p. 975/2.

1876 [Mr. Harrison of Chicago] is an excellent *watch-dog,* but he does not
bark when any of the family are around. He has been voting for a
consular and diplomatic bill without a roof, for a post-office appropriation without a roof, but when we come to the Chicago post-office,
where $3,000,000 worth of property are without a roof, then he rises in
a terrible way.—Mr. Foster of O., H. R., June 22: *Id.,* p. 4044/2.
[A bill "without a roof" allows an expenditure which is not definitely
limited; "the sky is the limit."]

1878 [Mr. Hanna of Ind.] comes from a State which has always kept here
a *"watch-dog upon the Treasury,"* never barking, I will admit, at an
Indiana claimant, but barking at every other.—Mr. W. P. Frye of Me.,
H. R., March 8: *Id.,* p. 1594/2.

[1879 Mr. Young of Tenn. described Mr. Baker of Ind. as "the great
apostle of economy in the House since my old friend Judge Holman
of his State left it." H. R., June 7: *Id.,* p. 1857/1.]

1890 Where is the *watchdog* from Aurora [Mr. W. S. Holman]? There
is a special call for him. Why does he lurk in his kennel when the
watchdog from Danville [Mr. J. G. Cannon] is found barking in the
wrong Keep?—Mr. A. J. Cummings of N. Y., H. R., July 30: *Id.,*
p. 7928/2.

1890 My friend from Iowa [Mr. Kerr] is trying to make himself a *watchdog of the Treasury.* . . Why sir the gentleman from Iowa told us the
other day that the claimants in this case came mostly from the East.
If they had come from the West, and especially if they had come from

Iowa, the watchdog might have remained in his kennel, and the approaching claimant could exclaim:—

'Tis sweet to hear the watchdog's honest bark
Bay deep-mouthed welcome as we draw near home.
—Mr. A. G. Caruth of Ky., H. R., Aug. 30: *Id.*, p. 9412/1.

[This quotation was applied to Mr. Holman (see Vol. II), and by Senator Hoar of Mass. to Senator Harris of Tenn., July 3, 1894: *C. R.*, p. 7108/2.]

1892 You may pile up *watchdogs of the Treasury* until they stand as high as the Washington Monument, and . . . no number of watchdogs will be able to prevent the millions poured into the Treasury by the robbery of the poor from slipping out again in extravagance and corruption.— Mr. T. L. Johnson of O., H. R., March 31: *Id.*, p. 102/1, App.

1893 All this was done by a Democratic House under the management of Judge Holman, . . . the famous *"watch dog of the Treasury."*—Mr. D. B. Henderson of Ia., H. R., March 3: *Id.*, p. 102/2, App.

1894 I want to say that the gentleman from Indiana (Mr. Holman), "the *watchdog of the Treasury*," has cost this Government millions upon millions in his leadership of the Democratic party.—Mr. J. H. Walker of Mass., H. R., March 9: *Id.*, p. 2791/1.

1894 Mr. Enloe:—I have seen . . . gentlemen vote for questionable appropriations for their own States and their own districts, but when it came to voting for just claims to other States and other districts the same gentlemen have stood up here and paraded before the country as economists and *watchdogs of the Treasury*. I wish we could kill off that breed of deceitful dogs. Mr. Reed:—Mr. Chairman, I would suggest . . . that the gentleman from Indiana is not now present. . . Mr. Enloe:—I want to say that I had no special reference to the gentleman from Indiana. I have seen quite a number of dogs here of that character . . . I have seen big dogs and little dogs, and dogs of every degree, who were false *watchdogs of the Treasury*. They never bark at those who feed them.—H. R., May 25: *Id.*, p. 5298/1.

1896 [The people of the U. S. will not support those Representatives] who seek to make a cheap record by wearing the old clothes of the gentleman from Indiana [Mr. Holman] and to pose as great reformers and *watchdogs of the Treasury* at the present time. The day of *watchdogs of the Treasury* has passed.—Mr. G. L. Johnson of Calif., H. R., Feb. 28: *Id.*, p. 2276/1.

1896 [Some of these examiners] dub themselves *"watchdogs of the Treasury,"* and begin to bark as soon as they see an old soldier or a soldier's widow. I have no objection to good, honest, faithful watchdogs, but deliver me from so many watch pups who do nothing but bark.—Mr. H. R. Gibson of Tenn., H. R., Feb. 29: *Id.*, p. 2309/2.

1897 [Mr. Holman's] very first speech in the House was a protest against an appropriation for a navy-yard. The economic streak in his character was ingrained. . . He began his career in the 36th Congress, but it was not until the short session of the 44th Congress that he first became chairman of the Committee on Appropriations. His friends claim that in that time he reduced the expenses of the Government $10,000,000, with no deficiencies to be made up thereafter. It was at this time that he became generally known as *"the watchdog of the Treasury."*—Mr. A. J. Cummings of N. Y., in his remarks on Judge Holman's decease, July 8: *Id.*, p. 2517/1.

1900 O ye shades of the immortal Holman, and other more modern *watchdogs of the Treasury*, what has become of your occupation?—Mr. J. A. T. Hull of Ia., H. R., March 28: *Id.*, p. 3456/2.

Water-bar. A ridge crossing a hill or mountain road, and leading aside water flowing down the road. (Century Dict.)

1880 They . . . were descending, with careful reining in and bearing back, the steep, long plunges,—for these mountain roads are like cataract beds, and travellers are like the falling water,—where the only break and safety were the *water-bars*, humping up across the way at frequent intervals.—Mrs. A. D. T. Whitney, "Odd or Even," ch. xiii. (Century Dict.)

Water-bound. Detained by a flood. [Cf. with "snowbound," shut in or blockaded by snow.]

1862 While *water-bound*, [the party] was attacked by guerrillas.—*N. Y. Tribune*, Apr. 30. (Century Dict.)

Water-chinkapin. The American lotus. "The American nelumbo, *Nelumbo lutea*, or primarily its edible nut-like seed." (Century Dict.) [Cf. **Chinquapin.**]

Water-devil. The dobson or hellgrammite.

Watered stock. See quotations.

1872 [The capitalists] have a method of creating fictitious capital, which is termed "*watering the stock*," and which enables them at pleasure to levy tribute on the country.—Mr. M. M. Walden of Ia., H. R., Feb. 17: *C. G.*, p. 1101/1.

1884 Talk about *watered stock*! What do you think it costs to build every mile of railroad in this country, *watered* or not *watered*?—Mr. R. G. Horr of Mich., H. R., June 13: *C. R.*, p. 5120/1.

1885 The Senator from New Jersey [Mr. Sewell] says . . . that he thinks the stock is not much *watered*, very slightly diluted.—Mr. C. H. Van Wyck of Neb., U. S. Senate, Jan. 16: *Id.*, p. 751/2.

1886 To give value to "*watered stock*" means in plain English to rob the public in extortionate transportation charges, etc.—Mr. Richard Coke of Tex., U. S. Senate, May 18: *Id.*, p. 4622/2. [See the rest of his speech.]

1888 Mr. Drew . . . dressed like a drover, having originally been employed in that capacity. By the way, the significant term of "*watering stock*" originated in the practice of Uncle Daniel giving his cattle salt in order to create a thirst in them that would cause them to imbibe large quantities of water, and thus appear bigger and fatter when brought to market.—Henry Clews, "Twenty-Eight Years in Wall St.," p. 121. (N. Y.)

1890 These men who allege themselves to have put money into a road when they really put in only "*water*."—Mr. John A. Anderson of Kan., H. R., June 11: *C. R.*, p. 5959/1.

Water-haul. A cheat, a swindle. A fisherman who makes a water-haul gets nothing but water instead of fish. [1882.]

1871 It occurred to me [that] the gentleman from California [Mr. Sargent] had made what fishermen call a "*water haul*."—Mr. W. E. Niblack of Ind., H. R., Feb. 17: *C. G.*, p. 1356/1.

1879 They sent out their committee, and, as the boys say about the fishermen, they made a *water-haul*.—Mr. James G. Blaine of Me., U. S. Senate, March 24: *C. R.*, p. 55/1.

Water privilege. A site bordering on water, which is adapted to the purposes of a mill; an exclusive grant of such to favored persons.

1815 [Doolittle mistakes "milliner" for "mill in her."] She must be as big as the nation, and have a wonderful *water privilege* into the bargain.—David Humphreys, "The Yankey in England," p. 53.

[1884 Mr. Allison:—Do I understand the Senator from Missouri that there are seven hotel locations in the [Yellowstone] park? Mr. Vest:—Yes, sir; seven *hotel privileges.*—U. S. Senate, May 27: *C. R.*, p. 4550/2.]

[1886 *Hotel privileges* have been granted [in the Yellowstone Park] to every reputable and respectable person who has asked for them.—Mr. H. M. Teller of Colo., U. S. Senate, Aug. 2: *Id.*, p. 7844/1.]

Water-turkey. 1. The anhinga or snake-bird, *Plotus anhinga*. 2. The wood-ibis, *Tantalus loculator*. Southern and Southwestern U. S. See Century Dict., which supplies cuts in each instance.

Waumus. A jacket of warm material. [1805-1854.]

1912 *Wammus.* A coat-like jacket worn by men in such work as threshing wheat. (Western Indiana.)—*Dialect Notes,* III, 592.

Way, for **Away.** [1866-1908.]

1873 My friend from Utah says that Utah is *way* in advance of the age in one respect: that female suffrage has been adopted there.—Mr. Clagett of Mont., H. R., Jan. 29: *C. G.,* p. 948/1.

1882 Instead of that, they go *way* out to Peoria, Illinois.—Mr. R. G. Horr of Mich., H. R., March 9: *C. R.,* p. 1758/1.

1888 He is *way* below . . . in mathematics; but he is very high in writing.— Mr. F. M. Cockrell of Mo., U. S. Senate, Oct. 3: *Id.,* p. 9122/1.

Way back, from. Humorously, for "from a long line of ancestry," or "from the founding of the country" or some such idea.

1886 The Thomas Cat, at Colby, preceded by about a year the organization of Thomas county. *The New York Sun* has an office cat; our Cat has the office. It is "a fighter from *way back,*" and "whoops it up" in a most lively manner.—"Kansas Hist. Colls.," III, 405.

1894 See HUSTLER.

Way station. An intermediate one. See Vol. II, **Way passenger.** [1799-1824.]

1881 [A] spiteful engineer saw somebody at a *way station* [whom] he did not like, and when that person wanted to get aboard as a passenger, the engineer put on additional steam, and ran by with great velocity.—Mr. D. W. Voorhees of Ind., U. S. Senate, Apr. 1: *C. R.,* p. 166/2.

1892 Mr. Owens:—Will the gentleman allow me to ask him a question? Mr. Brosius:—The gentleman will excuse me. On a fast schedule I can not stop at *way stations.*—H. R., March 23: *Id.,* p. 2462/2.

Ways, for **Way.** Distance.

1874 Practically you carry in the mails only the newspapers that go a great *ways.*—Mr. E. H. Roberts of N. Y., H. R., June 19: *C. R.,* p. 5207/2.

Weakfish. A sciænoid fish of the genus *Cynoscion* (formerly *Otolithus*), as the squeteague: so called because it has a tender mouth, and cannot pull hard when it is hooked. (Century Dict.)

Weatherboard. A board adapted to form lapped joints with boards above and below so as to shed water; a clapboard. (Webster.) American?

1768 [They] ripped off the *Weather boards* of the dwelling House and Stable.—Journal of House of Burgesses of Va., Apr. 12, p. 162. (Richmond, 1906.)

Webfoot. An inhabitant of Western Oregon. [1873-1878.]

1877 I have been informed . . . that the actual precipitation of moisture [in Oregon] is such that the population at some seasons of the year are practically amphibious, and that they exhibit a decided tendency to become *web-footed.*—Mr. John J. Ingalls of Kan., U. S. Senate, Feb. 27: *C. R.,* p. 1974/1.

1882 I should think that no State is so much scoffed at as Oregon on the score of wet weather. Our neighbors in California call us "*Web-feet,*" and the State is called "The *Web-foot* State."—Wallis Nash, "Two Years in Oregon," p. 164.

Weel. A fish-trap. Obs. in England.

1621 Fishing is a kind of hunting by water, be it with nets, *weeles,* baits, angling.—Burton, "Anat. of Melancholy." (Century Dict.)

1881 In our river Ishnia eel-pouts were caught, as well as crucians and crawfish; the last tumbled of themselves into the *weels* set for them, or into ordinary baskets.—*Harper's Mag.,* lxxviii, 379. (Century Dict.)

Well. Whole; healthy. [1850-1857.]

1879 I would not have made those remarks [concerning General Schenck] had I known he had not been *a well man.*—Mr. Saulsbury of Del., U. S. Senate, May 17: *C. R.*, p. 1425/1.

1886 He was a soldier, he was a *well* man, a healthy man.—Mr. J. B. Beck of Ky., U. S. Senate, May 18: *Id.*, p. 4630/1.

1893 He had the appearance of ruddy health, but he lacked the animation and vivacity and aggressive energy of a *well* man.—Mr. Charles W. Stone of Pa., H. R., Feb. 4: *Id.*, p. 1219/1.

1893 [This proposal] is too much like putting the plaster on the *well* leg.—Mr. W. P. Hepburn of Ia., H. R., Aug. 22: *Id.*, p. 633/2.

1897 He was not continuously employed in farming as a *well* man.—Mr. W. S. Knox of Mass., H. R., Jan. 22: *Id.*, p. 1082/1.

Western Reserve, The. A tract of land in Northern Ohio, reserved by the State of Connecticut for the purposes of a school fund, when it ceded (in 1800) its claims on western lands. [1822-1862.]

1869 [The grant of King James to Connecticut] was for the width of the State of Connecticut through, from ocean to ocean. When it reached the line of New York it was defeated by the prior claims of the Dutch, and after crossing the western line of Ohio, then Virginia territory, now known as the *"Western Reserve,"* it failed because of the rights claimed there by Spain.—Mr. B. F. Butler of Mass., H. R., Apr. 6: *C. G.*, pp. 559-60.

1872 See also the remarks of Mr. J. L. Strong of Conn., H. R., March 15: *Id.*, p. 1714.

Westminister, for **Westminster.** This vulgar distortion of the word is frequent, and should be checked.

1883 We still go to Europe for our literature; we still seek the authorities of *Westminister Hall,* and we still read the Pandects of Justinian.—Mr. Geo. F. Hoar of Mass., U. S. Senate, Jan. 29: *C. R.*, p. 1700/2.

West Pointer. A graduate of the United States Military Academy at West Point, N. Y. [1863.]

1866 Gentlemen, because of their admiration of the Volunteer corps and prejudice against *West Pointers,* are trying, etc.—Mr. A. J. Rogers of N. J., H. R., June 5: *Id.*, p. 2973/1.

1866 The volunteer army put down the late rebellion, and they could have done it as well if there had not been a single *West Pointer* in the whole army.—Mr. L. H. Rousseau of Ky., H. R., pp. 2973-4.

1896 As to the *West Pointers,* the 30th of June is the annual period, I believe, for their graduation, and their commissions date from that time.—Mr. W. B. Bate of Tenn., U. S. Senate, Feb. 18: *C. R.*, p. 1874/1.

1901 Some of the most conspicuous of our soldiers on both sides during the civil war were *Westpointers,* and some of the most conspicuous failures as commanders were *Westpointers.*—Mr. F. E. Warren of Wyo., H. R., Jan. 15: *Id.*, p. 1027/2.

Wet and Dry. "Wet" communities, states, etc. are in favor of liquor-drinking. "Dry" ones are in favor of prohibiting the drinking of liquor. ["Dry" also means **thirsty.**—Ed.]

1890 Mr. Springer:—The rule in [Neb.] and in other States is that every spring election there is a contest as to whether the town is to be *"wet"* or *"dry"*; sometimes a town is *"wet"* and sometimes *"dry."* Mr. Heard:—Does not the history of the case show that the elections go *"wet"* when the people are *"dry"*?—H. R., March 12: *C. R.*, p. 2172/1.

1890 Suppose that all the Atlantic and Gulf States and the State of California were to become prohibition States, and suppose that all the interior States were to become *"wet"* or drinking States.—Mr. J. B. Eustis of La., U. S. Senate, May 28: *Id.*, p. 5377/1.

1894   This was a grocery store. I do not know whether they were "dry" groceries or *"wet"* groceries that were sold there, but I am inclined to think they were *"wet"* groceries.—Mr. W. A. Jones of Va., H. R., Apr. 6: *Id.*, p. 3527/1. [See CORNER GROCERY.]

We-uns, You-uns. Colloquial for *we, you,* among illiterate persons in the South.

1885   "Grind some for *we-uns* ter-morrer?" asked Ab. "I'll grind yer bones, ef ye'll send 'em down," said Amos.—Mary N. Murfree, "Prophet of the Great Smoky Mts.," ch. ix. (Century Dict.)

Whale-back. A vessel of which the upper deck is rounded. It has a spoon bow, with the whole of the main deck arched and meeting the side in a continuous curve. These vessels were first used on the Great Lakes. (Century Dict.)

1894   That magnificent passenger *"whaleback"* steamer, the Christopher Columbus, plying last summer between the city of Chicago and the World's Fair grounds, and having a capacity of 5,000 passengers, was built in the city of Superior.—Mr. N. P. Haugen of Wisc., H. R., Jan. 26; *C. R.*, p. 1516/1.

What-is-it. Somewhere in the earlier eighties, a made-up mystery, which was alive, was exhibited under this name in a travelling show, and was largely advertised. Hence the term came into common use.

a. 1882   The two negro girls, who figure as *"what-is-its,"* are paid $200 a week.—*Phila. Times,* n. d.

1890   [This measure] is not to be a mandatory law; it is not to be a prohibitory law; it is to be a legislative *what-is-it,* and nothing else.— Mr. James B. Eustis of La., U. S. Senate, May 27: *C. R.*, p. 5330/2.

1892   In this strange combination, this congressional *"what is it,"* half horse, half alligator; in this congregation, part crying good Lord and the balance good devil, it is safe to predict that the miller will get all the corn, and the farmer all the chaff.—Mr. M. D. Harter of O., H. R., June 6: *Id.*, p. 568/2, App.

Wheat pit. The market in which wheat stocks are bought and sold.

1890   They may perchance go to the *"wheat pit"* in Chicago, and there, amidst the growling of the bears and the roaring of the bulls, presided over by "Old Hutch," they may find what has become of their wheat crops year after year.—Mr. G. G. Vest of Mo., U. S. Senate, Apr. 21: *C. R.*, p. 3599/1.

Wheeler. A wheel horse.

1890   [He] never left the Democratic party until he began his race for Congress, and even then he claimed to be a Democratic *"Wheeler."*— Mr. T. C. McRae of Ark., H. R., June 30: *C. R.*, p. 6802/2.

Whiffet. A small or insignificant person. Colloquial. (Webster.) Also, a yelping small dog. [1801-1839.]

1876   How [a tree] rebukes by its tough and equable serenity . . . this gusty-temper'd little *whiffet,* man, that runs indoors at a mite of rain or snow!—Walt Whitman, "Specimen Days" (1887), p. 139.

1883   Sneaks, *whiffets,* and surface rats.—*Phila. Times,* Aug. 1. (Century Dict.)

Whiffling. Wavering; frequently changing in opinion; using shifts and evasions in argument.

1865   Why shall we have this irresolute, this indecisive, this *whiffling,* changing kind of legislation?—Mr. James W. Grimes of Ia., U. S. Senate, Feb. 7: *C. G.*, p. 633/3.

Whig. One of a political party which grew up, in opposition to the Democratic party, out of the National Republican party. It was first called the Whig party in 1834. (Century Dict.) [1837-1862.]

1847   See B'HOY.

1862 I never took any other name than the honored name of *Whig*, until this secession business sprung up.—Mr. W. H. Wadsworth of Ky., H. R., March 12: *C. G.*, p. 1197/3.

Whip. To beat, to overcome in a contest or fight. [1815-1878.]

1605   Lorenzo, thou doost boast of base renowne,
      Why I could *whip* al these, were there hose downe
—Thos. Kyd(?) "Ieronimo," F2.

1868 See CHIVALRY.

1870 Tamerlane and Bajazet seem to have fought to see who could *whip*, and curiosity on the same point may have contributed largely to bring about the conflict between France and Prussia.—Mr. T. C. McCreery of Ky., U. S. Senate, Dec. 13: *C. G.*, p. 74/1.

1884 If my regiment was *whipped* at all, it was because the army of Chickamauga was *whipped* in 1863. If we were *whipped* then, my regiment and probably my division was *whipped*. But I give you my word of honor that I did not know it.—Mr. G. W. Steele of Ind., H. R., Apr. 4: *C. R.*, p. 2613/2.

1896 [It has been said] that the great United States could *whip* the world: that she had on two occasions *whipped* Great Britain; that she had *whipped* Mexico several times; that every time she got at leisure she would go out and *whip* the Indians: and finally the top and bottom of the map fell out, and she turned in and flogged herself, and that is what the last war meant.—Mr. W. T. Talbert of S. C., H. R., Apr. 4: *Id.*, p. 3597/2.

Whip one's weight (usually in wildcats). Extreme prowess in fighting is humorously indicated. [1829-1852.]

1844 They feel a comfortable assurance that every American can *"whip his weight in wild cats."*—Lydia M. Child, "Letters from New York," Second S., p. 174. (Lond., 1845.)

Whipsaw, v. To cut with a whipsaw; i.e. a frame saw, with a narrow blade. (Century Dict.) Hence, to cut or destroy by a backward and forward movement. [1901-1909.]

1892 Under the operation of this compensatory duty the wool-grower has not only been *whipsawed*, but the masses of the people who own no sheep have been left to the tender mercies of . . . the manufacturer. —Mr. D. D. Hare of O., H. R., July 8: *C. R.*, p. 462/1, App.

Whisky insurrection. An uprising, in 1793-1794, against Federal taxation. [1794-1864.]

1862 It would not be [fair] to charge upon the whole people of Pennsylvania the responsibility of a *whisky insurrection* which once occurred in that State.—Mr. Francis Thomas of Md., H. R., March 11: *C. G.*, p. 1177/1.

1866 If the combination of men that wages war is not the combination that forms the State, as in the cases of the Dorr rebellion and the *whisky insurrection*, then the State is not in rebellion.—Mr. J. M. Broomall of Pa., H. R., Jan. 27: *Id.*, p. 467/1.

Whisky ring. The organized liquor interests. See quotation, 1869.

1868 The *whisky ring*, which is robbing the Government of from fifty to one hundred million dollars annually.—Mr. Henry Wilson of Mass., U. S. Senate, Jan. 7: *Id.*, p. 353/2.

1868 It is the "money ring" which controls on that side, which has been charging that the *"whisky ring"* controls on the other.—Mr. Thos. C. McCreery of Ky., U. S. Senate, July 9: *Id.*, p. 3865/2.

1869 Gentlemen are always talking here about a *"whisky ring"*; but one half of them do not know what the phrase means. I will tell what it means. It means an association of whisky men leagued together in a secret organization, with a president, with an attorney, with agents sent here to this Congress.—Mr. John A. Logan of Ill., H. R., March 30: *Id.*, p. 381/2.

1879 We have had here in Washington rings, *whisky rings* reaching from Saint Louis, and connected, as it was said and believed, with men near those in place and power.—Mr. Kernan of N. Y., U. S. Senate, May 14: *C. R.*, p. 1323/2.

White Leagues, White Leaguers. See quotation.

1875 Prior to, and with a view to the late election in Louisiana, white men associated themselves together in armed bodies called *"White Leaguers,"* and at the same time threats were made in the democratic papers that the election should be carried against the republicans at all hazards.—Message from President U. S. Grant, Jan. 13: *C. G.*, 415/2. [See also the accompanying documents, pp. 416-422.]

White line, White liners. See quotations.

1875 As the convention was strictly *white line,* and as no negroes were nominated, and as the hankering after the negroes was pretty thoroughly squelched, how would it do to raise a little purse to buy a few bags of salt for the use of those who still want to try and catch black birds?—*Vicksburg Monitor,* quoted in *C. R.,* App., p. 22/1. [Jan. 1876.]

1876 There were some few men in that [Miss.] convention, and some others assembled there who were not members of the convention, who were what was termed *"white-liners"*; in other words, they took the position that, as the colored people under the lead of a few white men were all on one side, and antagonized the whites, the only course left was to organize the white people on the other side.—Mr. Singleton of Miss., H. R., July 25: *C. R.*, p. 4878/2.

1876 We have never seen men more terribly in earnest, and the democratic *White-Line* speech made to them by Colonel Lamar aroused them to white heat.—*Vicksburg Herald,* cited on p. 4879/2. [Col. Lamar did not speak with this intent. See his statement on same page.]

1876 In their party pow-wow [Mr. Lamar and his friends], declared by formal resolution against the *white-line policy.—Meridian* (Miss.) *Mercury,* July 29: see *C. R.,* Aug. 4, p. 5183/2.

White man. A decent person.

1890 Between the smoke of two railroads on the north and on the south [Washington will be] a place not fit for a *white man* to live in.—Mr. S. L. Milliken of Me., H. R., June 23: *C. R.*, p. 6392/2.

1892 See Dutchman.

White-wood. See quotation. Several trees are so named.

1872 Ohio has more *white-wood* perhaps than any other State. What the New England people call *white-wood* is our poplar.—Mr. A. G. Thurman of O., U. S. Senate, May 27: *C. G.*, p. 3899/1.

Whizzer. A centrifugal drying machine, which makes much noise. The connection with "hot air" is clear.

1900 [The stockmen's way] when a speech consists principally of abuse of the other side, . . . is to get up and go away. They regard that man as "trying to run a *whizzer* on them."—Mr. W. L. Stark of Neb., H. R., Jan. 10: *C. R.,* p. 22/1, App.

Who struck Billy Patterson? A ludicrous question admitting of no reply.

1848 Patterson was the man, every one was hunting for him, not considering that Billy had been knocked down, and that tradition gives no account of his ever arising.—Wilmington (N. C.) *Commercial,* Dec. 23, p. 2/5. (From the *Spirit of the Times.*)

Whole cloth. A tale which is a lie from beginning to end is said to be made up out of whole [uncut] cloth. [1843-1888.]

1864 A letter was presented from the Governor, denying [the telegram]. It was a lie out of the *whole cloth.*—Mr. Powell of Ky., U. S. Senate, June 28: *C. G.,* p. 3346/1.

1870 We came to the conclusion that [these statements] were all chaff and nonsense, *manufactured out of whole cloth.*—Mr. John F. Farnsworth of Ill., H. R., Jan. 14: *Id.*, p. 502/1.

1870 Did you not see [this report] contradicted in the very papers that published it, and the statement made that it was a canard made out of *whole cloth?*—Mr. Lyman Trumbull of Ill., U. S. Senate, Apr. 19: *Id.*, p. 286/2, App.

1872 This reverend gentleman's statement [is] a preposterous lie, *cut out* of *the whole cloth.*—Mr. J. H. Sloss of Ala., U. S. Senate, May 20: *Id.*, p. 572/2, App.

1874 [This firm] never had anything to do with the importing of leaden statuary and busts, and the story . . . as to them is made out of *whole cloth.*—Mr. Lyman Tremain of N. Y., U. S. Senate, June 19: *C. R.*, p. 5236/1.

1896 [It was said that Mr. Carlisle] was interested in sugar stock: that he had used his influence to aid the sugar trust; all lies *made out of the whole cloth.*—Mr. David B. Hill of N. Y., U. S. Senate, Apr. 16: *Id.*, p. 4050/1.

Whole-hog, adj. Without reservations. A more elegant expression for somewhat the same idea is "wholehearted." See **Go the whole hog.**

1836 Mr. Hendricks [of Indiana] has lately declared himself "a *whole hog* Van Buren man."—Raleigh (N. C.) *Standard*, Nov. 3, p. 2/1.

1912 *Whole-hog* standpatters and progressives. See STANDPAT.

Whole-souled. Wholehearted; generous; honest and frank. [1834-1908.]

1862 [I have read of] a good brother in a church, who had a habit of responding to everything which the minister said by a hearty, *wholesouled* "amen."—Mr. Willard Saulsbury of Del., U. S. Senate, March 25: *C. G.*, p. 1359/2.

1864 The rule which our fathers wrote in the Constitution saved me from your expulsion, and saved you from the stern and indignant rebuke which I would have brought back with me from my patriotic and *whole-souled* constituents.—Mr. B. G. Harris of Md., H. R., May 9: *Id.*, p. 2195/2.

1870 Your *whole-souled* sort, that swallow the whole animal, from scalp to tail, and that make any asseveration of fact, without regard to its truth.—Mr. Garrett Davis of Ky., U. S. Senate, Feb. 23: *Id.*, p. 1512/1.

Whoop it up, to. To stir matters up in a lively and noisy manner. Slang.

1888 His rival is a prominent politician, with an abundance of party workers to *whoop it up* for him.—*Century Mag.*, xxxviii, 156.

1897 When you needed help, Grover Cleveland and his cuckoos . . . took off their coats and "*whooped it up*" for you, did they not?—Mr. John E. Kelley of S. Dak., H. R., March 23: *C. R.*, p. 207/2.

1897 No amount of mere "*whooping up*," by press or otherwise, can make the mills appear to run, and society to seem prosperous.—Address of Mr. Charles A. Towne of Minn.: See *C. R.*, July 6, p. 2358/1.

Wide-Awakes, The. An association of "Black Republicans," formed in 1860. [1860-1861.]

1870 I remember being a very enthusiastic supporter of [General Frémont] in 1856. I remember the *Wide Awake Club* that I belonged to, and the *Wide Awake cape* that I wore.—Mr. W. Warner of Ala., U. S. Senate, June 23: *C. G.*, p. 4770/1.

Wild and woolly. A phrase applied to the Far West and its inhabitants. [1891-1909.]

1890 Mr. Ingalls:—I had supposed that these denunciations of culture and of scientific investigation were confined to the wild and lawless West.

Mr. Vest:—*The woolly West.* Mr. Ingalls:—"Woolly," as the Senator from Missouri says, speaking after the manner of the tariff.—U. S. Senate, June 20: *C. R.*, p. 6304/1.

1892 O you wise Bourbons of the Southland, pursuing the phantom of "cheap money," do you not see that . . . if you squeeze [this bill] as you would a sponge, the golden drips of subsidy will ooze and trickle from it into the open mouths of the silver kings of the *wild and woolly West?*—Mr. O. M. Hall of Minn., H. R., March 23: *Id.*, p. 2425/2.

1893 The West is growing. You will hear from it by and by,—"*the wild and woolly West.*" The wildness will be tamed, and the wool will be combed.—Mr. W. W. Bowers of Calif., H. R., Oct. 3: *Id.*, p. 2098/1.

1894 [Mine] is a district in which the voice of the cuckoo is hushed forever in death, but a district in which the song of the whippoorwill in the evening continues as a melodious refrain the harsher music of the factory whistles, a district in which the rush, roar, and bustle of the mills and other hives of industry are taken up and continued by the hum of harvest machines in the golden wheatfields of the surrounding farms; a district in which illiteracy is unknown, in which the brawn and brain of the *wild and wooly West* are arrayed in harmonious juxtaposition to the culture and refinement of the effete East.—Mr. G. B. Shaw of Wisc., H. R., Jan. 16: *Id.*, p. 904/2.

1896 See JUG-HANDLED.

1896 I am too old now, after having been born and reared in the *wild and woolly West*, where we have our own way to a great extent, to subordinate my own judgment, etc.—Mr. W. V. Allen of Neb., U. S. Senate, March 20: *Id.*, p. 3008/2.

Wildcat, Wildcatting. Wildcatting is prospecting for ores, oil or minerals generally, and a wildcat is something thus discovered.

1903 New territory has been opened up by unexpected *wild-cats* (oil wells).—*McClure's Mag.*, p. 399. (Century Dict.)

1904 Large oil producers do not prospect; they leave that dangerous business to the professional "*wild-catter*," and when he has located a new rich territory, they buy him out.—*Scientific Amer.*, June 18. (p. 474.)

1907 *Wildcatting* has been going on at a number of other points in the state, and some encouragement has been met, especially in Randolph and Macoupin counties. It seems not unlikely that . . . additional oil fields will be found.—*U. S. Geol. Survey*, p. 829.

Wildcat banks, money, etc. Those having a precarious existence or value. [1838-1909.]

1868 Treasury notes are not a "disordered currency." They do not belong to the class denominated as "*wild cat*" or "stump-tail."—Mr. S. F. Cary of O., H. R., Jan. 7: *C. G.*, p. 370/1.

1870 Ten years ago, the moneyed East knew not the richer West, save as the home of *wild cats, wild-cat financiers,* and *wild-cat banks,*—as a financial Botany Bay.—Mr. S. S. Burdett of O., H. R., March 26: *Id.*, p. 224/2, App.

1877 That dollar on Rhode Island Central [Bank] was the first money I ever earned or owned in my life. I went to sleep one night worth a dollar, but in the night-time the infernal thing turned to a *wild-cat*, and in the morning the bank was broken, and so was I.—Mr. G. L. Fort of Ill., H. R., Nov. 23: *C. R.*, p. 624/2.

1879 See STUMP-TAIL.

1881 See RED DOG. See SHYSTER.

1882 I say here frankly that the national banking system is the best banking system of any we have ever had, and I also say that the worst system we have ever had was the *wild-cat* State banking system.—Mr. Chas. N. Brumm of Pa., H. R., May 16: *C. R.*, p. 303/1, App.

1882 The first night of our journey was spent at Ashford, in Conn., where we arrived late in the evening; and here the bother of *wild-cat currency*, as it was afterwards called, was forced upon our attention.— Josiah Quincy, Jr., "Figures of the Past," p. 196. (Century Dict.)
1893 See DETECTOR.
Wild hogs. See quotation.
1884 A distinguished railroad king, who talks about this House as *"wild hogs"* in letters which are of record—I refer to Mr. Huntington.— Mr. T. R. Cobb of Ind., H. R., June 4: *C. R.*, p. 4821/1.
Wilmot provise, The. This compromise, proposed by Mr. Wilmot of Pa., Aug. 8, 1846, and not finally adopted, provided that slavery should be excluded from Texas. [1847-1862.]
1849 The most zealous advocate of the *Wilmot proviso* may vote for it on the construction that it surrenders to the North all lying north of the line, and leaves open to contest all south of it: while on the opposite construction, that it secures by implication the rights of the South to all lying south of the line, a zealous opponent of that proviso may vote for it.—John C. Calhoun, U. S. Senate, Aug. 12. ["Works" (1856), IV, 513.]
1869 The *Wilmot Proviso* was attached to an appropriation bill, and nobody thought of raising a point of order.—Mr. John Sherman of O., U. S. Senate, March 2: *C. G.*, p. 1793/3.
Wilson tariff, the. The tariff enacted in 1894, under the management of Mr. William L. Wilson of Va., modifying the McKinley tariff. It became law without President Cleveland's signature.
Wilt. To wither, to fade, to droop, to collapse. [1809-1888.]
1912 Even the members of the United States team, who are more accustomed to the sun than most of the competitors, were distressed by yesterday's heat, while the English runners entirely *wilted* and were unable to approach their ordinary records.—*N. Y. Evening Post*, July 15, p. 1/1.
Windjammer. A sailing-vessel or sailor. Colloquial. This word may be an importation from Australia. [See 1878.] In Western Indiana it means a braggart. (DIALECT NOTES, 1912, III, 593.) Also, a fluent speaker who uses high flown language.
1878 Towards the finish, Spofforth, the *"wind-jammer,"* as he is called in aquatically-disposed Sydney, was put on to give the people a show.— 'Cricket in Queensland,' "The Vagabond Papers," 5th S., p. 87: printed in Sydney, N. S. W.
1904 I went for a voyage in a sailing-ship once, for my health. What is it you call them? *Wind-jammers?*—Dolf Wyllarde, "Captain Amyas," ch. vi. (Century Dict.)
Wind-slash. A clearing, occasioned by a storm.
1886 All persons having occasion to burn a fallow or start a fire in any old chopping, *wind-slash*, bush or berry lot, swamp "viaie" or beaver meadow, shall give five days' notice.—*N. Y. Times*, Apr. 13. (Century Dict.)
Windy City, The. Chicago. [1898.]
1890 With an iteration that to a Chicago ear is grateful, we hear descriptions of a *"Windy City"* on the west shore of a lake which all know to be flat and low, with an atmosphere filled with smoke and soot, etc.—Magazine article quoted by Mr. G. G. Vest of Mo., U. S. Senate, Apr. 21: *C. R.*, p. 3598/1.
Winter-count. A painted mnemonic record of the history of an Indian tribe. See Century Dict., Supplement, which furnishes a picture.
1900 The paintings were executed by an aged shaman as a sort of personal record akin to the calendars or *winter-counts* which play so large, yet so obscure a rôle in Indian life.—*Smithsonian Rep.*, p. 67. (Century Dict.)

Wipe out. To destroy. [1861-1911.]

1856 The Governor would neither let the Missourians *"wipe out"* the Abolitionists on the one hand, nor etc.—G. D. Brewerton, "War in Kansas," p. 101.

1856 It would seem that the business of *"wiping out,"* as it is called, of the pro-slavery party has been commenced.—C. Robinson, "Kansas Conflict" (1892), p. 313.

1857 They demanded that the abolitionists should take away their tents and be off at short notice, or otherwise they would be *"wiped out."*—J. H. Gihon, "Geary and Kansas," p. 30.

1862 On the first of August 1838 the whole system [of slavery] was *wiped out*; there was not a slave left in the [British West Indies.]—Mr. John P. Hale of N. H., U. S. Senate, March 18: *C. G.*, p. 1267/3.

1867 [Senator Wilson of Mass.] wants to *wipe out* these provisional governments.—Mr. C. R. Buckalew of Pa., U. S. Senate, July 11: *C. G.*, p. 8/2, App.

1868 We propose that [three great tobacco concerns] shall not *wipe out* the western manufacturers.—Mr. John A. Logan of Ill., H. R., June 25: *Id.*, p. 3497/2.

1877 Let us declare war against Mexico at once, and *wipe her out.*—Mr. T. T. Crittenden of Mo., H. R., Nov. 8: *C. R.*, p. 301/2.

1879 I am not very partial to bills of this nature. I should prefer to *"wipe out,"* as the phrase is, the whole thing—to repeal the whole business.—Mr. S. S. Cox of N. Y., H. R., June 10: *Id.*, p. 1899/2.

Wipe up the ground with one. To demolish utterly. Slang. See **Swipe.**

1890 Dr. Harris . . . in a short but vigorous speech completely *wiped the ground up with the Colonel*, but in such a pleasant manner, complimenting him all the while, that he will probably get over it in time.—*Times-Union*, May 19. Quoted by Senator Call, June 2: *C. R.*, p. 550/1, App.

Wishtonwish. A prairie-dog. J. F. Cooper in "The Last of the Mohicans," ch. xxii (1826), erroneously supposed it to be a whip-poorwill.

1810 The *Wishtonwish* of the Indians, prairie dogs of some travellers, . . . reside on the prairies of Louisiana in towns or villages, having an evident police established in their communities . . . As you approach their towns you are saluted on all sides by the cry of *Wishtonwish*, from which they derive their name with the Indians, uttered in a shrill and piercing manner.—Z. M. Pike, "Voyage to the Sources of the Arkansaw," etc., p. 156. (Century Dict.)

Wokas, wokus. The name given by the Klamath Indians of Oregon to the yellow pond-lily of that region (*Nymphæa polysepalum*) and to the fruit furnished by its seeds.

1902 *Wokas* is harvested exclusively in boats of the kind known as a "dugout."—*Rep. U. S. Nat. Museum*, p. 728.

Wolfing. The occupation or industry of taking wolves for their pelts. Wolfing is extensively practised in winter in some parts of the U. S., as Montana and the Dakotas. The wolves are destroyed chiefly by poisoning with strychnine. (Century Dict.)

Woodbine. "To go where the woodbine twineth" is to sink into obscurity or perdition. Slang. [*Woodbine* is honeysuckle; also Virginia creeper.]

1870 The silk-button business in this country has gone *"where the woodbine twineth."*—Mr. S. W. Kellogg of Conn., H. R., Apr. 11: *C. G.*, p. 2601/2.

1870 It was said to be out of the question for Congress to be passing charters for everybody; . . . and consequently my bill went *"where the woodbine twineth."*—Mr. C. D. Drake of Mo., U. S. Senate, Apr. 29: *Id.*, p. 3096/1.

1888   When Fisk heard that Secretary Boutwell had ordered gold sold, he exclaimed that it would knock spots out of phantom gold, and send him and others with the long stuff *"where the woodbine twineth."*— Henry Clews, "Twenty-Eight Years in Wall St.," p. 184. (N. Y.)

1897   If the bill does not become a law at this Congress, then we have no further jurisdiction. It goes *"where the woodbine twineth."*—Mr. G. W. Hulick of O., H. R., Jan. 18: *C. R.*, p. 907/1.

Woodchuck.   A thickset marmot . . . of the U. S. and Canada;—called also *ground hog.*   (Webster.)

1864   A Scotch divine was once asked by an incredulous fox hunter how it was possible for Samson to catch three hundred foxes so easily . . . He replied that Samson probably had only half a dozen foxes, and all the rest were skunks and *woodchucks.*—Mr. Scofield of Pa., H. R., June 10: *C. G.*, p. 2864/3.

1890   It is a waste to train a 30-pounder Parrott gun on a *woodchuck.*— Mr. J. D. Sayers of Tex., H. R., March 21: *C. R.*, p. 2487/2.

Wooden nutmegs.   Certain Connecticut merchants were said to have exported wooden nutmegs, basswood hams, and horn gun-flints. [1826-1864.]

1867   Mr. Hubbard of Conn.:—I move to amend by adding the words "wooden knobs." Mr. Stevens of Pa.:—The gentleman must mean *"wooden nutmegs."* Mr. Hubbard:—No; "wooden knobs." Mr. Spalding of O.:—The gentleman ought to include *"wooden nutmegs"* also. Mr. Hubbard:—*Wooden nutmegs* are an article which defy [*sic*] all tax or tariff; and I have no doubt my successor, the celebrated P. T. Barnum, will be able next summer to sell cargoes of them to the constituents of the gentleman from Ohio. Mr. Spalding:—That is why I want them put on the free list.—U. S. Senate, Feb. 22: *C. G.*, p. 1480/3.

1890   Now these gallant chivalric gentlemen must lug in an old cheap joke about the *wooden-nutmeg* State. Why, Mr. President, I never saw but half a dozen *wooden nutmegs* in my life, and they were cut from the wood of the Charter Oak tree, which is one of our glories. Even if we did make *wooden nutmegs,* there was not a fool in New England that would buy them; they were sold elsewhere. . . I suspect these *wooden-nutmeg* stories originated in Virginia or somewhere along down there, because one of the citizens bought one of the *wooden nutmegs* and cracked it and tasted it, thinking it was a walnut, and then got mad and charged the *wooden nutmcgs* to us. . . The *wooden nutmeg* is a "chestnut."—Mr. J. R. Hawley of Conn., U. S. Senate, Aug. 20: *C. R.*, p. 8864/1.

1896   The charge made against our Connecticut forefathers, of having manufactured nutmegs out of basswood, may not be true, but it can not be denied that there is some proof of its truth in the fact that there are people in this country today who are adulterating and counterfeiting almost every manufactured article of food which is used.—Mr. S. S. Barney of Wisc., H. R., Apr. 10: *Id.*, p. 3849/2.

1897   If the gentleman had come from one of the New England States, where the boys serve apprenticeship in making *wooden nutmegs,* he would not etc.—Mr. G. A. Grow of Pa., H. R., Jan. 7: *Id.*, p. 574/1.

Wooden shoe.   Sabotage.

1913   It now remains for reliable outside rebels, skilled in the use of *the wooden shoe,* to drive home the lesson by getting onto the job and incessantly using *the shoe* at every point where this robber corporation is open to attack. . . A word to the wise is sufficient. Class conscious rebels, get on the job, apply *the wooden shoe* and thus pave the way for the final overthrow of the capitalist system by the militant working class.—*Industrial Worker* (Spokane, Wash.), July 3.

Woods, out of the. Out of a difficulty; or out of a long-continued series of difficulties.

1888 [He got a patent for his invention] and felt that he was *out of the woods.*—Mr. John T. Morgan of Ala., U. S. Senate, Dec. 12: *C. R.,* p. 184/2.

Wood up. To take in wood, especially on a river steamboat. See Vol. II, **Wood, Wood up.** [1829-1888.]

1848 A steamer stopped at a landing to *wood up.*—Wilmington (N. C.) *Commercial,* Aug. 29, p. 1/6.

Wool, v. To pull the hair; to rumple or tousle. [1854.]

1884 [Mr. Chandler of Mich. was] one of the ablest men we had in the Senate, and by no means purchasable with "British gold"; . . . for if ever there was a man who *wooled* the British lion, he was the man.—Mr. James B. Beck of Ky., U. S. Senate, May 5: *C. R.,* p. 3796/1.

Work a thing for all (that) it is worth. To get all out of it that can be had; to squeeze the orange dry.

1893 I have not the slightest doubt that [he] *worked the Pension Bureau for all it was worth.*—Mr. E. A. Morse of Mass., H. R., Sept. 25: *C. R.,* p. 1762/1.

Work like a beaver. To work busily and industriously. [b.1775-1888.]

1871 The blacks turned out promptly, and *worked like beavers* [to extinguish the fire.]—Mr. C. H. Porter of Va., H. R., Apr. 4: *C. G.,* p. 278/3, App.

1888 The calf-wrestlers, grimy with blood, dust, and sweat, *work like beavers.*—Theodore Roosevelt, *Century Mag.,* xxxv, 861.

World Power. A powerful factor in the world's politics.

1900 There is a notion that the nation has suddenly expanded into a *"world power,"* and thereby got beyond the Constitution. . . A *world power!* This is a phrase, a mere phrase.—Mr. D. A. De Armond of Mo., H. R., Feb. 27: *C. R.,* p. 95/2, App.

1901 There was no talk then of being a *World Power.—N. Am. Rev.,* Feb., p. 182. (N. E. D.)

World's people. A phrase originated by the Quakers, to signify persons not belonging to their society, and afterwards adopted by some other sects. [1714-1866.]

1848 My conscience [said the Rogerite, a man from Connecticut] will not permit me to marry her in the forms of *the world's people.*—Wilmington (N. C.) *Commercial,* Aug. 8, p. 1/6.

Wrathy. Angry. [1834-1888.]

1830 Jehu was *wrathy,* and the sheriff was positive.—*Am. Beacon* (Norfolk, Va.) Sept. 11, p. 4/3. (From the N. Y. *Constellation.*)

Y

Yank. To pull, to snatch; always expressive of quick movement. [1854-1901.]

1881 [Think of] this mighty stream [Dan River, Va.] being subjected to the commerce of the country by a chain anchored at the head and a line reaching down to the mouth, run by steam, so as to *"yank"* vessels up by the capstan!—Mr. Thos. Updegraff of Ia., H. R., Feb. 15: *C. R.,* p. 1658/2.

1888 I don't see the fun of being *yanked* all over the United States in the middle of August.—C. D. Warner, "Their Pilgrimage," p. 201. (Century Dict.)

1893 There is a . . . difference between an attachment proceeding, where the plaintiff has to give a bond for damages, and this method of *"yanking"* the debtor up [in bankruptcy].—Mr. Champ Clark of Mo., H. R., Oct. 25: *C. R.,* p. 2833/1.

1894 [They should accept] the sage advice of Josh Billings, to *"yank* a few feathers outen the wings of their imagination, and stick 'em in the tails of their judgment."—Mr. E. J. Hainer of Mich., H. R., Jan. 26: *Id.,* p. 1494/1.

Yankee. Properly a New Englander; but used in a general sense for "American." It is used also to denote persons from various parts of the Eastern United States, as indicated in quotation 1827, in Vol. II. [1760-1876.] The origin of the word is uncertain. For conjectures of Gordon, etc., see Century Dict.

1765 From meanness first this Portsmouth *Yankey* rose,
And still to meanness all his conduct flows.—"Oppression, a poem by an American," Boston. (Webster.)

1812 [I] present to you the sentiments of a *Yankee,* in *Yankee* style; and should you esteem them worthy of a place in your *"Yan-Kee"* paper, you are at liberty to insert them:—

> Shall *Yankies,* who in freedom glory,
> Nurs'd in the lap of liberty,
> Descend to truckle to a tory,
> Or to a traitor bend the knee?
>
> I ask, shall we full blooded *Yankies*
> To Kings and Nobles cringe with bows,
> Because they've crowns and crinkum-crankies
> Superbly bound about their brows?
>
> Or shall a set of puny traitors
> E'er make the *Yankie's* blood run chill?
> Heavens, no! Tho' they were all Decaturs,
> *Yankies* would be freemen still.
> —"The Spirit of Putnam," in the May *Yankee.*

1815 The application of the word *Yankey* has often been vague. It has sometimes been applied to Americans of the United States in general; sometimes to New England men in particular; and then to the inhabitants of the interior parts of New England, as distinguished by a peculiar idiom and pronunciation, as well as by a peculiarity of character. In this last sense it is here used.—"The Yankey in England," by David Humphreys, p. 14.

1848 For ourselves, we do not entertain a doubt that the sobriquet of *Yankees,* which is in every man's mouth, and of which the derivation appears to puzzle all our philologists, is nothing but a slight corruption of the word "Yengeese," the term applied to the English by the tribes to whom they first became known. We have no other authority for this derivation than conjecture, and conjectures that are purely our own; but it is so very plausible as almost to carry conviction of itself.—J. F. Cooper, "Oak Openings," p. 28. (Century Dict.)

1864 Mr. Smith is a *Yankee,* born of a *Yankee,* bred a *Yankee,* has taken the oath of allegiance, and is as true and loyal as you or I. He has not been in Canada at all; he tried in the fright and terror which prevailed in New Orleans to save his property in part.—Mr. Edwards Pierrepont to General B. F. Butler, Apr. 1: *C. G.,* Jan. 24, 1865, p. 396/3.

1866 Wherever money is to be made, there is the omnipresent *Yankee.*— Mr. Garrett Davis of Ky., U. S. Senate, Jan. 16: *Id.,* p. 251/1.

1866 I know the negro nature better than all the *Yankees* in this body, or that live upon this continent. I know that if [the negro] can live without work, he will not work.—The same, Jan. 24: *Id.,* p. 396/2.

1866 The gentleman has a *Yankee* way of answering one question by asking another —Mr. Randall of Pa., H. R., May 5: *Id.,* p. 2407/3.

1870 See SYMMES'S HOLE.

1872 [Mr. G. F. Hoar's idea], and it is a perfectly *Yankee* one, is that the object of education is to make a man cunning in diplomacy, artful and crafty in war; that it teaches him how to take advantage of his neighbor, helps a man to office, and much more of the same sort.—Mr. John B. Storm of Pa., H. R., Feb. 6: *C. G.*, p. 857/1.

1874 Will you tell me that a *Yankee*—and when I say a *Yankee* I mean an American—could not manage [an international exhibition]? Why, sir, we will take a contract to pick up one of these little European nations, and pack it in plant-pots, and bring it here and set it up for a show, if you want it.—Mr. J. R. Hawley of Conn., H. R., May 7: *C. R.*, p. 257/2, App.

1875 See LARIAT.

1876 Mr. Sargent:—Will the Senator allow me to answer him? Mr. Howe:—Certainly. Mr. Sargent:—I will answer him by asking another question. Mr. Howe:—No; answer the question, but do not ask another. Mr. Sargent:—I will answer the question by asking another, *which is my right by birth, being a Yankee.*—U. S. Senate, Apr. 12: *C. R.*, p. 2406/2.

1878 Although not a *Yankee* in the sense in which that word is sometimes used, implying particular sharpness in the making of bargains, . . . I believe it to be the duty of the Government . . . to make the very best bargain attainable.—Mr. Stanley Matthews of O., U. S. Senate, March 14: *Id.*, p. 1759/1.

1879 Mr. Hamlin:—The *Yankee* was there [when China was compelled to trade with other nations]. Mr. Matthews [who had introduced the word]:—I use it as a descriptive term applicable to myself, as to all of us. Mr. Hamlin:—But the *Yankee* was there, and did his part.—U. S. Senate, Feb. 13: *Id.*, p. 1275/2.

1879 My honorable friend from Connecticut [Mr. Eaton], with not only the wit but the mechanical contrivance of a *Yankee*, suggests etc.—Mr. Roscoe Conkling of N. Y., U. S. Senate, June 14: *Id.*, p. 2005/2.

1884 [Mr. Turner of Ky.] spoke about the *"Yankees."* What does he mean by that? The *Yankees!* Does he know the origin of the term *"Yankees"*? Does he know that it is a corruption from the Indian "Yengeese," their way of pronouncing the word "English"?—Mr. W. W. Eaton of Conn., H. R., May 1: *Id.*, p. 3674/1.

1893 Seen close and better known, the rebel brigadiers drink less blood than we were once told they did; and they, I believe, find us *Yanks* not so well provided with hoofs and horns, as they once were taught to think.—Mr. A. R. Bushnell of Wisc., H. R., Feb. 17: *Id.*, p. 62/2, App. [See also JOHNNY REB.]

1896 Mr. Cannon:—Now I will *play Yankee* with my friend. Mr. Wellington:—Do not do that. Mr. Cannon:—I will answer his question by asking another.—H. R., March 30: *Id.*, p. 3366/1.

Yankee notions. Things made, invented, or "raised" in New England; a comprehensive phrase. ["Notions" may be ideas, or they may be small useful articles.] [1819-1889.]

1815 See LONG SAUCE AND SHORT SAUCE.

1865 [When] that raft with a cheese-box on it [the Monitor] discharged her immense guns into the sides of the Merrimac, that vessel, gigantic as she was, found that she was entirely unable to cope with this diminutive, untried *Yankee notion.*—Mr. A. H. Rice of Mass., H. R., Feb. 3: *C. G.*, p. 44/2, App.

1870 Take off that duty [on lumber] and you aid [New Eng.] to export carriages, furniture, woodenware, and *Yankee notions.*—Mr. Jacob H. Ela of N. H., H. R., Jan. 21: *Id.*, p. 653/3.

1878 See BODY AND BREECHES.

Yard, v. To go into winter quarters.

1888 [The caribou] never *yards* in winter, as do the deer and moose.— *Harper's Mag.*, lxxvii, 506. (Century Dict.)

Yard, Yard up, v. To enclose in the fashion of a yard.

1887 In 1885 the largest catch of mackerel was made that had been made in 50 years and still gentlemen come here demanding that we shall *yard up* the Atlantic Ocean and prevent mackerel fishing for 3 months of the year.—Mr. Miller, U. S. Senate, Feb. 8: *C. R.,* p. 1487/2.

Yazoo men. Men concerned in the Yazoo land frauds. [1796-1805.]

1808 The old cry of *Yazoo* is raised against this [Massachusetts] memorial and its supporters. All are Yazoo speculators of course. Will any one say that I am a *Yazoo man?* The farthest from it of any person in the world.—Mr. Elliot in the H. R., Jan. 4: *Norfolk* (Va.) *Gazette,* Jan. 15, p. 2/2.

Yellow dog. As a type of worthless creature, this animal figures now and then in American talk and writing. [1840-1878.]

1873 [I pay no more heed to these insinuations] than I would to the barking of *a yellow dog* running down Pennsylvania Avenue.—Mr. R. B. Roosevelt, H. R., Feb. 11: *Id.,* p. 71/3, App.

1886 The *yellow-dog* Republicans, with the coal-oil bosses, have been baying gently . . . about the heels of Senator Logan.—*Cinn. Commercial,* quoted by Mr. Logan in *C. R.,* July 21, p. 7265/2.

1892 Any farmer . . . who would vote to put the protectionists in power would be apt to trade his farm for a three-legged mule, and the mule for a bob-tailed *yellow dog.*—Mr. M. D. Harter of O., H. R., March 29: *Id.,* p. 2652/1.

1894 If there is a *yellow-dog* of party, to snap and snarl at the heels of political decency, it is the New York Democracy.—*Chicago Times,* Jan. 25: cited in the *C. R.*: Jan. 29, p. 1599/1.

1896 They say that this year the Republicans can elect a *yellow dog* if we nominate one.—Senator W. E. Chandler, as quoted by Mr. H. A. Dinsmore of Ark., H. R., March 18: *Id.,* p. 2954/2.

Yellow journals. Those of a sensational, lying, and corrupt character.

1898 The thing that threatens our institutions more than any other is the existence of the great city so-called *"yellow journals."*—Mr. J. H. Walker of Mass., H. R., March 3: *C. R.,* p. 2432/2.

1898 Your bill admits to the pound rate of postage the silliest twaddle of *yellow journalism.*—Mr. W. D. Vandiver of Mo., H. R., March 3: *Id.,* p. 2434/2.

1898 This is a righteous war [with Spain]: and if the so-called *"yellow journals"* are responsible for it, it is greatly to their credit.—Mr. Marion Butler of N. C., U. S. Senate, June 4: *Id.,* p. 5529/1.

York shilling. 12½ cents; the same as a "bit" or a "levy." [1824-1861.]

1841 The [land] sales of this year do not exceed a million and a half of dollars, which would not leave more than a million for distribution: which among sixteen millions of people would be exactly fourpence half penny Virginia money, per head! A *fip* in N. Y., and a *picaillon* in Louisiana, precisely the amount which in specie times a gentleman gives to a negro boy for holding his horse a minute at the door. And for this miserable doit,—this insignificant subdivision of a shilling,—a *York shilling,*—can the demagogue suppose . . .?—Thos. H. Benton, U. S. Senate. Benton's "Thirty Years' View," II, 245/1. (1856.)

Young Hickory. A name applied to James K. Polk, by way of comparing him with Andrew Jackson. [1844-1847.]

1844 See the Speech of Mr. Bidlack of Pa., in defence of *"The Young Hickory,"* Jas K. Polk," p. 14. (Washington.) It has a cut representing a cabin, a hickory tree, a sheaf of grain, and a female holding up a liberty-cap on a pole.

You-uns. You. Southern. Cf. **We-uns.**

1897 The Federal said: "Well, Johnny, we fought on separate sides in the last war, but if another comes we will be found under the old flag, shoulder to shoulder." The Confederate said, "Well, we will, but *you-uns* won't." The Federal asked him ["Why so?" He] said, "Why, you can't; the pension roll shows that *you-uns* was all disabled."—Mr. John M. Allen of Miss., H. R., Dec. 9: *C. R.*, p. 66/1.

Z

Zee. The final letter of the alphabet. [1797-1883.] The following stanza of a parody on Poe's "Annabel Lee" shows the American pronunciation of the letter.

1854   I was at school and she was at school
           In the thriving city of C——
        But we fell in love, through a broken rule,
           I and my X.Y.Z.;
        And never a teacher in that grim school
           Of love had the least idee.
    —Wilmington (N. C.) *Journal*, Apr. 11, p. 2/4. (From the *Home Journal*.)

Zenith City of the Unsalted Seas. Duluth, Minn.

1868 The phrase was used, and apparently invented, by Dr. Thomas Foster, editor of the Duluth *Minnesotian*, in his Fourth of July oration, given at Minnesota Point, near Duluth. See that paper for May 1, 1869.

1880 From the mouth of the Mississippi to "*the Zenith City of the unsalted seas.*"—Mr. J. Proctor Knott of Ky., H. R., Feb. 17: *C. R.*, p. 950/2.

1888 Duluth, "*the Zenith City of the Unsalted Sea,*" with a population in 1870 of 2,000; in 1880 of 3,880; is now a substantial city, . . . with a population of 30,000.—"Lake Superior Region," Ashland, Wisc., Part 1.

ADDENDA*

Back country. s.v.
1754   Remembrancer (1778), V.490/2.
1755   Washington Writings (ed. Ford), I.145.
Back lands. s.v.
1683   Penn, Works (1782), IV.301.
1781   A. Hamilton Works (1886), VIII.34.
Back road. A road, usually an inferior one, through the remoter part
    of a district. (Webster)
1754   Remembrancer (1778), IV.488/2.
Back settlements. s.v.
1760   E. Lucas, Journals & Letters (1850), 26.
1763   W. Roberts, Nat. Hist. Florida, 98.
1777   A. Hamilton Works, VII.511.
1778   J. Carver Travels, 78.
Back side. The back, or rear, side of anything, including the rump.
1637   Boston Records, II.16.
1638   in T. Lechford Note-Book (1885), 11.
1640   Dedham (Mass.) Records, III.70.
1642   Boston Rec., II.69.
1646   Mass. Colony Records, III.102.
1677   W. Hubbard Indian Wars (1865), I.19.
1724   in G. Sheldon Hist. of Deerfield, Mass., I.425.
Boss. s.v.
1826   The Port Folio XXI.351/2.
Caboosis.
1874   If there be a colored man who is willing to recognize the necessity of
    putting Alabama under the rule of intelligence, he becomes our friend,
    and he should be preferred as tenant of our houses, *caboosis* on
    the farm, drayman upon the streets, etc.—*Opelika Times* (Ala.), Sept.
    30: see *C. R.*, Feb. 27, 1875, p. 1901/2.
Family pie. See quotation.
1818   *Family pye* is, in the New England dialect, nearly synonymous with
    mammoth pye.—Boston *Centinel*, Sept.
Fish-hedge. A weir.
1772   See Stop.
Jackass sense. Cf. **Horse sense.**
1898   Men who use more *jackass sense* than reason return to the Depart-
    ment the curt answer, "We refuse to review our decision."—Mr.
    Norton of O., *C. R.*, Feb. 4: p. 1459/2.

---

*These jottings were scattered among notes in the latest of Mr. Thorn-
ton's notebooks, and were discovered too late to be included in their places
alphabetically in the main text.—Ed.

439

Negro cloth. A material of coarse cotton, once used to make clothes for slaves.

1732 [He] had on a blue *Negro Cloth* Frock.—*So. Car. Gazette*, June 17, p. 4/1. (Advt.)

1732 Just imported, white and blue *Negro Cloth.*—*Id.*, Sept. 30, p. 4/2. (Advt.)

1769 *Negro cloth*, commonly called white and coloured plains.—*Boston Chronicle*, Aug. 3-10, p. 250/2. (N. E. D.)

1789 Had on when he went away a white *negro cloth* coat, breeches and boots.—*Augusta* (Ga.) *Chronicle*, Apr. 11, p. 4/1. (Advt.)

1803 Had on when he went away a pair blue broadcloth overalls, a *negro cloth* jacket &c.—*Georgia Republican*, Feb. 7, p. 1/2. (Advt.)

1803 A green cotton, *negro cloth jacket* and trowsers.—*Id.*, July 26, p. 4/4. (Advt.)

Negro Cottons. Probably much the same as *negro cloth*.

1818 NEGRO COTTONS. 10 Bales just received.—Norfolk (Va.) *Beacon*, Dec. 19, p. 1/4. (Advt.)

Negro house. A house built for plantation negroes. [1826.]

1734 To BE LETT, A Plantation Scituate on Wampee Savannah, most of it being rich Savana land, . . . whereon is a large Barn, a dwelling house, and *Negro houses.*—*So. Car. Gazette*, Oct. 19, p. 4/1. (Advt.)

New Lights. Followers of George Whitefield, English Methodist revivalist (1714-1770). See Vol. II, **Old Lights** [1781].

1830   When Whitefield, in long bygone days,
        Set all New England in ৭ blaze,
        His followers *New Lights* were named,
        And I to be a *New Light* claimed.

—*Am. Beacon* (Norfolk, Va.), Sept. 16, p. 4/1. (From the Boston *Courier*.)

Niggerheads. See quotation.

1900 The surface is pre-eminently swampy during the warmer periods of the year, and walking over it means either wading through the water or risking continuous jumps to and from the individual clumps of matted grass and moss,—the so-called *"nigger-heads."*—*Pop. Sci. Mo.*, p. 637. (Century Dict.)

Periogue, Pirogue. A large canoe. From Sp. *Piragua*. [1629-1853.]

1732 Run away, . . . a *Perriauger*-Man, belonging to Winyaw.—*So. Car. Gazette*, Nov. 18.

1732 Several *Pettyawgers* have received great Damage for want of a proper Mark at the White Point.—*So. Car. Gazette*, Mar. 25, p. 4/1.

Triple grinder. See quotation.

1842 There is not a tariff in the world half so dear to a coonskinner. Why, it is a *triple grinder.*—Mr. H. W. Beeson of Pa., H. R., July 9: p. 8/1 of speech as separately published.

APPENDIX

XLIII.* An Odd Sign.

Mr. Speaker,—in walking along D Street yesterday, I saw a very singular sign. I was forcibly reminded by that sign of the speech of the gentleman from Connecticut [Mr. Brandegee.] I ask the clerk to read it.

The clerk read as follows:—"New England Store: Established primarily for my own advantage, and partly to promote the interests of my customers."
—Mr. M. R. Thayer of Pa., H. R., June 7, 1866: *C. G.*, p. 3017/2.

XLIV. "Scrimmages" in Congress.

A former member of this House handed me a list of the Contests he had witnessed on this floor. . . . Among them was the scrimmage between Mr. Clingman and Mr. Stanley, of North Carolina, which resulted in some scratches and blows. Another was between Mr. Wilcox and Governor Brown of Mississippi, which he states was "a much prettier fight than the North Carolina one, and looked more like business." Another was a Tennessee fight. Mr. Churchwell of Tennessee drew a pistol on his colleague, General Cullom. General Cullom "went for" him, bounding over a desk, and denouncing him in a clear ringing voice, which could be heard in the remotest part of the galleries, as a coward and an assassin. Mr. Keitt of S. C., and Mr. Grow, says my authority, "opened their batteries on each other, and the engagement soon became pretty general along the whole line; Barksdale of Miss., Washburne of Ill., Ruffin of N. C., Covode of Pa., Reuben Davis of Miss., Potter of Wisc., and others, charging and retiring alternately."—Mr. Henry J. Raymond of N. Y., H. R., July 17, 1866: *C. G.*, p. 3877/1.

Within the last five or six years there have been three fights in the House. 1. *Turney and Bell*; 2. *Bynum and Rice Garland*; 3. *Wise and Stanley*. This last conflict called together a number of members, who, in attempting to separate the combatants, got at it themselves, and presented for a while quite a "battle royal," or what in legal parlance might be called a "riot." At length, however, my friend from Ala. [Mr. Lewis] strode into their midst, and with his herculean strength ended the scene, by lifting the antagonists entirely out of each other's reach.—Speech of Mr. Black of Ga. in the H. R., Feb. 12: p. 13/1 of the same as separately published.

XLV. A Scream from Iowa.

To become coequal members of our political family, [the Southerners] must open their eyes upon the party wrecks, the strewn and broken timbers which tell of the ignorant conservatism of captain and pilot. Conservatism! That of today offers neither a retreat for the man nor a pledge for the growth and virtue of his party. The idolaters of fossils, who on all occasions and with prolonged speech shout "Constitution," are akin to that class

---

* Mr. Thornton numbered these selections to follow the last one in Vol. II, Appendix.

described by the Virginian who declared unwittingly that when they said "Union" they meant nigger three times.—Mr. Josiah B. Grinnell of Ia., H. R., Jan. 4, 1867: *C. G.*, p. 287/2.

XLVI. The Protective System.

The farmer starting to his work has a shoe put on his horse with nails taxed 67 per cent, driven by a hammer taxed 54 per cent; cuts a stick with a knife taxed 50 per cent; hitches his horse to a plow taxed 50 per cent, with chains taxed 67 per cent. He returns to his home at night, and lays his wearied limbs on a sheet taxed 58 per cent, and covers himself with a blanket that has paid 250 per cent. He rises in the morning, puts on his humble flannel shirt taxed 80 per cent, his coat taxed 50 per cent, shoes taxed 35 per cent, and hat taxed 70 per cent; opens family worship by a chapter from his Bible, taxed 25 per cent, and kneels to his God on an humble carpet taxed 150 per cent. He sits down to his humble meal from a plate taxed 40 per cent, with knife and fork 35 per cent; drinks his cup of coffee taxed 47 per cent, or tea 78 per cent, with sugar 70 per cent; seasons his food with salt taxed 100 per cent, pepper 297 per cent, or spices 379 per cent. He looks around upon his wife and children, all taxed in the same way; takes a chew of tobacco taxed 100 per cent, or lights a cigar taxed 120 per cent, and then thanks his stars that he lives in the freest and best government under heaven.—Mr. S. S. Marshall of Ill., H. R., Mar. 29, 1870: *C. G.*, p. 240/1, App. [These remarks, based on the provisions of the "Morrill tariff," are obviously modelled after those of Sydney Smith in the *Edinburgh Review*, Jan. 1820.]

XLVII. Something about Duluth, Minn.

I was confident it existed somewhere, and that its discovery would constitute the crowning glory of the present century, if not of all modern times. I knew it was bound to exist in the very nature of things; that the symmetry and perfection of our planetary system would be incomplete without it; that the elements of material nature would long since have resolved themselves back into original chaos, if there had been such a hiatus in creation as would have resulted from leaving out Duluth. In fact, Sir, I was overwhelmed with the conviction that Duluth not only existed somewhere, but that wherever it was it was a great and glorious place. I was convinced that the greatest calamity that ever befell the benighted nations of the ancient world was in their having passed away without a knowledge of the actual existence of Duluth; that their fabled Atlantis, never seen save by the hallowed vision of inspired poesy, was in fact but another name for Duluth; that the golden orchard of the Hesperides was but a poetical synonym for the beer-gardens in the vicinity of Duluth. . . . Yet, Sir, had it not been for this map kindly furnished me by the Legislature of Minnesota, I might have gone down to my obscure and humble grave in an agony of despair, because I could nowhere find Duluth. Had such been my melancholy fate, I have no doubt that with the last pulsations of my breaking heart, with the last faint exhalation of my fleeting breath, I should have whispered, "Where is Duluth?"—Mr. J. Proctor Knott of Ky., Jan. 27, 1871: *C. G.*, p. 67/2, App.

XLVIII. The Glories of a High Tariff.

Your table is held together by taxed nails and hinges, and covered with a taxed cloth. Your breakfast is prepared by a cook or a good wife who is clad from the soles of her feet to the top of her head in taxed clothing. It is prepared in a stove made of taxed iron, on a fire made of taxed coal, kindled with a taxed match, and adjusted with taxed shovel and tongs. Your bread is leavened with taxed soda, saleratus, or yeast powders. Your victuals are served to you on taxed dishes, and eaten from taxed plates, or drunk out of taxed cups, saucers, or tumblers, with the aid of taxed knives, forks and spoons. . . . Your good wife is even compelled to seek culinary wisdom from a "cook-book" printed on taxed paper with taxed ink and taxed type.—Mr. M. C. Kerr of Ind., H. R., Mar. 16, 1872: *C. G.*, p. 1745/3.

XLIX. Lunar Observations from Wisconsin.

It is not wise to destroy a great party, freighted with precious hopes and struggling to noble ends, because it occasionally stumbles. It is not wise to silence a great teacher, in whose light a generation has walked and the human race has visibly grown, because of a single fault. It is not wise to drag the moon from the planetary system because there are a few spots on it. Of course, when the moon crumbles into ashes, and so flings dust and not light upon the beholder, it might as well be shoveled out of the system. When the teacher slips all the cables which moor him to truth, close reefs the hopes which waft him heavenward, and drifts out listless and rudderless upon the sea of unbelief, helplessly buffeted by all its waves, and hopelessly clapboarded by all its barnacles, the. sooner he goes to pieces the better. And when a party has sold itself to do evil, has coiled itself upon the path of human progress; when it no longer seeks to give nurse to but rather to nurse upon its country, all good men should abandon it and unite to take it to pieces.—Mr. Timothy O. Howe of Wisc., U. S. Senate, Feb. 8, 1876: *C. R.*, p. 940/1: remarks on the death of Senator Ferry of Conn. [It is fair to add that Mr. Howe did not usually mix up his metaphors in this manner.]

L. A Negro Legislature.

The door was opened, and we were permitted to look in upon the sacred temple wherein South Carolina law is made. It was a spectacle no intelligent man would defend, unless he fattened and battened on such meat. I cannot better express that Legislature than to say that it was *essentially negro*. There was visible but one white man in it; that was the speaker, Mackey. . . . In the hall of representatives they loll in listless indolence, with feet on top of the desks that look like scows upturned on the beach for repairs. . Numbers of them were smoking so furiously that, if a locomotive had rushed under full head of steam through the hall, it would not have sent up a much denser volume of smoke.—Mr. John F. Phillips of Mo., H. R., Feb. 21, 1877: *C. R.*, p. 103/1, App.

LI. A Character Sketch.

I am forbidden by decorum to call [Senator G. F. Edmunds] by name, but he comes in such questionable shape that I will call him the Saint Jerome of the Green Mountains. We have taken his measure and his gauge. He is an astute politician, a wily statesman, a man who can play thimble-rig with the law as cunningly as any prestidigitator ever did with my lady's thimble. He is a man who can play "now you see it and now you don't" with perfect accuracy. He is a man who can amuse an innocent inquirer after truth as cunningly as did his great prototype amuse sweet mother Eve from the bending bough of the primal apple-tree. He is capable of ground and lofty tumbling. O how he tumbled last winter when over yonder, in that hall dedicated to the . . . rendering of justice,—he proved first that white was black, and then bleached it out, and proved that black was white! In the case of that flowery land down South, the land where

> The orange and citron is fairest of fruit,
> And the voice of the mocking-bird never is mute,

with one fell blow of his legal hammer, he killed that veracious witness Mr. *Aliunde*, and would not let the people of this land have the man for whom they had voted [Mr. Tilden] to be their ruler. Then with one grand somersault, seventeen times turning while yet in the air, when he found himself in the forest mazes of that far-off region,

> Where rolls the Oregon, and hears no sound
> **Save his own dashing,**

he conjured up the ghost of Mr. *Aliunde*, and with his aid tore into shreds the Constitution of the land, and thrust through the crystal windows of the rear part of the Nation's Executive Mansion a ruler [Mr. Hayes] whom the majority of the voters had repudiated.—Mr. Carter H. Harrison of Ill., H. R., Oct. 24, 1877 : *C. R.*, p. 137/2.

LII.   The Mexicans on the Texas Frontier.

A population of mixed Indian and Spanish blood, a mixture which seems to have debased the original elements, it has neither the nobility of the Castilian nor the simple dignity of the Indian, and possesses all the vices of both and none of the virtues of either :—a set of men who gamble for an occupation, are filthy, unwashed, unkempt, unregenerated; who wear ragged gaberdines, their uniform being a *sombrero*, a blanket, and a pair of spurs; who eat red-pepper pies and dark-complected bread; who are one day in the army, the next day robbers on the frontier, the next *pronunciadores* (for a Mexican borderer, when he wishes to steal anything, pronounces for God and Liberty;) a set of men who curse the very soil on which they tread: a body of people so debased and. loathsome, that when they lie down to die, on the prairie even, the coyotes will not eat them.—Mr. W. A. Phillips of Kan., H. R., Nov. 9, 1877 : *C. R.*, pp. 325-6.

LIII.   "Rag money."

But, says another, your legal-tender note is "rag money." Hide from view your "rags"; listen and be charmed by the sweet music produced by the jingle of a single standard. Rag money, indeed! When that charge comes from the old Bourbon democrat who opposed its issue, I reply, "You are at least consistent; with you I will have no controversy." But, sir, I for one will not join in the effort to bastardize my own offspring . . . It was with these "rags" that you were enabled to build ships whose sails whiten every ocean. It was with these "rags" that you were able to arm and equip the grandest army that ever battled in defense of law. It was by virtue of these same "rags," to a great extent, that today the flag of our fathers floats in peace over the Capitol of a nation. These same "rags" have since the close of the war brought bread and comfort to the humble home of the widow and the orphan of the men who died in order that the Government which issued them might live to bless and ameliorate the condition of mankind. It is these same "rags" that every member on this floor, with cheerful smile, gladly accepts from the hands of the Sergeant-at-Arms.—Mr. William Hartzell of Ill., H. R., Nov. 15, 1877 : *C. R.*, p. 441/1.

LIV.   The early French Settlements.

The other element was the Arcadian peasant, a mixture of Indian inertia and French philosophic simplicity. There was old Kaskaskia, or as we used to call it "Kasky," Cahokia, Prairie du Rocher, Sainte Genevieve, Vincennes, Cape Girardeau. . . . I have heard the old Kaskaskians say that after St. Louis was started the people there came to "Kasky" to buy goods. Ah, these were the happy primitive days. They cultivated corn in the "big field", where each family had a few acres. They caught wild ponies on the point. They worshipped in a chapel almost as old as Philadelphia, when the bell rang. They celebrated holidays and saints' days, and would observe them for any saint kind enough to give them one. Their lives were not mathematical problems with everything carried and nothing over. They had leisure. They were not ground in the mill of Moloch. They danced in Pe-whingi to the music of Rafael Mart, and ran horse-races. Their wants were few, their labors light. They ate, they drank, they danced, and they died.—Remarks of Mr. W. A. Phillips of Kan., on the death of Senator Lewis Vital Bogy of Mo., Jan. 23, 1878: *C. R.*, p. 507.

LV. A Concise Vindication of the South.

When we of the South voted solidly with our Democratic brethren of the North, we were seeking to get possession of the Government, that we might overturn the Union. When we parted company with our northern Democratic brethren, and voted to sustain the electoral count, we were denounced as truckling to obtain Federal patronage. When we submitted to taunts and insults upon this floor, it was made the text for a glorification speech, and a nomination for the Presidency was claimed for the wonderful hero who was said to have taken the confederate brigadiers by the throat. When we have been insulted in the Senate, and refused to convert that august chamber into a fish-market, but proposed, like gentlemen, to settle our personal differences elsewhere, we were denounced for our plantation manners. When we have voted with the hard-money men of the East for Mr. Tilden, we were preparing to bankrupt the Government with southern claims and payment for our slaves. When we voted with the soft-money men of the West, we were seeking to disgrace the Government by debasing its currency. All these charges have been made against us.—Mr. J. R. Chalmers of Miss., H. R., Feb. 26, 1878: *C. R.*, p. 1348/1.

LVI. Building the Central Pacific Railroad Across the Sierras.

All iron, rails, and material, for the building of the Central Pacific, had to be sent round the Horn or across the Isthmus. Freights which are now $5 per ton cost from $25 to $33 per ton. The freight on a locomotive was $4,000, nearly its present price. Insurance was at war risks, 17 per cent. The road was built through an uninhabited and mountainous country, where was nearly no timber, water, fuel, food, or forage, the Pacific side thousands of miles distant from the real base of supplies. Even water had to be so hauled. It was the same with fuel, which had to be hauled eastward over six hundred miles for the use of trains. It is a standing wonder that the road was built at all, considering the engineering difficulties of the Sierras, the depreciation of the currency loaned, and the great cost of all necessary articles.

But after the track was laid across the mountains, it was a matter of doubt whether it could be kept open through the winter snows. Ten first-class engines were necessary to a single snow-plow in some storms. Forty miles of snow-galleries were built, as solid in construction as timber and iron could make them, story on story against the sides of the mountains, to catch and carry over the avalanches that swept from the heights above. The cost of these structures on the average was $100,000 per mile, making the cost of that forty miles, for snow-sheds alone, as much as building 250 miles of road would cost in a prairie country. Add to that the cost of the long tunnels, the deep cuts, the rock-ribbed mountains, which were deeply furrowed to make a bed for the iron track, with the expenses of equipment, stations, and other outlays, and some idea can be formed of the cost of the Central Pacific road across the Sierra Nevada mountains.—Mr. A. A. Sargent of Calif., U. S. Senate, Apr. 5, 1878: *C. R.*, p. 2304/2.

LVII. Proclamation Concerning a Fugitive Slave.

A Proclamation by the President of the United States.

Whereas information has been received that sundry lawless persons, principally persons of color, combined and confederated together for the purpose of opposing by force the execution of the laws of the United States, did, at Boston in Massachusetts, on the 15th of this month, make a violent attack on the marshal or deputy marshals of the United States for the district of Massachusetts, in the court-house, and did by force rescue from their custody a person arrested as a fugitive slave, and then and there lawfully holden by the said marshal or deputy marshals of the United States, and other scandalous outrages did commit, in violation of law:

Now THEREFORE, to the end that the authority of the laws may be maintained, and those concerned in violating them brought to immediate and condign punishment, I have issued this my proclamation, calling upon all well-disposed citizens to rally to the support of the laws of their country, and requiring and commanding all officers, civil and military, and all other persons, civil or military, who shall be found within the vicinity of this outrage, to be aiding and assisting, by all means in their power, in quelling this and other such combinations, and assisting the marshal and his deputies in recapturing the above-mentioned prisoner; and I do especially direct that prosecutions be commenced against all persons who shall have made themselves aiders or abettors in or to this flagitious offense; and I do further command that the district attorney of the United States, and all other persons concerned in the administration or execution of the laws of the United States, cause the foregoing offenders, and all such as aided, abetted, or assisted them, or shall be found to have harbored or concealed such fugitive contrary to law, to be immediately arrested and proceeded with according to law.

Given under my hand and the seal of the United States,
[L. S.]   this 18th day of February, 1851.
                    MILLARD FILLMORE.
                    DANIEL WEBSTER, Secretary of State.

LVIII. Congressional Amenities.

Mr. Samuel S. Cox of New York, on Jan. 22, 1880, made much fun of Mr. Roswell G. Horr of Michigan, a much larger man than himself, finally suggesting an epitaph for him:—

> Here lies the body
> of
> Congressman Horr:
> 'Tis Greece,
> but
> Living Grease
> no more!
> *Requiescat!*

On the next day Mr. Horr rejoined with an epitaph on Mr. Cox:—

> Beneath this slab lies the great Sam Cox;
> He was wise as an owl and grave as an ox.
> Think it not strange, his turning to dust,
> For he swelled and he swelled, till he finally 'bust.'
> Just where he's gone, or just how he fares,
> Nobody knows, and nobody cares;
> But wherever he is, be he angel or elf,
> Be sure, dear reader, he's puffing himself.

C. R., pp. 488, 507.

LIX. A Congressional Fisherman.

I have had some experience in fishing. May I be pardoned if I refer to the fact that I have fished under the shadow of our Sierras in Tahoe Lake and stream; that I have followed the mountain rivulet Restonica in Corsica.

where the waters blanch the boulders into dazzling whiteness, and the associations of the vendetta and the Bonapartes give a ruddy tinge to the adventure; that I have caught the cod in the Arctic around Cape Nord, under the majestic light of the midnight sun; that I have angled in the clear running Malaren Saltsjön, which circulates healthfully amid the splendid islets of stately Stockholm; that I have flecked the waters of the Bosphorus, in sight of the historic Euxine and the marble palaces and mosques of two continents; that I have been tossed in shallops along with the jolly fishers of the Bay of Biscay; that I have sauntered near the pillars of Iskanderoon, which were erected by a grateful Mediterranean people on the spot where Jonah was thrown ashore by the whale; but where'er I wandered, whether I cast my line

—under hanging mountains
Or by the fall of fountains,

my thoughts have always bounded o'er the main to ride the league-long rollers on the shores of New Jersey along with my favorite life-savers,—to see and feel the bluefish wriggling on the hooks. But, Mr. Speaker, notwithstanding these widespread endeavors, I am not prepared to say that there has been any perceptible diminution of the quantity of fishes in the waters of our planet.—Mr. S. S. Cox of N. Y., H. R., May 12, 1884: *C. R.*, pp. 314-15, App.

LX. A Restricted Challenge.

An individual in Buncombe County, North Carolina, rushed into the market-house on public square on court day, and swore he could whip any man there, their conditions and circumstances all being equal; he was forty-five years of age; lame in one leg, blind in one eye; married twice; had four children by his first wife, three by his second; two had died, and three then had the measles; and if anybody was similarly situated he was ready to fight him.—Mr. James B. Beck of Ky., U. S. Senate, Feb. 2, 1885: *C. R.*, p. 1160/1.

LXI. The Bed of the Mississippi.

If the Mississippi River were dry, and you started in a buggy to drive down its bed from Cairo to the Gulf, you would have a very up and down hill road to travel. In places you would be in a deep and narrow gorge, and again you would be on a hill-top, nearly up to the brink of the bank, and a broad expanse of sand would stretch out perhaps for miles on either side of you. You would then be up on a sand bar, while your previous position was where there had been a caving bend. Now suppose this bed to be filled again with a great flood. You readily see that when the water gets to the broad and shallow bar it spreads out, and loses a part of its velocity. The velocity is also diminished by the friction opposed to the water by this vast exposure of bottom surface. A part of the sediment that the river was able to carry, before it was thus retarded by dispersion and by friction, is, of course, dropped to the bottom. Thus the bar goes on building downstream, adding below what may be picked up at its head. But the water has a certain distance to fall before it reaches the Gulf, and it will make up for this almost no surface slope upon the bar by plunging headlong into the bend below, and in its new course it will pick up a new load of sediment from the bottom. This destroys the repose of the bank, and as soon as the sustaining pressure of the water is taken from the side of the bank, by the falling of the water, the bank will begin to cave in. . . . This new load of sediment will not be dropped until another wide place is reached, at which the river will again spread out, and the same operation will be repeated.

this new bar causing the same trouble below it that the previous bar has caused just above.—Mr. C. R. Breckinridge of Ark., H. R., Feb. 3, 1885: *C. R.*, p. 72, App.

LXII. Popular Government.

In 1830 Daniel Webster condensed the principles of the Declaration of Independence in these words:—The people's government, made for the people, made by the people, and answerable to the people.

In 1850 Theodore Parker adopted the idea in these words:—A government of all the people, by all the people, for all the people.

In 1863 the sentiment was repeated by Mr. Lincoln, who said:—And that a government of the people, by the people, for the people, shall not perish from the earth.—Mr. Joseph Wheeler of Ala., H. R., Mar. 31, 1886: *C. R.*, p. 478/2, App.

LXIII. The Tariff Again.

I will here insert a clipping which illustrates in a very forcible manner the burdens which the working man has to bear under the present tariff law. It is a true tariff story:—

"The American workingman returns at night from his toil, clad in a woolen suit taxed 55 per cent, stockings and undershirt taxed 75 per cent, a cotton shirt taxed 45 per cent, a woolen hat taxed 75 per cent, and perchance a pair of gloves in winter taxed 75 per cent.

"He carries in his hand his tin dinner-pail taxed 45 per cent, and greets his wife with a cheery smile as she looks at him through the window pane taxed 60 per cent, from which she has drawn aside the curtains taxed 40 per cent. . . .

"Hanging his hat on a brass pin taxed 45 per cent, he [suspends] his pail on a steel pin taxed 45 per cent, and proceeds to get ready for his supper. He washes his hands with castile soap taxed 20 per cent, in a tin basin taxed 45 per cent, and wipes them on a cotton towel taxed 45 per cent. He then goes to the looking-glass, taxed 45 per cent, and fixes his hair with a brush and comb taxed 30 per cent. . . ." [Long lists of other articles have been omitted.]—Mr. Charles E. Hogg of W. Va., H. R., June 1888: *C. R.*, p. 247/1, App.

LXIV. The Making of an Ambassador.

I am convinced that we shall never get . . . a really good, genuine, out and out, in and in American minister at the Court of St. James until we send a lay figure there, its legs made of good Alabama pig-iron, its arms of California live-oak, its abdominal recess filled with Mississippi cotton, its head of Eastern granite, and its auricular appendages tasseled ears of Illinois corn. Such a lay figure would certainly do us as much good as has been done by any minister we have sent for the past quarter of a century to that or any other court in the world.—Mr. William McAdoo of N. J., H. R., Jan. 12, 1889: *C. R.*, p. 719/1. [His malice was directed against Mr. James Russell Lowell.]

LXV. The Mississippi Valley.

I never saw the garden of Hesperides . . . I never saw that wonder of the ancient world, the hanging gardens of Babylon . . . But I have seen the garden of the modern world. In that marvellous basin which lies between the green tops of the Alleghanies and the lordly peaks of the Rockies, between the Great Lakes of the North and that summer sea which sings its love-songs to our beautiful Southland, lies the unchallenged and undisputed garden of the world. Climb yon mountain height, whose azure crown can be seen from the Capitol [of Missouri], and look out across this matchless garden.

which is also an empire, unrivaled by any upon which the lights of heaven shine. Yonder glimmering sheen is the Mississippi sweeping down from the Great Lakes, broad and beautiful, cleaving this fertile valley in twain. Yonder come the melted snows of the Rockies, and here go the turbid floods sent down from the green slopes of the Alleghanies. Yonder, in the very heart of the valley and in the very heart of the Republic, they glide gracefully one into the other, and thence pour on, their turbulent floods united, laving the feet of imperial cities on the way, until they are lost among the blue and laughing waves of the sea. Where can such a trio of great inland seas be elsewhere found upon the globe? Behold the checkered earth, crosscut in every direction by a vast, complete, wonderful web and network of rivers and railways. . . .

And here, right in the very center of this great valley; here, right at the center of our 60,000,000 of population; here, in the very center of that circle of noble cities and commercial capitals which girdle her with a golden chain; here, resting upon the beating heart of the Republic itself; here, upon the two shores of the great Father of Waters, midway between the emptying points of the Missouri and Ohio, planted upon the soil both of Missouri and Illinois, joint jewel of twin States, is the great city of St. Louis, a central star, and the proud capital of the great valley, whose 600,000 people throw wide her gates and invite the world to her hospitalities. . . . If it is to be a world's fair, we want our kith and kin of all tongues and degrees who come to us from other lands to see where the cotton they spin is grown, where the bread they eat is produced, where the juicy steaks broiled for their delicate palates in the coffee-houses of London and the cafés of Paris are fatted. We want our English cousins to see the blue-grass pastures of Kentucky, where the thoroughbreds are raised which win their Derby cup and the borrowed surplus of my noble lords. We want our Teutonic friends to inspect the great American hog on his native heath, and finding him fat, slick, and healthful as any porker dare be, go back prepared to silence envious tongues, and, if need be, to beard the iron chancellor in his den. We want our visitors from all the world to see our waste of agricultural wealth, and return to astonish their hungry constituents with stories of how they saw farmers in Kansas and Nebraska burn corn as common fuel, and thus induce their countrymen to come to us, as went the sons of Jacob to the fat land of Egypt, to buy our surplus. These things will not be seen, and these practical results will not be achieved, if the fair is held in New York or Washington, nor so well seen or so well achieved if it is held in Chicago; for, though Chicago may claim to be in the great valley, it is upon its uttermost northern outskirt.—Mr. William J. Stone of Mo., H. R., Feb. 20, 1890: *C. R.*, pp. 1567-8. [This was well enough in its way; but the "World's Fair" went to Chicago nevertheless.—R. H. T.]

LXVI. The burning of corn (maize) for fuel.

Our Democratic friends have been calling our attention to the fact that there is now stagnation in business in the West; that the farmers there are suffering, and that corn is being burned. Some gentlemen speak as if the burning of corn were a new thing. Why, Sir, I can remember that away out on the prairies corn has been burned at times for the last twenty years. Eighteen years ago, I myself burned a hundred bushels of corn in one winter. It is the height of folly for a man to go thirty or forty miles through a storm to sell a load of corn and buy a load of coal, and haul that coal back through the storm, when the load of corn will furnish fuel and heat for cooking just as long as the load of coal and just as cheap, besides saving the expense of the long haul.—Mr. Daniel Kerr of Ia., H. R., May 9, 1890: *C. R.*, p. 4409/1. [See the concluding part of the previous item.]

LXVII. A Yelp from Iowa.

Mr. Speaker, such men as the gentleman [Mr. Raines] would call states-men are no more to be compared with statesmen than the skunk-cabbage on the hills of New York to the giant redwood of the vales of California; no more to be compared to statesmen than the bleating calf to the roaring lion; no more to be compared to statesmen than the carrion crow to the bird of Paradise, or a dunghill to a diamond.—Mr. Walt H. Butler of Ia., H. R., Jan. 29, 1892: *C. R.*, p. 672/1.

LXVIII. "Marching Through Georgia."

Complete text given in *C. R.*, Feb. 16, 1891: p. 213/2, App.

LXIX. Concerning "Platforms."

We have a man in Kansas who made a study of platforms. He was once talking about platforms, and it happened to be about the Republican and Democratic platforms. The question was, what are they worth? He illus-trated it by stating that he boarded a car at one time, and got upon the platform for the purpose of entering the car. When the conductor came along, he told him to get off the platform. "Why," he says, "I want to ride on the train." The conductor replied: "All right, you can ride, but don't stand on the platform." "Why," he responded, "what are platforms made for?" The conductor said: "To get in . on, not to stand on."—Mr. John Davis of Kansas, H. R., Feb. 18, 1892: *C. R.*, p. 1298/1.

LXX. Razor-Backs.

Some years ago, a farmer in the State of Ohio made up his mind that he would change his place of residence and move to Arkansas—the reason why, nobody knows; history has never given us an explanation. It seems that a short time after he landed in Arkansas a county fair was held. He had taken with him from Ohio to his new home some very fine Chester White pigs—six in all—beauties every one of them. He thought it no more than right that he should encourage the industry of raising fine thorough-bred hogs in his new home; so he took to this county fair those six elegant Chester White pigs, and placed them on exhibition. After the awards had been made, the Ohio man discovered that the breed of hogs in which he had been dealing all his life were not appreciated in the State of Arkansas. The first premium ribbon was pinned upon a pen that contained six "razor-backed looking" hogs—hogs with long legs—hogs that looked more like greyhounds than any hogs ever before raised upon American soil. The man from Ohio was not very much chagrined because he had not received the first premium, but his curiosity was excited. So he called upon the chairman of the awarding committee, and asked him the reason why his hogs were rejected, while the pen containing the "razors" was recognized. The chair-man said to him, "My dear Sir, you must be a stranger in this part of the country. In Arkansas the people have no use for hogs that can not outrun a negro."—Mr. D. H. Mercer of Nebr., H. R., Jan. 22, 1894: *C. R.*, p. 1193/2.

LXXI. Queer currency.

The *Fort Wayne Times* gives a description of the currency of Indiana in 1843, which is instructive as to some doctrines of redemption . . . "White dog" was a State issue, to pay for canal repairs, and was receivable for certain lands at its face, and interest. . . . "Blue dog" was a State issue for canal extension, receivable for canal lands and canal tolls. . . . "Blue pup" was a shinplaster currency issued by canal contractors, and redeemable in "blue dog." Quotations, State bank being the standard, scrip, 85 to 90; bank scrip, 85; "white dog," 80 to 90; "blue dog," 40; "blue pup," anything you could get for it. The Ohio nomenclature was wider still, "yellow dog," "red cat," "smooth monkey," "blue pup," and "sick Indian."—Mr. John Dalzell of Pa., H. R., June 4, 1894: *C. R.*, p. 5735/2.

LXXII. What the Farmer knows and does not know.

He is no doubt ignorant of the difference between a "put" and a "straddle," but he knows as well as Sinbad when "the old man of the sea" has got straddle of his neck, and can not be made to let go. He may know little of the latest fashion in footwear, but he knows where his own shoe pinches, and proposes to relieve the pressure upon his bunions just at the present time. He may not follow correct forms in the creases in his trousers, but he knows mighty well the load he has to carry is big enough to put kinks in his back. His hat may be the worse for wear, and last year's style, but it covers a good quality of brains that he is not proposing to allow any political "flim-flam" fakirs (*sic*) to further fuddle. He may not wear a spike-tail coat after 6 o'clock, but such a one as he has does [button] over an honest, open heart.— Mr. J. C. Sibley of Pa., H. R., June 19, 1894: *C. R.*, p. 934/1, App.

LXXIII. A Theory Explaining the Influence of New England.

Take Thomas Jefferson, the greatest philosopher that ever lived, the profoundest thinker that ever devoted himself to the science of politics. Thomas Jefferson, Democrat, statesman, and friend of the human race, had not one-tenth the influence on mankind finally that John Adams had, though John Adams, if he had lived 1000 years, never would have had as much sense as Jefferson had in 15 minutes. The reason of the difference is that New England turned its attention to the business of writing books. . . . While Thomas Jefferson was creating States; while Calhoun, Hayne, and Loundes were expounding the Constitution; while George Rogers Clark was taking possession of a continent; while Taylor and Cass and Scott were fighting for a hemisphere; while Clay and Crittenden and Felix Grundy were electrifying the world with their eloquence; while John Sevier, Sam Houston, and their brethren in arms were taking an empire; while Thomas H. Benton was battling for the possession of the great Northwest; while Frank Blair was saving the Union; while John J. Crittenden was proposing compromises; while John C. Breckenridge and Judah P. Benjamin and the remainder of those . . . brilliant statesmen of the South were uttering polished sentences here that will never die, the schoolmasters up in New England were writing books about America.—Mr. Champ Clark of Mo., H. R., Dec. 10, 1894: *C. R.*, p. 183.

LXXIV. Tailoring in Mississippi.

A story was once told me about the way they [take] a man's measure down in Mississippi for a suit of clothes. The questions are asked about in this way: "Hip pockets?" "Yes." "How many?" "Two." "Four or six shooter?" "Six." "Inside coat pocket?" "Yes." "Pint or quart?" "Quart." And in that way they get the dimensions of a suit of clothes.—Mr. W. E. Mason of Ill., H. R., May 20, 1890: *C. R.*, p. 5028/2.

LXXV. The Harrison Campaign of 1840.*

The class of inducements addressed to the passions and imaginations of the people were such as history blushes to record. Log-cabins, coonskins, and hard cider were taken as symbols of the party, and to show its identification with the poorest and humblest of the people; and these cabins were actually raised in the most public parts of the richest cities, ornamented with coonskins after the fashion of frontier huts, and cider drank in them out of gourds in the public meetings which gathered around them; and the

---

* See Vol. II, Appendix, Nos. XXX and XXXI.

virtues of these cabins, these skins, and this cider were celebrated by travelling and stationary orators. The whole country was put into commotion by travelling parties and public gatherings. Steamboats and all public conveyances were crowded with parties singing doggerel ballads made for the occasion, accompanied with the music of drums, fifes, and fiddles; and incited by incessant speaking. A system of public gatherings was got up, which pervaded every State, county, and town; which took place by day and by night, accompanied by every preparation to excite; and many of [these] gatherings were truly enormous in their numbers.—Thomas H. Benton, "Thirty Years' View," II, 205. (1856.)

LXXVI. Tall talk from South Carolina, 1808.

Behold what has floated in pictured reality before us: the Imperial Bird, who had thrown his eyes upon the Sun, and was mounting in youthful vigour and with swift pinion towards the meridian of glory, whose flight was pushed, cheered, supported, and exulted in by the genius of federalism, has lowered his proud head, drooped and fallen, through the malevolent influence of the vapors engendered under the moon of Democracy. He has descended from the halo of his celestial heights, and been called to the ignominious sphere of chattering Pyes, and made to mingle with the fowl of marshes and lakes. The keepers, to whom we had committed him, were confounded with his lofty exaltation and towering wing, and have taken him under their closer tutelage, and to be cowed, pecked, and deplumed by the vultures and owls of Britain, France, and Spain. Let the contempt of the present age light upon us, and the execrations of posterity be sculptured on our tombs, if we suffer disgrace so foul to settle upon our glories!—"Adrastus," in the Charleston *Times*: *Norfolk* (Va.) *Gazette*, Jan. 6, p. 1/2.